Handbook of Action Research

EDITORIAL BOARD

Handbook of Action Research

The Concise Paperback Edition

edited by

PETER REASON AND HILARY BRADBURY

London • Thousand Oaks • New Delhi

First published 2001
Reprinted 2002, 2004

This edition first published 2006

SAGE Publications Ltd
1 Oliver's Yard
55 City Road
London EC1Y 1SP

SAGE Publications Inc
2455 Teller Road
Thousand Oaks, California 91320

SAGE Publications India Pvt Ltd
B-42, Panchsheel Enclave
Post Box 4109
New Delhi 110 017

British Library Cataloguing in Publication data
A catalogue record for this book is available from the British Library

ISBN 1 4129 2030 2

Library of Congress Control Number: 2005928564

Typeset by C&M Digitals (P) Ltd., Chennai, India
Printed in Great Britain by The Cromwell Press Ltd, Trowbridge, Wiltshire
Printed on paper from sustainable resources

Contents

Notes on Contributors ix

Preface xxi

Introduction: Inquiry and Participation in Search of a World Worthy of Human Aspiration 1
Peter Reason and Hilary Bradbury

PART ONE: GROUNDINGS **15**

1 Theory and Practice: the Mediating Discourse 17
Bjørn Gustavsen

2 Participatory (Action) Research in Social Theory: Origins and Challenges 27
Orlando Fals Borda

3 Action Research in the Workplace: the Socio-technical Perspective 38
William Pasmore

4 Infusing Race into the US Discourse on Action Research 49
Ella Edmondson Bell

5 Uneven Ground: Feminisms and Action Research 60
Patricia Maguire

6 Power and Knowledge 71
John Gaventa and Andrea Cornwall

7 Knowledge and Participatory Research 83
Peter Park

8 Exploring the Relevance of Critical Theory for Action Research: Emancipatory Action Research in the Footsteps of Jürgen Habermas 94
Stephen Kemmis

9 The Humanistic Approach to Action Research 106
John Rowan

10 The Relationship of 'Systems Thinking' to Action Research 117
Robert Louis Flood

PART TWO: PRACTICES 129

11 Action Science: Creating Communities of Inquiry in Communities of Practice 131
Victor J. Friedman

12 The Practice of Co-operative Inquiry: Research 'with' rather than 'on' People 144
John Heron and Peter Reason

13 Appreciative Inquiry: the Power of the Unconditional Positive Question 155
James D. Ludema, David L. Cooperrider and Frank J. Barrett

14 Large-group Processes as Action Research 166
Ann W. Martin

15 Ethnodrama: Constructing Participatory, Experiential and Compelling Action Research through Performance 176
Jim Mienczakowski and Stephen Morgan

16 Clinical Inquiry/Research 185
Edgar H. Schein

17 Community Action Research: Learning as a Community of Practitioners, Consultants and Researchers 195
Peter M. Senge and Claus Otto Scharmer

18 The Practice of Action Inquiry 207
William R. Torbert

PART THREE: EXEMPLARS 219

19 Working Together, Learning Together: Co-operative Inquiry in the Development of Complex Practice by Teams of Social Workers 221
Mark Baldwin

20 The Early Mothering Project: What Happened When the Words 'Action Research' Came to Life for a Group of Midwives 228
Penelope A. Barrett

21 Learning with *The Natural Step*: Action Research to Promote Conversations for Sustainable Development 236
Hilary Bradbury

22 Transforming Lives: Towards Bicultural Competence 243
Gloria Bravette Gordon

23 Action Research to Develop an Interorganizational Network 253
Rupert F. Chisholm

24 Participatory Research and Education for Social Change: Highlander Research and Education Center 262
Helen Matthews Lewis

25 Creative Arts and Photography in Participatory Action Research in Guatemala 269
M. Brinton Lykes, in collaboration with the Association of Maya Ixil Women – New Dawn, Chajul, Guatemala

26 The Art of Clinical Inquiry in Information Technology-related Change 279
Joe McDonagh and David Coghlan

27 Participatory Action Research in Southern Tanzania, with Special Reference to Women 286
Marja-Liisa Swantz, Elizabeth Ndedya and Mwajuma Saiddy Masaiganah

28 Six Street Youth Who Could . . . 297
Elizabeth Whitmore and Colette McKee

PART FOUR: SKILLS 305

29 Collaborative Off-line Reflection: a Way to Develop Skill in Action Science and Action Inquiry 307
Jenny W. Rudolph, Steven S. Taylor and Erica Gabrielle Foldy

30 On Working With Graduate Research Students 315
Peter Reason and Judi Marshall

31 The Mirror, the Magnifying Glass, the Compass and the Map: Facilitating Participatory Action Research 322
Yoland Wadsworth

32 Self-reflective Inquiry Practices 335
Judi Marshall

Conclusion: Broadening the Bandwidth of Validity: Issues and Choice-points for Improving the Quality of Action Research 343
Hilary Bradbury and Peter Reason

Index 352

Notes on Contributors

The Association of Maya Ixil Women – New Dawn is a non-governmental organization in Chajul, Guatemala. Since its previous inception as a Women's Committee in 1992, its more than 70 members have organized six community-based educational and economic development projects in Chajul. Twenty of its members, the women of PhotoVoice, have prepared, in collaboration with M. Brinton Lykes, a photo-text book, *Voices and Images: Maya Ixil Women of Chajul/Voces e Imágenes: Mujeres Maya Ixiles de Chajul* (Guatemala City, Guatemala: MagnaTerra, 2000), that describes the community's experiences of more than three decades of war and state-sponsored violence and their work as women to respond to these violations and build towards the future.

Mark Baldwin is Senior Lecturer in Social Work at the University of Bath in the UK. He teaches discrimination and empowerment, community profiling, and race and racism to undergraduates, and participative research methods to postgraduates. His research interests fall within a participative methodology and are focused upon the empowerment of people with learning difficulties and the facilitation of workers in health and social work as they struggle to maintain professional knowledge and values in the face of managerialism. His interest in cooperation is also there when making music with friends.

Frank J. Barrett, PhD, is Associate Professor of Systems Management at the Naval Postgraduate School in Monterey, California, where he is also Director of the Center for Positive Change. He also serves on the Faculty of Human and Organizational Development at Fielding Graduate University. He received his BA in Government and International Relations from the University of Notre Dame, his MA in English from the University of Notre Dame, and his PhD in Organizational Behavior from Case Western Reserve University. He has served on faculties at The Katholieke University of Leuven in Belgium, Pennsylvania State University Behrend College, Case Western Reserve University, Benedictine University, and Illinois Benedictine College. He has taught courses in management, organizational behavior, organizational theory, group dynamics and leadership, organizational design, organizational development, and organizational change.

Penelope A. Barrett, until recently, was employed as a registered nurse in Mental Health/Psychiatry at St John of God Hospital, North Richmond, on the outskirts of Sydney, Australia – a position that she has held since 2003. Prior to this, she was a lecturer in midwifery and nursing at the University of Sydney. She graduated with a PhD in Health Sciences from Southern Cross University in Lismore, northern New South Wales, and has a BEd in Nursing from the University of New England, Armidale, NSW. Penny was involved in midwifery since 1974, as a student, clinician and teacher, having worked in London, England and Thunder Bay, Ontario, Canada, as well as in Brisbane, Queensland and Sydney, New South Wales, Australia. She is interested in emotional care and factors that may impinge upon the provision of this, especially for mental health clients and new mothers. In November 2005 Penny was appointed as Associate Professor of Nursing at the University of Northern British Columbia in Prince George, BC, Canada.

Ella Edmondson Bell has been an advocate for and involved in action research as a practitioner and researcher beginning in the 1970s when she was a public school educator in New York City. Bell received her PhD in Organizational Behavior from Case Western Reserve University. Her research has focused on the career and life histories of professional Black and White women. She is currently an Associate Professor of Organizational Studies at the Tuck School of Business at Dartmouth University. *Our Separate Ways: Black and White Women and the Struggle for Professional Identity,* co-authored with Stella Nkomo, was published by Harvard Business School Press in 2001. Ella also writes 'Working It', a national column featuring careers advice for *Essence Magazine*.

Hilary Bradbury is an Associate Professor of Organizational Behavior at Case University and Director of the Weatherhead Institute for Sustainable Enterprise (WISE), www.weatherhead.case.edu/wise. Hilary also teaches business executives at University of Southern California and Pepperdine University. Her work explores the links among individual, organizational and social transformation. Her scholarship and teaching are oriented toward facilitating positive action in response to our need to move toward a more sustainable society. She has published numerous articles in journals such as *Academy of Management Executive*, *Organization Science*, *Journal of Management Inquiry*, *OD Practitioner*. She has received a National Science Foundation award, as well as awards for innovations in management teaching, writing and consulting. Hilary is founding editor, with Peter Reason, of the international journal *Action Research*. Hilary is Irish. She has lived and worked in Germany, Switzerland and Japan. She lives with her family in South Pasadena, California.

Gloria Bravette is a Senior Lecturer in the Human Resource Management Division of the Business School, South Bank University, London. Gloria specializes in research which enables both her and her students to engage in the process of 'personal inquiry' in their life-worlds leading to self transformation and renewal. Gloria's contribution to this handbook focuses on research (MBA and PhD) into one aspect of her humanity: the Black experience in the UK, drawing on cooperative inquiry, action research and action inquiry. She is of African-Caribbean descent, and has been educated and socialized in the UK context where she has lived for the majority of her life.

Rupert F. Chisholm (deceased 18 April 2004) was Professor of Management in the School of Public Affairs at the Pennsylvania State University at Harrisburg. He received his BSc in Business Administration and Social Science from Washington and Lee University; his MA in Industrial Relations from Cornell University, and his PhD in Organization Behavior from Case Western Reserve University. Before starting his academic career, Dr Chisholm worked for Esso, both in the United States and in Western Europe. His research interests included network and organization development, workplace design, quality of work life, job stress, and action research. He is the author of *Developing Network Organizations: Learning from Practice and Theory* (1998), which is part of the Addison-Wesley OD series.

David Coghlan teaches organization development and action research at the School of Business Studies, University of Dublin, Ireland. He has an MSc in Management Science from the Manchester School of Management (UK), a SM in Management from MIT's Sloan School of Management and a PhD from The National University of Ireland. He is co-author of *The Dynamics of Organizational Levels* (1994) in the Addison-Wesley OD series and has edited special issues of the *Journal of Managerial Psychology* on 'Action Science and Organizational Research' (1995), and the *Organization Development Journal* on 'Organization Development in Voluntary Organizations' (1996) and 'Grandmasters of Organization Development' (1997). *Doing Action Research in Your Own Organization, Second Edition*, co-authored with Teresa Brannick, was published by SAGE in 2004.

David L. Cooperrider is an Associate Professor of Organizational Behavior and Chair of the Social Innovations in Global Management (SIGMA) Program at the Weatherhead School of Management at Case Western Reserve University in Cleveland, Ohio. He co-authored *Organizational Dimensions of Global Change: No Limits to Cooperation* with Jane Dutton (SAGE, 1999), *Organizational Wisdom and Executive Courage* with S. Srivastva (New Lexington Press, 1998) and *Appreciative Leadership and Management* also with S. Srivastva (JAI Press, 1999). He is known for his seminal work in the area of appreciative inquiry.

Andrea Cornwall is a Fellow at the Institute of Development Studies, University of Sussex. A social anthropologist, she has worked in participatory development as a trainer and researcher for the last ten years, primarily in Africa and the UK. Her current research includes a critical assessment of the rhetoric and realities of participatory practice, and work on issues of difference in participatory development.

Orlando Fals Borda is Professor Emeritus at the National University of Colombia, Bogota, and Doctor Honoris Causa at the Central University of Venezuela,

Caracas, formerly Dean of Sociology. He has been involved in the development of participatory action research and territorial policies in Columbia, with emphases on rural problems, violence, and the social role of scientists. He was Vice-Minister of Agriculture, Deputy to the National Constituent Assembly of 1991, Visiting Professor and Research Director in several universities and institutions abroad, and recipient of the Kreisky Award (Austria) and the Hoffman Award (United Nations). He co-authored *People's Participation: Challenges Ahead* (IEPRI, 1998).

Robert Flood is currently an independent action researcher and Visiting Professor in Management at Monash University, Australia and at Maastricht School of Management, Netherlands. He previously held the Sir Q.W. Lee Chair in Management Sciences at the University of Hull, UK (1989–97). He was awarded Doctor of Science (Econ.) (1997, University of Hull) and Doctor of Philosophy (1985, City University, London). He is a Chartered Engineer and a Fellow of the Institute of Measurement and Control. Robert is the founding and current editor of the learned journal *Systemic Practice and Action Research*. He is the author of nine books, including *Rethinking the Fifth Discipline* (Routledge, 1999) and *Beyond TQM* (Wiley, 1993) which was nominated for the Management Consultants' Association Book of the Year.

Erica Foldy is Assistant Professor of Public and Nonprofit Management at the Wagner Graduate School of Public Service at New York University. She is also affiliated as a researcher with the Research Center for Leadership in Action, based at Wagner. She is also affiliated as a researcher with the Center for Gender in Organizations at the Simmons School of Management in Boston. Professor Foldy has published articles in a variety of journals and edited volumes, including *Public Administration Review* and *Journal of Applied Behavioral Science*. She also co-edited, with Robin Ely and Maureen Scully, *Reader in Gender, Work and Organization* (Blackwell, 2003). Her research interests include identity and diversity in organizations, organizational learning and reflective practice, and the interaction of individual, organizational and social change.

Victor J. Friedman is Senior Lecturer in Organizational Behaviour in the Department of Sociology and the Department of Behavioral Sciences at the Max Stern Emek Yezreel College, Israel. His work has focused on the application of action science to learning at the individual, group, organizational and community level with a special interest in promoting social inclusion. He holds an EdD in Counseling and Consulting Psychology from Harvard University, an MA in Applied Human Development and Guidance from Columbia University, and a BA in Middle Eastern Studies from Brandeis University.

John Gaventa is currently a Fellow at the Institute of Development Studies at the University of Sussex, where he coordinates the work of the Participation Group. Previously, he worked with the Highlander Research and Education Center in Tennessee. A political sociologist and adult educator, he has been involved in participatory action research for many years in the United States and in a number of other countries. His most recent work has been on participatory monitoring and evaluation, and on the uses of participatory methods for participatory governance.

Bjørn Gustavsen was educated as a lawyer at the University of Oslo and has a PhD in Sociology from the same university. He is a professor at the National Institute for Working Life in Sweden, a visiting professor at the University of Technology and the Natural Sciences in Norway, and a senior research fellow at the Work Research Institute in Norway. He has helped create several workplace development programs in Norway, Sweden and other countries, and has written extensively on the relationships between theory and practice, workplace democracy, the use of programs to create development effects and on labour-market institutions. His most recent works pertain to the notion of 'learning regions' where region is defined as a social landscape of actors with the ability to combine learning with the idea of critical mass. His most recent books include *Work Organisation and Europe as a Development Coalition*, co-authored with Richard Ennals (John Benjamins, 1998) and *The Role of Dialogue Conferences in the Development of Learning Regions: Doing From Within Our Lives Together What We Cannot Do Apart*, co-authored with John Shotter (Stockholm School of Economics, 1999).

John Heron is Co-director of the South Pacific Centre for Human Inquiry in New Zealand. He was Founder and Director of the Human Potential Research Project, University of Surrey, and Assistant Director, British Postgraduate Medical Federation, University of London. He is a researcher, author, facilitator and trainer in co-counseling, cooperative inquiry, educational development, group facilitation, management development, personal and transpersonal development, and professional development in the helping professions. His books include *Feeling and Personhood* (SAGE, 1992), *Group Facilitation* (Kogan Page, 1993), *Co-operative Inquiry* (SAGE, 1996), *Sacred Science* (PCCS, 1998), *The Complete Facilitator's Handbook* (Kogan Page, 1999) and *Helping the Client* (SAGE, 2001).

Stephen Kemmis is Director of Stephen Kemmis Research and Consulting Pty Ltd, and Professor Emeritus of the University of Ballarat. He held academic appointments at the University of Sydney, the University of Illinois, the University of East Anglia, Deakin University and the University of Ballarat. He has published widely on social and educational research methodologies (including philosophy of social and educational research, participatory action research, and case study methods). His recent work includes action research projects, projects on indigenous education, and university development (especially research development) in Australia, Finland, the UK and the USA.

Helen Matthews Lewis was on the staff of the Highlander Center from 1977 to 1997. She is a sociologist, writer and community activist who has taught in several colleges and universities in the Appalachian region: University of Virginia College at Wise, Virginia; Berea College, Kentucky; University of Tennessee; East Tennessee State University; and Appalachian State University, Boone, North Carolina. She is semi-retired and living in the North Georgia mountains, Morganton, Georgia but continues to consult, write and occasionally teach.

James D. Ludema is Professor in the PhD Program in Organization Development at Benedictine University. Jim's research focuses on appreciative inquiry, organization change and design, positive organizational scholarship, and whole system methodologies for strategic change. He is the author of numerous articles, book chapters, and books, including best-paper selections. His most recent book is *The Appreciative Inquiry Summit: A Practitioner's Guide for Leading Large Group Change* with Diana Whitney, Bernard J. Mohr, and Thomas J. Griffin (Berrett-Koehler, 2003). Jim is an internationally recognized organizational consultant who, for more than a decade, has been an innovator and thought leader in the field of appreciative inquiry. His practice focuses on the use of appreciative inquiry for large-scale corporate change initiatives, including strategy development, leadership development, core business redesign, culture change, and mergers and acquisitions.

M. Brinton Lykes is Professor of Psychology at the Lynch School of Education and Associate Director of the Center for Human Rights and International Justice at Boston College, Chestnut Hill, Massachusetts, USA. She is an activist scholar and teacher. From 1999 to 2001, she held a chair in psychology at the University of the Witwatersrand (Johannesburg, South Africa). Through participatory action research she works with local actors in developing community-based responses to the effects of war and state-sponsored violence. Her university-based teaching and research in culture and psychology, participatory action research, social and community psychology, and psychology of women and gender are complemented by the development of training programs and post-graduate diplomas for psychosocial trauma workers. She has published extensively about her work and is co-editor of several books, including *Myths about the Powerless: Contesting Social Inequalities* (Temple University Press, 1996).

Patricia Maguire is Associate Professor at Western New Mexico University, Gallup Graduate Studies Center, Gallup, New Mexico. For the past 16 years she has worked in the 'south' of the north as an educator and community activist in a team building and facilitating a culturally and socially relevant graduate education centre on the edge of the Navajo Nation and Pueblo of Zuni in the southwest United States. She is a community activist on issues of woman battering and child sexual assault. More recently she has focused on teacher training to meaningfully and equitably integrate web-based technologies in classroom education and to explore implications of current brain research for education practices and policies. Her best-known work is *Doing Participatory Research: A Feminist Approach* (University of Massachusetts, 1987). She has worked in South Africa, West Africa and Jamaica.

Judi Marshall is a Professor of Organizational Behaviour in the School of Management, University of Bath, UK. Her early research was on managerial job stress. Since joining Bath in 1978 her main research interests have been women in management (publishing *Women Managers: Travellers in a Male World* (Wiley, 1984) and *Women Managers Moving On: Exploring Career and Life Choices* (International Thomson Publishing, 1995)), organizational cultures, career development, change and education for sustainability. She has especially developed self-reflective sense-making and inquiry practices. She teaches on a range of academic courses, and is Director of Studies and a tutor for the action-research based MSc in Responsibility and Business Practice.

Ann W. Martin is an adult educator whose prime interest is in engaging people in dialogue that will allow them to learn from different perspectives and take actions informed by multiple views. For several years she has taught interest-based negotiation and conflict resolution strategies to labor and management, always with both parties in the same room. This work led to an interest in large-group planning processes that would include and take advantage of the interests of many participants. She is currently directing the Extension Division, in charge of adult education, for the School of Industrial and Labor Relations at Cornell University in Ithaca, New York. She holds an EdD in Adult Education from Columbia University and Masters degrees from the School of Industrial and Labor Relations at Cornell and the Harvard Graduate School of Education.

Mwajuma Saiddy Masaiganah trained as a fisheries training officer. She was a tutor in a fisheries training institute and has received further education in various branches of fisheries development and research in Tanzania, Kenya and Norway, and studied Professional Studies in Education at Walsall Education Campus in the UK. She has specialized as a participatory rural appraisal (PRA), gender facilitator and trainer, and has served in several large rural development programs. She has also developed women's training and district development programs through PRA. In 2001, she served as a Visiting Fellow with the Participation Group of IDS Sussex, UK. She is currently a Coordinator for the People's Health Movement (PHM) in East Africa, a member of the Global Steering Committee of PHM, and Steering Committee Member of EQUINET Southern Africa.

Joe McDonagh is Senior Lecturer in Business Studies at Trinity College Dublin where he also serves as Director of Executive Education. He holds a BSc (Comp.) and MA from the University of Dublin, an MBS (MIS) from the National University of Ireland, and a PhD (Business Studies) from the University of Warwick. He also holds MBCS and CITP qualifications from the British Computer Society. His work focuses on leading large-scale change in complex organizations, particularly change enabled by modern ICT systems. He has extensive international experience and advises governments and large corporations on the effective integration of ICT and organizational change.

Colette McKee has almost ten years of experience in working with street-involved youth. In addition to her job as a staff member at the Besserer St Drop-In Centre, a program of the Youth Services Bureau of Ottawa-Carleton, she is currently in the process of completing a BSW degree at Carleton University School of Social Work.

Jim Mienczakowski's doctoral studies developed a framework for reflexive action in health settings. His construct of critical ethnodrama (ethnographic research which influences practical change in health and other settings) has been internationally acknowledged as a new and important form of ethnographic practice. Beyond health research, Jim has been involved in important funded research in the emotional experience of cosmetic surgery and numerous State Government Social Impact reports on proposed industrial development and community change. In 1999, Jim was an invited expert witness for the Australian Health Care Complaints Commission report into cosmetic surgery. Professor Mienczakowski is Foundation Dean of the Faculty of Education and Creative Arts, Central Queensland University and Dean of the Central Queensland Conservatorium of Music.

Stephen Morgan has a BA in Psychology (Newcastle Upon Tyne) and a Masters degree in Education (La Trobe). He is a Registered Psychologist (Queensland) and a Registered Psychiatric Nurse (Queensland). In addition to developing innovative research frameworks in performance and representation, Steve currently lectures in counseling skills, communication, mental health and psychiatric assessment with the Faculty of Nursing and Health at Griffith University.

Elizabeth Ndedya is an agricultural officer specializing in Nutrition. She has served the Rural Integrated Project Support Programme in southern Tanzania as Development Field Officer (training in participatory methodologies to promote community planning in the agricultural sector, 1996–2000), Rural Development Facilitator (2000), Civic Development Facilitator (facilitating local democracy, civil society, rule of law and associational life – community-based organizations and NGOs, 2000–02), and Team Leader (2002–05).

Peter Park is on the Faculty of the Fielding Institute in the Human and Organization Program and Emeritus Professor of Sociology, University of Massachusetts (Amherst). He is the founder and president of the Center for Community Education and Action. He was born in Korea and holds degrees from Columbia (BA) and Yale (MA and PhD); and was a postdoctoral fellow at Harvard. He held visiting professorships at the universities of Rome (Fulbright), California (LA and Irvine) and Brandeis University. He has conducted research in Italy and Finland, and made short research visits to India, Korea, Japan, Hong Kong, Taiwan, Brazil, Nicaragua, and Cuba. His involvement in participatory research projects has mostly been with at-risk youths and disempowered communities. He is the co-editor of *Voices of Change: Participatory Research in the United States and Canada* (Bergin & Garvey, 1993).

William Pasmore is currently Senior Director in the Delta Consulting Group in New York. Prior to joining Delta, he spent 20 years on the Faculty of Case Western Reserve University, where he conducted action research in the study of sociotechnical systems and global social change.

Peter Reason is Professor of Action Research/Practice and Director of the Centre for Action Research in Professional Practice in the School of Management at the University of Bath, which has pioneered graduate education based on collaborative, experiential and action-oriented forms of inquiry. He has contributed to the literature on participative forms of inquiry, having edited *Human Inquiry: A Sourcebook of New Paradigm Research* with John Rowan (Wiley, 1981), *Human Inquiry in Action* (SAGE, 1988), and *Participation in Human Inquiry* (SAGE, 1994), and authored book chapters and journal articles. He is founding editor, with Hilary Bradbury, of the international journal *Action Research*. His major concern is with the devastating and unsustainable impact of human activities on the biosphere which, he believes, has origins in our failure to recognize the participatory nature of our relationship with the planet and the cosmos.

John Rowan co-edited *Human Inquiry: A Sourcebook of New Paradigm Research* with Peter Reason (Wiley, 1981). He has also written books on humanistic therapy (*The Reality Game, Second Edition*, Routledge, 1998), humanistic psychology generally (*Ordinary Ecstasy, Third Edition*, Routledge, 2001), transpersonal therapy (*The Transpersonal: Spirituality in Psychotherapy and Counselling, Second Edition*, Routledge, 2005), and male consciousness (*Healing the Male Psyche*, Routledge, 1997). He is on the editorial boards of four journals.

Jenny Rudolph is an Assistant Professor in Health Services at the Boston University School of Public Health with a joint appointment to the Center for Organization, Leadership and Management Research (COLMR) at the Boston VA Medical Center. Rudolph applies the principles of action inquiry to explore and transform individual and group performance in settings where the social and/or physical consequences of making mistakes are high. Working with clinicians and managers, she utilizes both high-fidelity simulation environments and real-life cases to explore the role of self-awareness and systems thinking in enhancing problem solving, safety, and reducing errors. Rudolph is a graduate of Harvard College, studied System Dynamics at the Sloan School of Management as a visiting scholar, and received her PhD in Management from the Carroll School of Management at Boston College.

Claus Otto Scharmer is a founding research member of the Boston-based Society for Organizational Learning (SoL). He has taught change management courses at the MIT Sloan School of Management and the University of Innsbruck, and consulted with multinational firms in the United States, Europe, and Japan. He is a faculty member of the Fujitsu Global Knowledge Institute, a McKinsey Research Fellow, and a research partner of the Centre for Generative Leadership.

His article 'Strategic leadership within the triad growth-employment-ecology' won the McKinsey Research Award. Book publications include *Ästhetik als Kategorie Strategischer Führung (Aesthetics as Category of Strategic Leadership)*, Urachhausverlag, 1991; *Reflexive Modernisierung des Kapitalismus (Reflective Modernization of Capitalism)*, Schäffer-Poeschel, 1995. He is currently writing a book on leadership in the new economy.

Ed Schein is the Sloan Fellows Professor of Management Emeritus from MIT's Sloan School of Management, where he taught from 1956 to 2005. He received his PhD in Social Psychology from Harvard in 1952 and has focused his research on process consultation (*Process Consultation Revisited*, Addison-Wesley, 1999), career dynamics (*Career Anchors, Second Edition*, Pfeiffer, 1995) and organizational culture (*Organizational Culture and Leadership, Third Edition*, Wiley, 2004). Through most of his career he has evolved the clinical approach to doing research which is the subject of his contribution to this handbook. His most recent book, *DEC is Dead, Long Live DEC* (Berrett-Koehler, 2003) is a good example of how clinical work with an organization over a long time reveals cultural and organizational patterns that are difficult to observe with the more traditional research methods.

Peter M. Senge is a Senior Lecturer at the Massachusetts Institute of Technology. He is also Chairperson of the Society for Organizational Learning (SoL), a global community of corporations, researchers and consultants dedicated to the 'interdependent development of people and their institutions'. He is the author of *The Fifth Discipline: The Art and Practice of the Learning Organization* (Currency, 1990) and, with colleagues Charlotte Roberts, Rick Ross, Bryan Smith and Art Kleiner, co-author of *The Fifth Discipline Fieldbook: Strategies and Tools for Building a Learning Organization* (Currency, 1994). He wrote *The Dance of Change: The Challenges to Sustaining Momentum in Learning Organizations* (Currency, 1999) and co-authored with George Roth *Schools that Learn* (Currency, 2000), a field book for educators, parents and others concerned about education. Peter received a BSc in Engineering from Stanford University, California, a Masters degree in Social Systems Modeling and a PhD in Management from MIT.

Marja-Liisa Swantz is the former Director and Director of Research of the Institute of Development Studies, University of Helsinki. She has been Senior Research Fellow at the University of Dar es Salaam, Lecturer in the Science of Religion and Acting Professor in Social and Cultural Anthropology at the University of Helsinki. Most recently she has been a Visiting Professor at the United Nations University/World Institute of Development Economics Research in Helsinki. She is a graduate of the University of Helsinki and Turku, Finland and received her PhD from the University of Uppsala, Sweden. Marja-Liisa has pioneered participatory action research in Tanzania and has made use of it in large research programs in the field of Anthropology and Development Studies.

Steven S. Taylor is an Assistant Professor in the Management Department at Worcester Polytechnic Institute in Massachusetts, USA. His research interests include organizational aesthetics and reflective practice in the action science/action inquiry traditions. These come together in his interest in the aesthetics of organizational actions. His work has been published in journals such as *Human Relations*, *Organization Studies*, *Action Research*, *Journal of Management Inquiry* and *Management Communications Quarterly*.

Bill Torbert is Professor of Management at Boston College's Carroll School of Management, where he earlier served as Graduate Dean and Director of the PhD Program in Organizational Transformation. He received his BA and PhD from Yale, and served on the faculties of Southern Methodist and Harvard Universities. He is the past-chair of the Academy of Management's Organization Development and Change Division and a widely published author (for example, *Managing the Corporate Dream*, Dow Jones-Irwin, 1987; and *The Power of Balance: Transforming Self, Society, and Scientific* Inquiry, SAGE, 1991). In addition to consulting, he currently serves on the board of Trillium Asset Management (the original and largest social investing advisor), and he is a founding research member of the new Society for Organizational Learning, and a founding Associate of the Integral Institute.

Yoland Wadsworth has worked as a research and evaluation practitioner, consultant and facilitator for 33 years and is author of Australia's best-selling introductory texts: *Do It Yourself Social Research, Second Edition* and *Everyday Evaluation on the Run, Second Edition* (both published by Allen & Unwin, 1997). She is Convenor of the Action Research Program in the Institute of Social Research at Swinburne University of Technology, where she is an Adjunct Professor. She is currently writing the third book in the trilogy, *Building It In: Research and Evaluation in Living Human Systems*, and has recently had accredited Australia's first generic postgraduate higher education course in social science in action research. She is currently also Vice President (International) for the international network association Action Learning, Action Research and Process Management.

Elizabeth Whitmore (aka Bessa) has conducted participatory evaluations in a variety of settings. She recently edited a *New Directions in Evaluation* volume entitled *Understanding and Practicing Participatory Evaluation* (Jossey-Bass, 1998). Working with street-involved youth was a new experience for her, as was adapting PRA techniques in this context. In her other life, she is an Associate Professor at the School of Social Work, Carleton University in Ottawa, Canada.

Preface

Welcome to the concise paperback edition of the *Handbook of Action Research*. By publishing most of the first edition of the handbook in this form we hope we are making these resources accessible to a wider group of people who are using and developing the ideas and practices of action research.

Since the original publication of the *Handbook of Action Research* we have seen a lot to make us think that the community of action research is flourishing. We see a growing unease with 'ivory tower' scholarship which increasingly is seen as a waste of intellectual and financial resources. We also see an increased recognition of the importance of participation in fields as different as economic development and medicine, not least because participative processes are more impressive in terms of the results they produce. We hope you will feel welcome to make your contribution to this new community.

In these pages you will be able to appreciate the sheer diversity of ideas and practices that makes up the family of action research. As we have engaged in the work of editing both the handbook and the journal *Action Research*, we have increasingly seen them as integrative publications which draw together the many streams of action research. And we have come to regard action research not so much as a *methodology* but as an *orientation toward* inquiry (Bradbury and Reason, 2003) and indeed a *orientation of* inquiry that seeks to create a quality of engagement, of curiosity, of question-posing through gathering evidence and testing practices.

Action research can be described conceptually, but is best grasped through illustration. So, for example, a report from Harvard's Hauser Center, itself an action research think tank, describes the action research of Mohammed Yunus, instigator of the Grameen Bank:

> Yunus tested the hypothesis that accountability to peers might replace collateral as an incentive for poor borrowers to repay small loans, and helped create the practice innovations for a micro-credit movement that now serves millions of borrowers around the world. (Brown, 2002: 32)

We find this to be a neat account, neat in the sense that it portrays quite non-traditional research in the familiar language of 'hypothesis testing', suggests an orientation to research that is aimed at improving participants' lives. We have learned that Yunus' work resulted from his personal experience. Returning after completing a doctorate in the United States, he was distraught by the poverty and helplessness in his native Bangladesh. He discovered that just a few dollars could change compatriots' lives but sought a sustainable solution. Rethinking the rules of how new enterprises are financed, Yunus went on to develop micro-financing and the Grameen Bank. In so doing he changed our theory of why loans are repaid and has profoundly influenced the lending practices of global bodies such as The World Bank, as much as those who had been heretofore left out of the economy altogether, especially women.

Through examples such as this, and others you will read in this book, action research demonstrates an inquiry-in-action that positively shapes the lives of literally hundreds of thousands of people everyday. Indeed we might respond to the disdainful attitude of mainstream social scientists to our work that action research practices have changed the world in far more positive ways than has traditional social science. However, significant action research can be quite small in scope, for example through the personal reflection of one person on their professional practice, or through convening a few people to create and reflect on positive change. As such, action research:

- responds to practical and often pressing issues in the lives of people in organizations and communities
- engages with people in collaborative relationships, opening new 'communicative spaces' in which dialogue and development can flourish
- draws on many ways of knowing, both in the evidence that is generated and diverse forms of presentation as we speak to wider audiences
- is strongly value oriented, seeking to address issues of significance concerning the flourishing of human persons, their communities, and the wider ecology in which we participate
- is a living, emergent process which cannot be pre-determined but changes and develops as those engaged deepen their understanding of the issues to be addressed and develop their capacity as co-inquiries both individually and collectively.

We describe action research as a 'family of approaches', a family which sometimes argues and falls out, whose members may at times ignore or wish to dominate others, yet a family which sees itself as different from other forms of research, and is certainly willing to pull together in the face of criticism or hostility from supposedly 'objective' ways of doing research. We have come to appreciate the richness and diversity of this family, and our motivation as editors to create communicative spaces where the different members can come together in conversation has increased. For some, action research is primarily an individual affair through which professionals can address questions such as, 'How can I improve my practice?' For others, action research is strongly rooted in practices of organization development and improvement of business and public sector organizations. For many in the majority world, action research is primarily a liberationist practice aiming to redress imbalances of power and restoring to ordinary people the capacities of self-reliance and the ability to manage their own lives – to 'sharpen their minds', as villagers in Bangladesh describe it. For some, the key questions are about how to initiate and develop face-to-face inquiry groups, while for others the primary issues are about using action research to create change on a large scale and influence policy decisions. And for some action research is primarily a form of practice in the world, while for others it belongs in the scholarly traditions of knowledge generation.

Our aim as editors is to honour and value all these different orientations. We want to insist that good action researchers will appreciate and draw on the range of perspectives and approaches that are available to them. It upsets us when we see action research as narrowly drawn; when, for example, we review an article that only sees action research as short-sighted consulting, seems to argue that one approach is the true form of action research, or traces action research back through just one discipline stream to one set of founding (usually masculine) authorities. We want you to delight in and celebrate the sheer exuberance and diversity that are available to you and be creative in how you use and develop them.

This of course also means there can never be one 'right way' of doing action research. We have addressed this question in the Introduction and the Conclusion by arguing that this diversity of action research opens up a wide range of choices for the conduct of inquiry. We argue that a key dimension of quality is to be aware of the choices, and to make those choices clear, transparent, articulate, to your selves, to your inquiry partners, and, when you start writing and presenting, to the wider world. This is akin to the 'crafting' of research that Kvale (1995) advocates, or following Lather, away from validity as policing toward 'incitement to dialogue'.

Those who involve themselves in the action research this handbook represents are aligned around three important purposes. The first purpose is to bring an action dimension back to the overly quietist tradition of knowledge generation which has developed in the modern era. The second is to expand the hold over knowledge held traditionally by universities and other institutes of 'higher learning'. The examples of action research in this book show how this can be done. At the same time our purpose is to contribute to the ongoing revisioning of the Western mindset – to add impetus to the movement away from a modernist worldview based on a positivist philosophy and a value system dominated by crude notions of economic progress, toward emerging perspectives which share a 'postmodern' sentiment (in the widest sense of that term). This handbook offers many grounding perspectives which contribute to this, including our own understanding of an emergent participatory worldview which we articulate in the Introduction.

We wish to address an audience of scholar-practitioners whether they are in or out of academia. We clearly want to influence academic practice. Over the past 25 years, post-positivist research has received a great deal of attention in graduate and professional education, as evidenced by the attention to postmodernism and by developments in qualitative research (Denzin and Lincoln, 2000b). Indeed the so-called 'campus paradigm wars' in the United States may be understood as a debate about how social science ought to be practised by inquiring into the role of the intellectual in a postmodern world. We wish to add to this debate by bringing to the foreground the many innovations in action approaches to social science, to delineate the possibilities for a 'turn to reflexive action' (Reason and Torbert, 2001) which offers new understandings of the relationship between ideas and practice. We also want to contribute to the development of new thinking about validity and quality in research, to show that good knowing rests on collaborative relationships, on a wide variety of ways of knowing, and an understanding of value and purpose, as well as more traditional forms of intellectual and empirical rigour (Reason, 2006).

One might ask, 'action for what?' We want to challenge those who espouse one form of practice, and show that there are many varieties of action research practice on which the practitioners may creatively draw. We want to show that ideas about language, about critical thinking, about democracy, about race and gender are also providing important new perspectives on practice.

Bringing scholarship and praxis back together, thereby drawing on long cultural traditions, our immodest aim is to change the relationship between knowledge and practice, to provide a model of social science for the twenty-first century as the academy seeks additions and alternatives to its heretofore 'ivory tower' positivist model of science, research and practice.

Synergy with qualitative methods

Action researchers design their projects overall in ways that are often very similar to qualitative designs that are also field based, longitudinal and engaged. Multiple qualitative research methods may be used (for example, interviewing, focus groups, social network data gathering) and combined, as deemed appropriate given the aims of people involved. In the course of inquiry, action researchers might also include network analysis and surveys (or other such quantitative anchors) depending on how best to accomplish practical and other outcomes deemed necessary by those involved in the research.

Action research, qualitative, especially constructivist, approaches to inquiry and critical theory overlap significantly, sometimes to the point of being inseparable. Each research paradigm seeks to empower research subjects to influence decision making for their own aspirations. They share a mandate for social justice and accept considerable rupture among traditional divisions of objectivity and subjectivity. As Denzin and Lincoln put it, contemporary qualitative research:

> asks that the social science and the humanities become sites for critical conversation about democracy, race, gender, class, nation-states, globalization, freedom, and community... We struggle to connect qualitative research to the hopes, needs, and goals of a free democratic society. (Denzin and Lincoln, 2000a: 3)

Key differences also lie in the way in which researchers from each paradigm work with others. In action research the distinction between researchers and subjects may become quite blurred in the course of what is usually a lengthy, collaborative relationship. Additionally, there is a different relative emphasis on the importance of action and its relationship to conceptual insight. These key differences allow for action research to offer an alternative to the trenchant gap between traditional research and its application (Susman and Evered, 1978; Torbert, 1981; Wells, 2000). Most efforts to describe the gap (Kirk, 1979), perhaps ironically, continually re-establish it, by underscoring the disconnect between research and application. Research has traditionally been assumed to occur in a different domain from application and is practised by 'practitioners', who, by definition, are not researchers.

Strategies for enhancing appropriate use of research stress the importance of new institutional emphasis on forging closer bonds between the fragmented spheres of knowledge generation and knowledge application. As action research is research *with*, rather than *on* practitioners, who in many instances become co-researchers themselves, in effect action research bypasses the traditional, constructed separation between research and application.

Accounting for action research epistemology through practice

Traditionally science has privileged knowing through *thinking* over knowing through *doing*. The Cartesian foundation for traditional science is based on the insight that, in doubting, a person can know he thinks and thereby know that he exists (i.e., 'dubito, cogito, ergo sum'). This account of reality privileges individual rationality as the premier vehicle of knowing and lays the centuries deep foundation for the differentiation of knower from what is known. More recent accounts of reality, developed especially in the schools of critical theory and pragmatism (Dewey, 1938; Habermas, 1971; James, 1978; Mead, 1932; Rorty, 1999), privilege experience and action over insight per se. They draw attention to knowing through doing (rather than doubting) and emphasize the social nature of all experience and action. For example, drawing particularly on Habermas' theory of communicative action, Kemmis (Chapter 8) draws out the emancipatory function of deliberative democratic dialogue, which is the most common format for action researchers to work, collaborate, gather and reflect on data.

Action research is therefore an inherently value laden activity, usually practised by scholar-practitioners who care deeply about making a positive change in the world. As such it is unlikely that we find comfortable homes inside academia with its norms of disinterest (or value on the status quo). Nonetheless, many action researchers work well with the creative tension of the boundary space between academia and practice.

First, Second, Third Person Research/Practice

One way of providing some order within the diverse field of action research is to identify three broad pathways of action research practice (Reason and Torbert, 2001):

- First person action research/practice skills and methods address the ability of the researcher to foster an inquiring approach to his or her own life, to act awarely and choicefully, and to assess effects in the outside world while acting. First person research practice brings inquiry into more and more of our moments of action – not as outside researchers but in the whole range of everyday activities.
- Second person action research/practice addresses our ability to inquire face-to-face with others into issues of mutual concern – for example in the service of improving our personal and professional practice both individually and separately.

Second person inquiry starts with interpersonal dialogue and includes the development of communities of inquiry and learning organizations.

- Third person research/practice aims to extend these relatively small scale projects so that 'rather than being defined exclusively as "scientific happenings" they (are) also defined as "political events"' (Toulmin and Gustavsen, 1996). Third person strategies aim to create a wider community of inquiry involving persons who, because they cannot be known to each other face-to-face (say, in a large, geographically dispersed corporation), have an impersonal quality. Writing and other reporting of the process and outcomes of inquiries can also be an important form of third person inquiry.

We suggest that the most compelling and enduring kind of action research will engage all three strategies: first person research practice is best conducted in the company of friends and colleagues who can provide support and challenge; such a company may indeed evolve into a second-person collaborative inquiry process. Although attempts at third person research which are not based in rigorous first person inquiry into one's purposes and practices are open to distortion through unregulated bias.

Since the original publication of the handbook these ideas have been taken forward in important ways. Judi Marshall and Geoff Mead have edited a collection of papers on first person inquiry and reflective practices (2005). The journal *Concepts and Transformation* published an exchange between Davydd Greenwood (2002) and Bjørn Gustavsen (Gustavsen, 2003a) concerning the unfulfilled promises of action research and its impact on large scale issues and public policy. Gustavsen argued that action research will be of limited influence if we think only in terms of single cases, and that we need to think of creating a series of events interconnected in a broader stream – which we can see as social movements or social capital (Gustavsen, 2003a; 2003b). He argues that to do this we have 'to use action research in a distributive way' and that this means it:

> becomes more important to create many events of low intensity and diffuse boundaries than fewer events that correspond to the classical notion of a 'case'. Instead of using much resources in a single spot to pursue things into a continuously higher degree of detail in this spot, resources are spread over a much larger terrain to intervene in as many places in the overall movement as possible. (Gustavsen, 2003a: 96–7)

This development of this perspective can be seen in work in the broad Scandinavian tradition of action research (Philips, 2004 for example). A subsequent issue of *Concepts and Transformation* (Volume 8 Issue 3) carried the debate forward in a dialogue forum.

However, the counter argument can be made that if we wish to do work of significance and to influence changes in society toward justice and democracy, we need not only to build large scale networks of inquiry but also to engage in transformations of consciousness and behaviour at personal and interpersonal levels. While it is true that we cannot make large scale change on the basis of small cases, neither can we build truly effective and liberating political networks of inquiry without developing significant capacities for critical inquiry in the individuals and small communities which constitute them (Reason, 2004).

In a related development Chandler and Torbert (2003) took the idea of first, second, and third person inquiry a conceptual step forward by pointing to the temporal dimension – inquiry can be concerned with past, present, and future – thereby creating '27 varieties' of action research practice which together allow a comprehensive vision of action research practices. What we are seeing in these contributions is debate at a leading edge of our emerging discipline, as action researchers strive in their thinking and practice to integrate the personal and the political, the micro and the macro, voices in the mainstream of policy debate with those from the margins.

As we suggested in the original handbook, structuration theory (Giddens, 1984) allows us to link the individual to social structures such that both are seen to be related as chicken and egg. As in any causal, recursive loop, change to the pattern of interaction can occur through influence either at the more micro, first and second person levels, or the more macro, third person or institutional levels. Following Giddens (1984), and Bourdieu (1977) we suggest that social and organizational realities may be understood to be outcomes of patterns of interaction between the members: in turn, the members' dispositions and practices are shaped by social and organizational procedures. A structuration perspective therefore offers theoretical support for seeking leverage for desired change at macro levels through intervention at the individual, and dyadic or small group micro levels and vice versa. While we do not naïvely misunderstand the power of systems as coterminous with that of aggregates of individuals, we do believe in the power of conscious and intentional change which can result from the action research work of individual and committed groups. Indeed, to paraphrase Margaret Mead and Jürgen Habermas, perhaps the only way that systemic change does occur is through the committed action of small groups of people.

Introduction to the sections and chapters

This handbook is divided into four sections which we have called *Groundings*, *Practices*, *Exemplars* and *Skills*. We review our purpose for each section below.

While the handbook consists of a series of separate sections, there are important streams of thinking and practice running throughout. One thing we have learned is that it is almost impossible to write about action research without providing examples. And it is equally difficult to provide an example without referring to the theory and practices on which it is based. So while this volume is divided into four sections, the reader will find that the sections on Groundings and Practices will also contain examples, and the Exemplars will continually refer back to theory and method. We have asked the contributors to indicate the links they see as important, and have provided some ourselves (we did this by building a website on which drafts of chapters were posted so each contributor could see how their work related to others).

Groundings

Groundings is intended to review the range of paradigms and metatheories, the perspectives, values and epistemologies, that inform the various practices of action research. Action research is informed by diverse streams of intellectual and political thought, which both inform practice and provide underpinnings in the philosophy of knowledge and social action.

The ordering of chapters in this section is to some extent arbitrary. We begin with three chapters which provide us with different historical accounts of the development of action research, and identify some of the key issues to which this historical process has led us. There follow chapters exploring four areas of concern – race, gender, power and epistemology. Finally, the contributions of three different fundamental meta-theoretical perspectives are described – critical theory, humanistic psychology and systems thinking.

Practices

This section includes chapters representing the diverse approaches to action research. While we eschew thinking about action research as a methodology, different 'schools' have articulated the action research orientation in different ways as specific sets of practices which emerge in the interplay between action researchers, context and ideas. Action researchers will draw from a range of methodologies, both those described here and, where appropriate, from recent innovations in qualitative and sometimes quantitative research. These chapters offer a sense of the diversity of practices which together constitute the family of action research approaches. It is perhaps unlikely that a reader new to the field will be able to read a chapter on, say, action science or large group processes, and start practising in the terms illustrated; we do hope that by presenting this range of practices readers will be able to make more informed choices about where to direct their further studies.

Exemplars

The chapters in *Exemplars* show how different researchers – both established contributors to this field and relative neophytes – have taken Groundings perspectives and Practices into their own work. We have tried to provide exemplars which demonstrate both a range of approaches and a range of fields of application. Action research practices have flourished in business organizations and in rural villages; with formally educated people and with those strong in indigenous knowledge; among professionals seeking to improve their practice and with people dealing with the everyday problems of living. We have made two choices here: one has been to show the diversity of practice, maybe at the expense of depth within a particular field; and another has been to devote considerable space to these examples because we believe that action research is best understood as a way of being and doing in the world, informed ideas and formal practices, but always free to respond creatively to the requirements of context. There is something here of the spirit of Lyotard's description of the postmodern artist:

> The postmodern artist or writer is in the position of a philosopher: the text he writes, the work he produces are not in principle governed by pre-established rules, and they cannot be judged according to a determining judgement, by applying familiar categories to the text or to the work. Those rules and principles are what the work of art itself is looking for. The artist and writer, then, are working without rules in order to formulate the rules of what will have been done. (Lyotard, 1979: 81)

One might say that the primary 'rule' in action research practice is to be aware of the choices one is making and their consequences; we return to these issues in the Introduction and Conclusion (see also Reason, 2006).

Skills

The Section we have called *Skills* begins to address some of the competencies that may be required to make these choices, the nature of the skills that may be needed for the initiation and conduct of action research. We touch here on the personal practices of action researchers, on supervisory practice with graduate students, and on the practice of facilitation in participatory research.

Looking forward

The handbook is addressed to those whose work allows for the integration of first, second and third person research/practice. Therefore it is addressed to individual actors, groups of action researchers as well as to institutions, especially those devoted to higher learning. This handbook is also addressed to the world of political realities outside academia – with the ambition of bringing activists and others drawing on action research into a closer dialogue with interested academic scholar-practitioners.

From the world of pressing political concerns we are moved by these words from the South African Truth and Reconciliation Commission

> It is particularly important to emphasise that the truth could not be divorced from the affirmation of the dignity of human beings. Thus, not only the actual outcome or findings of the investigation counted. The process whereby the truth was reached was itself important because it was through this process that the essential norms of social relations between people were reflected. It was, furthermore, through dialogue and respect that a means of promoting transparency, democracy and participation in society was suggested as a basis for reaffirming human dignity and integrity.
>
> Truth as factual, objective information cannot be divorced from the way in which this information is acquired; nor can such information be separated from the purposes it is required to serve. (Truth and Reconciliation Commission Report, 1998: Chapter 5 pt 42 and 44)

As we address individuals and action research groups, and maybe particularly students in the world of academia, we recall the words which John Rowan authored to conclude the Introduction to *Human Inquiry* in 1981:

> What we are contending for in this book is that you don't have to settle for second best. You don't have to accept projects you don't believe in and really don't want to do. You don't have to toe the line of an orthodoxy which is in *many* ways quite illusory. You can do research which is worth

> while for you yourself and for the other people involved in it. You can do research on questions which are genuinely important.
>
> Thousands of researchers down the years have started on projects they really believed in, and which embodied ideas they really cared about. But too often these projects got pared down and chopped about and falsified in the process of getting approval, and the researchers got progressively more disillusioned and frustrated as they have gone on. Thousands of researchers have ended their research soured and disappointed and hurt or cynical. It doesn't have to be this way. Research doesn't have to be another brick in the wall. It is obscene to take a young researcher who actually wants to know more about people, and divert them into manipulating 'variables', counting 'behaviours', observing 'responses' and all the rest of the ways in which people are falsified and fragmented. If we want to know about people, we have to encourage them to be who they are, and to resist all attempts to make them – or ourselves – into something we are not, but which is more easily observable, or countable, or manipulable.
>
> Someone has got to be the next generation of great social scientists – the women and men who are going to break the ground of new knowledge for human growth and development to the next stage. You, the reader, might be one of them – why not? But you will only be one of them if you care enough about what you are doing, and who you are, and who the people are who you are doing it with... (Reason and Rowan, 1981: xxiii–xxiv, emphasis in original)

We also note that action research practitioners repeatedly criticize institutional structures, especially universities, as being inappropriate vehicles for the kind of inquiry practices we advocate. Good action research, that is truly differentiated from traditional research, brings the re-patterning of institutional infrastructures in its wake, some quite embryonic, some surprisingly robust over the years. Yet the emphasis in the handbook on reinvigorating universities perhaps underscores the importance of the role of the university through the course of the development of action research. Today we find ourselves faced with complex systemic issues, perhaps the most pressing and inclusive of all being the pressure to move toward ways of being that afford more sustainable human, social-economic and ecological ways of living – climate change, ecological degradation, loss of species (see, for example, Worldwatch Institute, 2005; WWF, 2004). At this time, however, we find our universities continuing to increase the fragmentation of knowledge by rewarding specialization unmediated by a concern for 'the whole'. The focus on conceptual knowledge further relegates in importance the primacy of learning to better align our espoused theory with our actual undertakings. This fragmentation through specialization and dichotomizing action and research comes precisely at a time when 'seeing the whole' and acting appropriately in light of the insights is so important. We believe that action research has much to share with traditional ways of engaging with knowledge work and that action research can increase the relevance of universities and better use the marvellous intellectual resources which sometimes atrophy in increasingly fragmenting intellectual pursuits.

As debates about the limits of a 'disinterested' social science continue and while we wait for and work toward a world that is more just and sustainable than the one in which we find ourselves, constructive alternatives to science like the action research you find described in these pages are needed to fill the void.

So we invite you into this handbook, exploring participative inquiry and practice from the perspective of your first person research and practice, attending to what draws your attention, excites you and meets your developmental needs; your second person research and practice, attending to what will work for and liberate your co-researchers and others with whom you work; attending always to the wider third person cultural and political concerns which frame your work and which call for attention. Moreover we ask that you share your work with the community of your peers. Let us know how we can support you in that.

Thank you

It's so good to look back on the years since these chapters were painstakingly written and edited and know that the handbook has found a deservedly large and growing audience. Our collaboration – still inter-generational, inter-continental and inter-gendered – remains as productive as ever. In the years that have passed since the original handbook, a new journal of *Action Research* and a new edition of the handbook are coming into being. We each manage to catch the ball when the other drops it and to design all sorts of new projects while waiting to throw it back. To paraphrase Ecclesiastes: a good collaborator is worth their weight in gold. One of our talents is a capacity for inquiry and commitment to '*acompañamiento*' or 'accompanying the process' (see Whitmore and McKee, Chapter 28) of others in the action research community. We therefore ask that you share your candid reactions and we hope to see your work pop up in all manner of worthwhile endeavours and your accounts be shared with the community of action researchers.

Peter Reason, Centre for Action Research in Professional Practice,
University of Bath, England

Hilary Bradbury, Associate Professor
Organizational Behavior,
Weatherhead School of Management,
Case Western Reserve University, USA

References

Bourdieu, P. (1977) *Outline of a Theory of Practice.* Cambridge: Cambridge University Press.

Bradbury, H. and Reason, P. (2003) 'Action research: an opportunity for revitalizing research purpose and practices', *Qualitative Social Work,* 2 (2): 155–75.

Brown, L.D. (ed.) (2002) *Practice-Research Engagement and Civil Society in a Globalizing Society.* Cambridge, MA: Harvard University/The Hauser Center.

Chandler, D. and Torbert, W.R. (2003) 'Transforming inquiry and action by interweaving 27 Flavors of action research, *Action Research,* 1 (2): 133–52.

Denzin, N.K. and Lincoln, Y.S. (2000a) 'Introduction: The Discipline and Practice of Qualitative Research', in N.K. Denzin and Y.S. Lincoln (eds), *Handbook of Qualitative Research,* 2nd edn. Thousand Oaks: SAGE, pp. 1–28.

Denzin, N.K. and Lincoln, Y.S. (eds) (2000b) *Handbook of Qualitative Research,* 2nd edn. Thousand Oaks: SAGE.

Dewey, J. (1938) *Experience and Education.* New York: Macmillan.

Giddens, A. (1984) *The Constitution of Society: Outline of the Theory of Structuration.* Berkeley, CA: University of California Press.

Greenwood, D.J. (2002) 'Action research: unfulfilled promises and unmet challenges', *Concepts and Transformation*, 7 (2): 117–39.

Gustavsen, B. (2003a) 'Action research and the problem of the single case', *Concepts and Transformation*, 8 (1): 93–9.

Gustavsen, B. (2003b) 'New forms of knowledge production and the role of action research', *Action Research*, 1 (2): 153–64.

Habermas, J. (1971) *Knowledge and Human Interests; Theory and Practice; Communication and the Evolution of Society* (J.J. Shapiro, Trans.). Boston, MA: Beacon Press.

James, W. (1978, orig. 1908) *Pragmatism and the Meaning of Truth*. Cambridge, MA: Harvard University Press.

Kirk, S. (1979) 'Understanding Research Utilization in Social Work', in A. Rubin and R. Rosenblatt (eds), *Sourcebook on Research Utilization*. New York: Council on Research Utilization.

Kvale, S. (1995) 'The social construction of validity', *Qualitative Inquiry*, 1 (1): 19–40.

Lyotard, J.-F. (1979) *The Postmodern Condition: A report on knowledge* (G. Bennington and B. Massumi, Trans.). Manchester: Manchester University Press.

Marshall, J. and Mead, G. (2005) 'Special issue: self-reflective practice and first-person action research', *Action Research*, 3 (4): 233–332.

Mead, G.H. (1932) *Mind, Self and Society: From the Standpoint of a Social Behaviorist*. Chicago: University of Chicago Press.

Philips, M.E. (2004) 'Action research and development coalitions in health care', *Action Research*, 2 (4): 349–70.

Reason, P. (2004) 'Action research and the single case: a response to Bjørn Gustavsen', *Concepts and Transformations*, 8 (3): 281–94.

Reason, P. (2006) 'Choice and quality in action research practice', *Journal of Management Inquiry*.

Reason, P. and Rowan, J. (eds) (1981) *Human Inquiry: A Sourcebook of New Paradigm Research*. Chichester: Wiley.

Reason, P. and Torbert, W.R. (2001) 'The action turn: toward a transformational social science', *Concepts and Transformations*, 6 (1): 1–37.

Rorty, R. (1999) *Philosophy and Social Hope*. London: Penguin Books.

Susman, G.I. and Evered, R.D. (1978) 'An assessment of the scientific merits of action research', *Administrative Science Quarterly*, 23: 582–602.

Torbert, W.R. (1981) 'Why Educational Research has been so Uneducational: The Case for a New Model of Social Science Based on Collaborative Inquiry', in P. Reason and J. Rowan (eds), *Human Inquiry: A Sourcebook of New Paradigm Research*. Chichester: Wiley, pp. 141–52.

Toulmin, S. and Gustavsen, B. (eds) (1996) *Beyond Theory: Changing Organizations Through Participation*. Amsterdam: John Benjamins.

Truth and Reconciliation Commission Report. (1998) Retrieved April 2003, from www.truth.org.za.

Wells, K. (2000) 'Use of Research in Mental Health Practice and Policy', in D. Drotar (ed.), *Handbook of Research in Pediatric and Clinical Child Psychology*. New York: Kluwer Academic/ Plenum Publishers.

Worldwatch Institute (2005) *Vital Signs 2005*. Washington DC: Worldwatch Institute.

WWF. (2004) Living Planet Report. Retrieved July 2005, from www.panda.org/news_facts/publications/ general/livingplanet/index.cfm.

Introduction: Inquiry and Participation in Search of a World Worthy of Human Aspiration

PETER REASON AND HILARY BRADBURY

I do not separate my scientific inquiry from my life. For me it is really a quest for life, to understand life and to create what I call living knowledge – knowledge which is valid for the people with whom I work and for myself. (Marja-Liisa Swantz)

Knowledge is always gained through action and for action. From this starting point, to question the validity of social knowledge is to question, not how to develop a reflective science about action, but how to develop genuinely well-informed action – how to conduct an action science. (Bill Torbert)

I am not a social scientist interested in more participatory research, but an educator and activist exploring alternative paradigm research as one tool in the multifaceted struggles for a more just, loving world. (Pat Maguire)

Practical knowledge, knowing how, is the consummation, the fulfilment, of the knowledge quest ... it affirms what is intrinsically worthwhile, human flourishing, by manifesting it in action. (John Heron)

The aim of participatory action research is to change practices, social structures, and social media which maintain irrationality, injustice, and unsatisfying forms of existence. (Robin McTaggart)

Participatory research is a process through which members of an oppressed group or community identify a problem, collect and analyse information, and act upon the problem in order to find solutions and to promote social and political transformation. (Daniel Selener)

Action research can help us build a better, freer society. (Davydd Greenwood and Morten Levin)

We must keep on trying to understand better, change and reenchant our plural world. (Orlando Fals Borda)

Action, Participation and Experience

In this Introduction, we draw together some of the major threads that form the diverse practices of action research, to provide a framework through which the reader can approach this volume. We know that our readership is varied. You may be new to action research, wanting to know whether it has anything to offer you. You may already be an action research practitioner, maybe with allegiance to one of the schools included (or not included) in this volume, and wondering how we have presented the kind of work you are committed to. You may belong to an academic discipline which draws on more orthodox forms of inquiry, wondering how this action research animal can be understood as science. And of course you may be downright hostile to the idea of action research, and are reading this to show how misguided the editors and contributors are!

There is no 'short answer' to the question 'What is action research?'. But let us say as a working definition, to be expanded on in this Introduction and indeed the rest of this volume, that action research is a participatory, democratic process concerned with developing practical knowing in the pursuit of worthwhile human purposes, grounded in a participatory worldview which we believe is emerging at this historical moment. It seeks to bring together action and reflection, theory and practice, in participation with others, in the pursuit of practical solutions to issues of pressing concern to people, and more generally the flourishing of individual persons and their communities.

What we want to say to all our readers is that we see action research as a practice for the systematic development of knowing and knowledge, but based in a rather different form from traditional academic research – it has different purposes, is based in different relationships, and has different ways of conceiving knowledge and its relation to practice. These are fundamental differences in our understanding of the nature of inquiry, not simply methodological niceties. As we have studied the contributions to this volume over these past two

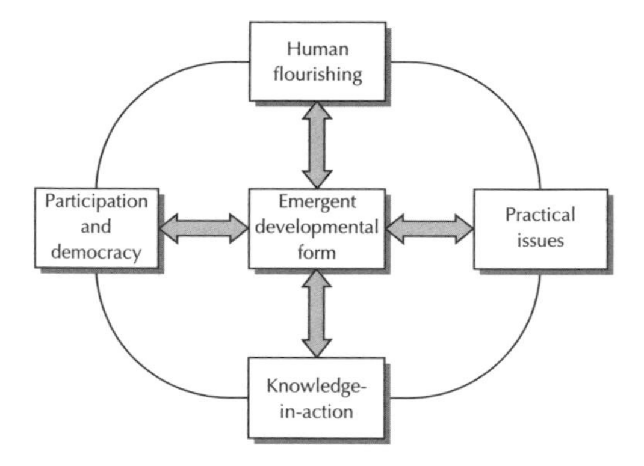

Figure 1 Characteristics of action research

years and more, we conclude that, while the field of action research is hugely varied and there are all kinds of choices to be made in practice, there are five broadly shared features which characterize action research which we show in Figure 1.

A primary purpose of action research is to produce practical knowledge that is useful to people in the everyday conduct of their lives. A wider purpose of action research is to contribute through this practical knowledge to the increased well-being – economic, political, psychological, spiritual – of human persons and communities, and to a more equitable and sustainable relationship with the wider ecology of the planet of which we are an intrinsic part.

So action research is about working towards practical outcomes, and also about creating new forms of understanding, since action without reflection and understanding is blind, just as theory without action is meaningless. And more broadly, theories which contribute to human emancipation, to the flourishing of community, which help us reflect on our place within the ecology of the planet and contemplate our spiritual purposes, can lead us to different ways of being together, as well as providing important guidance and inspiration for practice (for a feminist perspective would invite us to consider whether an emphasis on action without a balancing consideration of ways of being is rather too heroic).

As we search for practical knowledge and liberating ways of knowing, working with people in their everyday lives, we can also see that action research is participative research, and all participative research must be action research. Human persons are agents who act in the world on the basis of their own sensemaking; human community involves mutual sensemaking and collective action. Action research is only possible *with*, *for* and *by* persons and communities, ideally involving all stakeholders both in the questioning and sensemaking that informs the research, *and* in the action which is its focus.

Since action research starts with everyday experience and is concerned with the development of living knowledge, in many ways the process of inquiry is as important as specific outcomes. Good action research emerges over time in an evolutionary and developmental process, as individuals develop skills of inquiry and as communities of inquiry develop within communities of practice. Action research is emancipatory, it leads not just to new practical knowledge, but to new abilities to create knowledge. In action research knowledge is a living, evolving process of coming to know rooted in everyday experience; it is a verb rather than a noun. This means action research cannot be programmatic and cannot be defined in terms of hard and fast methods, but is, in Lyotard's (1979) sense, a work of art.

These five interdependent characteristics of action research emerge from our reflections on practice in this developing field. Together they imply an 'action turn' in research practice which both builds on and takes us beyond the 'language turn' of recent years: the language turn drew our attention to the way knowledge is a social construction; the action turn accepts this, and asks us to consider how we can act in intelligent and informed ways in a socially constructed world. Later in this Introduction we work towards the articulation of a participatory worldview as a grounding framework for these characteristics, and show how this draws our attention to the kinds of choices that action research practitioners need to make in the course of their work, choices which have implications for the quality and validity of their inquiries.

We start from these assertions – which may seem contentious to some of the academic community, while at the same time obvious to those of a more activist orientation – because the *purpose* of knowledge-making is so rarely debated. The institutions of normal science and academia, which have created such a monopoly on the knowledge-making process, place a primary value on pure research, the creation of knowledge unencumbered by practical questions. In contrast, the primary purpose of action research is not to produce academic theories based on action; nor is it to produce theories about action; nor is it to produce theoretical or empirical knowledge that can be applied in action; it is to liberate the human body, mind and spirit in the search for a better, freer world.

The Diverse Origins of Action Research

We doubt if it is possible to provide one coherent history of action research. Many writers on action research trace its origins back to the social experiments of Kurt Lewin in the 1940s, through the socio-technical experiments begun at the Tavistock Institute and in particular their application to practices of social democracy and organizational change (Greenwood and Levin, 1998; see also Gustavsen, Chapter 1 and Pasmore, Chapter 3). While we are clearly indebted to this tradition, there are others which deserve acknowledgement.

We may also see origins of action research in the contemporary critique of positivist science and scientism, in the movement to seek new epistemologies of practice. While all the contributions in our *Groundings* section address questions of the nature of knowledge, they are explored in particular by Park, Chapter 7 and Kemmis, Chapter 8 – as well as later in this Introduction. Others point out that important origins can be found in cultures which Eurocentric scholarship can overlook. Orlando Fals Borda asked in an email exchange

> … where are the Maya Aristotles who discovered the Zero and taught how to build the wonderful pyramids in Yucatán? How are their intellectual and technical contributions taken into account in our discourses and narratives?

Participatory forms of inquiry aimed at solving practical problems have existed forever in human cultures, and have contributed to all life-supporting human activities from plant and animal husbandry to political democracy (Hall, 2001).

We can also trace the evolution of action research back to the Marxist dictum that the important thing is not to understand the world but to change it, through the theorizing of Gramsci and others and the educational work of Freire, to the participatory research practice of those working for the liberation of the oppressed and underprivileged of this world (Fals Borda, Chapter 2; Selener, 1997). This is truly a living movement worldwide for which no one person or community can claim ownership: we see the inspiration of Freire meeting the pioneering work of Marja-Liisa Swantz and her colleagues in Tanzania (Chapter 27), the movement for popular education, as expressed for example at the Highlander Center (Lewis, Chapter 24; Horton and Freire, 1990) and institutions such as the Society for Participatory Research in Asia (Bhatt and Tandon, 2001). More recently, through practices such as participatory rural appraisal (Chambers, 1997), practices of participative research have become part of developmental institutions – governments, NGOs and supra-national bodies such as the World Bank – which raises important questions about people's participation in relation to institutionalized power (Gaventa and Cornwall, Chapter 6).

Other writers point first to the fundamental importance of liberating perspectives on gender and race as a foundation for action research. As Maguire points out (Chapter 5), feminisms in their fullest sense challenge the structures and practices of domination in all fields. And the feminist practice of consciousness-raising can in itself be seen as a form of experiential action inquiry. Bell (Chapter 4) also shows how the roots of action research were deeply embedded in progressive research on race.

Other roots of action research lie in the practices of experiential learning and psychotherapy. T-group training and encounter groups are, at their best, forms of mutual inquiry into the here-and-now development of group processes (Schein and Bennis, 1965). As John Rowan points out in Chapter 9, some forms of psychotherapy, particularly those informed by existential and humanist perspectives, can similarly be seen as mutual inquiries, as can a variety of forms of self-help groups such as co-counselling. In England humanistic approaches to learning and change led to experiments with learning communities based in humanistic education which directly informed the development of co-operative inquiry (Heron, 1971). All this interacted with the evolving practices of organizational development, which many would characterize as a form of action research in which the consultant's role is to facilitate reflective inquiry within the organization, for which Schein coined the term clinical inquiry (Chapter 16) and Senge and Scharmer describe as the development of a community of learning (Chapter 17).

While some approaches to action research have remained resolutely secular, others have seen some spiritual practices as inquiry (Torbert, Chapter 18; Bentz and Shapiro, 1998). The disciplines of mindfulness expressed in spiritual teachings from the Buddha to Gurdjief, and in practices such as Tai Chi and insight meditation, can make an important contribution to our understanding of inquiry – although, as Heron (2001) argues, these teachings and practices are often nested within authoritarian political structures from which they must be liberated.

Action research has been equally promiscuous in its sources of theoretical inspiration. It has drawn on pragmatic philosophy (Greenwood and Levin, 1998), critical thinking (Kemmis, Chapter 8; Carr and Kemmis, 1986), the practice of democracy (Gustavsen, Chapter 1; Toulmin and Gustavsen, 1996), liberationist thought (Fals Borda, Chapter 2; Selener, 1997), humanistic and transpersonal psychology (Rowan, Chapter 9; Heron and Reason, Chapter 12), constructionist theory (Ludema, Cooperrider and Barrett, Chapter 13), systems thinking (Flood, Chapter 10; Pasmore, Chapter 3) and, more recently, complexity theory (Reason and Goodwin, 1999). In its refusal to adopt one theoretical perspective it can be seen as an expression of a postmodern sentiment, or as Toulmin might have it, a re-assertion of Renaissance values of practical philosophy:

> Since 1945, the problems that have challenged reflective thinkers on a deep philosophical level … are matters of *practice*: including matters of life and death … The 'modern' focus on the written, the universal, the general, the timeless – which monopolized the work of most philosophers after 1630 – is being broadened to include once again the oral, the particular, the local and the timely. (Toulmin, 1990: 186, emphasis in original)

The diversity of sources that inspire action research are reflected in the arenas in which action research has taken root, which range from the problems of development in the majority world to questions of organizational change in the minority world; from practices which enhance inquiry as a personal practice in everyday life to attempts to engage whole societies as communities of inquiry; from intensely practical concerns such as the preservation of local fisheries to our experience of non-ordinary realities. From a disciplinary perspective action research practices can be found in community development, organization and business, education, healthcare and medicine, social work, the human social, psychological and transpersonal sciences.

Action Research, Paradigms and Worldviews

We will now turn to explore how the characteristics of action research we identified above can be seen as grounded in a participatory worldview which we believe is emerging at this historical moment. Let us say again that these characteristics are not simply questions of methodology. To be sure, we can argue that they lead to 'better' research because the practical and theoretical outcomes of the research process are grounded in the perspective and interests of those immediately concerned, and not filtered through an outside researcher's preconceptions and interests. But far more than that, when we assert the practical purposes of action research and the importance of human interests; when we join knower with known in participative relationship; as we move away from operational measurement into a science of experiential qualities (Reason and Goodwin, 1999), we undercut the foundations of the empirical-positivist worldview that has been the foundation of Western inquiry since the Enlightenment (Toulmin, 1990). In doing this, we are part of the current shift from a 'modern' to a 'postmodern' world, and we need to engage with the current debate about worldviews and paradigms. We need to look at the practical consequences of modernism; at the implications of the 'language turn' which has pointed to the importance of language in creating our world; and, in our view, point to a third possibility, a participatory worldview.

Many writers and commentators are suggesting that the modernist worldview or paradigm of Western civilization is reaching the end of its useful life. It is suggested that there is a fundamental shift occurring in our understanding of the universe and our place in it, that new patterns of thought and belief are emerging that will transform our experience, our thinking and our action. We have, since the Reformation, the beginning of the era of modern science, and the Industrial Revolution made enormous strides in our material welfare and our control of our lives. Yet at the same time we can see the costs of this progress in ecological devastation, human and social fragmentation, and spiritual impoverishment. So if we fail to make a transition to new ways of thinking our civilization will decline and decay. Gregory Bateson (1972a), one of the great original thinkers of our time, argued that the most important task facing us is to learn to think in new ways: he was deeply concerned with what he called the epistemological errors of our time, the errors built into our ways of thinking, and their consequences for justice and ecological sustainability. So the challenge of changing our worldview is central to our times.

The notion of a paradigm or worldview as an overarching framework which organizes our whole approach to being in the world has become commonplace since Thomas Kuhn published *The Structure of Scientific Revolutions* (1962). Kuhn showed that normal scientific research takes place within a taken-for-granted framework which organizes all perception and thinking, which he called a paradigm. However, from time to time the paradigm itself shifts in a revolutionary fashion as a new perspective is deemed to make better sense of the available knowledge. This idea of a paradigm in science can be transferred to the worldview of a whole culture, and the notion that the Western worldview may be in revolutionary transition has been part of intellectual currency for quite a while.

Research in the West has been integral with a positivist worldview, a view that sees science as separate from everyday life and the researcher as subject within a world of separate objects. In this perspective, there is a real world made up of real things we can identify, operating according to natural causal laws which govern their behaviour – laws which we can deduce by analysing the operation of the component parts. Mind and reality are separate: the rational human, drawing on analytical thought and experimental methods, can come to know the objective world. This is part of a modern worldview based on the metaphor of linear progress, absolute truth and rational planning (Harvey, 1990). Seeking objective truth, the modern worldview makes no connection between knowledge and power. We start from the position, well argued elsewhere (see for example Lincoln and Guba, 1985; Reason, 1994), that this positivist worldview has outlived its usefulness: as Habermas has announced, 'modernism is dead'.

Evolution of western thought

Stephen Toulmin's *Cosmopolis* (1990) provides a helpful account of the evolution of Western thought into and through the modernist period which prepares the ground for our discussion of an emerging participative worldview. Toulmin's argument is that the worldview which emerged with Descartes and Newton should not be seen as the first enlightened, rational correction of medieval superstition. Rather, that the break with the Middle Ages occurred considerably earlier, and that some important origins of modernity can be traced back to late sixteenth-century writers in Northern Europe. Toulmin refers to these writers as 'Renaissance humanists' (he refers particularly to Michel de Montaigne). Their 'theoretical inquiries were balanced against discussions of concrete, practical issues' (p. 24), and they 'displayed an urbane openmindness and skeptical tolerance … that led to honest practical doubt about the value of "theory" for human experience' (p. 25). They argued for a trust in experience, the courage to observe and reflect, a curiosity about the diversity of human nature.

Toulmin goes on to show that during the seventeenth century 'these humanist insights were lost', and there was an historical shift from a practical philosophy based on experience and particular practical cases to a theoretical philosophy concerned with the general, the timeless, and the universal. Toulmin argues that this happened at that time because the assassination of the tolerant Henri IV of France, the devastation brought about by the dogmatic religious struggles of the Thirty Years War and other economic and political difficulties brought about a 'counter-Renaissance' – a demand for a new certainty in the face of these appalling crises which neither humanistic scepticism nor religious dogma seemed able to meet. Thus the quest for certainty which led to the philosophy of Descartes was 'a timely response to a specific historical challenge – the political, social and theological chaos embodied in the Thirty Years War'.

> … the Cartesian program for philosophy swept aside the 'reasonable' uncertainties and hesitations of 16th-century skeptics, in favor of new, mathematical kinds of 'rational' certainty and proof … [F]or the time being, that change of attitude – the devaluation of the oral, the particular, the local, the timely, and the practical – appeared a small price to pay for a formally 'rational' theory grounded on abstract, universal, timeless concepts … Soon enough, the flight from the particular, concrete, transitory, and practical aspects of human experience became a feature of cultural life in general. (Toulmin, 1990: 75–6)

Toulmin continues the story to the present time. As different sciences developed, particularly in the eighteenth and nineteenth centuries, a more pragmatic and practical attitude developed: each new field of inquiry had to discover its own methodology, and the hard edges of the Enlightenment were softened. But just as Europe was beginning to rediscover the values of Renaissance humanism, the roof fell in again with the First World War, the inequitable peace and the Great Depression. Re-Renaissance was deferred: the intellectual response was a return to the formalism of the Vienna Circle and the monopoly of logical positivism. It was not until the 1960s that humanism could be re-invented and 'the dream of foundationalism – i.e. the search for a permanent and unique set of authoritative principles for human knowledge – proves to be just a dream, which has its appeal in moments of intellectual crisis, but fades away when matters are viewed under a calmer and clearer light' (Toulmin, 1990: 174).

As Toulmin argues, the way ahead is to draw on the twin legacies of the exact sciences and the humanities: a participative worldview does just this.

The linguistic turn

The linguistic and cognitive turn has swept the social sciences and humanities since the 1960s and brought to mainstream scholarship the Kantian differentiation between the world itself (*das Ding an sich*) and the phenomenon, or our interpreted experience of the world. The cognitive turn focused on the cognitive structures (schemata or mental models) which allow us to make sense of the world. The linguistic turn, rediscovering Nietzsche's sense of language as an 'army of metaphors', looked at the hitherto underestimated role of language in our construction of our world in which we are always seeking to make (or give) sense. It is now difficult to sustain a position of 'naïve realism'. In scholarly circles it is difficult to suggest that the world exists outside our construction of it (Gergen, 1994, 1999; Schwandt, 1994; Shotter, 1993).

> Language is auditioning for an a priori role in the social and material world. Moreover, it is a role that carries constitutional force, bringing facts into consciousness and therefore being. No longer then is something like an

> organization or, for that matter, an atom or quark thought to come first while our understandings, models or representations of an organization, atom or quark come second. Rather, our representations may well come first, allowing us to see selectively what we have described. (Van Maanen, 1995: 134)

We have probably left the idea of language as 'representation' behind us, even if it does linger in the discourse of modernism and positivism. So we may say that since the linguistic and cognitive turns, we have become more fluent in understanding the difference between phenomena and our interpretations of them. Postmodernism, indeed, is predicated on the insight about this differentiation, and sometimes threatens to collapse the distinction once again. No longer is the world to be thought of as naively 'out there', but in extreme constructionist positions the world is evoked always and only in a dance of signs (Derrida, 1981). Such a world perhaps, is one that is only 'in here'. But surely, even if phenomena such as gravity are not directly apprehended, but are understood within a cultural context mediated by language, there are 'deeper structures of reality' (Berry, 1999) which lie under and behind them.

The deconstructive sentiment lays bare our illusions of any kind of certainty and holds that we must be suspicious of all overarching theories and paradigms – incredulous towards meta-narratives, as Lyotard (1979) put it. It asserts that there is no accessible reality behind the 'text', the immediate expression of human understanding we have in front of us. Since all understanding is relative, despite the range of competing paradigms currently on the social science scene (Guba and Lincoln, 1994; Heron and Reason, 1997; Lincoln and Guba, 2000), there are in the end no foundations on which truth can be securely laid (Schwandt, 1996), and the postmodern perspective asks us to 'deconstruct' and 'transgress' beyond our taken-for-granted assumptions, strategies, and habits. As Lather puts it: 'we seem somewhere in the midst of a shift away from a view of knowledge as disinterested and toward a conceptualization of knowledge as constructed, contested, incessantly perspectival and polyphonic' (1991: xx).

The postmodern perspective points to the researcher's 'complicity in the constitution of their objects of study' and the 'interested nature of knowledge-making' (Calás and Smircich, 1999). It also emphasizes the intimate relationship between knowledge and power, how knowledge-making, supported by various cultural and political forms, creates a reality which favours those who hold power. Similarly, action researchers agree that objective knowledge is impossible, since the researcher is always a part of the world he or she studies, and point out that knowledge-making cannot be neutral and disinterested but is a political process in the service of particular purposes, and one which has been institutionalized in favour of the privileged (Hall, Gillette and Tandon, 1982). This close examination of the role of language in creating our shared reality is of great importance within the action research movement. Since action research is concerned with the development of democratic forms of knowledge it is concerned with the ways in which language is used in the service of those who hold power to define reality (Gaventa and Cornwall, Chapter 6; Lukes, 1974). As Selener puts it: 'One of the greatest obstacles to creating a more just world is the power of the dominant hegemony, the ideological oppression which shapes the way people think' (1997: 26).

In this volume, many contributors argue the need to see through the dominant worldview and its construction of reality, and to create new possibilities: this is particularly important in Bell's account of the infusion of perspectives from race into action research (Chapter 4) and Maguire's exploration of the significance of feminist perspectives (Chapter 5).

However, from the perspective of action research we find that the emphasis that deconstructive and poststructuralist perspectives place on the metaphor of 'text' is limiting. There is a lot of concern with discourse, text, narrative, with the crisis of representation, but little concern for the relationship of all this to knowledge in action. For example, Denzin's (1997) fascinating exploration of interpretive ethnography is full of references to text; and Calás and Smircich (1999) ask us to consider how the 'textuality' of our writings defines the nature of knowledge. Neither ask what the text is actually *for*. As Lather, also writing within the postmodern sentiment, points out: 'The question of action … remains largely under-addressed within postmodern discourse' (1991: 12).

While postmodern/poststructuralist perspectives help us immensely in seeing through the myth of the modernist world, they do not help us move beyond the problems it has produced. If we in the West were alienated from our experience by the separation of mind and matter introduced by Descartes, we are even more alienated if all we can do is circle round various forms of relativist construction: any sense of a world in which we are grounded disappears. We are particularly concerned about this in these times of approaching ecological crisis when appreciating our embeddedness in the more-than-human-world (Abram, 1996) is so critical. Our concern is that the deconstructive postmodern sentiment will exacerbate, rather than heal, the modern experience of rootlessness and meaninglessness. While acknowledging the postmodern suspicions of meta-narrative, we believe that all inquiry, and all of life, is necessarily framed by a worldview – and indeed that the postmodern/ poststructuralist perspective is just such a worldview, based on the metaphor of the world as text. We need to find a way of acknowledging the lessons of the linguistic turn while not ignoring the deeper structures of reality, and propose that a more creative and constructive worldview can be based on the metaphor of participation.

Towards a Participatory Worldview

The emergent worldview has been described as systemic, holistic, relational, feminine, experiential, but its defining characteristic is that it is participatory: our world does not consist of separate things but of relationships which we co-author. We participate in our world, so that the 'reality' we experience is a co-creation that involves the primal givenness of the cosmos and human feeling and construing. The participative metaphor is particularly apt for action research, because as we participate in creating our world we are already embodied and breathing beings *who are necessarily acting* – and this draws us to consider how to judge the *quality* of our acting.

A participatory worldview places human persons and communities as part of their world – both human and more-than-human – embodied in their world, co-creating their world. A participatory perspective asks us to be both situated and reflexive, to be explicit about the perspective from which knowledge is created, to see inquiry as a process of coming to know, serving the democratic, practical ethos of action research.

A participatory view competes with both the positivism of modern times and with the deconstructive postmodern alternative – and we would hold it to be a more adequate and creative paradigm for our times. However, we can also say that it also draws on and integrates both paradigms: it follows positivism in arguing that there is a 'real' reality, a primeval givenness of being (of which we partake) and draws on the constructionist perspective in acknowledging that as soon as we attempt to articulate this we enter a world of human language and cultural expression. Any account of the given cosmos in the spoken or written word is culturally framed, yet if we approach our inquiry with appropriate critical skills and discipline, our account may provide some perspective on what is universal, and on the knowledge-creating process which frames this account.

This places scientific work – our extraordinary knowledge about the world in which we live that is derived from natural sciences – in a new light. Of course, some in the natural sciences draw on participative perspectives to inform their work

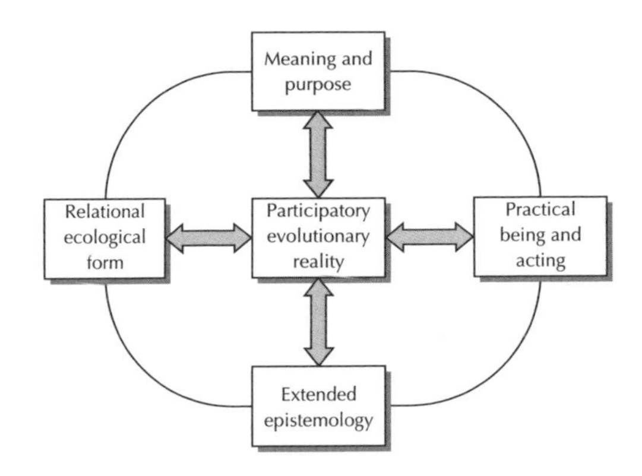

Figure 2 Dimensions of a participatory worldview

(Clarke, 1996; Goodwin, 1999; Ho, 1998). But apart from this, a participative worldview enables us where appropriate to draw on techniques and knowledge of positivist science and to frame these within a human context. Participative medical practitioners do not throw away medical training, but draw on it to work *with* patients in diagnosis and healing. Ecologists can draw on their scientific perspective to provide villagers with useful information about local forests and work with them towards better management. Scientists can, and have, claimed privileged knowledge; they can also see themselves as participants, with a particular set of skills and information, within a wider knowledge democracy.

While worldviews can be sketched out exclusively in simple cognitive terms, their nature is far richer. As Mumford put it:

> Every transformation of [the human species] ... has rested on a new metaphysical and ideological base; or rather, upon deeper stirrings and intuitions whose rationalised expression takes the form of a new picture of the cosmos and the nature of [humanity]. (1957: 179)

In seeking to articulate some of these 'deeper stirrings' we will sketch below the characteristics of a participatory worldview. We start with our intimations of the *participatory nature* of the given cosmos whose form is *relational and ecological*. Since we are a part of the whole, we are already engaged in *practical being and acting* (Skolimowski, 1994). Thus our science is necessarily an action science, which draws on *extended epistemologies* and continually inquires into the *meaning and purpose* of our practice. These dimensions of a participatory worldview (shown in Figure 2) echo the characteristics of action research we identified earlier (Figure 1). They also provide a basis for judgements of quality or validity in action research, which we touch on below and explore in more detail in our concluding chapter.

On the nature of the given cosmos

At the centre of a participatory worldview is a participatory understanding of the underlying nature of the cosmos we inhabit and which we co-create. We can only point towards this intuition here, drawing on Laszlo's (1996) evocative metaphor, that the cosmos is a 'whispering pond', a seamless whole in which the parts are constantly in touch with each other: 'Wherever scientists look and whatever they look at, they see nature acting and evolving not as a collection of independent parts, but as an integrated, interacting, self-consistent, and self-creative whole' (Laszlo, 2003).

It is now plausible to consider that the quantum metaphor, which points to space- and time-transcending interconnections between phenomena, is not confined to the sub-atomic world, but is applicable to the structure of the living world (Ho, 1998), to consciousness, and to the evolution of the cosmos itself (Laszlo, 2003). This suggests we are living as part of a cosmos which is far more interconnected than we have hitherto suspected, a cosmos of non-local correlations and coherence, organized in ways that cannot be explained either by classical or systemic models. Laszlo argues that 'evidence for space- and time-transcending connections is accumulating: the phenomena, investigated by physicists, biologists, consciousness researchers and cosmologists turn out to be non-locally correlated and coherently coevolving wholes' (Laszlo, 2003). Further, panexperientialist philosophers, developing the process philosophy of Whitehead, suggest that matter and consciousness are not ontologically separate, but are 'coeternal, mutually complementary realities' (de Quincey, 1999: 23; see also Griffin, 1998) and that '*Matter and psyche always go together* – all the way down' (de Quincey, 1999: 23, emphasis in original).

> Mind and matter are not distinct substances. The Cartesian error was to identify both matter and consciousness as kinds of substances and not to recognize them as phases in a process; that mind is the dynamic form inherent in the matter itself. Mind is the self-becoming, the self-organization – the *self-creation* – of matter. Without this, matter could never produce mind. Consciousness and matter, mind and body, subject and object, process and substance ... always go together. They are a unity, a nondual duality. (de Quincey, 1999: 24, emphasis in original)

As Griffin points out most thoroughly, this panexperientialist ontology radically confronts our assumptions about the nature of our world which, for modernists and postmodernists alike, assumes a separation of mind and matter. While panexperientialists are emphatically *not* arguing that rocks are conscious in the same way that are humans (Griffin, 1998: 95), they *are* arguing 'a form of reality of which mind is a natural part' (1998: 79). Similarly the quantum phenomena suggest a 'communicating universe in which all things are in instant and enduring communicative union – true communion – with each other' (Laszlo, 2003).

These suggestions are 'the strangest thing in a strange world', as Laszlo points out. They do not lead to an analytic paradigm anything like the classical Newtonian worldview, but an evolutionary, emergent and reflexive worldview in which the cosmos is continually self-ordering and self-creating. Within this perspective, human persons are centres of consciousness both independent and linked in a generative web of communion both with other humans and with the rest of creation (Heron, 1992). Our reality emerges through a co-creative dance of the human bodymind and the given cosmos: while this latter is fundamentally present we can only know it through our constructs and sensitivities. Human persons do not stand separate from the cosmos; we evolved with it and are an expression of its intelligent and creative force. As Thomas Berry puts it: 'the universe carries within it a psychic-spiritual as well as a physical-material dimension ... the human activates the most profound dimension of the universe, its capacity to reflect on and celebrate itself in conscious self-awareness' (1988: 132).

We live in a participatory world. There is a primordial givenness of being in which the human bodymind actively participates in a co-creative dance which gives rise to the reality we experience. Subject and object are interdependent. Thus participation is fundamental to the nature of our being, an *ontological given* (Heron, 1996a; Heron and Reason, 1997). As we are a part of the whole we are necessarily actors within it, which leads us to consider the fundamental importance of the practical.

On practical being and acting

Given our fundamental participation in the 'whole' we human persons are already engaged and are already acting (Skolimowski, 1994). All ways of knowing serve to support our skilful being-in-the-world from moment-to-moment-to-moment, our ability to act intelligently in the pursuit of worthwhile purposes. Human inquiry is necessarily practical and a participatory form of inquiry is an *action science*.

In arguing this we are following the Scottish philosopher John Macmurray, who argued long ago that 'I do' rather than 'I think' is the appropriate starting point for epistemology (1957: 84).

> ... most of our knowledge, and all our primary knowledge, arises as an aspect of activities that have practical, not theoretical objectives; and it is this knowledge, itself an aspect of action, to which all reflective theory must refer (p. 12).

However, as Macmurray also pointed out, the concept of 'action' includes the development of theory which may illuminate our action, guide it and provide it with meaning:

> In acting the body indeed is in action, but also the mind. Action is not blind ... Action, then, is a full concrete activity of the self in which all our capacities are employed (p. 86).

Greenwood and Levin (1998) follow Dewey, Rorty and other pragmatist philosophers to make a very similar point.

The concern for the 'full concrete activity of the self in which all our capacities are employed' invites us to articulate further the nature of knowing. It also invites us to consider our relationship with others with whom we act, and directs our attention to questions of what is worthwhile, what values and purpose are worthy of pursuit. We explore these questions in the next sections.

On the nature of knowing

A participative worldview, with its notion of reality as subjective-objective, involves an extended epistemology: we draw on diverse forms of knowing as we encounter and act in our world. As Eikeland points out this notion goes right back to Aristotle, while in modern times Polanyi (1962) described clearly his concept of tacit knowledge, a type of embodied know-how that is the foundation of all cognitive action. He rejected the notion of the objective observer in science or any other area of inquiry, expressing his belief in engaged practice that necessarily joins facts and values in a participatory mode of understanding.

Writing more recently, Shotter argues that in addition to Gilbert Ryle's distinction between 'knowing that' and 'knowing how' there is a 'kind of knowledge one has *only from within a social situation*, a group, or an institution, and thus takes into account ... the *others* in the social situation' (Shotter, 1993: 7, emphasis in original). It is significant that Shotter usually uses the verbal form '*knowing* of the third kind', to describe this, rather than the noun *knowledge*, emphasizing that such knowing is not a thing, to be discovered or created and stored up in journals, but rather arises in the process of living, in the voices of ordinary people in conversation.

Peter Park, writing in the context of participatory research and drawing on the emancipatory traditions of Freire (1970), Habermas (1972); see also Kemmis, Chapter 8) and others, argues that we must take an 'epistemological turn' and 'think of community ties and critical awareness, as well as objective understanding of reality, as forms of knowledge' (see Chapter 7). Thus he explores *relational* and *reflective*, as well as *representational* forms of knowledge. Representational knowledge provides explanation through identifying the relationship between discrete variables, or understanding through interpretation of meaning. Relational knowledge is the foundation of community life and its development fosters community ties as well as helping to crete other forms of knowledge (Bradbury and Liechtenstein, 2000). Reflective knowledge has to do with normative states in social, economic and political realms. It concerns a vision of what ought to be, what is right and what is wrong, and arises, Park argues, through the process of consciousness-raising, *conscientization*.

From a feminist perspective, Belenky, Clinchy, Goldberger and Tarule wrote of 'women's ways of knowing' (1986) which distinguished between connected and separated knowing: separated knowing adopting a more critical eye and playing a 'doubting game', while connected knowing starts with an empathic, receptive eye, entering the spirit of what is offered and seeking to understand from within. Feminist scholars generally have emphasized relational aspects of both knowing (e.g., Bigwood, 1993) and of the practice of management (Fletcher, 1998; Marshall, 1995).

Torbert (Chapter 18; also 1991) emphasizes the importance of a quality of attention which moment to moment is able to interpenetrate four territories of attention: an intuitive knowing of purposes; an intellectual knowing of strategy; an embodied, sensuous knowing of one's behaviour; and an empirical knowing of the outside world.

Heron and Reason (Chapter 12; see also Heron, 1996a) argue that a knower participates in the known, articulating their world in at least four interdependent ways: *experiential knowing* is through direct face-to-face encounter with a person, place or thing; it is knowing through empathy and resonance, that kind of in-depth knowing which is almost impossible to put into words; *presentational knowing* grows out of experiential knowing and provides the first form of expression through story, picture, sculpture, movement, dance, drawing on aesthetic imagery; *propositional knowing* draws on concepts and ideas; and *practical knowing* consummates the other forms of knowing in action in the world.

While all these descriptions of extended epistemologies differ in detail, they all go beyond orthodox empirical and rational Western views of knowing and assert, in their different ways, a multiplicity of ways of knowing that start from a relationship between self and other, through participation and intuition. They assert the importance of sensitivity and attunement in the moment of relationship, and of knowing not just as an academic pursuit but as the everyday practices of acting in relationship and creating meaning in our lives.

On relational ecological form

A participatory worldview is a political statement as well as a theory of knowledge. Just as the classical Cartesian worldview emerged in part from the political situation of the time (Toulmin, 1990) and found its expression not only in science and technology, but also in our political structures and organizational forms, so a participatory worldview implies democratic, peer relationships as the political form of inquiry.

This political dimension of participation affirms people's right and ability to have a say in decisions which affect them and which claim to generate knowledge about them. It asserts the importance of liberating the muted voices of those held down by class structures and neo-colonialism, by poverty, sexism, racism and homophobia. Throughout this handbook contributors from all perspectives have argued strongly the connections between power and knowledge.

Daniel Selener emphasizes that while a major goal of participatory research is to solve practical problems in a community, 'Another goal is the creation of shifts in the balance of power in favor of poor and marginalized groups in society' (Selener, 1997: 12). And as Greenwood and Levin assert, action research contributes actively to processes of democratic social change (Greenwood and Levin, 1998: 3).

The political imperative is not just a matter of researchers being considerate about their subjects or acting ethically: it is about the democratic foundations of inquiry and of society. In 1791 Tom Paine argued that it is specious to think about government in terms of a relationship between those who govern and those governed; what is important is the legitimacy of the existence of government itself. Since the people existed before the government:

> The fact therefore must be, that the *individuals themselves*, each in his own personal and sovereign right, *entered into a contract with each other* to produce a government: and this is the only mode in which governments have a right to arise, and the only principle on which they have a right to exist. (Paine, 1791, 1995: 123, emphasis in original)

We can draw direct parallels between the legitimacy of government and the legitimacy of research. To paraphrase Paine, *it is for people themselves, in their own right, to enter into agreements with each other to discover and create knowledge, and this is the only principle on which research and inquiry have a right to exist.*

So while we may be concerned to produce knowledge and action directly useful to a group of people, participation can also empower them at a second and deeper level to see that they are capable of constructing and using their own knowledge. It enables them to see through ways in which powerful groups in society tend to monopolize the production and use of knowledge for their own benefit. Thus participation is also a process of consciousness-raising or *conscientization* and is thus an *educative imperative*. Action research is at its best a process that explicitly aims to educate those involved to develop their capacity for inquiry both individually and collectively.

This pedagogy of the oppressed, to borrow Freire's term, must be matched by a 'pedagogy of the privileged': inquiry processes which engage those in positions of power, and those who are simply members of privileged groups – based on gender, class, profession, or nation. We need to learn more about how to exercise power and position legitimately in the service of participative relationships, to find ways in which politicians, professionals, managers can exercise power in transforming ways (Torbert, 1991), power with others rather than power over others (see Gaventa and Cornwall, Chapter 6; Park, Chapter 7). We also need to find ways of liberating ourselves from those elements of the Western worldview which prohibit this.

Relationships do not only mean those with other humans, but also with the more-than-human world. As we are increasingly aware that the damage that is being done to the planet's ecosystems and the resultant sustainability crisis (Brown, 1999) has some of its origins in our failure to understand the systemic nature of the planet's ecosystems, and humanity's participation in natural processes, we can also see that that participation is an *ecological imperative*. The links between ecological devastation and our worldview are well made by deep ecologists and ecofeminists (see for example Devall and Sessions, 1985; Diamond and Orenstein, 1990; Naess, 1987, 1989; Plant, 1989; Roszak, 1995). As Bateson wrote long ago:

> If you put God outside and set him vis-à-vis his creation and if you have the idea that you are created in his image, you will logically and naturally see yourself as outside and against the things around you. And as you arrogate all mind to yourself, you will see the world around you as mindless and therefore as not entitled to moral or ethical consideration. The environment will be yours to exploit …
>
> If this is your estimate of your relation to nature and you have an advanced technology, your likelihood of survival will be that of a snowball in hell. You will die

either of the toxic by-products of your own hate, or, simply, of over population and over-grazing. (Bateson, 1972b: 462)

On purpose and meaning: spirit and beauty

As the quotes at the beginning of this chapter indicate, while action research practitioners suggest slightly different emphases in their work – 'quest for life', 'make the world better', 'loving', 'freer' – there is broad agreement that the purpose of human inquiry is the flourishing of life, the life of human persons, of human communities, and increasingly of the more-than-human world of which we are a part. A participative worldview invites us to inquire into what we mean by flourishing and into the meaning and purpose of our endeavours, and this, as we will argue, is a key dimension of quality in inquiry. As Berry (1999) asks us, what is the 'great work' of humanity in our time, and how are our individual human projects aligned with it?

Participative consciousness is part of a re-sacralization of the world, a re-enchantment of the world (Berman, 1981; Berry, 1988; Skolimowski, 1993). Sacred experience is based in reverence, in awe and love for creation, valuing it for its own sake, in its own right as a living presence. To deny participation not only offends against human justice, not only leads to errors in epistemology, not only strains the limits of the natural world, but is also troublesome for human souls and for the *anima mundi*. Given the condition of our times, a primary purpose of human inquiry is not so much to search for truth but to *heal*, and above all to heal the alienation, the split that characterizes modern experience. For as R.D. Laing put it rather dramatically:

> … the ordinary person is a shrivelled, desiccated fragment of what a person can be …
>
> What we call normal is a product of repression, denial, splitting, projection, introjection and other forms of destructive action on experience … It is radically estranged from the structure of being. (Laing, 1967: 25–7)

As one of us wrote earlier:

> To heal means to make whole: we can only understand our world as a whole if we are part of it; as soon as we attempt to stand outside, we divide and separate. In contrast, making whole necessarily implies participation: one characteristic of a participative worldview is that the individual person is restored to the circle of community and the human community to the context of the wider natural world. To make whole also means to make holy: another characteristic of a participatory worldview is that meaning and mystery are restored to human experience, so that the world is once again experienced as a sacred place. (Reason, 1994: 10)

We need to beware of inflating the notion of the spiritual to some remote end state that can be attained only after immense effort. For while the discipline of spiritual practice is important, as John Heron points out (personal communication 1997), 'simple openness to everyday participative experience, feeling that subject and object are in an inseparable seamless field of imaging and resonance – a field with infinite horizons – is itself a spiritual experience'. Meister Eckhart described the spiritual path as 'beautiful and pleasant and joyful and familiar', and as Matthew Fox asks:

> Is there a haunting sense in which the creation-centred way conjures up childhood and other periods of truth in our lives? Is it because what is beautiful and pleasant and joyful is necessarily familiar …? Is Eckhart's way a familiar way because it is non-elitist? … Eckhart learned to trust his life and own life experiences … to be spiritual is to be awake and alive – the holiness of life itself absolutely fascinated Eckhart. (Fox, 1983a: 3–4)

Nor does attention to the spiritual mean that we lose concern for the political, for our outer work – actions in the world – are grounded in our inner work. As Heron points out (1996b), just as practical knowing derives its validity from its grounding in experiential knowing, practical knowing also *consummates* our experiential knowing in worthwhile action. Eckhart tells us we cannot use the inner work as an excuse for abandoning the outer:

> We ought to get over amusing ourselves with raptures
> for the sake of a greater love
> which is to administer to what people most need
> whether spiritually
> or socially
> or physically. (Fox, 1983a: 92)

But he also points out that:

> The outward work
> will never be puny
> if the inner work
> is great.
> And the outward work
> can never be great or even good
> if the inward one is puny and of little worth. (Fox, 1983a: 99)

Fox (1983b) offers us a creation-centred spirituality which begins in the 'original blessing' of awe and delight at the beauty and richness of creation. According to Fox, Adelaide of Bath taught that if we didn't appreciate the beauty of the cosmos we deserve to be thrown out of it! And while in the Middle Ages Thomas Aquinas described God as the most beautiful thing in the universe, Descartes threw out beauty as a philosophical category for the modern age – and so we lost the notion of beauty in both philosophy and theology. Fox argues that we must reassert that the experience of wonder, awe and beauty is the basis of our experience of our participation in the cosmos – through beauty we can feel our sense of belonging.

So a participatory worldview locates the practical response to human problems in its necessary wider, spiritual context – as does Lincoln and Denzin's 'fifth moment' in qualitative research (1994). If humanity can be seen as 'nature rendered self-conscious', as Bookchin suggests (1991: 313), and humans are a part of the cosmos capable of self-awareness and self-reflection (Swimme, 1984), then human inquiry is a way through which human presence can be celebrated; as Skolimowski puts it, we need to take the courage to imagine and reach for our fullest capabilities. Thus the practical inquiry of human persons is a spiritual expression, a celebration of the flowering of humanity and of the co-creating cosmos, and as part of a sacred science is an expression of the beauty and joy of active existence.

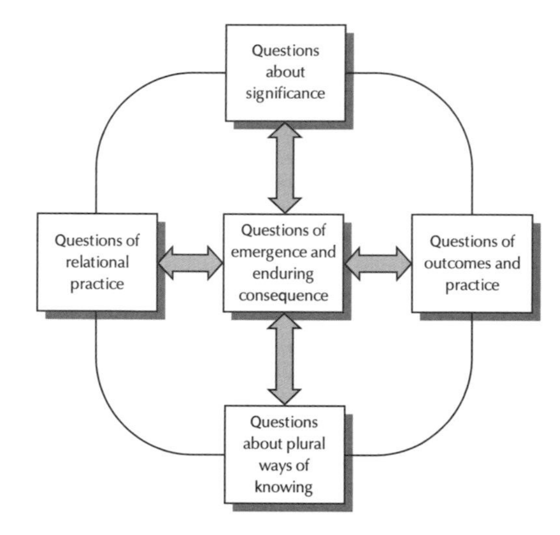

Figure 3 Questions for validity and quality in inquiry

From Participative Worldview to Quality in Inquiry

Early in this introduction we identified five characteristics of action research from our understanding of the varieties of practice in the field (Figure 1). In the previous section we have shown how these can be seen as rooted in an emergent participatory worldview (Figure 2), which we can begin to sense but cannot fully articulate. This leads us to ask five kinds of question about the validity and quality of action research practice (summarized in Figure 3), which we introduce briefly here and attend to in more depth in our concluding chapter.

Our considerations of the nature of the given cosmos, which we described as radically interconnected and evolutionary, draw our attention to the living process that is action research. Action research is best seen as an emergent, evolutionary and educational process of engaging with self, persons and communities which needs to be sustained for a significant period of time. This leads us to ask *questions about emergence and enduring consequence*.

Our emphasis on the importance of practical outcomes draws our attention to pragmatic *questions of outcomes and practice*. What are the outcomes of the research? Does it work? What are the processes of inquiry? Are they authentic/life enhancing? Our reflection on ways of knowing encourages us to ask what dimensions of an extended epistemology are emphasized in the inquiry and whether this is appropriate? It encourages us to consider the validity claims of the different forms of knowing in themselves and the relationship between different ways of knowing. These are *questions about plural ways of knowing*.

The relationship dimension draws our attention to the quality of interaction that has been developed in the inquiry and the political forms that have been developed to sustain the inquiry. These are *questions of relational practice*. How have the values of democracy been actualized in practice? What is the relationship between initiators and participants? What are the implications for infrastructure and political structures?

Finally, our questions about meaning and purpose encourage us to ask whether the inquiry process has addressed *questions about significance*. What is worthwhile? What values have been actualized in the inquiry? And at a wider level these questions invite us to connect our work to questions of spirituality, beauty – and whether we have created an inquiry process which is truly worthy of human aspiration.

Acknowledgement

We acknowledge Göran Carstadt's inspiration in our choice of the phrase 'in search of a world worthy of human aspiration'. Judi Marshall, Jack Whitehead, Lesley Treleaven, Alison Dyke and Peter Hawkins read and commented on drafts of this chapter; the proposals towards a participatory worldview were honed at a symposium sponsored by the Fetzer Institute in December 1999; the framework of the chapter was first presented and discussed at a graduate seminar in the Department of Organizational Behavior, Weatherhead School of Management, Case Western Reserve University; the quotations from the Peace and Reconciliation Commission were drawn to our attention by Ailish Byrn in her PhD dissertation. We appreciate all these contributions.

References

Abram, D. (1996) *The Spell of the Sensuous: Perception and Language in a More than Human World*. New York: Pantheon.

Bateson, G. (1972a) 'Form, Substance and Difference', in Bateson, G., *Steps to an Ecology of Mind*. San Francisco, CA: Chandler. pp. 423–40.

Bateson, G. (1972b) *Steps to an Ecology of Mind*. San Francisco, CA: Chandler.

Belenky, M., Clinchy, B., Goldberger, N. and Tarule, J. (1986) *Women's Ways of Knowing: the Development of Self, Voice, and Mind*. New York: Basic Books.

Bentz, V.M. and Shapiro, J.J. (1998) *Mindful Inquiry in Social Research*. Thousand Oaks, CA: Sage Publications.

Berman, M. (1981) *The Reenchantment of the World*. Ithaca, NY: Cornell University Press.

Berry, T. (1988) *The Dream of the Earth*. San Francisco, CA: Sierra Club.

Berry, T. (1999) *The Great Work: Our Way into the Future*. New York: Bell Tower.

Bhatt, Y. and Tandon, R. (2001) 'Citizen participation in natural resource management', in P. Reason and H. Bradbury (eds), *Handbook of Action Research: Participative Inquiry and Practice*. London: Sage Publications. pp. 301–6.

Bigwood, C. (1993) *Earth Muse: Feminism, Nature and Art*. Philadelphia, PA: Temple University Press.

Bookchin, M. (1991) *The Ecology of Freedom: the Emergence and Dissolution of Hierarchy* (revised edition). Montreal and New York: Black Rose Books.

Bradbury, H. and Liechtenstein, B. (2000) 'Relationality in organizational research: exploring the space between', *Organization Science*, 11 (5): 565–88.

Brown, L. (ed.) (1999) *State of the World 1999: a Worldwatch Institute Report on Progress Towards a Sustainable Society*. London: Earthscan.

Calás, M.B. and Smircich, L. (1999) 'Past postmodernism? Reflections and tentative directions', *Academy of Management Review*, 24 (4): 649–71.

Carr, W. and Kemmis, S. (1986) *Becoming Critical: Education, Knowledge and Action Research*. Basingstoke: Falmer Press.

Chambers, R. (1997) *Whose Reality Counts? Putting the First Last*. London: Intermediate Technology Publications.

Clarke, C.J.S. (1996) *Reality through the Looking Glass: Science and Awareness in the Postmodern World*. Edinburgh: Floris Books.

de Quincey, C. (1999) 'Radical nature and the paradox of consciousness', *ReVision*, 21 (4): 12–25.

Denzin, N.K. (1997) *Interpretive Ethnography: Ethnographic Practices for the 21st Century*. Thousand Oaks, CA: Sage Publications.

Derrida, J. (1981) *Dissemination*. Chicago, IL: University of Chicago Press.

Devall, B. and Sessions, G. (1985) *Deep Ecology: Living as if Nature Mattered*. Salt Lake City: Gibbs M. Smith.

Diamond, I. and Orenstein, G.L. (eds) (1990) *Reweaving the World: the Emergence of Ecofeminism*. San Francisco, CA: Sierra Club.

Eikeland, O. (2001) 'Action research as the hidden curriculum of the Western tradition', in P. Reason and H. Bradbury (eds), *Handbook of Action Research: Participative Inquiry and Practice*. London: Sage Publications. pp. 145–55.

Esteva, G. and Prakash, M.S. (1998) *Grassroots Post-Modernism*. London and New York: Zed Books.

Fletcher, J.K. (1998) 'Relational practice: a feminist reconstruction of work', *Journal of Management Inquiry*, 7 (2): 163–86.

Fox, M. (1983a) *Meditations with Meister Eckhart*. Santa Fe, NM: Bear and Co.

Fox, M. (1983b) *Original Blessing: a Primer in Creation Spirituality*. Santa Fe, NM: Bear and Co.

Freire, P. (1970) *Pedagogy of the Oppressed*. New York: Herder & Herder.

Gergen, K.J. (1994) *Realities and Relationships: Soundings in Social Construction*. Boston, MA: Harvard University Press.

Gergen, K.J. (1999) *An Invitation to Social Construction*. Thousand Oaks, CA: Sage Publications.

Goodwin, B. (1999) 'From control to participation via a science of qualities', *Revision*, 21 (4): 26–35.

Greenwood, D.J. and Levin, M. (1998) *Introduction to Action Research: Social Research for Social Change*. Thousand Oaks, CA: Sage Publications.

Griffin, D.R. (1998) *Unsnarling the World-Knot: Consciousness, Freedom and the Mind–Body Problem*. Berkeley, CA: University of California Press.

Guba, E.G. and Lincoln, Y.S. (1994) 'Competing paradigms in qualitative research', in N.K. Denzin and Y.S. Lincoln (eds), *Handbook of Qualitative Research*. Thousand Oaks, CA: Sage Publications. pp. 105–17.

Habermas, J. (1972) *Knowledge and Human Interests; Theory and Practice; Communication and the Evolution of Society* (trans. J.J. Shapiro). London: Heinemann.

Hall, B.L. (2001) 'I wish this were a poem of practices of participatory research', in P. Reason and H. Bradbury (eds), *Handbook of Action Research: Participative Inquiry and Practice*. London: Sage Publications. pp. 171–8.

Hall, B., Gillette, A. and Tandon, R. (eds) (1982) *Creating Knowledge: a Monopoly? – Participatory Research in Development*. New Delhi: Society for Participatory Research in Asia.

Harvey, D. (1990) *The Condition of Postmodernity*. Oxford: Blackwell.

Heron, J. (1971) *Experience and Method: an Inquiry into the Concept of Experiential Research*. Human Potential Research Project, University of Surrey, Guildford.

Heron, J. (1992) *Feeling and Personhood: Psychology in Another Key*. London: Sage Publications.

Heron, J. (1996a) *Co-operative Inquiry: Research into the Human Condition*. London: Sage Publications.

Heron, J. (1996b) 'Quality as primacy of the practical', *Qualitative Inquiry*, 2 (1): 41–56.

Heron, J. (2001) 'Transpersonal co-operative inquiry', in P. Reason and H. Bradbury (eds), *Handbook of Action Research: Participative Inquiry and Practice*. London: Sage Publications. pp. 333–9.

Heron, J. and Reason, P. (1997) 'A participatory inquiry paradigm', *Qualitative Inquiry*, 3 (3): 274–94.

Ho, M.-W. (1998) *The Rainbow and the Worm: the Physics of Organisms* (second edition). Singapore: World Scientific.

Horton, M. and Freire, P. (eds) (1990) *We Make the Road by Walking: Conversation on Education and Social Change*. Philadelphia, PA: Temple University Press.

Kuhn, T. (1962) *The Structure of Scientific Revolutions*. Chicago, IL: University of Chicago Press.

Laing, R.D. (1967) *The Politics of Experience*. New York: Ballantine Books.

Laszlo, E. (1996) *The Whispering Pond*. Rockport, MA: Element.

Laszlo, E. (2003) *The Connectivity Hypothesis: Foundations of an Integral Science of Quantum, Cosmos, Life and Consciousness*. Albany: State University of New York Press.

Lather, P. (1991) *Getting Smart: Feminist Research and Pedagogy with/in the Postmodern*. New York: Routledge.

Lincoln, Y.S. and Denzin, N.K. (1994) 'The Fifth Moment', in Y.S. Lincoln and N.K. Denzin (eds), *Handbook of Qualitative Research*. Thousand Oaks, CA: Sage Publications. pp. 575–86.

Lincoln, Y.S. and Guba, E.G. (1985) *Naturalistic Inquiry*. Beverly Hills, CA: Sage Publications.

Lincoln, Y.S. and Guba, E.G. (2000) 'Paradigmatic controversies, contradictions and emerging confluences', in N.K. Denzin and Y.S. Lincoln (eds), *Handbook of Qualitative Research* (second edition). Thousand Oaks, CA: Sage Publications. pp. 163–88.

Lukes, S. (1974) *Power: a Radical View*. London: Macmillan.

Lyotard, J.-F. (1979) *The Postmodern Condition: a Report on Knowledge* (trans. G. Bennington and B. Massumi). Manchester: Manchester University Press.

Macmurray, J. (1957) *The Self as Agent*. London: Faber and Faber.

Marshall, J. (1995) *Women Managers Moving On – Exploring Career and Life Choices*. London: International Thomson Publishing Europe.

Mumford, L. (1957) *The Transformations of Man*. London: Allen and Unwin.

Naess, A. (1987) 'Deep ecology', *Resurgence*, 123: 13.

Naess, A. (1989) *Ecology, Community and Lifestyle*. Cambridge: Cambridge University Press.

Paine, T. (1791, 1995) *Rights of Man, Common Sense, and other Political Writings*. Oxford: Oxford University Press.

Plant, J. (ed.) (1989) *Healing the Wounds: the Promise of Eco-Feminism*. London: Green Print.

Polanyi, M. (1962) *Personal Knowledge: Towards a Post-Critical Philosophy*. Chicago: University of Chicago Press.

Reason, P. (ed.) (1994) *Participation in Human Inquiry*. London: Sage Publications.

Reason, P. and Goodwin, B. (1999) 'Toward a science of qualities in organizations: lessons from complexity theory and postmodern biology', *Concepts and Transformations*, 4 (3): 281–317.

Roszak, T. (ed.) (1995) *Ecopsychology: Restoring the Earth, Healing the Mind*. San Francisco, CA: Sierra Club.

Schein, E.H. and Bennis, W. (1965) *Personal and Organizational Change through Group Methods: the Experiential Approach*. New York: Wiley.

Schwandt, T.A. (1994) 'Constructivist, interpretivist approaches to human inquiry', in N.K. Denzin and Y.S. Lincoln (eds), *Handbook of Qualitative Research*. Thousand Oaks, CA: Sage Publications. pp. 118–37.

Schwandt, T.A. (1996) 'Farewell to criteriology', *Qualitative Inquiry*, 2 (1): 58–72.

Selener, D. (1997) *Participatory Action Research and Social Change*. Ithaca, NY: Cornell Participatory Action Research Network, Cornell University.

Shotter, J. (1993) *Cultural Politics of Everyday Life: Social Construction and Knowing of the Third Kind*. Buckingham: Open University Press.

Skolimowski, H. (1993) *A Sacred Place to Dwell*. Rockport, MA: Element.

Skolimowski, H. (1994) *The Participatory Mind*. London: Arkana.

Swimme, B. (1984) *The Universe is a Green Dragon*. Santa Fe: Bear and Co.

Torbert, W.R. (1991) *The Power of Balance: Transforming Self, Society, and Scientific Inquiry*. Newbury Park, CA: Sage Publications.

Toulmin, S. (1990) *Cosmopolis: the Hidden Agenda of Modernity*. New York: Free Press.

Toulmin, S. and Gustavsen, B. (eds) (1996) *Beyond Theory: Changing Organizations through Participation*. Amsterdam: John Benjamins.

Van Maanen, J. (1995) 'Style as theory', *Organization Science*, 6 (1): 133–43.

PART ONE
GROUNDINGS

1
Theory and Practice: the Mediating Discourse

BJØRN GUSTAVSEN

CHAPTER OUTLINE

When the idea of action research was originally launched it was built on the assumption that practice can be shaped to reflect the structural properties of theory. Such a strong relationship, however, proved hard to maintain and today it is seen more as one of interdependence and mutual influence. This mutual influence must be mediated in discourse. Building on experience from Scandinavian work research, the chapter demonstrates how this discourse dynamic in itself has changed our notions of theory as well as of practice. The core contribution of research is to create relationships between actors, and arenas where they can meet in democratic dialogue.

Theory and Practice

The main pioneer of action research – Kurt Lewin – associated the idea of action research with the idea of doing experiments, albeit in the field rather than the laboratory. He required that an action research experiment must not only express theory but it must express theory in such a way that the results of the experiment can be fed directly back to the theory (Lewin et al., 1939). For this to be possible the experiment must be an expression of the theory, in principle in such a way that there is a one-to-one relationship between the concepts of the theory and the variables of the experiment. If such a direct relationship is lacking the experiment is no longer an experiment in quite the same sense. It can, of course, still be interpreted but the interpretation will be looser and more hermeneutic, leaving out much of the methodological force of a naturalist experiment; a force that emerged as a major point for Kurt Lewin.

In this way, the idea of 'action research' initially emerged out of the assumption that a theory can be rather directly expressed in action. One of the major paradoxes in the contemporary landscape is that this rather simple notion of action as some kind of direct reflection of theory is argued by very few action researchers while much *conventional* research must actually be seen as built on such an assumption. Most proponents of action research argue that theory alone has little power to create change and that there is a need for a more complex interplay between theory and practice.

But what is, more specifically, this interplay? The purpose of this chapter is to describe and analyse a specific action research tradition with a main emphasis on this issue.

Some Historical Points of Departure

In the 1960s, Norway saw the emergence of a series of field experiments with new forms of work organization, influenced by the Lewinian assumption of a strong relationship between theory and practice and seeing the action element as an extension of the idea of the experiment (Emery and Thorsrud, 1969, 1976; Gustavsen, 1996; Gustavsen and Hunnius, 1981). The Norwegian initiative was followed by similar efforts in a number of other countries, such as Sweden (Sandberg, 1982), Denmark (Agersnap, 1973), Germany (Fricke, 1975) and the USA (Duckles et al., 1977).

As pointed out by a number of participants and observers (i.e. Bolweg, 1976; Gustavsen and Hunnius, 1981; Herbst, 1974; Sandberg, 1982), these experiments were often quite successful but nevertheless led to limited diffusion. It took a long time to develop a full understanding of what the problems are with an experimental methodology but today there seems to be reasonable agreement on the following main point: using a theory-driven experimental approach implies the introduction of a new rationality in the workplace. Theory, however, is created in theoretical discourse while its use in a real-life setting implies a practical discourse and the logically structured scientific pattern of thought blocks practical discourse among those concerned (Gustavsen, 1996, 1998; Leminsky, 1997). The core point is not that the ideas – such as one kind or another of systems rationality – need to be considered wrong by the local actors. It is the very process of implementing theory which places strong restrictions on the participation of these actors. The difficulties of linking theory directly to practice were experienced in the first half of the 1970s and various new strategies emerged (for an overview, see Gustavsen, 1996). Space does not allow us to trace these developments. Instead we will turn to a theoretical perspective that came to play some role in this period; the perspective argued by Habermas in his discussion of theory and practice (1973).

Habermas perceives the creation of theory and the development of practice as rather *different* activities. While in constructing theory the aim is to reflect the truth or, with less pretensions towards being scientific, create the most adequate interpretation, the aim in developing practice is to achieve success in the real world. While a theory can certainly influence, or inform, practice and vice versa, there is no question of a *direct* relationship. The link is a discursive one where ideas, notions and elements from the theory can be considered in the development of practice but with no claims to being automatically applicable. The relationship between theory and practice can be seen as a relationship between three different but interdependent discourses – a discourse on theory, a discourse on practice and a mediating discourse on how to link them. This idea seemed quite well founded in our own experience by the early 1970s.

In seeing theory and practice as different discourses Habermas, however, goes one step further and rejects the notion of action research altogether (1973: 18). Participation in action will lock the researcher into the practical side of the equation in such a way that the ability to participate in theoretical discourse is lost. Habermas's platform in critical theory rests on the basic notion that society is ridden by extreme power and oppression, and that there is little prospect of new rational practices in the short run. A process of liberation has to start with theory, not practice. While a process of liberation cannot be a direct application of critical theory, critical theory can inform a process of enlightenment and out of this process can emerge new practices. This, of course, constituted a new challenge. Is this really a necessary conclusion? We will return to this later.

The New Focus: the Mediating Discourse

The problem of diffusing new forms of work organization throughout working life was experienced not only by researchers, but also by the labour market parties that had supported the first generation of experiments. In the early 1980s this joint concern opened up possibilities for collaboration around new approaches. In Norway as well as in Sweden the social partners decided to introduce new agreements specifically dealing with development (Gustavsen, 1985). In these agreements focus was placed not on content but on procedures: on *how to deal* with such issues as work organization and local co-operation (Ennals and Gustavsen, 1998; Gustavsen, 1992, 1996).

A core element in the Norwegian agreement was the introduction of *conferences*; meeting places for 'those concerned' where they could discuss what goals, ideas or visions they would like to pursue and how to go about doing it. In this way the mediating discourse was elevated to a core position and theory and what workplace practices to strive for were pushed more into the background.

The conference patterns introduced in Scandinavia in the 1980s are sometimes linked to the idea of 'search conference' (Emery, 1981; Martin, Chapter 14), and in actual practice there are overlapping areas. However, while the search conference was intended to discover the systems properties of the surroundings of the participants, the Norwegian dialogue conference evolved as a negation of classical procedures between the labour market parties. Ordinary negotiations are characteristically performed by representatives, over unequivocally defined objects (usually time and money) and in an adversarial fashion. In creating an agreement on development it was thought reasonable to apply the *opposite* principles: involve all concerned, accept less well-structured objects and create a co-operative setting. In this way the idea of dialogue conference emerged as a setting for discussing development and as an institutionalization of 'the mediating discourse'.

The Swedish agreement did not introduce such specific procedures, nor did it institute a set of specific bodies to carry it through. Rather, it relied on various mediating bodies, such as the R&D programmes organized by the Work Environment Fund (Oscarsson, 1997). However, much of the real development came to acquire the same characteristics. The first programme launched under the new agreement – the programme for new technology, work environment and work organization (Ford, 1987) – was not built on any specific theoretical platform but rather had as its core aim the re-establishment of co-operation between the labour market parties centrally and locally; a co-operation that had largely got lost in the politically turbulent 1970s. In the programme to follow – leadership, organization and co-operation (LOM) – the discourse idea from the Norwegian agreement was picked up and further elaborated (Gustavsen, 1992; Naschold, 1993).

The Idea of Democratic Dialogue

Within the context of the LOM programme a more elaborate set of dialogue criteria was developed (Gustavsen, 1992; Gustavsen and Engelstad, 1986):

- Dialogue is based on a principle of give and take, not one way communication.
- All concerned by the issue under discussion should have the possibility of participating.
- Participants are under an obligation to help other participants be active in the dialogue.
- All participants have the same status in the dialogue arenas.
- Work experience is the point of departure for participation.
- Some of the experience the participant has when entering the dialogue must be seen as relevant.
- It must be possible for all participants to gain an understanding of the topics under discussion.
- An argument can be rejected only after an investigation (and not, for instance, on the grounds that it emanates out of a source with limited legitimacy).
- All arguments that are to enter the dialogue must be represented by actors present.
- All participants are obliged to accept that other participants may have arguments better than their own.
- Among the issues that can be made subject to discussion are the ordinary work roles of the participants – no one is exempt from such a discussion.
- The dialogue should be able to integrate a growing degree of disagreement.
- The dialogue should continuously generate decisions that provide a platform for joint action.

Since there is a degree of resemblance between these criteria and 'the theory of communicative action' developed by Habermas (1984/1987; McCarthy, 1976), it is necessary to underline that they were not intended to be identical (Gustavsen, 1992).

First, the idea of democratic dialogue as outlined here refers to the mediating discourse, not to 'pure' theoretical or 'pure' practical discourse. It may be that the criteria for the various types of discourse can, or even have to, be merged, but when originally introduced the idea was to cover 'the ground in-between' without taking a stand on what criteria should guide the other discourses. In Habermas's conceptualization, our focus was the process of enlightenment, where theory and practice meet, not the generation of theory as such, nor the development of practical action, at least in so far as enlightenment and action can be kept apart.

A second point has to do with the relationship between theory and practice within the field of communication itself. Above, it is mentioned that Habermas breaks with the idea of a simple one-to-one relationship between theory and practice. When developing a 'theory of communicative action', however, Habermas (1984/1987) reintroduces just such a strong link through creating a theory of what is required for communication to function everyday – making certain implicit prerequisites explicit. However, given Habermas's earlier view on the relationship between theory and practice, it is not reasonable to make an exception for one type of theory: theory about how to communicate. Consequently, there was a need to see even this relationship as more open – to let the theoretical agenda be set stepwise as the new dialogues unfolded and in the light of where they brought us.

From where, then, did the above dialogue criteria come? Actually, they emerged largely out of practical experience. During the time that action research focused on implementing theory, the projects implied a lot of discussion: with managers, union representatives and workers. Initially these discussions were seen as background while the implementation of new forms of systems rationality was figural. What happened in this period was that the dialogues themselves moved into the foreground and were made subject to criteria in their own right.

While rejecting a theoretical 'foundation' of the type proposed by Habermas, his theory of communicative action could nevertheless provide inspiration and points to consider. Actually, this is, according to Shotter (1993), the way in which we should primarily use theory: not to try to establish the one and only true or right way – which theory can seldom do – but to test ideas, generate new associations and generally enrich our thoughts and actions. While a rather strong critique can be directed at Habermas's theoretical project, it remains that his perspective on communication as the constitutive force in social life is of great significance and of an immense *practical* importance. Since they were first introduced, both this author and others (McCarthy, 1996; Räftegård, 1998) have returned to consider the epistemological status of these criteria. We have progressively abandoned the idea of an unequivocal scientific-philosophical underpinning in favour of a pragmatic one, based on 'what works'. In a recent analysis (Shotter and Gustavsen, 1999) the word criteria is replaced by the term *orientational directives*, as more fitting the kind of use to which they are brought.

In addition to a set of discourse rules – generally referred to as democratic dialogue – a set of more specific design principles for conferences and similar events were also worked out (Gustavsen, 1992). We will return to some of them below.

To conclude, by the early to middle 1980s a new focus had emerged, centred on how to communicate about change rather than on what kind of rationality to strive for; in this focus, three 'poles' could be identified: a discourse on theory; a discourse on practical action; and a discourse on how to link them.

The Network Perspective

In the experimental period it was common to work with one single organization and to start change efforts within a limited area – a group area, a part of a factory, sometimes a whole factory. From this foundation, once the change was successfully established, documented and scientifically analysed, the process was intended to continue. This continuation could be horizontal, for example to include more of the production floor, and/or move upwards in the organization to encompass staff functions, higher levels of management and so on. The process had an essentially linear nature.

As we worked within the new agreement, experience taught us to break with this characteristic in two major ways: first, we moved away from the linear process inside each enterprise; and second, we stopped seeing organization development as mainly a process on the level of the single organization.

While about 450 conferences were organized in the period 1983–91, largely with individual organizations, relatively few cases of substantial change emerged. Towards the end of the decade, however, more and more of the enterprises that had used the agreement started development processes – to some extent it was possible to talk about a 'wave' emerging at this time (Ennals and Gustavsen, 1998; Gustavsen, 1993). And while each enterprise was only influenced by its own previous internal events to a limited extent, it seemed to be under quite a lot of influence from what happened in other enterprises. The fact that others were embarking on development processes seemed to count for more than 'internal dynamics'.

When organizations could recall conferences several years back it was not because of what had been said and what plans were laid at the time – this would be outdated anyway – but because of the *social relationships* that had been present during the conference. From managers, unionists and workers alike it was uniformly stressed that the possibility of meeting the others in a different forum and context was the core point. It was this potential for relating differently that was generally recalled when the development wheels started to turn faster. The need to focus more strongly on development emerged, however, in a process of interaction *between* enterprises. When the agreement on development was originally made, it was thought that the individual organization would be the main unit of development. As we recognized that processes across enterprise boundaries seemed to be important, we have directed more attention to networks and regions where enterprises from different industries work together or, if the enterprises come from the same industry, socio-geographical nearness is added as a main dimension. Nordvest-Forum, serving about 150 enterprises on the Northwest coast (Hanssen-Bauer, 1997), eventually became linked to the agreement as a member on line with branches. When the labour market parties, in co-operation with research, decided to launch a new development programme – Enterprise Development 2000 – the core emphasis was placed on networks, of which the programme works with several (Gustavsen et al., 1998).

When the LOM programme was launched in Sweden the core unit was no longer defined as a single organization but as a group of four organizations (Gustavsen, 1992). The main argument for this was not so much to make each group reach the level of 'critical mass' – which four organizations will seldom do – as to make them learn to work together. Out of such groups, or clusters, the idea was to help broader networks grow forth. Due, among other things, to the limited running time of the programme, this kind of network development could be initiated in a limited number of cases only. Some networks did, however, emerge: one in the Värmland region promoted by the University of Karlstad (Engelstad and Gustavsen, 1993; Gustavsen and Hofmaier, 1997; Räftegård, 1998); one in the Halmstad region with support from the local university (Engelstad and Gustavsen, 1993; Eriksson and Hauger, 1996; Gustavsen and Hofmaier, 1997; Lundberg and Tell, 1997); and one to promote equality between women and men in the workplace, unfolding in the Östersund area (Ekman Philips and Rehnström, 1996; Gustavsen and Hofmaier, 1997).

The most successful of these networks are characterized by a substantial number of participating organizations in combination with a number of different forms and levels of participation. The organizations range, furthermore, from industrial enterprises via service enterprises and municipalities to state agencies and civil organizations and movements. They form sub-groups and clusters within the broader network. Pluralism and manysidedness are the order rather than uniformity and single directedness.

In this way the network processes emerging out of Scandinavian work reform efforts start to resemble the patterns of economic-industrial development on a regional basis that is becoming a prominent feature in Europe. Links and bridges are starting to emerge between work reform and regional development (Ennals and Gustavsen, 1998). A major implication of this development is that 'the mediating discourse' can no longer be conducted mainly on the level of the single enterprise or workplace. This discourse acquires the major new dimension of having to be conducted on *the level of networks of different order*. But how do we do this? How do we conduct conversations with a network of organizations, and, or even a region or a country?

The Mediating Discourse and the Generation of Relationships

At this point we will draw upon the most recent generation of conferences – the so-called 'Learning region' programme in Sweden. This programme emerged in 1996 as a joint effort between the National Institute for Working Life and the Swedish Office for European Programmes, dedicated by the European Commission to lifelong learning. A series of conferences have been organized from the North to the South of Sweden where the main topic has been regional co-operation around learning and development. The more specific points of departure have been various programmes related to the European structural funds, such as for regional development, development of small and medium-sized enterprises, and the like. The implementation of these programmes presumes the existence of some kind of regional steering process in the form of co-operation between regional actors. Within the framework of the Objective 4 programme – aiming at enterprises with less than 50 employees – partnerships have been created in all the 24 Swedish administrative regions, generally including representatives for the regional authorities, regional representatives for the labour market parties, and the like. The conferences are documented in various ways: from all there are conference reports presenting the topics, the participation, the composition of the groups and the group reports. In some cases there are more thorough analyses; three of the conferences are included in a video, available with sub-titles in English, French and German.

Using this material this author has, together with John Shotter, taken a renewed look at the conferences (Shotter and Gustavsen, 1999). What are these conferences 'about' and how should they be understood?

Some of their characteristics follow from the design criteria, others follow from the ways in which the participants tend to act. In looking, for instance, at the video certain things are immediately apparent:

- the conferences function as meeting places
- where the participants are making points
- in discourse
- in groups
- with short reports in the plenary
- drawing on their experience
- in fluid and shifting relationships to others
- often seeking platforms for future co-operation
- about new practices.

It is important to note not only what is seen (or heard) but also what is not seen. Among the phenomena not seen are:

- lectures
- long stories
- told in monologue
- investigations besides the public proceedings
- feedback/evaluations from research
- mediation through a select group ('managers')
- highly original statements
- agreed-on general declarations or plans binding on all participants.

With some exceptions, the discussions take place in groups. Since the conference agenda generally consists of several topics (goals/visions, hindrances, ideas and further work), it gives rise to three to four group discussions and a corresponding number of plenaries. Since the learning regions conferences generally take place within the framework of only one – although full working day, the number of sessions has generally been limited to three. Each group discussion lasts for about one hour. Each group reports its main points, or conclusions, in the plenary: time frame about five minutes (for more detailed presentations of the conference pattern, see Gustavsen, 1992; Gustavsen and Engelstad, 1986; Shotter and Gustavsen, 1999).

With up to ten participants in each group it follows that the time allowed to each participant under the principle of equality is limited. When presenting his or her interests and experiences each participant has a limited 'window' through which to do it. There is consequently no room for long stories. Points must be formulated briefly and played into the discourse in a way that is natural and meaningful against the background given by how the discourse evolves.

Research helps to organize the event, put together the report and sometimes to give some comments. There are, however, no investigations going on in parallel to the public proceedings. Research has no other access to the participants than they have to each other. Care is taken to present comments and points in such a way that they emerge as natural elements in ongoing conversations. This underlines that research is a partner in a coalition, not a body that is to gain special knowledge or sit in judgement on the other actors. Nor does research undertake to summarize the conference, to tell 'what we have agreed on', and such like. Instead, the conferences always conclude with mutual commitments to further contacts and joint efforts between the participants. The outcome is a work agenda, not an analysis.

The conference report generally consists of the answers and statements summarizing the group discussions, plus lists of participants, divisions into groups and so forth. Modest interpretations are sometimes added, to the extent that research believes that the interpretations will help the process forwards. Beyond this, the report contains no analysis.

The Content of the Discussions

Above, the form of the discussions is outlined but what kind of content emerges within the framework of this form? As a brief illustration, some points from two group discussions emerging within a series of conferences held in Skåne, the southernmost part of Sweden, will be presented. Skåne constitutes a spearhead example of regional development, triggered off by the Øresund bridge between Malmö and Copenhagen.

In a conference on culture, one of the groups, in its response to the question of problems or hindrances, pointed at a series of differences that needed to be overcome such as between: geographical areas; state institutions and regional institutions; sectors, such as culture and economy; generations; municipalities in terms of policies and priorities; cultural institutions internally and between institutions and free actors. Even when it is reasonable to maintain institutional boundaries of the kind prevailing today, the need to improve communications was emphasized, such as across institutional boundaries, between interest groups, and so forth.

In a conference on transport and ecology, the following proposals for practical action were put forward from one of the groups: establish a local radio and TV station; get more 'regional news' into the media; create new dialogue arenas where representatives from different types of transport – railways, buses, bridges, ferries, roads, and so on – meet to discuss co-operation and interplay; promote better co-operation between the municipalities (there are altogether 33 in the region) in their planning; improve on co-operation between enterprises/branches and the regional political-administrative bodies; improve on co-operation between the regional authorities and the units within each municipality which are responsible for promotional activities in relation to enterprises and business; improve on co-operation between the regional politicians and the various agencies for environmental protection; create a system of specific agreements for actors who are willing to undertake responsibilities within the prevailing plans for protection and improvement of the environment; the co-ordination of all public transport in terms of connections, travel information, prices and ticket sales.

A striking aspect is that there is no unified, 'total' picture to be found, be it on the side of the 'diagnosis' or of the 'remedies'. As the points appear, they do not reflect any theoretically founded order. In a sense this is hardly surprising, since the rather low-profile kind of role that research assigns for itself is not intended to put much of a theoretical mark on the content of the discourse. One may, of course, imagine introducing a 'theoretical discourse' after the material has been generated, to give it an order after the event. Since research does not have access to other material than that which is publicly generated, the process of interpretation would, however, soon stop for lack of input. But are there other ways of relating to the material? Maybe there is no need for an order of the kind we traditionally tend to seek. Perhaps there is an order, but of a different kind?

What Kind of Order?

It is often assumed that the main purpose of a discourse is to get the participants to 'look in the same way' at something: a situation, an understanding, a plan of action. In Table 1.1, a conference with this aim is called a 'single product event' while its opposite is called a 'relationship-building event', a notion that will be further developed below.

In so far as it is meaningful to have a common story, single truth or common systems definition, it must also be meaningful not to have one, but to have a plurality. The same pertains to goals, or vision: to the extent that it is meaningful to have a shared vision, it is equally meaningful to have a number of visions. It may be, as Bakhtin pointed out (1984), that there are generalities collectively constituted in the sense that the sum total of all the contributions make up a coherent whole without any single individual being able to mentally grasp this whole. In both cases the right-hand column will be the expression. Consequently, a discourse fitting the right-hand column does not have to be a step on the way towards a unified understanding and a single master plan. Instead, it can, in itself, be the core activity. If we search for ability to process ideas along many lines rather than one, for overlapping networks rather than one-dimensional alliances, for giving a place to all actors rather than to 'those who agree (with me)', it is seen that the conference pattern indicated above is *the main constructive activity*. What emerges out of the event is an improved

Table 1.1 *Schematic comparison of a single product event and a relationship-building event*

Single product event	Relationship-building event
Discover the systems properties of a common environment.	Recognize a plurality of environments and environmental characteristics.
Discover the truth.	Create more potential for identifying and interpreting experiences.
Create a joint vision.	See what visions are present.
Agree on a plan.	Explore the possibilities for carrying through a number of plans.
Create a strategic alliance.	Create overlapping networks with the capacity for making real a number of plans simultaneously.
Organize a one-dimensional feedback and learning process.	See how different actors and actor groups can pursue their own learning needs while at the same time helping others to pursue their needs.
Create one single grand story that can be shared by all.	Create openings for a plurality of stories that can be linked to each other in different ways.

capacity for developing ideas, pursuing them into action and generally creating a rich landscape of different institutions, organizations and activities that can enter into fruitful and complementary relationships to each other.

In so far as there is an order, it is an *order of relationships*; an order that can be described in terms of who knows who, what work relationship structures exist, what joint arenas are available, and the like. The density and richness of relationships decide the capacity for developing and processing ideas, preferably many at the same time, the capacity for joining forces around major efforts when need be, and so on.

Table 1.1 *Schematic comparison of a single product event and a relationship-building event:* Single product event. Relationship-building event. Discover the systems properties of a common environment. Recognize a plurality of environments and environmental characteristics. Discover the truth. Create more potential for identifying and interpreting experiences. Create a joint vision. See what visions are present. Agree on a plan. Explore the possibilities for carrying through a number of plans. Create a strategic alliance. Create overlapping networks with the capacity for making real a number of plans simultaneously. Organize a one-dimensional feedback and learning process. See how different actors and actor groups can pursue their own learning needs while at the same time helping others to pursue their needs. Create one single grand story that can be shared by all. Create openings for a plurality of stories that can be linked to each other in different ways.

Against this background, the main purpose of the statements emerging in the conferences *is not to provide elements in an overall analysis but to present oneself.* The actors are in a situation where they must explore new relationships, find new partners, allies and co-actors. And how to do this? This is largely done through making statements that function towards declaring interests and defining issues and fields on which the participants want to focus. Participants make themselves known to the other participants through introducing points of concern. These points constitute something to which the others can relate. The development of these relationships can move along different trajectories. Sometimes people find new partners who share 'the same interest'. In other cases the sharing can be based on complementarity of interests: a businessperson can, for instance, pair up with an educator in an effort to improve on work-relevant competence. In further cases, actors agree to pursue interests that are completely new to them all, such as business actors agreeing to strengthen cultural dimensions so as to improve the quality of life in the region and its attractiveness as a business community. Possibilities for combinations of this kind are almost endless.

The need to declare interest, tell the others who 'I am', also explains another aspect of the lists of themes presented above: their lack of deep originality. They represent intelligent reflections on hindrances and development measures but hardly reflections or actions that are not argued and promoted in many other contexts as well, for instance in many of the now mushrooming efforts to strengthen regional relationships in Europe in general. Would it not have been more interesting if something had emerged that nobody had thought about before?

Participants confront a number of different contexts in terms of discussion partners. It is common, for instance, to conduct the discussion on visions in homogeneous groups, on hindrances in diagonal groups (people with different types of roles from different organizations, such as managers in one organization meeting workers in another), ideas in freely composed groups and what to do in the future in groups composed of those who need to work together after the conference. (With three sessions these compositions are to some extent modified.) In addition there are breaks for coffee and meals which are structured in such a way that people are encouraged to move around. Participants will, in principle, move through a number of discourses and each discourse takes place within a narrow time frame. This calls for simple and easily understood ways of presenting one's points. In building relationships, the issue is not to be original but to be understood. The understanding must, furthermore, be created within the framework of narrow 'windows'.

Obviously, one single conference can generally not create a major and forceful development process, be it on the level of a network of organizations or a region. There is generally a need for more – in terms, for instance, of more conferences cross-sectionally and in sequence, and for many other types of activity. The point, however, is that these measures generally have to be of the same *type* as the conferences: they need to make pluralism and the number of links and relationships grow; they need to strengthen the ability to process numerous plans and ideas simultaneously; they need to keep up and improve on the ability to form continuously new configurations of actors and relationships to keep up the dynamics. Ultimately, the success of the kind of action research described here is linked to our ability to help initiate and support processes that become long-term, self-sustaining and include a continuously growing number of actors and constellations of actors. The co-operation between research and the labour market parties in Norway – spanning close to 35 years – can be said to be of this kind, although the development has not been linear. To what extent the learning regions programme in Sweden, used as an example in this chapter, will become such a movement is not clear at the time. However, a more detailed analysis of these aspects falls beyond the framework of this chapter. (Some of the long-term lines of evolution in the interplay between research and the labour market actors can be found in Ennals and Gustavsen, 1998; and Gustavsen, 1992, 1996.)

Concluding Perspectives

When we compare this to the original focus of action research – the content of work roles, the systems properties of work organization, and the like – the change to a main focus on relationships is quite radical. Although research is welcome to make its contributions within fields like job design or the definition of an optimal traffic flow across the Øresund bridge, these issues are not core ones in the kind of action research described above. Instead, the focus is on those dimensions of social organization that decide the *capacity* for initiating, developing and putting ideas into effect.

Given that capacity is thought to be linked to scale – at least up to the level of what is today commonly referred to as 'region' – there is an emphasis on magnitude, or 'mass' – even 'critical mass' if one likes. However, the mass or scale dimension must not be interpreted as 'a mass of people' flocking around the same solutions to problems of how to organize, be it workplaces, enterprises or regions. Instead, mass, or scale, refers to the number of actors and relationships, to the complexities and qualities of these relationships, and to the ability to develop and make real a broad range of ideas in parallel. If there is any meta-idea that can be said to guide this kind of development it is the idea of being able to maximise the number and quality of the ideas that can be created and made real. In this way, these developments differ from the efforts to create diffusion networks around a specific form of systems rationality which characterize the socio-technical school of workplace development, at least in its original version (i.e. Emery and Thorsrud, 1976; Trist, 1982).

They differ, furthermore, from efforts at creating scale through working with, say, a number of small groups and then expecting the patterns worked out in these group contexts to be made subject to diffusion through the ordinary channels of conventional research, such as the written word and/or the education system. In the approach outlined above, the spearhead of the diffusion process is the continued expansion of network relationships between people, that is a new practical order, not a theory about what practical order should be.

In principle, the approach outlined here makes no distinction between 'primary events' and 'later diffusion'. We are talking about waves of continuous development where all events have the same status: in certain respects they are alike, in others they differ. One consequence of this is that it becomes of limited interest to have a very detailed description of some of the events in the expectation that what we learn can in some way or another be 'carried over' into other events to which we can, as researchers, have a less detailed approach. We will, for instance, not follow Argyris and colleagues (1985) into very detailed observations of the processes unfolding between the action researcher and small groups of co-actors. Instead, what we need to handle are processes with numerous events, somewhat diffusely shaped and linked to each other while still maintaining a long-term relationship-building perspective.

A main reason why a high degree of detailing of specific events is of limited interest is that dialogue situations are 'relational-responsive' events where each event has a strong constructive side to it. No event is a replication of a previous event, no new event is a printout of a theory constructed ahead of the event. However, for relational-responsive processes (with associated new social constructions to appear) to be possible, people need to be exposed to each other in relationship-building events.

If we return to Habermas's notion of three discourses, the relative weight between them has been radically shifted. Action research, as it originally emerged with actors like Kurt Lewin and the early Tavistock Group, was like raids into reality performed to verify grand theory. One may ask if there is much theory and associated research left in the position sketched above. Processes like those outlined here are essentially driven by an influx of practical problems and challenges to which research has to respond as well as it can. Maybe Habermas was essentially right in rejecting action research? If we really want to become involved in socially significant practical action with demands for long time horizons, for relating to numerous actors and engaging in highly complex activities, perhaps the notion of linking such involvement to research as traditionally conceived is futile.

Compared to a social science that aims at telling people what social facts 'exist' and why, there are some obvious differences. One is the strong emphasis on the setting in which research tells whatever it has to tell: these settings are 'moments of dialogue' where research is one of the actors and not a supreme authority. Another is to express the contribution of research through the design of the dialogue process itself.

It seems a reasonable assumption that if the social sciences want to help construct the future and not only interpret the past, we can hardly avoid embarking on a course which will, in important respects, differ from the descriptive-analytic tradition. What this means for such notions as 'research', 'science' and 'action research' is largely an open question. It may be, furthermore, that one should not seek general answers to this question. Embarking on general reflections may easily lead into just the terrain that should be avoided, the terrain where action research immediately comes under fire from the proponents of analytically generated decontextualized statements. Instead, issues like what kind of theory can be generated and what kind of role can research play may have to be answered in relational-responsive terms, that is from the context where each specific process of action research goes on. Shifting from a theory-driven way of working to a practice-driven way may imply facing and settling numerous questions on a new basis.

When leaving the assumption that there is one single, 'best theory', a question often emerging is: Do we then become complete relativists? Even with its limitations, do we not need theory to give at least some indication concerning the best and most preferable way to go? This was argued in the introductory comments of the editors of the special issue of *Human Relations* on constructivism (1998, no. 3), which contained an article by this author arguing some of the above points (Gustavsen, 1998). This argument builds on the misunderstanding that the ultimate choice concerning where to go and what to be is a *theoretical* issue. Looking at the history of theories – such as the role of violence in Marxism, the empty 'pattern variables' of Parsonian functionalism or the crude manipulation programme in Skinnerism, to mention but some examples – it is easily seen that we cannot let our choice be guided by *any* theory. The theory to guide our basic choices must fill some criteria beyond claiming to be a theory. But what criteria derived from where? It is the view of this author that ultimately these choices are questions of *practice*, not of theory. Our 'first choice' has to pertain to what kind of practices we will pursue in our constructive tasks, of whatever kind (Rorty, 1992). Such a choice does not, however, have to be purely subjective with a basis in individual feelings and preferences. If our purpose is to build social relationships that can embody a principle of equality for all participants, the choice that offers itself is *democracy*, taken as a set of historically validated practices that we can enter into and make our own. If there is a need for a 'foundation', democracy is, as foundations go, as good as any philosophical or scientific one. Actually, what made enlightenment possible was not the recognition that 'cogito ergo sum', nor that two parallel lines never cross, but the recognition that unless people can relate in a democratic way to each other, no new ideas, no just causes, or indeed any science, be it social or other, are possible.

Note

Thanks are due to Hilary Bradbury and Peter Reason for ideas and suggestions concerning content, as well as language and style of presentation, and to Otto Scharmer for critical but friendly comments on some of the main points of the chapter.

References

Agersnap, F. (1973) *Samarbejdsforsög i jernindustrien*. Copenhagen: Foreningenaf Verkstedfunktionrer i Danmark/Centralorganisationen af Metalarbejdere i Danmark/Sammensludningen af Arbejdsivere indenfor Jern-og Metalindustrien i Danmark.

Argyris, C., Putnam, R. and Smith, D.M. (1985) *Action Science: Concepts, Methods and Skills for Research and Intervention*. San Fransisco, CA: Jossey-Bass.

Bakhtin, M.M. (1984) *Problems of Dostoevsky's Poetics*. Minneapolis, MN: University of Minnesota Press.

Bolweg, J.F. (1976) *Job Design and Industrial Democracy: the Case of Norway*. Leiden: Nijhoff.

Duckles, M.M., Duckles, R. and Maccoby, M. (1977) 'Process of change at Bolivar', *Journal of Applied Behavioral Science*, 13 (3): 387–99.

Ekman Philips, M. and Rehnström, K. (1996) 'Workplace development, gender and communicative competence', in S. Toulmin and B. Gustavsen (eds), *Beyond Theory: Changing Organizations through Participation*. Amsterdam: John Benjamins. pp. 53–66.

Emery, F.E. (1981) 'Searching for common ground', in F.E. Emery (ed.), *Systems Thinking*. London: Penguin. pp. 5–22.

Emery, F.E. and Thorsrud, E. (1969) *Form and Content in Industrial Democracy*. London: Tavistock Publications.

Emery, F.E. and Thorsrud, E. (1976) *Democracy at Work*. Leiden: Nijhoff.

Engelstad, P.H. and Gustavsen, B. (1993) 'A Swedish network development for implementing a national work reform strategy', *Human Relations*, 46 (2): 219–48.

Ennals, R. and Gustavsen, B. (1998) *Work Organisation and Europe as a Development Coalition*. Amsterdam: John Benjamins.

Eriksson, K. and Hauger, M. (1996) 'Workplace development and research: two examples', in S. Toulmin and B. Gustavsen (eds), *Beyond Theory: Changing Organizations through Participation*. Amsterdam: John Benjamins. pp. 31–40.

Ford, W. (1987) 'The Swedish development programme for new technology, working life and management', *Australian Bulletin of Labour*, 3: 254–70.

Fricke, W. (1975) *Arbeitsorganisation und Qualifikation*. Bonn: Neue Gesellschaft.

Gustavsen, B. (1985) 'Technology and collective agreements. Some recent Scandinavian developments', *Industrial Relations Journal*, 16 (3): 34–42.

Gustavsen, B. (1992) *Dialogue and Development*. Assen: van Gorcum.

Gustavsen, B. (1993) 'Creating productive structures: the role of research and development', in F. Naschold, R.E. Cole, B. Gustavsen, and H. van Beinum, *Constructing the New Industrial Society*. Assen: van Gorcum. pp. 133–68.

Gustavsen, B. (1996) 'Development and the social sciences: an uneasy relationship', in S. Toulmin and B. Gustavsen (eds), *Beyond Theory: Changing Organizations through Participation*. Amsterdam: John Benjamins. pp. 5–30.

Gustavsen, B. (1998) 'From experiments to network building: trends in the use of research for reconstructing working life', *Human Relations*, 51 (3): 431–48.

Gustavsen, B. and Engelstad, P.H. (1986) 'The design of conferences and the evolving role of democratic dialogue in changing working life', *Human Relations*, 39 (2): 101–16.

Gustavsen, B. and Hunnius, G. (1981) *New patterns of work reform: the case of Norway*. Oslo: The University Press.

Gustavsen, B. and Hofmaier, B. (1997) *Nätverk som utvecklingsstrategi*. Stockholm: SNS Förlag.

Gustavsen, B., Colbjörnsen, T. and Pålshaugen, Ö. (eds) (1997) *Development Coalitions in Working Life. The 'Enterprise Development 2000' Program in Norway*. Amsterdam: John Benjamins.

Gustavsen, B., Hofmaier, B., Ekman Philips, M. and Wikman, A. (1996) *Concept-driven Development and the Organisation of the Process of Change*. Amsterdam: John Benjamins.

Habermas, J. (1973) *Theory and Practice*. London: Polity Press.

Habermas, J. (1984/1987) *The Theory of Communicative Action* (Vols. I–II). London: Polity Press.

Hanssen-Bauer, J. (1997) 'Networking to learn in Nordvest-Forum: optimizing the earning cycle of a regional learning network organization through action research', in B. Gustavsen, T. Colbjörnsen and Ö. Pålshaugen (eds), *Development Coalitions in Working Life: The 'Enterprise Develpment 2000' Program in Norway*. Amsterdam: John Benjamins. pp. 113–32.

Herbst, P.G. (1974) *Socio-technical Design: Strategies in Multi-disciplinary Research*. London: Tavistock.

Leminsky, G. (1997) 'On the relationship between social science, participation processes and changes in industrial work in Germany: observations from a trade-union perspective', *Concepts and Transformation*, 2 (3): 255–68.

Lewin, K. (1946) 'Action research and minority problems', *Journal of Social Issues*, 34–6.

Lewin, K., Lippitt, R. and White, R.K. (1939) 'Patterns of aggressive behavior in experimentally created social climates', *Journal of Social Psychology*, 10: 271–99.

Lundberg, L. and Tell, M. (1997) 'From practice to practice: on the development of a network of small and medium sized enterprises', *Concepts and Transformation*, 2 (1): 33–41.

McCarthy, T. (1976) *The Critical Theory of Jürgen Habermas*. Cambridge, MA: MIT Press.

McCarthy, T. (1996) 'Pragmatizing communicative reason', in S. Toulmin and B. Gustavsen (eds), *Beyond Theory: Changing Organizations through Participation*. Amsterdam: John Benjamins. pp. 159–78.

Naschold, F. (1993) 'Organization development: national programmes in the context of international competition', in F. Naschold, R.E. Cole, B. Gustavsen and H. van Beinum, *Constructing the New Industrial Society*. Assen: van Gorcum. pp. 3–120.

Oscarsson, B. (1997) *25 år för arbetslivetsförnyelse*. Stockholm: Rådet för Arbetslivsforskning.

Räftegård, C. (1998) *Pratet som demokratiskt verktyg*. Gothenburg: Gidlunds Förlag.

Rorty, R. (1992) 'The intellectuals at the end of socialism', *Yale Review*, 50: 1–16.

Sandberg, T. (1982) *Work Organization and Autonomous Groups*. Lund: Gleerup.

Shotter, J. (1993) *Conversational Realities*. London. Sage.

Shotter, J. and Gustavsen, B. (1999) *The Role of Dialogue Conferences in the Development of Learning Regions: Doing from within our lives together what we cannot do apart*. Stockholm: The Centre for Advanced Studies in Leadership, Stockholm School of Economics.

Trist, E.L. (1982) 'The evolution of socio-technical systems as a conceptual framework and as an action research program', in X. van de Ven and W.F. Jouce (eds), *Perspectives on Organization Design and Behavior*. New York: Wiley. pp. 58–71.

2

Participatory (Action) Research in Social Theory: Origins and Challenges

ORLANDO FALS BORDA

CHAPTER OUTLINE

The Majority World origins of participatory action research and subsequent conceptual and methodological developments are recalled. Tensions between theory/practice, subject/object and knowledge/reason are resolved on the basis of a philosophy of life committed to social renovation for justice. The quest for an alternative research paradigm is linked to postmodern liberationist perspectives. Some emergent tasks are identified which lead towards bridging the gap between academic science and popular wisdom which is a basic concern for PAR practitioners.

The last three decades witnessed a deliberate transition in the way many intellectuals have seen the relation between theory and practice. The well-known academic insistence on value-neutrality and aloofness in investigation, the incidence of problems in real life, plus the overwhelming recurrence of structural crises almost everywhere, made it compulsory to move on and take a more definite personal stand regarding the evolution of societies. These tensions led us to envisage knowledge and techniques effectively committed to social and political action in order to induce needed transformations. Conditions for such tasks were readily found in poor, underdeveloped regions where there was blatant economic exploitation and human/cultural destruction. Of course this tragic situation has continued.

This chapter is an attempt to describe the intellectual quest involved in those efforts from the standpoint of national groups of concerned scholars, mostly social scientists, the present author among them. Looking retrospectively, I will try to describe some of the main ways by which we converged into a participatory action methodology which at the same time aspired to be a fulfilling way of life. I will also point out some of the challenges that emerged from our World Congress which met in 1997 at Cartagena, Colombia.

1970: a Crucial Year

The year 1970 was the first in a series of turning points for those of us (mostly in sociology, anthropology, education and theology) who were increasingly preoccupied with life conditions which appeared unbearable in communities around us. We took for granted that these conditions were produced by the spread of capitalism and universalistic modernization which were destroying the cultural and biophysical texture of rich and diverse social structures well known and dear to us. We just could not be blind or silent when we were witnessing – and suffering – the collapse of positive values and attitudes towards humankind and nature.

This seemed to require a radical critique and reorientation of social theory and practice. Our conceptions of Cartesian rationality, dualism and 'normal' science were challenged, as we could not find answers or supports from universities and other institutions which had formed us professionally. Therefore, as we became more and more unsatisfied with our training and with our teaching, many of us broke the shackles and left the academies. During the course of the year 1970 some of us started to formalize alternative institutions and procedures for research and action focused on local and regional problems involving emancipatory educational, cultural and political processes.

Efforts at institutional reconstruction of this type went on independently and almost simultaneously in the different continents, without any one of us being aware of what our colleagues were doing. It was like telepathy induced by the urgency for understanding the tragic, unbalanced world being shaped, and by the stimulation of recent revolutions. Among those efforts of 1970 which had considerable effect in our subsequent work with Participatory (Action) Research (I will refer to it here interchangeably as P(A)R or PR), I can readily recall the following:

- The birth of Bhoomi Sena (Land Army) in Maharashtra, India, with a peaceful-disobedience land take-over led by Kaluram, a social scientist who never finished school but who helped in articulating the basic principles of PR (De Silva et al., 1979).[1]
- The establishment of one of Colombia's first NGOs, the Rosca Foundation for Research and Social Action, founded by a group of social scientists who had quit university posts and were proceeding to co-operate with poor peasants and Indians organized to fight *latifundia* (Fals Borda, 1979–86).[2]
- The completion of a five-year participant immersion project in Bunju village in Tanzania by Finnish scholar Marja-Liisa Swantz, which opened the gate to consider alternative ways of doing social research in Africa and other parts of the world (Swantz, 1986).[3]
- The civil resistance, underground organization in Brazil that facilitated reading, in manuscript form, Paulo Freire's classic work, *Pedagogy of the Oppressed* (1970), before it was published abroad during the same year. The exiled Paulo found an intellectual home at IDAC Documentation Centre at the World Council of Churches, Geneva, Switzerland, with educators Rosisca and Miguel Darcy de Oliveira.[4]
- Like in Brazil, in Mexico during the same year Guillermo Bonfil and a group of colleagues led critical operations inside the National Autonomous University to revise the role of anthropology (Bonfil, 1970; Warman et al., 1970).[5] Another one of those critics, Rodolfo Stavenhagen, was in Geneva at the Institute of Labour Studies finishing his epoch-making essay on 'Decolonialising applied social sciences', and getting ready to return to his country to found the innovative Institute for Popular Culture (Stavenhagen, 1971).[6]

Besides these dispersed efforts, in Paris, Geneva and Mexico there appeared during the same year, supporting materials on 'engagement' (commitment), subversion, heresy, liberation and the political crisis. They came out in the journal *Aportes*, in the Foyer John Knox lecture series, and in the new editorial house 'Nuestro Tiempo' (Agulla, 1970; Fals Borda, 1970a, 1970b, 1970c; Warman et al., 1970).[7] Not coincidentally, in the aftermath of the 1968 student revolts, well-known scholars like the members of the Frankfurt School, and Tom Bottomore, Henri Lefebvre and Eric Hobsbawm continued to push for change and challenged established institutions.

Especially noteworthy for us was the 1970 edition at the University of Minnesota of Paul K. Feyerabend, *Against Method*. This book, by a distinguished colleague of Thomas Kuhn (recognized for his work on the notion of paradigm shifts), gave additional documentary support for efforts at socio-political transformation in our respective societies, for its daring theses on the usefulness of anarchism to rebuild epistemology and to furnish a new base for scientific practice.

Some Initial Concerns

Soon after 1970, it became clear that the initial P(A)R 'crowd' was looking for new conceptual elements to guide fieldwork. We wanted to go beyond our tentative steps with social psychology (Lewin), Marxism (Lukács), anarchism (Proudhon, Kropotkin), phenomenology (Husserl), and classical theories of participation (Rousseau, Owen, Mill). But action or participation alone were not enough. We also felt that we had to continue to respect the immanent validity of critical methodology which implies one logic of scientific investigation, as Gadamer (1960) taught us. We wanted to perform these tasks with the same seriousness of purpose and cultivated discipline to which traditional university research has aspired.

Some urges in this regard were already in the air during the 1970s, from which our initial concerns came. Besides establishing a rigorous pertinent science, we also wanted to pay attention to ordinary people's knowledge; we were willing to question fashionable meta-narratives; we discarded our learned jargon so as to communicate with everyday language even with plurivocal means; and we tried innovative cognitive procedures like doing research work with collectivities and local groups so as to lay sound foundations for their empowerment. With the advantage of hindsight we can now say that we somehow anticipated postmodernism. At the time of our endeavours thinkers of this stream were just warming up to the subject. I believe we went beyond them in trying to articulate discourses to practical observations and experiences in the field. This has been a crucial difference from them.

From those practical concerns three broad challenges arose which were related to the scientific deconstruction and emancipatory reconstruction that we were trying to do. The first one touched on the relations between science, knowledge and reason; the second one, on the dialectics of theory and practice; and the third one on the subject/object tension. I will now shortly describe each one of these challenges and our attempts to face them.

On science, knowledge and reason

To deal with this challenge we began by questioning the fetish-like idea of science as truth which had been transmitted to us as a cumulative, linear complex of confirmed rules and absolute laws. We started to appreciate in fact that science is socially constructed, therefore that it is subject to reinterpretation, revision and enrichment. Although this may sound obvious, we postulated that its main criterion should be to obtain knowledge useful for what we judged to be worthy causes. Hence the painful confirmation of our own shortcomings for such a task, and the hopeful discovery of other types of knowledge from unrecognized worthy sources like the rebel, the heretical, the indigenous, and the common folk.

If we could discover a way to bring about a convergence between popular thought and academic science, we could gain both a more complete and a more applicable knowledge – especially by and for the underprivileged classes which were in need of scientific support. This convergence we found both possible and convenient. Intellectual harmonization was eased by appealing to those pioneers who had deviated somewhat from logical empiricism, positivism and/or functionalism. Thus from Kurt Lewin and Sol Tax we took their triangular concept of 'action research' (AR). From Daniel P. Moynihan's report on poverty for the Johnson Administration in the United States (1969; cf. Birnbaum, 1971) we learned that action research could be relevant for black communities and to do 'subaltern studies', while American educator Myles Horton struggled together with coal workers in Appalachia to found the Highlander Research and Education Center, a future bastion of PR (Lewis, 1997, Chapter 24; Horton and Freire, 1990).[8]

For discussing the evasive problem of purpose in science and knowledge we started with the concepts of rationality transmitted since the seventeenth century. There were Newton's operational rationality and Descartes' instrumental reason with which to understand and control nature. This had an implicit self-objective trend later identified with scientism. But on the other hand, there were Bacon's and Galileo's acknowledgements of practice and community needs to justify the existence of science and to explain the functions of everyday life. The two procedures are equally subject to cause-and-effect processes. They can be brought together; in fact, popular knowledge has always been a source of formal learning. Thus academic accumulation plus people's wisdom became an important theoretical guideline for our movement. This rule did not imply to give a blanket recognition to any infallibility for the people's wisdom. We rather tried to make a critical recovery of the popular and not to fall into the trap of populism.

We also confirmed our hunch that this cognitive process had an ethical strain. Instrumental rationality, by so often by-passing common life, has accumulated a deadly potential that could lead to genocide or world destruction, as we have seen in our century. Regular scientists may discover ways to travel to the moon, but their priorities and personal values may not permit them to solve the messy problems of the poor woman who has to walk each day for water for her home. The former is of primary interest for technical development as such; the latter is one of the persistent expressions of inhumanity. We therefore declared that the common people deserved to know more about their own life conditions in order to defend their interests, than do other social classes which monopolized knowledge, resources, techniques and power; in fact we should pay attention to knowledge production just as much as the usual insistence on material production, thus tilting the scales towards justice for the underprivileged.

In this way, science appeared in need of a moral conscience, and reason strived to be enriched with sentiment and feeling. Head and heart would have to work together. These challenges could not be resolved except with a personal ethical stand, with a balanced handling of the ideal and the possible, and with a holistic epistemology. Arguments related to efforts towards the construction of a more satisfactory scientific paradigm are explained below.

On theory and practice

As we understood more clearly how popular knowledge could be congruent with the heritage of academic science, we experienced the practical necessity to challenge the prophylactic definitions of 'commitment' which we had inherited. We felt that colleagues who claimed to work with 'neutrality' or 'objectivity' supported willingly or unwillingly the status quo, impairing full understanding of the social transformations in which we were immersed or which we wanted to stimulate. We rejected the academic tradition of using – and often exploiting – research and fieldwork mainly for career advancement. These preoccupations implied two painful, difficult and somewhat dangerous stages: (1) we needed to decolonize ouselves, that is, to discover the reactionary traits and ideas implanted in our minds and behaviours mostly by the learning process; and (2) to search for a more satisfactory value structure around praxis to give support and meaning to our work without forgetting scientific rules.

Our *praxis-inspired commitment* found bases in the iconoclastic presence and actions of Third World leaders like the sociologist-priest Camilo Torres in Colombia, an example of the 'moral subversive'; educator Paulo Freire and his 'dialogical conscientization' model in Brazil; Mahatma Gandhi and his practice of non-violent resistance in India; and Julius Nyerere, as the champion of 'ujamaa' policies for communities in need of justice and progress in Tanzania.

We learned that we were not alone in this practical struggle for social transformation. Besides the pioneering work of socialists like Peruvian José Carlos Mariátegui and Colombian Ignacio Torres Giraldo, in Latin America we reviewed the pertinent production of scholars like Brazil's L.A. Costa Pinto on resistance to change, and Mexico's Pablo González Casanova on the concept of exploitation. In Africa, economist Samir Amin stood out for his analyses of imperialism, as well as for some unique experiences on 'recherche-action' in Senegal.[9]

One specific problem, already alluded to, was rooted in the tendencies towards self-objectivity in the sciences. Scientism and technology, if left to themselves, could produce a mass of redundant information as happened in the USA with positivists, functionalists and empiricists gone berserk accumulating data to explain social integration. We tried instead to theorize and obtain knowledge enriched through direct involvement, intervention or insertion in processes of social action. This was a solution which eased the cyclical separation between theory and practice. It seemed also possible to rescue the utopian, active traditions of sociological founders like Saint-Simon, Fourier and Comte, as well as to learn from nineteenth-century socio-political movements like literacy, co-operativism, Chartism, feminism, and organized labour.

The contingent of praxis-committed popular educators and social workers became strategic at this point in our intellectual development. Following Freire's and Stenhouse's leads on the need to combine research and teaching and transcend pedagogical routines for the achievement of justice, ease of communication, and cultural awareness, Canada's International Council for Adult Education (ICAE) – under the leadership of Budd Hall – organized a PR network with nodes in Toronto, New Delhi, Dar-es-Salaam, Amsterdam and Santiago, and published the influential magazine *Convergence*. Almost simultaneously, at Deakin University in Australia, a group of professors headed by Stephen Kemmis started to work with Yothu-Yindi Aborigines. Seminal ideas like the PR 'spiral', the 'reflection action rhythm' and 'emancipatory research' resulted from their practice (Carr and Kemmis, 1986).

Finally, it was Bacon who solved for us again the theoretical tensions created by direct action and the primacy of the practical. In his 1607 booklet on 'Thoughts and Conclusions' we read: 'In natural philosophy, practical results are not only a way to improve conditions but also a guarantee for truth ... Science must be recognised by its works (like faith in religion). Truth is revealed and established more through the testimony of actions than through logic or even observation'. Thus we went ahead, adopting the guidelines that practice is determinant in the praxis-theory binomial, and that knowledge should be for the improvement of practice as emphasized by conscientizing educators.

On subject and object

We were careful to not extend to the social domain the positivist distinction between subject and object that is possible to establish in the natural sciences, and to avoid the commodification of human phenomena, as occurs in the traditional research experience and 'development' policies. Without denying immanent dissimilarities in social structures, it seemed counterproductive for our work to regard the researcher and the researched, the 'experts' and the 'clients' or 'targets' as two discrete, discordant or antagonistic poles. Rather, we had to consider them both as real 'thinking-feeling persons' ('sentipensantes') whose diverse views on the shared life experience should be taken jointly into account.

A resolution of this tension implied looking for what Agnes Heller (1989) called 'symmetric reciprocity',[10] for mutual respect and appreciation among participants, and also between humans and nature, in order to arrive at a subject/subject horizontal relationship. Moreover, the resolution of this tension was another way of defining authentic 'participation' away from liberal manipulative versions – like the dominant one offered by political scientists, for example Samuel Huntington – and as a manner of combining different kinds of knowledge. If applied in earnest, this participatory philosophy could produce personal behavioural changes as well as deep social/collective transformations and political movements, for example popular participation movements recognized by Colombia's new 1991 constitution.

All of this of course had practical consequences in our research tasks. Schedules or questionnaires, for example, had to be conceived and crafted differently, with full participation of the interviewees from the very beginning. Collective, group research became possible with advantages in obtaining more interesting, reliable, and cross-referenced results.

And the barrier between the intellectual 'crowd' and grassroots leaders and common folks could be overcome. One related idea was to convert into Antonio Gramsci's 'good sense', that common sense and information which we were gathering in collective meetings and group action. We recovered his advice to overcome the authoritarian tendencies of religion and common sense in order to arrive at free transformations for cohesion and social action with the people, by identifying ourselves with them as 'organic intellectuals'. We formed new 'reference groups' with grassroots leaders; they replaced the university professors who had been our referents during our formative years, even though 'organicity' did not necessarily imply partisanship.

Upon recognizing the symmetrical, living relationship of social research, we then invented the 'systematic restitution' or 'devolution' technique for communication purposes. The fundamental role of language was acknowledged. We had to change our ways of reporting to make them understandable mainly by the common persons who had furnished the data. We developed a communication differential according to the level of literacy. One consequence was to retrieve and correct official or elitist history and reinterpret it according to class interests. To this end we applied little-known techniques like 'trunk or family archives', oral tradition and collective memory. We practised imputation of persons and symbolic projection, and developed 'casettcsstories', illustrated historical booklets, popular protest music, spoken portraits and cultural maps.

The style of writing was also affected by these experiences as we promoted a 'Logos-Mythos technique' to combine hard 'core' data with imaginative, literary and artistic 'cortex' interpretation within cultural frames. We learned this two-language technique from the Latin American-born novelists Julio Cortázar, Alejo Carpentier, Gabriel García Márquez and Eduardo Galeano.[11]

P(A)R as a philosophy of life

During those years in the construction of PR we had the advantage of observing directly, within the processes, some of the results of our work. The processes were indeed slow, but whatever achievement was gained in improving local situations and in people's self-reliance and empowerment, it was always a wonder and a fulfilling experience, formative not only for the basegroup leaders but also for the outside/organic researchers. We saw that it is possible for the scientific spirit to show itself in the most modest and primitive circumstances, that work of importance and pertinence for our peoples need not be expensive or complicated. Consequently we found little use for scholarly arrogance and learned instead to develop an empathetic attitude towards Others which we called *vivencia*, meaning life-experience (Husserl's *Erfahrung*). With the careful, human touch of *vivencia* and its need for symmetry in the social relation, it became easy to listen to discourses coming from diverse intellectual origins or conceived with a different cultural syntax.

The crowning effort of this early search for a new type of scientific plus activist/emancipatory work arrived in 1977 with the first World Symposium of Action Research convened at Cartagena, Colombia.[12] It turned out to be a fruitful, encouraging exchange. At this Symposium we had our first epistemologist, Paul Oquist, who afterwards worked in co-operation as minister, with the Nicaraguan Sandinista Revolution. We heard the first claims for an alternative paradigm from German philosopher and educator Heinz Moser. There were sensible caveats from political scientists James Petras (USA), Aníbal Quijano (Peru) and Lourdes Arizpe (Mexico) on scientific work and political action. A bridge towards sceptical academicians was tended by Swedish professor Ulf Himmelstrand, future president of the International Sociological Association; and there were many other highly interesting contributions related to social values, people's power and political life.

Participatory research was then defined as a *vivencia* necessary for the achievement of progress and democracy, a complex of attitudes and values that would give meaning to our praxis in the field. From this time on, PR had to be seen not only as a research methodology but also as a philosophy of life that would convert its practitioners into 'thinkingfeeling persons'. Then our movement took on worldwide dimensions.[13]

Liberationist Perspectives and the New Paradigm

Once we deal with these existential challenges and review critical work done or in progress, we can ask ourselves: What do we do with the knowledge thus obtained? Here is our limited, decanted answer: there is not one way but many so we must keep on trying to understand better, change and re-enchant our plural world.

Such has been the implicit, and often explicit, altruistic theme of our eight world meetings.[14] These congresses – especially the one held in June 1997 at Cartagena, attended by about 2,000 delegates from 61 countries (cf. Fals Borda, 1998) – have condemned our messy world and proposed ways out of present uncertainties. Accumulated scientific knowledge and techniques, as well as socioeconomic policies, have not helped in solving critical local/regional problems. The Enlightenment heritage of rationality has not been sufficient, and national and international institutions in charge of development projects have found it necessary to look for alternatives. As demonstrated in our congresses and in the field, participatory research projects, among others, are clearly different, their language is 'politically correct' now, and they have proved successful. Hence developmentalists, experts, academicians and entrepreneurs have recently gone on a rampage to co-opt P(A)R.[15] Subversive approaches like those discovered in 1970 appear useful to give more play to a rationality based on a new articulation: the pluralistic utopia of Reason and Liberation.[16]

Of course, to speak of liberation today in a post-modern world carries a somewhat different meaning from the political intent of previous revolutions, starting with the French and culminating with the Cuban. National liberation as the prime result of taking over state power by force of arms appears to have little resonance at present, just as the Winter Palace syndrome of our formative years no longer holds. But old ideals of personal and social advance and political insurgency still live. The persistent ring of the insurgent, progressive challenge has been stated by Immanuel Wallerstein's idea of the 'two modernities' (1995), those of technology and liberation. According to him, this symbiotic pair forms 'the central cultural contradiction of our modern world-system, the system of historical capitalism ... leading to moral as well as to institutional crisis' (1995: 471–4).

Such is then the contemporary liberation call of substantive plural democracy and human fulfilment, an 'eternal modernity' which is ever present or latent among billions of persons in poor countries especially, as experienced by PR researchers. We feel there is still a need for active crusaders and heretics for the great adventure of peoples' emancipation, in order to break the exploitative ethos that has permeated the world with poverty, oppression and violence for much too long.

This great challenge has motivated the present generation of PR practitioners to *redefine commitment*. Another support from *vivencia*, different from praxis, is also necessary because it is not enough to be just an activist. Thus to the Marxist-Hegelian concept of praxis Aristotle's 'phronesis' is to be added, that is, wise judgement and prudence for the achievement of the good life. Phronesis should furnish serenity in participatory political processes; it should help to find the middle measure and the proper proportion for our aspirations; and to weigh the hermeneutic relations between 'core' and 'cortex' data provided by the Logos-Mythos technique.

This renovated, two-pronged commitment for liberation and service undergirds PR lifestyle and practice today. As stated above, participatory action research has not been just a quest for knowledge. It is also a transformation of individual attitudes and values, personality and culture, an altruistic process. Such may be the most intricate meaning of P(A)R as an historical project. Therefore, a liberationist/emancipatory ethos is clearly related to a new intellectual challenge: the construction of a practical and morally satisfying paradigm for the social sciences to make them congruent with the ideal of service.

When the possibility of an *alternative paradigm* was presented at the 1977 Symposium, there were doubts because we preferred the possibility of constructing P(A)R as an open project, distinct from the closed-circuit claim of the community of scientists who became guardians of the positivist paradigm. Twenty years later, at the 1997 World Congress, the feeling was different. There were encouraging opinions from prestigious colleagues who stated that the values usually accompanying the dominant paradigm (consistency, simplicity, scope, certitude, productivity) could be enriched with participatory ones like altruism, sincerity of intent, trust, autonomy and social responsibility; other delegates added elements from chaos and complexity theories, like fractality and serendipity.

In sum, the alternative paradigm appears to confirm previous PR work, especially in the South of the world, by combining praxis and ethics, academic knowledge and popular wisdom, the rational and the existential, the regular and the fractal. It breaks down the subject/object dichotomy. It is inspired in the democratic pluralist concepts of alterity and service, favouring to live with differences, and introducing perspectives of gender, popular classes and pluriethnicity into the projects.[17] But this paradigm does not appear like a final product, as the rich strategic challenge for an open PAR project seems to continue.

Participants at the 1997 World Congress felt that this sort of open paradigm would also help to focus on multidisciplines, that is the shaded areas of overlap between the formal boundaries of arts and sciences. This idea of mixing visions and methodologies with their several readings applies to universities to recover their critical mission, to shake up the tardy, tedious and departmentalized disciplinary world, and to put students and professors more in touch with real-life problems. It is not anti-academic. It also applies to our own internal work as participatory researchers because we have been experiencing dispersion. At the first Symposium, there appeared two trends already: one activist represented by the Latin American contingent, and another one of participatory elements represented by Canadian educators. To the former's contribution of 'action research' the others offered the idea of 'participation'. One result was to combine both with the formula, 'participatory action-research' (PAR) which went on to world recognition. Yet the two trends persisted until the discussion clarified that participation obviously included action elements and commitment (indeed Polanyi had said so during the 1970s), therefore PAR could be seen also as PR. To facilitate the transition I proposed (apparently without much success) to keep for awhile the 'A' (action) element in parenthesis.

However, for the 1997 World Congress the number of 'schools' or trends of PR-related work had grown to about 32, reflecting local realities and conditions. The gamut of divergences ran from the technical-aid approach of Robert Chambers' Participatory Rural Appraisal (PRA) to the theoretical sophistication of Yvonna Lincoln's Constructivist Research. Through an email exchange at the University of Calgary previous to the World Congress, an effort was made to induce some convergence of 11 such streams or 'schools'. This provided for one of the most positive and interesting sessions of the meeting.[18]

Though inconclusive, such convergence was upheld there by systems theorists following P.B. Checkland's action research and emancipatory theories (1991; Churchman, 1979; Flood, 1998; Flood and Jackson, 1996) on the basis of a pluralism of causes and effects, and an applicable holistic or extended epistemology (Levin, 1994; Reason, 1994). A group of Scandinavian colleagues, also present, was of the convergent opinion that PR is at once discovery and creation, thus unfolding in an epigenetic space in which 'what is' can only be defined in the context of 'what should be' (Toulmin and Gustavsen, 1996: 181–8).[19] This view reinforced, at the Congress, the ethical components of the new service-oriented paradigm as well as the praxis-plus-phronesis commitment, as explained.

Some Emergent Tasks

The 1997 World Congress helped us to articulate what can be considered an action agenda for the decades ahead, with the advantage that in Cartagena we had a fruitful dialogue among the several 'schools' of participatory research and action, with the good number of colleagues who were present.[20] Some of the main emergent tasks for the committed PR 'crowd' of today, as articulated at that Congress, appear to me to be the following.

1 Multidiscipline and institutional transformation

Through practice and by paying attention to innovators like Gregory Bateson, Fritjof Capra, Ilya Prigogine and others, we have learned the merits of multidisciplinary work. We have shown that this is important for schools and universities as well as for global trends, enterprises and companies. Is it an impossible dream to visualize participatory researchers, educators, philosophers and others working shoulder to shoulder with quantum physicists and biologists – and to continue it with systems theorists? If we feel more at home with them than with classical colleagues, if we enjoy combining our scientific work with literary and artistic expressions, and if our audience does too, can we stimulate these holistic processes and make deeper connections with diverse academic and technical communities and among internal institutional components? At least a more satisfying academic division of labour may accrue for the benefit of all, including the action research family itself. Besides, what about keeping on converging in order to develop from our own trends a more coherent AR, PR or P(A)R project for the grassroots and academia? (See below.)

2 Rigour and validity criteria

We know that rigour in our work can be gained by combining quantitative measures, when needed, with relevant, well-made qualitative and/or ethnographic descriptions and critique; that validity is not an autistic exercise nor just an internal discursive experience. Pertinent validity criteria can be derived as well from common sense, with inductive/deductive examination of results in practice, from *vivencia* or empathetic involvement in processes, and with the considered judgement of local reference groups. Moreover, critical evaluation can be done in the actual process of fieldwork without having to wait for the end of arbitrary prefixed periods. How then can we surmount the persistence of amateurism in much of our work and reports, except to work harder and more carefully? This is now more amply felt yet it should be better translated into action (cf. McTaggart, 1998).

3 Generalizable projects

For investigating symptoms of social pathology like anomie, violence, conflict and drug addiction, so common in today's world, we believe there are no better methods than those provided by P(A)R. Deep and respectful observation in localities is deemed essential. Considering the need to spread pertinent knowledge to combat those social ills, how are we to provide for studies of significant cases (including macro studies) whose theoretical-practical interpretations could be generalized without falling into the trap of traditional and usually failed 'pilot projects'? (Gustavsen, Chapter 1 and comments on large-scale inquiries).

4 Deconstruction of global uniformizations

We have perceived that global trends towards uniformity which are harmful to people's culture and the environment – such as those promoted by 'development' policies – can be subverted through local efforts of cultural and educational revival as well as through civic defence in specific regional and zonal levels. This should be a satisfying task for participant researchers. Yet the enemy is of such enormous proportions that little appears to be gained from isolated efforts. How are we going to continue towards deconstruction of developmentalism and other global trends adverse to people's interests? How are we going to set up limits to the self-devouring, entropic tendencies of capitalism?

5 Scientific research, education and political action

Education, information, research and scientific work have been geared to the upkeep of unjust power structures. Then, how can we privilege the production of responsible knowledge so that the common peoples who have been victims of capitalist exploitation and abuse become the main recipients and beneficiaries of research and schooling? Here we deal with the classic clash of intellectual responsibility and political expedience. The 1997 World Congress sided with the idea of assuming a sense of moral responsibility in research, teaching and action with clear political consequences. Otherwise it is difficult to see how unbearable situations can be resolved with people's countervailing power. Research, action and schooling politically committed to social justice and progress, inspired by a new humanism, appear to be close to the solutions because P(A)R necessarily involves democratization. Participatory democracy built from the bottom up with supporting social, political and cultural movements should be a natural result of our work.

6 Alleviation of conflict, violence and repression

We have seen that P(A)R can reveal well the imageries and representations underlying the logic of conflictual, violent and repressive acts. We know that we can provide keys to preventing or diluting such acts as no other methodology. We discover their sources in dire poverty, ignorance and hunger, abetted by economic systems which can be fought with means made available by the technological revolution. Can we push for meta-narratives like pluralistic socialism which real experiences have shown possible and convenient? How much longer can we tolerate going on a suicidal track by not resisting the inhuman trends implicit in Western systems of thought and action?

7 Construction of an ethnogenetic emancipatory ethos

This is the most general, overarching challenge that we face if we are serious in trying to mitigate the present ethos of uncertainty. Such a task may be doubly difficult because it requires deep conceptual preparation towards an alternative scientific paradigm, insightful and pointed discussion, and effective decisions to carry the resulting propositions into local practice where they count most.

Let's not be modest. Theoretical/practical skirmishes for a new paradigm and a satisfying ethos have been going on in this regard since the 1970s, as recalled here. We have moved together from eighteenth- and nineteenth-century participatory and utopian theories to the threshold of another set of theories on complexity, chaos and post-modernist liberation. We have done this with the guidance of, and impetus from, intellectual and political giants. Now alert philosophers of action, eloquent post-modernists and critical theorists could very well take hold of their theses and assimilate their deeds with the purpose of converting them into efficient tools for the liberation of peoples who are under the heel of oppressive power systems.

Can we therefore be participative students and agents of change and work together in order to assist in this intellectual and political movement for people's self-reliance and empowerment, for the defence of life and the pursuit of relevant, useful science? Can we commit ourselves as scholars and citizens to this epoch-making task?

The need to construct an altruistic ethos for heterogeneous forms of cultures, times, spaces and peoples implies a world-wide effort to combine intellectual, political and economic resources from North and South, East and West. For awhile, our concern for knowledge, power and justice and their relationships grew independently in our respective regions. Now those parallel developments have had an important consequence: we are merging with additional competence (cf. Chambers, 1998).

Our tasks as participatory scholars and practitioners seem to be more clear. In the last analysis, the effect of P(A)R work carries a liberating, political accent world-wide. The rising universal brotherhood of critical intellectuals – women and men – tends to construct open pluralist societies in which oppressive central powers, the economy of exploitation, monopolies and the unjust distribution of wealth, the dominance of militarism and armamentism, the reign of terror, abuse of the natural environment, racism, and other plagues will be proscribed. On these vital issues many of us appear to be like one, as we concur on insisting about the humanist utilization of science, knowledge and techniques. Such now appears to be our global commitment.

The merging ways in which we will be able to articulate our research and action will also determine the survival of our PR 'schools' and the promise of our efforts through application in local environments: in communities and cities, families, enterprises, churches, art and communication media, universities and colleges. As we arrive at a new millennium, it is great to think that P(A)R will be able to do its share to find better scientific, technical and social ways for improved living conditions, and for the enrichment of human cultures.

Notes

1 The Dag Hammarskjöld Foundation of Uppsala, Sweden, published a detailed report on this seminal experience written by a group of involved social scientists composed of G.V.S. De Silva and Ponna Wignaraja (from Sri Lanka), Niranjan Mehta (from India), and Md Anisur Rahman (from Bangladesh). They recorded that 'activists and cadres [of socialist inspiration] joined us as partners in research ... to give an intersection of perceptions and knowledge generated from two different life streams ... to create knowledge jointly'. They identified their method as 'participatory [beyond dialogical] research'.

2 The Rosca included the present writer, colleagues Augusto Libreros, Jorge Ucrós, Víctor Bonilla, Gonzalo Castillo, and many others who worked in several fronts. We were influenced by Marxist humanism, and we revived thinkers like Gramsci, Lukács and Mandel. Praxis, common sense and the subject–object dichotomy, then not very popular, were introduced and discussed. Dogmas like the 'science of the proletariat' were rejected for lack of field evidence. For comparative elaborations of participatory action research see Fals Borda and Rahman (1991), as well as other sources cited below. On our search for intellectual independence see Fals Borda (1970a).

3 Swantz's initial work was not closely linked with the university structure nor with political theory, but it carried its own impetus to bring knowledge to the support of neglected peoples in the region. The Massai pastoralists soon came next with the Jipemoyo (Tanzania) study done by her with colleagues Kemal Mustafa, Odhiambo Anacleti and others at the Ministry of Culture (Swantz, 1978), which was influential for developmental work and 'research-in-action'.

4 IDAC trilingual bulletins on PR had universal repercussions. There were considerable results in Mexico/Holland (Anton de Schutter), Chile/Venezuela (Francisco Vio Grossi, Marcela Gajardo), India (Rajesh Tandon, Smitu Kothari), Nicaragua/France/Holland (Guy LeBoterf, Mark Lammerink), Peru/Holland (Vera Gianotten, Ton de Wit), and elsewhere.

5 Another Mexican pioneer, anthropologist Ricardo Pozas, spoke about PR approaches at the 9th Latin American Congress of Sociology in Mexico in 1969, an extraordinary occasion for the radical ideas on social and academic transformation that it espoused.

6 Stavenhagen proposed 'activist [beyond participant] observation', claiming that scientists cannot 'refuse to take a stand' but rather 'to raise the issues and create new models in place of the ones he is obliged to discard, and if he can, to take the necessary action'. Of the eleven commentators of this article, eight sided with Stavenhagen. His presence at the 1997 Cartagena World Congress afforded one of the high points of the meeting.

7 In these books and articles reference is made to the 'sociology of liberation' spurred by the Cuban Revolution and the writings and deeds of the Colombian sociologist and guerrilla-priest Camilo Torres.

8 There were other supports: social sciences were already being criticized for their shortcomings by C. Wright Mills who insisted on the use of imagination, Alvin Gouldner for his idea of reflexive sociology as a work ethic, and Barrington Moore's rare analysis of injustice and democracy. Instead, economics came out badly for its baseless bent for scientific exactness, rightly penalized by Gunnar Myrdal and other humane economists.

9 Later on, in Europe, we discovered the critical study of 'counter-currents' in the sciences by Helga Nowotny and Hilary Rose; Karl Polanyi's critique of the detached observer; E.P. Thompson's workers' history; Jürgen Habermas's communicative action theory; André Gunder Frank's opus on 'development of underdevelopment'; Alain Touraine's theory of action and social movements; Pierre Bourdieu's concepts of 'habitus' and 'participant objectivation'; the demystifying lessons of Foucault, Lyotard and Todorov on the academic rhetoric supportive of institutional forms of domination and control. Their intellectual inputs gave us confidence in what we were doing, even though they were not members of our participatory strand.

10 In Heller's view, the central purpose of social science is 'to set us free', that is it has a liberating, emancipatory connotation. A considerable contribution in this field is Denzin and Lincoln (1994: Part V).

11 Such is the experiment contained in my two-column work, *Historia Doble de la Costa* (Fals Borda, 1979–86). This is further explained in Fals Borda (1996). A few other authors have done something similar (two-column books) in anthropology and medicine, in the English and French languages.

12 At this Symposium 32 papers were presented by delegates from 17 countries. They were sponsored by Fundarco Foundation (Simposio de Cartagena, 1979). This is considered a classic in our field. There was no English edition of this work, only of particular articles. A representative, partial translation into German came out in book form (Moser and Ornauer, 1978). For recent case studies and regional descriptions of P(A)R, see among others McTaggart, 1997; Park et al., 1993; Whyte, 1991.

13 The First Symposium of 1977 accelerated the adoption and spread of P(A)R throughout the world. Besides ICAE's PR international network, the European Association of Development Research and Training (EADI) evolved in 1978 from the institutional basic needs approach to PR thanks to Swantz's Jipemoyo Project in Tanzania. In 1979 the United Nations Research Institute for Social Development (UNRISD) at Geneva started with anthropologists Andrew Pearse and Matthias Stiefel a comprehensive series of studies and publications on people's participation. The International Labour Organisation

(ILO) and UNESCO did something similar with economist Md Anisur Rahman and the MOST Programme. The Research Committee on Social Practice and Social Transformation of the International Sociological Association opened a section on PR with the leadership of philosophers Peter Park and Y. Michal Bodemann. Important P(A)R centres were established in Toronto, New Delhi, Colombo, Santiago, Caracas, Amsterdam, and other cities. Teaching at universities started in Massachusetts, Calgary, Cornell, Caracas, Dar-es-Salaam, Campinas, Managua, Pernamabuco, Bath and Deakin.

The Society for International Development (SID), at the initiative of political scientist Ponna Wignaraja, organized an International Group for Grassroots Initiatives (IGGRI) in 1980, including Majid Rahnema, Gustavo Esteva, Marja-Liisa Swantz, Luis Lopezllera, Ward Morehouse, Rajni and Smitu Kothari, Paul Ekins, Manfred Max-Neef, Orlando Fals Borda, and others. The World Bank proceeded to organize its own Participatory Development Group, under the leadership of sociologists Michael M. Cernea and Anders Rudqvist.

The Latin American Council for Adult Education (CEAAL), with successive headquarters at Santiago de Chile and Mexico, played an important role in the PR field with the organization in 1981 of a special network coordinated by Brazilian educator Joao Francisco de Souza. This network has covered most countries of the region. For example, in Central America there are related institutions functioning under the leadership of scholar activists like Raúl Leis, Oscar Jara, Carlos Brenes and Malena de Montis. In Colombia: Gustavo de Roux, María Cristina Salazar, Ernesto Lleras, Elías Sevilla, Marco Raúl Mejía, Raúl Paniagua, Rosario Saavedra, Alejandro Sanz, and many others.

Besides Deakin, other Australian universities and organizations, like the Action Learning, Action Research and Process Management Association (ALARPM) stimulated the institutional adoption of these 'schools' with the leadership of Ortrun Zuber-Skerritt, Colin Henry, Ron Passfield, Yoland Wadsworth, Iaian Govan, and others.

14 Besides the 1977 Symposium, the other seven world congresses have been held in Ljubljana, Yugoslavia (1979) with support from the ICAE; Calgary, Canada (1989) with university sponsorship for the first time; Managua, Nicaragua (1989) with the leadership of the Latin American Council for Adult Education; Brisbane (1990, 1992) at Queensland University of Technology with the ALARPM Association; likewise at Bath (1994) at the University of Bath; and again at Cartagena, Colombia (1997) with ample governmental, academic, NGO, and international support. A ninth one has been convened by ALARPM for September 2000 at the University of Ballarat in Australia.

15 On the failures of development policies and co-optation of P(A)R by world organisms, NGOs and academic institutions, see the growing pertinent literature, among them the works of Arturo Escobar, Wolfgang Sachs and Majid Rahnema. Greenwood and Levin (1998) make a strong case on the point regarding the defensive role of orthodox academic vested interests. For a discussion of many of the elements pursued by participatory researchers in concrete conditions, facing the failures of development, see Apfel-Marglin (1998) and her Andean 'cultural affirmation' experience.

16 See note 7. Cf. Giulio Girardi (1997). On the theory of emancipatory research, see Carr and Kemmis (1986). On ethics and politics, see the insightful discussions of the 1997 World Congress workgroup, in Hoyos and Uribe (1998).

17 Cf. the Cartagena World Congress Report (Fals Borda, 1998: 189–91, 235–6). See related views of H.G. Gadamer on 'life experience' and 'fusion of horizons' in his *Truth and Method* (1960: 302–7, 567). For him, the proper hermeneutic reflection is 'a critical and emancipatory task'.

18 Among the 'schools' present at the Cartagena 1997 World Congress, the following 11 made a preliminary email exchange which proved immensely valuable: Participatory Rural Appraisal, Sussex (Robert Chambers); Critical Systems Theory, Hull (Robert L. Flood); Action Research, Cornell (Davydd Greenwood); Action Research, Scandinavia (Morten Levin); Constructivist Research, Texas (Yvonna S. Lincoln); Action Learning, Australia (Robin McTaggart); Cooperative Research, Bath (Peter Reason); Participatory Action Research, Germany/Peru (T. Tillmann, M. Salas); Action Research, Austria (Michael Schratz); Participatory Action Research, India (Rajesh Tandon); and Participatory Action Research, Calgary (Timothy Pyrch, co-ordinator). See reports in Pyrch (1998a, 1998b).

19 According to these authors, the unit of attention of P(A)R open systems is an observable constituent system with a structure ABX conformed by an epistemic subject A and an empirical object B in a social-research situation X. In the minds of those participating in the system, the structure becomes ABX:pox (the person, the other and X). This situation resembles that postulated in quantum physics with anthropic and indeterminacy principles. Hence its potential to enrich our discussions of a new paradigm for the sciences, from another point of view. This stimulating book also offers an example of a PR macro study on Turkey. Cf. Beinum (1998).

20 At the 1997 World Congress, besides the 'schools' mentioned in note 18, there were many other groups: on education, social and political organization, literature and arts, the economy, systems theories, communication, postmodernism, philosophy, process management, business administration, environment and natural resources. Interested persons may obtain catalogues and copies of papers and videos at the following address: iepri@-bacata.usc.unal.edu.co, or by writing to Apartado A. 52508, Bogotá, Colombia.

References

Agulla, J.C. (1970) 'Protesta, subversión y cambio de estructuras', *Aportes* (Paris), 15: 47–61.

Apfel-Marglin, F., with PRATEC (1998) *The Spirit of Regeneration: Andean Culture Confronting Western Notions of Development*. London/New York: Zed Books.

Beinum, H. van (1998) 'On the practice of action research', *Concepts and Transformation* (Amsterdam), 3 (1): 1–30.

Birnbaum, N. (1971) *Toward a Critical Sociology*. New York: Oxford University Press.

Bonfil, G. (1970) 'La antropología social en México: ensayo sobre sus nuevas perspectivas', *Anales de Antropología* (México), 7: 24–39.

Carr, W. and Kemmis, S. (1986) *Becoming Critical: Knowledge, Education and Action Research*. London: Falmer Press.

Chambers, R. (1998) 'Beyond "Whose reality counts?" New methods we now need', *Studies in Cultures, Organizations and Societies*, 4 (2): 279–87.

Checkland, P.B. (1991) *Systems Thinking, Systems Practice*. Chichester: Wiley.

Churchman, C.W. (1979) *The System Approach and its Enemies*. New York: Basic Books.

De Silva, G.V.S., Wignaraja, P., Mehta, N. and Rahman, M.A. (1979) 'Bhoomi Sena: a struggle for people's power', *Development Dialogue* (Uppsala), 2: 3–70.

Denzin, N.K. and Lincoln, Y.S. (1994) *Handbook of Qualitative Research*. London: Sage Publications.

Fals Borda, O. (1970a) 'La crisis social y la orientación sociológica', *Aportes* (Paris), 15: 62–76.

Fals Borda, O. (1970b) *Subversion and Development in Latin America*. Geneva: Foyer John Knox.

Fals Borda, O. (1970c) *Ciencia propia y colonialismo intelectual*. México: Nuestro Tiempo. (The third edition of this book in Bogotá: Carlos Valencia, 1986, underlined intellectual independence).

Fals Borda, O. (1979) 'The problem of investigating reality in order to transform it', *Dialectical Anthropology*, 4 (1): 33–56.

Fals Borda, O. (1979–86) *Historia Doble de la Costa* (4 vols). Bogotá: Carlos Valencia.

Fals Borda, O. (1996) 'A North–South convergence on the quest for meaning', *Collaborative Inquiry* (Bath), 18: 10–14.

Fals Borda, O. (ed.) (1998) *People's Participation: Challenges Ahead*. New York and London: Apex Press and Intermediate Technology Publications.

Fals Borda, O. and Rahman, M.A. (eds) (1991) *Action and Knowledge: Breaking the Monopoly with PAR*. New York and London: Apex Press and Intermediate Technology Publications.

Freire, P. (1970) *Pedagogy of The Oppressed* New York: Seabury.

Feyerabend, P.K. (1970) *Against Method*. Minneapolis, MN: University of Minnesota Press.

Flood, R.L. (1998) 'Action research and the management and systems sciences', in O. Fals Borda (ed.), *People's Participation: Challenges Ahead*. New York and London: Apex Press and Intermediate Technology Publications. pp. 131–56.

Flood, R.L. and Jackson, M.C. (eds) (1996) *Critical Systems Thinking*. Chichester: Wiley.

Gadamer, H.G. (1960/1994) *Truth and Method*. New York: Continuum.

Girardi, G. (1997) 'Investigación participativa popular y teología de la liberación', Paper 32, World Congress, Cartagena.

Greenwood, D. and Levin, M. (1998) 'Action research, science and the co-optation of social research', *Studies in Cultures, Organizations and Societies*, 4 (2): 237–61.

Heller, A. (1989) 'From hermeneutics in social science toward a hermeneutics of social science', *Theory and Society*, 18 (3): 304–5.

Horton, M. and Freire, P. (1990) *We Make the Road by Walking*. Philadelphia, PA: Temple University Press.

Hoyos, G. and Uribe, A. (eds) (1998) *Convergencia entre ética y política*. Bogotá: Siglo del Hombre.

Levin, M. (1994) 'Action research and critical systems thinking', *Systems Practice* (Hull), 7: 25–42.

Lewis, H.M. (1997) 'Myles Horton, pioneer in adult education', Paper 6, World Congress, Cartagena.

McTaggart, R. (ed.) (1997) *Participatory Action Research: International Contexts and Consequences*. Ithaca, NY: State University of New York Press.

McTaggart, R. (1998) 'Is validity really an issue for participatory action research?', *Studies in Cultures, Organizations and Societies*, 4 (2): 211–36.

Moser, H. and Ornauer, H. (1978) *Internationale Aspekte der Aktionsforschung*. Munich: Kösel Verlag.

Moynihan, D.P. (1969) *Maximum Feasible Misunderstanding*. New York: US Government Press.

Park, P., Brydon-Miller, M., Hall, B. and Jackson, T. (1993) *Voices of Change: Participatory Research in the United States and Canada*. Ontario: Oise Press.

Pyrch, T. (1998a) 'Action research', Special Issue, *Studies in Cultures, Organizations and Societies*, 4 (2): v–x.

Pyrch, T. (1998b) 'Mapmakers on mapmaking', *Systemic Practice and Action Research*, 11 (6): 651–68.

Reason, P. (ed.) (1994) *Participation in Human Inquiry*. London: Sage Publications.

Simposio de Cartagena (1979) *Crítica y política en ciencias sociales* (2 vols). Bogotá: Punta de Lanza.

Stavenhagen, R. (1971) 'Decolonialising applied social sciences', *Human Organization*, 30 (4): 333–44.

Swantz, M.L. (1978) 'Participatory research as a tool for training, the Jipemoyo Project in Tanzania', *Assignment Children*, UNICEF, 41: 93–109.

Swantz, M.L. (1986) *Ritual and Symbol in Transitional Zaramo Society* (second edition). Helsinki: Helsinki University.

Toulmin, M. and Gustavsen, B. (eds) (1996) *Beyond Theory: Changing Organizations through Participation*. Amsterdam: John Benjamins.

Wallerstein, I. (1995) 'The end of what modernity?', *Theory and Society*, 24 (4): 471–4.

Warman, A., Nolasco, M., Bonfil, G., Olivera, M. and Valencia, E. (1970) *De eso que llaman antropología mexicana*. México: Nuestro Tiempo.

Whyte, W.F. (ed.) (1991) *Participatory Action Research*. London: Sage Publications.

3
Action Research in the Workplace: the Socio-technical Perspective

WILLIAM PASMORE

CHAPTER OUTLINE

This chapter traces the evolution of action research and socio-technical systems thinking, demonstrating how the two came to be linked through persons and practice, and examining the emergent synergies produced by the union. Finally, the future of the action research paradigm is assessed, based on an analysis of the challenges it faces in shifting the dominant paradigm in research institutions, organizations and society.

The workplace is central to our existence. Hence, it is not surprising that social scientists have studied behaviour in the workplace in depth. The work of the socio-technical school (Pasmore, 1988; Trist, 1981; Weisbord, 1987) brought together Lewin's approach to action research with Bion's (1946) theories about leaderless groups, and von Bertalanffy's (1950) work on systems thinking to investigate and later intervene in a number of issues pertaining to workplace arrangements that could increase both human dignity and organizational effectiveness.

Kurt Lewin, in his classic formulation of field theory (Lewin, 1951), held that behaviour is influenced by its environment, the context within which it occurs. Therefore, it seems worthwhile to begin our exploration of the confluence of action research and socio-technical systems thinking by understanding the contexts which gave rise to Lewin's work on action research and to the work of members of the Tavistock Institute on socio-technical systems.

Origins of Action Research

Although there is rarely a single person who can be identified as the source of a novel perspective, credit for the earliest modern thinking about putting science to use in addressing practical social problems is often given to John Dewey, the American philosopher who wrote extensively about the need to democratize education. In his book, *How We Think* (1933), Dewey identified five phases of reflective thinking: suggestion, intellectualization, hypothesizing, reasoning and testing hypotheses in action. The stimulus for thinking (the suggestion) was a practical problem of concern to the scientist. After thinking about the problem in order to understand the dynamics at play, the researcher could begin formulating hypotheses regarding the nature of cause and effect operating among variables that shape the situation. Reasoning comes into play as the researcher identifies and creates theories regarding actions that can be taken to change the outcomes of the system by manipulating the variables. These theories are then tested through experimentation and observation to determine if the hypotheses are confirmed. For Dewey, practical problems demanded practical solutions. A solution to a problem could only be regarded as viable when it was demonstrated to produce desired outcomes in practice.

Dewey urged educators to teach students how to think, rather than teaching facts. He urged that education should be made a more collaborative process, in which students formulated hypotheses, which they could test in practice. In this way, he believed, education would better prepare students for life, which would present many problems for which there were no textbook solutions. Morten

Levin and Davydd Greenwood's discussion of Dewey's work shows two things: first, that Dewey's work remains as important today as when it was written; and secondly, that despite some experimentation with Dewey's ideas, universities approach learning in much the same way as they did in Dewey's time (Levin and Greenwood, 2001). At some point, it would be worth someone's time to examine why it is that good ideas don't always catch on.

Dewey didn't coin the term 'action research'. Credit for this is held jointly by two men working independently: John Collier and Kurt Lewin (French and Bell, 1984). Collier, a commissioner of American Indian affairs from 1933 to 1945, applied the term to his work in improving race relations between whites and native Americans. Problems in ethnic relations, he reasoned, could not be overcome by decree. Instead, a programme of collaborative research, in which representatives of the parties themselves participated, was needed to fashion acceptable solutions. Collier believed strongly that research was the most important tool in changing behaviour in ethnic relations, provided that the research was undertaken as a join effort of researchers and laypersons. Traditional research might produce interesting observations but those observations would be unlikely to change the deep-seated beliefs of participants. Engaging participants in dialogue without research would reveal differences of opinion but provide no means for the resolution of those differences. Collier reasoned that only a participative approach to research could create the conditions under which authentic improvements in race relations would occur.

Despite their similar views and the fact that they developed their thinking at almost the same time, Lewin is much more widely recognized than Collier among students of action research. Born in Prussia and educated in Berlin, Lewin experienced anti-Semitism first-hand. Although he had fought in the German army during the First World War, during which he began to formulate ideas that would later become the basis for his life's work in the area of field theory (Lewin, 1951), by 1933 he felt compelled to leave Germany for the USA to seek academic and personal freedom from oppression (Marrow, 1969; Weisbord, 1987). During his exodus, he stopped in Cambridge and was given a tour of the university by an aspiring literature student by the name of Eric Trist. Trist was taken by Lewin's ideas, switched his major to psychology, and began an association with Lewin which led to the incorporation of action research as a core methodology in the socio-technical school.

Upon reaching the USA, Lewin taught at Cornell and then Iowa and finally at MIT, but never in tenured positions. His work was discounted by some members of the scientific community who viewed it as too applied and he himself was sceptical of yielding to any institution which valued the same authoritarianism he had fled.

During the Second World War, Lewin collaborated with Margaret Mead in their now famous studies designed to reduce the civilian consumption of rationed foods. The researchers experimented with different methods of influencing behaviour: first, experts were used to explain why behaviour change was important and to exhort a group of housewives to change their cooking habits. Next, a second group of housewives was given the pertinent information and asked to discuss the problem of curtailing consumption among them in order to decide what could be done. The results of the participative approach to change were much more impressive, confirming Lewin's strong beliefs in democracy and more specifically in action research as a tool that could advance science while dealing with practical societal concerns.

Lewin's contributions to change in the workplace began shortly after the war. Alex Bevalas, one of Lewin's students at Iowa, worked with Alfred Marrow's Harwood manufacturing company to explore ways to enhance productivity by using action research methods in which workers participated in experimental changes in methods. The conditions they created resulted in what we would call a learning organization today; workers were encouraged to experiment with different methods, to discuss them among themselves, and to choose the methods which they agreed were most effective. Groups of workers increased their own quotas after discovering and employing new methods (Marrow, 1969).

Coch and French (1948) continued experimentation at Harwood, using participation as a means to reduce resistance to change, particularly when new products and production methods were introduced. They demonstrated clearly that participative management methods, in which workers discussed changes with their supervisors, were more effective than traditional approaches to change, in which industrial engineers specified the new processes workers should use.

Lewin also inspired his student Ronald Lippitt to investigate the effects of different styles of leadership (autocratic, democratic and laissez-faire) on conflict and performance within groups (Lewin, 1951). Autocratic groups were productive only in the presence of the leader and exhibited high levels of conflict. Laissez-faire groups showed signs of frustration, which also resulted in conflict and low productivity. Only democratic groups exhibited both high productivity and low levels of conflict. By changing the leadership styles of each group, Lewin and Lippitt were able to demonstrate that the behaviours observed were not due to the personalities of the group members; the effects of each leadership style were consistent regardless of the group. This confirmed Lewin's field theory, which states that:

B = f(p,e)

Or that the behaviour of an individual is a function of both personality and environment. Lewin's thinking was a challenge to Freudian psychology, the dominant paradigm at the time, which held that all behaviours could be explained by deep-seated aspects of the personality. Lewin's action research demonstrated clearly that behaviour varied across time and under the influence of different environmental forces. This theory and related findings became a central tenant of the socio-technical school as well, as it allowed for the possibility that by changing aspects of the workplace, behavioural changes could be produced. It would not be necessary to change the deep-seated personalities of workers in order to produce new behaviours; the potential for a wide range of behaviours, triggered by different environmental stimuli, already existed in the individual.

Towards the end of his career, and particularly during his association with Douglas McGregor at MIT's Research Center for Group Dynamics, Lewin became more interested in the effects of groups on the behaviour of individuals. Lewin and McGregor experimented with applications of action research to group dynamics in efforts to bring about changes in industry, educational institutions and society. One of these efforts, in connection with the Connecticut State Inter-Racial Commission, led to the founding of the NTL Institute for Applied Behavioral Science, which continues to offer training in group dynamics following the methods of open and honest participative inquiry among members of groups developed by Lewin over 50 years ago.

Thus, the context for Lewin's work was formed first by his personal experience as a Jew in Germany and then by the pressing issues of the Second World War and finally by issues of organizational and societal importance. These forces, following Lewin's own field theory, shaped his behaviour to pursue action research as a democratically-based approach to putting the power of science to use in understanding and changing human behaviour.

Origins of Socio-technical Systems

As mentioned, Eric Trist first met Kurt Lewin in 1933 during Lewin's visit to Cambridge, where Trist was a student. Trist continued his association with Lewin by studying in the USA under a commonwealth scholarship. Captivated by Lewin's thinking, Trist began his career as an applied psychologist, building upon and extending Lewin's work and theories in collaboration with his colleagues at the Tavistock Institute.

Shortly after finishing his studies, Trist joined the army and began working with members of the Tavistock Institute in treating mental casualties. The facilities available were woefully inadequate to care for the number of patients. Clearly, the traditional model of intense, one-on-one Freudian therapy would never meet the demand. A breakthrough in practice methodology was required. Wilfred Bion was experimenting with methods of self-directed group therapy, which is commonplace today but was unheard of at the time. Bion's ideas were considered radical and misguided by members of the academic establishment, but they fit perfectly with Lewin's collaborative approach to inquiry and behavioural change.

Bion convinced small groups of men to confront their problems rather than to run away from them. Once small groups were committed to discussing their problems and seeking solutions with one another, Bion called a meeting of between 100 and 200 men (some of the earliest large-group interventions on record) to discuss the management of the hospital wing. By taking responsibility for the management of their surroundings, the men began to regain a sense of control over their lives and responsibility for their own well-being. Using highly reflective and collaborative methods, the group began the process of addressing the treatment needs of its members and of selecting appropriate methods of intervention. Bion theorized that due to a number of conscious and unconscious forces, people build group and organizational structures that they do not find effective or satisfying but deep psychological resistance causes them to deny these negative effects. Once the effects are pointed out, paradigms can be shifted; then, democratic processes can be used to involve people in reconstructing their social arrangements to make them more effective, healthier, more responsive and more satisfying. The parallel here is notable with what Kemmis (Chapter 8) would call 'critical theory'.

Although successful, the first experiments by Bion were suspended after only six weeks because they were viewed as disruptive by the Department of Army Psychiatry (Bridger, 1990). It took another year for Bion to convince the Army to adopt his approach on a broader scale.

Trist then became involved in working with Hugh Murray on an officer selection process that would increase the number of applicants to officer training and improve the success of officers in the field, as measured by the survival rate of their troops (Murray, 1990). The traditional method of selecting candidates was for a highly experienced officer, called a military judge, to interview candidates briefly and to make selections based on their impressions and the candidate's records. The method devised by Trist and Murray is akin to what today we would call an assessment centre; candidates were interviewed by an interdisciplinary team, observed as they handled simulated leadership challenges, and assessed by virtue of paper and pencil psychological tests. Bion's leaderless group method was used to assess how the candidates would manage interpersonal relations, an important component of the officer's job. To increase the flow of candidates, the researchers devised a regimental nomination process, in which regiments that were in need of leaders nominated candidates from among their ranks. In this way, men chosen as leaders were assured the support of those they would command. The new methods were highly successful both in increasing the flow and quality of candidates. Other branches of the military adopted the procedures shortly thereafter, as did the British Civil Service following the war. Once again, the power of action research in dealing with pressing real issues had been demonstrated.

Following the war, Trist and his colleagues turned their attention to matters of national recovery. No longer supported by military funding, the work of the Tavistock group needed to become self-sustaining; there was a great deal of pressure for members of the Institute to demonstrate that their work held practical relevance. Trist's historical account of the early years of the Institute (Trist and Murray, 1990) makes it clear that intellectual productivity was born of need. Despite failures and miscalculations, the group persisted in advancing its thinking through practical experiments in real organizations involving significant and pressing problems. Trist could easily have joined a university faculty after the war but was perhaps influenced by Lewin in his desire to create an organization that would stand between academia and organizations, acting as a bridge between the two rather than a captive of either. Tavistock would be dedicated to action research and it would place equal emphasis on the advancement of knowledge and the resolution of practical problems.

The next major project of the Tavistock Institute was an observation of coal-mining practices (Trist and Bamforth, 1951). Coal was in short supply compared to the growing national demand for coal as a source of energy in the recovery of the industrial sector. New methods, based upon advances in above-ground industrial engineering (conveyor belts, Taylorism, job specialization) had been applied to the mines but had not yielded the results promised. Ken Bamforth, a fellow at the Institute, had knowledge of mines that used the new technology in novel ways in order to produce better outcomes. Trist was immediately interested and with the support of the British Coal Board, began detailed studies of the differences in work arrangements used in high-productivity and low-productivity mines. Using painstaking ethnographic methods, Trist began to formulate theories that would explain the differences in outputs he observed. Interviewing workers after hours in pubs and in their homes, he pieced together the tenets of what would later become socio-technical theory.

Workers in the highly productive, innovative mines operated more as self-managing groups. Their leaders, when confronted with the need to employ new technology, turned to the workers for advice in how to implement new methods rather than following the strict advice of industrial engineers who had never worked underground and who therefore didn't understand the myriad factors that made coal mining more challenging than above-ground production.

The miners devised systems that allowed them to be multi-skilled and self-directing, rather than highly specialized and dependent upon external leadership, as was the case in lower-productivity mines. The multi-skilled, self-directing arrangement made it easier for the group to adjust to conditions as they evolved, rather than trying to fit a mechanical process into changing underground conditions. Drawing on systems thinking, Trist, and later Flood (Chapter 10), was able to provide graphic evidence of how systems must possess requisite variety in order to adapt to changing external conditions (Ashby, 1960). He was also able to demonstrate that the social system and the technical system of an organization operated in an interdependent fashion. Because the basic technology in use in the mines was the same, the differences in performance could only be accounted for by the work arrangements employed. Through his ethnographic methods, Trist was able to deduce that the social systems used in the more productive mines were more consistent with the self-image of the miners and more able, in their view, to protect them from the many dangers that accompany work underground. In contrast, in the low-performance mines, workers felt alienated from their work, trapped in a system they could not influence, and constantly exposed to risks over which they had no control.

An interesting finding was that the incidence of mental illness was much higher in the low-performing mines than in the higher-performing mines. Given Trist's earlier involvement in the use of self-directing groups to cope with mental illness in the military, this finding didn't surprise Trist. Bion's theories of groups explained that when groups become dependent upon leadership for guidance they display unhealthy, 'basic assumption' behaviours, such as fight/flight, pairing or dependency, all of which interfere with the group's abilities to diagnose and deal constructively with its own issues (Bion, 1946).

In the underground situation, leaders could not supply all of the control necessary to guarantee safety; yet unaware of other choices, leaders continued to attempt to exert control through traditional means, such as blaming individual workers for problems, punishing workers for not meeting quotas, and providing additional rewards to workers whom they felt were loyal and supportive of their leadership. They failed to see that the work system itself made hierarchical control impossible; that the complex technology and fragmentation of roles had led to coordination needs that could not be met by supervisors in the dark, noisy, dangerous, ever-changing underground environment. No matter how advanced the technology, it would fail if not mated with a social system designed to operate the technology effectively. This principle, known as *joint optimization*, was to become the cornerstone of socio-technical systems theory:

> Inherent in the socio-technical approach is the notion that the attainment of optimum conditions in any one dimension does not necessarily result in a set of conditions optimum for the system as a whole ... The optimization of the whole tends to require a less than optimum state for each separate dimension. (Trist et al., 1963)

The key to the differences in mine productivity had to do with several factors. In the lower-performing mines, labour on each shift was specialized, so that problems created by previous shifts could only be dealt with by miners on those shifts. Whole cycles of mining were delayed while awaiting the return of shift workers with the specialized skills needed to address certain problems. Difficulties in communication across shifts, reliance on hierarchical methods of control and territoriality among specialties interfered with learning and performance improvement.

In the higher-performing mines, miners were committed to the design of work because they helped to create it, a point that Lewin would certainly have appreciated. Secondly, multi-skilling allowed workers to be responsibly self-directing, even in the face of tremendous complexity and difficulties in undertaking mining operations using the new technology. Thirdly, the workers decided on common pay tied to output, rather than the specialized wages paid to holders of different jobs in the low-performance mines. Finally, a commitment to maintain the productivity of the mine extended to relationships across shifts, which were vital to maintaining the advancement of the mining cycle.

The coal-mining studies laid the foundation for socio-technical systems theory but were not true examples of action research, since Trist and his colleagues were observers of naturally occurring experiments rather than collaborators in their planning and evaluation. When the researchers presented their findings to the Coal Board and suggested that they could use the results to help create more productive mines elsewhere, their work was blocked by traditionally thinking members of the Board. The continued blending of action research and socio-technical systems thinking would take place in experiments outside Britain, in Norway, India, Sweden, the USA and the Netherlands.

The work in India was undertaken by A.K. Rice in 1953 and described in his book, *Productivity and Social Organization* (1958). Rice became involved in the Indian weaving industry as a consultant, working with managers of the Calico Mills in Ahmedabad. An experimental loom shed was proposed by Rice which would involve multi-skilled teams who would hold the responsibility for the entire operation and maintenance of a bank of looms. Workers immediately accepted the proposal, and ironed out the details of team formation and individual roles and responsibilities literally overnight. As in the case of the coal mines, the socio-technically designed work system was far more successful than the traditional one-person, one-job set-up.

A paper written by Eric Miller recounts his visit to Calico Mills 17 years after the experiments by Rice were begun (Miller, 1975). Miller found the effects of the experiment to be robust in the experimental loom shed, which still operated in accordance with the design developed by Rice and detailed by workers, despite some changes in the products and market. Yet in other parts of the mill, where the concept of working in teams had been tried, there was evidence of regression to a traditional system of work.

Miller explained that the latter groups were not given sufficient support in the form of spare help and training to allow them to deal with the difficulties they encountered. Moreover, boundary conditions were not managed effectively, so that demands for increases in quality and the turnover of group members were not dealt with successfully. Miller concludes that a reversion to a more rigid structure can be taken as a symptom that the group as a social system has exceeded its capacity to accommodate external change. As the group's ability to self-regulate is exceeded, supervision steps in to provide support, but often, as in the case of the Calico Mills, ends up destroying the resilience of the group by fostering dependence on directive external leadership.

In Norway, a series of efforts that became known as the 'Norwegian Industrial Democracy Projects' was begun through collaboration between Trist and Einar Thorsrud, a frequent visitor to the Tavistock Institute during the 1950s. With a national culture that supported egalitarianism, stable labour relations, social welfare and work reform, Norway was the perfect place to investigate the diffusion of socio-technical systems thinking through action research (Weisbord, 1987). In 1962, the Norwegians undertook four field projects, which once again demonstrated the positive impact of introducing socio-technical arrangements in the workplace. Even in the positive Norwegian cultural climate, however, diffusion from the experiments was difficult due to politics and traditionalism. Eventually, the work in Norway would spread to Sweden, where many more experiments like Gustavsen's (Chapter 1) were undertaken during the next two decades. Later, the Dutch developed a distinct and strong school of socio-techical thinking that was widely embraced by managers in Dutch industries.

In the late 1960s, some of the first 'greenfield' (from the ground up) applications of socio-technical systems thinking occurred. These ideas were employed by Shell in the construction of a new refinery in the UK (Hill, 1971). In the USA, links between Tavistock researchers and their American colleagues led to the pioneering design of a pet food production facility in Topeka, Kansas (Walton, 1972). After these notable successes, diffusion of the socio-technical systems paradigm occurred rapidly, but always in the face of stiff resistance from those who preferred the comfort of traditional ways of managing.

Two other streams of work emanating from the Tavistock group are worth noting in light of the other chapters in this volume. First is the evolution of the search conference (Emery and Purser, 1996) which was born out of work in the 1950s to bring together a varied group of British government and industry officials to discuss the future of a troubled aircraft engine company. Recognizing from systems theory that organizations are influenced by their environments, Trist and his colleagues sought to influence the environment directly in order to make it more conducive to the company's survival. The success of that initial effort led to the refinement and reapplication of the search conference method to many other business and community applications. It is also partly responsible for the stream of work that today is known as large group interventions.

The second stream of work built upon Trist's recognition that the environment itself was changing (Emery and Trist, 1965) and that interventions in the environment would be required to create more positive human futures. Trist labelled this field of inquiry 'social ecology' (Emery and Trist, 1973). Again, the foundation for the development of Trist's thinking was action research, in this case led by studies in the 1950s and 1960s with the National Union of Farmers and the municipal government of Coventry. Later, when spending time with Russell Ackoff at Wharton, Trist came to believe that planning by central administrators was unlikely to resolve the complex social 'messes' (Ackoff, 1974) associated with post-industrial society. He sharpened his thinking about the usefulness of Ackoff's adaptive planning in societal transformation. Trist recognized that the traditional mode of societal planning, like the traditional mode of organizing work, was technocratically devised and centrally imposed from the top. A plan was supposed to show the path from the present state to a desired future state and it was supposed to be implemented by resources under the control of a hierarchy. As Trist explained, 'This represents closed systems thinking, the machine theory of organizing, the maximization of power – everything which the encounter with higher levels of complexity and uncertainty has shown to be unworkable' (Emery and Trist, 1973: 203).

Trist was on the leading edge of those proclaiming that planning in the current era is not a programme but a process – a social democratic process in which participation in planning leads to learning, which overcomes resistance to change, which leads to implementation. Effectiveness is increased both by engaging a wider variety of perspectives, requisite to dealing with the new environmental complexity and by creating commitment, by virtue of their participation, among those most directly concerned. Trist's involvement in communities in Jamestown, New York, Sudbury, Ontario and Craigmillar, Scotland, demonstrated the efficacy of bringing diverse members of communities together to take responsibility for planning their communities' futures:

> The combination of adaptive planning and action research, via collaboration between social actors and social scientists, enhances the likelihood that the process will not only produce action but also capability – increasing capability to be proactive in choosing and attaining one of the more desirable futures that await us. (Trist, 1979)

Many of the chapters in this volume address topics which would have resonated with Trist's own interest in improving the human condition through collaborative action research.

Socio-technical Systems Theory

While Trist, Rice and others were pioneering Tavistock's work in the field, Fred Emery, who joined Tavistock in 1951, was leading efforts to conceptualize theories that could explain what the group was discovering. In *Characteristics of Socio-Technical Systems* (1959), Emery conveyed important principles of socio-technical work design, hewn largely from the coal-mining studies and weaving experiments in the group's formative years. Drawing heavily on open systems theory, Emery explored the nature of technical systems, social systems, and the work relationship structures that bring the two systems together. Emery defined the dimensions of the technical system to include: the nature of the material being worked upon (e.g., physical properties of coal); the level of mechanization or automation; unit operations (steps that result in a physical transformation of the product); the degree of centrality of certain operations compared to others; required maintenance operations; supply operations; the spatial layout of the operation and the spread of the process over time; the immediate physical work setting; and the nature of interdependence among tasks. Each of these dimensions has the potential to affect the nature of roles and role relationships, and hence the level of productivity and quality of work life of the work system as a whole.

The dimensions of the social system, while less precisely defined than the dimensions of the technical system, were said to include: tasks and task interdependencies that constitute occupational roles; the grouping of roles into teams around tasks; the nature of co-ordination and control; the effectiveness of boundary management; the degree of delegation of responsibility; and the degree of reliance on the expertise of workers in making complex judgements and decisions.

Emery argued that because organizations employ whole persons, it is important to pay attention to human needs beyond those required for the regular performance of tasks dictated by the technology. His psychological requirements for individuals include: some control over the material and processes of the task; that the task itself be structured to induce forces on the individual towards aiding its completion; that the task have some variety and opportunity for learning; and that the task be continuously interesting and meaningful.

Emery's paradigm was in violent conflict with the master/servant relationship that characterizes many workplaces. Instead, Emery considered the creation of a more symmetrical relationship vitally important, a relationship in which management recognizes that no work can be accomplished without workers, and therefore values their contributions to decision-making. Some managers have mistaken this concern for the influence of workers in decision-making to be a veiled form of advocacy for communism. In fact, Emery was a staunch supporter of free market economies. His primary concern was with the effectiveness of work systems, not with who owned them.

Emery also helped us to understand that the continued extreme fractionation of work, best represented by the assembly line, can and often does exceed that level of fractionation which produces optimal results. Taking a systems perspective, Emery clarified that the fractionation of work creates an inability to control the system as a whole, rather than greater control, as assumed by designers of the system. Because the system seldom operates perfectly, even small problems can create large systemic impacts. In highly fractionated work systems, the single worker is powerless to correct the situation. Each person is 'tied to the job' or machine and cannot change the technical system to compensate for the disturbance. Instead, Emery proposed that the basic unit for design of socio-technical systems must itself be a socio-technical unit and have the characteristics of an open system. By this, he meant a small (8–10 person) self-managing group of workers who, among the members of the group, possess the skills and authority to control the operation of their technology.

At a larger system level, the success of each group would depend on the linkages among the groups, and the logic of control (in this case, self-control) behind those linkages. Three principles of design emerged from this analysis: first, that the best design for a productive system is one in which each part of the system embodies the goals of the overall system; secondly, that the parts should be self-managing to the point that they can cope with problems by rearranging their own use of resources; and thirdly, that members that make up the parts of the system are multi-skilled in ways that allow them to cope with anticipated needs to rearrange themselves around problems or opportunities that might arise.

Of the three design principles, the second has proven to be the most pivotal in distinguishing the socio-technical systems paradigm from other approaches to work. Emery distinguished between organization designs that address the problem of adapting to problems or change through either the redundancy of parts (each part/person is replaceable; when one fails, the other takes over) or through the redundancy of functions (aka, the second design principle).

But far more than simply allowing people to be more timely in their response to problems, Emery pointed out how only the second design principle permits adaptation to change, and hence fosters the democratization of work through adaptive planning, using highly participative methods. In organizations designed on a redundancy of parts, the limitations of individual jobs makes adaptation through learning difficult. This insight has tremendous implications for organizational inquiry and learning. Senge and Scharmer (Chapter 17) and Torbert (Chapter 18) also recognize that our thinking should be more prominent about these topics.

Thus, proponents of the socio-technical systems paradigm proved that action research could indeed lead to advancements in theory as well as producing positive and practical social change. More traditional, tightly controlled research methods or more purely theoretical approaches may have produced significant learning as well; but there can be no argument about the richness of thought and the applicability of methods conceived by the Tavistock pioneers using action research methods.

Emergent Synergies between AR and STS

The confluence of Lewin's action research school and the Tavistock's socio-technical systems thinking was hastened by the fact that Lewin and Trist remained in close contact, as did many other members of their groups. Each group was propelled forward by the need to invent methods and theories that could address practical problems of the day. Both groups were also highly committed to advancing scientific knowledge, particularly knowledge that would enable organizations and society to better themselves. A rough timeline of the events and ideas that shaped the history of each group is provided in Figure 3.1.

Each group started its work from the premise that change begins with the involvement of those directly affected. Each group, as it experimented with change in groups and organizations, came to see the need to address larger societal issues, requiring the evolution of more complex and inclusive change technologies, including large-group interventions. Each came to believe that the predominant paradigm of the time, which was based on expert hierarchical control of social systems, would never prove adequate to face the challenges of a modern, post-industrial society. Both felt that human dignity demanded that people have a role in setting the conditions that influenced the quality of their existence.

From a theoretical perspective, both groups embraced a form of open systems theory, in which the behaviour of actors was determined not just by their personalities but also by the environment or context within which the behaviour was observed. Both viewed involvement in decision-making as a means to enrich understanding and commitment to decisions, but moreover as a means to development and growth. While each school had its unique theories (Lewin's Field Theory and McGregor's Theory X and Theory Y, Emery's principles of work design and Emery and Trist's causal texture of environments), the theories were never incompatible. Indeed, the practical and theoretical contributions of the two groups were so closely aligned that it would be more sensible to describe them as one school of thought rather than two.

Looking towards the Future

What legacy have the pioneers of action research and socio-technical systems thinking left us, and

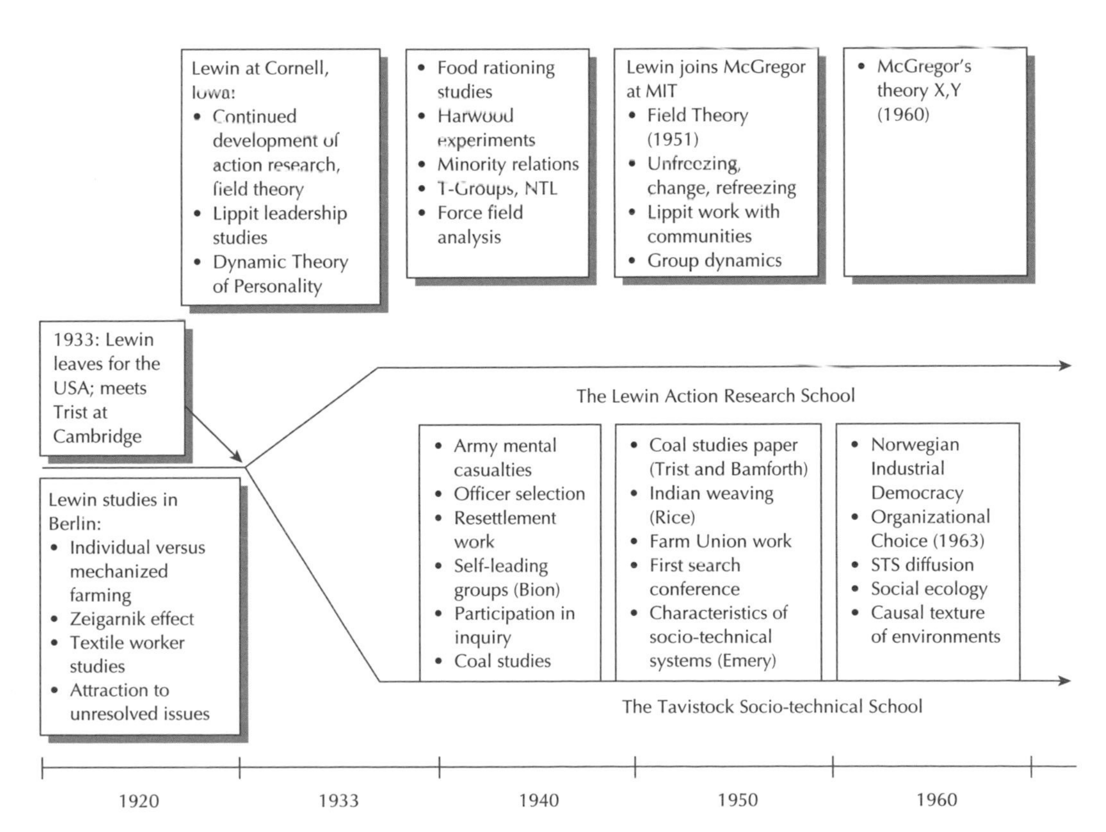

Figure 3.1 The confluence of action research and socio-technical systems thinking

what challenges remain for us to tackle? Is there important work yet to be done?

Lewin died suddenly in 1947 at the age of 57, at the height of his work. At that time, he was deeply concerned about overcoming individualism, which he viewed as a detriment to collaborative social learning and action.

Near the end of his life, Trist was disappointed with the rate of diffusion of socio-technical systems thinking. After nearly 50 years of work, he recognized that the paradigm of scientific management conceived by Taylor, linked with the control-oriented systems of bureaucratic management was still the dominant form of work organization. Democratic methods of management were still encountering stiff resistance, and even some successful demonstration projects had shown signs of regression in the face of traditional authoritarianism.

Both men had dedicated their lives to the betterment of organizations and society through the implementation of action research and democratic decision-making methods. Both were aware that despite their best efforts, powerful forces in society continued to provide resistance to their teachings. At this point, what can we say about the legacy they have left behind?

Lewin's work spawned a new approach to both inquiry and the management of change that has expanded its influence to applications that Lewin could never have envisioned. The chapters in this volume are perhaps the best testimony to the breadth of action research applications and the continuing interest in participative learning and decision-making. Whole fields (organization development, management development, community development, adult learning and global social change) have evolved using methods based on Lewin's thinking.

The impact of Trist's work is most visible in the methods of participation that have been built into decision-making in organizations and in the proliferation of large-group interventions to address organizational, community and global issues. To be certain, many individuals, organizations and communities have benefited directly or indirectly from the pioneering work of these two founding giants.

From a scientific perspective, action research methods are more accepted by mainstream scientists, especially in the study of complex systemic phenomena that do not lend themselves easily to reductionistic methods. Field experiments, ethnography and case studies appear much more frequently in social science journals today than they did in 1947, when Lewin and Trist collaborated in founding the journal *Human Relations* in order to have a publication outlet for their work.

So there have been scientific advances and impressive, lasting effects of the action research paradigm. But how should we assess its current state? Despite their idealism, Lewin and Trist were fundamentally realists. Their work was thoughtful but practical and their assessment of the state of action research today would probably be the same.

In the 70 years since Lewin began to think about action research as a tool for learning and change, and in the 50 years since Trist began building upon his ideas, expert-based, non-participatory methods of inquiry and change have remained the dominant paradigm. When action research, organization development, or participative methods of community development are invoked, they almost always face scepticism, despite their impressive record of success. More often than not, we continue to witness change driven from the top down, by the few with the power to control the many, without regard to the potential benefits of greater involvement by those who must implement the new way of operating. We continue to see failed efforts to improve organizational performance or community well-being followed not by efforts to involve people in learning what went wrong but instead by replacing leaders with others who repeat the same process over and over again.

In science, we continue to find journals full of one-sided, reductionistic research, correlational studies among a few variables, and fragmented insights offered in the prevailing genre of separate fields analysing parts of complex social systems. Strategists, social psychologists, industrial psychologists and operational researchers find little time to read each other's work and when they do, more often than not find reasons to deride what they see. Curriculums of business schools, social work schools and public policy schools are similarly fragmented, making it difficult for the values inherent in action research to emerge powerfully from the din of alternative claims to truth.

Yes, action research continues to exist and to be widely practised. But it also continues to be an alternative paradigm, competing for legitimacy in the face of the same traditional forces that forced Lewin to flee Nazi Germany to pursue academic freedom in the USA. Those with power still use it to overrule involvement in decision-making by students, workers and citizens whenever they feel threatened by the outcomes that involvement might produce. Involvement and chaos are viewed as closely linked by those who prefer to trust their own judgement regarding what is good for their classes, their workplaces or their communities. The majority of important organizational decisions continue to be made by 'experts', most jobs continue to be designed with too much specialization, and the fate of most communities continues to be determined by elected officials rather than by the people whose interests politicians purport to represent.

These challenges to action research demonstrate that we are still firmly caught in the grasp of technological determinism and scientific positivism.

Human needs continue to be secondary to technical and economic advancement as measures of the progress of society. If this course of events goes unchallenged, its way of thinking will block the development of solutions that could eventually shift the dominant paradigm to one which is more inclusive and egalitarian. To challenge the dominant view will require a paradigm shift that accomplishes the following ten objectives effectively.

1. The new paradigm would elevate the quality of total human experience above measures of economic progress as the primary measure for the advancement of society. Measures of economic progress would still be important, but secondary and in service of measures of the quality of human experience.
2. The new paradigm would devise ways of making expert knowledge readily available to those who need to draw upon it in order to make decisions that affect their systems.
3. The new paradigm would place the speed of learning and adaptation above costs and efficiencies as the ultimate measures of performance of a system.
4. The new paradigm would elevate environmental and community issues above the creation of wealth as the primary political concern. This would re-align societal goals with important shared interests and put power in the hands of the many rather than the few.
5. The new paradigm would restore human dignity as an important criterion for evaluating methods used in educational, organizational and political systems.
6. The new paradigm would call for enhanced diversity in scientific methods and ways of knowing. Positivism and reductionism would not be left behind; instead, more balance would be given to multiple ways of inquiring into important societal problems.
7. The new paradigm would ensure that information systems, productive systems and political systems are designed in accordance with the unique needs of those they serve and in such a way as to locate control over changes in their design to users rather than experts.
8. Since the boundaries of organizations, communities and even countries are becoming increasingly irrelevant, the new paradigm would target groups that share interests for intervention.
9. Recognizing that people working together globally will become as important as people working alone or locally, the new paradigm will develop ways for people to utilize diversity effectively.
10. The new paradigm would continue to explore ways for organizations and societies to develop, release and utilize the tremendous capabilities that are currently trapped in people operating within rigid structures. Rigid structures which are efficient in the short run are inherently inefficient in adapting to change. Structures themselves must be examined and re-invented to free organizations and communities from self-imposed limitations on the speed and direction of their development while at the same time devising methods to prevent anarchy and chaos.

Taken together, these challenges pose a formidable challenge to action researchers. Seventy years of successful experimentation, theorizing and attempts to change the dominant paradigm through practical demonstrations, publications and exhortation have failed to turn the tide. Yet, the alternative world that would be created by defaulting to the current dominant paradigm is all too easy to imagine. After 70 years of trying, is there value in continuing to work within the action research paradigm? One must answer, as Lewin and Trist did, with a vision in mind of the future one wishes to create.

References

Ackoff, R. (1974) *Redesigning the Future: a Systems Approach to Societal Problems*. New York: Wiley & Sons.

Ashby, W. (1960) *Design for a Brain*. New York: Wiley & Sons.

Bertalanffy, L. (1950) 'The theory of open systems in physics and biology', *Science*, 3: 22–9.

Bion, W. (1946) 'The Leaderless Group Project', *Bulletin of the Menninger Clinic*, 10: 77–81.

Bridger, H. (1990) *The Discovery of the Therapeutic Community: the Northfield Experiments*. Philadelphia, PA: The University of Pennsylvania Press.

Coch, L. and French, J. (1948) 'Overcoming resistance to change', *Human Relations*, 1: 512–33.

Dewey, J. (1933) *How We Think*. New York: Heath.

Emery, F. (1959) *Characteristics of Socio-technical Systems*. London: Tavistock Institute, Document #527.

Emery, F. and Trist, E. (1965) 'The causal texture of organizational environments', *Human Relations*, 18: 21–31.

Emery, F. and Trist, E. (1973) *Towards a Social Ecology: Contextual Appreciation of the Future in the Present*. London: Plenum Press.

Emery, M. and Purser, R. (1996) *The Search Conference*. San Francisco, CA: Jossey-Bass.

French, W. and Bell, C. (1984) *Organization Development: Behavioral Science Interventions for Organizational Improvement*. Engelwood Cliffs, NJ: Prentice-Hall.

Hill, P. (1971) *Towards a New Philosophy of Management*. New York: Barnes and Noble.

Levin, M. and Greenwood, D. (2001) 'Pragmatic action research and the struggle to transform universities into learning communities', in P. Reason and H. Bradbury (eds), *Handbook of Action Research: Participative Inquiry and Practice*. London: Sage Publications. pp. 103–13

Lewin, K. (1951) *Field Theory in Social Science: Selected Theoretical Papers*. New York: Harper & Row.

Marrow, A. (1969) *The Practical Theorist*. New York: Basic Books.

McGregor, D. (1960) *The Human Side of Enterprise*. New York: McGraw-Hill.

Miller, E. (1975) 'Sociotechnical systems in weaving, 1953–1970: a follow-up study', *Human Relations*, 28: 349–86.

Murray, H. (1990) *The Transformation of Selection Procedures: the War Office Selection Boards*. Philadelphia, PA: The University of Pennsylvania Press.

Pasmore, W. (1988) *Designing Effective Organizations: the Sociotechnical Systems Perspective*. New York: Wiley & Sons.

Rice, A. (1958) *Productivity and Social Organization: the Ahmedabad Experiment*. London: Tavistock.

Trist, E. (1979) 'New directions of hope: recent innovations interconnecting organizational, industrial, community and personal development', *Regional Studies*, 13: 439–51.

Trist, E. (1981) *The Sociotechnical Perspective: the Evolution of Sociotechnical Systems as a Conceptual Framework and as an Action Research Paradigm*. New York: Wiley & Sons.

Trist, E. and Bamforth, K. (1951) 'Some social and psychological consequences of the Longwall Method of coal-getting', *Human Relations*, 4: 3–38.

Trist, E., Higgin, G., Murray, H. and Pollock, A. (1963) *Organizational Choice: Capabilities of Groups at the Coal Face under Changing Technologies: the Loss, Rediscovery and Transformation of a Work Tradition*. London: Tavistock.

Trist, E. and Murray, H. (1990) *Historical Overview: the Foundation and Development of the Tavistock Institute*. Philadelphia, PA: The University of Pennsylvania Press.

Walton, R. (1972) 'How to counter alienation in the plant', *Harvard Business Review*, 50: 70–81.

Weisbord, M. (1987) *Productive Workplaces*. San Francisco, CA: Jossey-Bass.

4
Infusing Race into the US Discourse on Action Research

ELLA EDMONDSON BELL

CHAPTER OUTLINE

This chapter infuses race into the genre of action research and participatory inquiry, arguing that it has been implicitly absent so far. The chapter shares part of my journey, as a Black woman seeking ways to liberate Black people from social injustice and White racism. Using an historical lens from the 1960s to the 1990s, the evolution of Black liberation research and action research are blended, I show how the struggle for social justice and racial equality has informed action research. What emerges is a natural participative action research approach which suggests how we can address significant public and political events as inquiry.

My main purpose in offering this chapter is to infuse race into the dialogue on action research. In cooking, infusion is a technique of slowly introducing a new or uncommon ingredient to a dish. Infusing causes a subtle yet distinctive change in taste, and sometimes the texture of a dish, giving it layers of complexity. When infusing race into action research a similar result occurs. There is an interlocking complexity of social relations, social issues and social justice all infused with race, class and gender. I will begin by narrating how I, a Black woman, gradually infused myself into action research. Then I will describe how the Black struggle for civil rights infused the meaning of action research in the 1960s, and Black participatory inquiry in the 1990s.

My Journey towards Action Research and Participatory Inquiry

When I was in graduate school, I discovered a book with a very provocative title, *The Death of White Sociology* edited by Joyce Ladner (1973). For an historical reference point, the publication of this book followed on the heels of the tumultuous 1960s, leading right into the height of the Black Nationalist movement. The book consisted of a series of essays by both sociologists and psychologists, a majority of them being African-American. Their essays described the emergence of a critically radical way of thinking about social science research. The authors proclaimed a social science ideology that was proactive for liberating Black inner-city communities from the oppressive elements of racism, classism and poverty. Based on this ideology, research was a key tool for social liberation. They called the new ideology 'Black Sociology'. Ladner claimed the reasons for its importance as, 'a reaction to, and revolt against, the biases of mainstream bourgeois, liberal sociology; and as a positive step toward setting forth basic definitions, concepts, and theory-building that utilize the experiences and histories of Afro-Americans' (Ladner, 1973: xix).

The book made a big impact on me. I carried it around with me for months. Why? Because Ladner had the sass, the intellect and the nerve to challenge the White academic status quo, by putting the issue of racism squarely in their face. I admired her courage. Here I was a Black woman in my early twenties, having lived most of my early life in the South Bronx section of New York City. In the years since my childhood, South Bronx has earned a national reputation as the capital of inner-city ghettos. It was a neighbourhood where few had successfully made it out. But, I did. Returning to my old neighbourhood, I spent my days teaching Black and Latino children, who were bright and curious, but who were labelled uneducable by the system. My nights were spent at Teachers College, Columbia University, where I was working on a degree in urban education. In those days, my main goal was to dismantle an oppressive system. I desperately wanted to rebuild my community which had been broken emotionally, spiritually and physically. But being naive, impatient and unknowledgeable worked against even the best of my intentions. I soon discovered that working towards a degree in urban education was not leading me in the right direction. The programme's emphasis was on traditional research methods which had continually proven to disserve, alienate and undermine the Black community.

The Death of White Sociology opened my eyes to the idea that research could facilitate social justice and radical organizational change. Research when done in the hands of Joyce Ladner, Kenneth Clark, William Cross and Andrew Billingsley was a force for social equality and economic emancipation in the torn war zones of inner-city communities. It is no overstatement to say that reading this book deeply influenced my decision to one day further my graduate education. I wanted to follow in the footsteps of Ladner, Clark and DuBois. Some ten years later I enrolled in a doctoral programme in the School of Management at Case Western Reserve University. My new chosen field of study was organizational behaviour. Case's programme incorporated heavy doses of organizational development theories, adult learning and experiential teaching techniques. Its explicit underlying assumptions were on personal development, organizational change for greater democratization and societal involvement for those who had been traditionally marginalized. Dissertations were often studies of change efforts in organizations or communities. Both the programme's ideology and method were firmly planted in the fertile ground of action research.

Throughout my graduate school experience, I kept trying to integrate what I knew about Black sociology with the theories of Lewin (1951), Mitroff and Kilmann (1978), Freire (1970) and Wolfe (1980). Trying to weave these ideologies together was often frustrating. There was little, if any, acknowledgement of the scholarly work of Black social scientists in a management programme. Rarely did I find references made to critical race theory or acknowledgements given to Black social scientists for their contributions to the action research genre. The implicit message was that their work was not legitimate and did not fit into any organizational behaviour perspectives. My professors were unaware of the fact that one of the roots of action research was deeply embedded in the progressive research on race. This should not be surprising, since topics of race, racism and institutional racism have been ignored in the managerial literature until very recently (Cox and Nkomo, 1990; Nkomo, 1992).

Such invisibility was not the case for all marginalized voices. The linkage between gender and action research discourse has slowly, but surely, become evident. Several books on action research specifically credit feminist theory and the feminist voice in discussions on the evolution of this method (Heron, 1996; Reason and Rowan, 1981). For example, in *Voices of Change: Participatory Research in the United States and Canada* (Park et al., 1993) the authors include a section in their introduction entitled, 'the feminist advance', and they acknowledge the contributions of Patricia Maguire (1987), Dorothy Smith (1979) and Marja-Liisa Swantz (1982). Budd Hall (1992) credits Maguire for what he calls bridging 'feminist research approaches and participatory research' in her 1987 book, which points out what she called the 'androcentric filter' in participatory research writing. Women's voices were not heard in the writing on participatory research until 1981, when society was well into the women's movement (Hall, 1992; Maguire, 1987).

There may be other factors to consider for the invisibility of race in action research discourse. This discourse has been far more global than racial, particularly in relation to struggles for racial equality in America. Much of the writing available on action research represents its evolution in developing countries, such as in Latin America and in Africa (Hall, 1993; Park et al., 1993). These countries were the hot spots of social movements to dismantle colonialism. Yet, in the USA where the fight for racial equality has historically dominated the landscape, an eerie silence lurks when it comes to discussing action research techniques to dismantle racial oppression. There are a few exceptions.

Much of the writings on the civil rights and Black Nationalist movements, while firmly rooted in the action research tradition, often failed to make a direct link to action research approaches. Notable exceptions include writings produced by those individuals associated with the Highlander Research and Education Center (Adams, 1975; Glen, 1996; Horton, Horton and Kohl, 1990). The sociological and historical accounts of this era tell the powerful story of Highlander's critical role and involvement (Clark, 1965; Morris, 1984; Payne, 1995). I do not cover this material in my chapter, because Helen Lewis does an excellent job in her chapter on Highlander's story (Chapter 24). Since there is a literature linking the civil rights movement to action research, I have chosen another important historical moment, the early 1970s, when Black liberation research was making its debut in the social sciences. My intent is to reveal the nature of the relationship between them. The discourse between Black liberation research and participatory inquiry re-emerged in the early 1990s, albeit differently, as I will discuss in the following sections. By juxtaposing these two historical moments, I hope to illuminate the importance of social context in determining the dimensions of inquiry and the kinds of interventions generated when race is infused with action research.

Setting the Stage for the Birth of the Black Liberation Social Science Movement

The South Side of Chicago, Black Bottom, Detroit; Roxbury, Boston; Watts, Los Angeles; the Hough section of Cleveland; Fort Apache, South Bronx, Bedford-Stuyvesant and Harlem, all in New York City; these are some of the worst inner-city communities – urban homelands – in the USA. My use of the word homeland is intentional. Borrowed from the South African system of apartheid, homelands were government-designated areas of land to which people from varying Black ethnic groups were restricted. For me, the meaning of homeland has a different twist. Urban homelands denote not only a geographic place, but because communities undergo transitions, erode and sometimes even vanish, homelands also represent a given period of time. In the time between the 1960s and the 1970s, urban homelands were where a majority of African Americans lived, where they shared a collective history and held a common understanding of the world, particularly the White world. But, urban homelands in this country shared a dark commonality with their South African brethren. Inner-city ghettos were self-contained neighbourhoods. They were cut off – geographically, physically, economically and psychologically – from other areas of the city where Whites lived. Within these communities African-Americans established their own centres of commerce, selected their own community leaders and created their own cultural ethos, based on African-American values and traditions. Take Harlem, for example. Harlem was the birthplace for the renaissance of Black art and letters; it was home to the Marcus Garvey Movement – a Pan-Africanist strategy for Black economic and social advancement – and it was where Malcolm X preached on the corner of Lenox Avenue and 166th Street.

But there was the other side of urban homelands and inner-city life. In the early 1970s Harlem and other ghetto communities throughout the nation suffered from substandard housing, high rates of infant mortality, unemployment and inferior schools. The *New York Times* reported a growing disparity between Blacks and Whites living in New York City. In 1964 the median annual income for Blacks was $3,995 compared to $6,100 for Whites. In Harlem, 49 per cent of the housing was classified as substandard; the figure was only 15 per cent for the rest of the city. The infant mortality rate for Black infants was 45.3 per cent compared to 26.3 per cent for White infants. The unemployment rate was 15 per cent for Harlem residents and only 5 per cent for other New Yorkers. Robert Conote, author of *River of Blood, Years of Darkness* (1967), illuminated clearly some of the discriminatory barriers that faced ghettoized Blacks: 'A refrigerator that might cost $99 elsewhere, would go for $169, a stereo set selling for $600 in a store located where there was competition would be priced at $1,000' (1967: 26). These were stark reminders of the existence of an apartheid system, albeit American style.

In the wake of the riots, hope abounded for rebuilding ghettos. The spirit of Black nationalistic pride was captured in three simple words, 'Black is beautiful'. This was the historical moment in which Black liberation research was born. But, there was another factor, a significant one. A new wave of scholarly research written by White men on the minority experience in America made its debut in academic journals and public policy reports. Authors of these writings painted a dark, demeaning and ugly portrait of Black life. Inner-city communities were described as being crime-infested, drug-infested, and dirt-infested. Black people who inhabited ghettos were portrayed as deviants of every kind, especially when compared to White people. The Black family was the focal point of White researchers, however. In inner city communities family life, especially among the working poor, was described as disintegrating and disorganized (Glazer and Moynihan, 1965; Lewis, 1968; Moynihan, 1965; Rainwater, 1970). In his report, *The Negro Family: a Case for National Action* (1965), Daniel Moynihan characterized the Black family as a 'tangle of pathologies', that was 'at the heart of the deterioration of Negro society' (quoted in Martin and Martin, 1978: 106). His idea for uplifting the black community was 'large-scale government intervention for the rehabilitation and restructuring of lower-class black family life' (Martin and Martin, 1978: 107).

This particular genre of sociological investigation was labelled as the 'pejorative perspective' (Hill, 1972) or the 'pathology-disorganization perspective' (Martin and Martin, 1978). The pejorative method worked mainly through dichotomous thinking and objectification, with the object needing to be controlled and manipulated (Collins, 1990). And, as we shall soon learn, this perspective was a galvanizing force for young, newly trained African-American social scientists.

The Changing Tide

And when we speak we are afraid
Our words will not be heard
Nor welcomed

> But when we are silent
> We are still afraid
> So it is better to speak
> Remembering
> We were never meant to survive
> (Litany for Survival, Audre Lorde, 1984)

In the late 1960s and early 1970s, the tides of the pejorative tradition began to recede. Starting with the civil rights movement, then growing strong with the Black Nationalist, Black Students and Black Arts movements, the pejorative approach was being seriously challenged. For the first time in history, there was an ample cadre of Black intellectuals, community activists, lawyers and clinicians to take on the system. Moynihan's report was the lightening rod that unified Black voices. As Martin and Martin suggest, 'The Moynihan report aroused consternation among blacks because it came during a time when the black consciousness mood was sweeping the nation, when blacks were taking a positive view of themselves and were actively seeking liberation from racial oppression' (1978: 108).

The tide of change became dramatically visible in the academic world at the American Sociological Association meeting in 1968. At this meeting a group of Black sociologists organized the 'Caucus of Black Sociologists'. This group called for the decoupling of Black sociology from mainstream White sociology. Progressive Black sociologists understood that the Black family was being targeted as deviants. The situation was that Black families were being isolated from White society because they were perceived as a societal problem. Black researchers knew full well that family disorganization was not a problem solely relegated to the Black community. White communities had their fair share of dysfunctional families as well. A major point of contention was that White, mainstream social scientists never mentioned the oppressive economic and social web that had historically locked Blacks into poverty. Thus, a key question for Black sociologists was an action research type of question: 'How does Black social science contribute to the survival and development of Black people in the United States and in the Diaspora?' (Staples, 1973: 210).

The Black Liberation's Tenets and its Links to Action Research

The tenets of the Black liberation research approach are: (1) to move beyond traditional methods, by (2) creating knowledge for the sake of economic, political and social change in the Black community, and (3) without forsaking rigorous social investigation. Research was a tool to dismantle the master's house, and to achieve social justice. It was also to be used as a building block in the creation of Black social institutions (Walters, 1973: 206) Under these circumstances, the role of the Black social scientist was to be both scholar and social activist.

A strong principle was the call for collaboration between Black social scientists and members of the Black community. The traditional, positivist stance of distance and non-communication between researcher and subject was totally unacceptable. Or, as Black social scientists put it: the historically exploitative, oppressive position that a majority of White social scientists held towards minority groups would no longer be tolerated. The group called for the organization of community action committees to work with academics in planning and implementing projects. These committees also served an evaluative role. As political scientist Ronald Walters underscored, the community research review committee, 'was to screen actual research proposals and otherwise evaluate the project and finally to provide results to the community' (1973: 206). It would be community members who finally decided how to use knowledge gleaned from research. This stance of community members being responsible for building knowledge for the purpose of social equality and organizational change is one of the core values of action research. Today we would identify this collaborative problem thinking process as a form of participatory co-inquiry. As a research approach, co-inquiry emphasizes the research process as an elevating learning experience for all those involved in the research endeavour, stimulating dialogue between the researcher and participant in the creation of new knowledge (Argyris, 1970; Bell, 1990).

It is important not to overlook the fact that Black liberation research had support and comrades among White scholars, too. The political, social and ethical roles of social scientists were also being rethought and challenged among some White scholars. David Wellman, a member of the Union of Radical Sociologists, and Robert Blauner, author of *Internal Colonialism and Ghetto Revolt* (1969), are two White men who were actively involved in the liberation cause. Having conducted a study on the lived experiences of Black people, they were keenly aware of the hostility, resentment and distrust the Black community held towards White social scientists. What they understood was quite simple, 'People knew that sociologists have been used by government agencies to develop more sophisticated techniques for the control of poor people' (Blauner and Wellman, 1973: 322). Blauner and Wellman challenged traditional White positivist research on three dimensions: the inegalitarian nature of traditional research when it came to minority communities; the colonalized nature of the research process; and 'the intensification of these dynamics which stems from the structure of the university as setting and sponsor of social research' (p. 314).

Realizing the dire scope of the situation and the complexities involved, in terms of the Black community and White social science institutions, Blauner and Wellman called for 'new organizational formats: centers or institutes that integrate social action, change and community assistance with the theoretical and empirical goals of researchers' (pp. 327–8). Such centres would accommodate and support traditional researchers working alongside practitioners.

An explicit goal of Black liberation research was to gain a broader knowledge of Black life, as it was lived every day, by men and women, families and children. This called for thick analyses, combining research methods that enabled social scientists to inquire into the language, culture, traditions, social relations and political realities of the Black community. While rigour was considered to be important, it was equally important to use methods that allowed for collaboration, and equalized the relationship between researcher and participant. Blauner and Wellman put it this way, 'social scientists realize the need for a series of deep, solid ethnographies of Black and Third World communities' (p. 329). Within this group, there was also a general consensus that Blacks should serve in the role of principal investigators. After all, they had first-hand experience about the everyday realities of Black life because they were members of this community. Some believed 'White researchers [were] biased toward their own norms and standards, and their objectivity was often influenced by their vested interests ... maintaining a subservient working class for capitalist exploitation ...' (Harris and McCullough, 1973: 335). Through a scholarly lens, Black social scientists could more readily interpret Black life from a positive perspective, one that revealed the community's strength and resilience living under oppression.

Thus far, I have traced the evolution of the Black liberation research, and the case against the White positivist research tradition. I have described links between Black liberation research and action research. Next, several scholarly examples are presented to better illuminate the connection between Black liberation research and action research.

Examples of Research Taken from the Black Research Tradition

Kenneth Clark's *Dark Ghetto* (1965) has been cast by some as a work with pejorative overtones towards the Black community (Martin and Martin, 1978). While faulted for his harsh accounts of everyday life in Harlem, his goal was to produce a study with a balanced view of this community. Clark, having spent his childhood in Harlem and as a resident in adulthood, sought to portray in his work 'the feelings, the thoughts, the strengths and weaknesses of the people who lived in the ghetto' (Clark, 1965: xv). His study grew out of a planning report written for the government anti-poverty programme, HARYOU – Harlem Youth Opportunities Unlimited. The purpose of the initial report was to investigate the day-to-day realities of inner-city youth with the intention of using the data to design programming targeted for adolescents. Originally on HARYOU's planning staff, Clark decided a deeper study was merited.

Clark's underlying ideology is clearly one of an action research stance. He declares, 'I believe that to be taken seriously, to be viable, and to be relevant social science must dare to study the real problems of men and society, must use the real community, the market place, the arena of politics and power as its laboratories, and must confront and seek to understand the dynamics of social action and social change' (Clark, 1973: 409). And, involving the 'real community', was exactly what he did. When conducting his study, Clark involved members of Harlem's community, including young people. Adolescents from varying economic and educational backgrounds, were included in the planning and implementation of the study. The group of active participants became known as the HARYOU Associates. They served on committees, pretested research protocols, met with federal and city representatives and helped to develop ways to integrate the study into the fabric of the community. Their participation empowered them to be actively involved in reconstructing a different reality, and to change some of the conditions shaping their lives. According to Clark's own account, '[they] brought me into the vortex of the ghetto community' (Clark, 1973: 401). Understand that by involving members of the Harlem community in his research team, Clark's approach was highly unusual, especially for a psychologist in the 1960s.

Long before it was considered in vogue by some social scientists, Clark displayed the courage to discuss his own vulnerabilities and fears as the principal investigator of *Dark Ghetto*. He coined the term 'involved observer', to capture the way he straddled two worlds: that of the researcher and that of the Black man. Clark poignantly writes:

> I could never be fully detached as a scholar or participant. More than forty years of my life had been lived in Harlem. I started school in Harlem public schools. I first learned about people, about love, about cruelty, and sacrifice, about cowardice, about courage, about bombast in Harlem. For many years before I returned as an 'involved observer,' Harlem had been my home. My family moved from house to house, and from neighborhood to neighborhood within the walls of the ghetto in a desperate attempt to escape its creeping blight. In a very real sense, therefore, Dark Ghetto, is a summation of my personal and lifelong observations as

> a prisoner within the ghetto long before I was aware that I was really a prisoner. (1973: 402)

For Clark, involved observers are in some way, shaped by and connected to the individuals, groups or community they are studying. He distinguishes this kind of observer from a participant observer because the latter 'demands participation not only in rituals and customs but in the social competition with the hierarchy in dealing with the problems of the people he is seeking to understand' (1973: 403). Clark's involved observer is similar to Torbert's (1991) 'observant participant' and Ruth Behar's (1996) 'vulnerable observer'. Behar, an anthropologist, is referring to the researchers' emotional relationship with and involvement in their work. It is the researcher as data point: making it clear where she was coming from in doing the work; what got turned upside down and inside out in her world as a result of doing the work; and the surprising twists and turns she encountered along the way. Behar is describing the internal process of authorship. Clifford Geertz framed it as the 'burden of authorship' (1989: 5–6).

Two other scholarly works found in the Black liberation genre are also worth mentioning because of their links to action research. First, there is Joyce Ladner's *Tomorrow's Tomorrow: the Black Woman* (1971). The study is consistently noted in the literature as being among the first to use a 'strength–resiliency' perspective in understanding Black life in the USA (Hill, 1972; Martin and Martin, 1978; Stack, 1974). This perspective examines how African-American families survive, and in some cases even flourish, in spite of poverty and institutionalized racism. Questions Ladner sought to answer in her work were: 'What is life like in the urban Black community for the "average" girl? How does she define her roles, behaviors, and from whom does she acquire her models for fulfilling what is expected of her?' (1971: xxxi).

It is not clear exactly how much involvement Ladner's participants had in assisting her to shape the inquiry. She did spend four years interviewing the girls – ranging between 13 and 18 years old – and observing them. What is evident, however, is her commitment to establishing a strong bond with the girls. She worked very hard at entering and becoming an integral part of their world. Similar to Clark, Ladner too deeply struggles with her dual roles of researcher and Black woman. Ladner, unlike the Black girls from an inner city she interviewed, was raised in rural Mississippi. Even though the contexts were worlds apart, she had to identify with their feelings of anger and pain, but also their sense of hope and determination to survive. With candour and courage, she reflected on the challenges she encountered:

> As I became more involved with the subjects of this research, I knew that I would not be able to play the role of the dispassionate scientist, whose major objective was to extract certain data from them that would simply be used to describe and theorize about their conditions. I began to perceive my role as a Black person, with empathy and attachment, and, to a great extent, their day-to-day lives and future destinies became intricately interwoven with my own. This did not occur without a considerable amount of agonizing, self-evaluation and conflict over 'whose side I was on'. (Ladner, 1971: xxi–xxii)

Carol Stack's *All Our Kin* (1974), is the other example. Stack stands apart from both Clark and Ladner in two ways: she is an anthropologist and a White woman. While anthropologists are known to do fieldwork, Stack explicitly turned traditional anthropological method on its head. She credits Cicourel's (1964) work for helping her to develop alternative methodological devices in her own study. Forewarned by White colleagues and friends of the perils of a young White woman living in an inner-city neighbourhood, she moved with her young son to the poorest section of a Midwest urban, Black community. They remained there in a small apartment for three years, while she inquired into the 'collective adaptations to poverty of men, women, and children within the social-cultural network of the urban Black family' (Stack, 1974: 28).

In entering the community, Stack refused to build her informant base by customary means. She did not seek assistance from members of the old, established power hierarchy in the community – pastors and politicians – to gain access to the community. 'They were regarded as "uppity" individuals who thought they were too good to sit down on an old couch', she wrote (p. x). By 'uppity' she means those Blacks who were too identified with the White community. She perceived that their association would jeopardize her ability to establish relationships with the 'regular' folks. In time she built strong bonds in the community and earned the nickname 'White Caroline'.

Stack was extremely aware of being a researcher, White, female and middle-class, conducting an investigation on poor Black people. Her ideology was clearly grounded in an action research stance. She believed in the political, social and economic empowerment of Black people. In her eyes, Black people must be involved in determining the fate of their communities and families. She especially believed in those Blacks who were politically active and committed to improving the education, healthcare, economic development and day-to-day conditions of their community. She wrote, 'such persons may in the future decide whether a research study of their community may be conducted and by whom. They choose to censor the findings that they believe may be used to repress, harm, or manipulate those studied' (p. x).

Anthropologists are dependent on their informants for data. Informants also act as guides and translators in a unknown terrain. Stack chose another way. More than informants, she hired three research assistants from families she knew, 'who were interested in the study, and who were imaginative and critical thinkers' (p. xi). They collaborated throughout the course of her research, but particularly in considering different topics to explore, families to interview, scheduling and 'mapping out meaningful questions about daily life in the community' (p. xi).

Fade out the 1970s, Turn to the 1990s

When the Black liberation social science movement emerged there was much hope that the plight of the poor urban Blacks could be transformed. The focus of Black liberation social science was primarily macro: problems in the structures, policies and institutions that contributed to institutionalized racism. The goal was for Black researchers and members of the Black community to work together, to learn about their problems and to take collective action in solving them. Under these circumstances, a number of studies employing the 'strength–resiliency' model and action research devices were generated. Plus, there were other advances.

The Black liberation social science movement ignited a fire, the flames of which can still be seen today. The Caucus of Black Sociologists became a national organization, the Association of Black Sociologists, on 9 August 1976. This organization holds a national annual conference prior to the American Sociological Meetings, has a student paper competition and presents a Distinguished Career Award (Conyers, 1992). In acts of true democratization and social equality, the Black Caucus made major strategic inroads in changing both the culture and structures of the American Sociological Association.

According to sociologist, Doris Y. Wilkerson, '... there is agreement that the structures of the American Sociological Association had been transformed by the external sociopolitical climate and the collective activism of white women and black men and women sociologists who felt that the profession was not responsive to their intellectual and professional need and concerns at the time' (1992: 8). Collaborative efforts between the Black Caucus and the American Sociological Association resulted in the establishment of the following: the Committee on Racial and Ethnic Minorities in Sociology; the Minority Fellowship Program; the DuBois–Johnson–Frazier Award; and the Office of Executive Specialist, for managing issues of women and minorities. On a personal level, I can testify for the support, resources, training, networking and mentoring given to fellows of the Minority Fellowship Program. I am one of 395 Latino, Asian-American, Native American and African-American fellows, 214 of whom have received their doctorates in the 23-year history of the programme. Nationally, this programme has had the highest success record for helping minorities get through doctoral studies.

Unfortunately, newly created knowledge and organizational interventions could not change the horror of things to come. By the 1980s, the Republicans, starting with President Ronald Reagan and continuing with President George Bush, regained political office. The effect of this Republican era was particularly devastating on poor urban communities. Between increased joblessness in urban areas and deep slashes in federal spending, there was a strong economic decline for poor urban Blacks. This economic downswing was coupled with a mass exiting of middle-class Blacks who had the education, skills and financial resources to relocate to gilded suburban neighbourhoods. Black migration left only those without skills, little training and insufficient political savvy to do battle. And, this marked just the beginning of the tragedy. By the 1990s inner-city neighbourhoods were plagued by every social ill imaginable: Black on Black crime, female headed households, youth killing youth, crack cocaine addiction, AIDS, homelessness and joblessness (Ladner, 1995: xiv).

Once Again, the Tide Changes

> We will not be silenced ... We pledge ourselves to continue to speak out in defense of one another, in defense of the African American community and against those who are hostile to social injustice no matter what color they are. No one will speak for us but ourselves. (African American Women In Defense of Ourselves)

The early 1990s brought the first strong wave of the dismantling of affirmative action. Colour blindness, thanks to political correctness, was the term of choice to describe race relations, or should I say the lack of race relations. Race was no longer thought to be relevant by most of White America. After all, Blacks were represented in most sectors of government (with the exception of the Senate and the White House). Industry reported a modest share of them (with the exception of any in top-ranking executive positions). They were accepted in institutions of higher education (although fewer in numbers in elite schools). Whites and Blacks now lived in integrated housing developments (although they rarely socialize with one another). Blacks were seen in major films and on television (although they still play stereotypical roles). Why there had even been several Black Miss Americas, indicating a breakthrough in standards of beauty for American women. African-Americans had broken through all the apparent colour barriers. With obstacles behind them, issues of class were the hot topic for the 1990s. Enter Anita Hill.

Anita Hill appeared on the public scene on 11 October 1991, when she testified before the United States Senate Judiciary Committee that Clarence Thomas had sexually harassed her when she worked for him at the Equal Employment Opportunities Commission in the early 1980s. Thomas, a Black conservative, was nominated by President George Bush to replace Thurgood Marshall on the Supreme Court. Hill's testimony and Thomas's ardent denial were nationally televized live for all of America to witness. Coverage of the story made front-page news until after Thomas was finally sworn into the Supreme Court. The Hill–Thomas controversy created a race event, intersected with gender and sex, of mythical and epic proportions.

Hill, herself a conservative, was a well educated, Yale-trained lawyer turned professor, who reluctantly testified against Thomas. In response to her testimony, she was labelled with 'just about every psychopathic disorder known to womankind' (Bell, 1992: 365). Then there were the usual pathological stereotypes attributed to Black women: wanton, sexually promiscuous, insatiable, and out to demean any Black man just for the fun it. Thomas, knowing full well he was playing the cruelest of race cards, countered by proclaiming he was a victim of a 'high-tech lynching'. This time, however, the lynch mob was being led by a Black woman. 'Thomas and his supporters did not create a race and class context; they exploited it', proclaimed Elsa Barkley Brown (1995: 105). And, exploitation it was, for both Blacks and Whites. In the Black community Thomas's accusation conjured up old nightmares of Black men's lifeless bodies dangling from tree limbs. They circled their wagons against Hill in the name of 'race' comes first. In the White community, their Black guilt buttons were pushed, disempowering them to challenge Thomas further.

Hill's testimony both brought to light and broke Black women's code of silence that protected Black men and the Black community, even in times of abuse. Never before had the issue of sexuality between a Black man and a Black woman been played out before a national audience. In breaking the code, Hill was left to her own defence. To make matters worse, no one in Hill's camp, no one on the Judiciary Committee and no one in the media thought to bring in an expert who could offer an analysis on the intersection of race, gender, sexuality and class. In the end Thomas won. As Brown explains:

> When European American middle- and upper-class men harass and abuse European women, they are generally protected by white male privilege; when African American men harass and abuse European American women, they may be protected by male privilege, but they are likely to be subjected to racial hysteria; when African American men harass and abuse African American women, they are often supported by racist stereotypes that assume different sexual norms and different female value among African Americans. (1995: 104–5)

Distraught with frustration and anger at the invisibility of racialized sexism, not only in mainstream White America, but in Black America as well, Black professional women took collective action. Historians Elsa Barkley Brown and Barbara Ransby, and sociologist Deborah King, organized African American Women In Defense of Ourselves. Barbara Ransby maintained, 'There was no place for our anger or our insights. Ironically, an event that made a single Black woman more visible to more people than at any time in our recent memory simultaneously signified our collective invisibility' (1995: 46). There was an urgent need for Black women to make sense of the Hill–Thomas event, and come to terms about what could be learned from such a painful situation.

Brown, Ransby and King put out a call to Black women across the nation. They came up with the idea of placing a statement in the *New York Times* featuring Black women's position on the nomination of Clarence Thomas, the appalling treatment of Anita Hill by the all-White, male Senate Judiciary Committee, and President Bush's pathetic record on social equality and justice in the Black community. In addition, the names of Black women supporting the statement would be included as a part of the statement. Black women – academics, lawyers, school teachers, secretaries – came forth in bold numbers for the cause.

One thousand, six hundred and three women signed the full-page statement that appeared in the *New York Times* on 17 November 1991. In order to place the statement, the women collected over $10,000 in a six-week period. Donations came from Black women, but also sympathetic White women, and a number of Black men. In addition to the statement appearing in the *New York Times*, it was printed in 11 Black newspapers across the country. Deborah King remembers their strategy being to 'advertise in the *Times*, because it is a national paper of public record, but we also wanted to reach the Black community' (personal communication, 6 July 1999).

At least eight books were written on the Hill–Thomas epic, including edited books by Black intellectuals (Morrison, 1992; Smitherman, 1995), a two-volume special edition of *Black Scholar* (1991, 1992), and two round table discussions in *Tikkun* (1992). A democratic dialogue around race, gender, class, sexuality and the workplace took place in a way that had never before occurred in the USA. Black men and women were confronted with the very real reality of sexual harassment in their community, an issue that had remained, until Hill–Thomas, one of its dark secrets. White and Black women had to re-examine their relationship, taking into account how sexual harassment is racialized. Everyone, including White men, was challenged to consider the power, status and ignorance of elite, privileged, White men who served in elected offices. Executives and managers had to rethink and reinforce their policies, training programmes and procedures for handling sexual harassment cases.

Three years after the statement appeared in the *New York Times*, the first national conference on Black women in the academy was held at the Massachusetts Institute of Technology. 'Black Women in the Academy: Defending Our Name, 1984–1994' was a milestone event with well over 800 participants, representing every discipline, a number of different positions and a variety of universities. While there were no direct links between Brown, Ransby and King's initiative and the MIT conference, there can be no doubt that their work sparked the flame for the creation of such an important event for Black women in academe.

A Few Closing Thoughts

My intention in writing this chapter was to infuse race into the discourse of action research. What happens when the two are blended? The tradition emerges of employing an action research approach to understanding the life experiences of African-Americans, and their struggles to liberate themselves from poverty, institutional racism and White racism. In the late 1960s and early 1970s, the focus was primarily on dismantling oppressive institutional structures. Race was at the heart of the struggle. As a result, we witnessed large federal studies and smaller investigations, some with an action research orientation, inquiring into Black culture and life. By the 1990s much had changed in the struggle for social justice and equality in the Black community. Unlike the early 1970s, the 1990s triggered different forms of social change. The liberation for racial equality had expanded to embrace class and gender. What with cut backs in spending both from government and private sources, large-scale social science investigations were drastically decreased. Consequently, action research and participatory social inquiries on the micro level – first-person and second-person participatory inquiry – have emerged. Autobiographies, memoirs and self-reflexive writings by Black men and women are more plentiful than in the past.

The infusion of race into the action research dialogue brings home still another point. The everyday public dramas being played out in our communities and society must become our learning laboratories. For those of us doing race work, these racialized public moments are natural settings for action research. Remember the O.J. Simpson case? Now think of it as one huge participatory, action research field experience. We should have been the storytellers, directors of change and producers of knowledge in the Simpson drama, thereby generating a deeper understanding of race in the USA. We should have been the magicians in this drama, creating sturdy bridges that could enable Black and White America to cross racial lines, so people could engage in an authentic transformative dialogue.

In this new millennium we carry forward the unresolved issue of race in America. We must find new ways to dismantle both systemic and social dimensions of racial oppression, while at the same time addressing the interlocking forces of class, gender and sexual preference. By new ways, I am referring to action research techniques enabling us not only to get a broader and deeper understanding of oppression in all its manifestations, but to find better solutions for closing the gaps between humankind. Opportunities for change, I believe, are all around us. I think back on an observation I made while attending the play *Twilight: Los Angeles, 1992* in New York City. Anna Deavere Smith, the playwright and one woman virtuoso actress, offered her impersonations of the issues and people that triggered the Los Angeles riots. Her performance was extraordinarily powerful. After the show, Blacks, Whites, Jews, young, old, gay, straight, women and men sat silenced in their seats. We all looked at each other. My fantasy at that moment was that we were ready to do a little work, and a little talking about race, wealth and how we were all contributing to a very ugly reality. I suspect people did talk about this problematic situation, at home around the dinner table with their children, in bed with their significant others and at work with their colleagues. This is a start; a first step towards change for many. And, this experience reminds me of the exciting work in ethnodrama done by Jim Mienczakowski, who also has a chapter in this volume (Chapter 15). But it is only one technique. What are the other possibilities for us to consider?

Racialized public dramas, no matter how shocking, how disturbing, how painful or how frustrating provide us with moments to engage deeply in the work of dismantling oppression. Such incidents force us to question what it means to be Black. Or, how do I as a White person become aware of the privilege surrounding my life? And, in what ways does my status and position, regardless of my race, blind me to those who are less fortunate? These are important questions to ask. These racialized public occasions are opportunities to teach our children, not about hate, but about tolerance and acceptance, and to prepare them to be better citizens of the world. As practitioners and teachers we can use these moments as live action cases to deconstruct the forces of oppression and reveal how race, class and gender interlock. Finally, these incidents help us to identify allies, both within and across racial lines, who are also seeking ways to resolve the race question. Together we can build sturdy bridges between our communities. One thing is for certain, however. In the new millennium, we must consider as many techniques, strategies and interventions as possible, if we are ever to find constructive solutions to the struggle for social justice and racial equality in the USA.

References

Adams, F. (1975) *Unearthing Seeds of File: the Idea of High Lander Winston*. St Salem, NC: John & Black Publisher.

Argyris, C. (1970) *Intervention Theory and Method: Behavioral Science View*. Reading, MA: Addison-Wesley.

Behar, R. (1996) *The Vulnerable Observer: Anthropology that Breaks Your Heart*. Boston, MA: Beacon Press.

Bell, E.L. (1990) 'The bicultural life experiences of career-oriented black women', *Journal of Organizational Behavior*, 11: 459–77.

Bell, E.L. (1992) 'Myths, stereotypes, and realities of Black women: a personal reflection', *The Journal of Applied Behavioral Science*, 28 (3): 363–72.

Black Scholar (1991) Special edition, 'The Clarence Thomas confirmation: the black community response'. 22 (1) Winter.

Black Scholar (1992) Special edition, 'The Clarence Thomas confirmation: the black community response'. 22 (2) Spring.

Blauner, R. (1969) 'Internal colonialism and ghetto revolt', *Social Problems*, 16 (4): 333–57.

Blauner, R. and Wellman, D. (1973) 'Toward the decolonization of social research', in J.A. Ladner (ed.), *The Death of White Sociology*. New York: Random House. pp. 310–30.

Bogle, D. and Toms, C. (1994) *Mulattoes, Mammies, & Bucks: an Interpretive History of Blacks in American Films*. New York: Continuum.

Brown, E.B. (1995) 'Imaging lynching: African American women communities of struggle and collective memory', in G. Smitherman (ed.), *African American Women Speak Out on Anita Hill–Clarence Thomas*. Detroit, MI: Wayne State University Press. pp. 100–24.

Christian, B. (1985) *Black Feminist Criticism: Perspectives on Black Women Writers*. New York: Pergamon Press.

Cicourel, A. (1964) *Method and Measurement in Sociology*. New York: Free Press.

Clark, K.B. (1965) *Dark Ghetto: Dilemmas of Social Power*. New York: Harper & Row.

Clark, K.B. (1973) 'Introduction to an Epilogue', in J.A. Ladner (ed.), *The Death of White Sociology*. New York: Random House.

Collins, P.H. (1990) *Black Feminist Thought: Knowledge, Consciousness, and the Politics of Empowerment*. New York: Routledge.

Conote, R. (1967) *Rivers of Blood, Years of Darkness*. New York: Bantam Books.

Conyers, J.E. (1992) 'The Association of Black Sociologists: a descriptive account from an "insider"', *The American Sociologist*, 23 (1): 49–55.

Cox, T.J. Jr. and Nkomo, S.M. (1990) 'Invisible men and women: a status report on race as a variable in organization behavior research', *Journal of Organizational Behavior*, 11: 419–31.

Freire, P. (1970) *Pedagogy of the Oppressed*. New York: Seabury Press.

Geertz, C. (1989) *Works and Lives: the Anthropologist as Author*. Stanford, CA: Stanford University Press.

Glazer, N. and Moynihan, D.P. (1965) *Beyond the Melting Pot*. Cambridge, MA: MIT Press.

Glen, J. (1996) *Highlander, No Ordinary School*. Nashville, TN: University of Tennessee Press.

Hall, B. (Winter, 1992) 'From margins to center? The development and purpose of participatory research', *The American Sociologist*, 23 (4): 15–28.

Hall, B. (1993) 'Introduction', in P. Park, M. Brydon-Miller, B. Hall and T. Jackson (eds), *Voices for Change: Participatory Research in the United States and Canada*. Westport, CT: Bergin and Garvey. pp xiii–xxii.

Harris, J. and McCullough, W.D. (1973) 'Quantitative methods and black community studies', in J.A. Ladner (ed.), *The Death of White Sociology*. New York: Random House. pp. 331–43.

Heron, J. (1996) *Co-operative Inquiry: Research into the Human Condition*. London: Sage Publications.

Hill, R. (1972) *The Strengths of Black Families*. New York: Emerson Hall Publishers.

Horton, M., Horton, J. and Kohl, H. (1990) *The Long Haul: an Autobiography*. New York: Teachers College Press.

Ladner, J.A. (1971) *Tomorrow's Tomorrow: the Black Woman*. Lincoln, NB: University of Nebraska Press.

Ladner, J.A. (ed.) (1973) *The Death of White Sociology*. New York: Random House.

Ladner, J.A. (1995) *Tomorrow's Tomorrow: The Black Woman*, with a new introduction by the author. New York, Doubleday. pp. xx–xxxiv.

Lewin, K. (1951) *Field Theory in Social Science*. New York: Harper & Row.

Lewis, O. (1968) *A Study of Slum Culture: Backgrounds for La Vida*. New York: Random House.

Lorde, A. (1984) *Sister Outsider*. Trumansburg, NY: Crossing Press.

Maguire, P. (1987) *Doing Participatory Research: a Feminist Approach*. Amherst, MA: Center for International Education, University of Massachusetts.

Martin, E.P. and Martin, J. (1978) *The Black Extended Family*. Chicago, IL: The University of Chicago Press.

Mitroff, I.I. and Kilmann, R.H. (1978) *Methodological Approaches to Social Science: Integrating Divergent Concepts and Theories*. San Francisco, CA: Jossey-Bass.

Morris, A.D. (1984) *The Origins of the Civil Rights Movement: Black Communities Organizing for Change*. New York: The Free Press.

Morrison, T. (ed.) (1992) *Race-ing Justice En-gendering Power: Essays on Anita Hill, Clarence Thomas and the Construction of Social Reality*. New York: Random House.

Moynihan, D.P. (1965) *The Negro Family: a Case for National Action*. Washington, DC: United States Department of Labor, Office of Policy, Planning and Research.

Nkomo, S.M. (1992) 'The emperor has no clothes: rewriting race in the study of organizations', *Academy of Management Review*, 17: 487–513.

Payne, C.M. (1995) *I've Got the Light of Freedom: The Organizing Tradition and the Mississippi Freedom Struggle*. Berkeley, CA: University of California Press.

Park, P., Brydon-Miller, M., Hall, B. and Jackson, T. (eds) (1993) *Voices for Change: Participatory Research in the United States and Canada*. Westport, CT: Bergin and Garvey.

Rainwater, L. (1970) *Behind Ghetto Walls*. Chicago, IL: Aldine Publishing Company.

Rainwater, L. and Yancey, W.L. (1967) *The Moynihan Report and the Politics of Controversy*. Cambridge, MA: MIT Press.

Ransby, B. (1995) 'A righteous rage and a grassroots mobilization', in G. Smitherman (ed.), *African American Women Speak Out on Anita Hill–Clarence Thomas*. Detroit, MI: Wayne State University Press. pp. 45–52.

Reason, P. and Rowan, J. (1981) *Human Inquiry: a Source Book of New Paradigm Research*. New York: John Wiley.

Smith, D. (1979) 'A sociology for women', in J. Sherman and E. Bock (eds), *The Prison of Sex: Essays on the Sociology of Knowledge*. Madison, WI: University of Wisconsin Press. pp. 7–16.

Smitherman, G. (ed.) (1995) *African American Women Speak Out on Anita Hill–Clarence Thomas*. Detroit, MI: Wayne State University Press.

Stack, C. (1974) *All Our Kin*. New York: Basic Books.

Staples, R. (1973) 'What is black sociology? Toward a sociology of black liberation', in J.A. Ladner (ed.), *The Death of White Sociology*. New York: Random House. pp. 161–89.

Swantz, M.-L. (1982) 'Research as education for development: a Tanzanian case', in B. Hall, A. Gillette and R. Tandon (eds), *Creating Knowledge: a Monopoly*. New Delhi: Society for Participatory Research in Asia. pp. 113–26.

Tikkun (1992) 'Sexuality after Thomas/Hill: roundtable discussion', January–February.

Torbert, W. (1991) *The Power of Balance: Transforming Self, Society and Scientific Inquiry*. Newbury Park, CA: Sage Publications.

Walters, R. (1973) 'Toward a definition of black social science', in J.A. Ladner (ed.), *The Death of White Sociology*. New York: Random House. pp. 190–212.

Wilkerson, D.Y. (1992) 'Minorities and women in the liberation of the ASA (American Sociological Association), 1964–1974: reflections on the dynamics of organizational change', *The American Sociologist*, 23 (1): 3–7.

Wolfe, D.M. (1980) 'On the research participant as co-inquirer', Paper presented at the Academy of Management Annual Convention, August.

5

Uneven Ground: Feminisms and Action Research

PATRICIA MAGUIRE

CHAPTER OUTLINE

This chapter argues that feminist theorizing and practice is a relatively unacknowledged force at the heart of participatory forms of action research. Feminist scholarship remains unfamiliar ground to many in action research, which is unsettling given that feminism and feminist scholarship have always embraced the call to transformational action. The chapter explores core themes of feminism in relation to action research – gender, multiple identities and interlocking oppressions, voice, everyday experiences, and power. It concludes that any action research which continues to ignore, neglect or marginalize diverse feminist thought and its goals is simply inadequate for its supposed liberatory project.

For the new practitioner of action research or the veteran wanting to be refreshed, this chapter explores how feminisms have informed and grounded action research.[1] Because feminisms have been critical of abstract academic knowledge, to develop this chapter I took a turn, albeit small, to concrete, lived experience. To understand how feminisms have grounded action researchers' work, I simply began to ask them. As a parent of information-age daughters, I put out a call to action researchers via list serves, chat rooms, email, and a short-lived, web-based, threaded discussion site.[2] How, if at all, did they think feminisms had influenced action research as a field? How, if at all, had feminisms influenced their work? As a child of Gutenberg, I poured over action research reference lists, endnotes, footnotes and indexes in an attempt to quickly cut to the chase. How had feminist scholarship informed the work? The range of answers suggested the title, *uneven ground*.

Some action researchers express concern that 30 years into second-wave feminism and over a decade into third-wave feminism, feminist scholarship remains unfamiliar ground to many in the field (Bradbury, email, 21 July 1999; Greenwood and Levin, 1998). This may have been explainable historically, as older action research traditions were primarily associated with men, for example, Dewey, Lewin, Corey, Stenhouse, Argyris, Freire and Kemmis (Anderson, Herr and Nihlen, 1994: 23). Yet many recent primers still offer little discussion of how feminist scholarship informs action research (Calhoun, 1994; K. Collins, 1999; Kemmis and McTaggart, 1988; McNiff, 1993; Selener, 1997). Susan Noffke (1998) and Alison Bowes (1996) note that there are only rare instances of action research and feminist theory engaging each other. Lykes (email, 18 March 1999) observes, 'As I review the field and read in it regularly I continue to find that feminisms/womanist perspectives are marginal, on the edge ... it is a cutting edge'. Morwenna Griffiths (1999) proposes that the degree of feminist influence depends on the version of action research. She posts, '... there are quite instrumental versions which focus on technical improvement with very little reflection drawn from outside sources ... And there are versions calling themselves critical which somehow often manage to look carefully at power without noticing the feminist perspective on power'. She notes Gabby Weiner's (1989) critique of these brands of action research. Greenwood and Levin conclude that there are 'only a handful of systematic attempts to link' feminism and action research. They call for an 'intensification of the discussion about the relationship between feminism and action research as a necessary condition for the success of both' (1998: 185).

This chapter contributes to an intensified conversation by building on the concrete experiences of action researchers. What has grounding in feminisms meant for their practice? What could it mean for yours? You are invited to join, redirect and extend this conversation. Conversation implies an ongoing though not particularly fluid process, something in progress across time interrupted by life's daily demands. In this process, conversants listen, share, interrupt, question and challenge, interpret, shake their heads sideways in disagreement or nod in affirmation, get distracted, seek clarification and possibly end up somewhere initially unforeseen. This is aligned with Kemmis's (Chapter 8) conceptualization of action research as a process that opens communicative space, which '*brings people together around shared topical concerns, problems and issues* ... in a way that will permit people to achieve mutual understanding and consensus about what to do' (p. 103; original emphasis).

Action researchers are expected to take a 'turn to action'. This requires us to examine and change our behaviours, relationships, and the often unseen institutional and organizational structures and relations which shape the ways we live and work, love and play (Maguire, 1996). Embracing this call to transformational action, personal and structural, has always been a bedrock of feminism and feminist scholarship (Mies, 1983, 1986, 1991; Mitchell and Oakley, 1986; Russell, 1977). As Liz Stanley asserts, feminism is not merely a perspective (way of seeing) or an epistemology (way of knowing), it 'is also an ontology, or a way of being in the world' (1990: 14). How have feminisms influenced being and doing in the liberatory project of action research?

Feminist Groundings

By their own accounts, feminist theories, epistemologies, and methodologies have inspired and grounded many action researchers' work (e.g., Barrett, Chapter 20; Brydon-Miller, 1997; Flood, Chapter 10; Greenwood, email, 22 February 1999; Griffiths, 1999; Lykes, email, 18 February 1999; Martin, email, 7 March 1999; McIntyre, 2000; Park, Chapter 7; Reason, 1999; Rowan, email, 17 March 1999; Swantz, email, 24 March 1999; Wadsworth, email, 26 February 1999). The themes discussed here emerged first from cyberconversations with action researchers and were expanded by review of feminist and action research literatures (P. Collins, 1991; Cornwall, 1998; De Vault, 1999; Fine, 1992; Fonow and Cook, 1991; Gorelick, 1991; Greenwood and Levin, 1998; hooks, 1984; Lather, 1991; Lentin, 1993; Mies, 1983, 1986; Morawski, 1997; Reinharz, 1992; Wadsworth and Hargreaves, 1993).

Many action researchers acknowledge a diversity of feminist perspectives. Alice McIntyre (email, 26 April 1999) notes, '... feminist scholars have challenged the assumption that there is "a" universal feminist perspective ... their work complicates any notion that feminism is fixed, monolithic, and/or predictive of women's lives'. Hence the term feminisms (Kemp and Squires, 1997). There is no single method, methodology, or theoretical base of feminist scholarship, indeed there are competing theoretical foundations and varied methodologies (DeVault; 1999; Fonow and Cook, 1991; Reinharz, 1992). Differing feminist perspectives emerge from competing explanations of the basis of women's oppressions and recommended solutions for change.

For me, feminism posits that women, despite differences, face some form of oppression, devaluation and exploitation as women. Differences such as race, ethnicity, class, culture, sexual orientation, physical abilities, age, religion and one's nation's place in the international order create conditions for a web of oppression. Hence women, and men, with multiple identities, experience their oppressions, struggles and strengths in specific, changing, historical locations (Mohanty, Russo and Torres, 1991). Despite differing and interwoven experiences of oppression, feminism celebrates women's strengths and resistance strategies. Women are not, nor have been helpless and hopeless victims. Feminism requires a commitment to expose and challenge the web of forces that cause and sustain all and any forms of oppression, for both our sisters and brothers, our daughters and sons.

Nearly a quarter of a century ago, Michelle Russell (1977) challenged feminists in the Academy to consider how their work would alter oppressive conditions for women. Stanley says of feminist inquiry, 'Succinctly, the point is to change the world, not only to study it' (1990: 15). It is this commitment to a liberatory, transformational project that is essential to any definition of feminism and feminist scholarship. At its core, feminism and its scholarship is a political movement for social, structural and personal transformation. Feminist and action research share an avowed intent to work for social justice and democratization (Atweh, Kemmis and Weeks, 1998; Greenwood and Levin, 1998; Lather, 1991). Without a grounding in feminisms, what would action research liberate us from and transform ourselves and communities into?

Given diverse feminist perspectives, is there any common core that distinguishes feminism as it grounds action research? For this chapter, action researchers identified how feminism informs their work. The themes which emerged include gender, multiple identities and interlocking oppressions, voice, everyday experiences, and power – all components of feminist critiques of the traditional social science research paradigm.

Gender

Action and feminist research problematize systematic relations of power in the social construction of knowledge. Feminist inquiry is distinguished by analysis of the centrality of gender in such power relations (Hartsock, 1998; Lather, 1991; Morawski, 1997). Feminist scholarship has shifted from 'working on women' to 'theorizing gender' (Kemp and Squires, 1997: 11). Theorizing gender and promoting emancipatory goals distinguishes feminist scholarship from other traditions (Kirsch, 1999: 7). What has this shift meant for action researchers?

The shift has first foregrounded the concept of gender, pushing action researchers to grapple with its meaning. Early feminist scholarship established a distinction between sex, that is biologically-based differences between male and female, and gender, that is socially and culturally constructed differences, that is what is considered masculine/feminine (Oakley, 1972; Reiter, 1975). This distinction challenged underlying assumptions that sex roles and the sexual division of labour, hence women's secondary status, were biologically determined, therefore unchangeable (Reiter, 1975). The sex/gender distinction exposes gender as culturally and historically constructed, variable processes in which human traits and capacities are asymmetrically divided, ascribed and expected, some as feminine, others as masculine. Division, assignment, stratification and internalization of gendered identities serve as a mode of domination, in which 'masculinity' devalues and rejects what is assigned as 'feminine' while simultaneously trying to control it (Flax, 1997: 174–5; Knoppers, 1997: 119). The gender system embeds itself in power structures and institutional and interpersonal relations that translate difference into hierarchy and power asymmetries, positioning man as normal and woman as ab/normal; man as universal, woman as the other (Cornwall, 1998; Fine and Gordon, 1992; Knoppers, 1997).

The 'rules and regulations' of the gender system shift and change, with gender functioning in different ways in different times and places (Schiebinger, 1999). The sex/gender distinction gives purpose to feminist scholarship and activism to identify, unsettle and revise the complex set of gender relations and power asymmetries. Feminist-informed action research considers how gender arrangements are constructed, sustained, experienced, changed or ignored (Barrett, Chapter 20; Flax, 1997; Morawski, 1997; Treleaven, 2001). Cott (1986) calls this the 'paradox of feminism'.

> It requires gender consciousness for its basis, yet calls for the elimination of prescribed gender roles. These paradoxes of feminism are rooted in women's actual situation, being the same (in a species sense) as men; being different, with respect to reproductive biology and gender construction, from men. (1986: 49)

Feminist critique of Cartesian dichotomies or binaries points out the dangers of the gender/sex dichotomy (Harding, 1987). The binary is blurred by recent understanding of the ways experience shapes biology, even alters physiology or neurochemistry (Perry, 1996; Schiebinger, 1999; Treichler, 1997). Nonetheless, Harding concludes, '... we are forced to think and exist within the very dichotomizing we criticize ... These dichotomies are empirically false, but we cannot afford to dismiss them as long as they structure our lives and our consciousness' (1987: 300–1). The biological/ cultural and male/female binaries seem unavoidable in societies in which people are categorized primarily by their biological sex (Gatenby and Humphries, 1999: 5 on Butler, 1990). The sex/gender distinction has debunked what had been considered as immutable, unchangeable 'givens' of male or female.

Feminist scholarship's shift from studying women to theorizing gender as a central category of human experience has grounded many action researchers' work in women's lives and concerns, experienced in part as gendered beings. Barrett (Chapter 20), Treleaven (2001), Gatenby and Humphries (1999) and Katila and Meriläinen (1999) provide exemplars of action research unsettling taken-for-granted assumptions and binaries of gendered identities. These are instructive to an action research gaining popularity as a tool for organizational and educational change. This is particularly essential given the embeddedness of gender in power relations which have been largely ignored in school reform literature (Dantow, 1998) and management education (Marshall, 1995).

When gender has meant only women, it can provoke male resistance or backlash (Brooker et al., 1998) and make a ghetto of the gender agenda (Guijt and Shah, 1998). Action researchers are moving beyond the notion that only women have gendered identities (e.g., Marshall, Cobb and Ling, 1998). Rooney (1998) utilizes collaborative inquiry and feminist research methodologies with men's groups in which they explore their experiences as men and of men in the family/work nexus. Cornwall (1998), Bilgi (1998) and Debrabandere and Desmet (1998) describe innovative uses of participatory rural appraisal to help community and staff men understand gendered experience and give their support for community development efforts.

Despite the feminist shift from 'working on women' to 'theorizing gender', Flax says of male academics:

> Men tend to see themselves as free from or not determined by gender relations ... [M]ale academics do not worry about how being men may distort their intellectual work ... [T]o the extent that feminist discourse defines its problematic as 'women' it too ironically privileges men as unproblematic or exempted from determination by gender relations ... men and women are both prisoners of gender, although in highly differentiated but interrelated ways ... [I]n order for gender relations to be useful as a category of social relations, we must be as socially and self critical as possible ... or run the risk of replicating the very social relations we are attempting to understand. (1997: 175)

Davydd Greenwood offers part of his experience of 'theorizing gender:'

> I want to convey to you something I think I have observed in my classes since 1991. Most women are quicker to learn AR than most men. I don't attribute this to biology. AR requires the willingness to forego the authority of professionalism and the domination of situations through objectivity and validity tests ... I think the experience of being a woman in our society – unfortunately – is good preparation for AR. Learning how to manage without domineering, linking rather than coercing, respecting diversity and otherness rather than imposing sameness are lessons women often learn as a result of being coerced themselves. For a man to become interested in these matters often requires a different trajectory ... but more women are called to this research modality and I don't think it is an accident that those least well treated by current arrangements are attracted to approaches that seek to overturn them. (email, 22 February 1999)

While it is common for feminists to share how their experiences of gender, among other identities, have influenced their scholarship, activism, and development, it is less common for male researchers (Bravette, Chapter 22; DeVault, 1999; Kirsch, 1999; Roberts, 1981; Stanley and Wise, 1983). For example, Kemmis (Chapter 8) and Fals Borda (Chapter 2) trace influences on their intellectual and professional development as action researchers without mention of how their gendered identities might also have shaped their development and practice of action research.

As part of 'an intensified conversation', action research grounded in feminism considers how the complexities and diversities of both women and men's gendered identities and experiences influence its practice and practitioners. This requires personally political excavation work. Noffke (email, 23 March 1999) proposes that men in action research need to 'think through their positions of relative privilege'. To borrow Kohlstedt and Longino's (1997) question of science, how is maleness being reproduced or unsettled in action research?

Multiple Identities – Interlocking Oppressions

Feminists of colour, of the south, and lesbian women have pushed northern feminists to acknowledge women's diverse positions, struggles, oppressions and strengths that take place in a complex web of historical and cultural locations (Bravette, Chapter 22; P. Collins, 1991, 1998; hooks, 1984, 1989; Mohanty, Russo and Torres, 1991). Scholarship by and with lesbian women and women of colour has moved feminist activism and scholarship, action research and the social sciences towards scholarship of difference and race-gender scholarship (Dill and Baca Zinn, 1997; Young, 1990).

Recognition of the interlocking nature of oppression pervades Black feminist thought and scholarship of difference which treats race, class, and gender as basic analytical categories, with complex, interdependent and simultaneous effects on human behaviour (P. Collins, 1991; Dill and Baca Zinn, 1997). This intersection creates different opportunities, choices, privileges and inequalities, rewards and life styles for different groups of people. The resultant interlocking system of oppression is not simply additive as in double or triple oppression, but complexly interdependent (Dill and Baca Zinn, 1997: 45–50). This scholarship considers how the experiences of all people, women and men, as well as different racial groups and classes shape and mould each other (p. 50). What has this meant for action research?

Feminist grounded action research posits that *women and men*, given multiple locations, often experience their struggles, oppressions and strengths differently. Multiple locations and interlocking oppressions manifest themselves in the varied ways people name the world and their experiences of it. Some women may not identify gender as the central oppression in their lives. Therefore feminist-grounded action research is not limited to a struggle against gender oppression alone, as gender oppression is structured and experienced in the web of other oppressions. As hooks challenged, 'when we cease to focus on the simplistic stance, "men are the enemy", we are compelled to examine systems of domination and our role in their maintenance and perpetuation' (1984: 23). Lykes faced this challenge in her participatory action research in Central America.

> ... I have worked with indigenous women who deny that there is sexism among indigenous groups ... I think for me the tension, contradiction, bind has often been around who defines issues and how I negotiate my power and powerlessness in collaborative work that is constrained by racism, economic violence ... (email, 18 March 1999)

Voice and Silence

The metaphor of 'voice' is common to feminist and action research. The metaphor has had multiple feminist uses, for example, silence, secrets and lies (Rich, 1979), talking back (hooks, 1989), a different voice (Gilligan, 1982), disruptive voices (Fine, 1992), and contesting the voice of authority (Morawski, 1997). Drawing from Freire's (1970) work to pierce the culture of silence among marginalized groups, Budd Hall notes, 'Participatory research fundamentally is about the right to speak ... Participatory research argues for the articulation of points of view by the dominated or subordinated' (1993: xvii).

What has foregrounding 'voice' meant for action research? Similar to Freire, Shulamit Reinharz observes, 'By dealing in voices, we are affecting power relations. To listen to people is to empower them ... before you can expect to hear anything worth hearing, you have to examine the power dynamics of the space and the social actors' (1988: 15, quoted in Way, 1997: 706). Practitioner researcher Susan Noffke cautions action researchers in relatively privileged positions,

> ... regardless of how we see our positions, we do not 'give voice' to those in less powerful positions. Rather, we must see ourselves as part of the process of breaking apart the barriers for speakers and listeners, writers and readers, which are perpetuated through and act to support our privileged positions. (Noffke, 1998: 10–11).

The long-term preoccupation of feminist activism and scholarship with women speaking from and about their own experience has influenced action research (Gatenby and Humphries, 1999: 20; Kemp and Squires, 1997: 90; McIntyre, email, 26 April 1999; Reason, 1999). The telling of, listening to, affirmation of, reflecting on, and analysis of personal stories and experiences 'from the ground up' are potentially empowering action research strategies drawn from women's organizing. For example, through consciousness-raising (CR) groups and public speak outs, feminist activism of the 1960s and 1970s created spaces for women's diverse voices and personal experiences. Initially CR groups arose in opposition to men's skewed interpretation of, and exclusion of, women and their varied experiences from everything from the historical record to the New Left. Lesbian feminists and feminists of colour struggled to have their voices meaningfully influence the feminist movement itself (hooks, 1984). CR provided a means to transform experience through reflection, particularly on aspects of women's lives previously considered politically unimportant (Hartsock, 1974) or unspeakable, such as child sexual abuse, women battering and rape.

Supportive and challenging relationships facilitate silence breaking. Action research draws from the relational processes inherent in many feminist methodologies (Maguire, 1987, 1996; Park, Chapter 7; Stanley and Wise, 1983; Way, 1997). There is a profound connection between empowerment and relational processes, as feminists posit that people grow and change in the context of human relationships (Miller, 1986). As Sherry Gorelick asserts, 'the production of science is not an operation (or indeed an autopsy); it is a relationship' (1991: 460).

Feminist-grounded action research is immersed in this activist, relational tradition. Barrett's (Chapter 20) Midwives' Action Research Project illustrates feminist commitment to make women's voices more audible and facilitate women's empowerment through 'ordinary talk' and subsequent organizational action. Gatenby and Humphries's (1999) Career Project with female managers and students does likewise. Niobe Way (1997) utilized feminist, voice-centred, relational research approaches with urban, multi-racial adolescent boys. Their group work uncovered the hunger of boys for trusting, caring, reciprocal friendships, thus unsettling preconceptions of 'human' experience. By listening to boys' voices, feminist-grounded research reframes women and men's lives. It exposes the inadequacy of androcentric research and its partial, inaccurate and incomplete representation of gendered human experience when women are muted.

Attention to themes across personal stories helps identify gendering mechanisms. Gatenby and Humphries note: 'We suspect that examining silences in women's talk, and in talk about women, may reveal some of the myriad ways in which gender is accomplished' (1999: 3). Exposing and disrupting mechanisms, personal and organizational, which shape and sustain gendered power asymmetries is a task of feminist-grounded action research.

Because our voices and stories cannot be extracted from our social, cultural locations in the world, the interactions of gender, multiple locations, interlocking oppressions and voice become apparent (Way, 1997: 706; Cornwall, 1998: 48 on Mohanty, 1987). These interactions raise questions for feminist-grounded action research. Who is authorized to speak for which women and men? Why is it impossible to speak for all women by trying to essentialize 'women' through a generalized woman's standpoint (Yeatman, 1994)? How can we avoid a fragmentary science, which recognizes women's multiple identities yet seems to privilege some knowers over others (Gorelick, 1991)? Feminism gives new meaning to questions at the heart of the politics of knowledge creation. Whose perspective? Whose voice? Whose knowledge?

Action researcher Ann Martin explains how the feminist concept of voice influenced her:

> For me, the connection between feminism and action research begins with the concept of voice as I found it in the work of Belenky, Clinchy, Goldberger, and Tarule (1986) and the essays of Audre Lorde ... Many of us (women) have lived the transition from silence to voice and experienced the power gained in that transition ... it's only a small step from the experience of finding one's own voice to realizing that this finding of voice, this learning that one does know, applies to everyone. (email, 17 March 1999)

Martin's action research is usually in the context of labour management relationships, working with those perceived by others as powerful and already having voice. She continues, '... But this is not the voice of feminist research. This voice is more like a noise, saying what is expected, speaking the organizational creed, speaking because it is expected ... speaking to cover the silence of others. As an action researcher, I'm working on liberating a different kind of voice.'

Women's development of voice, the 'other side of silence', with its contribution to the development of a sense of empowerment and efficacy, is traced by Belenky, Clinchy, Goldberger and Tarule (1986). There is a point in a person's evolving sense of self as a knower at which multiple perspectives and diverse opinions are appreciated. 'Only then is the student able to understand that knowledge is constructed, not given; contextual, not absolute; mutable, not fixed' (Belenky et al., 1986: 10). The linkage of gaining voice to the recognition of knowledge as a social construction in the context of human relations is central to feminist-grounded action research.

DeVault and Ingraham (1999) contend however that Belenky, Clinchy, Goldberger and Tarule (1986) obscure the mechanisms which keep women from speaking. Socially constructed and maintained, active and complex silencing mechanisms include censorship, suppression, intimidation, marginalization, trivialization, ghettoization, other forms of discounting (1986: 178) and gatekeeping (Spender, 1981). Barrett (Chapter 20) describes these mechanisms in play by a Hospital Ethics Committee and Senior Medical Staff Committee, gatekeepers who can give or withhold permission to speak with women. Historic, hidden, taken-for-granted male control of local institutions, public forums and development processes has often silenced or marginalized women in action research (Guijt and Shah, 1998; Maguire, 1987). Feminist-grounded action research works to uncover and disrupt silencing mechanisms, subtle and overt, in knowledge creation and organizational change efforts.

Gendering and silencing practices often work in tandem. Guijt and Shah observe of participatory rural appraisal:

> This mythical notion of community cohesion continues to permeate much participatory work, hiding a bias that favours the opinions and priorities of those with more power and the ability to voice themselves publicly ... [R]arely does a thorough understanding of the complexity of gender relations help structure the process, analysis, and resulting community plans. (1998: 1)

Whether in the poorest villages of the world or at an esteemed World Congress of Participatory Action Research, predominant male control of institutions, networks, agendas and decision-making structures or processes can function to silence and marginalize women (Swantz, email, 24 March 1999; Wadsworth, email, 9 March 1999) or trivialize them (Fals Borda, 1998: 218). The dynamics of racism also interact with gendering and silencing. Gatenby and Humphries (1999) discuss the added burden on Maori women in the Career Project, at times expected to speak for all Maori women or to take on the responsibility of challenging racist assumptions of non-Maori women.

There can be consequences for speaking up (DeVault and Ingraham, 1999). These include figuratively killing one's career or love relationships and literally getting killed. Building on Judi Marshall's (1995) research with women managers, Gatenby and Humphries (1999) note the high toll extracted of women in management positions when they speak of workplace sexual harassment or gender discrimination. Naming the difficulties of organizational life for women might actually provide ammunition for those who want to keep women out of organizations and management (Gatenby and Humphries, 1999; Marshall, 1995). In response to the violence of a battering relationship (Maguire, 1987) or violent state-sponsored terror (Lykes, 1997), silence may be a consciously chosen survival strategy. Feminist-grounded action research affords participants the power and space to decide for or against action, for or against breaking silence.

What about the silences of the powerful? Their 'chosen silences' may be mechanisms to maintain control (DeVault and Ingraham, 1999). In her account of a participatory research project with a Canadian native community, Chataway (1997) discussed silencing herself to avoid influencing the research. Yet she notes, 'withholding information such as one's own opinion does not just allow space for the other to speak, it can also be an act of power that forces the other to carry the burden of speaking or acting if any relationship is to be maintained' (Chataway, 1997: 758).

Feminist academicians have undertaken the difficult political task of finding voice to influence disciplines resistant to the disruptive feminist voices (Brydon-Miller, 1997; Fine and Gordon, 1992). It has likewise been difficult for action researchers to transform the Academy (Levin and Greenwood,

2001). Yet Greenwood and Levin maintain, 'Without the feminist onslaught on the centers of power, we do not believe that the kind of space we occupy as action researchers would exist' (1998: 183). There are gendered differences of experience within that space for action researchers, whether in a village, a prestigious university, or an international Congress. A review of experience in the Academy might show that more male action researchers have been able to survive, indeed thrive, by moving up the academic ladder faster, higher, with more institutional privileges, power and resources, and in larger numbers than their female colleagues. Feminist-inspired action research challenges us to consider how we create spaces for all voices to be heard, as well as how we use our voices to unsettle power differentials wherever encountered.

Everyday Experience

Feminist scholarship has long prioritized women's everyday experiences (Hartsock, 1974). Based on profound mistrust of male authority and questioning male-generated 'truths' about women's proper place or essential nature, women in the 1960s and 1970s turned to their own feelings and experiences as a source of legitimate and politicizing knowledge (Sarachild, in Weiler, 1991: 457). 'When we think of what it is that politicizes people it is not so much books or ideas but experience' (Peslkis, in Weiler, 1991: 457). Action researchers have made similar observations (Gaventa and Horton, 1981).

Both action and feminist research have centred the voices of the marginalized and muted in knowledge creation processes by starting from their everyday experiences (Barnsley and Ellis, 1992; Callaway, 1981; Freire, 1970; Lykes, 1997; Tandon, 1981). Even though there is no unitary women's experience, feminist-grounded action research embraces experience as a source of legitimate knowledge (Barrett, Chapter 20; Gatenby and Humphries, 1999; Lather, 1991; Mies, 1983, 1991; Park, Chapter 7; Reason, 1999; Treleaven, 2001; Weiler, 1991). Weiler reminds us that it was the very turning to women's experiences that revealed profound differences and deep conflicts of women's multiple identities and locations and hence promoted movement solidarity and coalition-building based on articulation of difference rather than pretense of sameness (Weiler, 1991: 468–9). Attention to the everyday reveals the dynamics of multiple locations.

Feminist sociologist Dorothy Smith has strongly influenced action research attention to the everyday. Smith notes, 'My project is a sociology that begins in the actualities of women's experience ... It attempts to create a method of inquiry beginning from the site of being that we discovered as we learned to center ourselves as speaking, knowing, subjects in our experience as women' (1992: 88). Her method of inquiry '... in fact works to make a space into which anyone's experience, however, various, could become a beginning-place inquiry. Anyone ... My notion of standpoint doesn't privilege a knower ... it shifts the ground of knowing ...' (1992: 88–92). With the everyday a problematic of inquiry, the knower can excavate the social relations of knowledge and what Smith calls the 'relations of ruling' beyond the grasp of everyday experience. How *do* things work? How do gendering or silencing work in organizations? By beginning from lived experiences, it becomes possible to grasp social relations, 'in which we participate and to which we contribute, that have come to take on an existence and power over us' (Smith, 1992: 95).

Gaining voice and excavating direct experience has its limitations if they fail to attempt to expose the hidden or invisible relations, mechanisms and underlying structures of oppression (Gorelick, 1991; Harding, 1987; hooks, 1984; Smith, 1992). Feminist action research seeks to connect the articulated, contextualized personal with the often hidden or invisible structural and social institutions that define and shape our lives. How *do* things work? How do we contribute to the workings? How can we collectively change them? The community-based Women's Research Centre, in Vancouver, Canada, grounds action research in feminist principles of voice and prioritizing everyday experience. Barnsley and Ellis note, 'The key thing that action research makes possible is the development of strategies and programs based on real life experience rather than theories or assumptions ... The kind of research we're recommending provides an analysis of issues based on a description of how people actually experience those issues' (1992: 10–13). Feminist-grounded action research uncovers how gender and other locations influence people's voicing and visioning.

Power

Feminist and action researchers both seek to unsettle and change the power relations, structures and mechanisms of the social world and social science research. Unsettling power relations is multifaceted, ranging from redefining power to rethinking the very purposes of knowledge creation to reworking the relations of the research process itself. Feminists continually remind us that gender is embedded in power relations.

Second-wave feminists' experiences in the New Left prompted them to reconceptualize the concept of power, particularly as played out within the very organizations dedicated to creating political change.

Power was reframed as energy, strength, effective interaction, and access to resource mobilization for others and self, rather than power as domination of others, whether by money, force or the cult of personal leadership and ego (Hartsock, 1974). Starhawk (1987, in Park, Chapter 7) differentiates power-over, power-with and power from within. It was a short step from feminist reconceptualization of power and its motor mechanisms within movement organizations to reconceptualization of power and its mechanisms within social science research and the Academy (Oakley, 1981; Russell, 1977; Stanley and Wise, 1979).

A key feminist influence on action research has been restructuring the power dynamics of the research process itself. Feminists' impetus to redefine power and its manifestations in research emerged from lived experiences. Participatory researchers' impetus to redefine power in inquiry likewise came from experiences with the poor and marginalized in adult or popular education, community development and development assistance (De Koning and Martin, 1996; Fals Borda, 1998; Hall, 1981; Smith, Willms, and Johnson, 1997; Tandon, 1998). Turning the relationship between researchers and subjects inside out by promoting the approach of co-researchers in an effort to share or flatten power is at the heart of action research. Through reflexivity, feminist-grounded action researchers critique and change their own research practices, particularly regarding the nature and processes of empowerment (Bowes, 1996). Lather challenges us 'to develop a kind of self reflexivity that will enable us to look closely at our own practice in terms of how we contribute to dominance in spite of our liberatory intentions' (1991: 150).

Action research has been influenced by feminist efforts to make visible and rework the conditions of knowledge production (DeVault 1999; Fonow and Cook, 1991; Kirsch, 1999; Lather, 1991; Mies, 1983, 1991; Oakley, 1981; Stanley, 1990; Stanley and Wise, 1979, 1983). 'Conscious reflexivity' about feminist knowledge production processes is a strategy to avoid producing more alienated knowledge which leaves no trace of the conditions of its production or the social conditions from which it arose (Rose, 1983, in Stanley, 1990: 40).

Feminist scholars often disclose their biases, feelings, choices and multiple identities, clearly locating themselves within the research process. Rowan (email, 17 March 1999) characterizes this as 'the refusal to remain anonymous'. Feminists grapple with how their voices and those of participants are represented and interpreted (Patai, 1991; Stanley and Wise, 1979; Thompson and Barrett, 1997). Empowering approaches advocated by feminist action research put new demands on researchers (Reinharz, 1992) as well as on participants (Maguire, 1996). Feminist-grounded action research opens knowledge creation conditions to scrutiny, attempts to unsettle and equalize power relations between researchers and participants, facilitates conditions for empowerment and reciprocity, wrestles with dilemmas of representation and interpretation, and experiments with polyvocal research accounts (Kirsch, 1999).

Summary

What lessons can we glean from the experiences of action researchers informed by feminisms? The overarching lesson is that any action research which continues to ignore, neglect or marginalize diverse feminist thought and its goals is simply inadequate for its supposed liberatory project. Without grounding in feminisms, what would action research liberate us from? Jointly, feminist and action research can be powerful allies in the effort to harness research as one resource in the struggle to dismantle the interlocking systems of oppression and domination in our lives.

Feminist-informed action research theorizes gender for women and men, girls and boys and pushes us to examine the implications of our own gendered and multiple identities for our action research practices. How is gendering still at work within action research? Feminist-informed action research challenges and proposes alternatives to the gendered conditions within which we promote, teach or train, engage in, and write and conference about action research. It requires us to expose and unsettle gendering and silencing mechanisms wherever encountered and however they intersect with other oppressions. It pushes us to redefine and share power for the tasks at hand. Those training action research practitioners and documenting efforts must develop curriculums and materials which include exposure to diverse feminist thought and practices. New practitioners and old editors must demand it. We must make visible the conditions of knowledge production, lest we create more alienating knowledge.

Our work is always done in the context of relationships. Hence we must support and challenge each other as we implement more feminist-informed action research. We are deep in the long-haul struggle to create a world in which the full range of human characteristics, resources, experiences and dreams are available to all our children. It will be a world in which knowledge creation processes and products nurture and nourish us all. To accomplish this, we are pushed to explore the unfamiliar and often uncomfortable landscape at the edge. It's uneven ground. There we get glimpses of how we might each further transform ourselves as action researchers engaged in transforming the world.

Notes

1 The term action research includes the sister trends of action research, participatory action research and other schools of participative inquiry (Fals Borda, 1998; Greenwood and Levin, 1998).

2 I am grateful to the many action researchers who responded and gave permission to use their comments. While all of their responses shaped this work, space limitations prohibited directly quoting and acknowledging many contributions.

References

Anderson, Gary, Herr, Kathleen and Nihlen, Ann Sigrid (1994) *Studying Your Own School: an Educator's Guide to Qualitative Practitioner Research*. Thousand Oaks, CA: Corwin Press.

Atweh, Bill, Kemmis, Stephen and Weeks, Patricia (eds) (1998) *Action Research in Practice*. London: Routledge.

Barnsley, Jan and Ellis, Diana (1992) *Research for Change: Participatory Action Research for Community Groups*. Vancouver: The Women's Research Centre.

Belenky, Mary, Clinchy, Blyhe, Goldberger, Nancy and Tarule, Jill (1986) *Women's Ways of Knowing*. New York: Basic Books.

Bilgi, Meena (1998) 'Entering women's world through men's eyes', in I. Guijt and M.K. Shah (eds), *The Myth of Community: Gender Issues in Participatory Development*. London: Intermediate Technology Publications. pp. 93–9.

Bowes, Alison (1996) 'Evaluating an empowering research strategy: reflections on action research with South East Asian women', *Sociological Research Online*, 1, no. 1, *http://www.socresonline.org.uk/socresonline/1/1/1.html.*

Brooker, Ross, Smeal, Georgia, Ehrich, Lisa, Daws, Leonie and Brannock, Jillian (1998) 'Action research for professional development on gender issues', in B. Atweh, S. Kemmis and P. Weeks (eds), *Action Research in Practice*. London: Routledge. pp. 189–211.

Brydon-Miller, Mary (1997) 'Participatory action research: psychology and social change', *Journal of Social Issues*, 53 (4): 657–66.

Butler, Judith (1990) *Gender Trouble: Feminism and the Subversion of Identity*. New York: Routledge.

Calhoun, Emily (1994) *How To Use Action Research in the Self-renewing School*. Alexandria, VA: Association for Supervision and Curriculum Development.

Callaway, Helen (1981) 'Women's perspectives: research as re-vision', in P. Reason and J. Rowan (eds), *Human Inquiry*. New York: John Wiley. pp. 457–72.

Chataway, Cynthia (1997) 'An examination of the constraints on mutual inquiry in a participatory action research project', *Journal of Social Issues*, 53 (4): 747–66.

Collins, Kathleen (1999) *Participatory Research: a Primer*. Cape Town: Prentice-Hall South Africa (Pty) Ltd.

Collins, Patricia Hill (1991) *Black Feminist Thought: Knowledge, Consciousness, and the Politics of Empowerment*. New York: Routledge.

Collins, Patricia Hill (1998) *Fighting Words: Black Women and the Search for Justice*. Minneapolis, MN: University of Minnesota Press.

Cornwall, Andrea (1998) 'Gender, participation, and the politics of difference', in I. Guijt and M.K. Shah (eds), *The Myth of Community: Gender Issues in Participatory Development*. London: Intermediate Technology Publications. pp. 46–57.

Cott, Nancy (1986) 'Feminist theory and feminist movements: the past before us', in J. Mitchell and A. Oakley (eds), *What is Feminism*? New York: Pantheon Books. pp. 49–62.

Dantow, Amanda (1998) *The Gender Politics of Educational Change*. Washington, DC: Falmer Press.

Debrabandere, Regine and Desmet, Arnout (1998) 'Brides have a price: gender dimensions of objective-oriented project planning in Zimbabwe', in I. Guijt and M.K. Shah (eds), *The Myth of Community: Gender Issues in Participatory Development*. London: Intermediate Technology Publications. pp. 100–9.

de Koning, Korrie and Martin, Marian (1996) 'Participatory research in health: setting the context', in K. de Koning and M. Martin (eds), *Participatory Research in Health: Issues and Experiences*. London: Zed Books. pp. 1–18.

DeVault, Marjorie (1999) *Liberating Method: Feminism and Social Research*. Philadelphia, PA: Temple University Press.

DeVault, Marjorie with Chrys Ingraham (1999) 'Metaphors of silence and voice in feminist thought', in M. DeVault, *Liberating Method*. Philadelphia, PA: Temple University Press. pp. 175–86.

Dill, Bonnie Thornton and Baca Zinn, Maxine (1997) 'Race and gender: revisioning the social sciences', in M. Anderson, L. Fine, K. Geissler and J. Ladenson (eds), *Doing Feminism*. East Lansing, MI: Women's Studies Program, Michigan State University. pp. 39–52.

Fals Borda, Orlando (ed.) (1998) *People's Participation: Challenges Ahead*. Bogotá: FAIEP.

Fine, Michelle (1992) *Disruptive Voices: the Possibilities of Feminist Research*. Ann Arbor, MI: University of Michigan Press.

Fine, Michelle and Gordon, Susan Merle (1992) 'Feminist transformations of/despite psychology', in M. Fine (ed.), *Disruptive Voices*. Ann Arbor, MI: University of Michigan Press. pp. 1–26.

Flax, Jane (1997) 'Postmodernism and gender relations in feminist theory', in S. Kemp and J. Squires (eds), *Feminisms*. Oxford: Oxford University Press. pp. 170–8.

Flood, Robert (1999) *Rethinking the Fifth Discipline*. New York: Routledge.

Fonow, Mary Margaret and Cook, Judith (eds) (1991) *Beyond Methodology: Feminist Scholarship as Lived Research*. Bloomington, IN: Indiana University Press.

Freire, Paulo (1970) *Pedagogy of the Oppressed*. New York: Seabury Press.

Gatenby, Bev and Humphries, Maria (1999) 'Exploring gender, management, and careers: speaking in the silences', *Gender and Education*, 11 (3): 281–94.

Gaventa, John and Horton, Billy (1981) 'A citizens' research project in Appalachia, USA', *Convergence*, 14 (3).

Gilligan, Carol (1982) *In a Different Voice*. Cambridge, MA: Harvard University Press.

Gorelick, Sherry (1991) 'Contradictions of feminist methodology', *Gender and Society*, 5 (4): 459–77.

Greenwood, Davydd and Levin, Morten (1998) *Introduction to Action Research: Social Research for Social Change*. Thousand Oaks, CA: Sage Publications.

Griffiths, Morwenna (1999, 11 March) ACR500 Bulletin Board post. Article No. 9. http://web-ct.nmsu.edu:8900/SCRIPT/ACR500/scripts/student/serve_bulletin?ARTICLE+Main+9

Guijt, Irene and Shah, Meera Kaul (eds) (1998) *The Myth of Community: Gender Issues in Participatory Development*. London: Intermediate Technology Publications.

Hall, Budd (1981) 'Participatory research, popular knowledge, and power: a personal reflection', *Convergence*, 14 (3): 6–19.

Hall, Budd (1993) 'Introduction', in P. Park, M. Brydon-Miller, B. Hall and T. Jackson (eds), *Voices of Change: Participatory Research in the United States and Canada*. Westport, CT: Bergin and Garvey. pp. xii–xxii.

Harding, Sandra (1987) 'The instability of the analytical categories of feminist theory', in S. Harding and J.F. O'Barr (eds), *Sex and Scientific Inquiry*. Chicago: University of Chicago Press. pp. 283–302.

Hartsock, Nancy (1974) 'Political change: two perspectives on power', *Quest: a Feminist Quarterly*, 1 (1). Reprinted in *Building Feminist Theory: Essays from Quest* (1981). New York: Longman. pp. 3–19.

Hartsock, Nancy (1998) *The Feminist Standpoint Revisited and Other Essays*. Boulder, CO: Westview Press.

hooks, bell (1984) *Feminist Theory: from the Margin to Center*. Boston, MA: South End Press. pp. 17–31.

hooks, bell (1989) *Talking Back: Thinking Feminist, Thinking Black*. Boston, MA: South End Press.

Katila, Saija, and Meriläinen, Susan (1999) 'A serious researcher or just another nice girl – doing gender in a male-dominated scientific community', *Gender, Work, and Organization*, 6 (3): 163–73.

Kemmis, Stephen and McTaggart, Robin (1988) *The Action Research Planner* (third edition). Victoria, Australia: Deakin University Press. Reprinted, 1997.

Kemp, Sandra and Squires, Judith (eds) (1997) *Feminisms*. Oxford: Oxford University Press.

Kirsch, Gesa (1999) *Ethical Dilemmas in Feminist Research*. Albany, NY: State University of New York Press.

Knoppers, Annelies (1997) 'The construction of gender in physical education', in M. Anderson, L. Fine, K. Geissler and J. Ladenson (eds) (1997) *Doing Feminism*. East Lansing, MI: Women's Studies Program, Michigan State University. pp. 119–33.

Kohlstedt, Sally and Longino, Helen (1997) 'The women, gender, and science question', in S. Kohlstedt and H. Longino (eds), *Women, Gender, and Science: New Directions*. Osiris, 12. Chicago, Il: Chicogo University Press. pp. 3–15.

Lather, Patti (1991) *Getting Smart: Feminist Research and Pedagogy with/in the Postmodern*. New York: Routledge.

Lentin, Ronit (1993) 'Feminist research methodologies – a separate paradigm? Notes for a debate', *Irish Journal of Sociology*, 3: 119–38.

Lykes, Brinton (1997) 'Activist participatory research among the Maya of Guatemala: constructing meanings from situated knowledge', *Journal of Social Issues*, 53 (4): 725–46.

Maguire, Patricia (1987) *Doing Participatory Research: a Feminist Approach*. Amherst, MA: Center for International Education, University of Massachusetts.

Maguire, Patricia (1996) 'Proposing a more feminist participatory research: knowing and being embraced openly', in K. de Koning and M. Martin (eds), *Participatory Research in Health*. London: Zed Books. pp. 27–39.

Marshall, Judi (1995) 'Researching women and leadership: some comments on challenges and opportunities', *International Review of Women and Leadership*, 1: 1–10.

Marshall, Roger, Cobb, Alison and Ling, Chris (1998) 'Change in schools: practice and vision', in B. Atweh, S. Kemmis and P. Weeks (eds), *Action Research in Practice*. London: Routledge. pp. 163–88.

McIntyre, Alice (2000) *Talking Trash: Urban Youth Confront Life and Violence in the Inner City*. New York: New York University Press.

McNiff, Jean (1993) *Teaching as Learning: an Action Research Approach*. London: Routledge.

Mies, Maria (1983) 'Towards a methodology for feminist research', in G. Bowles and R. Duelli Klein (eds), *Theories of Women's Studies*. London: Routledge and Kegan Paul. pp. 117–39.

Mies, Maria (1986) *Patriarchy and Accumulation on a World Scale*. London: Zed Books.

Mies, Maria (1991) 'Women's research or feminist research? The debate surrounding feminist science and methodology', in M. Fonow and J. Cook (eds), *Beyond Methodology*. Bloomington, IN: Indiana University Press. pp. 60–84.

Miller, Jean (1986) *Toward a New Psychology of Women*. Boston, MA: Beacon Press.

Mitchell, Juliet and Oakley, Ann (eds) (1986) *What is feminism?* New York: Pantheon Books.

Mohanty, Chandra (1987) 'Under western eyes: feminist scholarship and colonial discourses', *Feminist Review*, 30: 61–88.

Mohanty, Chandra, Russo, Ann and Torres, Lourdes (eds) (1991) *Third World Women and the Politics of Feminism*. Bloomington, IN: Indiana University Press.

Morawski, Jill (1997) 'The science behind feminist research methods', *Journal of Social Issues*, 53 (4): 667–81.

Noffke, Susan (1998) 'What's a nice theory like yours doing in a practice like this? And other impertinent questions about practitioner research', Keynote Address, Sydney, Australia: Second International Practitioner Research Conference, 9 July.

Oakley, Ann (1972) *Sex, Gender, and Society*. London: Harper Colophon Books.

Oakley, Ann (1981) 'Interviewing women: a contradiction in terms', in Helen Roberts (ed.), *Doing Feminist Research*. London: Routledge and Kegan Paul. pp. 30–61.

Patai, Daphne (1991) 'US academics and third world women: is ethical research possible?', in S.B. Gluck and D. Patai (eds), *Women's Words: the Feminist Practice of Oral History*. New York: Routledge. pp. 137–53.

Perry, Bruce (1996) 'Incubated in terror', in J. Osofsky (ed.), *Children, youth and violence*. New York: Guilford Press.

Reason, Peter (1999, 23 February) ACR500 Bulletin Board post. Article No. 6. http://web-ct.nmsu.edu:8900/SCRIPT/ACR500/scripts/student/serve_bulletin?ARTICLE+Main+6

Reinharz, Shulamit (1988, February) 'The concept of voice'. Paper presented at meeting on Human Diversity. University of Maryland, College Park.

Reinharz, Shulamit (1992) *Feminist Methods in Social Research*. New York: Oxford University Press.

Reiter, Rayna Rapp (ed.) (1975) *Towards an Anthropology of Women*. New York: Monthly Review Press.

Rich, Adrienne (1979) *Lies, Secrets, and Silence: Selected Prose, 1966–1978*. New York: W.W. Norton.

Roberts, Helen (ed.) (1981) *Doing Feminist Research*. London: Routledge and Kegan Paul.

Rooney, Pat (1998) 'Men, work and family: the case for a subjective approach to an objective problem', *European Families and Work Network, New Ways*, pp. 10–12.

Rose, Hilary (1983) 'Hand, brain, and heart: a feminist epistemology for the natural sciences', *Signs*, 9: 73–90.

Russell, Michelle (1977) 'An open letter to the Academy', *Quest: a Feminist Quarterly*, 3 (4). Reprinted in *Building Feminist Theory: Essays from Quest*, (1981). New York: Longman. pp. 101–10.

Schiebinger, Londa (1999) *Has Feminism Changed Science*? Cambridge, MA: Harvard University Press.

Selener, Daniel (1997) *Participatory Action Research and Social Change*. Ithaca, NY: Cornell Participatory Action Research Network.

Smith, Dorothy (1992) 'Sociology from women's experience: a reaffirmation', *Sociological Theory*, 10 (1): 88–98.

Smith, Susan, Willms, Dennis and Johnson, Nancy (eds) (1997) *Nurtured by Knowledge: Learning To Do Participatory Action Research*. Ottawa: International Development Research Centre.

Spender, Dale (1981) 'The gatekeepers: a feminist critique of academic publishing', in H. Roberts (ed.), *Doing Feminist Research*. London: Routledge and Kegan Paul. pp. 186–202.

Stanley, Liz (1990) 'Feminist praxis and the academic mode of production: an editorial introduction', in L. Stanley (ed.), *Feminist Praxis: Research, Theory, and Epistemology in Feminist Sociology*. London: Routledge. pp. 3–19.

Stanley, Liz and Wise, Sue (1979) 'Feminist research, feminist consciousness and experiences of sexism', *Women's Studies International Quarterly*, 2 (3): 359–79.

Stanley, Liz and Wise, Sue (1983) *Breaking Out: Feminist Consciousness and Feminist Research*. London: Routledge and Kegan Paul.

Starhawk (1987) *Truth or dare. Encounter with power, authority, mystery*. San Francisco: Harper and Row.

Tandon, Rajesh (1981) 'Participatory research in the empowerment of people', *Convergence*, 14 (2): 20–7.

Tandon, Rajesh (1998) 'Struggle for knowledge: a personal journey', in O. Fals Borda (ed.), *People's Participation: Challenges Ahead*. Bogotá: FAIEP. pp. 95–104.

Thompson, S. and Barrett, Penelope (1997) 'Summary Oral Analysis (SORA): a method for interview data analysis in feminist qualitative research', *Advances in Nursing Science*, 20 (2): 55–65.

Treichler, Paula (1997) 'AIDS, identity, and the politics of gender', in S. Kemp and J. Squires (eds), *Feminisms*. Oxford: Oxford University Press. pp. 374–8.

Treleaven, L. (2001) 'The turn to action and the linguistic turn: towards an integrated methodology', in P. Reason and H. Bradbury (eds), *Handbook of Action Research: Participative Inquiry and Practice*. London: Sage Publications. pp. 261–72.

Wadsworth, Yoland and Hargreaves, Kaye (1993) *What is Feminist Research?* Melbourne: Action Research Issues Association.

Way, Niobe (1997) 'Using feminist research methods to understand the friendships of adolescent boys', *Journal of Social Issues*, 53 (4): 703–23.

Weiler, Kathleen (1991) 'Freire and a feminist pedagogy of difference', *Harvard Educational Review*, 61 (4): 449–74.

Weiner, Gabby (1989) 'Professional self-knowledge versus social justice: a critical analysis of the teacher–researcher movement', *British Educational Research Journal*, 15 (1): 41–51.

Yeatman, Anna (1994) *The Place of Women's Studies in the Contemporary University: Postmodern Revisionings of the Political*. New York: Routledge, Chapman, and Hall.

Young, Iris (1990) *The Ideal of Impartiality and the Civic Public. Justice and the Politics of Difference*. Princeton, NJ: Princeton University Press.

6
Power and Knowledge

JOHN GAVENTA AND ANDREA CORNWALL

CHAPTER OUTLINE

'Knowledge is power!' has long been a rallying cry for social activists. Various forms of action research hold within them implicit notions of the relationship between power and knowledge, one that is neither straightforward nor commonly understood. In this chapter, we will analyse and explore the complex connections between power and knowledge in action research processes. First, we review theoretical approaches to the concept of power, looking especially at their implications for knowledge and its production. Then, we explore how power is conceptualized and represented within the literature on action research, especially in the participatory action research (PAR) and participatory rural appraisal (PRA) traditions. Finally, we begin to examine issues of power and empowerment posed as participatory research is adopted by large and powerful institutions.

Participatory research has long held within it implicit notions of the relationships between power and knowledge. Advocates of participatory action research have focused their critique of conventional research strategies on structural relationships of power and the ways through which they are maintained by monopolies of knowledge, arguing that participatory knowledge strategies can challenge deep-rooted power inequities. Other action research traditions have focused more on issues of power and knowledge within organizations, while others still have highlighted the power relations between individuals, especially those involving professionals and those with whom they work.

Earlier understandings of power in participatory research tended to dichotomize the notion: 'they' (structures, organizations, experts) had power; 'we' (the oppressed, grassroots, marginalized) did not. Participatory research was a means of closing the gap, of remedying the power inequities through processes of knowledge production, which strengthened voice, organization and action.

In more recent years, the uses and understandings of participatory research have broadened considerably. Rather than being seen as an instrument only of the powerless, the language and methods of participatory research are being adopted by large and powerful institutions. The new legitimacy and acceptance of participatory research raises critical questions. What aspects of participatory practice are institutions like national governments and the World Bank taking up? Does this new incorporation represent co-optation, or does it represent new spaces for larger and more effective action? How are power relations mediated across agencies and actors as participatory practice moves to larger scale? What are the interrelationships of the uses of participatory research for social, institutional and individual change?

Power as Knowledge

Power and knowledge are inextricably intertwined. A starting point for situating our analysis of power and knowledge in participatory research is to map out some of the different ways in which power is conceptualized and their implications for research. In doing so, we draw on Gaventa's (1980) earlier work on quiescence and rebellion among mining communities in rural Appalachia. We take as our starting point the three dimensions of power elaborated by Lukes (1974) and built upon in Gaventa's analysis.[1] Adding a fourth dimension, the relational view of power emerging from the work of Foucault (1977, 1979) and his followers, we explore questions of power, knowledge and participation.

Lukes (1974) begins his argument by challenging the traditional view in which power is understood as a relationship of 'A over B': that is, power is the ability of A (the relatively powerful person or agency) to get B (the relatively powerless person or agency) to do what B might not otherwise do (Dahl, 1969). In this approach, power is understood as a product of conflicts between actors to determine who wins and who loses on key, clearly recognized issues, in a relatively open system in which there are established decision-making arenas. If certain voices are absent in the debate, their non-participation is interpreted as their own apathy or inefficacy, not as a process of exclusion from the political process.

Within this first dimension of power, knowledge or research may be conceived as resources to be mobilized to influence public debates. Practically, with this view, approaches to policy influence, knowledge and action relate largely to countering expertise with other expertise. The assumption is that 'better' (objective, rational, highly credible) knowledge will have greater influence. Expertise often takes the form of policy analysis or advocacy, both of which involve speaking 'for' others, based not on lived experience of a given problem, but on a study of it that claims to be 'objective'. Little attention is paid in this view to those whose voices or whose knowledge were not represented in the decision-making process, nor on how forms of power affected the ways in which certain problems come to be framed.

This pluralist vision of an open society, in which power is exercised through informed debate among competing interests, continues to affect many of our understandings of how power affects policy. However, this view has been widely challenged. Political scientists such as Bachrach and Baratz (1970) put forward a second understanding of power. They argued that the hidden face of power was not about who won and who lost on key issues, but was also about keeping issues and actors from getting to the table in the first place. Drawing upon the work of Schattschneider, they argued that political organizations 'develop a mobilization of bias ... in favor of the exploitation of certain kinds of conflict and the suppression of others ... Some issues are organized into politics while others are organized out' (Schattschneider, 1960: 71). The study of politics, Bachrach and Baratz argued, must focus 'both on who gets what, when and how and who gets left out and how' (1970: 105).

In this view knowledge, and the processes of its production, contribute very strongly to the mobilization of bias. Scientific rules are used to declare the knowledge of some groups more valid than others, for example 'experts' over 'lay people', etc. Asymmetries and inequalities in research funding mean that certain issues and certain groups receive more attention than others; clearly established 'methods' or rules of the game can be used to allow some voices to enter the process and to discredit the legitimacy of others.

From the second dimensional view, empowerment through knowledge means not only challenging expertise with expertise, but it means expanding who participates in the knowledge production process in the first place. It involves a concern with mobilization, or action, to overcome the prevailing mobilization of bias (see Gaventa, 1993). When the process is opened to include new voices, and new perspectives, the assumption is that policy deliberations will be more democratic, and less skewed by the resources and knowledge of the more powerful.

While the second dimension of power contributed to our understanding of the ways in which power operates to prevent grievances from entering the political arenas, it maintained the idea that the exercise or power must involve conflict between the powerful and the powerless over clearly recognized grievances. This approach was then challenged by others such as Steven Lukes who suggested that perhaps 'the most effective and insidious use of power is to prevent such conflict from arising in the first place' (1974: 24). The powerful may do so not only by influencing who acts upon recognized grievances, but also through influencing consciousness and awareness of such grievances in the first place.

In this approach, the control of knowledge as a way of influencing consciousness is critical to the exercise of power. Knowledge mechanisms such as socialization, education, media, secrecy, information control, and the shaping of political beliefs and ideologies, all become important to the understanding of power and how it operates. In this approach, power begins to resemble Gramscian notions of 'hegemony' (Entwistle, 1979) or Freirean ideas (1981) of the ways in which knowledge is internalized to develop a 'culture of silence' of the oppressed.

Countering power involves using and producing knowledge in a way that affects popular awareness and consciousness of the issues which affect their lives, a purpose that has often been put forward by advocates of participatory research. Here the discussions of research and knowledge become those involving strategies of awareness building, liberating education, promotion of a critical consciousness, overcoming internalized oppressions, and developing indigenous or popular knowledge. There are countless examples of how the transformation of consciousness has contributed to social mobilization, be they in the civil rights, women's, environmental or other movements. And, there are a number of intellectual traditions which may contribute to our understanding in this area. Increasingly, for instance, new social movement theory recognizes the importance of consciousness by raising such issues as the development of collective identity, and of the constructions of meaning and of culture in galvanizing citizen action (Morris, 1984; Mueller, 1992).

Each of these approaches to power carry with them implicit or more explicit conceptions of knowledge, and how it relates to power, as well as to strategies of empowerment. In the first view, knowledge is a resource, used and mobilized to inform decision-making on key public issues – issues of who produces knowledge, or its impact on the awareness and capacity of the powerless are less important. In the second view, the powerful use control over the production of knowledge as a way of setting the public agenda, and for including or excluding certain voices and participants in action upon it. In response, mobilization of the relatively powerless to act upon their grievances and to participate in public affairs becomes the strategy – one in which action research is an important tool. In the third dimension, the emphasis is more upon the ways in which production of knowledge shapes consciousness of the agenda in the first place, and participation in knowledge production becomes a method for building greater awareness and more authentic self-consciousness of one's issues and capacities for action.

Beyond the three dimensional view

While over the years this three dimensional framework has provided a useful way of understanding power and knowledge in research, it has also been critiqued from a number of differing perspectives. For some, the approach is limited in its understanding of power as a 'power over' relationship – whereas in fact power can be seen as a more positive attribute as well, as in the power to act. And, in some cases power is seen as an attribute growing from within oneself, not something which is limited by others. This 'power within' is shaped by one's identity and self-conception of agency, as well as by outside forces held by 'the Other' (Kabeer, 1994; Nelson and Wright, 1995; Rowlands, 1995).

All three dimensions of power focus on the repressive side of power, and conceptualize power as a resource that individuals gain, hold and wield. Building on work by Foucault, others have come to see power more as productive and relational. In this view, power becomes 'a multiplicity of force relations' (Foucault, 1979: 92) that constitute social relationships; it exists only through action and is immanent in all spheres, rather than being exerted by one individual or group over another. For Foucault, power works through discourses, institutions and practices that are productive of power effects, framing the boundaries of possibility that govern action. Knowledge is power: 'power and knowledge directly imply one another ... there is no power relation without the correlative constitution of a field of knowledge, nor any knowledge that does not presuppose and constitute at the same time power relations' (1977: 27).

Foucault's analysis of the micro-practices of power shows how the effects of knowledge/power create particular kinds of subjects, who are subjugated through 'regimes of truth' that provide a means of policing the boundaries around the categories that knowledge defines. By placing the power effects of knowledge at the heart of his analysis, Foucault opens up a perspective on power that has often been misinterpreted as unduly negative. Rather, by showing how knowledge/power produces and sustains inequalities, Foucault affirms 'the right ... to rediscover what one is and all that one can be' (1979: 145).

Recent work by Hayward draws on Foucault to argue for 'de-facing power' by reconceptualizing it as 'a network of social boundaries that constrain and enable action for all actors' (1998: 2).[2] She argues that freedom is the capacity to act on these boundaries 'to participate effectively in shaping the boundaries that define for them the field of what is possible' (1998: 12). This has a number of important implications for thinking about power and knowledge in participatory research. First, it shifts the analysis of power only from resources that 'A' holds or uses, to include other broader ways in which spheres of action and possibility are delimited. If power is shaped by discourse, then questions of how discourses are formed, and how they shape the fields of action, become critical for changing and affecting power relations.

Secondly, this approach recognizes that no human relationship is exempt from a power component. In so far as power affects the field of what is possible, then power affects both the relatively powerful and the relatively powerless. From this perspective, power involves 'any relationship involving two or more actors positioned such that one can act within or upon power's mechanisms to shape the field of action of the other' (Hayward, 1998: 15). Power can exist in the micro-politics of the relationship of the researcher to the researched, as well as in broader social and political relationships; power affects actors at every level of organizational and institutional relationships, not just those who are excluded or at the bottom of such relationships.

Finally, this broader approach to power includes the more positive aspects through which power enables action, as well as how it delimits it. Power in this sense may not be a zero-sum relationship, in which for B to acquire power may mean the necessity of A giving up some of it. Rather, if power is the capacity to act upon boundaries that affect one's life, to broaden those boundaries does not always mean to de-limit those of others. In this sense power may have a synergistic element, such that action by some enables more action by others. Challenging the boundaries of the possible may in some cases mean that those with relatively less power, working collaboratively with others, have more, while in other cases it may direct conflict between the relatively powerful and the relatively powerless.

Knowledge as Power

If, in this expanded view, freedom 'is the capacity to participate effectively in shaping the social limits that define what is possible' (Hayward, 1998: 21), then we can also more clearly situate knowledge as one resource in the power field. Knowledge, as much as any resource, determines definitions of what is conceived as important, as possible, for and by whom. Through access to knowledge, and participation in its production, use and dissemination, actors can affect the boundaries and indeed the conceptualization of the possible. In some situations, the asymmetrical control of knowledge productions of others can severely limit the possibilities which can be either imagined or acted upon; in other situations, agency in the process of knowledge production, or co-production with others, can broaden these boundaries enormously.

Throughout the literature on participatory action research, we find various theories and approaches which to some degree or another are premised upon the claim that democratic participation in knowledge production can expand the boundaries of human action. However, writers do not fall neatly into certain mutually exclusive categories, and there are great variations even within the schools. Increasingly, as was seen in the 'Convergence' conference in Cartagena in 1997, the schools and approaches are changing and overlapping with one another (Fals Borda, 1998).

Below we illustrate and explore some commonalities and differences that draw especially (but not exclusively) from the approaches which have influenced our thinking the most. These are those associated with the Freirean tradition of participatory action research, and those associated with more recent work around participatory rural appraisal, an approach which has spread very quickly in the 1990s with an enormous impact on development thinking and practice.[3]

The nature and locations of power

For those early writers on participatory action research (PAR), power is understood as relation of domination in which the control of knowledge and its production was as important as material and other social relations. As Rahman put it:

> The dominant view of social transformation has been preoccupied with the need for changing the oppressive structures of relations in material production – certainly a necessary task. But, and this is the distinctive viewpoint of PR (Participatory Action-Research), domination of masses by elites is rooted not only in the polarization of control over means of material production, but also over the means of knowledge production, including control over the social power to determine what is useful knowledge. Irrespective of which of these two polarizations set off a process of domination, one reinforces the other in augmenting and perpetuating this process. (1991: 4)

The knowledge that affects people's lives is seen as being in the hands of a 'monopoly' of expert knowledge producers, who exercise *power over* others through their expertise. The role of participatory action research is to empower people through the construction of their own knowledge, in a process of action and reflection, or 'conscientization', to use Freire's term. Such action against power over relations implies conflict in which the power of the dominant classes is challenged, as the relatively powerless begin to develop their new awareness of their reality, and to act for themselves (Selener, 1997: 23).

While in this earlier view of PAR, power is located in broad social and political relations, later work by Chambers, more often associated with PRA, puts more emphasis on domination in personal and interpersonal terms. Starting with a focus on 'hierarchies of power and weakness, of dominance and subordination' (1997: 58), Chambers outlines two categories: 'uppers', who occupy positions of dominance, and 'lowers', who reside in positions of subordination or weakness. In his account of 'uppers' and 'lowers', power is less fixed in persons than in the positions they inhabit *vis-à-vis* others: people can occupy more than one position as 'upper', and may occupy both 'upper' and 'lower' positions depending on context. This relational portrayal of power relations mirrors Foucault's view of power as residing not in individuals, but in the positions that they occupy and the ways in which discourses make these positions available to them.

Chambers's description of the ways in which what he describes as 'normal professionalism' creates and reproduces power relations can equally be read through a Foucauldian lens. By circumscribing the boundaries of what is knowable, Chambers argues, professionals replicate hierarchies of knowledge and power that place them in the position of agents who know better, and to whom decisions over action, and action itself, should fall. His description of the ways in which professionals impose their 'realities' on 'lowers', with power effects that obliterate or devalue the knowledge and experience of 'lowers', resonates with Foucault's (1977) account of the ways in which 'regimes of truth' are sustained through discourses, institutions and practices.

Departing from a 'power over' perspective, PRA is characterized as a means through which a zero-sum conceptualization of power can be transcended: 'lowers' speak, analyse and act, in concert with each other and with newly sympathetic and enabling professionals who have become aware of the power effects of their positions as 'uppers'. Through analysis and action, 'lowers' are able to lay claim to their own distinctive versions and visions, acquiring the 'power to' and 'power within' that restores their agency as active subjects. By listening and learning, 'uppers' shed the mantle of dominance:

> From planning, issuing orders, transferring technology and supervising, they shift to convening, facilitating, searching for what people need and supporting. From being teachers they become facilitators of learning. They seek out the poorer and weaker, bring them together, and enable them to conduct their own appraisal and analysis, and take their own action. The dominant uppers 'hand over the stick', sit down, listen, and themselves learn. (Chambers, 1995: 34)

While offering an optimistic view of the possibilities of individual change, this view has also been critiqued for failing to analyse broader sources of oppression (e.g., Crawley, 1998). At the same time, those involved with PAR have also been critiqued for offering a broad analysis of social power relations, without clear starting points for change at the micro and personal level. (Many of those involved in organizational action research might also emphasize an intermediate level, which examines power in the organization and group, as a mediating level between individual power and broader social relationships.)

Part of the difference in views here is found in the level of analysis. Rather than thinking about these approaches as necessarily competing, it is perhaps more useful to think of them of as complementary, each with a differing starting point in addressing mutually re-enforcing levels of power. In his comparative work on PAR, 'co-operative inquiry' and 'action inquiry', Reason also points to the necessary interlinkages of each of these levels and approaches. 'One might say that PAR serves the community, cooperative inquiry the group, and action inquiry the individual practitioner. But this is clearly a gross oversimplification, because each of the triad are dependent upon the others' (Reason, 1994: 336). If freedom, as defined earlier, is the capacity to address the boundaries of possibility which are drawn in multiple ways and relationships, then surely the multiple levels of change are each important.

Power and the nature of knowledge

While differing approaches to action research may have differing understandings of the location of power, they all share an epistemological critique about the ways in which power is embedded and reinforced in the dominant (i.e. positivist) knowledge production system. The critique here is several-fold. First, there is the argument that the positivist method itself distorts reality, by distancing those who study reality (the expert) from those who experience it through their own lived, subjectivity (Gaventa, 1993). Second is the argument that traditional methods of research – especially surveys and questionnaires – may reinforce passivity of powerless groups, through making them the objects of another's inquiry, rather than subjects of their own. Moreover, empirical, quantitative forms of knowing may reduce the complexity of human experience in a way that denies its very meaning, or which reinforces the status quo by focusing on what is, rather than on historical processes of change. Third is the critique that in so far as 'legitimate' knowledge lies largely within the hands of privileged experts, dominant knowledge obscures or under-privileges other forms of knowing, and the voices of other knowers.

Against this epistemological critique, participatory action research attempts to put forth a different form of knowledge. On the one hand, such research argues that those who are directly affected by the research problem at hand must participate in the research process, thus democratizing or recovering the power of experts. Secondly, participatory action research recognizes that knowledge is socially constructed and embedded, and therefore research approaches that 'allow for social, group or collective analysis of life experiences of power and knowledge are most appropriate' (Hall, 1992: 22).

Thirdly, participatory action research recognizes differing forms of knowing (see Park and the Introduction in this volume), and that feeling and action are as important as cognition and rationality in the knowledge creation process. While participatory research often starts with the importance of indigenous or popular knowledge (Selener, 1997: 25), such knowledge is deepened through a dialectical process of people acting, with others, upon reality in order both to change and to understand it.

Resonating with the feminist critique of objectivity (see Harding, 1986; Maguire, Chapter 5; Treleaven, 2001), writing on participatory research emphasizes the importance of listening to and for different versions and voices. 'Truths' become products of a process in which people come together to share experiences through a dynamic process of action, reflection and collective investigation. At the same time, they remain firmly rooted in participants' own conceptual worlds and in the interactions between them.

Knowledge, Social Change and Empowerment

While there is thus a certain amount of commonality in the various approaches in terms of their critique of positivist knowledge, and the liberating possibilities of a different approach to knowledge production, there are important differences across views as to what about participatory research actually contributes to the process of change. That is, what is it in participatory research that is empowering?

In our earlier analysis of three approaches to power, we saw that each carried with it a distinctive approach to knowledge, and how it affects power relations. Participatory research makes claims to challenge power relations in each of its dimensions through addressing the need for:

- knowledge – as a resource which affects decisions;
- action – which looks at who is involved in the production of such knowledge; and
- consciousness – which looks at how the production of knowledge changes the awareness or worldview of those involved.

However, in much of the literature, and indeed in the practical politics of participatory research, processes of empowerment, or of overcoming unequal power relations, tend to emphasize one or the other of the above approaches. To do so, as we shall discuss below, is limiting, for it fails to understand how each dimension of change is in fact related to the other, as Figure 6.1 illustrates.

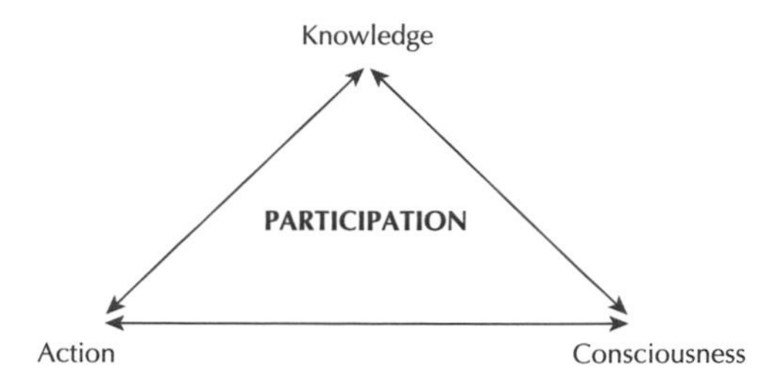

Figure 6.1 Dimensions of participatory research

Participatory research as an alternative form of knowledge

Undeniably one of the most important contributions of participatory action research to empowerment and social change is in fact in the knowledge dimension. Through a more open and democratic process new categories of knowledge, based on local realities, are framed and given voice. As Nelson and Wright suggest, based on an analysis of PRA approaches, the change process here involves 'an ability to recognize the expertise of local farmers as against that of professional experts; to find more empowering ways of communicating with local experts; and to develop decision-making procedures which respond to ideas from below, rather than imposing policies and projects from above' (1995: 57).

Similarly, Chambers (1997) argues for the importance of participatory processes as a way of bringing into view poor people's realities as a basis for action and decision-making in development, rather than those of the 'uppers' or development experts. A number of case studies of participatory research have clearly demonstrated how involving new participants in the research process brings forth new insights, priorities and definitions of problems and issues to be addressed in the change process (see, for example, case studies in Park et al., 1993 and others in this volume).

The importance of using participatory methods to surface more democratic and inclusive forms of knowledge, as a basis of decision-making, cannot be denied. At the same time, by itself, this approach to using participatory research for altering the boundaries of knowledge is fraught with challenges for several reasons. First, there is the danger that knowledge which is at first blush perceived to be more 'participatory', because it came from 'the community' or the 'people' rather than the professional researcher, may in fact serve to disguise or minimize other axes of difference (see critiques by Maguire, 1987, 1996 on PAR; Guijt and Shah, 1998 on PRA). In the general focus on the 'community', an emphasis on consensus becomes pervasive. Yet consensus can all too easily masquerade as common vision and purpose, blotting out difference and with it the possibility of more pluralist and equitable solutions (Mouffe, 1992). By reifying local knowledge and treating it as singular (Cornwall, Guijt and Welbourn, 1993), the possibility is rarely acknowledged that what is expressed as 'their knowledge' may simply replicate dominant discourses, rather than challenge them. Little attention is generally given to the positionality of those who participate, and what this might mean in terms of the versions they present. Great care must be taken not to replace one set of dominant voices with another – all in the name of participation.

Moreover, even where differing people and groups are involved, there is the question of the extent to which the voices are authentic. As we know from the work by Freire (1970), Scott (1986, 1990) and others on consciousness, relatively powerless groups may simply speak in a way that 'echoes' the voices of the powerful, either as a conscious way of appearing to comply with the more powerful parties' wishes, or as a result of the internalization of dominant views and values. In either case, participatory research implies the necessity for further investigation of reality, in order to change it, not simply to reflect the reality of the moment. Treating situated representations as if they were empirical facts maintains the dislocation of knowledge from the agents and contexts of its production in a way that is, in fact, still characteristic of positivism.

The dangers of using participatory processes in ways that gloss over differences among those who participate, or to mirror dominant knowledge in the name of challenging it, are not without consequence. To the extent that participatory processes can be seen to have taken place, and that the relatively powerless have had the opportunity to voice their grievances and priorities in what is portrayed as an otherwise open system, then the danger will be that existing power relations may simply be reinforced, without leading to substantive change in policies or structures which perpetuate the problems being addressed. In this sense, participation without a change in power relations may simply reinforce the status quo, simply adding to the mobilization of bias the claim to a more 'democratic' face. The illusion of inclusion means not only that what emerges is treated as if it represents what 'the people' really want, but also that it gains a moral authority that becomes hard to challenge or question.

Participatory research as popular action

For this reason, to fulfil its liberating potential, participatory research must also address the second aspect of power, through encouraging mobilization and action over time in a way that reinforces the alternative forms and categories of knowledge which might not have been produced.

Though the action component of the participatory action research process is developed in all schools, it has particular prominence in the work of Lewin, and those organizational action researchers who have followed in his tradition. Action research focuses first on problem-solving, and more secondarily on the knowledge generated from the process. The emphasis of the process is not knowledge for knowledge sake, but knowledge which will lead to improvement, usually, for the action researcher, taken to mean in terms of organizational improvement or for the solution of practical problems.

At the same time, while knowledge is not for its own sake, neither is action; rather, the process is an iterative one. Through action, knowledge is created, and analyses of that knowledge may lead to new forms of action. By involving people in gathering information, knowledge production itself may become a form of mobilization; new solutions or actions are identified, tested and then tried again. Thus, in action research, knowledge must be embedded in cycles of action-reflection – action over time (Rahman, 1991). It is through such a process that the nature of action can be deepened, moving from practical problem-solving to more fundamental social transformation (Hall, 1981: 12). The ultimate goal of research in this perspective is not simply to communicate new voices or categories, but

> the radical transformation of social reality and improvement in the lives of the people involved ... Solutions are viewed as processes through which subjects become social actors, participation, by means of grassroots mobilizations, in actions intended to transform society. (Selener, 1997: 19–21).

Participatory research as awareness building

Just as expressing voice through consultation may risk the expression of voice-as-echo, so too action itself may represent blind action, rather than action which is informed by self-conscious awareness and analysis of one's own reality. For this reason, the third key element of participatory action research sees research as a process of reflection, learning and development of critical consciousness. Just as PRA has put a great deal of attention on the 'knowledge' bit of the equation, and action research on the action component, PAR, which grew from pedagogical work of Freire and other adult educators, placed perhaps the greatest emphasis on the value of the social learning that can occur by oppressed groups through the investigation process.

Here again, however, it is important to recognize that reflection itself is embedded in praxis, not separate from it. Through action upon reality, and analyses of that learning, awareness of the nature of problems, and the sources of oppression, may also change. For this reason, participatory research which becomes only 'consultation' with excluded groups at one point in time is limited, for it prevents the possibility that investigation and action over time may lead to a change in the knowledge of people themselves, and therefore a change in understanding of one's own interests and priorities. Not only must production of alternative knowledge be complemented by action upon it, but the participants in the knowledge process must equally find spaces for self-critical investigation and analysis of their own reality, in order to gain more authentic knowledge as a basis for action or representation to others. Such critical self-learning is important not only for the weak and powerless, but also for the more powerful actors who may themselves be trapped in received versions of their own situation. For this reason, we need to understand both the 'pedagogy of the oppressed' (Freire, 1970) and the 'pedagogy of the oppressor', and the relation between the two.

The important point is to recognize that the approaches are synergistic pieces of the same puzzle. From this perspective, what is empowering about participatory research is the extent to which it is able to link the three, to create more democratic forms of knowledge, through action and mobilization of relatively powerless groups on their own affairs, in a way that also involves their own critical reflection and learning.

The New Context: from Margins to Mainstream and from Micro to Macro

In much of the literature on action research in the past, the assumption has been that this process of participatory action research was used primarily at the micro level, and often with or on behalf of relatively marginalized groups. Participatory action research was often associated with social movements, various forms of participatory rural appraisal with local planning and development projects, and forms of action research with organizational change. As we have seen, the links between knowledge, power and empowerment are complex and difficult, even at these levels.

During the 1990s, however, participatory research has faced a new challenge. Rather than being used only at the micro level, it has been scaled up and incorporated in projects or programmes working at regional, national or even global levels. Rather than being used by social movements or marginalized groups, its rhetoric and practice have been adopted by large and powerful institutions, including governments, development agencies, universities and multinationals.[4]

There are many examples. One is the 'Consultations with the Poor' project, commissioned by the World Bank in 1999, in preparation for the World Development Report on Poverty 2000/2001. This study used participatory research methods (mainly based on earlier experiences of participatory poverty assessments), to gain views from poor people about their priorities and concerns. Over 20,000 people were involved in the consultation process, in 23 countries. This represented the first time the World Bank had sought a report based on hearing from 'popular' voices, rather than on analysis by its inhouse experts.[5] Now, the World Bank and the IMF are even beginning to use participation as a new 'conditionality'. In order to receive debt relief under the new Highly Indebted Poor Countries programme, representing a key success of the global Jubilee 2000 Campaign, national governments will have to demonstrate not only that the funds will go towards poverty alleviation, but also that the poverty plan is 'participatory' in its approach.

In a number of countries, similar processes have been used for some time at the national level. In Uganda, for instance, a national Participatory Poverty Assessment Process involving government officials, NGOs and local communities is using participatory research approaches to gain information about the expressed priorities and needs of poor people, as well as for local action planning at the district level. The process represents the latest generation of Participatory Poverty Assessments (Holland, with Blackburn, 1998; Robb, 1999), which have now been used in a number of countries by governments and international agencies to ascertain the needs and priorities of poor people. A number of national governments have also begun to institutionalize participatory processes in various sectoral programmes. In Indonesia, for instance, building upon the success of farmer-to-farmer schools for integrated pest management approaches, the government has now made these approaches mandatory across the country. Similarly, in India, participatory methods of assessment have been required in the national watershed programme, requiring huge challenges of training to go effectively to scale (Blackburn, with Holland, 1998).

There are changes at the local level as well. In a number of countries such as India, the Philippines and Bolivia new local government legislation institutionalizes processes of participatory action planning, and of participatory monitoring through local vigilance committees. In other countries, such as the USA and the UK, processes for direct consultation, such as citizens' juries, are seen as new forms of direct democracy, supplementing past forms of representative democracy (Gaventa and Valderrama, 1999).

These and other examples raise new challenges for participatory action research and questions of power. How do we understand the dynamics of power when participatory methods are employed by the powerful? What happens when participatory research becomes incorporated as 'policy'? Whose voices are raised and whose are heard? And how are these voices mediated as issues of representation become more complex with the use of participatory methods in larger-scale planning and consultation exercises?

Here there are at least two possible positions, each of which has its proponents. On the one hand, there are those who argue that such adoption of participatory processes from above represents cooptation of its core concept and principles. And, the evidence is abundant that even if this is not the intent, the problems associated with rapidly taking participatory approaches to scale are abundant. Flexible approaches give way to blueprints;

participation has been rushed and superficial; methods and techniques have been overly stressed, rather than the purposes for which they are used, or the behaviours and attitudes which must also be present; hopes are raised, and follow-up has often been weak. The rapidly developing misuse and abuse of participatory approaches has raised serious questions of quality, and of the ethics of what constitutes good practice (see Chambers, 1998a: 12).

On the other hand, there is the argument that under such conditions new policies and programmes for participatory approaches create opportunities for change, and at a much more far-reaching and significant level than could be reached through local, micro action alone. Even if there are cases of misuse, the hope is that large-scale programmes create 'spaces' which can legitimate local action, through which relatively powerless groups can find new voice and gain capacity and leverage resources for more effective change. As Chambers writes, for instance,

> These conditions present huge opportunities. Bad practice is an opportunity to improve. Scale is an opportunity to have widespread impact. Potentials are not just for local level participation, but for changes at three levels: policy, institutional and personal. (1998b: 113)

The fact is that we know relatively little about what happens when participatory approaches are adopted on a large scale, or about the degree to which they are used to co-opt resistance and reinforce existing power relations, or the degree to which they provide new spaces and opportunities that strengthen change from below. At the Institute of Development Studies, several exploratory studies are beginning to pursue this question. While the answers are not yet fully conclusive, we can begin to suggest certain enabling factors which will help to maximize the change potential for participatory processes. Early lessons include:

- *The importance of organizational and institutional change:* Scaling-up of participatory approaches must mean more than simply adding a new set of tools and methods to existing institutions, which themselves may be hierarchical, inflexible and non-participatory. As those working with action research in organizations have perhaps realized for some time, effective promotion and use of participatory methods at the 'grassroots' by large organizations means changing the organizations themselves – addressing issues of organizational culture, procedure, incentives and learning. While in the past much attention has been paid to strengthening the capacity of local organizations and grassroots actors to conduct participatory research, the mainstreaming of the participation debate recognizes a 'second generation' agenda – that is how to build the capacity for institutional change at all levels (Tandon and Cordeiro, 1998). Such organizational change is most effective when there are high-level 'participation champions' who will support the process, who encourage middle managers to take risks and behave differently, who can interpret the new way of working for others.
- *The importance of personal attitudes and behaviour change:* Closely related to the importance of organizational change is the importance of personal attitude and behaviour change. While this may appear self-evident to those who have long used participatory methods for personal reflection and change, when participatory methods are adopted on a large scale, there is still a tendency to drift towards their use in a rote, checklist manner, even if they are used in arrogant or culturally insensitive ways. Approaches to training and dissemination must be found which also focus on changing personal values, ethics and commitments by those who are using the tools, again at all levels.
- *Taking time to go slow:* There is tendency when participatory approaches are adopted on a large scale to rush them into place quickly. Targets are adopted. Mass training must be done. Funds must be dispersed. The risk of course is that the bureaucratic needs will drive the process rather than allowing a slower more deliberate participatory process to take its course. Those programmes which have gone to scale most effectively, in fact, have done so horizontally – rather than vertically. That is, they have included processes of peer-to-peer sharing, of building demonstration projects which then spread to other areas, and of including time for learning, testing and continuous improvement in the process.
- *Links to social movements and local capacity:* Even if openings for change are created from above, such spaces must be filled by simultaneous movements and actions from below which can occupy the new spaces with different voices. Otherwise, there is always the danger that these openings for participation will simply mirror the status quo, and serve to strengthen and reinforce more dominant voices at every level. Filling such spaces 'from below' requires local capacity – organizations which are already empowered and aware, and who have the ability to use the new legitimacy that participatory policies can offer to challenge the status quo, to negotiate and to sustain their involvement over time. Where there are social movements in place which have helped to 'conscientize' and mobilize local voices, this is more likely to occur. Where there

is no prior organizational and mobilization experience of those 'at the bottom', it is unlikely that these new public spaces will be filled, though the new opportunities may help to stimulate and catalyse new local demands.

- *Creating vertical alliances and networks:* If a prior level of social capital is important for encouraging local groups to mobilize and to occupy political spaces created above, so too is there a need for new forms of trust and collaboration across levels of power. By definition, large-scale change must happen at multiple levels – changing global actors will not be done by the villagers, nor will village-level change be created by a staff person in a global organization. But change at both levels is important, for large-scale and meaningful change to occur. Such change processes can best be aligned, to create new synergies with one another, to the extent that actors at differing levels learn to engage critically across power differences. For this to happen, mediating organizations, processes and networks that vertically cut across hierarchies are critical – but so too are processes of meaningful representation and voice from one level to the other. While large-scale consultation processes begin to make this possible, transparency of how differing voices are being mediated, and by whom, must be present.
- *The importance of monitoring for quality and accountability:* Finally, it is clear that to do participatory research on a large scale also means constantly monitoring and holding to account the nature and degree of participation which is occurring. This argues for the need to evolve new concepts of validity in participatory research, ones which measure the quality of participation, as well as the quality of knowledge. This implies a new understanding of participatory research ethics – that goes beyond traditional ethical concerns regarding such things as confidentiality and protection of research subjects, to ask questions about who participates in and benefits from research processes, how information is used and by whom, and how the process transforms or supports power relations. How to evolve such quality standards, and how to use them to hold differing actors and institutions to account, represents one of the most important challenges facing participatory research today.

Such approaches to large-scale change begin to recognize, with Hayward and others, that power relations occur at every level and sphere, affecting the powerful as well as the powerless. Rather than seeing participatory research as only a tool for mobilizing the powerless against the powerful, this approach takes a more nuanced view, to explore how participatory methods can facilitate change at multiple levels, among multiple actors. Such an approach is not to wish away conflict – for conflict of interests and views will also be present within and between levels – but it is to suggest that to change the boundaries of the possible, especially in a highly globalized world in which actors and issues are so interrelated, means to bring about change in multiple spaces and arenas, and to link those processes of change through new and accountable forms of interconnection. This approach also argues that the potential for large-scale change through participatory research is determined as much by the quality of the relationships of one set of actors to another, and the extent to which they each address power relations, as by the capacity or strength of any one set of actors in the process.

Ultimately, developing and using new forms of participatory knowledge on a large scale is a question of promoting and creating new forms of participatory democracy, in which ordinary citizens use their knowledge and experience to construct a more just and equitable society. In a time in which inequality between the rich and the poor is greater than ever before, in which globalization threatens even the limited democracy of nation states, the challenges of going to broader scale with participatory research are enormous, but so also are the risks of failing to do so.

Notes

Our thanks to Kate Hamilton and Mel Speight for research assistance on this chapter.

1 This section draws heavily on Gaventa (1999).

2 Among the most interesting recent empirical studies of power we have seen, the study is based upon her dissertation on power in the schools in New Haven (Hayward, 2000).

3 PRA evolved through innovation and application in the South in the late 1980s and early 1990s, influenced by Rapid Rural Appraisal (RRA), applied anthropology, participatory action research, feminist research and agroecosystems analysis (Chambers, 1992; Guijt and Shah, 1998). Core methodological principles include iterative, group-based, learning and analysis, the use of visualization methods to broaden the inclusiveness of the process and enable people to represent their knowledge using their own categories and concepts, and an explicit concern with the quality of interaction, including a stress on personal values, attitudes and behaviour.

4 For reviews of some of these experiences of scaling up, see Blackburn, Chambers and Gaventa (1999), Gaventa (1998) and Chambers (1998b).

5 Further information on this project can be found on the World Bank web page at *http://www.worldbank.org/poverty/wdrpoverty/conspoor/index.htm*

References

Bachrach, P. and Baratz, M.S. (1970) *Power and Poverty: Theory and Practice*. New York: Oxford University Press.

Blackburn, J., with Holland, J. (eds) (1998) *Who Changes? Institutionalizing Participation in Development*. London: Intermediate Technology Publications.

Blackburn, J., Chambers, R. and Gaventa, J. (1999) 'Learning to take time and go slow: mainstreaming participation in development and the comprehensive development framework (CDF)'. Paper prepared for Operations Evaluation Department, World Bank. Brighton: Institute of Development Studies.

Chambers, R. (1992) 'Rural appraisal: rapid, relaxed and participatory'. *IDS Discussion Paper, 311*. Brighton: Institute of Development Studies.

Chambers, R. (1995) 'Paradigm shifts and the practice of participatory research and development', in N. Nelson and S. Wright (eds), *Power and Participatory Development: Theory and Practice*. London: Intermediate Technology Publications. pp. 30–42.

Chambers, R. (1997) *Whose Reality Counts? Putting the First Last*. London: Intermediate Technology Publications.

Chambers, R. (1998a) 'Foreword', in I. Guijt and M.K. Shah (eds), *The Myth of Community: Gender Issues in Participatory Development*. London: Intermediate Technology Publications. p. xvii.

Chambers, R. (1998b) 'Beyond "whose reality counts?" New methods we now need', in O. Fals Borda (ed.), *People's Participation: Challenges Ahead*. Bogotá: Tercier Mundo SA. pp. 105–30.

Cornwall, A., Guijt, I. and Welbourn, A. (1993) 'Acknowledging process: challenges for agricultural research and methodology'. *IDS Discussion Paper, 333*. Brighton: Institute of Development Studies.

Crawley, H. (1998) 'Living up to the empowerment claim? The potential of PRA', in I. Guijt and M.K. Shah (eds), *The Myth of Community: Gender Issues in Participatory Development*. London: Intermediate Technology Publications.

Dahl, R.A. (1969) 'The concept of power', in R. Bell, D.M. Edwards and R. Harrison Wagner (eds), *Political Power: a Reader in Theory and Research*. New York: Free Press. p. 80. Reprinted from *Behavioral Science*, 2: 201–5 (1957).

Entwistle, H. (1979) *Antonio Gramsci*. London: Routledge and Kegan Paul.

Fals Borda, O. (1998) *People's Participation: Challenges Ahead*. Bogotá: Tercier Mundo SA.

Foucault, M. (1977) *Discipline and Punishment*. London: Allen Lane.

Foucault, M. (1979) *The History of Sexuality, Part 1*. London: Allen Lane.

Freire, P. (1970) *Pedagogy of the Oppressed*. New York: Seabury Press.

Freire, P. (1981) *Education for Critical Consciousness*. New York: Continuum.

Gaventa, J. (1980) *Power and Powerlessness: Quiescence and Rebellion in an Appalachian Valley*. Urbana, IL: University of Illinois Press and Oxford: Clarendon Press.

Gaventa, J. (1993) 'The powerful, the powerless, and the experts', in P. Park, M. Brydon-Miller, B. Hall and T. Jackson (eds), *Voices of Change: Participatory Research in the United States and Canada*. Westport, CT: Bergin and Garvey and Toronto: OISE Press. pp. 21–40.

Gaventa, J. (1998) 'The scaling-up and institutionalization of PRA: lessons and challenges', in J. Blackburn with J. Holland (eds), *Who Changes? Institutionalizing Participation in Development*. London: Intermediate Technology Publications. pp. 153–66.

Gaventa, J. (1999) 'Citizen knowledge, citizen competence, and democracy building', in S.L. Elkin and K.E. Soltan (eds), *Citizen Competence and Democratic Institutions*. University Park, PA: The Pennsylvania State University Press. pp. 49–66.

Gaventa, J. and Valderrama, C. (1999) 'Participation, citizenship and local governance. Background note prepared for workshop on Strengthening Participation in Local Governance', IDS, Brighton, 21–24 June 1999.

Guijt, I. and Shah, M.K. (1998) 'Waking up to power, process and conflict', in I. Guijt and M.K. Shah (eds), *The Myth of Community: Gender Issues in Participatory Development*. London: Intermediate Technology Publications. pp. 1–23.

Hall, B.L. (1981) 'Participatory research, popular knowledge and power: a personal reflection', *Convergence*, XIV (3): 6–17.

Hall, B.L. (1992) 'From margins to center? The development and purpose of participatory research', *The American Sociologist*, 23 (4): 15–28.

Harding, S. (1986) *Feminism and Methodology*. Bloomington, IN: Indiana University Press.

Hayward, C.R. (1998) 'De-facing power', *Polity*, 31 (1): 1–22.

Hayward, C.R. (2000) *De-facing Power*. Cambridge: Cambridge University Press.

Holland, J., with Blackburn, J. (1998) *Whose Voice? Participatory Research and Policy Change*. London: Intermediate Technology Publications.

Kabeer, N. (1994) *Reversed Realities: Gender Hierarchies in Development Thought*. London and New York: Verso.

Lukes, S. (1974) *Power: a Radical View*. London: Macmillan.

Maguire, P. (1987) 'Towards a feminist participatory framework: challenging the patriarchy', in *Doing Participatory Research: A Feminist Approach*. Amherst: Center for International Education, University of Massachusetts.

Maguire, P. (1996) 'Proposing a more feminist participatory research: knowing and being embraced openly', in K. de Koning and M. Martin (eds), *Participatory Research in Health: Issues and Experiences*. London: Zed Books. pp. 27–39.

Morris, A. (1984) *The Origins of the Civil Rights Movement*. New York: Free Press.

Mouffe, C. (1992) 'Feminism, citizenship and radical democratic politics', in J. Butler and J. Scott (eds), *Feminists Theorize the Political*. New York: Routledge.

Mueller, C.M. (ed.) (1992) *Frontiers in Social Movement Theory*. New Haven, CT: Yale University Press.

Nelson, N. and Wright, S. (1995) 'Participation and power', in N. Nelson and S. Wright (eds), *Power and Participatory Development: Theory and Practice*. London: Intermediate Technology Publications. pp. 1–12.

Park, P., Brydon-Miller, M., Hall, B. and Jackson T. (eds) (1993) *Voices of Change: Participatory Research in the United States and Canada*. Westport, CT: Bergin and Garvey and Toronto: OISE Press.

Rahman, M.A. (1991) 'The theoretical standpoint of PAR', in O. Fals Borda and M.A. Rahman (eds), *Action and Knowledge: Breaking the Monopoly with Participatory Action-Research*. New York: The Apex Press and London: Intermediate Technology Publications. pp. 13–23.

Reason, P. (1994) 'Three approaches to participatory inquiry', in K. Denzin and S. Lincoln (eds), *Handbook of Qualitative Research*. Thousand Oaks, CA: Sage Publications.

Robb, C. (1999) *Can the Poor Influence Policy? Participatory Poverty Assessments in the Developing World*. Washington, DC: The World Bank.

Rowlands, J. (1995) 'Empowerment examined', *Development in Practice*, 5 (2): 101–7.

Schattschneider, E.E. (1960) *The Semi-sovereign People: a Realist's View of Democracy in America*. New York: Holt, Rinehart and Winston.

Scott, J.C. (1986) *Weapons of the Weak*. New Haven, CT: Yale University Press.

Scott, J.C. (1990) *Domination and the Arts of Resistance*. New Haven, CT: Yale University Press.

Selener, D. (1997) *Participatory Action Research and Social Change*. New York: The Cornell Participatory Action Research Network, Cornell University.

Tandon, R. and Cordeiro, A. (1998) 'Participation of primary stakeholders in the World Bank's project and policy work: emerging lessons'. Contribution to the International Conference on Mainstreaming and Up-scaling of Primary Stakeholder Participation – Lessons Learned and Ways Forward, Washington, DC, 19–20 November 1998.

Treleaven, L. (2001) 'The turn to action and the linguistic turn: towards an integrated methodology', in P. Reason and H. Bradbury (eds), *Handbook of Action Research: Participative Inquiry and Practice*. London: Sage Publications. pp. 261–72.

7
Knowledge and Participatory Research

PETER PARK

CHAPTER OUTLINE

In participatory research, ordinary people generate knowledge in addressing their concerns as members of society. This chapter identifies the forms of this knowledge as *representation*, *relational* and *reflective*. It argues that putting participatory research on an epistemological grounding forces us to think of community ties and critical awareness, as well as objective understanding of reality, as forms of knowledge. Knowledge is related to power, and people gain power of solidarity and confidence, as well as of control, in the process of pursuing these forms of knowledge. The implications of understanding knowledge and power in this way go beyond the conduct of participatory research; it allows us to liberate the limited conceptions of knowledge and power tied to the Enlightenment project of the West.

Participatory research is action-oriented research activity in which ordinary people address common needs arising in their daily lives and, in the process, generate knowledge. This chapter discusses the forms that knowledge takes by broadening conventional Western epistemological horizons to produce a more complete understanding of knowledge, not only in participatory research but also in our lives in general.

Participatory Research as People's Research

Participatory research differs from both basic and applied social science research in terms of people's involvement in the research process, integration of action with research, and the practice-based nature of the knowledge that is entailed. It sets itself apart even from other forms of action-oriented research because of the central role that non-experts play. In contrast to other forms of action-oriented research, in which outside parties have an important role in determining what problems to address, often taking charge of the research process and implementing action, in participatory research people who share problems in common decide what problems to tackle and directly get involved in research and social change activities (Park, 1999). Action-minded researchers with technical backgrounds often get involved in this process but mainly as facilitators (Swantz, Chapter 27; Wadsworth, Chapter 31). The reason for this emphasis on popular participation is that participatory research is not just a convenient instrument for solving social problems through technically efficacious means, but is also a social practice that helps marginalized people attain a degree of emancipation as autonomous and responsible members of society (Freire, 1982). It is allied to the ideals of democracy, and in that spirit it is proper to call it research of the people, by the people, and for the people (Park, 1997).

Participatory research deals with issues that affect classes of people in such wide-ranging areas as inner-city and rural poverty, health, education, agriculture, environment, housing, community development, mental health, disability, domestic violence, women's oppression, and immigration (*The American Sociologist*, 1992, 1993; Callaway, 1982; *Convergence*, 1981, 1988; Khanna, 1996; Merrifield, 1993; Park et al., 1993; Participatory Research Network, 1982; Selener, 1997). The more obvious purpose of participatory research is to bring about changes by improving the material circumstances of affected people. To this end, people engage in three different kinds of activity: inquiring into the nature of the problem to solve by understanding its causes and meanings; getting together by organizing themselves as community units; and mobilizing themselves for action by raising their awareness of what should be done on moral and political grounds. For this reason, gathering and analysing necessary information, strengthening community ties and sharpening the ability to think and act critically emerge as three main objectives of participatory research, requiring three different kinds of knowledge (Park, 1997).

For the first of these objectives, inquiry makes use of the more conventional quantitative and qualitative research methods. But often it also requires the use of non-canonical approaches, such as art, photography, video, theatre, oral history, storytelling, music, dance and other expressive media, to reveal the more submerged and difficult-to-articulate aspects of the issues involved. In all cases, however, group processes play an important role. Dialogue, in particular, looms large as an important methodological link among the activities pursued because of its existential significance for human life. More than a technical means to an end, it is an expression of the human condition that impels people to come together as thinking and feeling beings to form a common entity that is larger than its constituent parts (Freire, 1970). Dialogue occupies a central position as inquiry in pursuing the three objectives of participatory research, and the knowledge associated with them, by making it possible for participants to create a social space in which they can share experiences and information, create common meanings and forge concerted actions together.

An Epistemological Turn

Participatory research, when successful, produces an understanding of the world through research efforts that mirror key features of the classical natural sciences. I will refer to this kind of knowledge, or understanding, as 'objective' without necessarily implying that it refers to reality that is ontologically independent of the knower or that is epistemologically non-problematic. The term is simply a convenient, short-hand way of referring to a kind of knowledge that produces technically useful results by following certain methodological procedures. We can readily understand the creation of such knowledge in participatory research in epistemological terms. In addition to this, however, participatory research also has the objectives of seeking to strengthen community ties and to heighten transformative potential through critical consciousness, which can be thought of as forms of knowledge as well. Other social change efforts, such as community development projects that are not thought of as any kind of research, can also have such outcomes. But putting the activities aimed at these objectives in the context of research in effect gives the workings of participatory research an epistemological turn by forcing us to think of what they produce as knowledge since research is above all a knowledge-producing endeavour. This epistemological understanding is relatively non-problematic where objective knowledge is concerned since it is after all commonly referred to as such, notwithstanding the philosophical disputes surrounding the concept. However, we should also consider the activities undertaken in pursuit of the other goals of participatory research from an epistemological perspective, for two reasons. First, by explicitly putting these activities in an epistemological framework we are able to give them methodological rigour analogous to the procedures associated with the generation of the so-called objective knowledge. Secondly, participatory research begins with what people bring to this enterprise as everyday knowledge – their intimate familiarity with their environment, their knowledge of one another as members of a community, and their critical consciousness that their lives can change for better – and transforms that knowledge into a more organized form, turning common sense into good sense (Gramsci, 1971).

Forms of Knowledge

Knowledge occupies a prominent place in the theory and practice of participatory research, as even a casual perusal of the literature readily reveals (Fals Borda and Rahman, 1991; Gaventa, 1993; Hall, Gillette and Tandon, 1982; Smith, Willms and Johnson, 1997). In participatory research, people affected by social conditions use their insider knowledge, acquire information from existing public records, and generate new knowledge by means of analysis and systematization in order to arrive at satisfactory solutions to their problems without depending exclusively on the expertise of outside professionals (Cable and Degutis, 1997; Chambers, 1983; Fals Borda, 1982, 1988; Gaventa, 1993; Gaventa and Horton, 1981; Gibbs, 1998; Rocheleau, 1994; Rusmore, 1996).

The views concerning knowledge expressed in many discussions of participatory research are tied to an implicit epistemological bias that equates knowing with describing, explaining or understanding a phenomenon as an object, or what I referred to earlier as objective knowledge. This kind of knowledge is clearly valuable for dealing with human and social problems, as well as with the physical world, despite the fact that the success of its application in the social sciences has been less than spectacular. To the extent, however, that the self-understanding of participatory research limits itself just to this kind of knowledge, it falls short of its objective of creating new kinds of human and emancipatory knowledge (Gaventa, 1993). We need to broaden the existing epistemological horizons to include forms of knowledge associated with various human concerns. I will discuss these below as *representational*, *relational*, and *reflective knowledge* (Park, 1997, 1999).

Representational knowledge: functional subtype

One subtype of representational knowledge comprises the portrayal of a thing, a person, an event or an experience as being related as a variable to some other variable or variables in a functional manner, as in saying that one variable is a function of another in a mathematical sense; for example, powerlessness is a function of poverty. Correlational and causal relationships are good examples of such representational knowledge. These relationships ideally present themselves as general propositions, making up a theory with a logical structure that makes deductive, nomological explanation possible. The instrumental power of representational knowledge in this functional form lies in its capacity to make predictions by showing antecedent events leading to probable consequences, which makes it possible, in theory, to produce desired events or to prevent undesirable ones. Equipped with such knowledge, the actor is then in a position to control events, with varying degrees of success.

The methodological procedures for generating this species of knowledge prescribe, in principle, strict separation of the researcher as the knower from the object of inquiry, in both laboratory settings and social research involving questionnaires and standardized interviews. This separation criterion, however, is of limited utility when applied to social settings, because in order to obtain valid information from people there must be trust between the researcher and the researched, which can only come from human closeness, not separation (Oakley, 1981). The documented inability of the US government to collect accurate census data involving essentially simple head counts, which has resulted in missing millions of people in published statistics, graphically illustrates this methodological shortcoming. This is one of the mistakes that the positivistically-oriented social sciences have made in slavishly emulating the methodological procedures of the natural sciences.

Representational knowledge carries with it no guarantee of instrumental success, especially in human and social applications, and even worse, can be a threat to human freedom because of its potential for manipulative control. All the same, human beings do rely on the technical efficacy of this form of knowledge in their daily living to an important degree, for example, in trying to improve agricultural yields or figuring out what causes youth violence. It is for this reason that this kind of representational knowledge occupies a rightful place in participatory research.

Representational knowledge: interpretive subtype

The functional form, however, constitutes only one branch of representational knowledge. The other subtype is interpretive knowledge. Hermeneutics as a philosophy and a science of interpretation has generated insights into how this form of knowledge creates an understanding of texts, persons, events and situations (Bernstein, 1983; Gadamer, 1975; Palmer, 1969). Interpretive knowledge, in contrast to the functional subtype, manifests itself as understanding of meaning and requires that the knower come as close to the to-be-known as possible. This means taking into account the backgrounds, intentions and feelings involved both in understanding human affairs and textual and other kinds of artifacts that are human creations. For example, the local residents who participated in the landmark participatory research project in Appalachia read the courthouse records of several counties in the region, not as disinterested observers but rather as members of a community suffering from endemic poverty. As a result, they came to understand the inequitable distribution of tax burdens in Appalachia, which they saw as a personal affront (Gaventa and Horton, 1981).

In the interpretive process, there is no assumption that the individual is a detached observer unsullied by personal history and points of view, but rather a supposition that the knower inevitably comes to the task as a whole, living person with a past and a future, personal likes and dislikes, and enters into the phenomenon to know it on its own terms. This requires an attitude of openness and willingness to listen to the messages emanating from the object of interpretation. The knower and the known thus participate in the process of knowing, in which what they bring to the encounter merges together. This process assembles disparate pieces of information into a meaningful whole or pattern, rather than dividing it into analytical components as variables in a functional equation. Interpretive knowledge is synthetic and integrative, rather than analytic and reductive.

In coming to an understanding, the interaction between the knower and the known produces changes in both. In interpreting, we always encounter something new and unexpected, and we gain a new experience, by virtue of which we become altered (Rorty, 1979). This argument applies equally well to situations involving both humans and human creations, such as texts and events, since these things always come to us as products of previous understanding and will become altered in the meaning they emanate with each subsequent interpretation. Interpretive knowledge is representational in the sense that we as knowers 'redescribe' or re-present the object of knowing, as this in turn re-presents itself over and over again for interpretation (Fay, 1975).

As originally formulated, hermeneutics had more to do with non-human applications than human ones (Gadamer, 1975; Heidegger, 1962) and we find its historical prototypes in biblical studies and legal interpretation of written laws and legal precedents. These practice-oriented applications grew out of the need for guidance in religious and judicial action, respectively. Interpretation has also played an important role in the social sciences, at least for theoretical understanding, the most illustrative example being Max Weber's sociology of *verstehen* (understanding), although here the connection to practice has been more remote and attenuated. Nevertheless, interpretive knowledge as such has strong connections to practice, which is the reason why it deserves to be brought out here as a distinctive subtype of representational knowledge for participatory research.

Relational knowledge

Interpretive knowledge, when applied to human situations, has the potential for bringing people together in empathy and making it possible for them to know one another as human beings affectively, as well as cognitively, which constitutes relational knowledge. In everyday usage, when we say we know someone, we mean this in a very different sense from knowing a fact or theory, or knowing right from wrong; it has a distinctively relational meaning. In participatory research, this kind of knowing plays an important role in strengthening community (Geddis, 1997; Lynd, 1992; Maguire, 1987). And more broadly, the spirit of 'deep participation' that Reason (1994) situates in human inquiry shares much in common with this notion of relational knowledge. To ground the idea of relational knowledge theoretically in this chapter, I will first turn to suggestions from Habermas's critique of rationality and then take liberties with his theory of communicative action (Habermas, 1971, 1981, 1987) by using insights from feminist scholarship and classical Chinese linguistics and philosophy.

At the core of Habermas's critical theory is the proposition that for humans to be rational, or reasonable, means to act according to our knowledge of the so-called objective world that we approach as outside observers, the moral order that we constitute inter-subjectively, and the internal subjective state that we access as personal experience. Habermas calls the types of knowledge associated with rationality in these arenas of life, respectively, empirical theoretical, moral practical and aesthetic practical knowledge (Habermas, 1981). He thus broadens the prevailing notion of rationality, going beyond instrumental understanding tied to an ends-means calculus. By showing that human rationality also has components that relate to aspects of life other than the one that objectifies the world through technical means, Habermas creates action possibilities aimed at the improvement of not merely the technical but also the moral and expressive dimensions of social life.

Habermas bases his theory of rationality on his understanding of linguistics, which focuses on the pragmatic aspects of the speech act (Habermas, 1979). When we speak, Habermas observes, not only does what we say convey semantic meanings, but also the very act of speaking is a performance through which we simultaneously make three different kinds of illocutionary claim: that we have a right to speak; that we are sincere in wanting to be understood; and that we are speaking the truth. Since the speaker directs these claims to the listener, speaking necessarily brings the two together in interaction in which they engage, however tacitly or obliquely, in acts of questioning and justifying the warrant for the claims on the grounds of reasonableness. Rationality in this sense has to do with questions not only of fact but also of norms and feelings. It is a social accomplishment which derives from interpersonal relations revolving around the illocutionary claims embedded in the speech act. Rationality entails relationship.

While all three illocutionary claims involved in speaking have a role in generating interaction among actors, Habermas singles out sincerity as paradigmatic for creating a 'bonding' or 'binding' kind of relationship. In Habermas's theory, however, relationship is made up of communicative exchanges occasioned by the speakers' display of their subjective experiences whose claims to sincerity are subject to justificatory argumentation. It is a relationship that is not built on the sharing of feelings and experiences but rather on discursive consensus between the partners in communication concerning the reasonableness of the speaker's claim of sincerity. Thus Habermas's formulation of rationality that would account for all aspects of the lifeworld, including human relationships in their tenderest moments, stops short of fully embracing as rational our knowledge of others as human beings which is weighted with affective content and process. Habermas's attempt to rationalize the lifeworld is still very much tied to the cognitivist prejudices of Kantian philosophy of reason which is devoid of emotive content (Code, 1991). More generally, it carries baggage from Western Enlightenment philosophy, with its male biases, which does not admit affectivity in its epistemology (Jaggar, 1989; Lloyd, 1989). Furthermore, despite its name, Habermas's universal pragmatics (Habermas, 1979) which leads to the postulation of rationality in the three domains of life, is similarly constrained by the surface features of the Western language communities, which make it difficult to see fully the illocutionary force with which language creates relationships among people. In order properly to imbue relational knowledge with all-inclusive rationality, partly in response to the call for a more feminist voice in participatory research (Maguire, 1996; see also Chapter 5), we need to incorporate insights that restore the rightful place of affectivity in knowing, insights to which feminist scholarship has contributed significantly.

Affectivity in knowing others

Our shared experiences and feelings enable us to know the world as an object of cognition (Belenky et al., 1986; Braaten, 1995; Code, 1991; Shotter, 1993) and, more importantly for the present purpose, to know one another as friends and lovers. In coming to know others in these human ways, affective ties that bind and make community possible (Rousseau, 1991) become predominant. We establish relationships with our bodies and feelings, in pleasure and pain, in laughter and tears, and with shared experiences and stories. In knowing others relationally, we focus on their unique features as ends to be appreciated, in contrast with representational knowledge which places the particular in generalized contexts of understanding. Friendship in the Aristotelian sense involves knowing the second person as a particular entity, not as a representation of a universal principle (Gustavsen, Chapter 1; Nussbaum, 1991) and treating him/her as an equal with care, respect, admiration and trust (Code, 1991). In its most sublime form, relational knowledge expresses itself as love, in which people become one with each other in a union, which transcends and transforms the individuals involved. As Fromm argues, 'The only way of fully knowing lies in the *act* of love: this act transcends thought, it transcends words. It is the daring plunge into the experience of union' (1956: 31). Such knowing is primordial, since it is rooted in the relationship we establish with our first primary caretakers which contributes to the later development of relational knowledge of others (Richards, 1998). Some feminists have argued that in a paradoxical sense we experience our own separateness and identity as persons, in the creative tension generated in knowing others intimately (Dimen, 1989). Relational knowledge is also mutual since it is directed at and derives from each partner in relationship and stays with both to become part of them. This form of knowing is the real basis of solidarity and community and one of the cornerstones of human rationality (Braaten, 1995).

The Chinese language and mind/heart

In order to show how this kind of affectively-laden relational knowledge is produced in our daily lives, we can start with Habermas's pragmatic linguistics which argues that language plays an important role in producing interpersonal relations. But it is convenient to turn to classical Chinese to show that relational knowledge results not so much from the built-in sincerity claim in the speech act that can be redeemed by means of justificatory arguments, as Habermas would have it, but rather from an illocutionary force of language that is perfomative at a practical and affective level.

The basic building blocks in the Chinese language are not sentences, as in English, but strings of words, each of which we understand by knowing how to interpret it in terms of the scope of action it implies (Hall and Ames, 1987; Hansen, 1993). A word in Chinese functions very much like a graphic symbol, analogous to signs for, say, toilets in public places. Because each word in Chinese contains what is essentially this kind of performative instruction, a linked sequence of them, making up what can be regarded as a sentence (Graham, 1989), affects the way the speakers of this language relate to each other. These expressions are not primarily declarative or propositional and do not explicitly describe or explain reality as an object of depiction. As a consequence, in Chinese the pragmatic function overrides the semantic, such that expressions are prescriptive rather than descriptive. Knowledge made possible by this language functions less for conveying facts and abstract concepts than for shaping our behaviour. In Chinese, we know the meaning conveyed by language not by seeing its correspondence to reality, but by being able to carry out what it commands. In this respect, knowing in Chinese implies doing, as when we know how to read a musical score by being able to sing or play an instrument according to the instructions imbedded in it.

This performative characteristic of the Chinese language shows that the socially binding function of language not only lies in bringing about agreements concerning claims of truth, rightness or sincerity in our speech acts, as Habermas theorizes, but also derives from the power of language to directly create a relationship of reciprocity between speaker and listener. While we can more readily appreciate this illocutionary characteristic of classical Chinese because of its structure and usage, it is important to understand that we can detect it also in other languages, such as English. Speaking always contains an implicit invitation to carry out in action what the embedded performative meaning conveys. This performative meaning is more like reaching out, a kind of touching, that bids the listener to acknowledge and reciprocate. When someone speaks to me, the illocutionary meaning is a gesture, a kind of beckoning that starts the dance of relating. It is in accepting this invitation to action that we make interpersonal connections and we come to know in a relational way. And, as feminist scholars have taught us, we make these connections not just with our heads but with our hearts as well.

There has been a long tradition in the West of dichotomizing intellect and emotion, and, more generally, mind and body, associating knowing with the former. In Chinese philosophy, in contrast, this mind/body dichotomy is absent, for there is no concept of mind that is divorced from feeling. There is only one expression in Chinese, symbolized by one character, which means both mind and feeling. The usual English translation for this character is mind/heart, or mind-and-heart, because it refers to both cerebral and emotive functions (de Bary, 1989; Hansen, 1991). The same word means both mind, the thinking centre, and the heart, the biological organ that pumps blood and the psychological home of feelings. Thus, in Chinese we know with our head and heart simultaneously, with our mind and with our body. If we get to know our conversation partners in the process of talking that impels us to connect, this knowing is inherently not just an intellectual exercise, but an affect-laden action. That is, when we know relationally, we mobilize our feelings and our minds. In English, the verb 'to understand', when used in interpersonal contexts, also has both cognitive and emotive components, which gives us a glimpse into the concept of mind/heart in Chinese, and, by extension, into the affective component of relational knowledge imbedded in language.

Knowledge in relationship

Relational knowledge does not describe anything, nor does it consist of facts (Richards, 1998). Rather, it resides in the act of relating and shows itself in words, expressions, actions and other forms of doing relationship. In relationship, we know with feeling, and the knowing is in the feeling. In its primeval form, that knowledge resides in physical touching. We can reasonably argue that we get to know the world through our bodily sensations first, in the mother's womb (Buber, 1970). In general, knowing through senses comes before knowing through thinking. Because of this, relational knowledge is arguably prior to other kinds of knowing (Code, 1991). The most intimate form of knowing is also through touching, which we express most intensely in making love. Our deeply ingrained linguistic habit, going back to the biblical usage referring to intimacy, equates relationship with knowledge.

Although knowing a person representionally, especially through interpretive knowledge, may help us gain relational knowledge, it is not relational knowledge itself. Similarly, knowing someone relationally may help to access representational knowledge of that person as an object of depiction or understanding (Shotter, 1993), but the two forms remain conceptually distinct. The *raison d'être* for relational knowledge is not in putting that knowledge to use; rather, it is an end in itself. In knowing relationally, knowledge becomes part of us, in the same way that food nourishes us. It enriches us, and we become more whole because of it. Love, which is the prototype of relational knowledge, epitomizes these qualities.

Relational knowledge comes from connecting and leads to further connecting. It is reciprocal, not only in that the parties involved know each other, but also in that it grows from interaction. Forms of interaction may include touching, as in shaking hands or hugging, conversing, telling stories and communicating through other means, sharing things, engaging in activities together, experiencing common events, living together, and partaking in the same cultural and ethnic background. What makes conversation and other forms of interaction that lead to relational knowledge possible are respect, caring, sincerity, authenticity and trust. The attitude most conducive to promoting these traits in conversations is that of listening, for it is in listening that we come close to someone and we are with that person, as in putting our ear to someone's heart (Fiumara, 1990). Hence the significance of the 1960s' saying, 'I hear you'.

Relational knowledge endures and grows through a commitment on the part of the parties involved to persevere through good times and bad. It is this quality that sustains relational knowledge when interaction is interrupted due to material circumstances, as when, for example, intimate partners are separated from each other for periods of time. Relational knowledge grows out of active communal life and, conversely, it is relational knowledge that makes it possible to create and sustain a community. This is the dual import of relational knowledge for participatory research.

Reflective knowledge

The notion of reflective knowledge derives from the critical theory tradition which argues that meaningful human knowledge must not merely understand the world but also change it; it must be normative and oriented to action as well as descriptive or explanatory. Through the influence of critical theory, the creation of reflective knowledge has been an important feature of participatory research in both theory and practice (Carr, 1997; Comstock and Fox, 1993; Horton, 1993; Kemmis, Chapter 8; Park, 1992). One crucial tenet of critical theory is that the full realization of human life in society requires the mobilization of rationality that includes knowledge of moral values relevant in everyday living (Habermas, 1971, 1973, 1981, 1987). This kind of knowledge provides practical moral criteria for comprehending the social nature of the problems that affect classes of people and points to what people themselves can do in order to improve their situations. The concept of *conscientization*, which is at the heart of Paulo Freire's pedagogy of liberation (Freire, 1970), connotes both consciousness and conscience and thus captures the cognitive and normative processes that constitute this form of knowledge.

Concerted engagement in change-producing activity requires conscious reflection on the part of the actors involved, which is why I choose to call this form of knowledge reflective, in the spirit of critical theory (Geuss, 1981). Reflective knowledge involves actors themselves critically analysing and evaluating questions of morality and values relating to their life conditions and the proper actions to take (Mezirow, 1990). But this form of knowledge is also a product of group deliberation in which concerned parties present arguments for or against a moral stance, an understanding of the problematic situation or a course of action to be taken, and, ideally, discuss them according to criteria of rational discourse (Habermas, 1970). It is social and dialogic.

Reflective knowledge upholds the dignity of human beings as free and autonomous agents who can act effectively and responsibly on their own behalf in the context of their interdependent relationships. It is emancipatory in this sense, but with an emphasis on the social both in the practical ends to which it is directed and the process through which it is generated. It is constitutive of actors who are autonomous in a social sense, signifying not the individualistic self-determination, self-confidence, self-identity or self-reliance of independent actors, but rather the capacity to act with determination, confidence and resourcefulness that is made possible by, and expressed in, the interaction and interdependence embedded in human communities (Benhabib, 1986; Code, 1991). Reflective knowledge creates collective autonomy and responsibility.

Action is an integral part of reflective knowledge. One way of understanding the relationship between knowledge and action is to say that people with problems figure out what to do by first finding out their causes and then acting on insight. We can think of this kind of experiential learning in the language of scientific experiment (Dewey, 1991). In this view, we learn by seeing if our understanding of how things work actually makes a difference in trying to bring about change, which is in essence a form of hypothesis testing. In participatory research, we implement the solutions that we fashion through research, and then assess the results to see if the efforts have produced the desired effects. Through this process, which constitutes participatory evaluation research (Park and Williams, 1999), we learn, in effect, by testing the ideas that emerge from research in terms of efficacy in actual application.

The notion of praxis, in contrast, gives action, or practice, the primary role in the relationship between action and theory, such that theory is thought of as experience-based (Gustavsen, Chapter 1). Critical theory in the tradition of Marxian epistemology similarly understands the significance of action in the constitution of reflective knowledge in a way that gives primacy to the former (Bernstein, 1971). Praxis in this context speaks to the relationship between theory and practice in which human activity shapes history, produces an understanding of the world and thereby contributes to people's actualization as free social beings (Vazquez, 1977). Action thus plays the central role in generating our knowledge of the world in the course of bringing about material changes.

Action relates to reflective knowledge in still another sense, which has to do with critical engagement. Social action, whether it is, for example, participating in sit-ins (Starhawk, 1987) or engaging in the reorganization of a housing project (Heaney and Horton, 1990), produces in participants changes that go beyond intellectual understanding. Because such actions invariably entail modifying or going against existing social arrangements that actors perceive to be at the root of their problems, they elicit resistance on the part of the guardians of the status quo. In dealing with the social forces that stand in the way of change in such ways, the actors come to understand at the visceral and emotive level the workings and intransigence of social arrangements. This kind of understanding puts flesh on the bones of the abstract conceptual knowledge about social reality they gain through theoretical analysis and compels them to engage in political activities, such as petitioning, lobbying, advocating, negotiating, protesting and organizing. In the process, actors come to feel the power they gain by engaging in political actions as autonomous agents. Through action we learn how the world works, what we can do, and who we are; we learn with mind/heart. This is how we become aware and emancipated.

The second wave of the feminist movement succeeded in producing reflective knowledge of the kind discussed here in all its aspects, including research, analysis and action. In gathering force as a social movement containing diverse theoretical and practical concerns, feminism was able to bring about significant changes in the ways both men and women feel, think, talk and act at the individual level. More significantly, it has produced modifications in the structure of society and in cultural patterns, often through legal means, which has in turn had the effect of freeing both women and men from some of the abuses of the patriarchal social order. There remains much to be done in this respect, of course, but the point is that the feminist movement provides a concrete example of how an oppressed segment of society can organize to produce reflective knowledge and, in the process, empower themselves and change the world.

Knowledge and Power

As expressed in the saying 'knowledge is power', knowledge and power are intimately linked. If we conceive knowledge solely in terms of representational knowledge, we are likely to define power as the ability to dominate or benignly control nature and social relations by technical means that derive from this form of knowledge. But by broadening our epistemological framework to include relational and reflective knowledge, we can also think of other types of power that do not involve control. The conception of power that comes out of Starhawk's work as a feminist activist sees three different kinds, or dimensions, of power as being operative and necessary in community-based actions. They are 'power-over', 'power-with' and 'power-from-within' (Russell, 1998; Starhawk, 1987). Without being able to analyse and elaborate on Starhawk's ideas here, I would interpret her three terms to mean, respectively, power to control objectifiable reality, power of being in solidarity with others and power to act on moral values. With this formulation, it is possible to see associations between the dimensions of power and the forms of knowledge that are discussed here. There is no space here for me to elaborate on these linkages, but I would like briefly to point to the following fairly obvious knowledge–power relationships. Representational knowledge clearly provides the cognitive basis for building the competence needed for controlling our world, including our social environment. It is with relational knowledge that people come to feel that they are not alone but are part of a larger whole that sustains them as connected social beings. This is the power of solidarity. And finally, reflective knowledge builds up the normative foundation that gives actors value standards and the self-confidence to engage in social change activities. In short, these three forms, or dimensions, of power might be called power of competence, connection and confidence, respectively.

Conclusion

In participatory research, groups of people come together to grapple with serious social issues that affect them in their daily lives. To this end, they organize activities to understand those issues and strategize effective actions, with the intention of bringing to that enterprise seriousness, deliberateness, and a systematic approach to research. Participatory research is a social pursuit of human fulfilment in which rationality, understood in an expanded sense, dominates as a theme and orientation. Since the problems dealt with in this enterprise have roots in the social fabric, consisting of material conditions, human relations and the moral order, any rational endeavour attempting to provide satisfactory solutions must take all these factors into account. Participatory research as practice, on the one hand, simultaneously addresses questions of community relations and moral consciousness, as well as technical considerations having to do with material conditions as constituent activities. Critical theory, on the other hand, provides a broadened understanding of rationality that embraces technical, social and moral dimensions of life, providing a conceptual scheme for deriving different forms of knowledge needed for these tasks. My purpose here has been to join these two strands together to articulate a coherent and comprehensive epistemological framework. In the process, I went beyond Habermas's theory of communicative action to develop the notion of relational knowledge, as well as articulating representational and reflective knowledge which are also discernible in that theory.

This analytic exercise is needed because, if the goal of participatory research is production of knowledge, we cannot understand knowledge in terms of a narrow definition of rationality that recognizes only the technical. We cannot privilege knowledge inherited from positivistic sources. To do so is to limit our ability to talk of what we do in participatory research as a rational research activity. By conceptualizing the main dimensions of the activity involved in participatory research as forms of knowledge, we are better able to bring methodological mindfulness to our efforts. This, I hope, will enrich our understanding of what we do as participatory researchers and give a renewed direction to participatory research as rational human activity.

Participatory research is a form of praxis that mirrors the history of human evolution. It is praxis that helps us to actualize our potentials and develop ourselves as a human community in which rationality plays an active role. For this reason, it is relevant to think of what we do as agents of change in terms of the forms of knowledge presented here. That is, we need to be conscious of cultivating all three forms of knowledge whenever we engage in rational activities aimed at making our lives more whole and satisfying. Thus, the forms of knowledge discussed here have a significance for emancipatory human endeavours in general, not just for participatory research. This epistemological framework also helps us link up with a more liberating concept of power, which embraces solidarity and moral courage as well as control. It is through the exercise of power in this comprehensive and liberating sense that we become fully human and change both ourselves and our social institutions.

References

The American Sociologist (1992) 'Participatory research', Part I. 23 (4).

The American Sociologist (1993) 'Participatory research', Part II. 24 (1).

Belenky, M.F., Clinchy, B.M., Goldberger, N.R. and Tarule, J.M. (1986) *Women's Ways of Knowing: the Development of Self, Voice, and Mind*. New York: Basic Books.

Benhabib, S. (1986) *Critique, Norm, and Utopia: a Study of the Foundation of the Critical Theory*. New York: Columbia University Press.

Bernstein, R.J. (1971) *Praxis and Action*. Philadelphia, PA: University of Pennsylvania Press.

Bernstein, R.J. (1983) *Beyond Objectivism and Relativism: Science, Hermeneutics, and Action*. Philadelphia, PA: University of Pennsylvania Press.

Braaten, J. (1995) 'From communicative rationality to communicative thinking', in J. Meehan (ed.), *Feminists Read Habermas: Gendering the Subject of Discourse*. New York: Routledge. pp. 139–61.

Buber, M. (1970) *I and Thou*. New York: Simon and Schuster.

Cable, S. and Degutis, B. (1997) 'Movement outcomes and dimensions of social change: the multiple effects of local mobilization', *Current Sociology*, 46 (3): 121–35.

Callaway, H. (ed.) (1982) *Case Studies of Participatory Research*. Armsfoort, The Netherlands: The Netherlands Centre for Research and Development in Adult Education.

Carr, T. (1997) *Broadening Perspectives in Action Research*. Brisbane, Australia: Action Learning, Action Research and Process Management Association (ALARPM).

Chambers, R. (1983) *Rural Development: Putting the Last First*. London: Longman.

Code, L. (1991) *What Can She Know? Feminist Theory and the Construction of Knowledge*. Ithaca, NY: Cornell University Press.

Comstock, D.E. and Fox, R. (1993) 'Participatory research as critical theory: the North Bonneville, USA, experience', in P. Park, M. Brydon-Miller, B. Hall and T. Jackson (eds), *Voices of Change: Participatory Research in the United States and Canada*. Westport, CT: Bergin and Garvey. pp. 103–24.

Convergence (1981) 'Participatory research: developments and issues', 14 (3).

Convergence (1988) 'Focus on participatory research', 21 (2, 3).

de Bary, W.T. (1989) *The Message of the Mind in Neo-Confucianism*. New York: Columbia University Press.

De Koning, K. and Martin, M. (1996) *Participatory Research in Health Issues and Experiences*. London: Zed Books.

Dewey, J. (1938/1991) 'Common sense and scientific inquiry', in *John Dewey: the Late Works, 1925–53* (Vol. 12). Carbondale, IL: Southern Illinois University Press. pp. 66–85.

Dimen, M. (1989) 'Power, sexuality, and intimacy', in A.M. Jaggar and S. Bordo (eds), *Gender/Body/Knowledge: Feminist Reconstructions of Being and Knowing*. New Brunswick, NJ: Rutgers University Press. pp. 34–51.

Fals Borda, O. (1982) 'Participatory research in rural social change', *Journal of Rural Cooperation*, 10 (1): 25–41.

Fals Borda, O. (1988) *Knowledge and People's Power*. New York: New Horizons Press.

Fals Borda, O. and Rahman, M.A. (1991) *Action and Knowledge: Breaking the Monopoly with Participatory Research*. New York: Apex Press.

Fay, B. (1975) *Social Theory and Political Practice*. Boston, MA: Unwin Hyman.

Fiumara, G.C. (1990) *The Other Side of Language: a Philosophy of Listening*. New York: Routledge.

Freire, P. (1970) *Pedagogy of the Oppressed*. New York: Plenum.

Freire, P. (1982) 'Creating alternative research methods. Learning to do it by doing it', in B. Hall, A. Gillette and R. Tandon (eds), *Creating Knowledge: a Monopoly?* New Delhi: Participatory Research in Asia. pp. 29–37.

Fromm, E. (1956) *The Art of Loving: an Inquiry into the Nature of Love*. New York: Harper and Row.

Gadamer, H.G. (1975) *Truth and Method*. New York: Continuum.

Gaventa, J. (1993) 'The powerful, the powerless, and the experts: knowledge struggles in an information age', in P. Park, M. Brydon-Miller, B. Hall and T. Jackson (eds), *Voices of Change: Participatory Research in the United States and Canada*. Westport, CT: Bergin and Garvey. pp. 21–40.

Gaventa, J. and Horton, B. (1981) 'A citizens' research project in Appalachia, USA', *Convergence*, 14 (3): 30–42.

Geddis, S. (1997) 'Participatory research with tenants in public housing: "working together for change"'. Unpublished PhD dissertation. Toronto, Canada: University of Toronto.

Geuss, R. (1981) *The Idea of Critical Theory: Habermas and the Frankfurt School*. Cambridge: Cambridge University Press.

Gibbs, L.M. (1998) *Love Canal: the Story Continues*. Stony Brook, CT: New Society Publishers.

Graham, A.C. (1989) *Disputers of the TAO*. La Salle, IL: Open Court.

Gramsci, A. (1971) *Selections from Prison Notebooks*. New York: International Publishers.

Habermas, J. (1970) 'Towards a theory of communicative competence', in H.P. Drizzle (ed.), *Recent Sociology. No. 2: Patterns of Communicative Behavior*. New York: Macmillan. pp. 114–48.

Habermas, J. (1971) *Knowledge and Human Interests*. Boston, MA: Beacon Press.

Habermas, J. (1973) 'Dogmatism, reason, and decision: on theory and praxis in our scientific civilization', in J. Habermas, *Theory and Practice*. Boston, MA: Beacon Press. pp. 253–82.

Habermas, J. (1979) 'What is universal pragmatics?', in J. Habermas, *Communication and the Evolution of Society*. Boston, MA: Beacon Press. pp. 1–68.

Habermas, J. (1981) *The Theory of Communicative Action. Vol. 1: Reason and the Rationalization of Society*. Boston, MA: Beacon Press.

Habermas, J. (1987) *The Theory of Communicative Action. Vol. 2: Lifeworld and System: a Critique of Functionalist Reason*. Boston, MA: Beacon Press.

Hall, B.L. (1982) 'Breaking the monopoly of power: research methods, participatory research and development', in B.L. Hall, A. Gillette and R. Tandon (eds), *Creating Knowledge: a Monopoly*? New Delhi, India: Participatory Research in Asia. pp. 13–26.

Hall, D.L. and Ames, R.T. (1987) *Thinking through Confucius*. Albany, NY: State University of New York Press.

Hall, B.L., Gillette, A. and Tandon, R. (eds) (1982) *Creating Knowledge: a Monopoly*? New Delhi, India: Participatory Research in Asia.

Hansen, C. (1991) 'Language in the heart/mind', in R.E. Allinson (ed.), *Understanding the Chinese Mind: the Philosophical Roots*. New York: Oxford University Press. pp. 75–124.

Hansen, C. (1993) 'Term-beliefs in action: sentences and terms in early Chinese philosophy', in H. Lenk and G. Paul (eds), *Epistemological Issues in Classical Chinese Philosophy*. Albany, NY: State University of New York Press. pp. 45–68.

Heaney, T.W. and Horton, A.I. (1990) 'Reflective engagement for social change', in J. Mezirow and Associates, *Fostering Critical Education in Adulthood: a Guide to Transformative and Emancipatory Learning*. San Francisco, CA: Jossey-Bass. pp. 74–98.

Heidegger, M. (1962) *Being and Time*. New York: Harper and Row.

Horton, B. (1993) 'The Appalachian land ownership study: research and citizen action in Appalachia', in P. Park, M. Brydon-Miller, B. Hall and T. Jackson (eds), *Voices of Change: Participatory Research in the United States and Canada*. Westport, CT: Bergin and Garvey. pp. 85–102.

Jaggar, A.M. (1989) 'Love and knowledge: emotion in feminist epistemology', in A.M. Jaggar and S. Bordo (eds), *Gender/Body/Knowledge: Feminist Reconstructions of Being and Knowing*. New Brunswick, NJ: Rutgers University Press. pp. 145–71.

Khanna, R. (1996) 'Participatory action research (PAR) in women's health: SMARTHI, India', in K. De Koning and M. Martin (eds), *Participatory Research in Health Issues and Experiences*. London: Zed Books. pp. 62–71.

Lloyd, J. (1989) 'The man of reason', in A. Garry and M. Pearsall (eds), *Women, Knowledge, and Reality: Explorations in Feminist Philosophy*. Boston, MA: Unwin Hyman. pp. 111–28.

Lynd, M. (1992) 'Creating knowledge through theater. A case study with developmentally disabled adults', *The American Sociologist*, 23 (4): 100–15.

Maguire, P. (1987) *Doing Participatory Research: a Feminist Approach*. Amherst, MA: Center for International Education.

Maguire, P. (1996) 'Proposing a more feminist participatory research: knowing and being embraced openly', in K. De Koning and M. Martin (eds), *Participatory Research in Health: Issues and Experiences*. London: Zed Books. pp. 27–39.

Merrifield, J. (1993) 'Putting scientists in their place. Participatory research in environmental and occupational health', in P. Park, M. Brydon-Miller, B. Hall and T. Jackson (eds), *Voices of Change: Participatory Research in the United States and Canada*. Westport, CT: Bergin and Garvey. pp. 65–84.

Mezirow, J. (1990) 'How critical reflection triggers learning', in J. Mezirow and Associates, *Fostering Critical Education in Adulthood: a Guide to Transformative and Emancipatory Learning*. San Francisco, CA: Jossey-Bass. pp. 1–20.

Nussbaum, M. (1991) 'The speech of Alcibiades: a reading of Plato's *Symposium*', in R.C. Solomon and K.M. Higgins (eds), *The Philosophy of Erotic Love*. Lawrence, KS: University of Kansas Press. pp. 279–316.

Oakley, A. (1981) 'Interviewing women: a contradiction in terms', in H. Roberts (ed.), *Doing Feminist Research*. London: Routledge and Kegan Paul. pp. 30–61.

Palmer, R.E. (1969) *Hermeneutic Interpretation: Theory in Schleiermacher, Dilthey, Heidegger, and Gadamer*. Evanston, IL: Northwestern University Press.

Park, P. (1992) 'The discovery of participatory research as a scientific paradigm: personal and intellectual accounts', *The American Sociologist*, 23 (4): 29–42.

Park, P. (1993) 'What is participatory research?', in P. Park, M. Brydon-Miller, B. Hall and T. Jackson (eds), *Voices of Change: Participatory Research in the United States and Canada*. Westport, CT: Bergin and Garvey. pp. 1–20.

Park, P. (1997) 'Participatory research, democracy, and community', *Practicing Anthropology*, 19 (3): 8–13.

Park, P. (1999) 'People, knowledge, and change in participatory research', *Management Learning*, 30 (2): 141–57.

Park, P., Brydon-Miller, M., Hall, B. and Jackson, T. (eds) (1993) *Voices of Change: Participatory Research in the United States and Canada*. Westport, CT: Bergin and Garvey.

Park, P. and Williams, L. (1999) 'From the guest editors: a theoretical framework for participatory evaluation research', *Sociological Practice: a Journal of Clinical and Applied Sociology*, 1 (2): 89–100.

Participatory Research Network (1982) *Participatory Research: An Introduction*. New Delhi, India: Participatory Research in Asia.

Reason, P. (1994) 'Participation in the evolution of consciousness', in P. Reason (ed.), *Participation in Human Inquiry*. Thousand Oaks, CA: Sage Publications.

Richards, L.E. (1998) 'The heart of knowledge: an epistemology of relationship'. Unpublished PhD dissertation. Santa Barbara, CA: The Fielding Institute.

Rocheleau, D. (1994) 'Participatory research and the race to save the planet. Questions, critiques, and lessons from the field', *Agriculture and Human Values Society*, 11 (2, 3): 4–19.

Rorty, R. (1979) *Philosophy and the Mirror of Mind*. Princeton, NJ: Princeton University Press.

Rousseau, M. (1991) *Community: the Tie That Binds*. New York: Lanham.

Rusmore, B. (1996) 'Reinventing science through agricultural participatory research', Unpublished PhD dissertation. Santa Barbara, CA: The Fielding Institute.

Russell, S. (1998) 'Dimensions of power in the workplace: an ethnographic study'. Unpublished PhD dissertation. Santa Barbara, CA: The Fielding Institute.

Selener, D. (1997) *Participatory Action Research and Social Change*. Ithaca, NY: Cornell University Press.

Shotter, J. (1993) *Cultural Politics of Everyday Life: Social Constructionism, Rhetoric and Knowing of the Third Kind*. Toronto, Canada: University of Toronto Press.

Smith, S., Willms, D. and Johnson, N. (eds) (1997) *Nurtured by Knowledge. Learning To Do Participatory Research*. New York: Apex Press.

Starhawk (1987) *Truth or Dare: Encounter with Power, Authority, Mystery*. San Francisco, CA: Harper and Row.

Vazquez, A.S. (1977) *The Philosophy of Praxis*. London: Merlin Press.

Williams, L. (1997) 'From common sense to good sense: participatory research, power, knowledge and grassroots empowerment'. Unpublished PhD dissertation. Knoxville, TN: University of Tennessee.

8
Exploring the Relevance of Critical Theory for Action Research: Emancipatory Action Research in the Footsteps of Jürgen Habermas

STEPHEN KEMMIS

CHAPTER OUTLINE

This chapter recounts some highlights of a personal journey in the theory and practice of critical or emancipatory action research. The story aims to make connections between my changing view of action research and some theoretical work in critical theory. After considering aspects of my initial view of action research, it considers the relevance to action research of several contributions to critical theory by Jürgen Habermas – in particular, his theory of knowledge-constitutive interests, his theory of communicative action (including the theory of system and life-world), and his critique of the philosophy of the subject and the social macro-subject.

In the mid-1970s, I first encountered Habermas's work through his books *Theory and Practice* (1974) and *Knowledge and Human Interests* (1972). These books seemed to offer a promising way through some of the debates I had encountered about explanation and understanding in the social sciences, about the relationship between objective and subjective perspectives, the relationship between the individual and the social realms of cognitive and cultural realities, and the relationship between theory and practice.

As someone committed to improving educational practice as constituted by practitioners, I had been exploring research approaches capable of having an impact on practitioners' theories and practices – approaches which would involve practitioners *themselves* in researching the relationship between their theories and practices. Such research approaches would challenge the division of labour between professional researcher-theorists and the social and educational practitioners studied in much conventional social and educational research. Candidate approaches would be ones which did not separate the roles of teacher (for example) and researcher – as the responsibilities of separate professions and professionals – but which offered teachers a double role as both teachers and researchers into their own teaching. Such approaches would cast the practitioner as both subject and object of research, at different moments, by adopting and alternating between the contrasting attitudes of practitioner and critical and self-critical observer of her or his own practice. Action research, historically, had advocated such an approach in the fields of educational (see also Zeichner, 2001) and social research (see Friedman, Chapter 11).

With colleagues at Deakin University, where I was working by the end of the 1970s, I thus began a 20-year long exploration of the theory and practice of action research. Our Deakin action research group was firmly of the view that action research is first and foremost *research by practitioners* – something they do, not something done 'on' or 'to' them. This view gained widespread acceptance at a 1981 National Seminar on Action Research held at Deakin University (Brown et al., 1982). This conclusion had been forced upon me by Habermas's dictum that 'in a process of enlightenment there can be only participants' (1974: 40). That is, others cannot do the enlightening for participants; in the end, they are or are not enlightened in their own terms. (This point also applies to 'empowerment', another aspiration of many advocates of action research.)

Through this period, we worked on two fronts: on the one side, to develop a critique of educational research and evaluation methodologies which would properly locate action research in relation to other approaches to social and educational research; on the other, to explore some of the problems and possibilities of action research through a variety of projects in schools and other settings. *Becoming Critical: Education, Knowledge and Action Research* (Carr and Kemmis, first edition 1983; third edition 1986) and *The Action Research Reader* (Kemmis and McTaggart, first edition 1982; third edition 1986a) were the major outcomes of the former task; *The Action Research Planner* (Kemmis and McTaggart, first edition 1982; third edition 1986b) and a number of reports of action research in various settings – mostly in education – were among the outcomes of the latter.

The Theory of Knowledge-Constitutive Interests

Influenced by Habermas's (1972) theory of knowledge-constitutive interests, our research group had begun to distinguish *empirical-analytic* (or *positivist*), *hermeneutic* (or *interpretive*) and *critical* approaches in research theory and practice. Each had its own basic *raison d'être* in terms of the interests which guided its quest for knowledge: a *technical* or *instrumental* (or means-ends) interest in the case of *empirical-analytic* research – that is, an interest in getting things done effectively; a *practical* interest in the case of *interpretive* research – that is, an interest in wise and prudent decision-making in practical situations; and an *emancipatory* interest in the case of *critical* research – that is, an interest in emancipating people from determination by habit, custom, illusion and coercion which sometimes frame and constrain social and educational practice, and which sometimes produce effects contrary to those expected or desired by participants and other parties interested in or affected by particular social or educational practices.

At first, we had expected to locate our view of action research entirely within the third of these categories as a form of *critical* research guided by an *emancipatory* interest. As Shirley Grundy and I (Grundy, 1982; Grundy and Kemmis, 1981a, 1981b) soon came to recognize, however, the field of educational action research included all three kinds of research.

Much action research was – and is – of a *technical* form. It is oriented essentially towards functional improvement measured in terms of its success in changing particular outcomes of practices. There are literally thousands of examples of such work. Most aim to increase or decrease the incidence of particular outcomes (like decreasing classroom behaviour problems, or increasing the rate of production in factories, or decreasing the incidence of sexist behaviour, for example). This kind of action research is a form of problem-solving, and it is regarded as 'successful' when outcomes match aspirations – when the defined goal of the project has been attained. But such action research does not necessarily question the goals themselves, nor how the situation in which it is conducted has been discursively, socially and historically constructed. It takes a narrow, generally 'pragmatic' (in the ordinary-language use of the term) view of its purpose.

By contrast, there is a good deal of action research today that is best described as of a *practical* form. It has technical aspirations for change, but it also aims to inform the (wise and prudent) practical decision-making of practitioners. Much of the action research influenced by the work of Donald Schön (1983, 1987) is of this kind. On this view of action research, practitioners aim not only to improve their practices in functional terms, but also to see how their goals, and the categories in which they evaluate their work, are shaped by their ways of seeing and understanding themselves in context. The process of action research is a process of self education for the practitioner – though one which may also produce commentaries and reports aimed at helping others see things more clearly, too. Examples of this kind of action research include a variety of self-reflective projects, often involving practitioners telling stories and writing histories of the ways they have participated in making change. Unlike technical action research, however, practical action researchers aim just as much at understanding and changing themselves as the *subjects* of a practice (as practitioners) as changing the *outcomes* of their practice.

There is a smaller body of action research today which might reasonably be labelled *critical* or *emancipatory*. This form of action research aims not only at improving outcomes, and improving the self-understandings of practitioners, but also at assisting practitioners to arrive at a critique of their social or educational work and work settings. This kind of action research aims at intervening in the cultural, social and historical processes of everyday life to reconstruct not only the practice and the practitioner but also the practice setting (or, one might say, the work, the worker and the workplace). It recognizes that we may want to improve our achievements in relation to our functional goals, but also that our goals (as defined by particular individuals, or as defined by a particular organization) may be limited or inappropriate given a wider view of the situation in which we live or work. It recognizes that we may want to improve our self-understandings, but also that our self-understandings may be shaped by collective misunderstandings about the nature and consequences of what we do. So emancipatory action research aims towards helping practitioners to develop a critical and self-critical understanding of their situation – which is to say, an understanding of the way both particular people and particular settings are shaped and re-shaped discursively, culturally, socially and historically. It aims to connect the personal and the political in collaborative research and action aimed at transforming situations to overcome felt dissatisfactions, alienation, ideological distortion, and the injustices of oppression and domination. Examples of this kind of action research include many participatory action research projects undertaken in the context of social movements – for example, in the women's movement, in Indigenous education and in defence of Indigenous rights, in land reform, and in people's movements aimed at community development and improved civil rights.

We adopted an action research approach to our own teaching at Deakin University, leading not only to innovations in our own practice (for example, more collaborative relationships between teachers and students) but also to interventions in the educational policies of the institution (in debates about and changes to practices of curriculum development and evaluation, teacher appraisal and student assessment).

By 1986, at an invitational seminar on action research at Deakin (McTaggart and Garbutcheon-Singh, 1986), however, many participants came to the view that we should cease proselytizing for action research. That is, we believed that we should no longer set out to persuade others that they should undertake action research projects as a form of participatory, collaborative critical investigation aimed at critical reconstruction of the work, the worker and the workplace. We feared that our advocacy for critical action research had become a 'solution' looking for 'problems' – that we had an 'answer' to questions that people were not necessarily asking for themselves. Instead, we thought, we should be working with people already committed to addressing felt dissatisfactions and overcoming injustices in the settings in which they found themselves. It was not that we decided to abandon our advocacy for the practice of emancipatory action research – on the contrary. It was rather that we believed we could more readily develop the critical approach in contexts where people were already committed to taking action because they had begun to form a critical view about the nature and consequences of the practices in which they were engaged. Our role in helping with the development of the critical approach would be subsidiary to the end of addressing felt dissatisfactions and injustices, not as an end in itself (which might just be another way of saying 'our own self-interests').

In our action research work in the 1980s, we were powerfully compelled by the connection Habermas made between truth and justice – the notion that truth could only emerge in settings where all assertions are equally open to critical scrutiny, without fear or favour. This applied as much to the practices of social and educational research as to other processes of social and political debate and discussion. We were acutely aware that the processes of critical action research should aspire to be democratic in the sense that the requirement of authenticity (at the level of the individual) would be paralleled by a social and discursive criterion of validity – that participants should be committed to reaching *mutual understanding and unforced consensus about what to do*. Here, we steered in the light of Habermas's famous validity claims developed in his theory of communication in works including *Communication and the Evolution of Society* (1979). The four validity claims are questions which can be asked of any utterance, and which every utterance tacitly asserts (until challenged), and they provide a start for critical reflection by interlocutors. The four key questions are: 'Is this utterance comprehensible?' 'Is it true (in the sense of accurate)?' 'Is it right and morally appropriate?' and 'Is it sincerely (or truthfully) stated?' These questions help interlocutors to open critical doors on the nature, social and historical formation, and consequences of the ways they think and what they do. In short, the aim of the kind of critical social science we were developing was to help people to grasp the ways they are shaped by taken-for-granted assumptions, habit, custom, ideology and tradition, and to see what kind of collaborative social action might be necessary to transform things for the better. The general aspiration of our approach at that time could be summed up in terms of the 'basic scheme' of a critical social science as described by Fay (1987).

The Theory of Communicative Action and the Theory of System and Lifeworld

I was increasingly called upon to defend the emancipatory approach in action research as the 1980s wore on, as the possibility of progress through reason became the target of attacks on modernist theory from postmodernists and poststructuralists. At stake was whether it was any longer possible to hold on to the ideal of a form of reason capable of sustaining the critical and emancipatory aspirations of critical theory. Habermas had addressed such questions in *The Theory of Communicative Action*

(1984, 1987a) and *The Philosophical Discourse of Modernity* (1987b), and my study of these works began to lead to a fairly decisive turn in my thinking about action research. The very possibility of a critical social science was under threat from the postmodernist and poststructuralist challenges – and with it the notion of critical or emancipatory action research. I needed to think my way through these challenges, since a failure to respond to them would imply that the notion of critical, emancipatory action research as an ideal should be abandoned, though perhaps some more limited form of action research for improvement might still be justified. Some of my reflections on these topics emerged in two articles (Kemmis, 1993, 1995) in *Curriculum Studies*. In the first, I argued that, contrary to the despair induced by understanding evaluation technologies as social technologies understood in Foucauldian terms, Habermas's concept of communicative action offers humane, convivial and rational resources for the further development of the theory and practice of educational evaluation. In the second, I argued, against certain postmodernists, in favour of the continuing relevance of critical perspectives on education and educational and social change. In my view, a funeral for the emancipatory project would be premature.

Habermas's theory of communicative action was a decisive contribution to *substantive* social theory – it privileged the kind of reflection and discussion (communicative action) we do when we interrupt what we are doing (generally technical or practical action) to explore its nature, dynamics and worth. It seemed to me that the aspirations of communicative action could be written into or alongside the practices of reflection and discussion characteristic of action research. The theory of communicative action includes a substantive theory (the theory of system and lifeworld) which offers a new way of construing many of the problems critical action researchers worked on in projects with which I was familiar – problems which arise for participants in a setting when the personal, social and cultural processes that sustain the setting as a *lifeworld* collide with processes which characterize the setting as a *system* (the means-ends functionality of systems oriented to outcomes or success). Construing such problems in terms of (system–lifeworld) *boundary-crises* made sense of many of the social and educational issues being confronted by participants in action research projects.

In *The Theory of Communicative Action*, Habermas considers the strengths and weaknesses of systems theory and theories of social action. He criticizes both, and arrives, through a reconstruction of earlier social theories, at a 'two-level' social theory which explores the tensions and interconnections between system and lifeworld as two faces of the social world of modernity.

Seen from a *systems perspective*, modern society encompasses organizational and institutional structures (including roles and rules) and the functioning of these structures – in particular, their functioning as oriented towards the attainment of particular goals. Systems operate through *rational-purposive action* – that is, (instrumental, means-ends) action oriented towards success. They operate through definition of goals, the definition of criteria against which progress towards achieving the goals can be measured, the setting of targets for what will count as success (maximization of outcomes in relation to goals), and the monitoring of progress towards goals to evaluate and improve system efficiency defined in terms of the ratio of inputs to outcomes achieved. Since it is circumscribed by system structures and processes, and oriented towards achieving outcomes defined in terms of system goals, its central concerns are with systems functioning; hence it characteristically employs a form of reason which can be described as *functional rationality*.

Modern societies are characterized by advanced differentiation in a variety of dimensions, posing particular kinds of problems of social integration and system integration, with a variety of effects (including pathological effects) which the theory of communicative action aims to address. Habermas is particularly concerned with the nature, functioning, and interrelationships between *economic* and *political-legal* systems in modern societies (particularly capitalism and the state which have been linked together in particular mutually-compensating ways in the modern welfare state).

Seen from a *lifeworld perspective*, modern society encompasses the dynamics by which culture, social order and individual identity are secured. Drawing on a key insight from American sociologist George Herbert Mead that 'no individuation is possible without socialization, and no socialization is possible without individuation' (Habermas, 1992: 26), Habermas develops a more extensive conceptualization of the social matrix of lifeworlds, identifying three 'structural nuclei' of the lifeworld – culture, society and person – which are 'made possible' by three enduring and interacting sets of processes – cultural reproduction, social integration and socialization. He writes:

> Considered as a *resource*, the lifeworld is divided in accord with the 'given' components of speech acts (that is, their propositional, illocutionary, and intentional components) into culture, society, and person. I call *culture* the store of knowledge from which those engaged in communicative action draw interpretations susceptible of consensus as they come to an understanding about something in the world. I call *society* (in the narrower sense of a component of the lifeworld) the legitimate orders from which those engaged in communicative action gather a solidarity, based on belonging

Table 8.1 *Contributions of reproduction processes to maintaining the structural components of the lifeworld*

Structural components: / *Reproduction processes:*	***Culture***	***Society***	***Personality***
Cultural reproduction	Interpretive schemes fit for consensus ('valid knowledge')	Legitimations	Socialization patterns Educational goals
Social integration	Obligations	Legitimately-ordered interpersonal relations	Social memberships
Socialization	Interpretive accomplishments	Motivation for actions that conform to norms	Interactive capabilities ('personal identity')

Source: Habermas, 1987a: 142.

to groups, as they enter into personal relationships with one another. *Personality* serves as a term of art for acquired competences that render a subject capable of speech and action and hence able to participate in processes of mutual understanding in a given context and to maintain his own identity in the shifting contexts of interaction. This conceptual strategy breaks with the traditional conception – also held by the philosophy of the subject and praxis philosophy – that societies are composed of collectivities and these in turn of individuals. Individuals and groups are 'members' of a lifeworld only in a metaphorical sense.

The symbolic reproduction of the lifeworld does take place as a circular process. The structural nuclei of the lifeworld are 'made possible' by their correlative processes of reproduction, and these in turn are 'made possible' by contributions of communicative action. *Cultural reproduction* ensures that (in the semantic dimension) newly arising situations can be connected up with existing conditions in the world; it secures the continuity of tradition and a coherency of knowledge sufficient for the consensus needs of everyday practice. *Social integration* ensures that newly arising situations (in the dimension of social space) can be connected up with existing conditions in the world; it takes care of the coordination of action by means of legitimately regulated interpersonal relationships and lends constancy to the identity of groups. Finally, the *socialization* of members ensures that newly arising situations (in the dimension of historical time) can be connected up with existing world conditions; it secures the acquisition of generalized capacities for action for future generations and takes care of harmonizing individual life histories and collective life forms. Thus, interpretive schemata susceptible of consensus (or 'valid knowledge'), legitimately ordered interpersonal relationships (or 'solidarities'), and capacities for interaction (or 'personal identities') are renewed in these three processes of reproduction. (Habermas, 1987b: 343–4, original emphasis)

These relationships are summarized by Habermas in Table 8.1.

Habermas also relates the functions of communicative action – action oriented towards mutual understanding – directly to these structural nuclei of the lifeworld and their correlative reproduction processes, as in Table 8.2.

Table 8.2 summarizes the direct roles played by communicative action in the three processes of symbolic reproduction. Communicative action is the process by which participants test for themselves the comprehensibility, truth (in the sense of accuracy), truthfulness (sincerity) and rightness (in the sense of moral appropriateness) of the substantive content of these processes as it applies in their own situations. Only when they give their own unforced assent will they regard substantive claims raised in these processes as personally binding upon them – or perhaps it would be better to say that, when a doubt arises about any such substantive claim, it will not be regarded as binding until it is underwritten by communicative action (that is, action oriented towards mutual understanding and unforced consensus).

Under the conditions of advanced differentiation characteristic of late modernity, whole realms of social life are co-ordinated in terms of purposive-rational action and functional reason, with the requirement for mutual understanding and consensus being more or less suspended. Under the imperatives of systems functioning, people simply 'get on with the job', as it were, without requiring a justification for what they are doing in terms of authentic personal assent. This deferment, displacement or

Table 8.2 *Functions of action oriented towards mutual understanding*

Structural components: / *Reproduction processes:*	***Culture***	***Society***	***Personality***
Cultural reproduction	Transmission, critique, acquisition of cultural knowledge	Renewal of knowledge effective for legitimation	Reproduction of knowledge relevant to child rearing, education
Social integration	Immunization of a central stock of value orientations	Co-ordination of actions via intersubjectively recognized validity claims	Reproduction of patterns of social membership
Socialization	Enculturation	Internalization of values	Formation of identity

Source: Habermas, 1987a: 144.

distortion of the (validity) claims of mutual understanding and consensus is not cost-free, however: it puts the processes of symbolic reproduction under strain. If sufficiently severe, the strain becomes evident in various kinds of crises in the domains of culture, society and personality. Habermas summarizes these kinds of crises in Table 8.3.

These kinds of crises may be thought of as costs of systems rationalization to be borne by cultures, societies and individuals. The question arises of whether the costs can be minimized, and/or whether it is possible to reduce them by changing the way systems function *vis-à-vis* the lifeworld. Habermas addresses this question in *The Philosophical Discourse of Modernity* (1987b: 336–7), offering the possibility that self-organized groups in a revitalized public sphere can sensitize systems to their untoward effects in ways which may reduce burdens on cultures, societies and individuals. He comes to this conclusion by way of an exploration of two key theses about the nature of modernity: theses concerning (a) the 'uncoupling' of system and lifeworld, and (b) the colonization of the lifeworld by the imperatives of systems.[1]

(a) The thesis of 'uncoupling' of system and lifeworld

The thesis of the 'uncoupling' of system and lifeworld refers to the development of 'relative autonomy' in systems regulated by the distinctive steering media of money and administrative power. A principal line of argument in *The Theory of*

Table 8.3 *Manifestations of crisis when reproduction processes are disturbed (pathologies)*

Structural components: / Disturbances in the domain of:	**Culture**	**Society**	**Personality**	**Dimension of evaluation**
Cultural reproduction	Loss of meaning	Withdrawal of Legitimation	Crisis in orientation and education	Rationality of knowledge
Social integration	Unsettling of collective identity	Anomie	Alienation	Solidarity of members
Socialization	Rupture of tradition	Withdrawal of motivation	Psychopathologies	Personal responsibility

Source: Habermas, 1987a: 143.

Communicative Action is that modern societies are characterized by such an elaborate pattern of differentiation (for example, in contexts of production and the division of labour) that it is barely possible to secure collective social 'anchoring' in a shared culture, shared social order, and shared social identity. The burden of maintaining such societies against fragmentation and dissolution has been transferred from individuals and small face-to-face social groups to open social systems which provide co-ordination.

What is distinctive about late modernity, in Habermas's view, is that *steering media* characteristic of the economic and political-legal systems – money and administrative power, respectively – now do their work of co-ordination so smoothly that the systems have begun to operate 'relatively autonomously', that is, 'on their own terms'. This relatively autonomous functioning of systems in societies characterized by advanced differentiation involves an 'uncoupling' of system and lifeworld in the sense that systems appear to be 'objects' (reified) to the people who inhabit them, as if (but only as if) they functioned according to their own rules and procedures, in a disinterested manner indifferent to the unique personalities and interests of the individuals inhabiting them, and thus, in a manner which appears to be indifferent to the dynamics of cultural reproduction, social integration and socialization necessary for the development and reproduction of lifeworlds.

(b) The thesis of colonization of the lifeworld

Habermas's second thesis follows from the first. In societies characterized by advanced differentiation and the relative autonomy of economic and political-legal systems, he argues, individuals and groups increasingly define themselves and their aspirations in systems terms – in particular, so that their 'privatized hopes for self-actualization and self-determination are primarily located ... in the roles of consumer and client' (Habermas, 1987a: 356) in relation to the economic and political-legal systems respectively. This is 'colonization' in the sense that the imperatives of the economic and political-legal systems dislodge the internal communicative action which underpins the formation and reproduction of lifeworlds, providing in its place an external framework of language, understandings, values and norms based on systems and their functions. Under such circumstances, the symbolic reproduction processes of the lifeworld (cultural reproduction, social integration and socialization) become saturated with a discourse of roles, functions and functionality, reshaping individual and collective self-understandings, relationships, and practices. In some versions of systems theory (notably the systems theory of Niklas Luhmann criticized by Habermas[2]), it has even led to the characterization of the person as no more than a system in interaction with other systems, including other individuals and other kinds and levels of social, material and ecological systems. This is to say that from the perspective of systems theory, the very idea of the person has been assimilated 'without remainder' into a self-referential systems logic.

The effect of the colonization of the lifeworld by the imperatives of systems is that individuals and groups in late modernity increasingly identify themselves and their aspirations in systems terms. The theory of communicative action aims to offer a 'stereoscopic vision' which allows the effects of uncoupling and colonization to come into perspective. In doing so, it allows us to

> become conscious of *the difference between steering problems and problems of mutual understanding*. We can see the difference between systemic disequilibria and lifeworld pathologies, between disturbances of material reproduction and deficiencies in the symbolic reproduction of the lifeworld. We come to recognize the distinctions between the deficits that inflexible structures of the lifeworld can cause in the maintenance of the systems of employment and domination (via the withdrawal of motivation or legitimation), on the one hand, and manifestations of a colonization of the lifeworld by the imperatives of functional systems that externalize their costs on the other. Such phenomena demonstrate once more that the achievements of steering and those of mutual understanding are resources that cannot be freely substituted for one another. Money and power can neither buy nor compel solidarity and meaning. In brief, the result of the process of disillusionment is a new state of consciousness in which the social-welfare-state project becomes reflexive to a certain extent and aims at taming not just the capitalist economy, but the state itself. (Habermas, 1987b: 363)

From this conclusion, Habermas proceeds to examine the possibilities for revitalizing a public political sphere which has side-lined mutual understanding in favour of system self-regulation through the steering media of money and power, and which is now paying a high price in terms of the withdrawal of motivation and legitimacy from those systems – as a result of 'the intolerable imperatives of the occupational system [and] the penetrating side effects of the administrative provision for life' (1987b: 364). In short, the economic and political-legal systems have become insensitive to the imperatives of mutual understanding on which solidarity and the legitimacy of social orders depends. He suggests that a possible way forward is through the formation of autonomous, self-organized public spheres capable of asserting themselves with 'a prudent combination of power and intelligent self-restraint' against the systemically integrating media of money and power.

> I call those public spheres autonomous which are neither bred nor kept by a political system for purposes of creating legitimation. Centres of concentrated communication that arise spontaneously out of microdomains of everyday practice can develop into autonomous public spheres and consolidate as self-supporting higher-level intersubjectivities only to the degree that the lifeworld potential for self-organization and for the self-organized means of communication are utilized. Forms of self-organization strengthen the collective capacity for action. Grassroots organizations, however, may not cross the threshold to the formal organization of independent systems. Otherwise they will pay for the indisputable gain in complexity by having organizational goals detached from the orientations and attitudes of their members and dependent instead upon imperatives of maintaining and expanding organizational power. The lack of symmetry between capacities for self-reflection and for self-organization that we have ascribed to modern societies as a whole is repeated on the level of the self-organization of processes of opinion and will formation. (Habermas, 1987b: 364–5)

It might be argued that grassroots movements and self-organized groups conducting participatory and collaborative action research in system settings (for example, in education, social welfare and community development) are examples of such 'autonomous public spheres' at the local level. It is certainly the case that, where they are successful in bringing about changes in institutional practices, it is generally through indirect rather than direct means, by sensitizing systems to previously unnoticed effects – especially when projects draw attention to circumstances under which participants withdraw motivation or legitimacy from system operations.

Communicative Action and Action Research

The theory of system and lifeworld provides a theoretical discourse clarifying a significant shift in the social conditions of late modernity. It allows us to articulate problems which have emerged in late modernity as social systems have become more extensive, and as problems of integrating different kinds of social organizations and systems have emerged. It provides a useful framework from which to view changes in schooling – for example, the functional integration of schooling with political-legal and economic systems. It also provides a new perspective on action research.

Instead of taking the interpretive perspective according to which participants themselves are meant to be the sources of *all* theoretical categories arising in a research project (though usually with the mediating assistance of a researcher not indigenous to the setting), the theory of system and lifeworld offers a way of understanding participants' perspectives as structured by the contrasting and sometimes competing imperatives of social systems and the lifeworlds participants inhabit. As a co-researcher with others in an action research setting, one could, on the one hand, explore *with* participants how they were engaged in three kinds of *lifeworld process* in the settings they daily constituted and reconstituted through their practices:

- the process of *individuation-socialization* (by which practitioners' own identities and capacities are formed and developed);
- the process of *social integration* (by which legitimately-ordered social relations among people as co-participants in a setting are formed and developed); and
- the process of *cultural reproduction and transformation* (by which shared cultures and discourses are formed and developed).

Alongside this exploration, one could also investigate how practices in the setting enmeshed participants in *systems functioning* – the exchanges and transformations taking place to yield outcomes of interest to those involved, to the systems of which they are part, and to the wider environment beyond. On this view, the overall task of a critical social science, including critical action research, is *to explore and address the interconnections and tensions between system and lifeworld aspects of a setting as they are lived out in practice.*

It seemed to me that critical action research could help to create the circumstances in which communicative action among those involved could be encouraged, enabled, sustained and made generative in terms of personal, social and cultural development in and around the setting. In particular, this communicative action could be focused on the boundary-crises which arise at the intersection of system and lifeworld aspects of the setting, as they are realised in the immediacy and under the exigencies of daily practice.

In my current work consulting on university development and facilitating action research projects in a variety of settings, I have been exploring these possibilities, though always at the pace participants themselves will permit. I find the theory of system and lifeworld immensely powerful and generative, and I believe the insights it produces are regarded as significant and compelling by many in the settings where I work – though of course I do not expect anyone in those settings to be familiar with the theory of communicative action. The power and generativity of the theory is such that it produces an almost visceral reaction in many participants, as they see how one side of their organization (the system side) operates on one set of principles and dynamics, while another side of the social setting (the lifeworld side) operates in terms of quite different dynamics and principles (the three key lifeworld processes of individuation-socialization, social integration and cultural reproduction and transformation). As the relationship between the two aspects begins to be teased out, a number of boundary-crises become *comprehensible* to participants, though it is not always clear what should be done about them. But talking about them does encourage people towards communicative action – discussion aimed at mutual understanding and consensus about what could and should be done.

The kind of response this sort of analysis encourages is illustrated in many university development projects I have worked on in recent years. It quickly becomes clear to university teachers in Australia these days that their work is increasingly monetarized. Their work is extremely tightly monitored and regulated in terms of the resources generated (income per equivalent full-time student unit) and expended (salaries, other expenditure). In a situation of substantially declining resources for higher education, costs are being cut to the point where teaching and learning, and university research, are under threat in terms of the values traditionally associated with teaching and research. Their work is also increasingly juridified – brought under control of university-wide policies and administrative procedures aimed at achieving greater control and uniformity of work across departments, faculties and universities. This also challenges previous taken-for-granted assumptions and principles about academic freedom and academic work.

Alongside this first analysis of system functioning, I encourage participants to consider how their work and their values have been shaped by the material conditions of former times, before the contemporary funding crisis – for example, how funds were previously provided for administrative support, teaching and research. It quickly becomes apparent that participants' ideas and ideals of university life and work were formed under very different material conditions than those that have come to apply in recent years.

Organizationally, many departments, faculties and universities have been obliged to rationalize their work to meet the resource requirements of the new conditions in Australian higher education. In many places, this has meant cutting costs, courses, some kinds of research activities, and staff (especially contract staff – and frequently up-and-coming members of a rising generation of scholars). Not surprisingly, these rationalization processes are perceived by many as undermining the work of the institution, as an assault on academic values, and as an assault on the work and professional lives of staff. In short, participants experience – very sharply – the boundary-crisis of changes to system functioning as they impact on the lifeworld processes of individuation-socialization (identity formation in the job), social integration (and dealing with increasing interpersonal and organizational conflict), and cultural reproduction and transformation (changing the culture of the university and even the discourses by which its work is understood). Some become alienated; some become cynical about self-preservation in the face of organizational change; some even leave the university. At the same time, most try to find new ways to understand the nature and 'core values' of their work, and to find new ways of bringing in resources to support it. That is, they try to find new accommodations between systems functioning and the lifeworld processes by which the university is constituted as a place for academic work and life. But it is frequently difficult to find spaces for this work, especially under heavy pressure to cut costs from senior staff of the university, and when middle managers are expected to manage departments and faculties more directly, to meet increasingly explicit outcomes within increasingly constrained budgets.

It must be said, however, that these transformations are not achieved easily or without stress and conflict. Conditions of fear do not readily favour creative approaches to organizational, personal, social and cultural development – the kind of playfulness that supports transformative work. A major task for projects of the kind I have been working on in recent times is to help participants recover a sense of playfulness through development work aimed at reinforcing core values and ideals by reconstructing the work that expresses them.

The Critique of the Philosophy of the Subject and the Notion of the Social Macro-subject

Habermas has continued to develop the theory of communicative action. In his *Between Facts and Norms* (1996) he examines law and the philosophy of law (not only in its own terms but also in relation to social theory). In *The Philosophical Discourse of Modernity* (1987b), he indicated that *praxis theory* (the theory that underwrote the revolutionary ideals of Marxian theory and critical theory as one of its successors) had been premised on the notion of a social whole capable of regulating itself – a nation, a state, or some other social totality. One side of his critique in *The Philosophical Discourse of Modernity* had been 'the philosophy of the subject' – the view that truth is something that can be apprehended by a single mind (so the eye of the individual, human cognitive subject replaces the eye of God). His critique suggested that, despite their differences – objective versus subjective – systems theory and theories of social action were in accord about this notion of truth. His post-metaphysical philosophy, which locates truth in discourse, not in the minds of individual subjects, is a response to what he sees as the failures of the philosophy of the subject.

Late in *The Philosophical Discourse of Modernity* he identifies a problem parallel to the problem of the philosophy of the subject: the problem that much thinking about social change and social issues (especially praxis philosophy and the social theories it informs) is based on the idea of a 'social macro-subject' – the notion of a self-regulating social whole. Yet systems theory and many of the developments of postmodern and post-structuralist theory rightly persuade us that this notion of a social whole is illusory. There are no 'whole' societies, or 'whole' systems, or 'whole' states which are the addressees of social theory or practice. There are just interwoven, interlocking, overlapping networks of social relations which galvanize power and discourses in different directions and in different ways in relation to the personal, the social and the cultural realms.

In *Between Facts and Norms*, Habermas (1996) takes this argument further. Among other things, he revisits the argument about the fiction of the self-regulating, self-organizing state or society. He revisits the notion of the public sphere, to show how it is an open realm of intersecting discourses. But this realm (rooted in lifeworlds as much as in the organization of social systems) is crucial for *legitimacy* – for laws or policies or principles to be regarded as legitimate norms. Laws and policies are endured as impositions rather than felt to be organic to the people to whom they are addressed unless they develop legitimacy; and they will only be regarded as legitimate when they gain authentic personal assent (the level of the person), are seen as morally-right and socially-integrative in their effects (at the level of the society), and are regarded as discursively valid in cultural and discursive terms (at the level of the culture). The democratic process of communicative action in the public sphere makes it possible for ideas to circulate freely and to be explored sufficiently for them to attain legitimacy. Just as the theory of communicative action transfers the category of truth from the individual cognitive subject to the domain of debate and discussion in which communicative action occurs, so it now transfers legitimacy from the social macro-subject (for example, the state) to the fluid communicative networks of the public sphere.

It might not be an exaggeration to say that in these developments, Habermas has identified a third feature of communicative action. Formerly, it was described as being oriented towards (first) *mutual understanding* and (second) *unforced consensus about what to do*. To these, a third feature has been added: *making communicative space*. A previously unnoticed aspect of communicative action was that it *brings people together around shared topical concerns, problems and issues* with a shared orientation towards mutual understanding and consensus. To recognize that this as an element of communicative action is to acknowledge that the orientation to mutual understanding and consensus arises in all sorts of ways, around all sorts of practical problems and issues, and that people must *constitute* a communicative space (in meetings, in the media, in conversations with friends and colleagues, etc.) before they can work together to achieve mutual understanding and consensus. As Habermas shows, such communicative spaces are open and fluid associations, in which each individual takes an in-principle stand to participate, but does so knowing that a variety of forms of participation are available – to use the meeting metaphor, as a speaker or listener, at the podium or in the gallery, as an occasional participant or as a fully-engaged advocate, or even as the person who finds the discussion irrelevant and slips away by a side door.

Much of my advocacy of action research had been premised upon the prior existence of groups of people (an action research group in a school or community, for example) willing to work together on shared concerns. Because when we met them in real circumstances, they were composed of some number of actual people – though they might aim to involve others interested in and affected by the social or educational practices of the group – we could think of them as 'whole' and finite. A by-product of this way of thinking was that we began to see groups as self-organizing or potentially self-organizing social 'wholes' – as social macro-subjects (as Habermas described them). So it seemed appropriate that strictures about democratic debate and decision should be binding on the whole group – even when the group was confronted by the evident lack of interest of some participants and potential participants. This contradiction was thrown into sharp relief in the light of Habermas's redefinition of the public sphere – 'the group' turns out to be fluid (as action research project groups tend to be), and permits a range of different kinds of communicative role (speaker and listener, permanent and passing membership – as happens in most action research projects). The first step in action research turns out to be central: *the formation of a communicative space* which is embodied in networks of actual persons, though the group itself cannot and should not be treated as a totality (as an exclusive whole). A communicative space is constituted as issues or problems are opened up for discussion, and when participants experience their interaction as fostering the democratic expression of divergent views. Part of the task of an action research project, then, is to open communicative space, and to do so in a way that will permit people to achieve mutual understanding and consensus about what to do, in the knowledge that the legitimacy of any conclusions and decisions reached by participants will be proportional to the degree of authentic engagement of those concerned.

It seems to me helpful to think about action research without a 'social macro-subject' – to think instead about how it constitutes a communicative space in which people can come together to explore problems and issues, always holding open the question of whether they will commit themselves to the authentic and binding work of mutual understanding and consensus. In the light of this insight, we may think differently about how rigorously to require that debate and decision-making be binding on all participants; instead, we may want to think more about how the debate itself can become more open and engaging, as a basis for arriving at perspectives and decisions where necessary, in the (overlapping) organizational and lifeworld settings in which people live and work together.

Concluding Comment

In this chapter, I have described a broad journey through the territory of critical action research, informed by perspectives from the critical theory of Jürgen Habermas. In the first stage, my view of the action research group was of a 'critical community', bound together to work on some common problems or issues in their own situation. I viewed each participant as an authentic person, whose own views were paramount in determining what a 'problem' or an 'issue' or a reasonable interpretation of reality might be. In this stage, my thinking about action research drew particularly on Habermas's works *Communication and the Evolution of Society* (1979), *Knowledge and Human Interests* (1972), and *Theory and Practice* (1974).

In the second stage, my view of the action research group was changing. It was defined less in geographical or local terms, and more in terms of shared engagement in communicative action. Nevertheless, the concrete image of a face-to-face group of 'members' continued to inform my thinking, despite Habermas's critique of the possibility of a self-organizing 'social macro-subject'. During this stage, I had begun to view each individual participant as a conversation partner in communicative action, but I still regarded the conversation as principally internal to the group. Some of Habermas's works engaging my attention in this stage were *The Theory of Communicative Action* (1984, 1987a) and *The Philosophical Discourse of Modernity* (1987b).

In the third stage, the critique of the social macro-subject began to have real force in my thinking about the action research group. I have come to see a critical action research project as more open and fluid, as a 'self-constituting public sphere', and to see those who participate in the shared project of a particular programme of action research as engaged citizens committed to local action but with a wider critical and emancipatory vision for their work. The critical action research group might thus be understood in relation to, and as a contribution to, wider processes of social movement. My thinking in this stage has been informed particularly by Habermas's *Between Facts and Norms* (1996).

My reading in critical theory, and especially the work of Habermas, has been a programme of continuing study through most of my professional life. I believe that it is useful – that it is *important* – to show that theory is a powerful resource for developing insight and understanding, and that critical theory of the Habermasian kind is especially relevant to contemporary discussion and debate about the nature of action research. The point is not to claim credence for a view of critical action research by appeal to authority – in this case the authority of Habermas as a leading social theorist of our times. It is to show that some central problems of contemporary social theory have clear resonances for our work as action researchers. Problems about the nature of practice, the relationship between theory and practice, the relationship between systems theory and theories of social action, tensions and interconnections between system and lifeworld, the relationship between the critique of the philosophy of the subject and the critique of the social macro-subject (so crucial to praxis philosophy) – all these (and others) are highly relevant to a contemporary understanding of the potential and limitations of our theories and practices of action research. These profound issues cannot be ignored as we develop our field of action research through *our* communicative action in the fluid communicative space constituted by our networks and communications in the international community of action researchers. Addressing such issues requires that we draw deep from the well of available theoretical resources.

Notes

1 System and lifeworld are not separate realms of social existence in which the expansion of the one (system) threatens to obliterate the other (lifeworld), so that we are in danger of becoming social automatons whose lives are merely realizations of the functional requirements of systems. The Habermasian theses of the uncoupling of system and lifeworld, and the colonization of the lifeworld by systems perspectives and values, are based on no such bifurcation. On the contrary, system and lifeworld aspects of sociality continue to co-exist in interconnection, creating mutually-constitutive conditions for one another, though admittedly

with some rather one-sided (functionally integrative) effects as we live through the consequences of late modernity. System and lifeworld need to be understood as dialectically-related aspects of social formation in late modernity, not as two separate entities at odds with one another.

2 See for example, Habermas, 1987b: 353–5, 368–85.

References

Brown, L., Henry, C., Henry, J. and McTaggart, R. (1982) 'Action research: notes on the National Seminar', *Classroom Action Research Network Bulletin*, 4 (Summer): 1–6.

Carr, W. and Kemmis, S. (1986) *Becoming Critical: Education, Knowledge and Action Research* (third edition). London: Falmer Press. (First edition, 1983; Deakin University Press, Geelong.)

Fay, B.S. (1987) *Critical Social Science: Liberation and its Limits*. Cambridge: Polity Press.

Grundy, S. (1982) 'Three modes of action research', *Curriculum Perspectives*, 2 (3): 23–34.

Grundy, S. and Kemmis, S. (1981a) 'Social theory, group dynamics and action research'. Paper presented at the Annual Conference of the South Pacific Association for Teacher Education, Adelaide, July.

Grundy, S. and Kemmis, S. (1981b) 'Educational action research in Australia: the state of the art (an overview)'. Paper presented to the Annual Meeting of the Australian Association for Research in Education, Adelaide, November.

Habermas, J. (1972) *Knowledge and Human Interests* (trans. Jeremy J. Shapiro). London: Heinemann.

Habermas, J. (1974) *Theory and Practice* (trans. John Viertel). London: Heinemann.

Habermas, J. (1979) *Communication and the Evolution of Society* (trans. Thomas McCarthy). Boston, MA: Beacon Press.

Habermas, J. (1984) *The Theory of Communicative Action. Vol. 1: Reason and the Rationalisation of Society* (trans. Thomas McCarthy). Boston, MA: Beacon Press.

Habermas, J. (1987a) *The Theory of Communicative Action. Vol. 2: Lifeworld and System: a Critique of Functionalist Reason* (trans. Thomas McCarthy). Boston, MA: Beacon Press.

Habermas, J. (1987b) *The Philosophical Discourse of Modernity* (trans. Frederick Lawrence). Cambridge, MA: The MIT Press.

Habermas, J. (1992) *Postmetaphysical Thinking: Philosophical Essays* (trans. William Mark Hohengarten). Cambridge, MA: The MIT Press.

Habermas, J. (1996) *Between Facts and Norms* (trans. William Rehg). Cambridge, MA: The MIT Press.

Kemmis, S. (1982) 'Introduction: action research in retrospect and prospect', in S. Kemmis and R. McTaggart (eds), *The Action Research Reader*. Geelong, Victoria: Deakin University Press.

Kemmis, S. (1993) 'Foucault, Habermas and evaluation', *Curriculum Studies*, 1 (1): 35–54.

Kemmis, S. (1995) 'Emancipatory aspirations in a postmodern era', *Curriculum Studies*, 3 (2): 133–67.

Kemmis, S. and McTaggart, R. (eds) (1986a) *The Action Research Reader* (third edition). Geelong, Victoria: Deakin University Press. (First edition, 1982.)

Kemmis, S. and McTaggart, R. (1986b) *The Action Research Planner* (third edition). Geelong, Victoria: Deakin University Press. (First edition, 1982.)

McTaggart, R. and Garbutcheon-Singh, M. (1986) 'New directions in action research (notes on the 1986 Deakin University 'Fourth generation action research' seminar)', *Curriculum Perspectives*, 6 (2): 42–6.

Schön, D. (1983) *The Reflective Practitioner: How Professionals Think in Action*. New York: Basic Books.

Schön, D. (1987) *Educating the Reflective Practitioner: Toward a New Design for Teaching and Learning in the Professions*. San Francisco, CA: Jossey-Bass.

9

The Humanistic Approach to Action Research

JOHN ROWAN

CHAPTER OUTLINE

The chapter explores the kind of consciousness characteristic of the humanistic and existential worldview, and applies this to science. The concept of a universal research cycle then helps us to see where the humanistic approach to research fits in among other approaches, and how it applies to action research in particular. Characteristic features of the humanistic inquiry are identified: scepticism towards roles (including a discussion of the Real Self); scepticism towards the he-man (with a bow to feminist thinking in this area); and research as if people were human (including some ethical issues).

Centaur Consciousness

Consciousness has always been an important concept in social science, but it is such a slippery notion that none of the approaches which are familiar have been quite acceptable. Whether it be seen in terms of ideology (Marx, Mannheim, Popper, Aron, Arendt, Walsby, etc.) or whether it be seen in terms of different levels of consciousness (Freud, Jung, Lewin, Maslow, Mahrer, etc.), the theories all seemed to pass on one side somehow, and not to be used very much. In recent years much more interest has been taken in it, and the *Journal of Consciousness Studies* has been a focus for this interest. One of the most outstanding papers which has appeared in that journal came from Ken Wilber. He suggested (Wilber, 1997b) that there were currently at least 12 schools of thought with different approaches to consciousness, and presented his own integration of all of them, showing how they could all be valid and worth pursuing.

Part of this integration involves positing a series of levels, using a four-quadrant model to show that similar levels occur as an intentional field, as a behavioural field, as a social field and as a cultural field (Wilber, 1997b: 74). It is the fourth of these which I want to concentrate on here. It is the one which informs the book for which Wilber is perhaps best known, *The Atman Project* (Wilber, 1996). This describes in some detail a sequence of stages which he claims are universal structures of consciousness.

What he says is that there is a process of psycho-spiritual development which we are all going through, both as individuals and as members of an historically-located culture. He has outlined this process, and shows that we are very familiar with its early stages. The later stages are much more controversial, but follow the same form.

The easiest way to describe this model seems to be by going through Figure 9.1.

It can be seen from this that there are three broad sections, labelled as prepersonal, personal and transpersonal. One of Wilber's most insistent themes is that we tend to suffer from the pre/trans fallacy – that is, we confuse what is prepersonal with what is transpersonal. Some do it (like Freud) by saying that the transpersonal does not really exist – it is just a projection from the prepersonal; others do it (like Jung) by saying that the prepersonal does not really exist – anything beyond the personal must be transpersonal.

The term 'transpersonal' is still unfamiliar enough so that it needs some explanation. I like Grof's succinct description, where he says it is concerned essentially with 'experiences involving an expansion or extension of consciousness beyond the usual ego boundaries and beyond the limitations

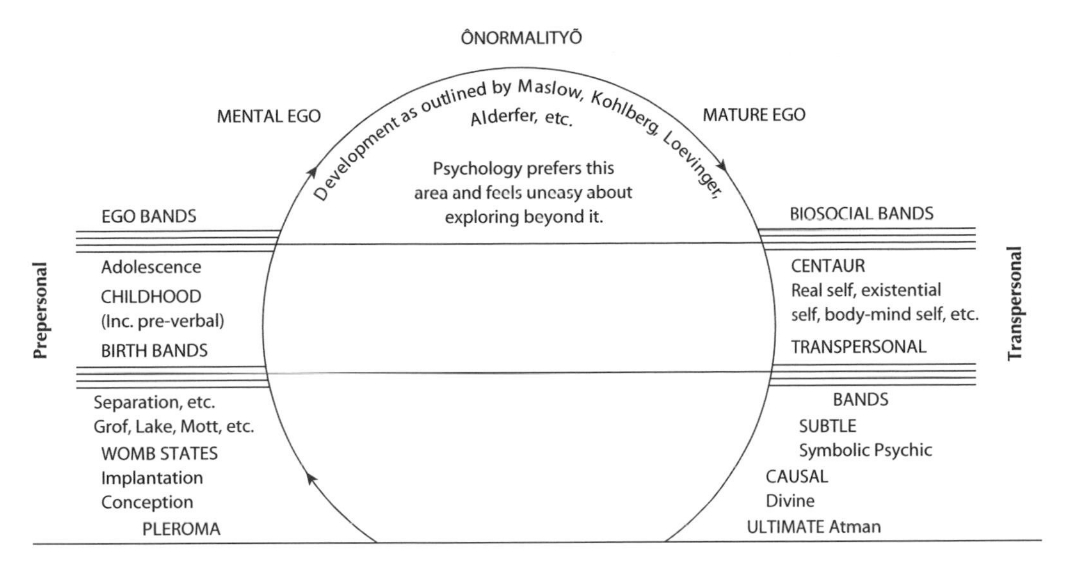

Figure 9.1 Ken Wilber's map
Source: Revised and consolidated by John Rowan in April 1982 and approved by Ken Wilber in May 1982.

of time and/or space' (Grof, 1979: 155). Many of us have had moments at least of this kind of experience – surveys show that something like one-third of the population have had peak experiences at one time or another (Hay, 1990). These can be experiences where, as Maslow says, 'the whole universe is perceived as an integrated and unified whole' (Maslow, 1970: 59) and where the ego boundaries seem to be stretched or removed. Such an experience can sometimes be remembered for the rest of a person's life, and can have a profound effect on how the person lives that life. Many people working in this field feel that the proportion of the population experiencing such events is probably much higher, except that people push the experience away as too disconcerting, and do not like the idea of changes in consciousness which go this far (Davis, Lockwood and Wright, 1991).

Now what Wilber says is that these experiences are really intimations of a possible transition from one level of consciousness to another. What is so reassuring about Wilber is that he says this is no great leap into the deep waters of spirituality (or religion or occultism), but a change no greater than that which we have experienced several times before, in the course of our development so far. We have already gone from symbiosis with the mother to separation, and from body-self as an infant to membership-self as a child, and from there through adolescence to the mental ego. At each of these transitions we had to revise our whole notion of who we were, and even what kind of self we were. So we know what it is like to revise our self-definition. The move from mental ego to the Centaur stage is just another such change, and peak experiences are a very common harbinger of this particular transition. Incidentally, the name Centaur was chosen to mark the contrast with the Mental Ego stage, where the basic image is of a controlling rider (the intellect) on a controlled horse (the emotions and body), separate and distinct. At the Centaur stage we think in terms of bodymind unity instead.

Now the movement from the mental ego to the Centaur (sometimes called Real Self) can be quite a wrenching move. It usually happens as a result of some crisis, such as a partner leaving, loss of a valued job, death of a loved one and so forth, which brings us into therapy. It is the stage where we say in effect – 'I know how to play my roles very well, and to get esteem from others to quite a reasonable extent, but it all seems to be about them: how about me? How about the person behind all the roles? I know all about playing parts in other people's dramas: how about writing my own dramas?' Usually this thought does not occur at the beginning – at the start we are very often lost in some problem which seems overwhelming – but it starts to dawn as the journey progresses.

But the movement does not have to start like that. Nowadays it can start in a much more positive way, where we say in effect – 'I know I can do my stuff adequately, but maybe I can do more than that. I am able, but maybe I can be more able.' This is the line of personal growth, rather than of problem-solving. It can also be linked with starting to take training in counselling or psychotherapy, and finding that one's own therapy is obligatory. But however it starts, the movement is away from role-playing and towards authenticity.

It is very important to note, however, that this Centaur, this Real Self, is still regarded as single and bounded. It has definite limits, a habitation and a name. People at this level often talk about community, but their actions are in fact very individualistic. Wallis (1985), in a sociological analysis, describes this whole way of looking at the world as epistemological individualism.

The actual experience of the real self is, I have argued, a mystical experience. This is the feeling of being in touch with my own centre, my inner identity, my true self, my authenticity – that self which lies behind or beyond all self-images or self-concepts or sub-personalities. It is what Assagioli (1975) calls the 'I' – the centre point of the whole personality. It is what Wilber (1996) calls the complete bodymind unity. It is a developmental step, principally discontinuous, involving step-jump rather than gradual form (Boydell and Pedler, 1981). We can now say 'I am I', and it means something to us. The existential tradition has a great deal to say about how it works. Martin Buber quotes from the tales of the Hasidim: 'Before his death, Rabbi Zusya said: "In the coming world, they will not ask me: 'Why were you not Moses?' They will ask me: 'Why were you not Zusya?' " ' (Buber, 1975: 251). This is the classic existential insight, that we are responsible for being ourselves, and this is a high and deep responsibility indeed. If we take responsibility for ourselves, we are fully human.This seems to me a very important step in psychospiritual development, because it is a gateway to the realization that we *must have spiritual experiences for ourselves*, we cannot get them from someone else. This is the basic attitude of the mystic in all religious traditions – to get inside one's own experience, to commit oneself to one's own experience, to trust one's own experience. Everything now seems clear and true, and there is no fear any more.

How Does This Apply to Science?

What I now want to say is that the humanistic approach to science comes from this particular state of consciousness. The great exemplar of this was Abraham Maslow (1969) who arranges his book into ten sections, each one dealing with a dilemma which faces everyone trying to work on research with human beings. In most cases he resolves this dilemma by grasping both sides of it.

(1) *Humanism vs mechanism*. Science is often seen as mechanistic and dehumanized. Maslow sees his work as about the rehumanization of science. But he conceives this to be not a divisive effort to oppose one 'wrong' view with another 'right' view, nor to cast out anything. He tells us that his conception of science in general and of psychology in general, is *inclusive* of mechanistic science. He believes that mechanistic science (which in psychology takes the form of behaviourism, of cognitive science and of the empirical approach generally) is not incorrect but rather too narrow and limited to serve as a *general* or comprehensive philosophy (Maslow, 1969: 5).

(2) *Holism vs reductionism*. If we want to do psychology, in the sense of learning about people, we have often in practice to approach one person at a time. What is the state of mind in which this is best done? This is one of my favourite quotes from Maslow:

> Any clinician knows that in getting to know another person it is best to keep your brain out of the way, to look and listen totally, to be completely absorbed, receptive, passive, patient and waiting rather than eager, quick and impatient. It does not help to start measuring, questioning, calculating or testing out theories, categorizing or classifying. If your brain is too busy, you won't hear or see well. Freud's term 'free-floating attention' describes well this noninterfering, global, receptive, waiting kind of cognizing another person. (Maslow, 1969: 10–11)

If we adopt this approach, Maslow says, we have a chance of being able to describe the person holistically rather than reductively. In other words, we can see the *whole* person, rather than some selected and split-off aspect of the person. But this depends crucially on the *relationship* between the knower and the known. We have to approach the person as a person:

> This is different from the model way in which we approach physical objects, i.e. manipulating them, poking at them to see what happens, taking them apart, etc. If you do this to human beings, you *won't* get to know them. They won't *want* you to know them. They won't *let* you know them. (Maslow, 1969: 13, original emphasis)

My own view is that this is a basic point which has to be taken on board by anyone studying people.

(3) *I-Thou vs I-It*. Maslow was way ahead of his time in recognizing the importance of Martin Buber's distinction between two ways of approaching another person. It is only today that this idea is being taken up by many other people as important for research. Maslow never mentions Merleau-Ponty, but the thinking is clearly related to phenomenological ideas (Valle, 1998).

(4) *Courage vs fear*. Most research and most knowledge, he says, comes from deficiency motivation. That is, it is based on fear, and is carried out to allay anxiety; it is basically defensive. There is a very good recent discussion of 'wishful and fearful

thinking' in Griffin (1998); but we can see that Maslow enumerated 21 cognitive pathologies which emanate from this basic stance in the 1960s (Maslow, 1969: 26–9).

(5) *Science and sacralization.* Science is notorious for the way in which it seems to oppose religion and also such emotions as reverence, mystery, wonder and awe. Maslow suggests that deficiency-oriented science has a need to desacralize as a defence.

The question Maslow wants to ask is: Is it in the intrinsic nature of science or knowledge that it must desacralize, must strip away values in a way that Maslow calls 'countervaluing', or not? On the contrary, says Maslow. And in this he is close to the recent thinking of Ken Wilber, who in his book *The Marriage of Sense and Soul* (1998) is making some very similar points (see also Bentz and Shapiro, 1998; Braud and Anderson, 1998).

(6) *Experiential knowledge vs spectator knowledge.* The world of experience can be described with two languages: a subjective (first-person) one and an objective (third-person) one. 'In his presence I feel small' is first-person, while 'He's trying to dominate me' is third-person. This question of first-person knowledge is now being explored in detail in the *Journal of Consciousness Studies*. Mitroff and Kilmann (1978) speak of 'authenticity' in relation to the kind of scientist we are now considering. If we want to know more about how to do the other kind of science (the experiental kind) we can go to Taoism and learn about receptivity.

> To be able to listen – really, wholly, passively, self-effacingly listen – without presupposing, classifying, improving, controverting, evaluating, approving or disapproving, without dueling with what is being said, without rehearsing the rebuttal in advance, without free-associating to portions of what is being said so that succeeding portions are not heard at all – such listening is rare. (Maslow, 1969: 96)

But if we can do it, says Maslow, these are the moments when we are closest to reality. Contemplation is something which is hard to learn, but it can be learned, and it is an essential moment in the scientific process as Maslow sees it. And again recent thinkers such as Anderson and Braud (1998) agree with him.

(7) *The comprehensive vs the simple.* Scientific work has two directions or poles or goals: one is towards simplicity and condensation, the other towards total comprehensiveness and inclusiveness. Both of these are necessary, but we should distrust simplicity as we seek it. We should also not value simplicity and elegance to the exclusion of richness and experiential truth.

(8) *Suchness vs abstraction.* There are two different kinds of meanings, which are complementary rather than mutually exclusive. Maslow calls one 'Abstractness meaning' (classifications) and the other 'Suchness meaning', having to do with the experiential realm. One tends to reduce things to some unified explanation; the other experiences something in its own right and in its own nature. There may be two kinds of scientists: the cool, who go most for abstraction and explanation; and the warm, who go for suchness and understanding. But great scientists integrate both.

(9) *Values and value-free science.* If we say that science can tell us nothing about why, only about how; if we say that science cannot help us to choose between good and evil, we are saying that science is only an instrument, only a technology, to be used equally either by good men or by villains. But Maslow believes that science can discover the values by which people should live.

(10) *Maturity vs immaturity.* Science is incredibly 'masculine', in the sense of idealizing the stereotyped image of the male. Maslow sees this as a sign of immaturity, much more to do with the adolescent boy who desperately wants to be accepted as a man, rather than with the mature man, who may have many 'feminine' traits.

It can easily be seen in these ten points how the Centaur consciousness comes through again and again. It also does so in the work of Alvin Mahrer (1978). The connection I want to make with the next section is that if we are sceptical about the either/or, as Maslow clearly is throughout his writings, we have to find models which enable us to reconcile apparent oppositions.

How Does This Apply to Research?

All through this handbook we can see in chapter after chapter the complex and multitudinous nature of research, even within the general category of action research. Now we shall take the opposite tack, and say that research is also very simple. We can reduce it to simplicity by saying that there is a research cycle, and that all the forms of research mentioned in this book conform to it. In this way we shall be able to see how alienated research, which arouses critical responses in so many of the contributors to this handbook, relates to authentic research, which is what many of us favour.

If we look at a representation of the basic standard research cycle (Figure 9.2), we can see that it has a very definite form, with some unavoidable stages within it (Rowan, 1981: 97–105). We normally start over on the left-hand side, just Being. We are working

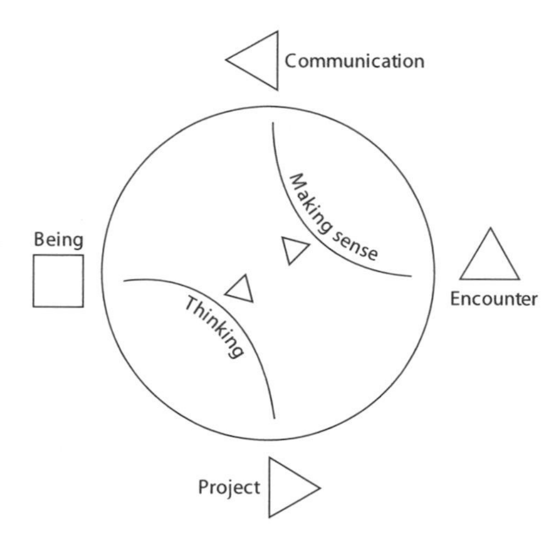

Figure 9.2 The standard research cycle

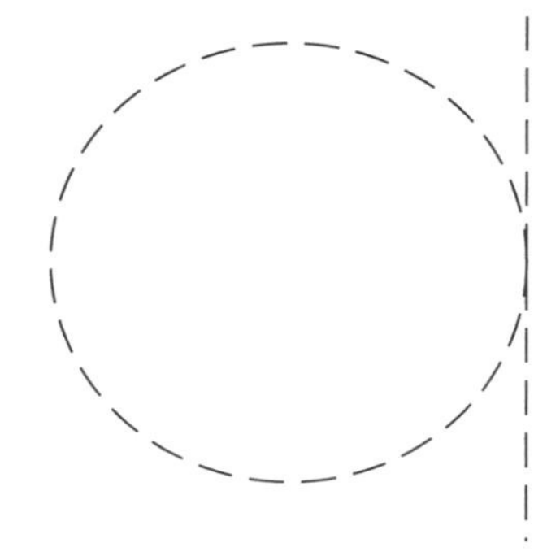

Figure 9.3 A quantatitive empirical research cycle

happily away in our field, when some disturbance arises. It may be negative, in that we have to solve some problem in order to survive; or it may be positive, in that we see an opportunity and take it. There are many possibilities as to why we should need to take action. But when we do so, the first thing we do is to get more information. This is the phase I have called Thinking. During this stage we are taking in material and processing it, in order to find whether there is some answer already, so that we do not need to do research. We survey the literature, we make telephone calls, we pick people's brains, we keep our antennae out, we lay ourselves open to receiving ideas and information. During this process, we become clearer as to what our research question really is.

At a certain point, when we are sure that we do have a question but do not have an answer, we stop doing that and start inventing a Project. Projects are very important: Sartre once said that people are known by their projects. A project is a plan of action, a statement that if we do this, we shall get the answers we need. We may revise the project, scrap the project and start again, amend the project in the light of advice from experienced people in the field, and so on. The project may be invented by one person, or be the result of much consultation with a number of people, but it has to be a plan of some kind.

But at a certain point, we need to abandon planning and actually get out into the field and do something. Here comes the Encounter with reality. Here comes the test of all our planning and plotting. We open ourselves up to the possibility of disconfirmation. We lay ourselves open to the possibility of learning something, genuinely and for ourselves. And there is a paradox here: the more planning we have done, the more spontaneous we can be in responding to the needs of the new situation as it presents itself.

Again, at a certain point the involvement has to stop. We have to stand back and assess where we have got to, and bring all the results together, and Make Sense of them. Some of this is done by contemplation and soaking ourselves in the data, and some of it is done by thinking and analysing and systematizing the results obtained. We may do it on our own, or as part of a research group, or with the participants in the research itself.

And eventually we arrive at something communicable, and we put it out in some form. We write or co-write a report, we go on television, we speak to journalists, we go on chat shows, whatever seems to be appropriate and possible. This is the stage of Communication. And when we have delivered ourselves of all we have to say, we go back to being again, in our field, as before but not as before. Once more around the spiral.

Now that we have this general schema for what research is, we can use it in an interesting way. Suppose we represent alienation by a dotted line, and non-alienation by a solid line. And suppose we represent the researcher by the circle, and the people whose experience is being studied by a line making some sort of contact with the circle. Then pure basic research, quantitative empirical research, would look like Figure 9.3.

The circle represents the researcher being alienated and role-bound, and the line represents the subject meeting the researcher, only at a tangent, at the point of Encounter, or in other words only during the experiment or observation or survey. We can show another style of research in Figure 9.4.

Here the solidity of the line means that neither the researcher nor the subject is alienated, but the two only meet even now at one point on the cycle. The researcher is genuinely open to the subject, and is setting or making use of a situation in which the subject is genuinely open to the researcher, but is not otherwise involving the subject in the whole research process.

It is also possible to show the extent of the involvement between researcher and subject. Figure 9.5 illustrates research in which there is a greater degree of participation.

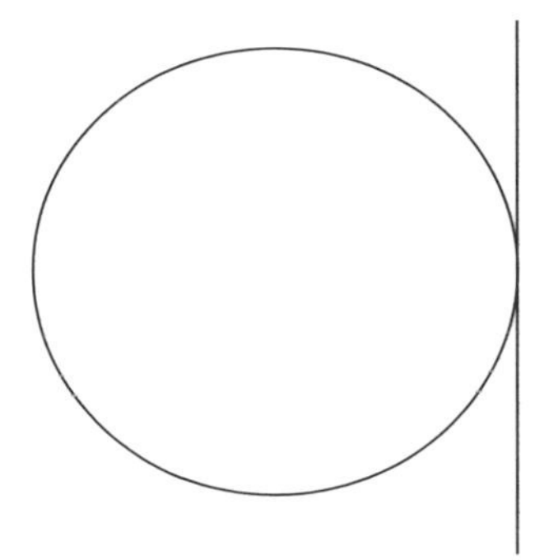

Figure 9.4 Non-alienated research

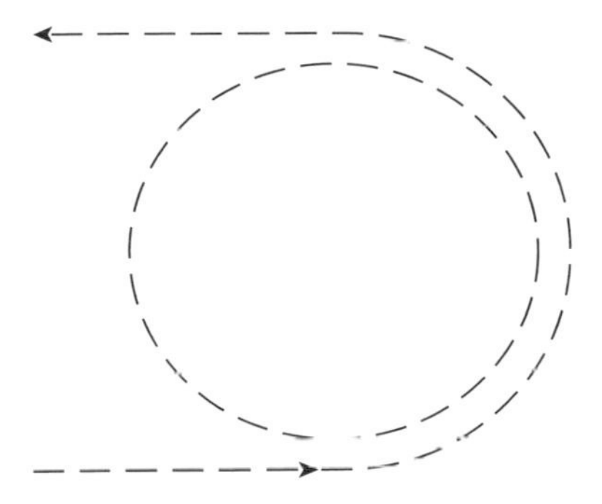

Figure 9.5 Participative research

Here the dashed line indicates that the degree of alienation varies, depending on the people involved and the social context. But the crucial difference is that the research subjects are also involved in the Project stage and the Communication stage. This means that they are involved in planning the research, and also involved in the final interpretation of what the research outcomes meant. We can show more authentic types of research which both decrease the amount of alienation and involve the subjects at more points on the cycle. In terms of the diagram, it looks like Figure 9.6:

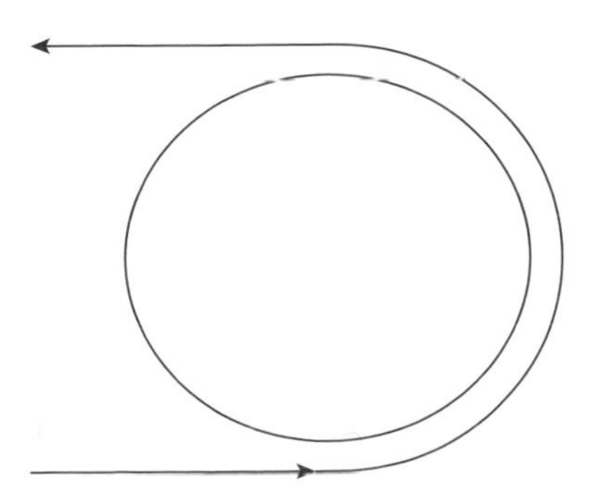

Figure 9.6 Fully automatic research

This is the kind of more humanistic research which is represented in many of the examples in this handbook, where all are authentically engaged on most points of the research cycle. In some cases the Being and Thinking points are also involved, particularly if the researchers engage in more than one cycle of inquiry. This kind of research can be seen, for example, in many of the chapters in the *Exemplars* section. This model is useful because it can be used to sketch out a research project at the planning stage, or as a means of checking the quality of interaction.

Some Implications

Scepticism towards roles

We saw right at the start that the humanistic approach comes from a particular state of consciousness. What all the humanistic forms of psychotherapy, management theory, research theory and so forth come from is an outlook first described by Abraham Maslow (1987), and later added to by people like Ken Wilber. It was named by Maslow as self-actualization or the discovery of the real self. Let us look at some of the implications of this.

What this achievement of integration brings with it is a great sense of what the existentialists have called 'authenticity'. And indeed the existentialist thinkers have done a great deal to outline this stage in some detail. According to general existential thought, when an individual's self is taken fully as autonomous, he or she can assume responsibility for being-in-the-world. And if we do this we can, as Sartre put it, choose ourselves. Carl Rogers is one of the great fathers of humanistic psychology, and he certainly saw the matter in this way, as can be seen in all his writings. Here is a passage in which he is most explicit about this:

> I have been astonished to find how accurately the Danish philosopher S¢ren Kierkegaard pictured the dilemma of the individual more than a century ago, with keen psychological insight. He points out that the most common despair is to be in despair at not choosing, or willing, to be one's self; but that the deepest form of despair is to choose 'to be another than himself'. On the other hand 'to will to be that self which one truly is, is indeed the opposite of despair', and this choice is the deepest responsibility of man. (Rogers, 1961: 110)

What we are saying, then, is that the Real Self which we are aiming at in humanistic psychotherapy is not something very abstract and hard to pin down – it is situated very concretely both in the empirical realm of psychological research and in the conceptual realm of philosophy. It is contrasted very sharply and clearly with the aims of other forms of therapy, though it is closest to existential psychotherapy, as described by Edgar Friedenberg:

> the purpose of therapeutic intervention is to support and re-establish a sense of self and personal authenticity. Not mastery of the objective environment; not effective functioning within social institutions; not freedom from the suffering caused by anxiety – though any or all of these may be concomitant outcomes of successful therapy – but personal awareness, depth of real feeling, and, above all, the conviction that one can use one's full powers, that one has the courage to be and use all one's essence in the praxis of being. (Friedenberg, 1973: 93–4)

Getting close to the Real Self, then, almost inevitably brings with it feelings which have to do with extreme good and extreme evil, with Heaven and Hell, with death and destruction as well as with life and growth. And in fact, contact with the Real Self is often experienced as a breakthrough. Finding suddenly that we are able to let go of all those false pictures of ourselves which the mental ego took for granted, can bring feelings of bliss or ecstasy.

The Real Self, then, is not an ultimate stage of development. It is not strange, alien or mystical. It is just the innermost and truest part of the separate individual, seen still as a separate individual. It can be described as the existential self, or the integrated bodymind centaur. And as such it offers a centre for the full integration of the person, as has been very thoroughly discussed in Mahrer (1978), particularly in his chapter on the 'optimal state'. What this means is that the usual splits which are found in so many people, between body and mind, intellect and emotions, duty and inclination, top-dog and underdog and all the rest, can now be healed very simply. It may take a little time to work through all the implications of this healing of the splits, and there may be some painful choices to be made along the way, but the essential blocks to full integration have now been removed, and the process is not so hard as all that.

And this means that the person now experiences a sense of personal power (Rogers, 1978) which is quite different from the old kind of power associated with the mental ego. Power at the mental-ego stage is always power over other people; power at the real-self stage is power with others, or power from within. And this means that the whole person is acting at once, with no splits, no reservations and no holding back; this is the 'spontaneous will' described by Rollo May (1969).

But what is also clear is that we are not into any automatic or unthought-out role-playing at this level. We are sceptical about roles because they may distract us from the Real Self and pretend to be more important than the Real Self. In the worst cases we can get lost in them, and in our self-image.

There is at this point, however, a question which humanistic psychology has to answer. It has to do with the challenge of social constructivism, social constructionism, deconstruction and postmodernism (e.g., Danziger, 1997; Gergen, 1997; Greer, 1997; Stenner and Eccleston, 1994). Its most acute point, it seems to me, is at the question of the self. All of these challenges say in their different ways that there is no 'real self' in the sense usually proposed by humanistic psychologists. Therefore there is no such thing as being authentic (true to oneself) or autonomous (taking charge of one's life) or self-actualization (being all that one has it in oneself to be). If this is true, then humanistic psychology is obsolete, overtaken by a postmodern wave which has passed it by. It is incumbent on those of us who call ourselves humanistic psychologists to answer this challenge.

This kind of critique, it seems to me, is very effective in undermining and even sometimes demolishing our taken-for-granted assumptions. But does it undermine or demolish our idea of a Real Self? At first it seems that it must. Is not the truth of the Real Self just the sort of truth which social constructionism is here to destroy?

But there seem to be at least four lines of thought which can lead in different ways to the reinstatement of the Real Self. The first of these, and the most obvious, is simply to put the Real Self into quotes. Then we could say that the 'real self' is simply the way the self appears in certain contexts, and that humanistic discourse favours this way of talking. This would enable us to continue to use the term 'real self' with the approval of social constructionists. However, this usage might not be acceptable to many of those within humanistic psychology, because it is difficult to think of oneself as something in quotes.

The second position we could take up is to say that the Real Self is real only in a particular context. If we participate in the humanistic psychology language community, we can very easily talk about the Real Self, because it makes sense in terms of other constructs like self-actualization, authenticity and autonomy, all of which form part of that field of discourse. We would not be claiming universal or exclusive validity for that field, but simply saying that it was as legitimate as any other. This would be taking very much the Wilber (1997b) line that what we have is a series of nested truths, none of which can stand alone, each of which depends on others. We would be arguing that the real self was a text in a context, and in that sense valid and meaningful.

A third position we might take up is to make a point which Wilber (1997a) makes about holons. I think he would say that the self is a holon: that is, it is a whole in relation to lesser parts or sub-parts of the person – and also, at the same time, a part in relation to a larger field. In other words, we are at the same time a unit in ourselves and a function of a larger field. Quite a number of people at the moment (Sapriel, 1998; Wheeler, 1998; Wheway, 1998; Yontef, 1993) are trying to say that a person is just a function of a field, and should not be regarded as an individual. But this is an indefensible either-or. The idea of a holarchy rescues us from this unnecessary dichotomy.

A fourth line to take would be to say that the Real Self is not a theoretical construct. In fact, as we can see quite easily in issue after issue of the *Journal of Humanistic Psychology*, no one has ever come up with a good theoretical description or empirical investigation of the Real Self. I suggest that this is because the Real Self is not a concept but an experience. When we have a breakthrough into the Centaur stage of psychospiritual development, we have an experience of the Real Self, an experience of authenticity. We relate to others in an authentic way; we own our bodies in a new way; other people experience us as clear and direct and truthful. It is basically an ecstatic experience, and I believe it is a mystical experience, although on the foothills of mysticism, rather than on the great heights. After it, we are more likely to say that we *own* our experience in a new way (Bugental, 1981).

Like all mystical experiences, it is ineffable. That is, it goes beyond the categories of our ordinary discourse. It can only be described in paradox, or in poetry. If we try to bring it down into everyday discourse, the language of the Mental Ego (the previous and much more familiar psychospiritual stage of development in Wilber's model), we can only distort and misrepresent it.

I am not sure that there is any great contradiction between the four positions I have outlined. I have some respect myself for all of them. No doubt there are others which could be put forward.

Scepticism towards the he-man

Just because the humanistic approach is so sceptical towards roles in general, it is of course sceptical about sex roles – or gender positions, as they are more often now called. Bob Connell (1987) has taught us about hegemonic masculinity and its complementary form of femininity, which he called emphasized femininity, and how oppressive they both can be.

It is clear that there are pressures on men to be masculine. But this is not quite as simple a statement as it may seem. It has often been pointed out that we should speak of many masculinities rather than just one masculinity, because there are many ways of being a man, not just one. There is now in fact a good journal called *Men and Masculinities*. It is surprisingly hard to define what a man actually is.

> A pair of the wiser men began to debate. One had said that 'masculinity is whatever you have to do to look like a man,' while the other thought that "masculinity is whatever you have to do to feel like a man.' (Pittman, 1993: 8)

It seems to make more sense to speak, with Wittgenstein, of a 'family resemblance' than of distinguishing features. In a family, we can often see that the members look like each other, but there may be no one feature that they all have in common. Similarly, it may be possible to find all sorts of things that define men, but any one particular man may have some of them missing. Judith Lorber (1994) has put together a whole book of exceptions and difficult intermediate cases, which make it hard indeed to point to any one thing and say 'This is what defines a man'. Even the favourite touchstone of the conservative man, testosterone, is not exempt from this. I remember a young man on the Oprah Winfrey show saying that when he was 15 years old he was 'a walking hormone' – meaning that he was perpetually randy. But it is not about hormones, it is about assumptions and expectations which are socially induced. Similarly with aggression and violence, which are popularly supposed to be the result of high levels of testosterone.

However, it is still true, in the dominance system which we live in today, that there is one dominant masculinity, and many subordinate masculinities. The hegemonic pattern requires clarity and simplification to be effective. What this means in practice is that men are pressured into being masculine in just one way. To be a proper man, a man who is successfully masculine, is to be constrained into quite a narrow band of expectations. These expectations have been outlined well by Robert Brannon (1976), who has extracted four themes or dimensions that seem to be valid across all specific manifestations of hegemonic masculinity:

- *No sissy stuff.* Anything feminine must be avoided. It is important not to be seen as feminine in any way. To do otherwise is to run the risk of being ridiculed or devalued by other men.
- *The big wheel.* There is a need to be seen to be high in status, or to be connected directly to people or organizations with high status. It is important to be important.
- *The sturdy oak.* One must be independent and self-reliant, and be ready to support others. This support may be physical or material: if it is emotional there is a risk of being seen as feminine.
- *Give 'em hell.* Always be ready to respond to threat. Do not avoid violence if it is appropriate. Protect one's image and one's loved ones. Take risks and take the lead.

What men want when they take up these images is a woman who will complement them. This woman will have what Bob Connell (1987) has called 'emphasized femininity' – that is, a corresponding pattern with the complementary values. Such a woman will want a manly man, will go for someone with social power (and possibly urge him on in his advancement), will behave in a dependent manner, not challenging the status of the man, and will praise a man for standing up to the various threats in the environment. So in this kind of system, there will be pressure on men to conform to this pattern of masculinity, and on women to conform to this pattern of femininity.

So the humanistic approach is sceptical of the he-man, and of all the over-masculine posturings in the field of research so well described by Ian Mitroff (1974).

Research as if People Were Human

What we can now say very clearly is that humanistic psychology has promoted a view of research which entails treating people as if they were human. This means that as researchers we do not hide behind roles. We take reflexivity seriously; and by this we mean that what we find out in research may be applied to us too. It also means that we do not exclude ourselves from the research process. We refuse to be alienated.

This puts us in a critical role in relation to much of the research at present being conducted by psychologists. It puts us very definitely in the qualitative camp, which is quite problematic, as Gill Aitken (1996) has pointed out in no uncertain terms. This does not mean that we are opposed to quantitative research: it just means that we do not often resort to quantitative research until and unless we have done enough qualitative research to know what the research means when it is carried out. However, the whole of this book takes off from the insight that action research is more than just qualitative research. It is even more in line with the humanistic forms of thought than is qualitative research. After all, much which goes under the label of qualitative research is just old empiricist research without the numbers.

Are there some general things we can say from the humanistic view we have now outlined? Take this statement from David Berg and Kenwyn Smith. They say that for them good research with human beings entails:

(1) direct involvement with and/or observation of human beings or social systems;
(2) commitment to a process of self-scrutiny by the researcher as he or she conducts the research;
(3) willingness to change theory or method in response to the research experience *during* the research itself;
(4) description of social systems that is dense or thick and favours depth over breadth in any single undertaking; and
(5) participation in the social system being studied, under the assumption that much of the information of interest is only accessible to or reportable by its members. (Berg and Smith, 1988: 25)

What is humanistic about this? It has the qualities of non-defensiveness, of openness, of authenticity, which are characteristics of the Real Self. And the following statement shows that we are not just concerned with the individual, but also with the social field. 'Resistance to enculturation' (Maslow, 1987) may be crucially necessary, in particular, before we can step outside the usual frameworks to engage in research along these lines. Someone who is simply taking for granted the usual cultural roles and values cannot do this.

1 Researchers recognize that all research carries with it the ideological assumptions of the researcher, reflective of his or her time in history and position of power within a culture and subcultures.
2 An honest evaluation is made of how these assumptions affect all phases of the research inquiry, including the choice of topic, methods and analysis employed, and generalizations extending from the analysis, as well as the choices made in properly presenting the results to the professional community and to the public.
3 As a result of this analysis, balancing points of view are considered and employed. Where balance is not completely feasible, researchers disclose their assumptions, as well as aspects of the research procedures and conclusions that favour the view of any one group, culture, or subculture over another.
4 When the research uses the experience of past research, each successive research inquiry is more balanced in empowering the silenced voices of society and thereby attempts to rectify the imbalances of past research and more fully explicate and understand the phenomenon being studied.
5 Taking seriously the power of knowledge in culture, researchers work individually and collaboratively to balance the hierarchical structures inherent in research and to create better structures for the benefit of all people. (Anderson and Braud, 1998: 248)

And this means that we may have to take much more seriously the question of research ethics. Empirical quantitative research does not raise any very difficult ethical issues. All the ethical requirements laid down by existing authorities apply very well. But with these more deeply engaged types of research, we find more and more new ethical challenges arising, as David Berg and Kenwyn Smith (1988) pointed out some years ago, and as Laura Brown (1997) has been arguing more recently.

In research where the researcher and the other participants come much closer, and are more deeply involved with one another, the personal and social implications become far more complex. Ethical statements by people concerned with such areas of research start to talk about interpersonal ethics – the care with which one treats another equal person – and social ethics, the concern with the results of one's research and the unintended consequences which may ensue. This kind of research actually makes a difference to the people involved – all of them – and to ensure that horrible mistakes are not made is a duty. Such points have been well made both by Braud and Anderson (1998) and by Bentz and Shapiro (1998).

The issue of self and other turns out to be central to all this, as Michelle Fine (1994) has well argued, and it is humanistic psychology which has most to offer in understanding the self. Its concept of the Real Self offers a point of reference from which authenticity can be understood. It offers a set of values which are helpful to all researchers in this new situation. I am not trying to say that humanistic psychology got there first, or that humanistic psychology has all the answers, or even that everyone needs to study humanistic psychology. All I am saying is that by understanding the humanistic value system which underpins Centaur consciousness, we can understand what actually needs to operate in the most demanding types of research, and particularly in action research.

References

Aitken, Gill (1996) 'The covert disallowing and discrediting of qualitative research', *Changes*, 14 (3): 192–8.

Anderson, Rosemarie and Braud, William (1998) 'Additional suggestions, ethical considerations and future challenges', in W. Braud and R. Anderson (eds), *Transpersonal Methods for the Social Sciences*. Thousand Oaks, CA: Sage Publications. pp. 238–55.

Assagioli, Roberto (1975) *Psychosynthesis*. Wellingborough: Turnstone.

Bentz, Valerie Malhotra and Shapiro, Jeremy J. (1998) *Mindful Inquiry in Social Research*. Thousand Oaks, CA: Sage Publications.

Berg, David N. and Smith, Kenwyn K. (1988) 'The clinical demands of research methods', in D.N. Berg and K.K. Smith (eds), *The Self in Social Inquiry*. Newbury Park, CA: Sage Publications. pp. 21–34.

Boydell, T. and Pedler, M. (1981) *Management Self-development*. Farnborough: Gower.

Brannon, Robert (1976) 'The male sex role: our culture's blueprint for manhood, what it's done for us lately', in D. David and R. Brannon (eds), *The Forty-nine Percent Majority: the Male Sex Role*. Reading, MA: Addison-Wesley.

Braud, William and Anderson, Rosemarie (eds) (1998) *Transpersonal Methods for the Social Sciences*. Thousand Oaks, CA: Sage Publications.

Brown, Laura S. (1997) 'Ethics in psychology: *Cui Bono*?', in D. Fox and I. Prilleltensky (eds), *Critical Psychology: an Introduction*. London: Sage Publications. pp. 51–6.

Buber, Martin (1975) *Tales of the Hasidim: the Early Masters*. New York: Schocken Books.

Bugental, James F.T. (1981) *The Search for Authenticity* (enlarged edition). New York: Irvington.

Connell, R.W. (1987) *Gender and Power*. Cambridge: Polity Press.

Danziger, Kurt (1997) 'The varieties of social construction', *Theory & Psychology*, 7 (3): 399–416.

Davis, J., Lockwood, L. and Wright, C. (1991) 'Reasons for not reporting peak experiences', *Journal of Humanistic Psychology*, 31 (1): 86–94.

Fine, Michelle (1994) 'Working the hyphens: reinventing self and other in qualitative research', in N.K. Denzin and Y.S. Lincoln (eds), *Handbook of Qualitative Research*. Thousand Oaks, CA: Sage Publications. pp. 70–82.

Friedenberg, Edgar Z. (1973) *Laing*. London: Fontana.

Gergen, Kenneth J. (1997) 'The place of the psyche in a constructed world', *Theory & Psychology*, 7 (6): 723–46.

Greer, Scott (1997) 'Nietzsche and social construction', *Theory & Psychology*, 7 (1): 83–100.

Griffin, D.R. (1998) *Unsnarling the World-knot: Consciousness, Freedom and the Mind–Body Problem*. Berkeley, CA: University of California Press.

Grof, Stanislav (1979) *Realms of the Human Unconscious*. London: Souvenir Press.

Hay, David (1990) *Religious Experience Today: Studying the Facts*. London: Mowbray.

Lorber, Judith (1994) *Paradoxes of gender*. New Haven, CT: Yale University Press.

Mahrer, Alvin R. (1978) *Experiencing: a Humanistic Theory of Psychology and Psychiatry*. New York: Brunner/Mazel. (Republished in 1989 by the University of Ottawa Press.)

Maslow, Abraham H. (1969) *The Psychology of Science: a Reconnaissance*. Chicago, IL: Henry Regnery.

Maslow, Abraham H. (1970) *Religions, Values and Peak Experiences*. New York: Viking.

Maslow, Abraham H. (1987) *Motivation and Personality* (third edition). New York: Harper & Row.

May, Rollo (1969) *Love and Will*. New York: W.W. Norton.

Mitroff, Ian I. (1974) *The Subjective Side of Science*. Amsterdam: Elsevier.

Mitroff, Ian I. and Kilmann, Ralph H. (1978) *Methodological Approaches to Social Science*. San Francisco, CA: Jossey-Bass.

Pittman, F. (1993) *Man Enough: Fathers, Sons and the Search for Masculinity*. New York: Perigee.

Rogers, Carl R. (1961) *On Becoming a Person*. London: Constable.

Rogers, Carl R. (1978) *On Personal Power*. London: Constable.

Rowan, John (1981) 'A dialectical paradigm for research', in P. Reason and J. Rowan (eds), *Human Inquiry: a Sourcebook of New Paradigm Research*. Chichester: John Wiley. pp. 93–112.

Sapriel, Lolita (1998) 'Can Gestalt therapy, self-psychology and intersubjectivity theory be integrated?', *British Gestalt Journal*, 7 (1): 33–44.

Stenner, Paul and Eccleston, Christopher (1994) 'On the textuality of being', *Theory & Psychology*, 4 (1): 85–103.

Valle, Ron (ed.) (1998) *Phenomenological Inquiry in Psychology: Existential and Transpersonal Dimensions*. New York: Plenum Press.

Wallis, Roy (1985) 'Betwixt therapy and salvation: the changing form of the human potential movement', in R.K. Jones (ed.), *Sickness and Sectarianism*. Aldershot: Gower.

Wheeler, Gordon (1998) 'Towards a Gestalt developmental model', *British Gestalt Journal*, 7 (2): 115–25.

Wheway, John (1998) 'Dialogue and intersubjectivity in the therapeutic relationship', *British Gestalt Journal*, 6 (1): 16–28.

Wilber, Ken (1996) *The Atman Project* (second edition). Wheaton, IL: Quest.

Wilber, Ken (1997a) *The Eye of Spirit*. Boston, MA: Shambhala.

Wilber, Ken (1997b) 'An integral theory of consciousness', *Journal of Consciousness Studies*, 4 (1): 71–92.

Wilber, Ken (1998) *The Marriage of Sense and Soul: Integrating Science and Religion*. New York: Random House.

Yontef, Gary (1993) *Awareness, Dialogue and Process: Essays on Gestalt Therapy*. Highland, NY: The Gestalt Journal Press.

10
The Relationship of 'Systems Thinking' to Action Research

ROBERT LOUIS FLOOD

CHAPTER OUTLINE

The chapter traces the development of 'systems thinking' since the 1920s and illustrates how each phase of development yields a distinct intellectual framework of ideas, which in turn gives rise to action-oriented methodological principles for the improvement of social and organizational contexts. In particular the importance of systemic thinking is emphasized as part of a holistic or spiritual quality to human existence that envelops the entire human experience and consequently everything that happens within that experience, including methodological principles.

Systems thinking emerged in the twentieth century through a critique of reductionism. Reductionism generates knowledge and understanding of phenomena by breaking them down into constituent parts and then studying these simple elements in terms of cause and effect. With systems thinking the belief is that the world is systemic, which means that phenomena are understood to be an emergent property of an interrelated whole. *Emergence* and *interrelatedness* are the fundamental ideas of systems thinking. An emergent property of a whole is said to arise where a phenomenon cannot be fully comprehended in terms only of properties of constituent parts. 'The whole is greater than the sum of its parts', is the popularized phrase that explains emergence. 'Synergy' is the sexy label for it. With systems thinking, then, it is argued that valid knowledge and meaningful understanding come from building up whole pictures of phenomena, not by breaking them into parts.

How to go about building up whole pictures of social phenomena is a big question that has led to much controversy in social systems thinking. One idea borrowed from the natural sciences assumes that all phenomena are real systems. The social world therefore comprises many interrelated social systems. A systems approach, it follows, entails qualitative and/or quantitative modelling of these social systems. Models are then employed as research tools to describe or explain a social phenomenon, or as decision-making tools that predict events and suggest actions to take today to achieve improvement some time later.

Another idea states that while the social world is intuitively assumed to be systemic, that is, characterized by emergence and interrelatedness, we cannot go on boldly to assume that it comprises real social systems. After all, any understanding we have of social phenomena is by way of interpretation made through cognitive processes of the human brain. A systems approach therefore will employ concepts like emergence and interrelatedness to interpret social phenomena, rather than attempt to represent systems as if they exist in the world (Checkland, 1981). Such a systems approach might be particularly empowering in this endeavour of meaning construction if the world is indeed systemic. That is, such a systems approach promises to construct meaning that will resonate strongly with people's experiences within a systemic world.

Systems thinking in the social sciences can be categorized, albeit rather crudely, into the two schools of thought sketched out above. The first I will refer to in this chapter as *systems thinking*, since it advocates thinking about real social systems as if they exist in the world. The second I will refer to as *systemic thinking*, because it assumes only that the social construction of the world is systemic. Each view offers its own fundamental knowledge for practice. This chapter explores some of the intricacies of each view, with each one offering grounding for the form of practice that we know as action research. The chapter places greater emphasis on systemic thinking, which is consistent with its greater importance to contemporary action research.

From Reductionism to Systems Thinking

Systems thinking came to the fore when research into living things encountered limitations to the concepts and principles of reductionism (see the collection of papers in Emery, 1981). A counter-position in biology took on a coherent form by the mid-1920s. Several scientists began to think in a new way. Paul Weiss, Walter B. Cannon (credited with homeostasis) and, in particular, Ludwig von Bertalanffy, came to the fore. Von Bertalanffy demonstrated that concepts of reductionism were helpless in appreciating dynamics of organisms. Existence of an organism cannot be understood solely in terms of behaviour of some fundamental parts. Parts are interrelated and influence each other. The end result is a whole organism that exhibits emergence. In other words, an organism demonstrably behaves in a way that is 'more than the sum of its parts'. Biology therefore required new ideas to explain happenings like interrelatedness and emergence.

In this regard, von Bertalanffy (1950) developed a theory of open systems. *Open systems theory* employs functional and relational criteria to study the whole, rather than principles of reductionism to study simple elements. An organism as a whole is said to co-exist in relation to an environment. Its functions and structure diversify or are maintained by management of a continuous flow of energy and information between organism and environment. Flows occur in an organism through its many interrelated parts. Parts are interrelated through feedback loops. *Feedback* is another key idea of systems thinking.

There are two types of feedback, one is known as negative feedback with balancing loops and the other as positive feedback with amplifying loops (see for example Forrester, 1968; Kim, 1993; Richardson, 1991; Wolstenholme, 1990). *Balancing loops* describe well naturally occurring control processes such as temperature and acidity. If conditions in an organism move out of the tolerable range of naturally occurring control parameters, then control action is taken through balancing loops to re-establish normal conditions. For example, when you feel hot, control action triggers off sweating that leads to cooling through convection, keeping your body temperature below life threatening levels. *Amplifying loops* on the other hand lead to a growth in a trend. This may be desirable or undesirable. Diversification in the growth of an embryo might be considered desirable. Addiction where more and more heroin is needed to achieve the same impact may be considered undesirable. An organism achieves a steady-state, or normal condition, through the interplay of balancing and amplifying feedback loops. The end result is an emergent whole with an overall integrity, albeit a finite one.

Von Bertalanffy (1956, 1981) generalized the open systems concept for other fields of study in what he called general systems theory. The lasting impact of his ideas, however, became known as systems thinking. Systems thinking was readily taken up as the basis of a new form of social theory.

Taken into the field of organizational analysis, for example, systems thinking observes organizations as complex systems made up of interrelated parts most usefully studied as an emergent whole. An organization is open to its environment. Management action is taken to hold the organization in a steady-state through management functions that control activities and information within the organization, and between the organization and its environment. The primary aims are to ensure survival and then to secure desirable growth, by transforming inputs and by adapting to changes when they occur. Since parts comprise people, management is concerned with the needs of people at work. Parts, or subsystems, have lists of needs that must be met. Individual motivation therefore requires attention. For example, jobs can be enriched leading to increased productivity and satisfaction. A whole organizational structure that reflects the interrelated nature of its subsystems holds greater potential for participation. System orientated leadership, therefore, is more able to encourage people's involvement, to enable democracy, and to provide conditions for autonomy.

Cybernetic theory is a stream of systems thinking that came together around the same time as von Bertalanffy's path-breaking research. The core ideas relevant to action research are presented in the next section.

Cybernetic Theory

Cybernetics is traditionally defined as the science of communication and control in man (*sic*) and machine. It shares an interest in many of the concepts of systems thinking such as feedback and control. Cybernetic models represent dynamic phenomena conceptually, diagrammatically and/or mathematically, employing balancing and amplifying loops. Cybernetics found its home in the management sciences, for example, in the guise of control theory, systems engineering and, more recently, information theory. The field took shape after the Second World War in the famous Macy conferences on cybernetics held in the USA. Key participants in these conferences included John von Neumann, Warren McCulloch, Margaret Mead, and Norbert Weiner. Another founding participant was Gregory Bateson (see 1973, 1979) and he has attracted considerable interest in the literature of action research.

Bateson, in partnership with Margaret Mead, undertook studies in anthropology and the dynamics of social relationships. They all but discovered cybernetic theory before its articulation at the Macy conferences. In the 1930s in New Guinea they observed social entropy where in certain social contexts opposition dialectically heightened between people lead to a breakdown in relations. This can be likened to von Neumann's game of competitive maximization, which is an amplifying loop. In Bali in the 1940s they observed balance through propriety in social relationships, providing an example of balancing loops at work.

Bateson subsequently hypothesized a general theory of cybernetics as his studies broadened into psychiatry and evolution. He envisioned unity in structure, for example, where structure in plants is found in the construction of sentences. This is similar to von Bertalanffy's general systems theory. Bateson examined all sorts of patterns and order and linked them to modes of organization and communication. He employed organic analogies as dynamic models to facilitate learning. He drew no defining line between natural and social arrangements and ultimately concluded that patterns and order in nature come together in certain ways in mental activity. The human mind thus is both a part of nature and a distinct thing.

This chapter so far has assisted the reader to become familiar with the origins and main concepts of systems thinking. With these sorts of ideas firmly in mind, open systems theory and cybernetics began to influence practice and this endeavour became generally known as applied systems thinking.

Applied Systems Thinking

I first turn to Peter Checkland's (1985) general model of the organized use of rational thought. It offers a means of understanding applied systems thinking and a mode for its comparison with other systems approaches presented later on in the chapter. Checkland argues that research may be thought of as entailing three elements. These are (a) some linked ideas in a framework, (b) a way of applying these ideas in a methodology, and (c) an application area. After employing a methodology there is reflection on what has been learned about the three elements. Modifications might be called for. We will see this to be the case as the chapter unfolds, revealing modifications that eventually lead to a better understanding of the potential of the systems idea in a liberating praxis.

The framework of ideas that characterizes applied systems thinking makes the assumption that there are systems in the world. Applied systems thinking tends to concentrate on the structure of functional units. It focuses on the intrinsic or relative stability of structures. The number of subsystems could be important in the framework of ideas. A typical concern is, how and under what conditions system transformation will occur? Another asks, what is the impact of internal stability on relations with other systems? It follows that the application area is characterized by management problems that occur in these systems. When a problem crops up, it is necessary to enter the system to carry out an intervention on it. The methodology then is an intervention that begins with problem identification and concludes with some final solution, perhaps with an expectation that things will attain a desirable condition. The challenge is to find the most efficient means to achieve this predefined end. Often, systems models are constructed with the aim of predicting consequences of intended actions and in this way they support choice of an optimal action to meet a desired solution (known as feedforward control). Many examples of systems intervention are built on these principles (e.g., Atthill, 1975; Jenkins, 1969; M'Pherson, 1981). The contribution of MIT's Jay Forrester, more than most, has left a giant-sized impression on the applied systems map.

Jay Forrester (1961, 1968, 1969, 1971) created a strand of systems thinking originally known as industrial dynamics, but nowadays referred to as system dynamics. System dynamics is concerned with creating models of real world systems, studying their dynamics, and improving problematic system behaviour located through the models (Wolstenholme, 1990). Early applications were industrial but subsequently broadened into large-scale studies and even global behaviour (e.g., Meadows, Meadows and Randers, 1972).

System dynamics creates diagrammatic and mathematical models of feedback processes. Models represent levels of resources that vary according to rates at which resources are converted between these variables. Delays in conversion and resulting side effects are included in models so that they capture in full the complexity of dynamic behaviour. Model simulation using special software then facilitates learning about dynamic behaviour and predicts results of various tactics and strategies when applied to the system of interest.

Peter Senge studied system dynamics under Jay Forrester at MIT. Recently, however, Senge (1990; Senge et al., 1994), through his book *The Fifth Discipline*, achieved mega-popularization of system dynamics for its contribution to organizational learning. A learning organization is one that continually expands its capacity to create its own future. Senge argues that five disciplines underpin learning organizations: systems thinking, personal mastery, mental models, shared vision, and team learning. The fifth discipline is systems thinking that provides substance to the other four disciplines and hence to the learning organization as a whole.

Systems thinking in personal mastery helps us continually to see our connectedness to the world and to more and more of the interdependencies between our actions and our reality. Systems thinking in mental models exposes assumptions we make and tests if these are systemically flawed, for instance, by identifying feedback not previously accounted for. Systems thinking in shared vision clarifies how vision radiates through collaborative feedback processes and fades through conflictual feedback processes. Systems thinking in team learning identifies positive and negative synergy in discussion and dialogue where, respectively, the whole becomes greater or less than the sum of its parts.

Senge's ideas and other more recent studies in system dynamics arguably cross the border from systems thinking to systemic thinking. Unfortunately I have insufficient space to explore this claim. It is time to move on and concentrate now on the relationship of systems thinking to action research. Systems thinking found its way into action research, initially yielding what has been called a socio-ecological perspective.

Socio-Ecological Perspective

The socio-ecological perspective is a derivative of and is sometimes known as the open systems thinking school. While growing out of open systems theory, it is shaped by psychoanalytic thinking and an action orientation (Greenwood and Levin, 1998). Greenwood and Levin, in a helpful summary of the historical roots of the socio-ecological perspective, locate its origins in research carried out by The Tavistock Institute of Human Relations. Working with Tavistock, Trist and Bamforth (1951), in their famous study on the longwall coal-mining method, showed the importance of understanding interrelatedness between production technology and work organization. The longwall method fragmented the work cycle on each shift in a reductionist manner. This lessened rather than improved productivity. There was a lack of compatibility between demands created by the technology and needs of the workers as a group of interrelated human beings. Interrelatedness had been neglected and an impoverished outcome emerged.

Greenwood and Levin go on to explain how the industrial democracy movement came out of this and other early Tavistock studies. Further developments involved Kurt Lewin's (1948) concept of natural experiments and action research, which feature strongly in methodologies derived from the Tavistock programme of research. A Norwegian, Einar Thorsrud, and an Australian, Fred Emery, also made significant contributions. It is the contribution to action research made through the partnership of Emery and Trist that I concentrate on below (the Emery-Trist paradigm, see Baburoglu, 1992; Trist, Emery and Murray, 1997).

The socio-ecological perspective takes the open systems principle as its intellectual framework of ideas. It characterizes this principle in a particular way (see Barton and Selsky (1998) which is drawn upon in the following discussion). A system is defined by the 'system principle' (i.e., the organizing principle), which can be used to characterize the intra- and interrelationships existing in and between a system and its environment. These relationships are referred to as 'lawful relationships' reflecting the view that systems and individuals are capable of knowing about their environments (task environments and extended fields) in contrast to von Bertalanffy's view that environments are essentially random. Of particular interest to the socio-ecological perspective is the notion of a shared social field of organizational action, understood in terms of lawful relationships.

The socio-ecological perspective posits that the environment has an identifiable 'causal texture'. The four-step classification of these textures is presented in a classic paper by Emery and Trist (1965) that culminates in the most volatile texture, the turbulent field. Turbulence comes about through decisions and actions of managers in specific firms from a particular industry. These create mutually reactive chains as decision-makers respond and adapt to each other's decisions. Decision-makers mobilize their own competitive tools to pursue their own objectives. Behaviour is constrained by tacit agreements about the rules of competition, where rules are what decision-makers can expect of each other. A situation (system and environment) can become particularly volatile when unintended consequences of individual actions build up, become linked in unexpected ways, and change the character of the environment itself. This is likely to occur in politicized, pluralistic and fragmented circumstances.

An important focus in socio-ecological thinking is what emerges at system levels larger than an organization. Pollution, poverty, and economic and political stability are obvious examples. Organizations may respond to such occurrences in many ways. In turbulent conditions that prevail today, the socio-ecological perspective suggests that collaborative arrangements, in which resources can be pooled among dissimilar kinds of organization sharing an environment, may quell turbulence.

The socio-ecological framework of ideas manifests in a number of methodologies referred to in the literature of action research, including active-adaptive planning (Baburoglu, 1992), participative design workshops (Emery, 1989) and search conferences (Emery and Purser, 1996). The process of these methodologies aims to establish a common understanding between participants based on the framework of ideas just introduced.

Greenwood and Levin (1998) rightly point out that there are many interpretations of these methodologies and no one approach is correct. Each one has its own version of the framework of ideas, methodology and action area. Indeed, Greenwood and Levin's mode of operating a search conference suggests something quite different in these three elements than so far discussed. They propose a form of liberating praxis that reflects systemic thinking. Nevertheless, I intend to continue the discussion for now in the mould of systems thinking so that I can illustrate how it has been employed as an approach to action research.

An organization-oriented search conference based on systems thinking typically begins by establishing preliminary boundaries of the system and its environment. This enables things to move forward. Boundaries may be updated at any stage, as understanding of the system becomes clearer. Boundary identification focuses on interrelatedness of actors. A simple 'actor archetype' might include shareholders, employees, suppliers, competitors and governmental agencies. The next step is to articulate lawful relationships between actors in the system, between the system and the environment, and in the environment. Value propositions are formulated. For example, a customer value proposition could focus on price, image and personal relationships (Kaplan and Norton, 1996). A search conference seeks to achieve alignment of value propositions by referencing to ideals through dialogue, but note, this cannot be achieved without first negotiating a clear value set that co-joins actors of the system. The process of discourse about value propositions surfaces things that need attending to and results in solid strategies and action plans.

Although offering an important development in human thought, the concepts and principles of systems thinking as such have been subjected to considerable criticism. The next section very briefly outlines some key questions raised about the validity of systems thinking in social organizational contexts. It sets the context for the emergence of systemic thinking and my subsequent presentation of two main systemic approaches.

Systems Thinking in Social Organizational Contexts

One of the main concerns with systems thinking is that a social model built on biological concepts places too much emphasis on structure and function. (We might exclude here the Emery–Trist paradigm that is based on a contextualist rather than organic root metaphor, where the unit of analysis arguably is 'the historical event', not 'the organism'; see Pepper, 1943.) Very little is said about processes that go on in social affairs, such as cultural activities, political trading and power struggles. Perhaps the biological view offers some contribution in terms of a social arrangement that might be particularly suited to one situation or another. However, there are many alternative views that promise to yield even more insight into social affairs (see Morgan, 1986). That is, there is a wealth of different ways of defining human activity. Many texts have dealt with these and other criticisms of systems thinking (e.g., Checkland, 1981; Jackson, 1991).

Thus, results arising from systems thinking, such as organizational boundaries and purpose, inevitably turn out to be controversial. Choice of the most efficient means to achieve some given end (purpose) will also hit choppy waters. Admittedly, this criticism assumes that systems models are employed as representational tools purporting to represent reality, whereas they could be used as hermeneutic tools in meaning construction. In principle this defence may hold. In practice, however, it has to be said that for as long as people operate with a view of the world, or, in Checkland's terms, an intellectual framework of ideas, in terms of real social systems, systems models are bound to be used as representational tools. The view of the world must change first.

Systems thinking is a most influential mode of thought that today remains the commonly held and much maligned view of what the systems idea has to offer. As we now go on to discover, that view is far from an accurate or fair assessment of what systemic thinking has to offer. With systemic thinking there is growing rejection of the belief in a concrete social world that comprises real social systems, as people come to appreciate a quite different systemic quality to their existence. Writers such as Peter B. Checkland, C. West Churchman, as well as many others, began to argue from a systemic perspective that 'human systems' are different. Checkland (1981), from a soft systems viewpoint, contends that 'human systems' are better understood in terms of emergent systems of meaning people ascribe to the world. Systemic thinking is thus useful in meaning construction. Churchman (1968, 1979), from a critical systemic perspective, pleads that it is not possible to think about 'human systems' as emergent systems of meaning without encountering serious moral dilemmas. To appreciate 'human systems' in action research therefore requires learning and understanding about emergent systems of meaning and moral dilemmas that emerge when they interplay through human interaction. These are important themes that come through with force in the remainder of this chapter.

Soft Systems Thinking

One way of distinguishing systems thinking from systemic thinking is that the former takes an objective stance while the latter assumes a subjective position. Systems thinking is objective in believing that there are systems in the world that can be identified and improved. Systemic thinking is different.

Soft systems thinking is a form of systemic thinking that understands reality as the creative construction of human beings (Jackson, 1991). It sees social reality as the construction of people's interpretation of their experiences. In this way it is firmly linked to interpretive theory. Soft systems thinking therefore generates and works with an evolving appreciation of people's points of view and intentions. Systems concepts are employed in the process of meaning construction, reflecting an intuitive assumption that the world is indeed systemic.

Soft systems thinking is concerned with situations as they are defined through action concepts (Checkland, 1981; Checkland and Scholes, 1990). Its intellectual framework of ideas might be described in the following way. People have intentions that lie behind each action that they perform. Neither observation nor theory provides sufficient understanding to be sure of those intentions, that is, what is happening. For example, a high level of excitement observed in a person's actions might be theorized as threatening or conversely joyous behaviour. It is necessary to progress beyond observation and theory to come up with an 'authentic' explanation about what is going on in the minds of involved people and hence meaningful action that might be taken.

Soft systems thinking argues that a specific action concept becomes transparent only in the deeper context of a certain set of social rules. It is in these terms that an actor can be said to be doing some particular thing. Social rules lead to a social practice, that is, ways in which people live and work together. Lying behind social practice is constitutive meaning. Constitutive meaning 'puts in' meaning to the social practice, since it is the fundamental assumption that underlies what is done and what makes it meaningful. An 'authentic' understanding of people's actions may be constructed in this way.

To get to grips with the whole therefore involves the construction of understanding in terms of constitutive meaning, social practices and actions taken. Systems models or indeed any other model may be employed in heuristic fashion to see if they generate insight and assist in the construction process. With soft systems thinking, however, models must never be taken as representations of reality. Each model is employed like 'a pair of spectacles' through which we can 'look at and interpret reality'. Such interpretive thinking is systemic in outlook, not when it employs systems models, but when it helps all involved to interpret people's lives as an emergent whole by uncovering what is meaningful to them in terms of social rules and practices and underlying constitutive meaning. Of course, the argument goes on to say that systems models are likely to be particularly useful in achieving meaningful understanding.

Furthermore, to achieve a meaningful understanding of any situation, it is necessary both to study the cultural aspects of the context as well as the interpretations and perceptions that people form within the cultural context. Soft systems thinking therefore states that an 'authentic' understanding of any action context requires participation of all stakeholders, that is, all people involved in taking action as well as people affected by those actions. This may be achieved only if people enter into an action context as both an actor and a researcher. Participation of and with stakeholders is a recommendation of soft systems thinking that is also a pillarstone of action research. It is an important example of a deep relationship that exists between systemic thinking and action research.

Soft systems thinking provided the intellectual foundations for a number of methodologies relevant to action research (apart from Checkland's work, see for example Ackoff, 1974, 1981; and Mason and Mitroff, 1981). I have chosen to review soft systems methodology in the next section as an important representative of this tradition.

Soft Systems Methodology

The most thoroughly documented and discussed methodological example of soft systems thinking is soft systems methodology (SSM) (Checkland, 1981; Checkland and Holwell, 1998; Checkland and Scholes, 1990). It is thus an important representative of the soft systems tradition. SSM is normally introduced as a seven-stage process in the fashion rehearsed below.

Stage 1 suggests that a problem situation (the action area) might arise with which a number of people feel uncomfortable. They wish to explore the situation with a view to making some improvement. The problem situation is expressed with Stage 2, attempting to avoid structuring the problem situation that would close down original thinking and hence learning. In Checkland's view, conceiving the problem situation as a system in the manner a search conference would, put structure to thought before learning had had a chance to unfold in a creative fashion. Rich pictures are advocated as one suitable means of expression. They are cartoon type representations that allow people to express their experiences and, as is the case with cartoons, accentuate points that stand out in their minds.

Stage 3 recommends systemic thinking about the real world. The transition to Stage 3 is made by naming possible human activity systems that may offer insight into the problem situation, and may generate debate leading to action to improve the problem situation. A human activity system is a systemic model of the activities people need to undertake in order to pursue a particular purpose. Stage 3 develops root definitions of relevant systems. Root definitions are built around the worldview that states the constitutive meaning underpinning the purpose of a human activity system. The transformation process is then conceptualized. Customers, actors and owners are subsequently named. Environmental constraints are taken into account. Construction of root definitions therefore embraces customers (C), actors (A), transformation processes (T), worldview (W), owners (O), and environmental constraints (E) – that can be recollected with the CATWOE mnemonic.

Stage 4 elaborates on root definitions by drawing up conceptual models. Conceptual models in the first instance are the minimum set of verbs (action concepts) necessary to describe the actions of the human activity system, that was seeded in a relevant system and grown in the root definition. The verbs are ordered systemically, drawing out the feedback loops that describe the interactions of the human activity system. Conceptual models, which are the result of systemic thinking about the real world, are taken into the real world in Stage 5, where they are compared to the problem situation expressed in Stage 2. Debate is generated whereby worldviews inherent in conceptual models are thoroughly questioned and their implications understood. The conceptual model is also employed to surface possible change proposals.

With Stage 6, the change proposals are thought through in two ways. First, the *desirability* of the human activity system captured in the systems model is raised and discussed. Secondly, the issue of *feasibility* is explored in the context of the problem situation, attitudes and political interactions that dominate. Stage 7 seeks to explore possible accommodation between contrasting opinions and interests that surface in the process of SSM. Implementation of agreed upon change proposals gives rise to another problem situation and so the process of SSM continues.

As Checkland's action research programme continued, a maturing appreciation of a framework of ideas, methodology and action area became evident. Checkland and Scholes (1990) separated out two modes of SSM in action. Mode 1 SSM is as just described. It is the explicit application of SSM to guide action research. However, Checkland and Scholes reasoned that practitioners are immersed in an organizational context on a day-by-day basis, and surely could benefit from SSM principles in this greater portion of their working lives? SSM is not just about one-off action research; it may also help people to make sense of the rough and tumble of everyday affairs. If internalized, SSM affords the opportunity for action researchers to reflect on their experiences and to make some sense of them. There is a need for Mode 2 SSM.

Mode 2 SSM is a conceptual framework to be incorporated in everyday thinking. The main feature of Mode 2 SSM is recognition of two equally important strands of analysis – a logic-based stream of analysis and a stream of cultural analysis. The *logic-based* stream of analysis encourages practitioners to investigate the situation they are in, to look for new opportunities, and to seek ways to achieve accommodation between people, thus closing the gap that may exist between them. The stream of *cultural analysis* is an intertwined inquiry into the action research itself. It is both a 'social systems' analysis and a 'political systems' analysis. Three things are focused on. First is the action research itself, exploring the role of the client, problem owners and problem solvers. Secondly, 'social systems' analysis looks at roles, norms and values as they influence behaviour. Thirdly, 'political systems' analysis investigates political interaction, coalitions and the use of power as it makes an influence on decision-making.

Soft systems thinking and methodologies like SSM that are consistent with interpretive thinking have made a considerable contribution to practice. Concerns have been raised, however, that systemic thinking suggests more than just streams of cultural and political analysis. The next section recounts some of the main points that have been raised.

Soft Systems Thinking in Social Organizational Contexts

Soft systems thinking makes a clear break with the idea of systems of structure in the world. Instead, the entire effort becomes a matter of coming to terms through systemic concepts, with meaning construction. In so doing, it confines change in social situations to changing people's worldviews. However, systems thinking may yet have a point to make. A strong case can be made that structures in the world do exist, such as economic and political ones, and that these are responsible for the perpetuation of social arrangements. It may be necessary if change is desired to recognize these structures, and then to transform them in advance of, or at least in conjunction with, changing people's worldviews.

Furthermore, any approach that arguably is embedded in interpretive thinking as its intellectual framework of ideas is in the firing line of criticisms aimed at relativism. That is, if meaning is purely a matter of interpretation, then every viewpoint must be considered equally valid. In that case, exploring worldviews to generate mutual understanding can and perhaps should go on forever. The troubling question that this observation leads to is how then can we move from debate to a pragmatic action research? What seems to be inevitable is that closure of debate leading to action will come from prevailing power structures reflected in the dominant culture of the organizational arena in which debate is undertaken (Jackson, 1991).

Following on, the main criticism of soft systems thinking is that it neglects certain difficulties in achieving open and meaningful debate. Critics note, for example, that SSM has little to say in its principles about knowledge-power and the way that this distorts the outcome of debate (Flood and Jackson, 1991a; Jackson, 1991). Checkland offers some response to the criticism. He recommends 'political systems' analysis as part of the 'cultural stream of analysis'. Still, this adaptation barely touches upon the notion of knowledge-power and social transformation. It fails to acknowledge the full potential of systemic thinking for a liberating praxis. A new approach to systemic thinking called critical systems thinking emerged in the 1980s with these concerns firmly on its agenda.

Critical Systems Thinking

Critical systems thinking (CST) is a term recently established in the systems community that refers to a wide range of research and practice (see Flood and Jackson, 1991a; Flood and Romm, 1996). There is no single approach or set of principles that defines what is CST. However, critical systems thinkers find integrity in their diversity through a number of core commitments. The first of course must be a commitment to *the systems idea*. Ways in which the systems idea is employed in critical systems thinking is multifarious and unravels in the presentation below. Critical systems thinking embraces five other major commitments (Jackson, 1991): critical awareness, social awareness, human emancipation, theoretical complementarity and methodological complementarity.

Critical awareness comes in two forms. The first is by surfacing and questioning assumptions and values inherent in any systems design (e.g., Ulrich, 1983). The second explores the strengths and weaknesses and theoretical underpinnings of systems methodologies and associated methods and techniques (e.g., Flood and Jackson, 1991b).

Social awareness is about appreciation of social rules and practices that make acceptable, or not, modes of practice in society. For example, it recognizes dominance in Western societies of the scientific method and its insistence on learning through generalizations. The cultural mode that is science creates an obstruction to action research and its way of handling learning, which comes by transfer and adaptation of research findings from one context to another.

Human emancipation expresses a concern for people's well-being as well as development of their potential. These two qualities of human existence can become severely restricted in modern-day societies. First, people may feel that they have become instruments of re-engineering in today's drive for efficiency and effectiveness. Secondly, people may feel that there is little meaning to them in participatory work practices when intrapsychic forces (Argyris and Schön, 1996) and cultural forces invisibly shape outcomes. Thirdly, people may sense limits to and unfairness in the roles predefined for them by the might of knowledge-power.

Theoretical complementarity must follow the concerns of human emancipation for two very good reasons. First, critical systems thinking must not itself slip into the knowledge-power trap creating its own conventional wisdom. Secondly, the scope of issues raised in the last paragraph cannot easily be addressed by just one systems approach. The brief critiques of systems thinking and soft systems thinking from earlier in this chapter illustrate that there are limitations to any one framework of ideas. What is required is a complementary and informed development of all varieties of the systems approach (Flood, 1990; Jackson, 1991; Mingers and Gill, 1997).

Methodological complementarity sits side by side with theoretical complementarity. As Checkland (1985) argues, each framework of ideas brings with it methodological principles for action. Critical systems thinking recognizes the need for different sets of methodological principles for each of the three concerns raised above about human emancipation (e.g., Flood and Jackson, 1991b).

Making something of these commitments in the domain of practice presents a considerable challenge. Thankfully, the six commitments of critical systems thinking sit strong in the minds of a community of researchers who continue to explore ways and means of realising the commitments in practice (e.g., see the collection of papers in Mingers and Gill, 1997). I have selected 'total systems intervention' (TSI) as an illustration, in part because I am obviously familiar with it, but also because the approach is well documented, including case studies, and has generated discussion (see Flood, 1995, 1999; Flood and Jackson, 1991b; Flood and Romm, 1996; Jackson, 1991: these references cover a number of interpretations and developments of TSI).

'Total Systems Intervention'

Let me first state that the name 'total systems intervention' (TSI) is unfortunate in every respect in the context of action research. May I simply say that 'local' would be preferable to 'total', 'systemic' to 'systems', and 'action research' to 'intervention'? The name however has stuck and so I will work with it below.

TSI offers an example of a commitment to methodological complementarity. The argument is that there will never be a super methodology capable of addressing all the concerns of human emancipation summarized in the last section. However, prior to TSI, the trend in systems research appeared rather like a search for the super methodology. Arguments on this score ironically fragmented systems research, which otherwise purported to be the science of holism. TSI offered to this debate a new holistic research agenda. The agenda suggests that we accept that there is diversity in the issues and dilemmas that confront decision-makers. Therefore, it makes sense to continue to develop an equally rich variety of methodologies, but it also makes sense to handle them in a systemic fashion. The TSI principle of complementarity demonstrates a commitment to critical awareness and social awareness by continually raising the question, which methodologies should be used, when, and why?

An ideal type categorization is employed by TSI to facilitate critical awareness. The intention of the ideal type is to stimulate debate, to generate insights, and to enhance learning. Debate is encouraged about issues and dilemmas that characterize an action area. At the same time, debate is encouraged about a variety of methodologies and the potential they hold for managing the issues and dilemmas. Insights and learning that are forthcoming enter into a continuous process of unique methodology design. In this way, action researchers learn their way into the future and continually influence how this future might unfold.

Several versions of the ideal type categorization are found in the references already given. The version introduced below comes from Flood (1999). It suggests that organizational life, that is issues and dilemmas and ways of managing them, might be made sense of in terms of the following four categories: systems of processes, of structure, of meaning, and of knowledge-power. The prefix 'systems of' indicates only a desire to be systemic with respect to that category. The four categories help to locate types of issue and dilemma encountered in organizational life as well as methodological principles that might be drawn upon to manage the issues and dilemmas. Systems of processes is a category concerned with efficiency and reliability of flows of events and control over flows of events. Systems of structure is a category concerned with effectiveness of functions, their organization, coordination and control (Stafford Beer's trilogy on organizational cybernetics, surprisingly not yet mentioned, makes an important contribution here: 1979, 1981, 1985). Systems of meaning is a category concerned with people's viewpoints on the meaningfulness to them of improvement strategies, such as improved efficiency and/or effectiveness. Systems of knowledge-power is a category concerned with fairness in terms of entrenched patterns of behaviour where what is said to be valid knowledge and proper action, such as preferred modes of efficiency and effectiveness, is decided by powerful groups.

Methodology design unfolds and subsequent action is then taken, depending on what is learned by employing the ideal type. Methodology design might be based on one or more of the following strategies. If there is inefficiency or unreliability in processes, then action might be taken on the processes. This might take the form of continuous incremental improvement or radical change and quantum improvement. If there is ineffectiveness resulting from an inappropriate structure, then action might be taken in terms of strength of emphasis placed on rules and procedures and ways in which this might shape functions and their organization.

If, on the other hand, people experience a lack of meaningfulness because of disagreement about action required, then steps might be taken to address the disagreement. Disagreement might arise from polarized viewpoints or a plethora of viewpoints, which need to be tackled in different ways. And if people experience unfairness in chosen actions, then there may be a need to do one or both of the following. Steps might be taken to emancipate privileged people from their ideologies and power structures that lead to unfair treatment for less privileged people. Also, steps might be taken to unshackle underprivileged people from dominant ideologies and power structures.

Clearly, if TSI is to be followed, it is important for action researchers to become familiar with a range of methodologies that cover all four categories introduced above. The task is demanding, but the result promises to be rewarding. The outcome is a liberating praxis that takes into account many aspects of human emancipation. That is, people are less confined if actions in which they are involved are efficient rather than inefficient, and effective rather than ineffective. (Consider the frustrations of inefficiency and ineffectiveness in your life.) People are freer if actions that involve them are experienced as meaningful. And people are liberated if forces of knowledge-power are transformed, making for a fairer existence for them.

In summary, the argument of this section is that systemic thinking, when taken to its practical conclusion from a critical systemic perspective, offers to action research a somewhat unique liberating praxis. The liberating praxis, however, will remain a hollow one in the absence of a certain kind of spiritual awareness that is suggested by wholeness.

Beyond Fragmentation

The preceding sections are very much oriented towards an appreciation of systemic thinking in everyday action research. However, when focused on human existence as such, systemic thinking helps people to sense a deep holistic or spiritual quality to human existence. In other words, with systemic thinking we may attain a deeper sense of how we fit in with the scheme of things. C. West Churchman (1982) intuitively sensed this in his writings on systemic thinking, wisdom and hope, that many people have found inspirational. The spiritual quality of systemic thinking, however, became easier to grasp in an everyday sense with the recent materialization of a new form of systemic thinking called complexity theory (e.g., Cilliers, 1998; Coveney and Highfield, 1995; Waldrop, 1992). Complexity theory explains that the vastness of interrelationships and emergence in which people are immersed is beyond our ability to establish full comprehension. Complexity theory thus offers a systemic logic that purports to explain why human understanding will forever be enveloped in mystery. It leads us to know of the unknowable (Flood, 1999). Once this idea is grasped, a systemic appreciation of spiritualism then envelops the entire human experience and consequently everything that happens within that experience, including action research. We can learn more about spiritualism in systemic thinking by revisiting discussions on reductionism.

Reductionism, let us be reminded, advocates analysis of phenomena, which means breaking them down into constituent parts and then studying these simple elements in terms of cause and effect relationships. The reductionist way arguably has demonstrated a relevance to the physical world. That part of the world we know as non-living things to an extent can be learned about in terms of physical relationships of cause and effect. Scientific knowledge of this sort has made possible new ways of living moulded by technological developments in an era of modernization. Science and technology aim to bring things under control, to achieve 'progress', in order to improve the human condition. Some of these developments might well be considered impressive. Yet, 'technological progress' has led to changes in our biological and social behaviour that some people experience as oppressive. For example, it seems that some people are doomed to a life of drudgery as a result of monotonous work in mechanized factories and computerized offices. Oppression of this kind often results from managers' obsession with technology under their control, rather than the technology itself. These technocrats have lost touch with people and this includes their own self. Modern living it turns out has in certain senses led to impoverishment rather than improvement of the human condition.

What this all boils down to, is that science through reductionism has in our minds fragmented the world, our existence, and our thoughts about how we might manage ourselves. The richness and mystique of life and living are deflated to a mental model with an unrealistic and mind-blowing simplicity of the type, 'A caused B'. This alienates so-called parts, for example you and me, from patterns and rhythms of life in which we participate. It separates so-called 'problems', apparently caused by you or me, from the complex dynamics of each unique context. As a result we become subjects of language and observations like, 'I know that you caused this problem'. People are blamed in this way and are then found guilty in the kangaroo court of reductionism. Meanwhile, the blame mentality is further consolidated in NIMO denial, that is, 'the cause of that problem was Not In My Office'. People, especially those with formal power, find it convenient to detach themselves from patterns of interrelationships and emerging 'problems' to which they in fact have a systemic relationship and moral responsibility (people in power can decide what happens to other people). Reductionism, so the argument goes, leaves people out of touch with their own self, other people, and indeed any sense of the human spirit.

A systemic view may assist in healing people from this kind of wretched alienation (Reason, 1994). A systemic view recognizes a spiritual quality that modern living lacks. In its essence, a deep systemic view pictures each person's life as a flash of consciousness, in existence, and of existence. What a person is, is what everything else is. Thus, a person looking out at the world is in a sense the world looking at itself. Such a view leads to a perception of wholeness, not of individuals and objects. Yet, wholeness cannot easily be analysed and then logically explained because, taking our definition of analysis from the Introduction, that involves reduction, which of course will denature any sense we have of wholeness. Very quickly we will lose touch with wholeness in a trivialized account of its assumed-to-be-properties. So, let us just say that wholeness begins with an intuitive grasp of existence reflected in the words of this paragraph and take things from there.

A most convincing intuitive grasp of existence and hence wholeness is located in the opening chapter of Peter Reason's *Participation In Human Inquiry* (1994). Reason captures the reader's attention using as a backdrop Thomas Berry's *The Dream of the Earth* (1988). Berry, we are shown, writes of a systemic existence in a mood of spiritualism as he observes that, 'we bear the universe in our being as the universe bears us in its being' (1988: 132). Berry remarks that, 'the two have a total presence to each other and to that deeper mystery out of which the universe and our selves have emerged' (1988: 132). Reason enriches the scene as he observes that the human race is indeed no alien species suddenly transported to this universe and deposited on Earth. In a quite literal sense, human beings come from Earth. Because of this, he observes, 'phenomena as wholes never can be fully known for the very reason that we are part of them, leading us to acknowledge and respect the great mystery that envelops our knowing' (1994: 13). In other words, not only might you and I know of ourselves and the world in terms of wholeness, but also, our grasp of wholeness will be bounded, partial and subjective. For that reason our lives forever will be shrouded in mystery.

Therefore, seeking absolute mastery over our lives as science and technology do, misses the point of wholeness and takes away our human spirit. It turns the magic of mystery in our lives into the misery of failed mastery over our lives. The point is that complexity emerges in our lives over which the human mind is no master. In fact, the human mind is both the creator and the subject of complexity, not an externally appointed master over it and all its parts. That is why it makes no sense to separate action from research in our minds or in our practice.

So, there is a need in everyday living and at work to maintain a balance between mystery and mastery. This entails operating somewhere between the hopelessness of the belief that we are unable to understand anything and, at the other extreme, the naiveté of the belief that we can know everything. Balancing mystery with mastery means to know of, yet to learn and act within, the unknowable that is wholeness (Flood, 1999). And here, with these words, I finally locate what I believe to be the conceptual convergence of systemic thinking and action research. It is through systemic thinking that we know of the unknowable. It is with action research that we learn and may act meaningfully within the unknowable. Where these two arcs of reasoning converge, we witness the incredible genesis of a conceptual universe that opens up otherwise unimaginable ways in which people may live their lives in a more meaningful and fulfilling manner.

I will now briefly round off this chapter.

Conclusion

Systemic thinking is a mode of thinking that keeps people in touch with the wholeness of our existence. It helps to keep in mind that human thought is not capable of knowing the whole, but it is capable of 'knowing that we don't know'. This is a pretty significant step forward in human understanding. Such recognition spotlights the futility, let alone the hostility, of traditional forms of practice based on prediction and control, which are so prominent in today's social organizational arrangements. It is futile because any social dynamic will always remain beyond control. It is hostile because it attacks people's spiritual well-being by isolating us and treating us as separate objects, rather than appreciating patterns of relationship that join us all together in one dynamic.

Systemic thinking clarifies these and other matters. However, systemic thinking is not an approach to action research, but a grounding for action research that may broaden action and deepen research. That is, action research carried out with a systemic perspective in mind promises to construct meaning that resonates strongly with our experiences within a profoundly systemic world. If systemic thinking delivers on this promise, then people may at last sense of our existence on Earth that we belong here, together, perhaps not in idyllic harmony, but at least with thoughtful tolerance.

Note

The section on the 'socio-ecological perspective' benefits from unpublished notes provided by, and subsequent communications with, John Barton and John Selsky. It also takes into account ideas that developed at a round table discussion held in July 1999 between myself, Merrelyn Emery and Eric Wolstenholme, a video of which is available from the Department of Management at Monash University, Australia.

References

Ackoff, R.L. (1974) *Redesigning the Future*. New York: Wiley.

Ackoff, R.L. (1981) *Creating the Corporate Future*. New York: Wiley.

Argyris, C. and Schön, D. (1996) *Organisational Learning II*. New York: Addison Wesley.

Atthill, C. (1975) *Decisions: West Oil Distribution*. London: BP Educational Services.

Baburoglu, O. (1992) 'Tracking the development of the Emery–Trist systems paradigm', *Systems Practice*, 5: 263–90.

Barton, J. and Selsky, J. (1998) *An Open-systems Perspective on Urban Ports: an Exploratory Comparative Analysis*. Working Paper 78/98. Melbourne: Monash University.

Bateson, G. (1973) *Steps to an Ecology of Mind*. St Albans: Granada.

Bateson, G. (1979) *Mind and Nature: a Necessary Unity*. New York: Dutton.

Beer, S. (1979) *Heart of the Enterprise*. Chichester: Wiley.
Beer, S. (1981) *Brain of the Firm*. Chichester: Wiley.
Beer, S. (1985) *Diagnosing the System for Organisation*. Chichester: Wiley.
Berry, T. (1988) *The Dream of the Earth*. San Francisco, CA: Sierra Club.
Bertalanffy, L. von (1950) 'The theory of open systems in physics and biology', *Science*, 11: 23–9.
Bertalanffy, L. von (1956) 'General Systems Theory', *General Systems*, 1: 1–10.
Bertalanffy, L. von (1981) *A Systems View of Man: Collected Essays*. Violette, P.A. (ed.). Boulder, CO: Westview Press.
Checkland, P.B. (1981) *Systems Thinking, Systems Practice*. Chichester: Wiley.
Checkland, P.B. (1985) 'From optimising to learning: a development of systems thinking for the 1990s', *Journal of the Operational Research Society*, 36: 757–67.
Checkland, P.B. and Holwell, S. (1998) *Information, Systems, and Information Systems*. Chichester: Wiley.
Checkland, P.B. and Scholes, J. (1990) *Soft Systems Methodology in Action*. Chichester: Wiley.
Churchman, C. West (1968) *The Systems Approach*. New York: Delta.
Churchman, C. West (1979) *The Systems Approach and its Enemies*. New York: Basic Books.
Churchman, C. West (1982) *Thought and Wisdom*. Seaside, CA: Intersystems.
Cilliers, P. (1998) *Complexity and Postmodernism: Understanding Complex Systems*. London: Routledge.
Coveney, P. and Highfield, R. (1995) *Frontiers of Complexity Theory*. London: Faber and Faber.
Emery, F.E. (ed.) (1981) *Systems Thinking* (2 vols). Harmondsworth: Penguin.
Emery, F.E. and Trist, E. (1965) 'The causal texture of organisational environments', *Human Relations*, 18: 21–32.
Emery, M. (ed.) (1989) *Participative Design for Participative Democracy*. Canberra: Australian National University.
Emery, M. and Purser, R (1996) *The Search Conference*. San Francisco, CA: Jossey-Bass.
Flood, R.L. (1990) *Liberating Systems Theory*. New York: Plenum.
Flood, R.L. (1995) *Solving Problem Solving*. Chichester: Wiley.
Flood, R.L. (1999) *Rethinking the Fifth Discipline: Learning within the Unknowable*. London: Routledge.
Flood, R.L. and Jackson, M.C. (eds) (1991a) *Critical Systems Thinking: Directed Readings*. Chichester: Wiley.
Flood, R.L. and Jackson, M.C. (1991b) *Creative Problem Solving: Total Systems Intervention*. Chichester: Wiley.
Flood, R.L. and Romm, N.R.A. (eds) (1996) *Critical Systems Thinking: Current Research and Practice*. New York: Plenum.
Forrester, J.W. (1961) *Industrial Dynamics*. Cambridge, MA: MIT Press.
Forrester, J.W. (1968) *Principles of Systems*. Cambridge, MA: MIT Press.
Forrester, J.W. (1969) *Urban Dynamics*. Cambridge, MA: MIT Press.
Forrester, J.W. (1971) *World Dynamics*. Cambridge, MA: MIT Press.
Greenwood, D. and Levin, M. (1998) *Introduction to Action Research*. Thousand Oaks, CA: Sage Publications.
Jackson, M.C. (1991) *Systems Methodology for the Management Sciences*. New York: Plenum.
Jenkins, G.M. (1969) 'The systems approach', in J. Beishon and G. Peters (eds), *Systems Behavior*. New York: Harper and Row. pp. 78–104.
Kaplan, R.S. and Norton, D.P. (1996) *The Balanced Scorecard*. Boston, MA: Harvard Business School Press.
Kim, D.H. (1993) *Systems Archetypes: Diagnosing Systemic Issues and Designing High Leverage Interventions*. Cambridge, MA: Pegasus Communications.
Lewin, K. (1948) *Resolving Social Conflicts*. New York: Harper.
Mason, R.O. and Mitroff, I.I. (1981) *Challenging Strategic Planning Assumptions*. New York: Wiley.
Meadows, D.M., Meadows, D.L. and Randers, J. (1972) *Limits to Growth*. New York: Universe Books.
Mingers, J. and Gill, T. (1997) *Multimethodology*. Chichester: Wiley.
Morgan, G. (1986) *Images of Organisation*. Beverly Hills, CA: Sage Publications.
M'Pherson, P.K. (1981) 'A framework for systems engineering design', *Radio and Electronic Engineer*, 51: 59–93.
Pepper, S.C. (1943) *World Hypotheses*. Los Angeles, CA: University of California Press.
Reason, P. (ed.) (1994) *Participation in Human Inquiry*. London: Sage Publications.
Richardson, G.P. (1991) *Feedback Thought in Social Science and Systems Theory*. Philadelphia, PA: University of Pennsylvania Press.
Senge, P. (1990) *The Fifth Discipline*. New York: Doubleday.
Senge, P., Kleiner, A., Roberts, C., Ross R.B. and Smith B.J. (1994) *The Fifth Discipline Fieldbook*. London: Nicholas Brealey.
Trist, E. and Bamforth, K.W. (1951) 'Some social and psychological consequences of the Longwall Method of coal-getting', *Human Relations*, 4: 3–38.
Trist, E., Emery, F. and Murray, H. (1997) *The Social Engagement of Social Science – a Tavistock Anthology. Vol. III: The Socio-Ecological Perspective*. Philadelphia, PA: University of Pennsylvania Press.
Ulrich, W. (1983) *Critical Heuristics of Social Planning*. Berne: Haupt.
Waldrop, M.M. (1992) *Complexity: the Emerging Science at the Edge of Order and Chaos*. London: Viking.
Wolstenholme, E.F. (1990) *System Enquiry: a System Dynamics Approach*. Chichester: Wiley.

PART TWO

PRACTICES

11
Action Science: Creating Communities of Inquiry in Communities of Practice

VICTOR J. FRIEDMAN

CHAPTER OUTLINE

Action science is an approach to action research which attempts to bridge the gap between social research and social practice by building theories which explain social phenomena, inform practice and adhere to the fundamental criteria of a science. The chapter identifies and describes four distinguishing features of action science: creating a community of inquiry within a community of practice; building theories in practice; combining interpretation with rigorous testing; and creating alternatives to the status quo and informing change in light of values freely chosen by social actors.

The objective of this chapter is to provide researchers and practitioners with a concise introduction to 'action science', an approach to action research which integrates practical problem-solving with theory-building and change (Argyris, Putnam and Smith, 1985: x). This approach was first set forth by Chris Argyris, Robert Putnam and Diana Smith in order to articulate 'the features of a science that can generate knowledge that is useful, valid, descriptive of the world, and informative of how we might change it' (1985: x). Although action science has been cited as one of the most popular 'action technologies' in use today (Raelin, 1997), it has also been cited as being difficult to understand and to practise (Edmundson, 1996: 586; Raelin, 1997). As a student of Argyris, who was present at the birth of action science and participated in the seminar described by Argyris, Putnam and Smith (1985), my own understanding of action science emerged very gradually through 15 years of experimentation and reflection. In that sense this chapter represents an interpretation of action science filtered through my own personal experience.

The chapter begins with a definition of action science and a brief discussion of the problem action science is meant to address. It then presents four main features of action science and illustrates them through a case study. The chapter concludes with a discussion of barriers to the practice of action science and how they may be overcome.

What is Action Science?

It is difficult to find a single, comprehensive definition of action science in the literature. However, a fairly good picture can be constructed from the following quotations:

> Action science is an inquiry into social practice, broadly defined, and it is interested in producing knowledge in the service of such practice. (Argyris et al., 1985: 232) The action scientist is an interventionist who seeks both to promote learning in the client system and to contribute to general knowledge. (Argyris et al., 1985: 36)

> An action science would concern itself with situations of uniqueness, uncertainty, and instability which do not lend themselves to the application of theories and techniques derived from science in the mode of technical rationality. It would aim at developing themes from which, in these sorts of situations, practitioners may construct theories and methods of their own. (Schön, 1983: 319)

> [Action science] focuses on creating conditions of collaborative inquiry in which people in organizations function as co-researchers rather than as subjects. (Argyris and Schön, 1996: 50)

From these quotations it is possible to define action science as *a form of social practice which integrates both the production and use of knowledge for the purpose of promoting learning with and among individuals and systems whose work is characterized by uniqueness, uncertainty and instability.*

The Gap between Social Science and Social Practice

Action science attempts to address the widening gap between social science theory/research and social science-based professional practice. Schön (1983, 1987) described this gap as the 'rigor vs. relevance' dilemma, in which both practitioners and researchers face the choice between remaining 'on the high ground where [they] can solve relatively unimportant problems according to prevailing standards of rigor or ... descend to the swamp of important problems and nonrigorous inquiry' (1987: 3). Schön (1983, 1987) attributed this dilemma to the dominance of the 'technical rationality' model, according to which pure science produces basic knowledge (theory) which applied science uses to create techniques (technology) for solving real-world problems. These two kinds of science make up the fundamental knowledge-base of practitioners, who receive their training through professional education.

Technical rationality has worked extremely well in engineering and medicine, but not in social work, education, psychotherapy, policy, urban planning and management (Schön, 1983, 1987). Effective practice in these fields is often attributed to intuition and personal attributes rather than the skilful application of scientific knowledge. As a result, the gap between theory and practice is often accepted as the natural state of affairs. According to the action science account, there is nothing natural about this gap. Rather, the problem stems from features of mainstream, or 'positivist', social science which render the knowledge it produces of limited use to practitioners (Argyris et al., 1985).

These features of positivist science include the requirement for completeness and precision, for observing causal relations under conditions of control, for maintaining distance as an important safeguard of objectivity, and a focus on means rather than ends. They produce theories that are too complex to be used by practitioners who must function in real time (Argyris et al., 1985: 41–3) and are difficult to reproduce in practice situations where all the variables are changing at once (Argyris, 1980). They also introduce threats to validity such as distortion, withholding of information and defensiveness (Argyris et al., 1985: 61), and prevent social science from addressing goal and value problems which are of central importance to social practice (Argyris et al., 1985; Schön, 1983, 1987). Thus, the rules that produce valid positivist explanations of social problems cannot produce the knowledge needed to do something about them. Applied science fails to bridge this gap because it functions according to the same positivist rules and standards as basic science.

From the perspective of action science, phenomenological and interpretive research methods offer a useful approach to practitioners who require theories which explain problems within the context of particular settings and systems of meaning. The problem with this approach, however, is that there is no technical or rational way of coming to agreement over the validity of different interpretations (Argyris et al., 1985: 26–8). Practitioners must act and action requires making choices among different interpretations of a particular situation (Keeley, 1984).

Key Features of Action Science

'Action science' attempts to bridge the gap between social research and social practice by building theories which explain social phenomena, inform practice, and adhere to the fundamental criteria of a science. Argyris, Putnam and Smith (1985) discussed in great depth action science and its philosophical underpinnings; the following discussion identifies what I consider to be its four key distinguishing features.

Creating communities of inquiry within communities of practice. According to action science, there need be no division of labour between those who produce knowledge (i.e., scientists) and those who use it (i.e., practitioners). The role of the researcher is to create conditions under which practitioners (e.g., teachers and/or schools, social workers and/or social welfare agencies, managers and/or organizations) can build and test 'theories of practice' (defined below) for the purpose of learning. Thus, the goal of action science is research *in* practice, not research on practice. Argyris, Putnam and Smith expressed this integration as the creation of 'communities of inquiry in communities of social practice' (1985: 34). They defined a community of practice as professionals – such as engineers, physicians, teachers, psychotherapists, managers, social workers, scientists – who share a common 'language of practice' learned in the course of their education and apprenticeship (1985: 30). The term language is used here both literally and figuratively to represent a set of values, knowledge, terminology and procedures through which members of the community frame practice problems and connect them to a range of acceptable solutions. The common language constitutes the boundary of a particular community of practice, making action intelligible and acceptable to members of the community, but not necessarily to outsiders. Science represents a 'community of inquiry' – a special kind of community of practice whose central activity is the creation of knowledge (Argyris et al., 1985: 29).

The goal of action science inquiry is to help practitioners discover the tacit choices they have made about their perceptions of reality, about their goals and about their strategies for achieving them. The fundamental assumption of action science is that by gaining access to these choices, people can achieve greater control over their own fate (Argyris et al., 1985). If people can find the sources of ineffectiveness in their own reasoning and behaviour, or their own causal responsibility, they then possess some leverage for producing change. Data are collected first and foremost for the purpose of helping people understand and solve practice problems of concern to them.

Creating communities of inquiry within communities of practice means that both researchers and practitioners must redefine their roles and develop a set of common values, norms, terminology and procedures. Practitioners are not simply problem-solvers, but also researchers committed to critically examining their practice. Action scientists not only study social phenomena, but also critically inquire into their own scientific practice. They need to be able to acknowledge and correct their own errors and to model skills of public reflection.

Building 'theories in practice'. Action science assumes that human beings are theory-builders who mentally 'construct' theories of reality, which they continually test through action (Argyris and Schön, 1974; Dewey, 1966; Friedman and Lipshitz, 1992; Senge, 1990). The difference between researchers and practitioners is that the former are 'explicit' theoreticians whereas the latter are 'tacit' theoreticians. The objective of action science is to make these tacit theories explicit so that they can be critically examined and changed.

The basic building blocks of action science are 'theories of action' (Argyris and Schön, 1974, 1978) which take the following form:

1 in situation X (conditions)
2 then do Z (strategy)
3 to achieve Y (goal)

Theories of action can be used as a tool for analysing and representing the rules underlying observed behaviour. According to Argyris and Schön (1974, 1978), human behaviour is *guided* by theories of action which people hold in their minds. Groups and organizations also possess theories of action for accomplishing their tasks and for solving problems. However, people and organizations are often unaware of the theories that drive their behaviour (Argyris and Schön, 1974, 1978, 1996). Thus, action science aims at helping practitioners infer theories of action from observed behaviour so they can be critically examined and changed.

A theory in practice consists of a set of interrelated theories of action for dealing with problems typical to practice situations. The work of action science involves constructing and testing theories in practice by inquiring into the actors' behaviour and the reasoning behind it:

- How do actors perceive the situation or the problem?
- What results do they wish to achieve (i.e., objectives)?
- What strategies do they intend to use in order to achieve these objectives?
- What strategies do they actually produce in action?
- What were the actual outcomes of these strategies?
- To the extent that these outcomes were unintended (i.e., did not match the desired results), what might account for this mismatch?

This line of inquiry can yield detailed, context-rich theories in practice which reflect recurrent patterns of individual and/or organizational behaviour. Theories in practice predict that actors will employ the same strategies whenever they are trying to reach given goals under similar sets of conditions. These patterns can be graphically illustrated in the form of 'maps' (e.g., Argyris and Schön, 1978; Argyris et al., 1985; Friedman and Lipshitz, 1994; Weick and Bougon, 1986). In the case study cited later in this chapter such a map is used to illustrate the interaction of two generic theories of action for dealing with conflict in a particular organization and how this interaction made the conflict particularly intractable.

Argyris and Schön (1974, 1978, 1996) observed that all problem-solving behaviour in situations involving ambiguous information and psychological threat could be reduced to a limited number of patterns or strategies. They explained these patterns by positing the existence of an underlying, universal theory of action which aims at maximizing unilateral control, protection of self and others, and rationality (Argyris and Schön, 1974, 1978, 1996). This theory of action, which they called 'Model I', accounts for much individual and organizational ineffectiveness and lack of learning. In order to facilitate learning, Argyris and Schön (1974, 1978, 1996) proposed 'Model II', a theory of action aimed at maximizing valid information, free and informed choice and internal commitment.

Combining interpretation with 'rigorous' testing. Action science attempts to integrate the descriptive, context-rich power of the interpretive approach with the rigorous testing of validity demanded by the positivist mainstream (Argyris et al., 1985: 54). In this sense it strives to produce what Argyris, Putnam and Smith defined as the 'core features of science': 'hard (directly observable) data, explicit inferences connecting data and theory, empirically disconfirmable propositions subject to public testing, and theory that organizes such propositions' (1985: 12).

Action science addresses the problem of multiple interpretations by requiring both practitioners and researchers to make their own interpretation processes explicit and open to public (intersubjective) testing. Theories in practice are empirically tested in the action context. For example, Argyris and Schön (1974) made a critical distinction between 'espoused theories' and 'theories-in-use'. Espoused theories represent what actors say or think they do. Theories-in-use are inferred from observed behaviour. Espoused theories can be tested by (1) asking practitioners to articulate what they intend to do in particular situations in order to achieve their desired outcomes, (2) asking them to 'produce' their theories by actually taking action either in real situations or through role plays or simulations, and (3) observing what behaviour they actually produce and what outcomes result. An espoused theory is 'disconfirmed' when actors produce unintended behaviours or unintended outcomes. When theories of action are made explicit they can be used to predict the behaviour that should result if all of the conditions of the theory hold true. If predictions are not realized, then the theory can be said to be disconfirmed and the action scientist needs to return to the data in order to come up with a more valid explanation.

Action science addresses the problem of multiple interpretations by asking people to reflect critically on their own reasoning processes. Since action science assumes that people act upon the basis of reality images which they themselves construct, no one can claim ultimate, unmediated knowledge of 'reality' (Berger and Luckmann, 1966; Friedman and Lipshitz, 1992). Rather what people 'know' should be regarded as hypotheses about reality rather than as facts. Thus, when people disagree about their interpretations of a situation, they can engage in the process of jointly testing their reality images.

Action science uses a metaphor called the 'ladder of inference' as a means of addressing the problem of testing (Argyris et al., 1985: 57). This metaphor posits that people construct their reality images through a series of inferences made from observed phenomena. This construction process begins at the bottom of the ladder with the most concrete, directly observable data (e.g., the words that were actually spoken) and a literal interpretation of the data. It then builds to ever-increasing levels of abstraction such as attributions and evaluations, and finally theories of these phenomena.

People who disagree about the meaning of an event can 'go down the ladder' until they discover the point where their interpretations diverged and then inquire into what led to the divergence. They can ask themselves how their interpretations are connected to the directly observable data. In the process they may discover considerable gaps between the observable data and the inferences that were drawn from the data. They may also discover that some of their inferences were unreasonable or that other inferences make more sense. They may also reveal assumptions of which they were unaware and, if tested, could change the meaning of the phenomena. Finally they may seek additional data that could disconfirm one, or both, of the interpretations.

The point of testing is not to get down to the 'facts' but to move from more abstract interpretations to more concrete (i.e., 'directly observable') interpretations. This process can never guarantee that observers will agree or arrive at the 'right' interpretation. However, the ladder of inference represents a method for determining that some interpretations are more reasonable than others (Weick, 1979).

Action science strives to enact an approach to testing consistent with Popper's (1959) idea of 'falsifiability' (Argyris, 1993: 284). It assumes that all knowledge of reality is partial and indeterminate. Theories in practice can never be 'proven', but they can be maintained as long as they withstand disconfirmation. Thus, action science testing depends largely on the participants' willingness and ability to formulate their claims in ways which leave them open to being proven wrong. Furthermore, they need to be strongly motivated, even passionate, about seeking out information which can lead to disconfirmation (Argyris, 1993: 284). Model II values are important because striving for disconfirmation goes against the desire to prove oneself right and to stay in control. In mainstream science, 'rigour' in testing can be achieved through the use of clearly defined procedures. From an action science perspective, however, rigour requires behaving as if discovering one's own errors were more important than 'winning'.

Creating alternatives to the status quo and informing change in light of values freely chosen by social actors. Action science takes a particular interest in the more intractable conflicts and difficult dilemmas faced by social practitioners. It explicitly aims at helping practitioners change systems and 'transform their world' (Argyris et al., 1985: 71). As opposed to social engineering, which applies scientifically-based solutions to particular problems, action science is a form of ongoing social *experimentation* (Schön, Drake and Miller, 1984). It claims no a priori solutions but does lay claim to procedures for discovering or inventing them. Changing the status quo not only serves social ends but also knowledge production, following in the tradition of action research (Lewin, 1948, 1951).

From an action science perspective the meaning of change is more closely associated with a never-ending process of learning and movement rather than in achieving new equilibria or 'stable states' (Schön, 1971). In doing so it draws on Dewey's (1938) concept of inquiry:

> [Inquiry is] the intertwining of thought and action that proceeds from doubt to the resolution of doubt. (Argyris and Schön, 1996: 11)

> [Dewey] thought that inquiry begins with an indeterminate, problematic situation, a situation whose inherent conflict, obscurity, or confusion blocks action. And the inquirer seeks to make that situation determinate, thereby restoring the flow of activity. (Argyris and Schön, 1996: 31–2)

As indicated above, doubt is the experience of being blocked or stuck. The resolution of doubt means more than helping practitioners understand why they are ineffective or why systems cannot change. Rather it means enabling them to take action which moves them closer to their goals or to changing their goals.

Action science takes into account the fact that people tend to avoid doubt by systematically making themselves unaware of inconsistencies in their own behaviour (Argyris, 1982, 1990; Argyris and Schön, 1974, 1978, 1996; Kelly, 1971). Therefore, action scientists consciously attempt to induce doubt as a stimulus for change by making people aware of gaps, contradictions and errors in their reasoning and behaviour. For example, the point of testing espoused theories in action is not to 'catch' people in their inconsistencies, to show them that they are Model I, or to prove that one interpretation is right and the other wrong. Rather, it is intended to bring into awareness gaps and contradictions that may lead them to experience doubt and, as a result, engage in inquiry. Essentially the role of the action scientist is to identify practice 'puzzles' and help practitioners probe deeply (i.e., inquire) into their reasoning and behaviour in order to make sense of them.

Change can stem from any one of the three components of a theory of action: initial conditions, strategy, goals. According to Argyris and Schön (1974), the easiest and most common changes occur at the level of strategies or 'single-loop learning'. Upon discovering error, individuals or organizations try different ways of achieving their goals in a given situation. However, simply changing strategies is often insufficient for solving more intractable problems and dilemmas and may even make the situation worse. Under these conditions the action scientist looks at altering actors' reality images, assumptions, goals and/or values. Change at this level has been called 'double-loop learning' (Argyris and Schön, 1974).

Action science treats 'the intelligent choice of ends' as well as means as objects of inquiry, especially in the face of intractable conflicts and dilemmas (Argyris et al., 1985: 70). In making choices about goals and values explicit, action science not only helps practitioners clarify what they wish to achieve, but also leads them to question why they hold these goals/values and why they are important (Rothman, 1997).

Exposing goals and values to inquiry involves serious risk because actors may not be able to resolve the conflicts that emerge. Action science proposes that discourse based on Model II values enables people both to act on the basis of deeply held beliefs and to expose those beliefs to doubt, thus avoiding the imposition of absolute values or giving in to an extreme relativism.

An Illustration of Action Science: the Case of Open House

The previous section identified the four distinguishing features of action science: creating community of inquiry within a community of practice, building theories in practice, combining interpretation with testing, and changing the status quo. The following section presents a case study to illustrate these features. This case study involves an organizational conflict in which the author played the role of outside consultant.

The conflict took place at Open House (a pseudonym), which described itself as a 'politically alternative volunteer organization within the community health system'. Located in a large American city, it was founded in the 1960s by a minister who opened his home to young people who had taken to the streets and were in physical or emotional stress. The minister eventually recruited volunteers to provide counselling services and later initiated one of the first 'hotlines' in the USA. In the early 1970s Open House moved to its own building and developed an ambulance service, a drop-in counselling centre, and a day centre for the homeless. Since the Open House ideology held that a caring nonprofessional was preferable to professional services, all services were provided free-of-charge by approximately 100 volunteers.

The organization was administered by a small, poorly paid staff, consisting of the director, the fundraiser, the business manager, an administrative assistant, and three service co-ordinators. All but one of them began as volunteers before assuming staff positions and they continued to work as volunteers. None of them considered themselves professional managers but rather saw their management role as a service to the organization. The staff reported to the 'Steering Committee' which was meant to be the highest governing body, representing the entire organization. Every volunteer was free to attend steering committee meetings, raise an issue, question a decision of the staff, and vote. There was a great deal of warmth and friendship among the volunteers and staff, who all referred to Open House as 'the community'.

In the fall of 1983 I was invited into the organization to help them deal with a series of conflicts among the staff. The staff functioned according to a norm of consensual decision-making, so when conflicts went unresolved, decisions were not made. My interventions consisted mostly of on-line attempts to help the staff confront each other's behaviour and to communicate more effectively. I provided training in basic theory of action concepts such as the ladder of inference, testing and Model II (Argyris, 1982; Argyris and Schön, 1974). At first these interventions succeeded in de-escalating conflicts and seemed to generate progress towards better working relationships. The explosion, however, came about a year after my entry into the organization when the three service co-ordinators issued a written 'warning' to the director. They criticized him for 'lack of foresight and ability to plan ahead, a lack of attention to the internal workings of the organization, and an inability to work as a member of a consensual collective'. The warning demanded 'a demonstration of ... more familiarity with all of the aspects of the organization' as well as 'respect and support for the staff and their knowledge and opinions'. This document was presented to the Steering Committee and openly posted in the organization.

The director was taken completely by surprise and issued a written response condemning this 'trial by public accusation as unjust, invalid, and shameful', arguing that these charges 'were presented as if their truth had been established' and that 'little interest was shown at the Steering Committee in [their] content or accuracy'. He expressed his feelings of deep 'personal hurt and insult', saying that the service co-ordinators had chosen 'to destroy the trust we had painstakingly built up over the course of months of dialogue'. Furthermore, he expressed sadness that they had acted 'in a way so contrary to and destructive of the "humane" spirit of Open House'.

This incident left the entire staff angry, but also deeply shaken and feeling trapped in a dynamic which seemed impossible to stop. I too was shaken by this incident, which took me completely by surprise and which cast doubt on the value of the work done so far. It convinced me that the solution could no longer be framed in terms of improving communication and building trust at the interpersonal level. In subsequent meetings, I began to explore together with the staff what other factors might be driving the conflict.

One issue that emerged was the relationship between mistrust and the high degree of ambiguity about authority throughout the organization. The director wanted to act relatively autonomously on matters he considered important without the service co-ordinators looking over his shoulder. Because his role and his authority were ill-defined, however, it was almost impossible for him to carve out an area of autonomy. The service co-ordinators interpreted his attempts to act autonomously as acting unilaterally (i.e., he does what he wants even when the staff has decided upon something else), which led to mistrust and increased surveillance.

Upon deeper inquiry, it became clear that a similar dynamic occurred in the relationship between the staff and the volunteers. Although the staff espoused participative values, volunteers were generally uninvolved in governance and the staff enjoyed its autonomy. Occasionally, however, volunteers strongly objected to a staff decision and tried to have it overturned. In order to protect its autonomy the staff tended to restrict the flow of information, which eventually led to suspicion and mistrust on the part of some volunteers.

Another discovery was that the interpersonal conflicts reflected a conflict between two sub-groups in the staff. On almost every issue the staff split between the director, fundraiser and business manager on one side and the service co-ordinators on the other. One of the service co-ordinators pointed to a fundamental 'difference in philosophies' between the director and herself (and the other service co-ordinators). The service co-ordinators believed that the primary mission of the organization was to offer an alternative to the established social service system. According to this perspective, every facet of organizational life – service, governance, fundraising, decision-making, etc. – should reflect the organization's values and ideology. The other staff members maintained that the primary objective of the organization was providing social services to inadequately served populations. According to this perspective, co-operating with the establishment in order to obtain resources for survival was more important than maintaining ideological purity. I termed the former group 'alternativists' and the latter group 'pragmatists'.

Making these two perspectives explicit provided a new frame through which the staff could view the conflict. They could see that it involved a deeper substantive issue and that there was a degree of validity in each other's perspective. These insights provided an avenue for further inquiry by focusing on two central puzzles: What accounted for the split in these two 'philosophical' camps? What led this conflict to escalate and become so difficult for staff members to manage?

The solution to these puzzles emerged from discussions with former volunteers who recalled that a similar 'alternativist' and 'pragmatist' split had occurred among them even though the personalities and the specific issues were completely different. Through discussions with veteran volunteers, I was able to piece together what appeared to be a cycle of conflict that repeated itself at least over the two previous 'generations' of staff and was manifesting itself again.

The cycle began with a major organizational crisis which left the organization with a leadership vacuum. In order to prevent the organization from collapsing, volunteers stepped forward to assume staff positions. Because they had no management experience and received almost no guidance from their predecessors, the new staff had to define their own roles and learn how to perform them. At some point staff members began experiencing conflict around pragmatist– alternativist lines, which was not something they had experienced as volunteers in the organization. As it became increasingly difficult for them to come to consensus, these conflicts escalated, increasing interpersonal tensions and frustration. Eventually an issue would arise that caused the conflict to spill over into the organization as a whole, where it was even more difficult to arrive at consensus. Finally the staff cohort dissolved, either through schism or burnout, and the cycle repeated itself. The traumatic circumstances of the staff transitions diminished the chance of learning from past experience, reinforcing the high degree of ambiguity around role and authority.

About a year after the 'warning' I was able to put all of these pieces of the puzzle together into a comprehensive 'causal map' of the conflict (see Figure 11.1):

- *Initial conditions*. The environmental, structural and cultural conditions which the staff regarded as the main givens of their situation.
- *Primary interface*. The different staff roles which emerged as a central determinant of the pragmatist–alternativist split.
- *Worldviews*. Each side's understanding of the organization's identity, goals and their preferred ways of working.
- *Choice points*. Specific decisions which became the focus for a clash between worldviews.
- *Strategies*. The way each side framed the problem and advocated its position.
- *Perceptions*. Each side's evaluation of the other's behaviour and motivations.
- *Short-term consequences*. Similar consequences for both sides, including each side's blindness of its impact on the other. These consequences also reinforced the initial conditions, strategies and perceptions (or at least left them unchanged).
- *Second-order strategies*. Each side's way of dealing with the conflict that had been created.
- *Second-order perceptions*. Each side's increasingly negative evaluation of the other.
- *Middle-term consequences*. Common, highly negative consequences for both sides which created a feedback loop of escalation and polarization.
- *Long-term consequences*. The historical consequences of these dynamics and thus a prediction as to where things were headed.

The map was presented to the staff, who were asked whether it accurately reflected their experience of the situation, and changes were made on the basis of their reactions. For instance, in the original map the alternativist worldview said 'survive with what we can get without the establishment', but the staff changed this to 'enhance the organization without being dependent on the establishment'. In general the staff confirmed that the map accurately captured the dynamic of the conflict.

The map enabled the staff literally to 'see' a dynamic of which they had been unaware. Each member of the group had some of this map in his or her mind, but no single member of the staff possessed the entire map. The mapping process elicited these pieces and put them together in a way that allowed the staff to grasp the problem as a whole. It provided the staff with their first comprehensive and coherent picture of their dysfunctional dynamics and the causes behind them.

In addition the map provided a basis for the staff members to test their own interpretations of the problem. They could see that the problem could not be reduced to personalities or philosophies alone. Furthermore, the map illustrated for staff members how their individual and collective strategies drove the conflict and made it increasingly unmanageable. The map enabled the staff members to see clearly their own blindness and to see that each side did to the other what it felt the other did to it. Thus, it became difficult for each side to perceive itself as 'right' and the other side as 'wrong'.

Finally, the map provided the staff with a basis for redesigning their theories of action. The map indicated where the situation was headed even though no one intended or wanted such outcomes. By bringing the implications of their actions into awareness, the map enabled them to interrupt the negative dynamics and to ask themselves where they really wanted to go. In this way it functioned as a powerful 'unfreezing' mechanism (Friedman and Lipshitz, 1992; Lewin, 1951; Schein, 1969).

Staff members identified specific points in the map where their particular behavioural strategies or perceptions led to an escalation of the conflict. For

Initial conditions →		Worldview →	Action Strategies →	Perceptions
Ambiguous organizational identity stemming from multiple goals. Uncertainty over role definitions, tasks and standards. High uncertainty over obtaining essential financial and human resources.	*External role interface:* Director, Treasurer, Fundraiser.	*Pragmatists* – Co-operate with the establishment to get resources. – OH is primarily a social service organization. – Services should meet current social needs. – Rationalize organizational structure and roles.	*Pragmatists* Define problems in terms of survival. Appeal to reason and rationality. State 'facts' to prove points.	*Pragmatists see alternativists as:* • dogmatic • unreasonable • unrealistic • irresponsible • motivated by personal agendas.
Conflicting organizational norms such as a high degree of personal autonomy coupled with a consensus rule for decision-making. Stressful, hard work, long hours, and low monetary rewards.	*Internal role interface*: Service co-ordinators.	*Alternativists* – Obtain resources without depending on the establishment. – OH is a community. – OH exists in order to stimulate social change. – Services should reflect OH's unique values. – We can make the existing, non-hierarchical process work.	*Alternativists* Define problems in terms of organizational identity and *raison d'être.* Appeal to values, ideology and tradition. Tell stories to prove points.	*Alternativists see pragmatists as:* • money driven • insensitive • out of touch with the community • condescending • motivated by personal agendas.

Figure 11.1 Map of conflict at Open House

Consequences →	Second-order Strategies →	Second-order Perceptions →	Second-order Consequences →	Long-term Consequences
Each side feels invalidated by the other and becomes increasingly blind to the validity of the other side's views.	*Pragmatists* Humour the alternativists but act unilaterally when something important is at stake.	*Pragmatists see alternativists as:* • nagging • childish • vindictive.		Schism (members form a new or breakaway organization).
Each side feels unappreciated and becomes increasingly blind to the contributions of the other side.	Reinterpret organizational tradition to support the pragmatist view.		Little mutual trust.	
	Withdraw to sub-group (i.e., other pragmatists) for support and validation.		Issues drag on unresolved.	or
Each side feels that the other side's actions threaten the organization's fundamental well-being and becomes entrenched more deeply in its own position.	*Alternativists* Demand input on every decision and closely scrutinize the pragmatists' actions.	*Alternativists see pragmatists as:* • secretive • unilateral • untrustworthy.	Increased polarization of sub-group positions.	
	Mobilize community support behind key alternativist symbols and values. Withdraw to sub-group (i.e., other alternativists) for support and validation.		Tension and emnity covered up conviviality.	Staff burnout (current staff quits *en masse*, inexperienced members take their place, and history repeats itself).

Figure 11.1 (*Continued*)

instance, the tendency to turn inward to the sub-group rather than communicate with members of the other side, reinforced a closed loop of increasingly negative evaluation and polarization. The deeper each side became entrenched in its negative views and the worse it felt about the other side, the more difficult it became to talk directly and sort things out. Once staff members of both groups identified this specific dynamic, they set an alternative rule for themselves: before discussing a problem with a member of your sub-group, first present the issue to a member of the other group and ask for clarification.

Because of the hard feelings and each side's tendency to seek confirmation, this redesigned strategy was not easy to produce. However, staff members were aware of the consequence of not confronting the other side directly. This self-imposed dissonance between doing what came naturally and being aware of the negative consequences enabled staff members to employ the new strategy enough of the time to check, or at least slow, the dynamics described in the map.

The map did not necessarily improve interpersonal relations, instill feelings of trust or create cooperation. However, the map did provide the staff members with greater control over their behaviour. Rather than experience themselves as victims or as subject to forces beyond their control, the staff members could see that they made choices which had unintended consequences. At least some of these choices were under their direct control, giving them some leverage to change the situation.

The map illustrated that the conflict was embedded in the organization's identity and self-definition. As long as the organization was dependent upon the establishment and held on to alternativist values it would find itself in conflict, which received expression in the alternativist–pragmatist split. Since the staff did not wish to abandon these fundamental values, the question became how to design ways of more constructively engaging in this ongoing conflict. One condition the staff members were able to influence more directly was that of role ambiguity and lack of autonomy. They began to experiment with ways of granting each other more authority to carry out their roles. They also openly confronted the issue of organizational governance and their desire to exercise more authority *vis-à-vis* the volunteers.

Conflicts continued to erupt but they never reached the peak of intensity experienced prior to the map. Furthermore, the staff were able to arrive at stable compromises more often. One critical juncture occurred when the director announced his intention to resign. The search for a new director initially engaged the negative dynamics, as each side lobbied for a new director who would strongly identify with its worldview. Eventually, however, the staff realized that they were playing out the map and where it would lead them. As a result, both the pragmatists and the alternativists agreed to look for a director who could satisfy both sets of demands. Eventually they succeeded in finding such an individual, creating a smooth leadership transition.

The case of Open House illustrates the four main features of action science in varying degrees.

Creating a community of inquiry within a community of practice. My intervention in the organization can be seen as developing through three stages, each about one year in length. In the initial stage I provided a common language and a theory of action concepts, but the staff acted as a community of inquiry in a very limited way, focusing mainly on its inability to make decisions and on interpersonal conflict. The shock of the 'warning' incident served as an impetus for staff to inquire more deeply into the sources of stuckness. This process was more like detective work than systematic analysis. As issues arose in the staff or in the organization, we examined them and gathered data. I then pieced together the data, looked for important patterns and presented these to the staff, often in the form of maps. This stage culminated with the formulation of the comprehensive map (Figure 11.1). Once the map provided them with a valid 'theory' of the problem, they entered the third stage: designing and testing out ways of changing the map.

Building theories in practice. The map itself represents a theory of conflict in this particular organization constructed from the components of theories of action: a description of the situation, objectives and action strategies, and the causal links between them. In this particular situation, however, these fundamental building blocks were shaped into a more complex picture including additional components such as worldview and perceptions.

The map can be read as a kind of story created from a series of linked 'if ... then' propositions (e.g., if the staff members carry out strategy X, under conditions Y, they will produce outcome Z) that moved through time. It simplified and abstracted from a very complex reality in order to identify the essential elements of the conflict and the causal links between them. Staff members could identify their own theories of practice within the map but the map itself was more comprehensive than any one person's perception of the problem.

Although this theory was developed on the basis of a single case involving conflict in a particular kind of organization, it can be generalized to other similar situations. It predicts that organizations facing similar initial conditions are likely to produce similar conflictual dynamics. Indeed most organizations with democratic, non-hierarchical structures and values are likely to experience similar dynamics. For example, I have presented it to many kibbutz managers who have reported that it accurately captures the conflictual dynamics in their organizations.

Thus, action science conducted in one setting to help members of that setting can produce knowledge that is generalizable to other settings. Generalizability in action science means 'seeing-as':

> To see this site as that one is not to subsume the first under a familiar category or rule. It is, rather, to see the unfamiliar, unique situation as both similar to and different from the familiar one, without at first being able to say similar or different with respect to what. (Schön, 1983: 138)

In other words, action science theories become explicit parts of a practitioner's 'repertoire' that can be used as templates for reflecting on new experience. The key is not only to see the similarities but also 'the difference that makes a difference' (Bateson, 1979).

Action science theories and normal science theories may complement each other. In this particular case, for instance, Dearborn and Simon's (1958) concept of selective perception would have predicted the role-determined differences in worldview, but it would have only accounted for one part of the problem. Action science theories, on the other hand, attempt to capture a problem dynamic as a whole while being simple enough for practitioners to grasp and use in the action context.

Combining interpretation with 'rigorous' testing. Through much of the first stage and part of the second stage, staff members tended to attribute the conflict to each other's personality or hidden motivations. However, in most cases neither side saw its behaviour as problematic. Similarly, when one of the service co-ordinators hypothesized that there was a fundamental difference in philosophy, the director denied that his fundamental beliefs were any different. In many cases staff members provided directly observable data to illustrate and test their points, but these interchanges rarely led to resolutions.

On the other hand, the process of inquiry and theory-building in the second stage led to an alternative interpretation of the problem. The map portrayed individual behaviour and differences in philosophy (worldview) not only as causes, but also as effects of contradictory organizational goals and the influence of role on philosophy. Thus, the map provided a more reasonable explanation of the conflict than personalities or philosophies.

I tested the map with the staff, who confirmed its validity after some minor revisions. Subsequently staff continued to test its validity as they observed themselves reproducing it in their actions. They were able to locate themselves in the map and predict where they would end up if they did not interrupt the dynamic.

Creating alternatives to the status quo and informing change in light of values freely chosen by social actors. From the beginning the intervention was intended to produce change. At first these changes were focused on individual reasoning and behaviour. One of the significant shifts that occurred after the presentation of the map was a reduction in attempts at changing each other's behaviour. Since the map clearly illustrated the causal responsibility of both sides, it pushed them to focus more on changing their own behaviour and the conditions which exacerbated the conflict (i.e., roles and structures). Although the intervention did not resolve the pragmatist–alternativist conflict, it did enable the staff to alter their way of enacting the conflict, making it less destructive for themselves and for the organization.

Overcoming Obstacles to Action Science

Despite the claim that action science represents one of the two most popular action technologies (Raelin, 1997), a review of the literature revealed relatively few discussions or applications of action science (Edmondson, 1996; Friedman, 1997; Greenwood and Levin, 1998; Raelin, 1997; Rothman, 1997). The limited practice of action science may be attributed to both a lack of conceptual clarity (Edmondson, 1996) or a tendency to view action science primarily as a method of intervention rather than research (Raelin, 1997).

Another obstacle to the practice of action science is the need to acquire complex skills of reasoning and behaviour, such as Model II, which require considerable time, effort, commitment, skilful instruction and a very special set of conditions which rarely exist in academic or organizational settings (Argyris, 1993; Friedman and Lipshitz, 1992). Learning Model II not only means developing skills, but also internalizing and enacting new values. This difficult learning process may lead to a sense of 'hopelessness' and present a significant barrier to entry into action science (Edmundson, 1996: 586; Raelin, 1997). One of the central challenges for action science is to develop ways of more effectively teaching these competencies and creating conditions for learning in the action context.

One important question, however, is whether Model II is essential. Personally I have found Model II tremendously useful for helping me to learn and to teach others under conditions of ambiguity and psychological threat. However, I believe the essence of action science is the ability to (1) treat one's knowledge of a situation as hypotheses rather than facts and (2) actively test these 'hypotheses' through inquiry and action. There are probably different names for and ways of acquiring Model II-like values and competencies, such as 'dialogue' (Isaacs, 1993; Schein, 1993; Senge, 1990).

Action science makes high demands on both action scientists and practitioners. Practitioners need to be committed enough to learn to devote the time and effort required to engage effectively in the process. Entry into a setting is also a problem since practitioners rarely know what they are getting into and explanations are often inadequate. Collecting action science data is difficult. Tape recording interactions is not always possible or practical. Finally, because action science conforms to an unorthodox set of rules and standards, it may be difficult to publish in mainstream journals.

Despite these barriers, I am optimistic about the potential for action science to grow and to make significant contributions to knowledge. The gap between mainstream social science and social practice continues to grow, leading both practitioners and researchers to seek alternatives that enable them to manage the dilemma of rigour versus relevance. Forces such as technological and social change, globalization and the spread of democracy make it increasingly important for science to address ends as well as means. The explosion of interest in organizational learning and reflection have brought the work of Argyris and Schön to the attention of researchers and practitioners in a wide variety of fields. From an action science perspective, the barriers themselves represent opportunities or stimuli for inquiry, learning and change. In addition to addressing practice problems in target fields, researchers and practitioners need to experiment and produce knowledge about the practice of action science.

References

Argyris, C. (1980) *Inner Contradictions of Rigorous Research*. New York: Academic Press.

Argyris, C. (1982) *Reasoning, Learning, and Action: Individual and Organizational*. San Francisco, CA: Jossey-Bass.

Argyris, C. (1990) *Overcoming Organizational Defenses: Facilitating Organizational Learning*. Boston: Allyn and Bacon.

Argyris, C. (1993) *Knowledge for Action: a Guide to Overcoming Barriers to Organizational Change*. San Francisco, CA: Jossey-Bass.

Argyris, C., Putnam, R. and Smith, D. (1985) *Action Science: Concepts, Methods, and Skills for Research and Intervention*. San Francisco, CA: Jossey-Bass.

Argyris, C. and Schön, D.A. (1974) *Theories in Practice: Increasing Professional Effectiveness*. San Francisco, CA: Jossey-Bass.

Argyris, C. and Schön, D.A. (1978) *Organizational Learning: a Theory of Action Perspective*. Reading, MA: Addison Wesley.

Argyris, C. and Schön, D.A. (1996) *Organizational Learning II: Theory, Method, and Practice*. Reading, MA: Addison Wesley.

Bateson, G. (1979) *Mind and Nature*. New York: E.P. Dutton.

Berger, P. and Luckmann, T. (1966) *The Social Construction of Reality*. New York: Doubleday, Anchor Books.

Dearborn, D. and Simon, H. (1958) 'Selective perception: a note on the Department Identifications of Executives', *Sociometry*. Reprinted in H.L. Tosi and W.C. Hammer (eds) (1976) *Organizational Behavior and Management: a Contingency Approach*. Chicago: St Clair Press. pp. 204–207.

Dewey, J. (1938) *Logic: the Theory of Inquiry*. New York: Holt, Rinehart & Winston.

Dewey, J. (1966) *Democracy and Education*. Toronto: Free Press.

Edmondson, A. (1996) 'Three faces of Eden: the persistence of competing theories and multiple diagnoses in organizational intervention research', *Human Relations*, 49 (5), 571–95.

Friedman, V.J. (1997) 'Making schools safe for uncertainty: teams, teaching, and school reform', *Teachers College Record*, 99 (2), 335–70.

Friedman, V.J. and Lipshitz, R. (1992) 'Shifting cognitive gears: overcoming obstacles on the road to Model 2', *Journal of Applied Behavioral Science*, 28 (1): 118–37.

Friedman, V.J. and Lipshitz, R. (1994) 'Human resources or politics: framing the problem of appointing managers in an organizational democracy', *Journal of Applied Behavioral Science*, 30 (4): 438–57.

Greenwood, D.J. and Levin, M. (1998) *Introduction to Action Research: Social Research for Social Change*. Thousand Oaks, CA: Sage Publications.

Isaacs, W. (1993) 'Dialogue, collective thinking, and organizational learning', *Organizational Dynamics*, 22 (2): 24–39.

Keeley, M. (1984) 'The impartiality and participant interest theories of organizational effectiveness', *Administrative Sciences Quarterly*, 29: 1–25.

Kelly, H. (1971) *Attribution in Social Interaction*. Morristown, NJ: General Learning Press.

Lewin, K. (1948) *Resolving Social Conflicts*. New York: Harper & Row.

Lewin, K. (1951) *Field Theory in Social Science*. New York: Harper & Row.

Popper, K. (1959) *The Logic of Scientific Discovery*. New York: Harper & Row.

Raelin, J. (1997) 'Action learning and action science: are they different?', *Organizational Dynamics*, 26 (1): 21–34.

Rothman, J. (1997) 'Action evaluation and conflict resolution training: theory, method, and case study', *International Negotiation*, 2: 451–70.

Schein, E.H. (1969) 'The mechanisms of change', in W.G. Bennis, K.D. Benne and R. Chin (eds), *The Planning of Change*. New York: Holt, Rinehart & Winston. pp. 98–108.

Schein, E.H. (1993) 'On dialogue, culture, and organizational learning', *Organizational Dynamics*, 22 (2): 40–51.

Schön, D.A. (1971) *Beyond the Stable State*. New York: W.W. Norton.

Schön, D.A. (1983) *The Reflective Practitioner*. New York: Basic Books.

Schön, D.A. (1987) *Educating the Reflective Practitioner*. San Francisco, CA: Jossey-Bass.

Schön, D.A., Drake, W.D. and Miller, R.I. (1984) 'Social experimentation as reflection-in-action', *Knowledge Creation, Diffusion, and Utilization*, 6 (1): 5–36.

Senge, P. (1990) *The Fifth Discipline: the Art and Practice of the Learning Organization*. New York: Doubleday Currency.

Weick, K. (1979) *The Social Psychology of Organizing* (second edition). Reading, MA: Addison Wesley.

Weick, K. and Bougon, M. (1986) 'Organizations as cognitive maps: charting ways to success and failure', in H.P. Sims and D.A. Gioia (eds), *The Thinking Organization: Dynamics of Organization Social Cognition*. San Francisco, CA: Jossey-Bass.

12

The Practice of Co-operative Inquiry: Research 'with' rather than 'on' People

JOHN HERON AND PETER REASON

CHAPTER OUTLINE

This chapter outlines a way of doing co-operative research with people on matters of practical concern to them, a well-considered way of closing the gap between research and the way we live and work together. The authors identify the prime features of co-operative inquiry and the four phases of the research cycle with a variety of illustrative examples. They distinguish between various formal features of inquiry groups and inquiry cultures, and consider how four ways of knowing, consummated in practical knowing, are integrated in the inquiry process, and the sorts of skills and validity procedures involved in this integration. They end with some guidelines about initiating and launching an inquiry group.

Co-operative inquiry is a way of working with other people who have similar concerns and interests to yourself, in order to: (1) understand your world, make sense of your life and develop new and creative ways of looking at things; and (2) learn how to act to change things you may want to change and find out how to do things better.[1] Research is usually thought of as something done by people in universities and research institutes. There is a researcher who has all the ideas, and who then studies other people by observing them, asking them questions, or by designing experiments. The trouble with this kind of way of doing research is that there is often very little connection between the researcher's thinking and the concerns and experiences of the people who are actually involved. People are treated as passive subjects rather than as active agents. We believe that good research is research conducted *with* people rather than *on* people. We believe that ordinary people are quite capable of developing their own ideas and can work together in a co-operative inquiry group to see if these ideas make sense of their world and work in practice.

A second problem with traditional research is that the kind of thinking done by researchers is often theoretical rather than practical. It doesn't help people find how to act to change things in their lives. We believe that the outcome of good research is not just books and academic papers, but is also the creative action of people to address matters that are important to them. Of course, it is concerned too with revisioning our understanding of our world, as well as transforming practice within it.

So in traditional research on people, the roles of researcher and subject are mutually exclusive: the researcher only contributes the thinking that goes into the project, and the subjects only contribute the action to be studied. In co-operative inquiry these exclusive roles are replaced by a co-operative relationship, so that all those involved work together as co-researchers and as co-subjects. Everyone is involved in the design and management of the inquiry; everyone gets into the experience and action that is being explored; everyone is involved in making sense and drawing conclusions; thus everyone involved can take initiative and exert influence on the process. This, as we have said, is not research on people or about people, but research with people. We summarize the defining features of co-operative inquiry – on which we elaborate as the chapter proceeds – as follows:

- All the active subjects are fully involved as co-researchers in all research decisions – about both content and method – taken in the reflection phases.
- There is intentional interplay between reflection and making sense on the one hand, and experience and action on the other.
- There is explicit attention, through agreed procedures, to the validity of the inquiry and its findings. The primary procedure is to use inquiry cycles, moving several times between reflection and action.
- There is a radical epistemology for a wide-ranging inquiry method that integrates experiential knowing through meeting and encounter, presentational knowing through the use of aesthetic, expressive forms, propositional knowing through words and concepts, and practical knowing-how in the exercise of diverse skills – intrapsychic, interpersonal, political, transpersonal and so on. These forms of knowing are brought to bear upon each other, through the use of inquiry cycles, to enhance their mutual congruence, both within each inquirer and the inquiry group as a whole.
- There are, as well as validity procedures, a range of special skills suited to such all-purpose experiential inquiry. They include fine-tuned discrimination in perceiving, in acting and in remembering both of these; bracketing off and reframing launching concepts; and emotional competence, including the ability to manage effectively anxiety stirred up by the inquiry process.
- The inquiry method can be both informative about, and transformative of, any aspect of the human condition that is accessible to a transparent body-mind, that is, one that has an open, unbounded awareness.
- Primacy is given to transformative inquiries that involve action, where people change their way of being and doing and relating in their world – in the direction of greater flourishing. This is on the grounds that practical knowing-how consummates the other three forms of knowing – propositional, presentational and experiential – on which it is founded.
- The full range of human capacities and sensibilities is available as an instrument of inquiry.

A co-operative inquiry cycles through four phases of reflection and action. In Phase 1, a group of co-researchers come together to explore an agreed area of human activity. They may be professionals who wish to inquire into a particular area of practice; couples or families who wish to explore new styles of life; people who wish to practise in-depth transformations of being; members of an organization who want to research restructuring it; ill people who want to assess the impact of particular healing practices; and so on. In the first part of Phase 1, they agree on the focus of their inquiry, and develop together a set of questions or propositions they wish to investigate. Then they plan a method for exploring this focal idea in action, through practical experience. Finally, in Phase 1, they devise and agree a set of procedures for gathering and recording data from this experience: diaries, self-assessment rating scales, audio or video recordings, feedback from colleagues or clients, etc.

For example, a group of health visitors in south-west England were invited by one of their colleagues to form an inquiry group to explore the sources of stress in their work (Traylen, 1994). After some resistance to the idea that they could be 'researchers', the group decided to explore the stress that comes from the 'hidden agendas' in their work – the suspicions they had about problems such as depression, child abuse, and drug taking in the families they visit which are unexpressed and unexplored.

In Phase 2 the co-researchers now also become co-subjects: they engage in the actions they have agreed; and observe and record the process and outcomes of their own and each other's action and experience. They may at first simply watch what it is that happens to them so they develop a better understanding of their experience; later they may start trying out new forms of action. In particular, they are careful to notice the subtleties of experience, to hold lightly the conceptual frame from which they started so that they are able to see how practice does and does not conform to their original ideas.

The health visitors first explored among themselves their feelings about their 'hidden agendas' and how they were managing them at that time. They then decided to experiment with confronting them. Through role play, they practised the skills they thought they would need, and then agreed to try raising their concerns directly with their client families.

Phase 3 is in some ways the touchstone of the inquiry method. It is a stage in which the co-subjects become fully immersed in and engaged with their action and experience. They may develop a degree of openness to what is going on so free of preconceptions that they see it in a new way. They may deepen into the experience so that superficial understandings are elaborated and developed. Or their experience may lead them away from the original ideas into new fields, unpredicted action and creative insights. It is also possible that they may get so involved in what they are doing that they lose the awareness that they are part of an inquiry group: there may be a practical crisis, they may become enthralled, they may simply forget. It is this deep experiential engagement, which informs any practical skills or new understandings which grow out of the inquiry, that makes co-operative inquiry so very different from conventional research.

The health visitors' experience of trying out new ways of working with clients was both terrifying and liberating in ways none of them had expected. On the one hand they felt they were really doing their job; on the other hand they were concerned about the depth of the problems they would uncover and whether they had adequate skills to cope with them. In particular, the woman who had initiated the project was anxious and had disturbing dreams. The group members found they had to keep in good contact with each other to provide support and reassurance as they tried out new behaviours.

In Phase 4, after an agreed period in Phases 2 and 3, the co-researchers re-assemble to share – in both presentational and propositional forms – their practical and experiential data, and to consider their original ideas in the light of it. As a result they may develop or reframe these ideas, or reject them and pose new questions. They may choose, for the next cycle of action, to focus on the same or on different aspects of the overall inquiry. The group may also choose to amend or develop its inquiry procedures – forms of action, ways of gathering data – in the light of experience.

The health visitors came back together and shared their experience, helping each other understand what had taken place and developing their strategies and skills at confronting hidden agendas. After several cycles they reflected on what they had learned and wrote a report which they circulated to their managers and colleagues.

So the cycle between reflection and action is repeated several times. Six to ten cycles may take place over a short workshop, or may extend over a year or more, depending on the kind of questions that are being explored. These cycles ideally balance divergence over several aspects of the inquiry topic, with convergence on specific aspects, so that there is a refined grasp of both the whole and its parts. Experiential competencies are realized; presentational insights gained; ideas and discoveries tentatively reached in early phases can be checked and developed; skills are acquired and monitored; investigation of one aspect of the inquiry can be related to exploration of other parts; the group itself becomes more cohesive and self-critical, more skilled in its work.

Repeat cycling enhances the validity of the findings. Additional validity procedures are used during the inquiry: some of these counter consensus collusion and manage distress; others monitor authentic collaboration, the balance between reflection and action, and between chaos and order. We discuss these below.

Some Examples of Co-operative Inquiry Groups

Accounts of co-operative inquiry practices can be found in this handbook by Mark Baldwin and Penny Barrett (Chapters 19 and 20), as well as in John Heron's account of transpersonal inquiry (Heron, 2001). Here we sketch some other examples to show the potential breadth of the approach.

A group of general medical practitioners formed a co-operative inquiry group to develop the theory and practice of holistic medicine (Heron and Reason, 1985; Reason, 1988c). They built a simple model of holistic practice, and experimented with it in practice, exploring a range of intervention skills, power sharing with patients, concern for the spiritual dimensions of doctoring, as well as attention to their own needs as medical practitioners. Each reflection phase took place over a long weekend, after six weeks of holistic practice, the whole inquiry lasting some eight months. The experience of this inquiry contributed to the formation of the British Holistic Medical Association. The study was taken forward when a group of general and complementary medical practitioners worked together in a further inquiry group to explore how they might effectively work in an interdisciplinary fashion (Reason, 1991; Reason et al., 1992).

A group of co-counsellors met to refine, through aware practice together over several weekends, a description of the experiences and practices of the self-directed client (Heron and Reason, 1981). Another group met for five hours once a week to reflect together on effective skills, practised during the week in their daily lives, for handling irrational responses to life-situations arising from past trauma and conditioning (Heron and Reason, 1982).

A group of obese and post-obese women explored their experience together, looking in particular at how they were stereotyped in society, and how it was difficult for them to obtain appropriate attention from doctors and other medical people (Cox, 1996). We think there is great potential for inquiries in which groups of people with a particular physical or medical condition work together to take charge of how their condition is defined and treated. For example, an inquiry is being initiated with people with diabetes to explore their relationship to the services designed to support them.

Two black social work teachers established inquiry groups of black social work students, practitioners and managers to explore their experience. They looked at relationships between black people at work, particularly the experience of black managers and subordinates working together; and how a creative black culture could be generated (Aymer, in preparation; Bryan, in preparation).

Other groups have formed to explore questions of gender, in particular the experience of women and men at work. One inquiry looked at how black women might learn to thrive, as well as survive in British organizations (Douglas, 1999). A woman management undergraduate student used co-operative inquiry in her course work to explore the experience of young women managers in primarily male organizations (Onyett, 1996), stimulating a continued co-operative inquiry at the University of Bath (McArdle, in preparation). Another inquiry has recently been started to explore questions of masculinity and leadership within the police force (Mead, in preparation).

Different Forms of Co-operative Inquiry

Some groups are convened by one or two initiating researchers, familiar with the method, who choose an inquiry topic, invite others who are interested to join, and initiate these co-opted members into the inquiry procedures. Others are bootstrap groups, who learn of the method through the literature, and engage in a peer initiation process.

Some initiating researchers may be internal to the inquiry topic, that is, they are fully engaged with the field of study. As a black woman living and working in UK organizations, Carlis Douglas is clearly fully engaged with the inquiry topic, and in an inquiry by youth workers into how people learn, the initiator was herself a youth worker (DeVenney-Tiernan et al., 1994).

In other cases, initiating researchers are external to the particular culture or practice that is the research focus of the group, and so cannot be full co-subjects. There are, however, certain to be important areas of overlapping interest and practice, which enable them, to a greater or lesser degree, to be analogous or partial co-subjects. So the initiating researchers of the holistic medicine inquiry were not doctors, but they were both at the time practitioners in psychotherapy, and became analogous co-subjects, in the action phases, in this form of practice (Heron and Reason, 1985; Reason, 1988c). The initiators of an inquiry into an organizational culture were not members of the culture, but were academics with a lot of experience in the field, and were partial co-subjects as participant, ethnographic visitors to the culture (Marshall and McLean, 1988).

Many inquiries focus on practice within a given social role. A same role inquiry is one in which co-inquirers all have the same role, such as doctor or health visitor, and are researching aspects of their practice within that role. In a reciprocal role inquiry, the co-inquirers are two or more people who interact intensively within a role of equal status, such as spouse, partner, friend, colleague, and inquire into that interaction. Peer relationships of this kind can readily be turned into ongoing co-operative inquiries, thus entirely closing the gap between research and everyday life.

A counterpartal role inquiry is one in which the co-inquirers include, for example, both doctors and patients, or health visitors and some members of the families they visit, and the inquiry is about the practitioner–client relationship and what it is seeking to achieve. We have not yet heard *of* any full counterpartal role inquiries (although Marcia Hills was developing a proposal for elders to work with their physicians, and for an example of a consultant surgeon's attempts to turn outpatient consultations into mini-inquiries, see Canter, 1998), but they are extremely promising and are bound to occur sooner or later in the interests of client empowerment and practitioner deprofessionalization.

A mixed role inquiry is one that includes different kinds of practitioner. If they do not work together, then they may explore similarities and difference in their several modalities of practice. If they collaborate, then they may focus on aspects of this, as in the inquiry involving general medical practitioners and various complementary therapists exploring issues of power and conflict involved in their collaboration (Reason, 1991).

A further distinction depends on where the action phase is focused. Inside inquiries are those in which all the action phases occur in the same place within the whole group: they include group interaction inquiries and group-based inquiries. A group interaction inquiry looks at what goes on within the inquiry group: members are studying their individual and collective experience of group process. Thus one of us launched a three-day inquiry into the phenomenon of group energy (Heron, 1996a). A group-based inquiry is rather more varied in its format. All the action phases occur when the whole group is together in the same space, but some phases may involve each person doing their own individual activity side-by-side with everyone else; or there may be paired or small group activities done side-by-side. Other action phases may involve the whole group in a collective activity. A transpersonal inquiry used this sort of combination: of the six action phases, two involved people doing individual activities side-by-side, and four involved collective activity (Heron, 1988b).

An outside inquiry is about what goes on in group members' working and/or personal lives, or in some special project, outside the group meetings.

So the group come together for the reflection phases to share data, make sense of it, revise their thinking and, in the light of all this, plan the next action phase. Group members disperse for each action phase, which is undertaken on an individual basis out there in the world. In the example of the social workers' inquiry reported by Mark Baldwin in Chapter 19, the group members, having agreed on the aspects of their practice they would explore, attended to their experience in everyday work situations, bringing their observations back to the inquiry group for reflection and sensemaking on a regular basis.

Inquiries can be further distinguished by their having open or closed boundaries. Closed boundary inquiries are concerned entirely with what is going on within and between the researchers and do not include, as part of the inquiry, interaction between the researchers and others in the wider world. Open boundary inquiries do include such interaction as part of the *action phases* of the inquiry. The youth worker inquiry into how its members learn had a closed boundary: the inquirers focused exclusively on their own learning processes in sub-groups and the whole group (De Venney-Tiernan et al., 1994). The inquiry into health visitors' practice in working with families had an open boundary (Traylen, 1994), as did the holistic medicine inquiry in which general practitioners were engaged with the practice of holistic medicine with their National Health Service patients (Heron and Reason, 1985; Reason, 1988c).

The main issue for open boundary inquiries is whether to elicit data and feedback from people with whom the inquirers interact in the action phases, but who are not themselves part of the inquiry. If no data is generated, a valuable source of relevant feedback and information is ignored. If the data is generated, but the people by whom it is generated remain outside the inquiry and have no say in how it is explained and used, then a norm of co-operative inquiry is infringed. The radical solution is to include some of them, or their representatives, within the inquiry group. A second is to engage with them in dialogue, creating as it were a series of mini-co-operative inquiries, as occurred to some extent in the teachers' inquiry reported by Marcia Hills (2001). A third approach is for the co-operative inquiry group to take the initiative to establish one or more 'sibling' groups, as for example the midwives' group, reported by Penny Barrett in Chapter 20, whose experience of establishing a supportive group suggests how useful such a group would be for early mothers.

Some inquiries have an open boundary in *the reflection phases*. In the holistic medicine inquiry we invited visiting luminaries to several reflection meetings to give a talk to the whole group, to participate in the reflection process and give us feedback on it. These luminaries were invited 'to inject new perspectives, refresh our thinking, contribute to our programme design, and challenge the limitations of our inquiry' (Reason, 1988c: 105).

> With external participation, it is possible to avoid several of the implicit dangers of collaborative inquiry. Participants are not assumed to fully resource their own inquiry but are able to draw on knowledges beyond the group. External voices can also present a challenge to the paradigms within which the inquiry/co-researchers are located. (Treleaven, 1994: 156)

Inquiry Cultures

We have found it useful to distinguish between two complementary and interdependent inquiry cultures, the Apollonian and the Dionysian (Heron, 1996a). Any effective inquiry will have some elements of both cultures, even when the emphasis is tilted towards one pole rather than the other. The Apollonian inquiry takes a more rational, linear, systematic, controlling and explicit approach to the process of cycling between reflection and action. Each reflection phase is used to reflect on data from the last action phase, and to apply this thinking in planning the next action phase, with due regard to whether the forthcoming actions of participants will be divergent or dissimilar and convergent or similar. The whole person medicine inquiry is a classic example of this genre (Heron and Reason, 1985; Reason, 1988c).

The Dionysian inquiry takes a more imaginal, expressive, spiralling, diffuse, impromptu and tacit approach to the interplay between making sense and action. In each reflection phase, group members share improvisatory, imaginative ways of making sense of what went on in the last action phase. The implications of this sharing for future action are not worked out by rational pre-planning. They gestate, diffuse out into the domain of action later on with yeast-like effect, and emerge as a creative response to the situation. A Dionysian inquiry is described by John Heron (2001); and the Dionysian spirit is explored in relation to chaos and complexity by Reason and Goodwin (1999).

A more fundamental cultural distinction, is whether it is *informative* or *transformative*. Will the inquiry be descriptive of some domain of experience, being informative and explanatory about it? Or will it be exploring practice within some domain, being transformative of it? The descriptive and the practical are interdependent in various ways. Holding a descriptive focus means you have to adopt some practice that enables you to do so. Here the information you are seeking to gather about a domain determines what actions you perform within it. Having a practical focus throws into relief a lot of descriptive data. Here the transformative actions within a domain are your primary intent and the information you generate about their domain will be a secondary offshoot of them.

If the inquiry is mainly descriptive and explanatory, the primary outcomes will be propositions and/or aesthetic presentations about the nature of the domain. Secondary outcomes will be the skills involved in generating the descriptive data. If the inquiry is mainly practical, the primary outcomes will be practical knowing, the skills acquired, plus the situational changes and personal transformations they have brought about. Secondary outcomes will be propositions and/or aesthetic presentations; and the propositions will (1) report these practices and changes, and evaluate them by the principles they presuppose; and (2) give information about the domain where the practices have been applied, information which is a consequence of this application. And of course an inquiry may aim to be both informative and transformative, one before or after the other.

Our view, based both in experience and in philosophical reflection (Heron 1996a, 1996b; Heron and Reason, 1997) is that, if your primary intent is to be practical and transformative within a domain, you will get richer descriptions of the domain than you will if you pursue descriptions directly. Practical knowing consummates the other three forms of knowing and brings them to their fullness.

Ways of Knowing and the Inquiry Process

Among the defining features of co-operative inquiry listed at the outset, we mentioned a radical epistemology involving four different ways of knowing. We also call this an 'extended epistemology' – a theory of how we know, which is extended because it reaches beyond the primarily theoretical, propositional knowledge of academia. *Experiential knowing* is through direct face-to-face encounter with person, place or thing; it is knowing through the immediacy of perceiving, through empathy and resonance. *Presentational knowing* emerges from experiential knowing, and provides the first form of expressing meaning and significance through drawing on expressive forms of imagery through movement, dance, sound, music, drawing, painting, sculpture, poetry, story, drama, and so on. *Propositional knowing* 'about' something, is knowing through ideas and theories, expressed in informative statements. *Practical knowing* is knowing 'how to' do something and is expressed in a skill, knack or competence (Heron, 1992, 1996a).

In co-operative inquiry we say that knowing will be more valid if these four ways of knowing are congruent with each other: if our knowing is grounded in our experience, expressed through our stories and images, understood through theories which make sense to us, and expressed in worthwhile action in our lives. This was so for the doctors, the health visitors, the women in academia, and others, in their lived inquiry together.

We have found it valuable, in the reflection phases when the co-inquirers are busy with sense-making, to use the expressive forms of presentational knowing – both verbal and non-verbal symbols and metaphors – as a first step to ground descriptive and explanatory propositional knowing more fully in what has gone on in the prior action phase (Reason and Hawkins, 1988).

If the primary focus in co-operative inquiry is on action, on transformative practice that changes our way of being and doing and relating, and our world, then it follows that the primary outcome of an inquiry is just such a transformation, that is, our practical knowing, our transformative skills and the regenerated experiential encounters to which they give rise, together with the transformations of practice in the wider world with which the inquirers interact. The emphasis, with regard to research outcomes, shifts from the traditional emphasis on propositional knowledge and the written word to practical knowledge and the manifest deed.

Inquiry Skills and Validity Procedures

Co-operative inquiry is based on people examining their own experience and action carefully in collaboration with people who share similar concerns and interests. But, you might say, isn't it true that people can fool themselves about their experience? Isn't this why we have professional researchers who can be detached and objective? The answer to this is that certainly people can and do fool themselves, but we find that they can also develop their attention so they can look at themselves – their way of being, their intuitions and imaginings, their beliefs and actions – critically and in this way improve the quality of their claims to fourfold knowing. We call this 'critical subjectivity'; it means that we don't have to throw away our personal, living knowledge in the search for objectivity, but are able to build on it and develop it. We can cultivate a high-quality and valid individual perspective on what there is, in collaboration with others who are doing the same.

We have developed a number of inquiry skills and validity procedures that can be part of a co-operative inquiry and which can help improve the quality of knowing (Heron, 1996a). The skills include:

- *Being present and open.* This skill is about empathy, resonance and attunement, participating in the way of being of other people and the more-than-human world. And it is about being open to the meaning we give to and find in our world by imaging it in sensory and non-sensory ways.

- *Bracketing and reframing.* The skill here is holding in abeyance the classifications and constructs we impose on our perceiving, so that we can be more open to its inherent primary, imaginal meaning. It is also about trying out alternative constructs for their creative capacity to articulate an account of people and a world; we are open to reframing the defining assumptions of any context.
- *Radical practice and congruence.* This skill means being aware, during action, of its bodily form, its strategic form and guiding norms, its purpose or end and underlying values, its motives, its external context and defining beliefs, and of its actual outcomes. It also means being aware of any lack of congruence between these different facets of the action and adjusting them accordingly.
- *Non-attachment and meta-intentionality.* This is the knack of not investing one's identity and emotional security in an action, while remaining fully purposive and committed to it. At the same time it involves having in mind one or more alternative behaviours, and considering their possible relevance and applicability to the total situation.
- *Emotional competence.* This is the ability to identify and manage emotional states in various ways. It includes keeping action free from distortion driven by the unprocessed distress and conditioning of earlier years.

The co-operative inquiry group is itself a container and a discipline within which these skills can be developed (Reason, 1994a, 1999a). These skills can be honed and refined if the inquiry group adopts a range of validity procedures intended to free the various forms of knowing involved in the inquiry process from the distortion of uncritical subjectivity.

- *Research cycling.* It should be already clear that co-operative inquiry involves going through the four phases of inquiry several times, cycling between action and reflection, looking at experience and practice from different angles, developing different ideas, trying different ways of behaving. If the research topic as a whole, and different aspects of it singly and in combination, are taken round several cycles, then experiential and reflective forms of knowing progressively refine each other, through two-way negative and positive feedback.
- *Divergence and convergence.* Research cycling can be convergent, in which case the co-researchers look several times at the same issue, maybe looking each time in more detail; or it can be divergent, as co-researchers decide to look at different issues on successive cycles. Many variations of convergence and divergence are possible in the course of an inquiry. It is up to each group to determine the appropriate balance for their work.
- *Authentic collaboration.* Since intersubjective dialogue is a key component in refining the forms of knowing, it is important that the inquiry group develops an authentic form of collaboration. One aspect of this is that group members internalize and make their own the inquiry method so that an egalitarian relationship is developed with the initiating researchers. The other aspect is that each group member is fully and authentically engaged in each action phase; and in each reflection phase is – over time – as expressive, as heard and as influential in decision-making as every other group member. The inquiry will not be truly co-operative if one or two people dominate the group, or if some voices are left out altogether.
- *Challenging consensus collusion.* This can be done with a simple procedure which authorizes any inquirer at any time to adopt formally the role of devil's advocate in order to question the group as to whether one of several forms of collusion is afoot. These forms include: not noticing, or not mentioning, aspects of experience that show up the limitations of a conceptual model or programme of action; unaware fixation on false assumptions implicit in guiding ideas or action plans; unaware projections distorting the inquiry process; and lack of rigour in inquiry method and in applying validity procedures.
- *Managing distress.* The group adopts some regular method for surfacing and processing repressed distress, which may get unawarely projected out, distorting thought, perception and action within the inquiry. The very process of researching the human condition may stir up anxiety and trigger it into compulsive invasion of the inquiring mind, so that both the process and the outcomes of the inquiry are warped by it. If the co-researchers are really willing to examine their lives and their experience in depth and in detail, it is likely that they will uncover aspects of their life with which they are uncomfortable and at which they have avoided looking. So the group must be willing to address emotional distress openly when it arrives, to allow upset persons the healing time they need, and to identify anxieties within the group which have not yet been expressed. (See in addition the several chapters in this handbook which explore 'first-person' inquiry practices: Bill Torbert in Chapter 18, Gloria Bravette in Chapter 22, Peter Reason and Judi Marshall in Chapter 30, Yoland

Wadsworth in Chapter 31 and Judi Marshall in Chapter 32.)

- *Reflection and action.* Since the inquiry process depends on alternating phases of action and reflection, it is important to find an appropriate balance, so that there is neither too much reflection on too little experience, which is armchair theorizing, nor too little reflection on too much experience, which is mere activism. Each inquiry group needs to find its own balance between action and reflection and, within the reflection phase, between presentational and propositional ways of making sense. The appropriate balance will largely depend on the topic being explored.
- *Chaos and order.* If a group is open, adventurous and innovative, putting all at risk to reach out for the truth beyond fear and collusion, then, once the inquiry is well under way, divergence of thought and expression may descend into confusion, uncertainty, ambiguity, disorder and tension. When this happens, most if not all co-researchers will feel lost to a greater or lesser degree. So a mental set is needed which allows for the interdependence of chaos and order, of nescience and knowing, an attitude which tolerates and undergoes, without premature closure, inquiry phases which are messy. These phases tend, in their own good time, to convert into new levels of order. But since there is no guarantee that they will do so, they are risky and edgy. Tidying them up prematurely out of anxiety leads to pseudo-knowledge. Of course, there can be no guarantee that chaos will occur; certainly one cannot plan it. But the group can be prepared for it, tolerate it, and wait until there is a real sense of creative resolution.

Initiating an Inquiry Group

Many inquiry groups are initiated by one or two people who have enthusiasm for an idea they wish to explore, and who recruit a group by some form of circular letter. For example, the black social workers mentioned earlier invited social work managers, practitioners and students to a day long meeting to discuss mutual interests and to propose the establishment of inquiry groups. Groups of up to twelve persons can work well. A group of fewer than six is too small and lacks variety of experience.

When experienced co-operative inquiry researchers initiate an inquiry there can be no absolute parity of influence between them and their co-opted inquirers. They can move from appropriately strong and primary influence to significant peer consultant influence; and on the way may degenerate into either over-control or under-control. It is a mistake to suppose that there can be a simple parity of influence and to try to achieve it, or to imagine that parity has ever been fully achieved in an inquiry involving from five to eight full research cycles. What undoubtedly can be achieved as the inquiry proceeds is a sufficient degree of inter-dependent collaborative reflection and management, for the research to be genuinely *with* people, and not about them or on them.

The initiating researchers have, from the outset, three closely interdependent and fundamental issues to consider:

- the initiation of group members into the methodology of the inquiry so that they can make it their own;
- the emergence of participative decision-making and authentic collaboration so that the inquiry becomes truly co-operative;
- the creation of a climate in which emotional states can be identified, so that distress and tension aroused by the inquiry can be openly accepted and processed, and joy and delight in it and with each other can be freely expressed.

The first of these is to do with cognitive and methodological empowerment, the second with political empowerment, and the third with emotional and interpersonal empowerment. Initiating researchers need some skills in all these three ways of empowering others (Heron, 1996a).

At the induction meeting, the initiating researchers will be wise to make clear that the three strands are basic to the inquiry process, and to invite only those to whom the three strands appeal to join the project. Then they seek a contract in which everyone who wants to join makes a commitment to bring the strands into being. It is important that this contract is not the result of either rapid conversion or persuasive coercion. It needs to be a fully voluntary and well-informed agreement to realize the values of autonomy, co-operation and wholeness which underlie the three strands. A co-operative inquiry is a community of value, and its value premises are its foundation. If people are excited by and attuned to these premises, they join, otherwise not. Getting clear about all this at the outset makes for good practice later (Reason, 1995, 1997).

It is also really important at the induction meeting that, as far as is possible, people have an opportunity to help define the inquiry topic, the criteria for joining the inquiry, the arrangements for meeting structure and related matters. The following is a possible agenda for such a meeting:

- Welcome and introductions, helping people feel at home.
- Introduction by initiators: the broad topic of inquiry to be considered.
- People discuss what they have heard informally in pairs, followed by questions and discussion, leading to possible modifications of the inquiry topic.

- Introduction to the process of co-operative inquiry, the three strands mentioned above, and whether the proposed inquiry is likely to be Apollonian or Dionysian, and informative or transformative.
- Pairs discussion followed by questions, whole group discussion, with an airing of views on the three strands.
- Clarification of criteria for joining the inquiry group.
- Practical discussion: number of cycles, dates, times, venues, financial and other commitments.
- Self-assessment exercise in pairs. Individuals use the criteria to assess whether they wish to include themselves in the group or not.

We have found that this is a very full agenda for one meeting; it is better to hold a second introductory meeting to ensure understanding and agreement than to rush through all the items.

Groups will devise a programme of meetings arranged so there is sufficient time for cycles of action and reflection. A group wishing to explore activities that are contained within the group, such as meditation skills, may simply meet for a weekend workshop which will include several short cycles of practice and reflection. But a group which involves action in the external world will need to arrange long cycles of action and reflection with sufficient time for practical activity. The holistic doctors group met to reflect for a long weekend after every six weeks of action on the job, the health visitors for an afternoon every three weeks or so. An inquiry into interpersonal skill met for a weekend workshop at the home of two of the participants and then for a long afternoon and evening every month to six weeks, finishing with another residential weekend workshop.

Once the inquiry is under way, it is helpful to agree early on how roles will be distributed. If it makes sense for the initiator also to be group facilitator for the early reflection meetings, this should be made clear. Later on, the group can decide if it wishes to be fully democratic and eventually rotate the facilitator role, or if it would prefer one or two people to facilitate throughout. It may be helpful to identify who has skills in facilitating the methodology strand, the collaboration strand, and the emotional and interpersonal strand, and share out roles appropriately. Inquirers may wish to craft groundrules, particularly to preserve confidences within the group (Reason, 1988b).

It is helpful to decide early on what the primary outcomes of the inquiry are to be. For informative inquiries, then the primary outcomes will be presentational or propositional, or some combination of the two. For transformative inquiries, the primary outcomes are transformations of personal being, of social processes, or of the environment, and the various skills involved. Aesthetic presentations or written reports will be secondary: the primary outcomes may best be shared by demonstrations or portrayals of competent practice, or by training others to acquire and get the feel of such competence.

It is important for co-operative inquirers not to fall foul of the propositional compulsion of academia: the outcomes of inquiries do not have to be confined to the traditional written report. They can pioneer aesthetic presentations as informative outcomes, and find action-oriented ways of sharing transformative outcomes.

Regardless of the way in which the presented outcome is provided for others, the group needs to decide who will produce it. Thus if there is to be a written report or article, a decision is required on who will write it and on what basis. Will all members of the group contribute to it, edit it and agree to it before it is sent out? Or is it acceptable for one or two people to write their own report based on the group experience. While some form of co-operative report is consonant with the inquiry method, we have also found it helpful to adopt the rule that any individuals can write whatever they like about the group, so long as they state clearly who the author is and whether or not other group members have seen, approved, edited or contributed to the text.

Notes

Thanks to Marcia Hills for a careful reading of this chapter.

1 Our individual and separate accounts of co-operative inquiry over the past 27 years can be found in Heron, 1971, 1981a, 1981b, 1982, 1985, 1988a, 1988b, 1992, 1996a, 1996b, 1998; Heron and Reason, 1981, 1982, 1984, 1985, 1986, 1997; Reason, 1976, 1988a, 1988b, 1988c, 1991, 1993, 1994a, 1994b, 1995, 1996, 1998a, 1998b, 1999a, 1999b; Reason and Goodwin, 1999; Reason and Heron, 1995; Reason and Rowan, 1981.

References

Aymer, C. (in preparation) 'The regeneration of black culture'. PhD dissertation, Centre for Action Research in Professional Practice, School of Management, University of Bath.

Bryan, A. (in preparation) 'The experience of black students and professionals in higher education'. PhD dissertation, Centre for Action Research in Professional Practice, School of Management, University of Bath.

Canter, R.J. (1998) 'Clinical decision-making in a surgical outpatients: relating the science of discovery with the science of implementation'. Unpublished PhD, University of Bath, Bath.

Cox, J.S.A. (1996) 'A perspective view of the 'affect' and 'effects' of obesity and its treatment'. Unpublished MSc, Brunel University, Uxbridge.

De Venney-Tiernan, M., Goldband, A., Rackham, L. and Reilly, N. (1994) 'Creating collaborative relationships in a co-operative inquiry group', in P. Reason (ed.), *Participation in Human Inquiry*. London: Sage Publications. pp. 120–37.

Douglas, C. (1999) 'From surviving to thriving: black women managers in Britain'. PhD dissertation, Centre for Action Research in Professional Practice, School of Management, University of Bath.

Heron, J. (1971) *Experience and Method*. Guildford: University of Surrey.

Heron, J. (1981a) 'Philosophical basis for a new paradigm', in P. Reason and J. Rowan (eds), *Human Inquiry: a Sourcebook of New Paradigm Research*. Chichester: Wiley. pp. 19–35.

Heron, J. (1981b) 'Experiential research methodology', in P. Reason and J. Rowan (eds), *Human Inquiry: a Sourcebook of New Paradigm Research*. Chichester: Wiley. pp. 135–66.

Heron, J. (1982) *Empirical Validity in Experiential Research*. Guildford: University of Surrey.

Heron, J. (1985) 'The role of reflection in co-operative inquiry', in D. Boud, R. Keogh and D. Walker (eds), *Reflection: Turning Experience into Learning*. London: Kogan Page. pp. 128–38.

Heron, J. (1988a) 'Validity in co-operative inquiry', in P. Reason (ed.), *Human Inquiry in Action*. London: Sage Publications. pp. 40–59.

Heron, J. (1988b) 'Impressions of the other reality: a cooperative inquiry into altered states of consciousness', in P. Reason (ed.), *Human Inquiry in Action*. London: Sage Publications. pp. 182–98.

Heron, J. (1992) *Feeling and Personhood: Psychology in Another Key*. London: Sage Publications.

Heron, J. (1996a) *Co-operative Inquiry: Research into the Human Condition*. London: Sage Publications.

Heron, J. (1996b) 'Primacy of the practical', *Qualitative Inquiry*, 2 (1): 41–56.

Heron, J. (1998) *Sacred Science: Person-centred Inquiry into the Spiritual and the Subtle*. Ross-on-Wye: PCCS Books.

Heron, J. (2001) 'Transpersonal co-operative inquiry', in P. Reason and H. Bradbury (eds), *Handbook of Action Research: Participative Inquiry and Practice*. London: Sage Publications. pp. 333–9.

Heron, J. and Reason, P. (1981) *Co-counselling: an Experiential Inquiry*. Guildford: University of Surrey.

Heron, J. and Reason, P. (1982) *Co-counselling: an Experiential Inquiry 2*. Guildford: University of Surrey.

Heron, J. and Reason, P. (1984) 'New paradigm research and whole person medicine', *The British Journal of Holistic Medicine*, 1 (1): 86–91.

Heron, J. and Reason, P. (1985) *Whole Person Medicine: a Co-operative Inquiry*. London: British Postgraduate Medical Federation.

Heron, J. and Reason, P. (1986) 'Research with people', *Person-centered Review*, 4 (1): 456–76.

Heron, J. and Reason, P. (1997) 'A participatory inquiry paradigm', *Qualitative Inquiry*, 3 (3): 274–94.

Hills, M. (2001) 'Using co-operative inquiry to transform evaluation of nursing students' clinical practice', in P. Reason and H. Bradbury (eds), *Handbook of Action Research: Participative Inquiry and Practice*. London: Sage Publications. pp. 340–7.

Marshall, J. and McLean, A. (1988) 'Reflection in action: exploring organizational behaviour', in P. Reason (ed.), *Human Inquiry in Action*. London: Sage Publications. pp. 199–220.

McArdle, K. (in preparation) Work toward a doctoral dissertation, Centre for Action Research in Professional Practice, School of Management, University of Bath.

Mead, G. (in preparation) Work toward a doctoral dissertation, Centre for Action Research in Professional Practice, School of Management, University of Bath.

Merleau-Ponty, M. (1962) *Phenomenology of Perception*. London: Routledge and Kegan Paul.

Onyett, S. (1996) 'Young women managers: a co-operative inquiry'. Unpublished coursework project, University of Bath.

Reason, P. (1976) 'Explorations in the dialectics of two-person relations'. PhD dissertation, Case Western Reserve University, Cleveland, Ohio.

Reason, P. (ed.) (1988a) *Human Inquiry in Action*. London: Sage Publications.

Reason, P. (1988b) 'The co-operative inquiry group', in P. Reason (ed.), *Human Inquiry in Action*. London: Sage Publications. pp. 18–39.

Reason, P. (1988c) 'Whole person medical practice', in P. Reason (ed.), *Human Inquiry in Action*. London: Sage Publications. pp. 102–26.

Reason, P. (1991) 'Power and conflict in multidisciplinary collaboration', *Complementary Medical Research*, 5 (3): 144–50.

Reason, P. (1993) 'Reflections on sacred experience and sacred science', *Journal of Management Inquiry*, 2 (3): 273–83.

Reason, P. (ed.) (1994a) *Participation in Human Inquiry*. London: Sage Publications.

Reason, P. (1994b) 'Co-operative inquiry, participatory action research and action inquiry: three approaches to participative inquiry', in N.K. Denzin and Y.S. Lincoln (eds), *Handbook of Qualitative Research*. Thousand Oaks, CA: Sage Publications. pp. 324–39.

Reason, P. (1995) 'Participation: Consciousness and Constitutions'. Paper presented at the American Academy of Management Conference, Organizational Dimensions of Global Change: No Limits to Cooperation.

Reason, P. (1996) 'Reflections on the purposes of human inquiry', *Qualitative Inquiry*, 2 (1): 15–28.

Reason, P. (1997) 'Revisioning inquiry for action: a participatory view'. Paper presented at the American Academy of Management, Boston, MA.

Reason, P. (1998a) 'Co-operative inquiry as a discipline of professional practice', *Journal of Interprofessional Care*, 12 (4): 419–36.

Reason, P. (1998b) 'Political, epistemological, ecological and spiritual dimensions of participation', *Studies in Cultures, Organizations and Societies*, 4: 147–67.

Reason, P. (1999a) 'Integrating Action and Reflection through Co-operative Inquiry', *Management Learning Special Issue: the Action Dimension in Management: Diverse Approaches to Research, Teaching and Development*, 30 (2): 207–27.

Reason, P. (1999b) 'General medical and complementary practitioners working together: the epistemological demands of collaboration', *Journal of Applied Behavioral Science*, 35 (1): 71–86.

Reason, P. and Goodwin, B. (1999) 'Toward a science of qualities in organizations: lessons from complexity theory and postmodern biology', *Concepts and Transformations*, 4 (3): 281–317.

Reason, P. and Hawkins, P. (1988) 'Storytelling as inquiry', in P. Reason (ed.), *Human Inquiry in Action*. London: Sage Publications. pp. 79–101.

Reason, P. and Heron, J. (1995) 'Co-operative inquiry', in J.A. Smith, R. Harre and L.Van Langenhove (eds), *Rethinking Methods in Psychology*. London: Sage Publications. pp. 122–42.

Reason, P. and Rowan, J. (eds) (1981) *Human Inquiry: a Sourcebook of New Paradigm Research*. Chichester: Wiley.

Reason, P., Chase, H.D., Desser, A., Melhuish, C., Morrison, S., Peters, D., Wallstein, D., Webber, V. and Pietroni, P.C. (1992) 'Toward a clinical framework for collaboration between general and complementary practitioners', *Journal of The Royal Society of Medicine*, 86: 161–4.

Traylen, H. (1994) 'Confronting hidden agendas: cooperative inquiry with health visitors', in P. Reason (ed.), *Participation in Human Inquiry*. London: Sage Publications. pp. 59–81.

Treleaven, L. (1994) 'Making a space: a collaborative inquiry with women as staff development', in P. Reason (ed.), *Participation in Human Inquiry*. London: Sage Publications. pp. 138–62.

13
Appreciative Inquiry: the Power of the Unconditional Positive Question

JAMES D. LUDEMA, DAVID L. COOPERRIDER AND FRANK J. BARRETT

CHAPTER OUTLINE

This chapter describes appreciative inquiry as a positive mode of action research which liberates the creative and constructive potential of organizations and human communities. Appreciative inquiry contrasts with problem-focused modes of inquiry using deficit-based questions, which lead to deficit-based conversations, which in turn lead to deficit-based patterns of action. A case illustration is offered to show how appreciative inquiry uses the power of the unconditional positive question to overturn the tyranny of deficit-based vocabularies and opens up new alternatives for conversation and action.

In their original formulation of appreciative inquiry, Cooperrider and Srivastva (1987) argue that action research, especially in the guise of organizational development, has largely failed as an instrument for advancing 'second order' social-organizational transformation (where organizational paradigms, norms, ideologies or values are changed in fundamental ways) because of its romance with critique at the expense of appreciation. To the extent that action research maintains a problem-oriented view of the world it diminishes the capacity of researchers and practitioners to produce innovative theory capable of inspiring the imagination, commitment and passionate dialogue required for the consensual reordering of social conduct. If we devote our attention to what is wrong with organizations and communities, we lose the ability to see and understand what gives life to organizations and to discover ways to sustain and enhance that life-giving potential. While not all forms of action research are unquestioned in their commitment to a problem-oriented view, in this chapter we make figural this distinction in order to clarify the particular contribution of appreciative inquiry.

Cooperrider and Srivastva (1987) call for a social and behavioural science that is defined in terms of its 'generative capacity' (Gergen, 1982), that is, its 'capacity to challenge the guiding assumptions of the culture, to raise fundamental questions regarding contemporary social life, to foster reconsideration of that which is "taken for granted" and thereby furnish new alternatives for social action' (Gergen, 1982: 136). They offer appreciative inquiry as a mode of action research that meets these criteria.

> More than a method or technique, the appreciative mode of inquiry … engenders a reverence for life that draws the researcher to inquire beyond superficial appearances to deeper levels of the life-generating essentials and potentials of social existence. That is, the action-researcher is drawn to affirm, and thereby illuminate, the factors and forces involved in organizing that serve to nourish the human spirit. (Cooperrider and Srivastva, 1987: 131)

This chapter illustrates how appreciative inquiry, as a constructive mode of action research, can unleash a positive revolution of conversation and change in organizations by unseating existing reified patterns of discourse, creating space for new voices and new discoveries, and expanding circles of dialogue to provide a community of support for innovative action. It all begins with the unconditional positive question (Cooperrider and Whitney, 1999) that guides inquiry agendas and focuses attention towards the most life-giving, life-sustaining aspects of organizational existence.

The power of the unconditional positive question is premised on the notion that organizations are open books, which are continuously in the process of being co-authored. Past, present and future are endless sources of learning, inspiration and interpretation (similar to an inspiring piece of poetry or a good text) and, consequently, we as action researchers and organization members are free to study virtually any topic related to human experience in any human system. We can inquire into the nature of alienation or joy, stress or vitality, conflict or co-operation, and the topics we choose and the questions we ask are fateful. They set the stage for what we later 'find' and 'discover'. The concept of the unconditional positive question assumes that whatever positive topic we want to study, we can study it unconditionally and, in so doing, significantly influence the destiny of our organizations and of our social theory. In the next section of this chapter we briefly outline some of the relational consequences of the critical social and organizational sciences before turning in subsequent sections to a deeper exploration of appreciative inquiry.

The Relational Consequences of the Critical Social and Organizational Science

Scholars and practitioners alike are becoming increasingly disillusioned with the destructive consequences of the critical approach to scholarship (Brown, 1994; De Bono, 1992; Freire, 1994; George, 1989; Hazelrigg, 1989; Marcus, 1994; Rorty, 1980; Weick, 1982; Wollheim, 1980). Gergen (1994a) claims that while the initial purpose of this work was to attack the assumptions of empiricist foundationalism – such as cumulative knowledge, value-free theoretical formulations, unbiased observation, knowledge through hypothesis testing and objective measurement of human processes – more recently it has expanded to include critique of all kinds. Expressing the pervasiveness and viciousness of critical scholarship, Gergen uses the language of war to describe it. He writes:

> We now stand with a mammoth arsenal of critical weaponry at our disposal. The power of such technology is unmatched by anything within the scholarly traditions of longstanding. There is virtually no hypothesis, body of evidence, ideological stance, literary cannon, value commitment or logical edifice that cannot be dismantled, demolished, or derided with the implements at hand. Only rank prejudice, force of habit, or the anguished retaliation of deflated egos can muster a defense against the intellectual explosives within our grasp. Everywhere now in the academic world the capitalist exploiters, male chauvinist pigs, cultural imperialists, warmongers, WASP bigots, wimp liberals and scientistic dogmatists are on the run ... The revolution is on, heads are rolling everywhere, there is no limit to the potential destruction. (Gergen, 1994a: 59–60)

Gergen goes on to identify five consequences of the critical effort that destroy or erode human communities and the production of generative knowledge.

Contains conversation

The first consequence of the critical approach is the *containment of conversation*. Critique gains both its purpose and its intelligibility from a preceding declaration. An assertion must first be put forward in order for its negation to have any meaning. In this sense, critique operates to establish a form of binary – a discursive structure in which this is opposed to that. For example, if the assertion is that 'command-and-control management is necessary', critique is bound to a linguistic domain in which 'command-and-control/not command-and-control' serves as the critical defining structure. This form of argumentation is by nature conservative because it confines conversation to the terms of the binary. Words, sentences, images and ideas that lie outside of the binary are ignored. Thus, organizationally, critique limits possibilities for invention. It erects artificial boundaries that curtail the exploration of new knowledge and forecloses opportunities for breakthrough discoveries.

Silences marginal voices and fragments relationships

Once a binary has been established, the critic's voice operates so as to reify the terms of the binary and thereby silence other voices. As arguments proceed within the terms of the binary, other realities, values and concerns are removed from view. At the same time, the act of critique leads to rhetorical incitement. Particularly in the Western tradition, to criticize another's view is not a mere linguistic exercise, it is to invalidate the other. Thus it is no surprise that the posture of one who is targeted for criticism is anything other than defensive. Gergen writes 'There are, then, myriad means of ambiguating, complexifying, doggerelizing or transforming any utterance to imbecility. Resultantly, there is no principled end to argumentation ...' (1994a: 64). Fighting ensues and relationships are destroyed.

Erodes community

A fourth concern with the rhetorical impact of critique is the erosion of community. Language serves to sustain communal patterns of conduct. As communities reach normative consensus, their patterns of relationship stabilize. When critique is inserted into a community, a category is created, and all those who fit within that category are placed under attack. Those under attack close ranks, reaffirm their relationships, reiterate the value of their positions, and search for ways to mount effective counterattacks. In turn, the critics increase the intensity of their attacks, reaffirm solidarity within their ranks, and proselytize for further strength. Labels such as good and bad, right and wrong, rich and poor, smart and dumb are used to create distinctions between groups. Each group sanctions its members for attempting to fraternize with members of the other groups ('the crab crawling out of the barrel is pulled back down by the other crabs'). The result is a polarizing split within the community as a whole. Division along ideological lines ensues, and mutually exclusive realities ('incommensurable paradigms') solidify with little means of reconciliation.

Creates social hierarchy

At the same time, the critical impulse serves to support patterns of social hierarchy (Gergen, 1994b). It has long been recognized that approaches to social and organizational inquiry are premised on certain assumptions about the cultural ideal (Hartmann, 1960; Masserman, 1960). Vocabularies of deficit are simply careful and exacting ways to describe those who somehow do not measure up to the ideal. The existence of these vocabularies contributes to the proliferation of subtle but pervasive hierarchies by locating people and organizations on implicit axes of good and bad. The greater the number of categories of deficit, the greater the number of ways in which one can be made inferior in comparison to others.

Ironically, the propensity to create hierarchy is particularly strong in the critical social and organizational sciences because their very purpose is to examine, expose, demystify and debunk the accounts of the opposition. Armed with a vast arsenal of negative questions, the critic embarks on an intentional and rigorous search for most glaring deficits, deficiencies and offending characteristics of the opponent. Based on these inquiries, entire streams of theory are developed that reinforce hierarchy by describing 'the ideal' and then detailing the inadequacies of those who do not compare favourably. Organizationally, the proliferation of hierarchy dramatically limits individual potential and diminishes overall organizational capacity (not to mention its effect on morale and job satisfaction). As Berger and Luckmann point out, organizational members are continuously socialized through language into acting according to the roles and identities granted to them by their institutional 'subworlds' (1966: 138). As people begin to lock each other into negative descriptions, the 'space' granted for acting in ways that are recognized as positive, helpful or constructive becomes diminished or eliminated.

Contributes to broad cultural and organizational enfeeblement

There is a growing awareness that critical social and organizational science leads to what Gergen calls 'broad cultural enfeeblement' (1994b: 148). As applied to the field of organizational action research, the process proceeds as follows. First, the discipline of critical action research is formed and begins to create categories of 'cultural and organizational deficit'. Secondly, a collection of critical action research professionals emerges and commissions itself with the task and responsibility of identifying and describing the multiple forms of deficit as defined by its members. Thirdly, action research professionals create increasingly sophisticated vocabularies, models and theories to explain the deficits and then disseminate these explanations into the broader culture by means of universities, conferences, consulting projects, books, journals, magazines and other media. Fourthly, the vocabularies of deficit become absorbed into common organizational language and become the basis for the construction of everyday reality. In essence, then, organizations learn how to be deficient and problematic. Writes Gergen, 'Furnish the population with the hammers of [organizational] deficit, and the world is full of nails' (1994a: 158).

By containing conversation, silencing marginal voices, fragmenting relationships, eroding community, creating social hierarchy and contributing to cultural enfeeblement, scientific vocabularies of deficit establish the very conditions they seek to eliminate. As people in organizations inquire into their weaknesses and deficiencies, they gain an expert knowledge of what is 'wrong' with their organizations, and they may even become proficient problem-solvers, but they do not strengthen their collective capacity to imagine and to build better futures. The ability to foster constructive change relies on the capability of a group or organization to see and produce alternative realities through language. Vocabularies of deficit offer few resources for generating appealing and sophisticated options. In the next section of this chapter we introduce appreciative inquiry, a mode of action research that moves beyond the limitations of the critical effort to discover, understand and foster social and organizational innovations through language.

Appreciative Inquiry and the Power of the Positive Question

Appreciative inquiry distinguishes itself from critical modes of research by its deliberately affirmative assumptions about people, organizations and relationships. It focuses on asking the *unconditional positive question* to ignite transformative dialogue and action within human systems. More than a technique, appreciative inquiry is a way of organizational life – an intentional posture of continuous discovery, search and inquiry into conceptions of life, joy, beauty, excellence, innovation and freedom.

Our experiences suggest that human systems grow and construct their future realities in the direction of what they most persistently, actively and collectively ask questions about. If, for example, our interest is in developing an organization that instills and nurtures enthusiasm, would it be better to do a low morale survey documenting the root causes of low morale and then try to intervene to fix the problem, or might it be more effective to mobilize a system-wide inquiry into moments of exceptional enthusiasm and then invite organization members to co-create a future for their system that nurtures and supports even more enthusiasm? Appreciative inquiry is premised on the belief that it is much faster and more straightforward to go through the front door of enthusiasm. Going through the back door to study low morale on the way to a future of enthusiasm is an unnecessary detour that simply makes no sense.

As a method of organizational intervention, the underlying assumption of appreciative inquiry is that organizing is a possibility to be embraced. The phases include: (1) topic choice, (2) discovery, (3) dream, (4) design, and (5) destiny (see Figure 13.1 for a diagram of the appreciative inquiry 4-D model). Selecting a positive topic to explore is an essential starting point. Appreciative inquiry is based on the premise that organizations move in the direction of what they study. For example, when groups study human problems and conflicts, they often find that both the number and severity of these problems grow. In the same manner, when groups study high human ideals and achievements, such as peak experiences, best practices and noble accomplishments, these phenomena, too, tend to flourish. In this sense, topic choice is a fateful act. Based on the topics they choose to study, organizations enact and construct worlds of their own making that in turn act back on them.

The purpose of the discovery phase is to search for, highlight and illuminate those factors that give life to the organization, the 'best of what is' in any given situation. Regardless of how few the moments of excellence are, the task is to zero in on them and to discuss the factors and forces that made them possible. Valuing the 'best of what is' opens

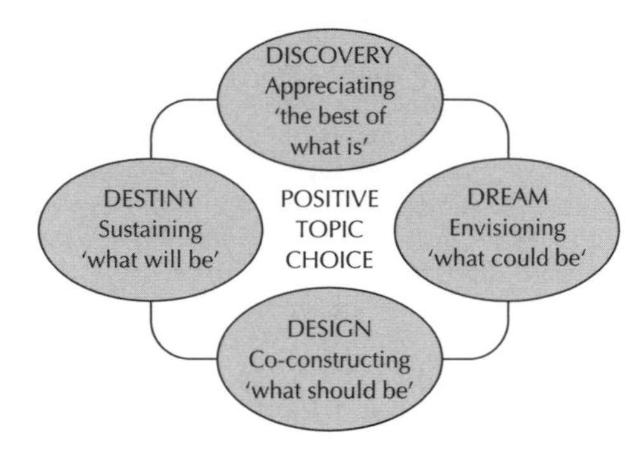

Figure 13.1 Phases of appreciative inquiry – The 4–D model

the way to building a better future by dislodging the certainty of existing deficit constructions. By asking organizational members to focus, even if only for a moment, on the life-giving aspects of organizational life, appreciative inquiry creates enough uncertainty about the dominance of deficit vocabularies to allow organizational members to consider new possibilities.

The second phase is to dream about what could be. As alternative voices enter the conversation, new ways of seeing and understanding the world begin to emerge. Because these perspectives have been cued by the asking of unconditional positive questions, the vocabularies used to describe and envision social and organizational reality are creative and constructive in the sense that they invite new, positive alternatives for organizing. By generating words, phrases and stories that illustrate the organization at its best and paint a compelling picture of what the organization could and should become, the dream phase liberates organizational members from the constraining power of existing reified constructions and offers positive guiding images of the future.

The third phase is to design the future through dialogue. It is a process of finding common ground by sharing discoveries and possibilities, dialoguing and debating, and finally getting to the point where everyone can say, 'Yes this is an ideal or vision that we value and should aspire to. Let's make it happen.' It is through dialogue that personal conversations evolve into organizational discourse and individual ideals become co-operative or shared visions for the future. The key to this phase is to create a deliberately inclusive and supportive context for conversation and interaction.

The final phase, destiny, is an invitation to construct the future through innovation and action. Appreciative inquiry accomplishes this by including ever-broadening circles of participants to join in the conversation. Each inquirer brings additional linguistic resources and helps to build a language that creates broader and deeper possibilities for action.

Together, organizational members live into the systems they have designed in ways that translate their ideals into reality and their beliefs into practice.

In the next section of this chapter, a case illustration is shared in which appreciative inquiry is used to transform the discourse between 120 non-governmental organizations (NGOs) worldwide. The case shows how the positive questions of appreciative inquiry can be used to release a virtual explosion of new vocabularies through which social and organizational innovations can be constructed. In the final section of the chapter, five positive relational consequences of the appreciative approach are developed and a call is extended to the field of action research to further create a positive revolution of learning and change by experimenting with appreciative modes of inquiry yet to be discovered.

Transforming Paternalism into Partnership – the Case of the Global Inquiry

The Global Relief and Development Organization (GRDO) is an NGO based in the USA and Canada that works with about 120 partner organizations around the world. When we first began to work with GRDO, they came to us with the following story.

> We have a system of building and measuring organizational capacity that is the envy of virtually every Northern NGO that has seen it. The system allows us to evaluate the organizational capacity of our partner organizations every six months according to five key criteria: their governance, managerial, technical, financial, and networking capabilities. We then use this information to design interventions – like training, consulting, systems improvements, finding new sources of funding, etc. – to strengthen their capacity. We also use the data to rate them and make informed decisions about how much we want to invest in them, both in terms of human and financial capital. In many ways, it's a perfect system. And yet, many of our partner organizations and even our own staff do not like it. They consider it to be an imposition, and they find it tedious, irrelevant, and in some cases, demeaning. We want to do a worldwide appreciative inquiry to find out what's wrong with the system and fix it!

It is important to point out that GRDO and its partners were entrapped in many embedded layers of deficit vocabularies (two of which we will mention here) that restricted their ability to accomplish their dreams. At the level of organizational architecture, GRDO's system for measuring organizational capacity was designed from a deficit perspective. It established a uniform global standard for a 'healthy' organization and then evaluated partner organizations to discover the areas in which they were weak. Thus, the system itself created a context in which deficit vocabularies and negative blaming attributions dominated.

GRDO and its partners were also entwined in a more complex and pervasive discourse of deficit that had to do with paternalism and dependency between the Northern and Southern worlds. GRDO harboured the implicit belief that its organizational knowledge was superior to that of its Southern partners because it was from the more advanced North. GRDO was also a source of funding for its partner organizations and therefore felt it had to be in a policing or monitoring role when it came to money. Thus, it was virtually impossible for GRDO to see itself in the role of an equal partner and learner in the capacity-building process. It simply did not have the vocabulary to describe itself in that way.

Topic choice

Resolute in our conviction that the seeds of change are implicit in the very first question we ask, we tried to discover the deeper yearning contained in GRDO's 'problem statement'. We asked something like, 'What do you *really* want from this process? When you explore your boldest hopes and highest aspirations, what is it that you ultimately want?' Quickly their vision began to unfold. They said that they wanted to see a wildfire of organizational capacity-building spread around the world in such a way that thousands of NGOs would be enabled to co-operate effectively with millions of marginalized communities to increase dramatically and sustain a dignified standard of living. They dreamed of an end to poverty and world hunger; social, political, and economic vibrancy; and the kinds of relationships between the Northern and Southern hemispheres that approached nothing short of global community.

Based on this image of the future, we, along with GRDO and its partners, launched a three-year global appreciative inquiry into the topic of 'Best Practices of Organizational Capacity-building from around the World' (see Johnson and Ludema, 1997). The purpose of the inquiry was twofold: first, to learn from each other about how to build strong, healthy, vibrant NGOs; and second, to discover new ways to work together in a partnership of equals. The inquiry was designed to follow a customized 4-D appreciative inquiry process, allowing the positive voice and experience of all the participating organizations to shape the learning and the outcomes of the study. (See Table 13.1 for the stages of the GRDO initiative juxtaposed to the four phases of appreciative inquiry.)

Table 13.1 *Stages of the GRDO initiative juxtaposed to the four phases of appreciative inquiry*

	DISCOVERY		*DREAM*	*DESIGN*		*DESTINY*
Stage One	***Stage Two***	***Stage Three***	***Stage Four***	***Stage Five***	***Stage Six***	***Stage Seven***
Global design team is formed and meets to design and launch the study.	The first round of large-group conferences with GRDO staff and partner organizations is held in East Africa, West Africa, Asia and Latin America to introduce appreciative inquiry, craft the unconditional positive questions and plan the 'listening tour' process.	GRDO staff and partner organizations engage in 'listening tours' with hundreds of organizations and community groups worldwide to discover the core forces and factors that support organizational capacity in each country and context.	The second round of large-group conferences with GRDO staff and partner organizations is held in East Africa, West Africa, Asia and Latin America to share stories and best practices, envision possible futures and create a new, radically participatory capacity-building system.	GRDO holds a global summit meeting with its partners to integrate learning from around the world, strengthen relationships by means of an appreciative inquiry into 'exceptional partnerships' and launch new initiatives for inter-organizational capacity-building.	GRDO staff and partner organizations return to their respective countries and regions of the world to field test new participatory capacity-building approach and launch capacity-building initiatives that have been ignited by the appreciative inquiry process.	The third round of large-group conferences with GRDO staff and partner organizations the is held in East Africa, West Africa, Asia and Latin America to share experiences with the new capacity-building approach and launch follow-up initiatives.
YEAR ONE				***YEAR TWO***		***YEAR THREE***

Discovery

In the first year of the inquiry, the discovery phase was carried out. It began with the formation of a global design team that included representatives from all of the different regions engaged in the study – East Africa, West Africa, Asia, Latin America and North America. Once the design team was in place, large-group retreats that lasted four days were held in each of the regions to familiarize GRDO and its partner organizations with appreciative inquiry, create an interview protocol and launch the study. Appreciative inquiry asks two basic unconditional positive questions:

1 What in this particular setting or context makes organizing possible? What gives life to our organization and allows it to function at its best?
2 What are the possibilities, latent or expressed, that provide opportunities for even better (more effective and value-congruent) forms of organizing?

Building on these two core questions, the inquiry participants developed variations on the following protocol as a guide for their inquiry:

Appreciative Interview Protocol

1 Think of a time in your entire experience with your organization when you have felt most excited, most engaged and most alive. What were the forces and factors that made it a great experience? What was it about you, others and your organization that made it a peak experience for you?
2 What do you value most about yourself, your work and your organization?
3 What are your organization's best practices (ways you manage, approaches, traditions)?
4 What are the unique aspects of your culture that most positively affect the spirit, vitality and effectiveness of your organization and its work?
5 What is the core factor that 'gives life' to your organization?
6 What are the three most important hopes you have to heighten the health and vitality of your organization for the future?

During the remainder of the year, each of the 120 partner organizations went back to its respective country and engaged in 'listening tours' with members of the communities in which it worked. The inquiry was made as broadly participatory as possible. For example, in East Africa, 22 GRDO staff and members of 31 partner organizations were trained in appreciative inquiry at the first regional conference. They in turn used the same process with the 888 communities in which they work. An average of two people from each group attended each conference or workshop. Thus, in East Africa alone, over the course of the inquiry, as many as 1,800 voices were included in the conversation. The total number of participants world-wide is estimated to have reached as high as 5,000 persons.

Dream

In year two, the dream and design phases began. At the beginning of the year, a second round of large-group retreats was held between GRDO and its partners. The retreats provided a forum in which the organizations could share with each other the stories and best practices they discovered in their interviews with community members, articulate their dreams for the future, and begin to re-design their approach to building and measuring organizational capacity.

For example, a woman from Senegal told of how she and a friend started an initiative to combat the rampant spread of AIDS in their country. From the beginning it was an uphill battle. Government ministries denied there was a problem, Muslim and Christian clerics denounced their efforts publicly, organized prostitute rings threatened their lives, and they had no money. Five years after they began, however, they had made remarkable progress. They formed a board of supportive government, religious, medical and community leaders; they equipped a staff of over 40 women to provide AIDS and health education throughout the country; in collaboration with the government, they started a centre for AIDS treatment and research; and they attracted an increasing amount of financial support from both domestic and international sources. When asked what were the forces and factors that made this exceptional growth possible, they highlighted six core ingredients: their own deep sense of call, the compelling sense of hope held by the victims of AIDS and their families, the unwavering support of key individuals and organizations, the unique gifts and contacts of their board, the dedication and skill of their staff, and the grace of God.

During the second regional conference in West Africa, this story was told and woven together with literally hundreds of other 'peak experience' stories from Senegal, Mali, Niger, Guinea, Nigeria and Sierra Leone. While all this was unfolding in West Africa, similar processes were underway in East Africa, Asia, Latin America and North America. A virtual explosion of positive stories was being shared, and the way GRDO and its partners talked about themselves, each other and their joint work was beginning to shift from a conversation of deficit to a conversation of possibility. Previously, GRDO and its partners rarely heard these compelling stories and rarely explored the core life-giving forces of their organizations, simply because they rarely asked the positive questions to elicit them.

As they entered the dream phase, many organizations described their image of the future in metaphorical terms. A group from Honduras imagined its ideal organization as a winding river carrying with it nutrients of all kinds, thus bringing life and vitality to an entire region. In West Africa, the participants described their organizations as fruit trees deeply rooted in the soil of African culture and tradition. They identified eight essential capacities that serve as 'water, fertilizer, and sunlight' to support the healthy development of their organizations in the unique cultural contexts of West Africa: servant leadership, participatory management, organizational development, resource development, community empowerment, technical expertise, networking and partnership, and spiritual resilience. Then they began to wonder what would happen if these capacities were thriving to the fullest in their organizations.

Design

The design stage began as members started to explore systematically what kinds of social architecture would most powerfully translate their dreams and visions into day-to-day reality. Over the course of the second year of the inquiry, hundreds of gatherings took place world-wide in which participants developed a series of locally relevant 'provocative propositions' that, based on their best experiences from the past and their highest hopes for the future, described their 'ideal' organizational architecture. A provocative proposition is a statement that bridges the best of 'what is' with what 'might be'. These propositions then became the basis for a new, radically-dispersed and broadly-participatory system of organizational capacity-building. In collaboration with its neighbours and with GRDO staff, each community and each NGO participating in the study developed its own criteria and process for developing capacity in its unique local context. For example, in West Africa, provocative propositions of the ideal, similar to the example below, were developed for each of the eight essential capacities mentioned above.

Provocative Proposition – Networking and Partnership

We are highly networked organizations, broadly and deeply. We have strong, supportive, mutual relationships with each other, other NGOs, our donors, government officials and the communities where we work. We celebrate our similarities and differences, understand each other's values, respect each other's cultures, and learn as much as we can from one another. We admit our needs and contract to help each other grow. We deliberately solicit and rely on each other's input, and we support each other in serving other parts of the world. In every way possible we strive to complement one another.

It was also during this second year that GRDO's language began to shift around partnership as a result of listening to the voices of its partners. Midway through the year GRDO convened a global summit meeting at which representatives from each of the regional conferences convened to integrate learning at a global level. In his opening remarks, GRDO's CEO led with the following words that reflect the organization's change in perspective:

> Through the appreciative inquiry process we have begun to realize that of all the crucial characteristics of organizational capacity building, none is more important than the need for mutual partnership between organizations. Organizational capacity is essentially an inter-organizational activity, a condition that occurs when organizations enter into mutually edifying relationships with one another to carry out their respective missions in the world more effectively. This kind of transformative growth and development flourishes most fully in relationships between equals. We hope you will help us discover the possibilities as we move forward.

This is language that previously GRDO simply could not hear let alone articulate because they and their partners were locked into a form of deficit-based linguistic binary whose terms included 'our system of capacity building/not our system of capacity building'. Within the conditions of the binary, 'good' partners where those who used the system and 'bad' partners were those who refused. It was not until GRDO and its partners began to inquire into the good, the beautiful, the better and the best that this language of possibility, previously invisible, could spring into view and offer itself as a resource for the social construction of the future.

Destiny

In year three, the destiny phase was launched. Because the restrictive grip of deficit vocabularies had been loosened and vocabularies of possibility had been unleashed, energy for action was immediately boosted within the system. People began to feel a sense of hope, excitement, co-operation and ownership about the future, and they began to unleash a veritable revolution of positive change and innovation. At the third round of large-group retreats these new initiatives were shared and a range of new joint activities were launched. While it is beyond the scope of this chapter to list all of the accomplishments, the following examples provide a flavour.

> An NGO in Bangladesh, having gained a new appreciation for the importance of networking, invited community members and its funding agencies into its strategic planning process. As a result, it doubled its budget and more than quadrupled the number of families it served in less than two years.
>
> In East Africa, the NGOs that participated in the appreciative inquiry banded together to form an East Africa NGO network that would provide training, consultation, advocacy and new sources of funding. A similar network was started in West Africa.
>
> On a global level, GRDO launched a new initiative to link business entrepreneurs with NGOs to bring their products into the global economy. In its first two years, this initiative raised more than three million dollars and established over 30 relationships between groups of entrepreneurs and local NGOs.
>
> GRDO and its partner organizations have also begun to hold regular organizational summit meetings every three years to provide a forum for strengthening relationships, finding common ground around visions for the future, and jointly enacting agendas for change.
>
> GRDO radically re-designed its organization to support their new understanding of partnership. It moved to a team-based structure, reduced layers of hierarchy from nine to three, and formed regional teams to manage its operations. The new design has shifted the locus of power (and therefore control, learning and innovation) from a central point in North America to multiple interdependent points through out the world.
>
> Finally, and perhaps most importantly, GRDO and its partners invented a new broadly participatory approach to organizational capacity-building that far exceeded their expectations, and indeed their individual imaginations. As a result of this new system, more than 100 NGOs and thousands of communities have dramatically improved their capacity to increase and sustain a dignified standard of living.

Hundreds of social innovations similar to these emerged around the world as a result of the appreciative inquiry. But undoubtedly the most important result, and the one that enabled all the others, was the shift from vocabularies of deficit to conversations of possibility that was unlocked by the unconditional positive questions that guided the inquiry.

The Relational Consequences of Appreciation

This case illustration demonstrates how appreciative inquiry can be used as a positive mode of action research to dislodge reified vocabularies of human deficit and liberate the socially constructive potential of organizations and human communities. By unlocking existing deficit constructions, creating spaces for new voices and languages to emerge, and expanding circles of dialogue to build a supportive relational context, appreciative inquiry allows for the positive construction of social reality. There are at least five ways in which it makes this possible.

Releases positive conversation within the organization

Relational patterns in industrial-era hierarchies and bureaucracies are often held in place by problem-focused theories, assumptions, beliefs and ideas that have been created and transmitted through language. The first and perhaps most important consequence of appreciative inquiry is that it releases an outpouring of new constructive conversations that refocus an organization's attention away from problems and towards hopeful, energizing possibilities (Ludema, Wilmot and Srivastva, 1997).

These positive conversations are crucial to the evolution of healthy and vital organizations. Human beings are continuously creating the future through the images they project, and in turn these images of desirable future events foster the behaviour most likely to bring about their realization (Polak, 1973). By asking unconditionally positive questions, appreciative inquiry draws out and highlights hopeful and empowering stories, metaphors, dreams, wishes that embrace a spirit of vitality and potency – musings that typically remain unexpressed or underexpressed in organizational conversation. These positive questions allow organizational members to inquire into the 'realm of the possible', beyond the boundaries of problems as they present themselves in conventional terms, and prefigure the very future they will later create.

Builds an ever-expanding web of inclusion and positive relationships

Appreciative inquiry is a collaborative effort to discover that which is healthy, successful and positive in organizational life. By definition, such a project is a radically participatory approach, designed to include an ever-increasing number of voices in conversations that highlight strengths, assets, hopes and dreams. Whereas the critical impulse attempts to undermine the knowledge claims of others, the act of appreciation leads to a heightened sensitivity to multiple ways of knowing and an acceptance of a wide array of diverse experiences (Kolb, 1984). It supports open, respectful, productive dialogue between seemingly 'incommensurable paradigms' and encourages a posture of empathy rather than attack when confronting differing points of view.

At the same time, momentum for change in any human system requires large amounts of positive affect and social bonding – including experiences of hope, inspiration and the sheer joy of creating with one another. Our experience in a variety of change efforts leads us to one unmistakable and dramatic conclusion: the more positive the questions that guide an inquiry and shape a conversation, the stronger will be the relationships and the more long-lasting and effective will be the change. By inviting participants to inquire deeply into the best and most valued aspects of one another's life and work, appreciative inquiry immediately enriches understanding, deepens respect and establishes strong relational bonds.

Creates self-reinforcing learning communities

As positive vocabularies multiply, people strengthen their capacity to put those possibilities into practice on an everyday basis. Organizational members develop increasingly textured and sophisticated vocabularies for doing things in new ways. Consider for a moment a young boy who aspires to be a basketball star. At an early age, he will have many ways to describe a poor shot – a brick, a squib, a rainbow, or an air ball – but few words other than 'good' to describe a skilful shot. As he grows older and learns by watching the pros, listening to his coaches, talking with his teammates and monitoring his own successes, he develops an ever more textured and sophisticated vocabulary for describing a 'good shot'. He discovers that balance, timing, elevation, extension, wrist action, focus and follow through are all essential ingredients in shooting a good shot, and all this language opens up whole new worlds of possibility for him and for those around him. He now has 'new knowledge' that will allow him to improve his own game, and he has an expanded capacity to see and encourage the positive strengths of others.

In this sense, there is a self-reinforcing cycle that develops as positive vocabularies multiply and people are drawn into relationships where they are invited to discover, see and affirm the good and the possible in each other. Our capacity to see and to grow in healthy ways is developed in and through language. As the richness of our positive vocabularies increases, we become ever more able to see the strengths and potential of others, and the capacity of the whole system is multiplied.

Bolsters democracy and self-organizing throughout the system

A third important consequence of appreciative inquiry is that it dynamically promotes egalitarian relationships. In our experience, as organization members inquire into the best of one another and dream about their hopes for the future, it inevitably leads to the creation of images of less hierarchy and more equalized power and decision-making. People talk about values of respect, partnership and coming to 'the table' as equals. They talk about breaking down silos between functions, transcending traditional boundaries and going directly to the source to build futures that matter. Never, in all of our years of learning with appreciative inquiry, have we ever seen a group dream of increased hierarchy, greater power distance between individuals, or more command and control in the system.

Organizations that engage in appreciative inquiry enhance the collaborative competence of the entire system to self-organize (Barrett, 1995). It is as though there is a direct and simultaneous link between the way we know and the kinds of organizational forms we create. Each organizational form – the rational bureaucracy and the self-organizing human system – has also an underlying way of knowing that operates at a foundational level to provide a logic for its existence. Self-organizing systems, characterized by equal distribution of power and self-management, are marked by an epistemic stance of liberation, freedom, solidarity and social construction, in which organizational members are released to co-create the worlds and realities in which they live. Similarly, they are distinguished by a deep appreciation for the miracle and mystery of organizational life, which allows members to create the future based on the strengths, assets, hopes and dreams that they cherish the most. It may well be as we move into a new era of organizing, that appreciative inquiry is to self-organizing systems what deficit-based approaches to research have long been to command and control bureaucracies.

Provides a reservoir of strength and unleashes a positive revolution of change

Just as the vocabularies of deficit of the critical social and organizational sciences contribute to broad cultural enfeeblement, so do the vocabularies of possibility and hope sparked by the unconditional positive questions of appreciative inquiry lead to widespread social imagination and invention. One of the basic theorems of appreciative inquiry is that it is the image of the future that in fact guides what might be called the current behaviour of any organization. Organizations exist, in the final analysis, because people who govern and maintain them share some sort of common discourse or projection about what the organization is, how it will function, and what it is likely to become. As organizations inquire ever more deeply into their strengths, achievements, assets, values, traditions, wisdoms, inspired emotions, they develop what could be called the organization's 'positive core' (Cooperrider and Whitney, 1999). This core is like the core of an atom that unleashes unbelievable power. It furnishes the organization with a deep sense of history, identity, continuity and strength that provides calming stability in the midst of turbulence. And yet, this reservoir of inspirational stories also serves as a source of energizing power that can be drawn upon to mobilize imagination and motivate creative actions. The more an organization experiments with crafting and asking the unconditional question, the more it will unleash new textured vocabularies of potentiality that contain within them possibilities for a truly desired future.

Conclusion

Ever since Descartes, the Western intellectual tradition has suffered from a form of epistemological schizophrenia (Popkin, 1979). Its intent of building knowledge to enhance the human condition is a noble one, yet its methodological starting point of doubt and negation undermines its constructive intent. Appreciative inquiry recognizes that inquiry and change are not truly separate moments, but are simultaneous. Inquiry *is* intervention. The seeds of change – that is, the things people think and talk about, the things people discover and learn, and the things that inform dialogue and inspire action – are implicit in the very first questions we ask. It may well be that our most important task as action researchers (and as organizational leaders) is continuously to craft the unconditional positive question that allows the whole system to discover, amplify and multiply the alignment of strengths in such a way that weaknesses and deficiencies become increasingly irrelevant. For, the questions we ask set the stage for what we 'find', and what we find becomes the knowledge out of which the future is conceived, conversed about, and constructed.

References

Barrett, F.J. (1995) 'Creating appreciative learning cultures', *Organization Dynamics*, 24 (1): 36–49.

Berger, P.L. and Luckmann, T. (1966) *The Social Construction of Reality: a Treatise in the Sociology of Knowledge*. New York: Anchor Books (Doubleday).

Brown, H.B. (1994) 'Reconstructing social theory after the postmodern critique', in H.W. Simons and M. Billig (eds), *After Postmodernism: Reconstructing Ideology Critique*. London: Sage Publications. pp. 12–37.

Cooperrider, D.L. and Srivastva, S. (1987) 'Appreciative inquiry in organizational life', in W.A. Pasmore and R.W. Woodman (eds), *Research in Organizational Change and Development* (Vol. I). Greenwich, CT: JAI Press. pp. 129–69.

Cooperrider, D.L. and Whitney, D. (1999) *Collaborating for Change: Appreciative Inquiry*. San Francisco, CA: Barrett-Koehler Communications.

De Bono, E. (1992) *Handbook for the Positive Revolution*. New York: Penguin.

Freire, P. (1994) *Pedagogy of Hope: Reliving Pedagogy of the Oppressed* (trans. R.R. Barr). New York: Continuum.

George, J. (1989) 'International relations and the search for thinking space', *International Studies Quarterly*, 33: 179–269.

Gergen, K.J. (1982) *Toward Transformation in Social Knowledge*. New York: Springer-Verlag.

Gergen, K.J. (1994a) 'The limits of pure critique', in H.W. Simons and M. Billig (eds), *After Postmodernism: Reconstructing Ideology Critique*. London: Sage Publications. pp. 58–78.

Gergen, K.J. (1994b) *Realities and Relationships: Soundings in Social Construction*. Cambridge, MA: Harvard University Press.

Hartmann, H. (1960) *Psychoanalysis and Moral Values*. New York: International Universities Press.

Hazelrigg, H. (1989) *Claims of Knowledge: On the Labor of Making Found Worlds*. Tallahassee, FL: The Florida State University Press.

Johnson, S. and Ludema, J.D. (1997) *Partnering to Build and Measure Organizational Capacity: Lessons from NGOs around the World*. Grand Rapids, MI: CRC Publications.

Kolb, D.A. (1984) *Experiential Learning*. Englewood Cliffs, NJ: Prentice-Hall.

Ludema, J.D., Wilmot, T.B. and Srivastva, S. (1997) 'Organizational hope: reaffirming the constructive task of social and organizational inquiry', *Human Relations*, 50 (8): 1015–52.

Marcus, G.E. (1994) 'What comes (just) after "post?" The case of ethnography', in N.K. Denzin and Y.S. Lincoln (eds), *Handbook of Qualitative Research*. Thousand Oaks, CA: Sage Publications. pp. 563–74.

Masserman, J. (1960) *Psychoanalysis and Human Values*. New York: Grune and Stratton.

Polak, F. (1973) *The Image of the Future* (trans. and abridged E. Boulding). San Francisco, CA: Jossey-Bass.

Popkin, R.H. (1979) *The History of Scepticism: From Erasmus to Spinoza*. Berkeley, CA: University of California Press.

Rorty, R. (1980) *Consequences of Pragmatism (Essays: 1972–1980)*. Minneapolis, MN: University of Minnesota Press.

Weick, K.E. (1982) 'Affirmation as inquiry', *Small Group Behavior*, 13: 441–50.

Wollheim, R. (1980) *Art and Its Objects* (second edition). Cambridge, MA: Cambridge University Press.

14
Large-group Processes as Action Research

ANN W. MARTIN

CHAPTER OUTLINE

This chapter makes a distinction between large-group processes designed for political and cultural purposes and those designed for organizational learning and social change. After describing three actual large-group interventions, the author elaborates on the conditions that she thinks are essential for a large-group process to achieve the learning and democratization goals of action research.

Large-group processes that include diverse stakeholders in planning are being used increasingly to cope with the complexity of modern organizational and community life. Many of these processes are designed for political or cultural purposes to inform and include stakeholders. Such designs seldom lead to social change, even though they may be meaningful to the participants. It is possible, however, to design a large-group process that will generate learning and social change. A large-group process structured for action aimed at 'a better, freer society' (Greenwood and Levin, 1998: 3) can be modelled on action research. In this chapter, I will distinguish between those multi-stakeholder processes designed for political/cultural purposes and those designed to be consistent with the values and goals of action research.

The large-group interventions or processes I refer to are events designed to engage representatives of an entire system, whether it be an organization or a community, in thinking through and planning change (Bunker and Alban, 1997); what distinguishes them from other large meetings is that the process is managed to allow all participants an opportunity to engage actively in the planning.

To be sure, the distinction between such processes designed for political and cultural purposes and those designed for organizational learning and change is not an easy one to make. An example of the former is a one-day event that brought all 600 employees of a manufacturing plant together to talk about potential plant improvements and to listen to the CEO of the company tell them he cared. To hear participants tell it, it was a memorable event, but no difference in operating assumptions – for managers or union members – emerged as a result. Lists of possible actions that resulted from the day of discussions were reproduced for later use, and some of these informed re-design of operations, but life and business went on as usual in the following months. Another example, also a one-day event, involved 35 people in a search conference-like event planned to develop the commitment of middle-level managers to a team approach. Concrete action plans were formed; some of these were even followed, but the purpose was to align the culture of the organization with the plant manager's vision, not to generate new knowledge. Participants engaged in the process were not asked to use critical thinking skills, but rather to develop ways to accomplish the mission already spelled out by company leaders.

On the other hand, a large-group process, even when it is a brief event, can be designed as a form of action research that exposes collective knowledge and assumptions and uses these to generate the knowledge and power that lead to change. The activity becomes, as Bhatt and Tandon (2001) say in describing the tribal forest movements in the Jharkland region of India, a learning process that triggers collective social action. There is the potential for learning in every large-group process, where the mix of knowledge is great, but to qualify as action research, learning and the generation of new knowledge should be conscious, if not explicit.

At the end of this chapter, I lay out a conscious approach in the form of conditions I believe are necessary for a large-group process to succeed as action research. Before doing that, I elaborate on what I mean by large-group processes in this context and describe the qualities of action research that are relevant. I will use three brief cases as references in illustrating the limitations and possibilities of large-group processes.

What Is Meant by Large-group Processes?

Bunker and Alban (1997) describe 11 large-group designs, all of which are used, though not exclusively, in corporate settings. These range from the Search Conference and the Future Search, two multi-day events in which participants undertake a series of small and whole-group discussions to design their future, to Work-Out, a process of cross-functional/cross-level group discussions to address workplace problems, to Open Space, described by its originator as a conference that is 'all coffee breaks' – freely flowing voluntary discussions of issues of importance to the participants. I describe a couple of specific designs in this chapter and Bjørn Gustavsen (Chapter 1) reflects on two-day dialogue conferences.

As advertised in the literature, the advantage of large-group interventions in the organizational context is that they provide the opportunity for a large number of organizational members to understand the need for and develop ideas for change as well as to support and take part in the implementation of change. The bringing together of diverse perspectives within an organization can address political issues of acceptability and acceptance. Exposure of the critical mass of people to problems in the internal and external environments can heighten the sense of need for change and lead to greater understanding. A large participative event may signify a cultural shift to a more open management style; the message sent by the event may have as much or more significance than the event itself. Getting more information and thinking focused on the system can generate more appropriate as well as more acceptable solutions. In the rationale Bunker and Alban present for large-group processes, these purposes are largely in support of managerial agendas: 'If an organization values ownership, commitment, alignment, and speed, it might consider using one of these large-scale, participative approaches' (Bunker and Alban, 1997: xvii). Jacobs (1994) reveals why this approach is advantageous in a complex corporate environment. It is consistent with the shift in business thinking to 'multi-minded ... getting a lot of points of view and feelings on the table and coalesced ... Just issuing a corporate directive isn't enough anymore' (Jacobs, 1994: 51–2).

In the national and local government arena, community dialogues bring together many voices and perspectives. Here these processes can serve a liberatory agenda as we see in the Chicali Forest story told in Bhatt and Tandon (2001). In the case described, community members identified the value of the forest to their lives and committed themselves to radical actions on their own behalf to save the forest.

Perhaps the most promising potential in large-group processes is learning, whether it is learning about organizational or community matters, about other individuals, or about oneself. In the Preface to this handbook, Reason and Bradbury describe three pathways to action research, each with the potential for learning leading to social good. Such learning supports political and cultural purposes, of course, but it is also what generates a more complete view of the system. The integration of perspectives that occurs in large-group processes is not just about making sure different perspectives are treated as valid (Emery, 1999); it is about a more accurate picture of reality than can be generated by any individual (Jacobs, 1994).

I believe we can take this notion one step further and assert that what may become available in such a setting is a multiple-party-constructed reality, or realities, that provide the foundation for inclusive and, therefore, sustainable planning. Bjørn Gustavsen (Chapter 1) draws a contrast between one single great story that is shared by many people and multiple stories of many people, stories that can be linked to produce different views of reality. He makes the specific point that distinguishes the potential learning value of large processes. It is not the mass of people agreeing on one idea that is of value, but rather, the number, complexity and quality of ideas that can be generated among a number of people. It is this aspect of large-group processes that nourishes the learning agenda.

What Is Meant by Action Research?

Greenwood and Levin (1998) set high standards for an action research process. In a relationship of 'symmetric reciprocity' (Fals Borda, Chapter 2) participants and professional researchers together define the problems to be examined, co-generate relevant knowledge about them, learn and execute social research techniques, take actions and interpret the results of actions based on what they have learned. One could argue that good designers and facilitators of any large-group process do much of this: they define the problems with process participants and teach and use social research techniques (for example, social mapping, focus-group interviews, environmental scanning) to design a process that produces relevant knowledge leading to action. Even granting that such action research activities can be found in good large-group design, the last, interpretive step in Greenwood and Levin's definition is infrequently taken. As I understand this interpretive step, it requires that learning is intentional and explicit, and, furthermore, that the process of learning has been learned. Not only have participant and researcher learned, but they are conscious of their learning. In Greenwood and Levin's definition, the action/social change that is the goal of action research is 'not just any kind of change. Action research aims to increase the ability of the involved community or organization members to control their own destinies more effectively and to keep improving their capacity to do so' (1998: 6). In other words, they have developed their capacity to continue learning.

By this definition, learning is an explicit objective in action research, and learning to learn is part of that objective. In another definition of action research, Carr and Kemmis remind us of Lewin's continuous spiral – planning, acting, observing, reflecting, and planning again – which creates 'the conditions under which learning communities may be established ... communities of enquirers committed to learning about and understanding the problems and effects of their own strategic action' (Carr and Kemmis, 1986: 164). This reflective spiral has not figured in North American discussions of large-group processes (Bunker and Alban, 1997; Emery and Purser, 1996; Jacobs, 1994; Weisbord, 1992) or in the practice as I have watched it over a few years. However, it is learning to learn that will enable participants in group processes to continue to improve their capacity to control their own destinies.

When I speak of learning and learning to learn in the context of action research, I have in mind reflective learning as described by Jack Mezirow (1991). Mezirow builds on the work of Habermas and distinguishes instrumental learning, akin to problem-solving, and communicative learning, learning to understand and be understood by others, from transformative learning. Transformative learning occurs when fundamental mental frameworks are questioned and revised. This third form of learning is dependent on a reflective review of what we have learned in the past or know and an openness to question whether our premises and assumptions are warranted. In action research, reflection leads to the uncovering of new interpretations and perspectives. As participants engage in inquiry, they are invited to challenge prior beliefs and understandings and reframe what they know. This new knowledge fosters action to bring social reality into alignment with what is understood.

This generation of knowledge in action research is supported by the conscious assumption by the researcher-facilitator of the role of the self-reflective and critical educator who fosters self-reflection and a self-critical approach in the participant community (Carr and Kemmis, 1986). Torbert (Chapter 18) calls for a commitment to engage in self-questioning-and-consciousness-raising and to self-and-other transforming types of dialogue which seek to create 'generating power' that is mutual among external and internal researchers.

Commonly, once the initial planning for a large-group process is done, the role of the designer-facilitator is to attend to group dynamics, guard the process and protect the rights of participants to speak and be heard (Bunker and Alban, 1997; Emery, 1999). Although this is not always treated as such, it is an opportunity to lead with critical reflection. In my search conference work, there are opportunities in the planning phase to engage the system in critical reflection regarding desired outcomes (for example, 'Why involve 100 people if you know what you want to do?') and participants ('If the goal is success for students, who is it most important to include in the process?'). But unless the facilitator works as critical educator and co-researcher during the conference, there is little chance for the larger participant group to become the critically reflective community for which Carr and Kemmis call.

Three Large-Group Interventions: Some Examples for Reference

One way to consider the action research question is to look at three real-life large-group interventions. Two of them are search conferences, after the practice of Merrelyn and Fred Emery (Emery and Purser, 1996) and one a Real Time Strategic Change (Jacobs, 1994). In each case, the search managers were conscious of research as they designed and managed the intervention. Each of the interventions is being actively researched apart from and in addition to any action research co-conducted with participants, which raises an important distinction. There is action research and there is research on action research. In the former, external researcher and participants define the research agenda. In the latter, the external researcher defines the agenda. In the former, action for change is an objective. In the latter, generalizable knowledge not aimed at specific action is the objective. The examples follow.

The North Country Community Food and Economic Security Search Project

This project included search conferences in six counties in the rural, mostly poor North Country region of New York State. One participant estimated that at the beginning of the twentieth century, 85 per cent of the people in the area lived on farms and were sustained on the produce of the region. By the late 1990s most of the farms were gone, and food in the region was purchased from national chainstores. Many of the poor came to subsist on welfare and food stamps.

The six conferences were held throughout the area to explore regional collaboration on food and nutrition matters as a means to promote community food security and strengthen local food systems. Funded by the US Center for Disease Control and managed by a team of university researchers, the project was designed as an experiment in a collaborative approach to improved food security. It was not thought of as an action research project so much as a research project on action research. Each conference included as participants 30–50 food system stakeholders, for example food producers, processors, retailers, consumers, clergy, anti-hunger advocates and government representatives, while the planners for the conference were representatives of local extension and community action agencies.

The two-and-a-half-day conferences followed a pattern of introduction, shared history, a visioning session or desirable future, a probable future should no actions towards the desirable future be taken, and action planning. Almost a year after the conferences, close to half of the original 34 task forces consider themselves active, working on ideas developed at the conferences. According to the university project leaders, some of the things they are working on are 'modest', others are 'impressive'. Extension and community agencies in the region have not shown an interest in following up, however, and almost none of the participants have volunteered to participate in reflection on the outcomes of the project.

The university research team is uncertain about the project as research or learning from participants' point of view. There are strong indications of individual learning, reported by people who learned about food security or the plight of farmers, and there are at least a few individuals taking on new roles and actions that involve risk. But the researchers won't predict whether these individual efforts will continue or whether there will be a continuing collective effort towards food security or further learning for action.

Going Home from Hospital, a whole system event

This event, which ultimately involved 170 people, had its history in an earlier search conference and the efforts of one small working group that emerged from that conference. The small group, first listening to the story of an unsatisfactory hospital discharge, set itself the task of finding out how to make going home from hospital a positive experience. The researchers reporting on this shift in attention identify its significance (Pratt and Kitt, 1998) as moving the focus from the patient to what others, sharing responsibilities, can do to make the system better. This very change in how a problem or issue is viewed may have its roots in the learning at the original search conference; certainly it is the kind of reframing that is part of search conference design (Emery, 1999).

The small group found others, generating a group of 40 or so, who met for half-days at a time and mapped the process of going into and out of hospital; this led, in turn, to new understandings of the role of family, community, and many organizations in a successful homegoing. The larger group produced a list of outcomes that separated into fundamental values, guiding principles and rules about what should be done when a patient goes home from hospital. Together these three comprised a possible strategy for a positive return home at the end of a hospital stay.

After this collective research, the group planned the Whole System Event, based on Real Time Strategic Change (Jacobs, 1994), in order to test their draft strategy. This was the group of 170, a far broader and more diverse group of people – service users, elders and their caregivers, doctors, agency workers – who at the outset committed themselves to carrying on with specific work at the end of the event. The results were not all as hoped, but researchers report an improved climate of co-operation among agencies, greater readiness of elders to become involved with the organizations, a reduction in blame for faults in the system, and a continuing pattern of communication among voluntary agencies and with others. What is perhaps most interesting from the perspective of this discussion, is that the learning was generated through collaborative research carried out in response to participant requests for more knowledge, research that included academic presentation and participant identification of gaps in what is known.

Vision for a Rural School District

This large-group event was designed specifically with action research in mind. This was a straightforward search conference in which 55 participants – community members, students, administrators, teachers, clerical and support staff, board of education members and parents – worked together for two-and-a-half days to confront a new and demanding environment for a small rural district. Elements of the new environment included radically more stringent state assessment standards for students graduating in the year 2005, an influx of urban people with sophisticated expectations for their children's schooling, and the virtual end of farming as the community's economic base.

This event failed as action research in the planning stage. Several months of planning with a representative group of participants still yielded a participant group that, everyone agreed afterwards, did not include the lower socio-economic sector of the community or the parents of or students in the group most 'at risk' under the new standards. And although the problem to be examined related directly to student performance, teachers were never asked as a group to help define the problem; this meant they never owned the premise of the search conference.

Nine task forces emerged from the conference with energy and determination to address a broad set of changes in the district: career opportunities, enrichment, early childhood intervention, self-governance for students, community–parent involvement, flexible structuring, staff development, technology, and data-driven decision-making. In concerted action, a co-ordinating committee of representatives from each of these reported out to the entire community of teachers and to the community at large and solicited additional participants in the changes planned. Another 40 to 50 people signed up to help with the various projects, which suggests that a broader group in the system may take ownership of the problems and actions to address them. But without ongoing inquiry into their assumptions, these action groups may never represent effectively the needs and interests of the at-risk population or of the teachers who must teach such students. While this conference was successful as action planning, the actions may not lead to significant change.

Conditions for Action Research in Large-group Design

For a large-group process to foster continuous reflection, it must be designed with that in mind. The conditions under which a large-group process can evolve as action research fall within four general areas of design: conceptualization of the task (the initial decisions about the goals and the desired outcomes), the framing of the event (who should be included, what ground rules should be followed, what role should process facilitators take), the design of the event itself (how the large group will be engaged and in what specific tasks), and, finally, the plans for follow-through.

Conceptualization

The initial phase of planning any large-group process is critical. It is essential for action research, but consistent with all good process that the facilitator-researcher engage potential participants in discussion to clarify the purpose and desired outcomes of the event. Without this exploration with insiders (what Yoland Wadsworth, Chapter 31 describes as 'compass work'), an external facilitator may operate on false assumptions that lead to an inappropriate process, or, equally dangerous, the participants themselves may enter into a process without a thorough understanding of where it might lead. Three dimensions of conceptualization are especially important. In these the role of external researcher as critical educator is most important.

1 Clarify the purpose

The researcher-facilitator takes a role in helping system representatives clarify the question to be addressed and expected outcomes. Sometimes this means asking again and again why this process is appealing and what the participants believe is needed. I once insisted that a group of traffic planners describe why traffic safety mattered and to whom before I agreed to design a large-group event with them. The questions led to broader inclusion than they had anticipated and to an awareness of the cultural dimensions of traffic safety that, at the event, made for a rich environmental scan. In another setting, a potential search conference client came to see that the large-group process she wanted for political reasons had disastrous potential because she could not accept the necessity for action on outcomes she could not predict. She had wanted to involve a broad group of people in designing a new system, but wanted to retain control of the ultimate outcome in case the plans made were opposed by a board of directors. The researcher- facilitator contribution here need not be in the content area, in school curriculum or services for the elderly or manufacturing teams, for example, but in asking the right questions to develop mutual understanding of what needs to be addressed.

2 Define the problem or issue collaboratively

Action research in large-group interventions raises a dilemma here, because in the interest of practicality, planning cannot be undertaken and the problem cannot be defined with the entire participant group. This dilemma led to the lack of ownership of high school teachers in the Rural School District search conference because these teachers were not adequately represented in the planning group and, as a result, their cynicism about a new superintendent and a 'flavor of the month' attitude towards state education department mandates remained largely undiscussed. Had the range of stakeholders been represented in the planning, this might have been avoided.

Table 14.1 *Conditions for large-group designs as action research*

Conceptualization	1 Clarify purpose – researcher as critical educator. 2 Define the problem or question – researcher and participants together. 3 Understand whose voices will be heard – and for whose action.
Framing the event	1 Establish learning as explicit objective. 2 Clarify responsibility for action – participants and researcher. 3 Decide who comes (the participants in the research).
Design of event	1 Establish ground rules for dialogue. 2 Design for multiple perspectives. 3 Prepare for power imbalance.
Continuation of reflection and action (follow-up)	1 Continue reflection on learning. 2 Offer social science tools to empower. 3 Ensure system support. 4 Shift responsibility for research to participants.

3 Whose voices and whose action?

An assumption of action research is that human beings have useful knowledge that can and should inform the shaping of their organizational and community lives. As Greenwood and Levin put it, 'action research rests on the belief and experience that all people – professional action researchers included – accumulate, organize, and use complex knowledge constantly in everyday life' (1998: 4).

This assumption is consistent with the democratic approach in most large-group processes. The strategy is to encourage the ideas and thinking of a diverse group of players in the system; events are set up to avoid expert speeches or executive directions. An exception is Real Time Strategic Change, which may include a report by the large group to an executive function, but the executive function then returns and negotiates with the large group, so that the democratic process is not a sham. It is not enough to invite people to think about and make plans for their future if the plans are ultimately little more than advice to some other 'real' decision-making body or individual. But hastily conceived large-group processes can do just that. In the Rural School District search conference, we took great care to avoid dominant roles for board members or school administrators. Their message to the conference group was a call for help: 'We know how to prepare students for exams, but we need your help to prepare students for life.'

However, the liberatory agenda of action research goes beyond the opportunity to participate genuinely in a democratic discussion. The expectation instead is to increase the ability of system members to control their own destinies. In Western capitalist society, such an agenda challenges the expectations of most organizational and community leaders. The participants in a conference to refine teamwork are not free, for example, to alter the fundamental nature of their work. The participants in the Going Home from Hospital work have no control over state licensure or regulatory requirements. Nonetheless, a point in conceptualizing the large-group process as action research would be to explore this question of control. Some measure of control over what will happen in the end is essential, or the exploration for action will be hollow.

Framing the event

Once the expectations for the process are clarified and grounded in mutual understanding, the process itself should be framed to support both the action and research goals. It must also be framed to support the capacity-building that characterizes action research. There are three key elements in this pre-event planning.

1 Establish learning as an explicit objective.
2 Clarify responsibility for action.
3 Decide who comes (the participants in the research).

1 Make learning objective explicit

Whatever the question to be addressed, a large-group process that is action research should have learning as an explicit goal and the role of reflection as an explicit component of the event. This differs dramatically from almost all large-group processes.

Translated into a design element in a large-group process, this means organizers of such a process must themselves be prepared to learn and see themselves as well as the broader group of participants as co-generators of new knowledge. Here is where it is important to understand Torbert's point (Chapter 18) that first-, second-, and third-person forms of research are 'mutually necessary'. Of course, there is risk involved because outcomes in such mutual research cannot be predicted. This is a significant difference from large-group processes designed to achieve alignment with a desired organizational culture or acceptance for decisions already in place.

2 Clarify responsibility for action

Certain large-group processes, such as Open Space, are so open to whatever agenda may develop that action may or may not result. Such a process can generate important new understandings among participants, but it cannot be counted on to lead to system change. In search conferences and Real Time Strategic Planning, the goal is clearly action, and the event is presented to potential participants as an opportunity to drive change in the organizational or community system in question. But action plans themselves do not define an action research project, and, as seen in the Rural School District search conference, a distinction should be made regarding *who* is to take action.

In action research, the participant researchers themselves undertake action. If the process is designed to inform a management team or even a designated design team, then responsibility for action lies with them and not ultimately with the participants.

3 Deciding who comes and how they will be invited

A third element in the framing of a large-group event is in the expectation about who gets to come and once there, whose voice will matter. An expressed rationale for large-group processes is that contemporary organizations are too complex and environments too uncertain for one person or group to have all the answers (Bunker and Alban, 1997), but framing a process as one in which all voices will matter must go beyond rhetoric.

With an action research goal in mind, it becomes vitally important that those who will engage in system change participate in the learning, planning process. Getting the right people in the room is worth a great deal of thought, and the social mapping that this entails is well worth the time. To do this, the facilitator-researcher engages the planning group in a series of questions, using questions about the components of the system, who will need to be involved in its change and, again and again, who is likely to be disenfranchized within the system. Members of the committee then seek volunteers from each group in the map. This process is not foolproof, as was the case in the Rural School District search conference. There were efforts by the planning group to open the process to the families of at-risk students, but they were not successful. And although there was discussion about including at-risk high school students, it may be that in the end the planning group feared their participation, for none were invited. As facilitator-researcher (and critical educator), I should have taken a much stronger role in pushing the planning committee on this issue. Part of the external researcher's role as critical educator is in getting the planners to step out of their usual social frameworks as in this case, where they would have been reaching out to an unfamiliar social group.

If learning from multiple perspectives is a goal for the process, it is not sufficient to include one person, or sometimes only a few people, whose voices are not usually heard. A disenfranchized group of people needs to be there in sufficient numbers so they feel free to speak. Four out of 55 participants in the Rural School District search were students. They were heard clearly only once, when they reported their small-group work on the environment in the school; not one of them spoke up again in the large group.

Design of event

Presumably researcher-facilitator and participant-researchers designing any large-group event will structure small- and large-group activities that:

- fit within a timeframe (though I caution on limiting the time; there is little time for reflection, even when you have been explicit about its value, in a one day event);
- begin with joint exploration;
- focus on what should be created;
- close with preliminary plans for action.

For action research purposes, there are three non-structural components that should be included:

1 Establish ground rules for dialogue.
2 Design for multiple perspectives.
3 Prepare for power imbalance.

These non-structural components are means to establish and practise inquiry and dialogue as the form of discourse within the event (Bohm, 1996; Isaacs, 1993). Care should be taken that the discourse is open and that people feel able to disagree and to state minority perspectives. The purpose of dialogue is to heighten the learning by making listening both to oneself and to others a conscious act. The Scandanavian dialogue conferences described by Bjørn Gustavsen (Chapter 1) have as their primary purpose mediating discourse, which leads to new ways of relating within the organization.

Establish ground rules for dialogue

Ground rules begin with an assumption that informs all the Emery search conferences, that all perceptions are valid (Emery and Purser, 1996). But additional ground rules serve as principles to allow those perceptions to be present in the event itself. A list of ground rules, then, might be:

- All perceptions are valid.
- Ask questions to clarify, not to challenge.
- Speak to be understood, not to score a point.
- Listen to understand. Listen to yourself listening.
- Treat difference as an opportunity to learn.
- Make sure everyone has a chance to speak.

Design for multiple perspectives

There are additional strategies to invite the inclusion of multiple perspectives. One I use in the context of search conferences is a shared history that begins with people in pairs, talking, then asks them literally to draw what they have talked about. As researcher-facilitator, I walk everyone through the mural, asking that each individual tell the story in his or her picture. Two messages are clear when this is done: (1) history is a social construction, an experience of our multiple realities, and (2) in individual stories we tell our truths. This history provides a new view of the whole and lays the foundation for reflective learning.

Secondly, when groups report to the large group on their discussion, I encourage them to present their differences as well as what they have agreed on. This enriches the content of the event and, again, encourages both the expression and consideration of different perspectives as participants struggle to make meaningful plans. It is more likely that organizational undiscussables will be mentioned in small-group discussions than in the larger group. This practice of bringing differences from the small groups into the large group creates a safe window for their exposure in the larger arena.

Prepare for power imbalance

The final point, to address power imbalance, is most difficult of all. No matter how much a researcher-facilitator professes that 'all perceptions are valid', if the participant-researcher group truly represents the whole system, there will be participants who perceive themselves as less powerful than others. Such perceptions often reflect the identity politics of the system itself; gender, job, race, socio-economic status, age, sexual orientation are not shed when we enter a room proclaiming that we each bring valuable knowledge to the discussion. People have to learn that their knowledge will be heard as valuable, which is hard to do in a single event. The ground rules begin, the history or some comparable exercise contributes, the tone and reiteration of the value of different perspectives help. An additional tool that may help is the use of a critical incident questionnaire (Brookfield, 1995) at the end of the first full day of the conference. This is a simple instrument that asks participants the points in the discussions in which they felt most and least engaged, what surprised them the most, what they found most puzzling or confusing, and what most affirming or helpful. The researcher-facilitator collects written responses and begins the following morning with a reflection on what she/he has learned from them and questions participant-researchers about the significance of some of the common responses. The questionnaire supports individual reflection, but in the feedback and discussion, it can also open the group to awareness of what others experience as well as invite into the group voices that have not been heard.

Continuation of reflection and action

Planning for follow-up is critical in a large-group process designed as action research. The spiral of action and reflection continues as participant-researchers take actions for change. Four conditions to foster that continuation are:

1. Make the expectation for a continuing spiral of action and reflection explicit.
2. Teach techniques and appropriate social science strategies that will enable and empower people to carry on with their work.
3. Ensure that system leadership is committed to ongoing action and learning.
4. Hand over responsibility to the local participant groups soon enough so they take on themselves the responsibility for learning.

Make explicit the expectation for a continuing spiral of action and reflection

The hope is that in the experience of the large-group event, participants have not only gained vital system data, but have learned new ways to frame problems, as occurred in the Going Home from

Hospital project. Learning to reflect on action is much more likely to occur in the additional time that follows the event. This can be modelled and taught as the facilitator-researcher engages with task forces to follow up on the actions they planned. It is not uncommon to have reunions of large-group events (Bunker and Alban, 1997; Weisbord, 1992). In the Rural School District search conference, reunions allow the entire group to track a strategic timeline that includes all the changes proposed for the district. Whether or not there are frequent large-group meetings, individual task forces can be encouraged to conduct their work in a process of ongoing action and reflection. The dialogue conferences in Scandinavia are expected to be repeated or replicated in a series of conferences that build on the first conference. As Gustavsen (Chapter 1) suggests, a single conference is not expected to provide answers; one can proceed by seeing what configurations emerge.

Teach techniques and appropriate social science strategies

As people leave large-group events with action plans in hand, there is a critical need for techniques and strategies to carry on their work. Often the first mission of a task group is to gather more specific data, for example, information on early childhood intervention practices in public schools or knowledge about careers represented in the community. Participant-researchers may need help putting together surveys, searching the World Wide Web, holding focus-group discussions, understanding resistance to change, or reaching consensus in a systematic way. They may need basic planning strategies, and they almost always need a systematic approach to evaluate their own work. More mature groups can use systematic approaches to question assumptions and uncover the undiscussable (Argyris, Putnam and Smith, 1985). This is not a list of requirements; it is, instead, a list of possibilities that a conscientious facilitator-researcher can only raise if she or he continues actively in the action research process.

Ensure that system leadership is commited to ongoing action and learning

While a goal of action research is that participants learn in ways that allow them to gain some control over their own destiny, it is hard in the aftermath of large-group events for participants to initiate and continue action without support from somewhere in the system. In an organizational setting, such as the Rural School District, that support can come from the top administration. In a community setting, that may need to be a unique, possibly informal, structure or network to serve as a central clearing-house for information and funding. It is wise to establish the expectation for this sort of support even before the large group convenes. In retrospect, the university researchers in the North Country Food Security see that they did not anticipate this need. The sponsoring agencies expected to assist with and participate in the conferences, but they did not anticipate a continuing role. As a result, simple co-ordinating tasks are not taken up, so groups struggle to carry on.

Hands-off responsibility

This leads to the final point that in action research, the facilitator-researcher must at some point let go and allow the participants to take responsibility for their own actions and learning. The groups that emerged from the North Country project will or will not develop regional collaboration on food systems; they will or will not find ways to increase regional economic security. What they have learned may mean they take greater control of their collective destiny. Their university partners worked with them along the way, and even wonder if they should have been more active in the immediate follow-up stage (Asher et al., 1999), but ultimately it is the participant partners who must drive change from within the system.

Conclusion

It would be unfair to leave the impression that the design of a large-group intervention as action research is a matter of following a recipe. Like any process dependent on collaboration and understanding among diverse perspectives, designing an action research large-group intervention requires negotiation and patience on the part of researchers and diverse participants. Participant groups seeking the cultural and political benefits of large-group work may be entirely uninterested in a broadly shared agenda, and their leaders may be unable to conceptualize the process as one in which they learn as well. Each setting presents its own challenges, a reality that is humbling. Taken as part of the action research process, however, the opportunities and obstacles in each are the substance that keeps action researchers so acutely sensitive to their own learning in the process.

Note

I am grateful to Bjørn Gustavsen for his thoughtful critique of this chapter. It may have improved the chapter, but it certainly contributed to my learning.

References

Argyris, C., Putnam, R. and Smith, D.M. (1985) *Action Science*. San Francisco, CA: Jossey-Bass.

Asher, K., Kraak, V., Lapido, P., McCullum, C. and Pelletier, D. (1999) Unpublished interview on North Country Community Food and Economic Security Search Conference.

Bhatt, Y. and Tandon, R. (2001) 'Citizen participation in natural resource management', in P. Reason and H. Bradbury (eds), *Handbook of Action Research: Participative Inquiry and Practice*. London: Sage Publications. pp. 301–6

Bohm, D. (1996) *On Dialogue*. London: Routledge.

Brookfield, S. (1995) *Becoming a Critically Reflective Teacher*. San Francisco, CA: Jossey-Bass.

Bunker, B.B. and Alban, B.T. (1997) *Large Group Interventions: Engaging the Whole System for Rapid Change*. San Francisco, CA: Jossey-Bass.

Carr, W. and Kemmis, S. (1986) *Becoming Critical: Education, Knowledge and Action Research*. London: Falmer Press.

Crombie, A. (1987) 'The nature and types of search conferences', *International Journal of Lifelong Education*, 4 (1): 3–33.

Emery, M. (1999) *Searching: the Theory and Power of Making Cultural Change*. Amsterdam: John Benjamins.

Emery, M. and Purser, R. (1996) *The Search Conference*. San Francisco, CA: Jossey-Bass.

Greenwood, D. and Levin, M. (1998) *Introduction to Action Research*. Thousand Oaks, CA: Sage Publications.

Isaacs, W.N. (1993) 'Dialogue, collective thinking, and organizational learning', *Organizational Dynamics*, July: 24–39.

Jacobs, R.W. (1994) *Real Time Strategic Change: How to Involve an Entire Organization in Fast and Far-reaching Change*. San Francisco, CA: Berrett-Koehler.

Kraak, V., Pelletier, D. and Rich, R. (1999) *The Forces and Events that Shaped the Food Systems of New York's North Country Region*. Ithaca, NY: Cornell University Division of Nutritional Sciences.

Mezirow, J. (1991) *Transformative Dimensions of Adult Learning*. San Francisco, CA: Jossey-Bass.

Pratt, J. and Kitt, I. (1998) 'Going home from hospital – a new approach to developing strategy', *British Journal of Health Care Management*, 4: 391–5.

Weisbord, M.R. (1992) *Discovering Common Ground*. San Francisco, CA: Berrett-Koehler.

15
Ethnodrama: Constructing Participatory, Experiential and Compelling Action Research through Performance

JIM MIENCZAKOWSKI AND STEPHEN MORGAN

CHAPTER OUTLINE

Through the use of illustrative script and other data drawn from a number of emancipatory research projects, this chapter endeavours to portray the construction of a new form of participatory and 'interactional' theatre that negotiates and constructs understandings and meanings in conjunction with its participants and audiences. In this context, critical ethnography has been combined with performance to construct the new form of theatre which we have labelled *ethnodrama*. The ethnodramas described seek to translate action research into reflexive, reflective performances which are both educational tools for teaching nursing and medical students and a form of 'voicing' to service providers by health consumers.

Using script and other data drawn from a number of *ethnodrama* projects, this chapter seeks to illustrate how critical ethnography has been combined with performance to construct a new form of action research which utilizes participatory and 'interactional' theatre to negotiate and construct understandings and meanings with its participants and audiences. Since 1992 we have been part of a team constructing critical ethnodramas with an increasing acceptance and understanding of the power of this mode of action research to influence participants and audiences. Our recognition of the potential to effect meaningful change is a paramount consideration in our work. Within this team we have also become profoundly aware of the inevitable consequences of utilizing this approach without proper caution or understanding. We have included examples of ethnodramas that seek to translate action research into reflexive, reflective performances as educational tools for teaching, nursing and medical students. Research scripts, which are also utilized as a form of 'voicing' to service providers by health consumers, are used to illustrate participatory research in health, institutional and educational settings. We have drawn from data within scripts and performances to demonstrate and describe a range of research settings through which this approach integrates 'action with knowing'.

Starting with a large-scale production concerning changing attitudes towards schizophrenia, we have moved through distinct phases of research into reflection upon experiences of drug and alcohol abuse and detoxification on to trajectories of recovery from sexual assault. With each research project we have refined the theoretical, practical and methodological approach to research and performance of research findings which has now become widely known as the 'ethnodrama' process. Using the umbrella of action research as a methodological approach, we have developed two phases to our data collection and validation processes. Initially we work very intensely with healthcare informants to gather data in an informant-led process that provides the raw data for our draft scripts [or research report]. The accuracy of this data is then validated through consensual agreement in discussion groups so that what is included in performance scripts and performances reflects the agreed views of all involved: healthcare patients, healthcare professionals, actors and research team. The second phase of our adaptation of the action research process is the actual performance(s) which is deliberately designed and performed to encourage interaction between the audience and performers.

Throughout 1994 and 1995, we challenged other arts practitioners, researchers, ethnographers, educators and academics to add to debate in this area and experiment with this form of 'performed research' in an endeavour to motivate wider community analysis, discussion and dissemination of issues affecting and informing health informants' lives and healing potential. Currently, allied national and international groups have taken up that interdisciplinary challenge and are contributing to the debate with work upon experiences of acquired brain injury (Appleby, 1995) and metastasis support groups (Gray, 1997). Other groups, to mention but a few here, have further turned towards this mode of representation to analyse a range of subjects outside health, including attitudes towards women and technology (Diaz, 1997), experiences of menarche (Fox, 1997) and understanding the motivations of theatre students who yearn for fame (Saldana, 1998). Some professional theatre companies (i.e., Triangle Theatre, Coventry, UK) are now recognizing the ability of research understandings to influence audiences and consequently utilize modes of ethnographic interpretation to authorize personal narratives and to move 'emotively' audiences' perceptions and aesthetic understandings.[1] As a mode of inquiry which further seeks to influence change among participants and audiences, while retaining the potential to construct new understandings, the approach is viable and flourishing.

In Australia, in line with federal funding opportunities to promote health intervention and health education, theatre companies have, of late, found financial inducement in the pursuit of anti-youth suicide educational performance pieces. Many of these health performance approaches claim some of the remit of action research as part of their agenda. First, they seek to inform, contest and promote changes in the perceptions, behaviours and lives of participants and audiences through research-based understandings. Secondly, the notion of research-based presentations is often used to legitimate and lend authority to their on-stage representations and post-performance audience interactions. We have been actively involved as auditors for a number of health agencies and community support groups who have sponsored such ventures and are aware of unwarranted and predictably negative outcomes from such works (Morgan, Mienczakowski and King, 1999). These implications will be discussed later in the chapter.

Critical Ethnodrama – a Process

It should be stated from the outset that the collection of data for critical ethnodrama is an informant-led process in that it is the informants who decide the purpose of the inquiry. Starting with intensive and traditional qualitative research, the ethnodrama process requires the gathering of ethnographic accounts, participant observation and, usually, a grounded-theory approach to data. We conduct ethnographic research in our chosen settings and benefit from the medical staff, student nurses or others in the team all conducting interviews and contributing data related to the experience of living and working in a particular setting. Usually, and to date we have been fortunate enough in this respect, our work is sponsored by particular health agencies who wish to promote certain aspects of health consumption. This also ensures access to the required setting.

Once data have been gathered, triangulated and returned to informants for additional comment, informant groups are asked specifically 'What do you want to tell an audience of medical health workers, health service providers, care-givers or young people about the experience of schizophrenia or alcoholism or sexual assault or cosmetic surgery or acquired brain injury or cancer or unemployment or suicide or whatever the subject of the research is?' From there we begin to compile a list of key informant themes. That is, we have adapted the principles of the phenomenological reduction of themes as proposed by Giorgi (1985) to gather, clarify and incorporate data through informant-led discussion sessions and feedback. Using the information uncovered, we are then able to prioritize the relevance of the material gathered to compile a list of scenario categories for the data. This list of themes is then subject to informant validation before scripting begins.

The critical edge of the theme production is that informants have control over how their health consumption will be publicly represented. Our application of action research to theatrical presentations may thus be viewed as a mode for questioning, reframing or providing the propositional. Critical ethnodrama presupposes interaction stemming from performance. An example that we have previously used to explain this (Mienczakowski and Morgan, 1993) is the notion of informants from the *Busting* project (alcohol-related illness) wishing to overcome the derision, abuse and ostracization generally related to their stigmatized association with a particular pathogen – in their case, alcoholism. Essentially, when they were publicly inebriated they believed themselves to be misunderstood.

> When you see a bloke falling down drunk and he's pissed legless remember he's ill not just drunk. He is ill. (Interview data, Brisbane, April 1993)

> Look around here. [A residential detox unit.] Where are all of the get-well cards? We are in here because we are sick but you don't see any grapes, flowers and get-well cards do you? (Detox Unit, Central Brisbane)

Consequently, a key ambition of the project was to depict informants not simply as human beings (rather than characterizations of pathogens), but to give them voice in the explanation of their lived realities. However, in order to represent the working realities of health professionals in that field of care appropriately we were also obliged to reflect upon the difficulties they encountered when dealing with behaviours related to distressed and intoxicated detoxees. The finding of such balance in the representations we make has always been through informant and project-group consensus and the polyphonic voicing of informants. Logically, in terms of research performance, a polyphonic narrative is the means by which disempowered health consumers might gain voice within the community while also giving rise to the potential to run counter narratives and divergent narratives drawn from health professionals and health agencies along with the superordinate informant narrative. We believe that recontextualizing and reconstructing informant words to appease the aesthetic conventions of academic and literary traditions would have further reduced the significance of the voices of our informants, thereby acting to disempower them.

Scripting and Performance

Where possible, an ethnodrama script will incorporate as much verbatim narrative as possible. Characters may speak the words and thoughts of several informants and fictionalized passages may also be included. However, *no* fictional characters, dialogue or scenarios are permitted unless they can be validated by informants and researchers as reasonable, likely, typical and representative of the range of behaviours and outcomes experienced in the setting. That is to say we do not create fictional accounts to serve a form of poesis or to satisfy aesthetic or dramatic need. The consumption of health is fraught with drama as it is! In all events, this is not theatre for artistic pretention, aesthetic appeasement or entertainment (Mienczakowski, 1998; Mienczakowski, Smith and Sinclair, 1996). We simply adapt a small repertoire of character devices integral to all narrative and performance work with the clear intention to involve audiences in the issues presented through performance for debate at the close of the performance. It is this reconstructive and reflective post-performance debate that separates ethnodrama from other health theatres and versions of verbatim theatre, which perform to, rather than discuss with, their audiences.

Furthermore, ethnodrama and other health theatres, our experience and research show us, attract predominantly health audiences (Mienczakowski, 1994, 1995, 1996).[2] In many ways, we anticipate performing our research narratives to 'expert audiences' (Mienczakowski, 1996) or informed audiences (Denzin, 1997). Consequently, we must gain their confidence that we understand and have credibility in our depiction of the research setting and its implications (from the perspectives of both professional nurses and health consumers) before we can engage them in reflecting upon their professional and personal relationship to the representations we make. As we have also performed our work in university settings and have invited local schools to performance seasons, we have, perhaps, artificially widened the nature and consistency of some audiences. With student groups we seek viable health promotion opportunities and with informed audiences the professional reflexivity that Coffey and Atkinson (1996) attribute to our work. To alleviate the potential for misunderstanding or contention prior to a performance, audiences are *cued* to it and the action research methodology from which it evolved via detailed programme booklets which also act as supplementary educational tools. In all cases we seek debate and to inform further our data, which is continually under construction. Each performance is considered an opportunity to add further data to the report.

Scenes, scenarios and dialogue are repeatedly returned to informant groups for comment and validation before inclusion in the script. The entire production is performed to, and validated by, host and non-associated expert health groups in a closed validation performance prior to any public performance of the project work. At that time, should the validating audience decide that the representations are damaging, inaccurate, inappropriate or insufficient, the performance will be reworked, postponed or abandoned. Consequently, throughout the ongoing ethnodramatic discourse performers, researchers and, to a lesser degree, audiences are provided with the opportunity to interact in an intentionally participatory assemblage. With student casts of 35 and production teams of around 50 nurses, teaching and theatre students, every effort is made to avoid falling at this important validatory hurdle. To date, happily, our consensual route to construction has served us well and we have never been forced to make major changes so close to a season of public performances.

It is at the performance stage that audiences are invited to discuss the implication of the performances with cast, health academics and educators and community health representatives at the close of performances. Sometimes audiences are also surveyed or asked to telephone questions and comments to the debriefing team when and if they desire to. Relevant health counsellors are always on hand (in private consultation rooms) to assist in debriefing audience members, and health promotion agencies have, in past years, provided a range of services such as free alcohol and penalty-free breath alcohol tests to audience members, health literature and advice, and of course financial and structural support for these projects.

One of the significant potentials of this approach is its ability to act as a reflective, reflexive tool for service providers represented in the projects. The passage below is such an example. It publicly suggests, among other things, the inadequacy of provision and police training in dealing with victims of assault.

> [*Briefing room, Canungarra Regional Police Station. Queensland. 1.15 am. Col, a Detective Inspector, is briefing Rob, a new recruit to the Sexual Assault Squad.*]
>
> *Col:* ... We have a lady just come in making a sexual assault complaint. The duty officer has taken details. She's been to A & E but didn't stay. She is in an interview room awaiting the arrival of the doctor and the forensic team. We'll interview her to get a quick statement and then again after she's been seen by the forensic team – providing she agrees to the examination, of course. Right? Many don't. Now you might find this interesting, this woman is complaining of being raped outside a nightclub by a guy she had been dancing with and had never met before. (Pause.) Now why would that be slightly unusual? ... Because most rapes are committed by relatives or friends.
> *Rob:* Do you think she'll go on with it? The complaint?
> *Col:* About 30% usually withdraw when they realize what court will involve.
> *Rob:* So, what do we do?
> *Col:* We get a short statement from her. If we know who the baddy[3] is we get him out of circulation fast. My philosophy is that we play it softly: we are kind, polite, thoughtful, caring and considerate to victims, but we want to process the victim quick in order to get enough evidence to get the offender. We must focus on the evidence.
> *Rob:* Will we offer support? Counsellors, Sexual Assault Services? You know?
> *Col:* Robert, in my experience the system supports a woman best by finding a perpetrator guilty which means we have to get the evidence and quickly. We have got a special room for this stuff downstairs. It's got a video and triple deck tape recorder. I like to get them giving evidence on video – so that if we need to – we can get that as evidence we can see her give her story – the expression on her face – see how she feels about it – see if she breaks down and cries. When that goes to a jury 'kerpow!' We will also have to ask about the nitty-gritty. So, Robert, what did they tell you on your two week training about the way we conduct interviews? (Mienczakowski and Morgan, 1998a)

In the above extract from an ethnodrama tracing the trajectories of recovery of victims of sexual assault, the dialogue of the Detective Inspector (Col) is an almost entirely unaltered verbatim account. The dialogue of the junior officer, Rob, is a combination of interviewer's prompt questions and rhetorical responses to the real-life officer's comments. This was done in order to assist the audience in their interpretation of the scene. But ethnodrama requires more than the presentation of ethnographically based research – it is influenced by a series of critical constructs that seek to influence and change the perspectives and understandings of both audiences and participants.

The theoretical focus of critical ethnodrama revolves around emerging moments and insights. Founded upon a combination of Habermasian (1987) notions of communicative consensual competence, that is, the simultaneous application of people's commonly understood language and thought processes to create meaning, ethnodrama is then refracted through Alberoni's (1984) suggestion of nascency, or the embryonic moment. These are moments, Alberoni glumly suggests, in which enlightenment may be achieved as a momentary insight swiftly followed with the realisation that the individual inevitably moves from circumstances of oppression through enlightenment into new circumstances of oppression. Nascency, in many ways, is the beginning or recognition of a moment of insight or enlightenment. Insight and enlightenment may even follow some time later than the moment of nascency. In ethnodrama the oppressive circumstances of illness, for example, may not be politically located and the remit to seek political upheaval through the form of enlightenment produced through dramatic research performances is not a coherent ambition. However, nascency is seen as a form of latent insight or potential. Nor can we be certain that nascency for our audiences will be a momentary experience. It is unlikely that ethnodrama will lead to political ambition but as it has the power to evoke simultaneously both emotional and intellectual understanding and insight, its effects might be somewhat more enduring. In sum, the ephiphanal (Denzin, 1989, 1997) nature of the cathartic constructs of ethnodrama, along with other forms of confrontational theatre (Mienczakowski, Smith and Sinclair, 1996), present ideal grounds to invoke empathetic understanding and learning. Furthermore, they provide circumstances for individuals to recognize themselves in the scenarios presented and to be confronted by the multiple interpretations and ramifications of those representations.

Baddies, Grubs and the Nitty-Gritty (an element of a current performance research project dealing with issues surrounding possible recovery from sexual assault) explains to audiences police officers' attitudes towards offenders and victims. Expressly, the one-hour performance piece further represents a detailed scenario of women's experiences of reporting sexual assault to police seen from the frank perspectives of serving officers in the

Sexual Assault Squad. In the following section of the research work, the police explain their motives and their attitudes towards dealing with victims.

Col: The [forensic] evidence can be got in a couple of hours. But the victims are naturally keen to get cleaned up. Another thing is we need to get this done quickly in order to get to the baddy before he gets a story lined up or gets away.
Rob: So we have a female cop for this interview then?
Col: No. Not one available today. Look, I might as well put you straight on this. I reckon that this woman – woman stuff is all bullshit. I am a professional person and so are you, the lawyer, the doctor even ... I can't guarantee a jury of women only so why start now? Strewth, if this was a rape-murder and we were looking at the naked body of a deceased female victim nobody would be expressing these sensibilities?

I want to be there when they gather evidence, if I'm allowed, to be able to direct the investigation. To be able to say 'photograph that bruise'; 'what's made that scar?' 'Take a shot of that.' Her body is a crime scene and I'm gathering evidence – to try and piece the story together and make sure it fits. Anything at all to get enough evidence for a watertight case. Think of another crime where you have to ask permission to gather evidence or gather it second hand through a connie?[4] Sometimes I'm allowed in, sometimes I have to get a connie to go in my place. It makes me sick. I don't like it. It's bad police-work.

(Scene iv)

Col: How would you feel to be describing a horrific personal violation to strangers? You've been violently, sexually assaulted. Terrified and abused. Traumatized. And now you have to face a strange group of police officers, doctors and forensic scientists as well as tell us all the details about something you are trying your hardest to forget. This is information that will be used in court and later the details of your violation will be in the hands of journalists and your relatives, neighbours and even your Mum and Dad will be reading about what, exactly, was done to you. Your best hope is if a baddy confesses and we can save you from going to court. And to do that we have to put pressure on with the amount of evidence we have – so victims refusing the examination is a disaster if we want a conviction. But – either way we do it nicely with the grub. We are nice to them to soften them up, to get them to confess. Two-faced folk – that's what we gotta be. So we treat the baddies like Lord Muck from Turd Island. And it makes me sick, underneath, of course. We apologise for having to pull them in. We are blokish about it. Give it the old 'nudge nudge'. [*Returns to stage where Rob is reading a newspaper.*]

[*The scene moves into a demonstration of a suspect interview scenario constructed from verbatim data contributed by a Senior Inspector of the Sexual Assault Investigations Unit.*]

The attitudes and pragmatism of the police officer's aim to provide social therapy through conviction are interspersed during the performance with verbatim data drawn from the contributions of sexual assault victims and sexual assault service counsellors. In this way the 'offence' and its procedural and judicial treatment are constantly related to their human consequences for victims.

It was very intimidating, and the police officer I saw, er, whilst he befriended me, um ... he actually eventually crossed the line of his professional role, ah ... Started to come around ... we eventually had a relationship for a while. I think he found my vulnerability and dependence, all of those things, he found them erotic.

When I went to the police ... I wasn't ... It wasn't offered to me to see a woman, and retelling the whole saga took eight hours. The first four hours ... oh shit ...

Finally I saw him, I think I saw him about a week after it had occurred. He took me into an interview room and ah ... didn't record or anything the door was open. I had to come back the next day and make my statement in a public office and you could have heard a pin drop – so it was quite intimidating really. Everyone could hear and there were lots of interruptions. He very kindly came in on his day off, the next day, to take my statement 'cause he saw my genuine distress. Ah, it was still pretty intimidating I would have much preferred to talk to someone ... a woman in an office in a sexual assault clinic.

Look, the first positive thing I did after the assault was to go to the police, well before that the first positive thing was to physically run away and hide from my assailant, the second positive thing was to go to the police. That was a really big step because it was putting all of my eggs in one basket and publicly saying 'its not my fault' in front of a lot of uniformed men. So I think it was a big step in the healing process ... and going through with the stalking charges was a big step too, because it meant that I was saying that I count and have rights and the law should protect me. (Verbatim informant account, Mienczakowski and Morgan, 1998a)

Inevitably, what is constructed here is an opening of competing issues and interests for audiences to debate and for further data to be added to the performance scripts. This all takes place in a controlled environment in which informants, participants and informed audiences can negotiate a consensual post-performance position and understanding of the import of the performance research. At times medical practitioners have claimed to have seen themselves within representations of medical behaviours and have declared that they have been moved to alter and inform their future professional behaviours. Other audiences have been stimulated to take the health education into their places of professional work – in one notable case instigating a campaign for alcohol awareness in a large national organization. The overriding appeal of this mode of research representation is that it is written in the public voice (Agger, 1991) and attracts far wider and greater audiences than we might achieve with less contemporary research approaches. When a theatre auditorium is nightly crowded with people who are about to hear a research report, we think back to our first ethnographies (no less weighty in construction or so we then thought) that were probably read by no more than a handful of people.

What is to be Done Anew

Having re-travelled the basic structures of ethnodrama it is imperative that we now turn to recognition of how action research might produce unwanted or unwarranted responses from audiences and participants. Latterly, we have become aware that the performance process can provide opportunities for unpredictable responses from participants. Although we do not use informants as performers (hence avoiding, at informants' suggestions, placing health consumers under performance duress or having them seen as performing pathogens [Mienczakowski, 1995, 1996]), we are overtly concerned with implications for young performers and vulnerable performers (Mienczakowski and Morgan, 1998b).

The use of performance modes is easily recognized as being of significance to studies in Symbolic Interactionism. Indeed, ethnodrama is established upon the notion that reality is symbolically represented upon the stage, with the consequence that understanding of the social world may be influenced and negotiated through social accessing of the symbolic through exposure to skilled performance. Missing from the dynamic are the tangible elements of constructive or negative emotional influences that performance research reporting may uncontrollably produce for certain audiences. Artaud's early theatre of cruelty for example – a theatre which intentionally challenged the psychological and emotional positioning of audiences in order to bring about a cathartic form of therapy (Artaud, 1970) – is a strong example of experimentation with the emotional positioning of audiences. It remains highly questionable whether his theatrical works were ever capable of producing what we have described as a 'constructive catharsis' (Mienczakowski, Smith and Sinclair, 1996). Without doubt, Artaud's performance genre represents a desire to produce deep emotional turmoil (Sontag, 1976) and cathartic responses from audiences (Artaud, 1976); that aside, he has often been accused of providing opportunities for psychological and emotional destruction as well as constructivity (Grotowski, 1986). Recently members of our team have moved towards exploration of the ethical dimensions of constructing research-based theatre and catharsis.

Although identifying strongly with this emergent trend in research representation, we suggest that the theoretical and practical advances in research theatre must be framed within consideration of previously unanticipated and accompanying ethical difficulties that inescapably co-exist with the opportunities performance research provides. Therefore we are drawn to consider a range of unwanted, and easily overlooked, outcomes. While these may be seen as relatively marginal, in that they are occurring in only one or two individuals or small groups, they are nonetheless greatly significant for the persons so affected and for the ethical conduct and representation of ethnographic research (Mienczakowski and Morgan, 1998b). We propose that ethnographic performance must pursue a harmonious relationship between researchers, participants and audiences, remaining responsive and aware of the rights and responsibilities of each.

Woods (1996) acknowledges the potential of poetics to access audiences previously left unmoved by more traditional research approaches. However, Woods further calls for the endorsement of a supporting supplementary narrative to validate the poetic-narrative or interpretative text. Woods believes that the inclusion of such (academic) text might assist claims of veracity and confirm authority by demonstrating examples of validated data while concomitantly revealing how a given literary text was constructed. Woods suggests that validity claims might subtly be supplanted with quality checks to aid navigation and rigour within research. Textually this might have implications for the construction of research narratives but its implications for ethical efficacy are less certain. The ethical difficulties I am about to describe in the following three examples (which we have emphasized elsewhere) reflect unintentional consequences that are unlikely to have been resolved through a textual parody narrative. They are unwanted consequences nonetheless.

1 Impact upon performers

Recently, we (Mienczakowski and Morgan, 1998a), in a semi-confessional tale, related how unwittingly we placed a mature-age student actor (who possessed firm but unpronounced and unrecognized fundamentalist religious beliefs) in a situation of personal vulnerability. This student actor came face to face with a patient in full-blown psychosis during the performance of a work on schizophrenia in a psychiatric institution. The patient mounted the stage and confronted her – she was playing the part of a psychiatrist and he had some specific questions and comments about his own medical scenario. However, to the student, her belief system stipulated that persons who were in schizophrenic psychosis were possessed by the devil and were the embodied mouthpieces of the devil. To this student he was the devil. Her scene ground to a halt and she, much troubled, fled out of the auditorium into the night.

Notably, student nurses in the cast were unfazed by the audience interactions but student actors (out of their typical audience–performer relationship) were much disturbed by this special audience's running commentary and unplanned participation in the play. Of course, the student nurses were in their professional habitus, performing research as part of their learning about the consumption and provision of mental health services. The student actors in the cast, and some of the production team, were caught off-guard because this audience had no notion of 'artistic integrity' or of the self-identity concepts of the performers as actors/artists. In effect, some actor students professed aggression towards the audience for marring their endeavours whereas the nursing student actors, taking themselves less seriously, adlibbed with the audience and escorted wandering patients back to their seats without breaking role or dropping the pace of the performance.

2 Audiences and health consumption

During a validation performance of the play *Busting* (Mienczakowski and Morgan, 1993), a nurse-actor portraying professional nursing routines surrounding standard vitamin injections for detoxees spilled the contents of a syringe box as a plot device for raising issues of nursing vulnerabilities in alcohol and drug detox settings. Some audience members from a local rehabilitation halfway house immediately demonstrated drug-related needle-fixation and became obsessed with the needles – leaving their seats to examine them. After the performance these audience members confessed to becoming agitated and obsessed with the needles after having seen them on stage. Our question has to be that our representation was validated as authentic but at what cost to the recovery processes of our audience? (Morgan and Mienczakowski, 1999).

3 The impact of fictionally-constructed suicide

Due to our early work in promoting this research area, team members have become increasingly involved in the evaluations of health-related performance projects produced by others. In response to the significant funding opportunities made available for anti-suicide health promotion in Australia, many theatre groups now access health funding in order to pilot health theatre – with an alleged critical research edge – in the area of youth suicide prevention. A Brisbane-based theatre production in which our team was involved in evaluating illustrates another and serious ethical difficulty.

> The evaluation indicated that exposure to the performance was the source of some likely harm or distress to a small number of audience members and performers (and possibly fatally). In addition it is possible to recognise the manner in which the topic of suicide was reconstrued by audiences in a new light, this possibly to the effect of contributing to imitative suicide or suicide contagion. (Morgan and Mienczakowski, 1999: 11)

It differed significantly from our own ethnodramatic approach in the respect that the group that constructed the play also largely performed it – but with professional directorial and performance assistance. An experienced mental health professional also produced the work and guided the group and its script production. While on one level the play was of educational value, revealing experiences and realities about living with schizophrenia, the performance also involved some elements of concern in relation to suicide. The play was dedicated to a group associate who had recently committed suicide, contained a song that may have indicated a suicidal intent, contained a graphic which depicted a hanging suicide and concluded with a final night post-performance hanging suicide of one of the writers. This was followed within one week by the hanging suicide of an associate of the group, although we are not able fully to verify attendance. Although tautologous, the difficulty in validating suicide-related data is a significant issue that affects the ability to make assertive causal statements, as noted in detail by Schmidtke and Haffner (1989).

In this way, it must be noted, there is no way of ascertaining the role that the dramatic performance played in any of the actual suicides, especially given the presence of other likely indicators to increase suicidal risk, such as schizophrenia. The point is simply that the potency of dramatic representation may be a contributing factor and that the representation of, or direct referring to, suicide within dramatic performance (Morgan, Rolfe and Mienczakowski, 1999) or educational forums (Kalafat and Elias, 1995; Taylor, 1998) is worthy of particular reservation. If suicide is a topic worthy of consideration prior to representation, then what other topics need to be similarly considered? (Morgan, Mienczakowski and King, 1999).

In response to these new understandings, we have moved towards the notion of guidelines to aid dramatists in the suicide area. These guidelines have already been proposed by Morgan, Rolfe and Mienczakowski (1999) and have been utilized within Australian contexts. However, the issues raised by a broad-based adoption of performed action research methodologies by unwary groups or by those unattuned to the notion of attracting and working with 'health' audiences remain problematic.

From the examples given, it seems evident that there have been clear and recognizable negative effects upon certain audiences and performers. Furthermore, it is distinctly possible that the performed representations and scenarios prompted negative effects among audiences and performers – influencing their social actions. In one case, associated with the Brisbane-based health theatre performances, it is feasible that the performance encouraged or prompted actual suicide. The ethical dilemma, for example, of presenting strong research-based representations of suicide or sexual violence or sexual abuse to young or vulnerable audiences is painfully clear. Audiences require a series of considerations and warnings in order to assist in the screening of both subject matter and audience vulnerability – where possible. This is most pertinent in the presentation of research-based interpretations to school audiences. For these reasons we maintain and advocate a rigorous adherence to action research containment within our methodology and that of other practitioners of critical ethnodrama. We consider that this should be viewed as an integral reflective practice.

Ethnodrama's contribution to action research lies in its potential to engage actively healthcare recipients, healthcare professionals and audiences in the consensual deconstruction and dissemination of knowledge. Through its employment of the validation of data through consensual processes of triangulation, the ethnodramatic practice ensures that data is constantly being reviewed and updated. It also aims to encourage interaction between the research team and healthcare informants by focusing their activities on the creation of an informed performance script.

The potential of performance to impact upon audiences is not to be underestimated and must be realized as a pre-condition of all ethnodrama performance ethnographies. Research ethics are a well-trammelled tenet of most research activity. However, the ethical dilemmas of performed research are less well recognized or understood. Performance, ethnodrama and health theatre are important facets of health education and health promotion and to embrace their worth fully researchers need to embrace and develop a fuller understanding of the ethical ramifications and potentials of this emerging mode of research performances. Beyond the containment of action research this mode of performance of research represents a challenge to audiences' emotions. Consequently, we are in new territory and this is the ethical dilemma.

Notes

We would like to extend our thanks and gratitude to Jim's Research Associate, Lynn Smith, for her support, linguistic gymnastics, crazy sense of mischief, resourceful researching techniques and prowess at the keyboard in getting this chapter finished.

1 In particular we refer to Carran Waterfield's performance in 'My Sister, My Angel' (1998) in which she combined auto-ethnography with informant dialogue (in this case her mother's recorded voice) to tell of the death of a sibling in childhood.

2 Surveying of our audiences suggests that most audiences for health performances consist of care-givers, health consumers, professional nurses, medical doctors and health service providers as well as health educators. Performances with a health and health research remit seem less likely to attract 'general' audiences. Many audiences of our work are not regular theatre-goers and attend the performances because of professional or subject interest. Emphatically, research-based understandings in this area require close attention to accuracy. We have witnessed first hand the wrath of health consumers and health support groups who several years back attended some colleagues' performance foray into representing mental health consumption which, for the sake of artistry, aesthetics and plot convenience took both licence and liberty with the performed construction of mental illness. The traditional and embracing aims of theatre clashed with the distinct social, political and cultural sensitivities of health consumer rights and needs.

3 In the argot of Queensland Police a 'baddy' is a serious offender – usually a rapist or paedophile. A 'grub' is the terminology reserved for the worst and cruellest of sex offenders. The 'nitty-gritty' refers to detailed victim statements concerning the exact nature, circumstances and events of their abuse and/or attack. Such statements are central to presenting a sustainable case for prosecution and are often pivotal in the alleged attackers' cases for defence.

4 Connie is a female police officer.

References

Agger, B. (1991) 'Theorising the decline of discourse or the decline of theoretical discourse?', in P. Wexler (ed.), *Critical Theory Now*. New York and London: Falmer Press. Chapter 5.

Alberoni, F. (1984) *Movement and Institution* (trans. P.A. Delmoro). New York: Columbia University Press.

Appleby, P. (1995) *A Good Smack in the Head* (Acquired Brain Injury Performance Group). Headway Gold Coast, Pty. Gold Coast: Griffith University.

Artaud, A. (1970) *The Theatre and Its Double* (trans. V. Corti). Signature Series 4. London: John Calder.

Artaud, A. (1976) *Antonin Artaud: Selected Writings* (Introduction by Susan Sontag; trans. H. Weaver). New York: Farrar, Straus & Giroux.

Coffey, A. and Atkinson, P. (1996) *Making Sense of Qualitative Data: Complementary Research Strategies*. Newbury Park, CA: Sage Publications.

Denzin, N.K. (1989) *Interpretive Interactionism*. Newbury Park, CA: Sage Publications.

Denzin, N.K. (1997) *Interpretive Ethnography: Ethnographic Practices for the 21st Century*. Thousand Oaks, CA: Sage Publications.

Diaz, G. (1997) 'Turned on/turned off (a clarion call)', *Qualitatives '97* OISE. Toronto, ON: Desktop Publication, Muzzin, L. et al. (eds), August 1997. ISBN 0–9682062–0–4.

Fox, K. (1997) 'First blood: rituals of menarche', *Qualitatives '97* OISE. Toronto, ON: Desktop Publication, Muzzin, L. et al. (eds), August 1997. ISBN 0–9682062–0–4.

Giorgi, A. (1985) *Phenomenology and Psychological Research*. Pittsburgh, PA: Duquesne University Press.

Gray, R. (1997) 'Handle with care? Living with metastatic breast cancer'. An ethnodrama production by the research team of the Toronto-Sunnybrook Regional Cancer Centre, Ontario.

Grotowski, J. (1986) *Towards a Poor Theater*. New York: Simon & Schuster.

Habermas, J. (1987) *Knowledge and Human Interests* (trans. J.J. Shapiro). Cambridge: Polity Press.

Kalafat, J. and Elias, M. (1995) 'Suicide in an educational context', *Suicide and Life Threatening Behavior*, 25: 123–33.

Mienczakowski, J. (1994) 'Theatrical and Theoretical Experimentation' in Ethnography & Dramatic Form', *ND DRAMA*, UK 2: 16–23.

Mienczakowski, J. (1995) 'The theatre of ethnography: the reconstruction of ethnography into theatre with emancipatory potential', *Qualitative Inquiry*, 1 (3): 360–75.

Mienczakowski, J. (1996) 'An ethnographic act', in C. Ellis and A. Bochner (eds), *Composing Ethnography: Alternative Forms of Writing*. Thousand Oaks, CA: Sage Publications. Chapter 10.

Mienczakowski, J. (1998) 'Reaching wide audiences: reflexive research and performance', *NADIE Journal (NJ)*, 22 (1): 75–82.

Mienczakowski, J. and Morgan, S. (1993) *Busting: the Challenge of the Drought Spiri*. Brisbane, Queensland: Griffith University Reprographics.

Mienczakowski, J. and Morgan, S. (1998a) *Stop! In the Name of Love & Baddies, Grubs and the Nitty-Gritty*. Society for the Study of Symbolic Interaction (SSSI), Couch Stone Symposium, 22–24 February 1998. University of Houston, University Hilton Hotel Complex, Houston, TX.

Mienczakowski, J. and Morgan, S. (1998b) 'Finding closure and moving on', *Drama*, 5: 22–9.

Mienczakowski, J., Smith, R. and Sinclair, M. (1996) 'On the road to catharsis: a theoretical framework for change', *Qualitative Inquiry*, 2 (4): 439–62.

Morgan, S. and Mienczakowski, J. (1999) *Ethical dilemmas in performance ethnography: Examples from ethnodrama and theatre*. Couch Stone Symposium, SSSI, Society for the Study of Symbolic Interactionism, Las Vegas, NV, February 1999.

Morgan, S., Mienczakowski, J. and King, G. (1999) 'The dramatic representation of suicide: issues, concerns and guidelines'. Suicide Prevention Australia, Melbourne Convention Centre, 25 March 1999. Published as an audiotape by Suicide Prevention Australia, Melbourne.

Morgan, S., Rolfe, A. and Mienczakowski, J. (1999) 'Exploration! Intervention! Education! Health Promotion!: a developmental set of guidelines for the presentation of dramatic performances in suicide prevention', in S. Robertson, K. Kellehear, M. Teeson and V. Miller (eds), *Making History: Shaping the Future: the 1999 Mental Health Services Conference*. Rozelle, NSW: Standard Publishing House.

Saldana, J. (1998) 'Ethical issues in an ethnographic performance text: the dramatic impact of juicy stuff', *RIDE* (UK), 3 (3): 74–100.

Schmidtke, A. and Haffner, H. (1989) 'Public attitudes towards and effects of the mass media on suicidal and self-harm behaviour', in R.F.W. Diekstra, *Suicide and Its Prevention*. Leiden: World Health Organisation.

Sontag, S. (1976) 'Introduction', in A. Artaud, *Antonin Artaud: Selected Writings* (trans. H. Weaver). New York: Farrar, Straus & Giroux.

Taylor, B. (1998) *Educating for Life: Guidelines for Effective Suicide Prevention Programs in Secondary Schools*. Melbourne: Taylor Education.

Woods, P. (1996) *Researching the Art of Teaching Ethnography for Educational Use*. London: Routledge.

16
Clinical Inquiry/Research

EDGAR H. SCHEIN

CHAPTER OUTLINE

The clinical approach to research is elaborated in this chapter by contrasting it to various other ways of obtaining information from human systems. The basic argument is that if researchers base their inquiry on the needs of the client system, and if they work on developing a helping relationship with that system, they will obtain deeper and more valid information. Depth and validity are preferable to the broader but more superficial kinds of data that are obtained by the more traditional research methods.

The basic purpose of this chapter is to show that useful data can be gathered in situations that are *not* created by the researcher. Gathering data, building concepts and developing theory are the result of a research *attitude*, a desire to clarify what is going on and communicate that clarification to other researchers. It is my argument that some of the best opportunities for such inquiry actually arise in situations where the setting is created by someone who wants help, not by the researcher deciding what to study. Gathering useful data in settings that are defined by 'clients' who are seeking help is what I mean by Clinical Inquiry/Research (Schein, 1987a).

Many would argue that 'action research' is precisely geared to this point. However, the original definition of action research is to take research subjects or targets of change programmes and turn them into researchers by involving them in the research process. The research agenda is defined by the researcher or change agent, and the 'subjects' or 'targets' become involved as a result of researcher initiatives. The researcher's skills in gathering and analysing data are the primary bases for the quality of the outcome. Clinical Research, by contrast, involves the gathering of data in clinical settings that are created by people seeking help. The researcher in these settings is called in because of his or her *helping* skills and the subject matter is defined by the client. It is my argument that if the helper takes an attitude of inquiry, this enhances not only the helping process but creates the opportunity for using the data that are produced to build concepts and theory that will be of use to others. The best examples come from medicine, particularly psychotherapy, where the publication of analyses of selected cases builds knowledge for fellow practitioners.

To clarify what Clinical Inquiry or Clinical Research (CR) means conceptually and operationally I need to locate CR among various other forms of traditional research and action research. My goal is to show that in each of these types of research a somewhat different psychological contract develops between the researcher and the subject (client) which has consequences not only for the kinds of data that can be gathered and for issues of reliability and validity, but also for the welfare of the subjects.

Three basic dimensions differentiate various kinds of research with human systems, as shown in Figure 16.1: (1) whether the initiative for the inquiry is launched by the participant or the researcher; (2) the degree to which the researcher/inquirer becomes personally involved in the inquiry process; and (3) the degree to which the participant in the research becomes personally involved in the process.

These dimensions produce eight different kinds of inquiry model and psychological contract. I will briefly describe each of these cells and give illustrations of the kinds of research or inquiry that characterize them. CR will then stand out in sharp contrast to the other models of inquiry and it is this contrast that most clearly defines the characteristics of CR.

Researcher/consultant initiates the project

		Subject/client involvement: Low	Subject/client involvement: High
Researcher involvement	Low	1. Demography	2. Experiments and surveys
	High	3. Participant observation and ethnography	4. Action research

Subject/client initiates the project

		Subject/client involvement: Low	Subject/client involvement: High
Researcher involvement	Low	6. Internship	7. Educational interventions and facilitation
	High	5. Contract research and consulting	8. Process consulting and clinical inquiry

Figure 16.1 Types of researcher/consultant/subject/client relationships

Researcher Initiated Inquiry

The four kinds of research that will be described below have in common that it is the *researcher* who makes the initial decision to get connected to some members of an organization, who advertises for 'research subjects' or who begins to make unobtrusive observations of some phenomenon he or she is interested in. If the research is to take place in an organizational context, the major up-front issues are how to get 'entry' into the organization and how to elicit the co-operation of organization members so that they will become willing research subjects. How these issues are resolved depends on how involved the subject becomes in the inquiry process and how involved the researcher becomes with the participants.

Cell 1: Low researcher and low subject involvement – demography

In this form of inquiry a researcher decides on a topic and finds a way of gathering data that, at the extreme, may not involve the participants at all. At the same time the researcher attempts to be objective and distances him- or herself from the data. Examples would be to work with demographic variables or records. For example, when I was a consultant with Ciba-Geigy in the late 1970s my primary client was the head of management development. He was asked at one point to make some recommendations about the relative importance for executive development of cross-functional and international assignments. He had records of the actual movement of all of the top executives for the past 20 years so we jointly decided that the 'research' would be an analysis of these records to determine whether actual patterns of greater or lesser movement were related to career outcomes of various sorts. This required coding the records and statistical analysis which revealed clear patterns that later became the basis of recommendations for future executive career management.

The essence of this kind of research is that the participant may never be involved at all and the researcher takes a fairly uninvolved role. It is the research question, the data and the research methods that drive the process and that define the 'quality' of the research. Joseph Campbell's analyses of heroic myths and David McClelland's analyses of achievement motivation in different cultures based on analysis of their art and literature would be good examples.

Cell 2: Low researcher but high participant involvement – experiments and surveys

This form of research also starts with the researcher formulating the question, issue or problem but differs from Cell 1 in that the method chosen requires some direct involvement of the participants. The researcher develops a design that minimizes researcher bias such as a double-blind experiment, but the participant has to display some behaviour, opinions or feelings that become the primary data to be analysed. In the organizational context experiments are rare, though Kurt Lewin was a genius in setting up experimental situations that enabled us to perceive what the dynamics were of different kinds of leadership and group climates (Lewin, 1947/1952, 1939/1999). Similarly, Muzapher Sherif, in his studies of boys' clubs, showed us clearly what some of the dynamics of inter-group competition are (Sherif et al., 1961).

In this form of research the participants are usually not privy to the purpose of the study though some form of debriefing is usually considered to be part of the psychological contract with the participant. It is this form of research that led to the evolution of consent forms for research subjects because experimenters became ethically blind to some of the consequences of the research process itself. Subjects were asked to engage in behaviour or reveal feelings that altered the subjects' self-image in non-reversible ways, raising a host of issues about the degree to which the experiment was actually an intervention, not just pure inquiry. Of course, signing consent forms may not solve this problem because when subjects are asked to sign consent forms they rarely know what the consequences of participation will be, which puts the ultimate ethical burden back on to the researcher.

Consumer or employee surveys conducted by the market research department or the human resources function are further examples of this kind of research if the purpose is primarily to learn what employees or consumers think before any decisions are made on how to act on the data. Some feedback of results might be promised as an incentive to participate but the primary purpose is for the researcher to draw conclusions and make recommendations about future programmes or policies. Particularly in climate and culture surveys, we seem to remain ethically blind to the issue of unintended intervention in asking employees all kinds of questions that have consequences for how they think and feel. Providing feedback is then a further intervention, which can alter but not undo the effects of taking the survey in the first place.

Cell 3: High researcher but low subject involvement – participant observation and ethnography

The classic form of this kind of research is participant observation or ethnography. In its pure form the assumption is made that the researchers become totally involved while, at the same time, trying to remain objective and to minimize their impact on the participants. If we recall the Hawthorne studies, a big issue was made of the fact that putting the observer into the Bank Wiring Room had an initial effect but the researchers argued that after some time he became simply part of the 'woodwork' and the data could therefore be trusted as being free of his influence (Homans, 1950). It is important for ethnographers to be able to argue that their time spent in the culture did not influence the culture, hence their data could be trusted to be 'objective'.

In this kind of inquiry researchers have to work actively with the participants to gather the data even as they are concealing the purpose of the inquiry and the way in which the data will be analysed (Whyte, 1943; Van Maanen, 1979). The evolution of projective tests can, in fact, be related to the need to have a measurement tool that the subject is unable to decipher, and may be used in either Cell 2 or Cell 3 as part of the inquiry process.

Cell 4: High researcher and high subject involvement – type 1 action research

Kurt Lewin's dictum that you cannot understand an organization until you try to change it is perhaps the clearest theoretical justification for the kind of research that occurs in this cell and that led to the label 'action research'. It is worth re-telling the story of how a group of researchers at an early group dynamics workshop at Bethel, Maine, were sitting around one evening to analyse their group observations of that day. A number of participants drifted into the room and started to listen to what the researchers were talking about. At one point some of these participants heard analytical comments that did not fit what they remembered as having happened so they intervened and said that they wanted to tell their view of what had gone on. This led to a joint analysis of the data by both researchers and participants, which proved to be much richer than what the researchers had come up with themselves. Such joint analysis then came to be seen as a legitimate form of inquiry even though by Cell 1 standards it could be viewed as 'contaminating' the data.

The discovery that greater insight could be obtained by joint analysis of the data between researcher and participant led both to the concept of 'action research' and to the invention of the training group (T-Group) that became a major way of helping participants to get in touch with intrapsychic, interpersonal and group dynamic phenomena (Schein and Bennis, 1965). Paradoxically, while joint inquiry when launched by the needs of the researcher led to the evolution of action research, T-groups designed to help participants to learn about themselves and about group dynamics were not viewed as producing 'research data'. Instead, outside researchers were hired to study what went on in T-groups and to evaluate the results of this kind of training.

But, of course, the staff members or 'trainers' in these groups were often professionally trained researchers whose observations led to the development of concepts and theories that informed the training field. But for some reason this form of inquiry was not viewed as a legitimate research method. Yet it is in these settings that I first encountered the power of what I later defined as 'Clinical Research'. What distinguishes it most clearly is that the joint inquiry is launched by the needs of the participants who now become 'clients' not research subjects. The trainer/consultant now can observe both the process and content of what goes on in trying to help the client to learn and can use these data to build and test theory in the clinical process itself.

In this kind of action research the researcher remains in control and defines the goals of the inquiry as in 'survey-feedback'. The research process is governed by getting valid data and the involvement of the participants is justified primarily by the assumption that the data will be that much better if they are involved. Subsequently, the researcher may train various managers to give feedback to the employees in order to initiate remedial action. Metaphors such as 'cascading the data down the organization' are used to highlight the action research elements and to show how the involvement of the participants in the data analysis will lead to improved organizational performance.

This form of action research differs from Cell 3 research in that the goal of the Cell 3 researcher is to gather data as a basis for action, whereas the Cell 4 researcher acknowledges that until the participants become involved in the gathering and analysis of the data we do not know enough to take the right kind of action and get the intended result. But this type of action research is also blind to the fact that the administration of the initial survey is itself already an intervention whether or not the data are fed back to the participants. The goal in this cell remains a focus on gathering valid data, developing reliable and valid methods of obtaining opinions and feelings, and using appropriate statistical methods to massage the data. The involvement of the participants is motivated primarily by the desire to validate the data. The focus remains primarily on the researcher's need to uphold the standards of research and only secondarily shifts to the consequences for the participants of doing the research at all. Participants remain 'subjects'; they do not become 'clients'.

In summary, when the researchers choose the focus of the research, they have the problem of gaining entry into the research site and eliciting the co-operation of the research subjects. Even if they are only to be observed, they must agree to the researcher's presence and hopefully ignore the researcher sufficiently to allow the assumption that what is observed is not influenced in a major way by the researcher's presence. The researcher offers as his or her contribution to the psychological contract that the results will be fed back to the participants in some form or another, that the results may be helpful to the participants and, most importantly, that the participants will not be harmed. Hence confidentiality is promised and the researcher may offer to let the participants see what will be published about them. What remains unstated and often unexplored by either researcher or participants is the consequences of participation itself. Most researcher-initiated research in all of the above cells assumes that the research process itself is more or less benign, that it 'precedes' intervention, and that the research process if anything will benefit the participants in that it gets them to inquire into their own processes.

The bottom line is that most researchers operating in this mode have little or no training in how to assess the consequences of their research interventions for the participants. The assumptions that research is benign allow researchers to proceed without worrying too much about the effects they may have on the participants.

Client Initiated Inquiry

If an individual in a group or organization needs some kind of help or solicits some research to be done in the organization, the psychological contract is much more complex. We can no longer think of research 'subjects'; the participants now become 'clients' who will pay for the services rendered. Some level of entry into the organization is guaranteed, but the person invited in to help must have helping skills and must focus, at least initially, on the areas of concern defined by the client. For many helpers, professional consultants or therapists, these considerations limit their self-concept to that of helper. They do not consider the possibility of gathering valid data in the helping context, and this self-perception is reinforced by the academic journal stance of not honouring case descriptions and other forms of qualitative research as legitimate. My argument is that not only should data-gathering based on helping be considered legitimate research, but such data are often deeper and more valid than any data gathered in the researcher initiated models (Cells 1–4).

On the one hand, the helping relationship limits the degree to which the helper can define a research agenda on top of the primary helping agenda. On the other hand, the fact that the client has asked for help legitimizes for the helper/researcher all kinds of inquiry possibilities. Questions that could never be asked by the researcher in the researcher-initiated model because they would be viewed as an invasion of privacy can be asked if it is deemed necessary by the helper to gather that kind of information in order to be helpful.

What this means, in essence, is that client-initiated inquiry is restricted in scope but is potentially much 'deeper'. It also means, however, that the research component must be governed by the *ethics of intervention*. If the helping process compromises the data and/or if certain kinds of data-gathering would not be helpful, they must be abandoned. The researcher must find ways of checking reliability and validity within the parameters of the intervention model and must build the research agenda around the possibilities that the client makes available.

As we will see, the boundaries between the four cells in this domain are not as clear-cut. Clinical research becomes possible to some degree in each cell. Nevertheless it is useful to distinguish some of the consequences of different degrees of involvement by the client and the researcher.

Cell 5: High researcher, low client involvement – contract research and expert consulting

One variant of this kind of inquiry results when the *client decides the research agenda and hires a researcher to implement it.* The client defines the problem, decides that some formal research is the way to solve it, decides who the researcher is to be and then empowers the researcher to proceed. Externally conducted employee or customer surveys, benchmarking studies of kinds such as salary surveys and various other kinds of 'contract' research would fit this model. Recently, I have had many inquiries around the question of whether or not I could come into an organization and do a cultural assessment for them, implying that I would gather the data, analyse them, and provide feedback on the culture of that organization.

What the client wants is data and information. The helper/consultant is hired to be an expert in providing it. If the data are primarily gathered outside the organization, the model resembles traditional research. However, if the data are to be gathered inside the organization, such as in an attitude survey, the issue of client involvement becomes complicated because the data-gathering is itself an intervention of unknown consequences. One part of the client system launches an inquiry process that has possibly unknown and unintended consequences for other parts of the client system. Whereas an outside survey is justified to 'help some outside group gather information', if the outsider is doing the survey on behalf of some group inside the organization, the participant has to wonder what is going on inside the organization that has motivated this activity.

In terms of consulting models, this cell would include both what I have called 'purchase of expertise' where the consultant is hired to provide information and advice, and the 'doctor' model in which the consultant is hired to provide both diagnosis and a prescription (Schein, 1999a). The project is often defined as 'finished' when the consultant has delivered a recommendation and, in fact, some consulting models consider the delivery of a recommendation to be the very essence of consultation.

The ethical issue is especially sharp in this cell because the researcher has the licence to gather data without having to worry about the consequences for the client because it is the client who has launched the inquiry. Contract researchers, if they are to be helpful, must understand the impacts of their data-gathering methods and must educate clients to those impacts before they undertake the data-gathering. Otherwise there is a risk that not only will parts of the client system be harmed by the research, but that the data may not be valid because of distortions introduced by employees who feel treated like 'guinea pigs'. They may be overly negative because 'finally someone is listening to us', or overly positive because 'even though they promised us confidentiality we better be careful what we say'. In either case management's decision to do the research signals their self-perception as having the right to gather such data which in itself may be new information to the employees about their own culture. All too often employees have learned that this kind of inquiry is a prelude to some form of restructuring or reorganization which invariably involves layoffs. And, as much experience has shown, the expert or doctor often ends up delivering information and prescriptions that the client rejects because they do not fit the culture in some way or another, something the expert did not discover in the rush to do the contract research.

Cell 6: Low researcher, low client involvement – internship

This kind of inquiry is really a variant of the Cell 5 but involves data-gathering that is basically less involving to the helper/inquirer. Examples might be where the client asks for an analysis of demographic information or invites a graduate student to come in as an intern to 'learn' a bit about the organization or to do some 'exploratory research'. The client stays in control of what will be done and how, thereby limiting the involvement of the researcher.

Cell 7: Low researcher, high client involvement – educational interventions and facilitation

The potential for clinical research increases as the client's involvement in the total process of inquiry and getting help increases. If the client wants more than data and information, if he or she is willing to let the researcher enter the organization to a greater degree, even into settings where 'real work' is getting done, the helper can begin to observe 'real' organizational phenomena.

The prototype of this level of inquiry is when the helper/consultant is brought in to facilitate a meeting or to make an educational intervention like running a workshop or giving a lecture to a group of executives. The helper is licensed to observe what is going on but not licensed to influence the situation beyond what the client has contracted for.

In my own experience, being the trainer in a T-group was the setting where I first encountered the power of this form of inquiry. I had extensive training in small-group research yet discovered as I sat more or less silently in the group that most of what was really going on was not covered in the traditional research literature, yet seemed more real and relevant to group theory than what was in the literature.

Years later I was working with a group of colleagues when the question came up of what material we used in teaching about organizational phenomena. We discovered that each of us used illustrations from our consulting experience to a much greater extent than 'findings' from traditional research. The traditional research informed our thinking and provided models for what to observe, but the reality of what was going on usually went far beyond those models and forced us to develop new concepts and theories.

When we make educational interventions like running a seminar for managers, we learn about them in part from their reaction to the material we provide. For many academic researchers such exposure to members of organizations serves as their primary data base about what goes on in organizations. We enhance those data by putting participants through role plays or simulations and thereby learn a lot about how the participants think, but unless we are dealing with teams from the same organization we cannot learn much about organizational dynamics *per se*. The client implicitly or explicitly limits the domain by choosing the focus of the educational intervention, but also opens the door to the helper who may wish to gather more information about the organization in order to design a better educational programme. In that inquiry the helper can seek all kinds of information about the organization legitimately.

Cell 8: High researcher and high client involvement – process consultation and clinical inquiry

The clearest form of CR occurs when the client and helper work together to decipher what is going on in the context of some problem that the client is trying to solve. On the surface this resembles the kind of action research that was described in Cell 4, but it differs greatly because it is driven by the client's agenda, not the researcher's.

The critical distinguishing features of this inquiry model are (1) that the data come *voluntarily* from the members of the organization because they initiated the process and have something to gain by revealing themselves to the clinician/consultant/researcher, and (2) that the helper consultant actively involves the client in the inquiry process itself not to improve the quality of the data (as in Cell 4) but in order *to improve the quality of the helping process* (Schein, 1969, 1987b, 1999a). If the helping process is successful, the client is motivated to reveal more, hence the depths and validity of the data improve as the helping process improves. Valid data are the *result* of effective helping rather than the basis for choosing interventions.

Furthermore, as pointed out before, in the inquiry process the consultant/clinician is psychologically licensed by the client to ask relevant questions which can lead directly into joint analysis and, thereby, allow the development of a research focus that is now owned jointly by the helper and the client. Both the consultant and the client become fully involved in the problem-solving process and the search for relevant data becomes, therefore, a joint responsibility. The helper is committed to a joint inquiry and joint decisions on further interventions. In Cell 7 the helper can privately learn what he or she needs to know to produce a good educational intervention. In this cell the helper wants to build joint knowledge so that the client not only learns inquiry techniques but becomes a co-researcher which enables both the research and helping processes to go much deeper.

The consultant/clinician is not, of course, limited to the data that surface in specific diagnostic activities such as individual or group interviews. In most consulting situations there are extensive opportunities to hang around and observe what is going on, allowing the helper/researcher to combine some of the best elements of the clinical and the participant observer ethnographic models. The clinician can also gather demographic information and measure various things unobtrusively, but if the 'subjects' are to be involved at all, they must be involved on their own terms around problems they have identified.

The clinical model reveals most clearly the power of Lewin's dictum *that one can understand a system best by trying to change it*. Repeatedly I have found both in group training and in organizational consulting that most of the relevant data surfaced as a *consequence* of some specific intervention I made. In this model, intervention and diagnosis become two sides of the same coin. Everything the helper/clinician does is an intervention and, at the same time, every intervention reveals new data.

The power of this process is revealed as one uncovers causal phenomena that lie in deeper levels of group and organizational dynamics, and that lead to real 'insights' both on the part of the clinician and the client. And as the client becomes an active inquirer he or she sees areas of relevant data to be collected that may never have occurred to the researcher.

The study of culture provides a good contrast of these approaches (Schein, 1992, 1999b). The client has asked for a culture assessment and is prepared to pay for the research on a contract basis. If the researcher accepts the contract and initiates the study, ethnography, formal surveying or individual interviewing with or without projective tests might be the methods of choice. The researcher would then take all the data and write a description of the culture which might or might not be checked with participants, but the researcher would remain in control. In the process consultation model I would first want to know what kind of help the client was looking for. What issues, problems or aspirations motivated the request for a cultural assessment in the first place? I would point out the likelihood that the contract research model might reveal accurate data but data irrelevant to the issues the client wanted to deal with. I would also point out that it would be much quicker and more efficient to work inside the client system as a helper around the questions that motivated the culture inquiry in the first place. If we involved the participants in deciphering their own culture, this would help them to decide for themselves what kind of culture interventions might be appropriate. I would also argue that if they become co-inquirers we could go deeper into the culture and test the validity of what we find as we go along. Not only would it be more helpful to do the joint inquiry, but the research data would be more valid and deeper.

Illustration No. 1: Collaborative Interactive Action Research

My colleague, Lotte Bailyn, and a team of researchers set out to study and intervene on work–family interactions in organizations under the auspices of a Ford Foundation grant (Bailyn and Rapoport, 1998). Initially the project appeared to fall in Cell 2 as being researcher initiated with low involvement of the researchers in the organizations studied but high involvement of the subjects who would have to reveal information about their work–family relationships. However, it was the intention of the researchers to intervene in client organizations to improve gender equity in work relations, placing the project into Cell 8 if they could get client involvement.

Several organizations were approached at high executive levels and permission was granted to study work–family relationships and gender equity in selected portions of these organizations. Permission and entry were secured through processes involving the human resource contacts and the managers of the groups who were to become both the research subjects, to be interviewed and observed, and clients. Bailyn and her team gained access to several engineering groups in a large corporation and launched their collaborative interactive action research in those groups.

In one group the research findings were that the engineers did not have enough time because of their demanding work schedule and the heavy overtime that they already put in just to get their regular work finished. When these data were fed back and worked on by both the clients and the researchers it was discovered that the engineers viewed 'work time as infinite' in the sense that the engineers worked until their work was done even if that cut into family time. The relationship was not reciprocal, however, in that family time was bounded by the norm that you cannot skip work just because your 'family duties are not finished'.

The researchers, with the consent of the clients, then shifted the emphasis to the question of why the work schedule was so heavy in the first place? Working collaboratively with the researchers, who intervened primarily by being a mirror around the data collected, the engineers realized they had come to believe that high rates of interaction and teamwork were important, and that to facilitate such interaction they had to be available to each other *at all times*. This norm led to frequent meetings, people wandering in on each other all hours of the day, constant use of the telephone, and other interactive activities that prevented them from getting their individual work done until late in the day and on overtime.

With this insight there occurred a further shift in the role of the researchers towards becoming process consultants by beginning to work with the engineers on what might be done about the stressful situation they were experiencing. They jointly realized that the structure of the workday was negotiable, that the engineers did not have to be available to each other all day long. They decided on an experiment to declare certain hours during the 9–5 workday as private time where no phone calls, meetings or interruptions were allowed. To their own and the researchers' amazement they were able to get all of their work done in the normal workday, which, parenthetically solved the work–family conflict.

What is significant about this example is that there was not a step in the middle where results were published showing how work group norms of time management can become dysfunctional. The researchers moved seamlessly into a clinical role and, in that process, produced an intervention that changed the way the organization worked, which, in turn revealed the significant data that the actual workload was manageable within the normal workday.

What this story highlights is that the research and clinical agendas often overlap and that researchers have to be prepared to move into clinical roles just as much as clinician helpers have to be ready to gather data and put on researcher hats.

Illustration No. 2: Deciphering a Technology Non-implementation

For several years I was a process consultant to a senior manager in a bank operations department, helping him with a variety of projects. One of his main goals was to introduce an effective new technology for handling various financial transactions. Several years had already been spent on developing the technology and contract research had been done to determine the feasibility of introducing the technology to the clerical workforce.

As the new technology was being installed, it became evident that many fewer clerks would be needed and it was then discovered that the bank had a powerful unbreakable norm that it would not lay anybody off. At the same time it was discovered that my client would not be able to relocate the many persons who would be displaced by the new technology. The existence of the 'no layoffs' norm was well known, but no one had any idea of how powerfully held it was until the technological change was attempted, and no one realized how overstaffed all the other departments of the bank were. The new technology was at this point abandoned as impractical.

In the traditional research model the existence of this norm would be a sufficient explanation of the observed phenomenon that a potentially useful technology failed to be adopted. But what I learned as a consultant to the head of this unit 'deepens' our understanding considerably. Once we discovered that the no layoffs norm was operating, I began inquiries about the source of the norm and learned that it was strongly associated with my client's boss for whom 'no layoffs' was a central management principle that he had made into a sacred cow. I had assumed from prior knowledge of social psychology that norms are upheld primarily by group members themselves. I found, instead, that in this situation it was the boss's fanaticism that was really the driving force, an insight that was confirmed three years later when he retired. All the attitudes about layoffs changed rapidly, the department was ready to lay off people but, surprisingly, the new technology was still not introduced. Our previous two explanations would both have been *wrong*.

It should also be noted that, as a traditional researcher, I would not have been allowed to hang around for so long, so I would not even have discovered that the constraint on the new technology was something other than the no layoffs norm and the presence of its powerful originator.

To explain further what was happening I had to draw on some other knowledge I had gained as a member of the design team for the initial change. I remembered that the group had had great difficulty in visualizing what the role of the new operator of such a computer programme would be and what the role of that person's boss would be. The group could not visualize the career path of such an operator and could not imagine a kind of professional organization where such operators would be essentially on their own. I asked a number of people about the new technology and confirmed that people did not see how it could work, given the kinds of people who were hired into the bank and given the whole career and authority structure of the bank.

So what was really in the way of introducing the innovation was not only the norm of no layoffs, but some deeper conceptual problems with the entire socio-technical system, specifically an inability to visualize a less hierarchical system in which bosses might play more of a consultant role to highly paid professional operators who, like airline pilots, might spend their whole career in some version of this new role. In fact, the no layoff norm might have been a convenient rationalization to avoid having to change deeper cultural assumptions about the nature of work and hierarchy in this bank.

What the clinical process revealed was that the phenomenon was over-determined, multiply caused and deeply embedded in a set of cultural assumptions about work, authority and career development. We were dealing with a complex system of forces, and once this system was understood as a system, it became obvious why the bank did not introduce the new technology. Attributing it to the boss with his norms of no layoffs would have been a misdiagnosis even though all the surface data indicated that this was a sufficient explanation.

The clinical process also revealed the interaction of forces across hierarchical boundaries, the operation of power and authority, the role of perceptual defences, the linkages of forces across various other organizational boundaries, and the changing nature of those forces as the situation changed. Human systems are complex force fields and many of the active forces are psychological defences and cultural assumptions that will not reveal themselves easily to uninvolved observers, surveyors, testers or experimenters. It is too much to ask of the traditional research process to reveal this level of dynamics, yet without understanding organizations at this level how can we possibly make any sense of what we observe around us?

How Valid are Clinically Obtained Data?

Hanging around organizations in a clinical consultant role reveals a lot, but is this shaky knowledge? How do clinician researchers know when they know something? I think the most basic answer to this question is that if one is observing dynamic processes, one confirms or disconfirms one's hypotheses continuously. As a matter of training, one should operate with self-insight and a healthy scepticism so that one does not misperceive what is out there to make it fit our preconceptions. But if we are reasonably careful about our own hypothesis formulation and well trained in observing what is going on, we should be able to generate valid knowledge of organizational and cultural dynamics throughout any period of interaction with an organization.

If dynamic 'on line', 'here and now' confirmation or disconfirmation is not enough, a second criterion of validity is replicability. If other observers see the same phenomenon that I do and if it occurs under conditions similar to the ones where I first observed it, that adds confidence that I am observing something real. In the cultural arena especially, important assumptions surface clearly and consistently to anyone observing from the inside, yet may be quite invisible to the outsider or to the surveyor with the questionnaire.

For me the only disadvantage of clinical data is that it is often not relevant to what I might like to study. The psychological contract with my client entitles me to go deeper, but not really to change the subject and broaden it to some research concerns I might have. On the other hand, seeing organizational processes at work first hand seems more relevant to me than trying to infer them from more superficial data. I would hypothesize, by the way, that good participant observers and ethnographers discover that the quality of their data improves as they become helpful to the organization in which they are working. It is inevitable that the insiders will not want someone to hang around who is not at least fun to talk to, to trade points of view with, and even to get advice from. In other words, good participant observation and ethnography inevitably become CR though that aspect is often not written about or even admitted because we are so wedded to discrediting clinically derived data.

Does Clinical Emphasis Bias Us towards Pathology?

A number of my colleagues are concerned about the word 'clinical' in that it focuses on pathology. It does focus us that way but is that not what our clients are already focused on? Whether they ask us to do contract research, support basic research or hire us as consultants, are they not always trying to make things better, which clearly implies that they see something that is wrong or unsatisfying? It is almost the essence of life in organizations to overcome things that are not working as well as they could be, to achieve goals that are beyond what is possible in the present, in other words, to overcome the small and large pathologies of organizational life. By not using the word clinical we are not avoiding the existence of pathology or its effects; we are only denying our own ability to face pathology squarely, analyse it and deal with it.

Implications for Education and Training

If we take this point of view seriously, what does it say about our graduate education and training. I would not wish to abandon the teaching of research as a logical process of thinking, nor do I want to abandon empiricism. In fact, in my view, clinical research, in that it deals with immediately observed organization phenomena, is *more* empirical than much research that basically massages second- and third-order data. What is needed, then, is better training in how to be helpful and how to be a genuinely observant, inquiring person so that organizations will want our help and open themselves up to us more.

Some suggestions come to mind. Why don't we send all our graduate students off into organizations early in their graduate training with the mandate to find something where they can be helpful? Would it be that hard to locate organizations that would take interns for six months to a year not to subject themselves to research but have an intelligent energetic extra hand to work on some immediate problems? The more immediate and practical the problems the better. Students would learn helping and inquiry skills fairly fast if they knew they would need them during their internship.

Why don't we teach our students basic interviewing and observational skills at the beginning of their graduate training? Instead of learning how to analyse tests or surveys, students might spend more time analysing the everyday reality they encounter in a real organization. Particularly in the area of interviewing, I have found most of my colleagues to be very naive about the dynamics of this process, the degree to which researchers ask essentially rhetorical questions, and the degree to which they try to remain mysterious and distant from the subjects.

Why don't we use more clinical materials in our graduate programmes, books by Levinson, Trist, Rice, Kets de Vries, Miller, Hirschhorn and others who try to lay out more systematically some of the dynamic processes they have observed? It is shocking that so little of the clinical tradition that was started in the Tavistock Institute studies in the 1940s has influenced US organizational research.

Finally, why don't we put much more emphasis on self-insight so that future clinician researchers can get in touch with their biases early in their career as a way of clarifying their vision?

Conclusion

The bottom line to all this, then, is that we need clinical skills for generating relevant data, for obtaining insights into what is really going on, and for helping managers to be more effective. We need more journals and outlets for clinical research, for case studies that are real cases, not demonstration cases to make a teaching point. We need to legitimate clinical research as a valid part of our field and start to train people in helping skills as well as in research skills. And we need more insight into our own cultural assumptions to determine how much they bias our perceptions and interpretations of what is going on.

We need to be clear in our thinking that there are different forms of inquiry and research, and that it makes a major difference who initiates the inquiry and for what reason. All the forms of research discussed in Figure 16.1 are legitimate and have their place, but they need to be matched to the goals of the researchers and consultants. What needs to be avoided is an imperialistic view that some forms of research are valid and others are not, and that research is an objective, neutral, non-political process. If there is one thing I have learned from my own clinical experience, it is that the research process in any form is an intervention. We have to understand better the consequences of different forms of intervention and to make sure that our research process does not unwittingly harm our subjects and/or clients.

My feeling when I look at journals and at meeting programmes and at tenure review processes is that the positivistic research paradigm is imperialistic, yet has shown itself all too often to be an emperor with no clothes. It is time to try something new. And that something new is to go back to good old-fashioned observation and genuine inquiry in situations where we are trying to be helpful. The ultimate challenge for researchers is to find roles for themselves in which they can be helpful, and the ultimate challenge for graduate education in our field is to train our doctoral and masters students in how to be helpful. Certainly our organizations need help. Isn't it more important to try to help them and learn in the process than to make a sacred cow out of a research paradigm that produces neither valid knowledge nor help?

References

Bailyn, L. and Rapoport, R. (1998) 'Moving organizations toward gender equity: a cautionary tale', in L. Haas (ed.), *Organizational Change and Gender Equity*. London: Sage Publications.

Hirschhorn, L. (1988) *The Workplace Within*. Cambridge, MA: MIT Press.

Homans, G. (1950) *The Human Group*. New York: Harcourt Brace.

Kets de Vries, M.F.R. and Miller, D. (1984) *The Neurotic Organization*. San Francisco, CA: Jossey-Bass.

Kets de Vries, M.F.R. and Miller, D. (1987) *Unstable at the Top*. New York: New American Library.

Levinson, H. (1972) *Organizational Diagnosis*. Cambridge, MA: Harvard University Press.

Lewin, K. (1947/1952) 'Group decision and social change', in G.E. Swanson, T.N. Newcomb and E.L. Hartley (eds), *Readings in Social Psychology* (revised edition). New York: Holt.

Lewin, K. (1939/1999) 'Experiments in social space', *Reflections: The Journal of the Society for Organizational Learning*, 1 (1): 7–13. (Reprinted with permission of the American Psychological Association Copyright 1997.)

Miller, D. (1990) *The Icarus Paradox*. New York: Harper Business.

Rice, A.K. (1963) *The Enterprise and its Environment*. London: Tavistock.

Schein, E.H. (1969) *Process Consultation: Its Role in Organization Development* (second edition, 1988). Reading, MA: Addison Wesley.

Schein, E.H. (1987a) *The Clinical Perspective in Field Work*. London: Sage Publications.

Schein, E.H. (1987b) *Process Consultation: Lessons for Managers and Consultants*. Reading, MA: Addison Wesley.

Schein, E.H. (1992) *Organizational Culture and Leadership* (second edition). San Francisco, CA: Jossey-Bass.

Schein, E.H. (1999a) *Process Consultation Revisited: Building the Helping Relationship*. Reading, MA: Addison Wesley Longman.

Schein, E.H. (1999b) *The Corporate Culture Survival Guide*. San Francisco, CA: Jossey-Bass.

Schein, E.H. and Bennis, W. (1965) *Personal and Organizational Change through Group Methods: the Experiential Approach*. New York: Wiley.

Sherif, M., Harvey, O.J., White, B.J., Hood, W.R. and Sherif, CA. (1961) *Intergroup Conflict and Cooperation: the Robber's Cave Experiment*. Norman, OK: University Book Exchange.

Trist, E.L. et al. (1963) *Organizational Choice*. London: Tavistock.

Van Maanen, J. (1979) 'The self, the situation, and the rules of interpersonal relations', in W. Bennis, J. Van Maanen, E.H. Schein and F. Steele (eds), *Essays in Interpersonal Dynamics*. Homewood, IL: Dorsey.

Whyte, W.F. (1943) *The Street Corner Society*. Chicago, IL: University of Chicago Press.

17
Community Action Research: Learning as a Community of Practitioners, Consultants and Researchers

PETER M. SENGE AND CLAUS OTTO SCHARMER

CHAPTER OUTLINE

The challenges facing industrial age institutions are overwhelming if faced in isolation. Co-operation in fostering organizational transformations is essential. Community action research offers one approach to such co-operation, based on an underlying theory of learning communities that integrates research, capacity building and practice and on shared understanding of why such integration is both important and difficult. Operationalizing this theory requires guiding ideas that elevate aspirations beyond self-interest, innovations in infrastructures, and compelling common work. Experience over the past ten years leads us to believe that such co-operation not only supports sustaining significant change processes but also creates a context for bringing forth important new theory closely connected to the deepest challenges of change.

This chapter presents an emerging approach to building knowledge for large-scale transformational change. Lying behind this approach is a core premise: that Industrial Age institutions face extraordinary challenges to evolve which are unlikely to be met in isolation. Collaboration and joint knowledge-building are vital. Competition, which fuelled the industrial era, must now be tempered by co-operation. Without this balance, organizations of all sorts will be unable to survive the hyper-competition of today's global marketplaces. While competition and competitiveness remain the mantra of traditional market advocates, the frenzy for optimal return on financial capital today threatens health and sustainability on all levels, not only of individual institutions but of their members and indeed the larger social and natural systems in which they are embedded.

Community action research represents an approach to collaborative knowledge creation with which we have been engaged now for some ten years. Community action research builds on the tradition of action research by embedding change-oriented projects within a larger community of practitioners, consultants and researchers. Like action research, community action research confronts the challenges of producing practical knowledge that is useful to people in the everyday conduct of their lives (Reason and Bradbury, Introduction to this volume). Like action research, community action research values knowing-in-action, embracing Humberto Maturana's dictum that 'all knowing is doing, all doing is knowing'. But, unlike traditional action research, community action research focuses on:

- fostering relationships and collaboration among diverse organizations, and among the consultants and researchers working with them;
- creating settings for collective reflection that enable people from different organizations to 'see themselves in one another';
- leveraging progress in individual organizations through cross-institutional links so as to sustain transformative changes that otherwise would die out.

For example, Gustavsen's (Chapter 1) account of cross-institutional democratic dialogues in Sweden in order to develop 'learning regions' is a good example of what we refer to as community action research. In short, community action research places as much emphasis on building cross-organizational learning communities as on undertaking action research projects.

Such communities grow from common purpose, shared principles and common understanding of the knowledge-creating process. The purpose, building knowledge for institutional and social change, defines why the community exists. Shared principles establish deep beliefs and ground rules for being a member of the community. Understanding the knowledge-creating process enables everyone to see how their efforts fit within a larger system – a continuing cycle of creating theory, tools and practical know-how – and how they inter-depend on one another.

Today, this knowledge-creating system is profoundly fragmented in the fields of management and institutional change. The consequences are ivory tower university research disconnected from practical needs (Levin and Greenwood, 2001), consulting projects that generate intellectually appealing change strategies that never get implemented, and 'flavour of the month' management initiatives that lack any underlying theory or long-term strategic coherence and engender more cynicism than commitment within organizations. The ultimate consequence of this fragmentation is the inability of Industrial Age institutions of all sorts – corporations, schools and universities, and public and non-profit organizations – to adapt to the realities of the present day. Especially in times of deep change, sustaining adaptive institutional responses requires better theory, method *and* practical know-how.

But bringing the theory of community action research to life involves conditions that are only just now being understood. It starts with genuine commitment on the part of a group of managerial practitioners from diverse organizations, consultants and researchers to work together. It further requires an agreed upon system of self-governance and learning infrastructures that enable relationship-building, collaborative projects, and sharing of insights across the entire community and beyond. Lastly, it entails appreciating and encouraging emergent learning networks that arise in ways that can be neither predicted nor controlled.

The aim of this chapter is to present the basic ideas underlying community action research and illustrate their potential to produce both organizational impact and new knowledge. While building such communities is challenging, the alternative is continued reliance on traditional, fragmented consulting and academic research, and on episodic organizational change programmes driven by top management's latest ideas. We believe this status quo will never produce the breakthroughs in theory and practice needed to re-invent Industrial Age institutions.

A Brief History of One Effort at Community Action Research: From the MIT Center for Organizational Learning to SoL (the Society for Organizational Learning)

In 1991, a group of large, primarily US-based corporations came together to found the MIT Center for Organizational Learning.[1] The collaboration originated from interest in applying the 'five discipline' tools and principles for organizational learning (Senge 1990; Senge et al., 1994) and from a belief that sustaining progress with such tools required deep and extensive change, and that this was more likely with a group of organizations willing to work together, providing examples, help and inspiration to one another (Senge, 1993).

During the early 1990s, the collaboration gradually grew into the beginnings of a community. This incipient community was evident in enthusiasm for early successful projects (e.g., see Roth and Kleiner, 1996; Senge et al., 1994) and for support extended to those involved in projects that ran into difficulties (e.g., Wyer and Roth, 1997). For example, when managers left firms that were not prepared to sustain innovations they had initiated, they immediately began helping other consortium companies who were not so cautious.

But, as the MIT Organization Learning Center (OLC) community grew to include about 20 member companies and many change projects within those companies, basic problems became evident (Bradbury, 1999). It became increasingly awkward to be organized as a research centre at MIT. As responsibility for the success of the community became more widely shared, in a sense the 'centre' became increasingly distributed. Ambiguous power relationships developed. Dealing with the crosscurrents of a 'de-centring' organization diverted increasing amounts of time away from research and initiating new projects. Revenue growth slowed and staff expansion to serve the growing community was deferred. At the same time, despite slowing growth, the overall revenue volume was several times what it had been when the Center was founded and there was pressure from the MIT administration for a larger share of the Center's revenue to go to traditional faculty research.

Beginning in 1995, a design team was formed, composed of 25 people, including representatives from member companies, senior consultants and researchers, including several MIT faculty. The task was to rethink the OLC. It was clear to all that the promise of this emerging learning community was being lost amid growing complexity and confusion.

A Theory of Learning Communities

The OLC redesign team met for almost two years. What some had hoped would be a quick identification of solutions became instead a deep and demanding process of reflecting on who we were and why we were here. We were fortunate to be guided in this process by VISA founder Dee Hock. Dee's ideas on 'chaordic organizations', radically decentralized organizations which consistently generate order out of chaos, inspired the group to imagine that there might be a viable alternative to the centralized organization structure of the OLC (Hock, 1999).

Eventually, we realized that where the MIT OLC had succeeded, the success arose from three sources: a talented group of people committed to linking deep change at the personal and organizational levels, employing powerful tools based in deep theory, and a common aim to better integrate research and practice. In effect, there existed a common purpose although we had never articulated it: building knowledge for organizational transformation. There also existed an implicitly shared understanding of what we meant by knowledge and knowledge creation: advancing theory, tools *and* practical knowhow. What we had never addressed was how best to organize to support this common aim.

In the second year, a guiding image emerged which catalysed the shift from reflecting on our past to creating our future. We began to think of the knowledge creation process metaphorically as a tree. The roots symbolize underlying theory, below the surface – yet, though invisible to many, the ultimate determinants of the health of the tree. The branches symbolize tools and methods, the means whereby theory is translated into application. The fruit of the tree is the practical know-how whose tangible benefits ultimately prove the value of the knowledge.

The tree is a living system. It continually regenerates itself, creating new roots, branches and fruit. This self-creating arises from the interdependence of the elements. Can you imagine new branches being created in a tree without roots? Or fruit that arises without branches? Moreover, the system as a whole nurtures itself. What happens if all the fruit is consumed and none falls to the ground? Of course, there will then be no new trees.

This simple metaphor of living interdependence has powerful implications for thinking about knowledge creation. In contrast to this model of living interdependence, the present managerial knowledge-creating system is deeply fragmented. Academics create theory with little connection to practice. Consultants develop tools that are often unrelated to theory. Managers focus exclusively on practical know-how and results. Members of the OLC redesign team observed that, in their eagerness to 'eat all the fruit', managers may actually undermine future advances in theory, method and, ultimately, new know-how and results. 'The picture of the tree showed me that I had a personal responsibility for better theory, which was a completely new awareness', says David Berdish, director of process leadership and learning at Ford's motor company.

Lastly, the tree as a living system embodies a transformative process that has deep parallels with the transformative nature of genuine learning. For the tree, this transformative process is photosynthesis, whereby complex carbohydrates are produced from the 'fixing' of atmospheric carbon dioxide with water and nutrients drawn up through the tree's roots. These carbohydrates are the building blocks for the tree's fruit. Just so, at the heart of all learning is a deep, transformative process that creates new awarenesses and new capabilities, the building blocks for new practical know-how. The by-products of this transformative process are especially interesting. Carbon fixing releases oxygen, without which life as we know it would not exist. So too does genuine learning release the life and spirit that pervades an organization where people are growing.

The tree's transformative process is driven by energy from the sun, just as the learning process is driven by the energy of committed people. Thus, it was natural that, when it came time to pick a name for the new organization that emerged from rethinking the MIT OLC, we chose the Society for Organizational Learning, SoL, Spanish for 'sun'.

Over this two-year period, the simple picture of the tree emerged as an icon for the OLC redesign team. It also became a springboard for articulating a theory of what constitutes a learning community. A learning community is a diverse group of people working together to *nurture and sustain a knowledge-creating system*, based on valuing equally three interacting domains of activity.

- *Research*: a disciplined approach to discovery and understanding, with a commitment to share what is learned.
- *Capacity-building*: enhancing people's awareness and capabilities, individually and collectively, to produce results they truly care about.
- *Practice*: people working together to achieve practical outcomes.

Such a community continually produces new theory and method, new tools and new practical know-how.

Figure 17.1 shows the three domains of activity and their consequences (the activity streams or flows are represented by the solid arrows; the rectangles represent accumulated consequences of activity streams, stocks increased or decreased by the flows arising from these activities; the lighter, curved arrows represent causal connections among and between the different domains).

The activity of research produces a flow of new theory and method, which accumulates in a stock of theory and method. But general method, the sorts of approaches taught to graduate students, differs from practical tools, tested and refined extensively in real

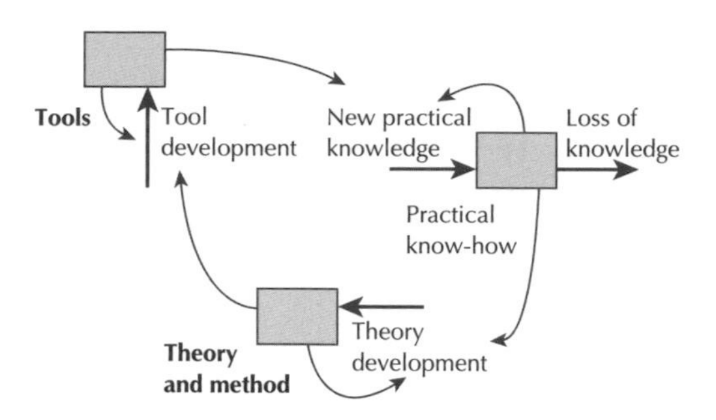

Figure 17.1 A stock-flow diagram of the knowledge-creating system

work situations (the second set of stocks and flows in the diagram). This is typically the work of consultants who develop reliable approaches to address practical problems. Tools and methods do not just help in solving problems, they also help in developing new capabilities. Hammers are essential to carpentry but they are equally essential to creating carpenters. In the words of the genial Buckminster Fuller (cf. Fuller, 1976): 'If you want to change how people think, give them a tool the use of which will lead them to think differently.' So, creating and using tools is the core activity in the domain of capacity-building, the ultimate result of which is new practical know-how (the third set of stocks and flows in the diagram). This is the domain of managerial practice. Because practical know-how is inseparable from the practitioners who embody that know-how, it can disappear when those who embody it leave the system: 'knowledge [is] primarily tacit ... deeply rooted in an individual's action and experience' (Nonaka and Takeuchi, 1995: 8). Thus, the stock of practical know-how must be continually replenished through new knowledge creation.

In a new field, the cycle of theory creation and its extension into practical tools and ultimately into a broad base of practical know-how may take many years. If this new knowledge represents a deep shift in prevailing ways of thinking and problem-solving, it may take generations. Consider, for example, that the Quality Management movement begun in Japan in the 1950s and gradually spread worldwide by the1980s had its roots in theory established in the first half of the nineteenth century, Poisson's law of large numbers and Quetelet's binomial or 'normal' curve. By the turn of the century, basic statistical theory and method were taught widely in university sciences classrooms and, by the 1920s, were being applied by statistics experts to analyse variation in production lines. But, the Quality Management revolution really only started after the Second World War, when people like Deming and Juran, building on earlier work by Shewhart (1931), led the movement to translate the philosophy and method into ideas and tools like control charts that could be understood and used by non-experts. This then led to capacity-building and practical know-how and results on a significant scale. One interesting feature of this example is the critical role of consultants in developing and applying the tools that bridged theory and practice through capacity-building – Deming's personal letterhead said, simply, 'consultant in statistics', and he frequently credited other consultants and managerial practitioners with crucial ideas and practical insights in his writings (e.g., Deming, 1982).[2]

But, why does the knowledge-creating cycle take so long? Can it be accelerated? To address such questions we need to understand how this knowledge-creating system becomes fragmented. This arises through breakdowns in each of the major linkages that interconnect the three domains. Sources of these breakdowns can be found in the taken-for-granted attitudes and activities of each of the respective professional communities. In effect, while incomplete learning cycles within organizations usually can be traced to cognitive or structural causes (Kim, 1993; March and Olsen, 1975), differing cultures and institutional norms create additional sources of fragmentation for the larger knowledge-creating process. In short, the worlds of academia, professional consulting firms and managerial practice, in both business and non-profit organizations, differ in ways that make greater integration extremely difficult.

For example, the development of new theory and method is isolated from the larger system through breakdowns in both 'outputs' and 'inputs'. In particular, assessment of most academic research is dominated by peer review. While peer review is a valid source of outside critique of new theory or analysis, it rarely considers the practical consequences of research. As a result, the outputs of most academic research, journal articles, have little impact outside self-defined academic communities. Although the array of journals continues to expand, this is driven by the growing number of academic researchers needing to publish, and most are readable only by the initiated. The fundamental problem with this entire publication-review-promotion system is that it is self-referential. The academic paper mill tends to produce a growing number of papers in increasingly narrow fields (Levin and Greenwood, 2001).

Most academic research is equally fragmented in its 'inputs'. Few academics spend enough time in work organizations to appreciate the actual challenges confronted by managerial practitioners and to engage in mutual learning. Those who attempt to do so find that they confront significant dilemmas. For example, to understand deeply what is going on within a work situation, it is necessary to gain the confidence of the practitioners in that setting. This often takes more time than academic researchers can give, and it also takes establishing a perception of adding value. As Edgar Schein puts it, managers are unlikely to tell an outsider what is really going on unless that outsider can offer real help (Schein, Chapter 16). Researchers there to 'study' what is going on are rarely seen as providing much help, so people are not likely to share with them the most important, and problematic, aspects of what is happening. Connecting practitioners' knowledge, much of which is tacit, to developing better theory and method requires a genuine sense of partnership between researcher and practitioner based on mutual understanding and on embracing each others' goals and needs. This rarely occurs in academic research.

The consulting profession generates its own forces of fragmentation. For example, most consultants aim to solve problems, not to develop new capabilities on the part of their clients. They practise what Schein (1999) calls 'expert consulting,' selling technical solutions to technical problems. But most difficult problems in work organizations are not purely technical. They are also personal, interpersonal and cultural. The consequence is that expert consultants' solutions often prove difficult to implement. Large consulting firms are driven by 'billable hour' business models that require common problem-solving frameworks that can be applied by large numbers of expert consultants. These firms are naturally conflicted about teaching manager clients how to do what they do, because they regard their problem-solving skills as the key to their competitive advantage. In short, although expert consultants may develop new tools, they usually do not employ these tools to build their client's practical know-how.

Lastly, managerial practitioners play their own part in fragmenting the larger system through defining their work as producing results not knowledge. For example, with today's emphasis on short-term results, they look for consultants who can provide quick-fix solutions to pressing problems rather than challenge prevailing assumptions and practices. This often results in a kind of co-dependence between consultants and corporations. Consultants get better and better at quick fixes. But these quick fixes only mask deeper issues. The deeper issues remain unaddressed, which means that new, often more difficult, problems will arise in the future. These then require more quick-fix consulting. Some firms, like AT&T, realizing just how strong this reinforcing cycle has become, have even declared temporary moratoriums on external consulting, in an extreme move to stop the vicious spiral (Lieber, 1997).

The net effect of these breakdowns is that the knowledge-creating system is dominated by the 'minor connections' that link each stock back to its

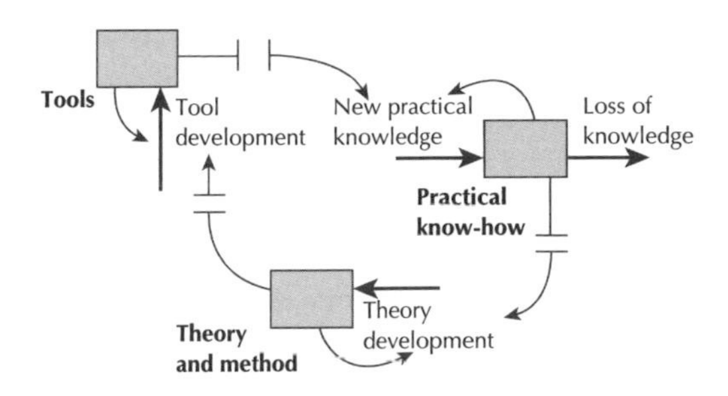

Figure 17.2 Breakdowns in major linkages; minor connections dominate

own respective in-flow, as suggested in Figure 17.2. In other words, theory begets theory: new theory development is driven primarily by current theory, rather than by wrestling with the dilemmas and challenges of managerial practice – as academics talk mainly to other academics. Similarly, consultants continually extend their tools in order to remain competitive, but with little connection to articulating and testing new theory – for that would mean exposing private theory to public scrutiny. And practitioners continually share their views and tacit knowledge with one another. As with the other minor linkages of the knowledge-creating system, this sort of 'single loop' learning is important (Argyris and Schön, 1996). But it rarely leads to breakthroughs in new capabilities. For this new theory, method and tools that challenge current assumptions and practices are needed.

In summary, the sources of fragmentation arise due to self-referential, self-reinforcing activities in each of the three professional worlds of academia, consulting, and managerial practice. Each creates its own separate island of activity rather than contributing to research, capacity-building and practice as interacting domains within a larger system. These breakdowns in the overall knowledge-creating system do not result in no growth in theory, tools and practical know-how; rather, they result in fragmented and superficial growth. These are the challenges to be confronted in building learning communities. They require a kind of meta-knowledge, knowledge of the knowledge-creating process itself. Building such knowledge is the fundamental task of community action research.

Operationalizing the Theory: Guiding Ideas, Infrastructure and Common Work

Within the SoL community, we have approached this challenge of reintegrating the knowledge-creating system on three levels:

1 Establishing a shared statement of purpose and a shared set of guiding principles.
2 Developing infrastructures that support community-building.
3 Undertaking collaborative projects that focus on key change issues and that create concrete contexts for further deepening common purpose and improving infrastructures.

Guiding ideas

Leading management thinkers from Deming to Drucker have pointed to the importance of constancy of purpose and mission as the foundation for any enterprise. Retired CEO Bill O'Brien, an influential elder within the SoL community, has argued that the core problem with most corporations is that they are governed by 'mediocre ideas' (O'Brien, 1998). Dee Hock says that it took two years to develop the purpose and principles that led to VISA's innovative decentralized design (Hock, 1999). So, it was not entirely surprising that the OLC redesign team took almost as long to articulate its guiding ideas (Carstedt, 1999; SoL, 1997; and SoL web page www.solonline. org), such as

> SoL is a global learning community dedicated to building knowledge for fundamental institutional change (who we are) – specifically, to help build organizations worthy of people's fullest commitment (why we are here) – by discovering, integrating, and implementing theories and practices for the interdependent development of people and their institutions (how we make it happen).

In addition, The SoL *Constitution* incorporates a set of 14 core principles like:

- people learn best from and with one another, and participation in learning communities is vital to their effectiveness, well being and happiness in any work setting (*learning is social*); and
- it is essential that organizations evolve to be in greater harmony with human nature and with the natural world (*aligning with nature*).

The potential impact of such guiding ideas comes from the depth of the commitment to them, and from how they become the foundation for day-to-day practices. Commitment comes alive in what we do, not what we say. For this reason, much of the effort in the past two years has focused on developing the learning infrastructures that can help leaders at all levels to succeed in their change efforts and learn from and share their experiences.

Infrastructure for community-building

There is a dramatic difference in the speed and likelihood of new ideas moving into practice in different fields, depending largely on the infrastructures that exist. For example, new knowledge in areas like electronics, biotechnology and engineering materials moves much more quickly from laboratory to commercialization than does new knowledge in management. One reason is the infrastructure created by venture capital firms, which enables people continually to search out promising new technologies and financially to support practical experimentation in the form of new companies and new products. By contrast, in the social sciences and management there is infrastructure to support research (e.g., foundations like the National Science Foundation) but little to support practical experimentation. This is the gap that the SoL community is seeking to fill, knowing full well that it may be inherently more challenging to 'move' from concept to capability when instituting social innovations than when instituting technological ones.

To date, there have been efforts to develop three types of infrastructure that better interconnect learning and working within the SoL community:

Type 1: Intra-organizational learning infrastructures

These revolve around specific projects and change efforts within individual organizations. For example, in 1996 a large US-based oil company, OilCo, established a Learning Center. The intent was not only to support many education and training efforts but to be a catalyst and hub for a variety of research projects on learning and change. As one illustration, the Learning Center supported a learning history study of the 'transformation' process at OilCo that began in 1994 (Kleiner and Roth, 1997). The aim of the study was to help the 200 or so leaders directly involved and many others within the company to make sense of a complex array of changes in philosophy, management practices and organization structure (Kleiner and Roth, 2000). Unlike the typical 'roll out' of corporate change efforts, leaders at the OilCo Learning Center sought to encourage broad-based inquiry into the interactions among personal, team and organization changes involved in the multiyear process. The study focused on tough and complex issues, such as pursuing a new business model, diversity, establishing a new governance system that broke apart the traditional corporate power monopoly, and developing new management behaviours. The OilCo Learning Center continues to engage in a variety of studies on the multiple levels of significant change processes, including a recent study of the impact of 'personal mastery' education programmes (Markova, 1999).

In many SoL company projects, innovations in infrastructure are the heart of the project. For example, many teams have created 'learning laboratories' as a core element of their change strategy. These are intended as 'managerial practice fields' where people can come together to inquire into complex business issues, test out new ideas and practice with new learning tools (Senge, 1990). To illustrate, several years ago, sales managers at Federal Express created the 'global sales learning lab', a learning environment aimed at bringing together FedEx people and key customers to explore complex global logistics issues (Dumaine, 1994). Similarly, product development teams have created learning laboratories so that engineers from diverse expert groups can better understand how their best efforts at local solutions often end up being sub-optimal for the team as a whole, and the overall development effort (see Senge et al., 1994: 554–60; Roth and Kleiner, 1996, 1999).

These and many similar experiences have underscored the crucial role of innovations in learning infrastructure in successful change processes. Managers everywhere struggle with how to integrate working and learning. Perhaps the most common symptom of this struggle is the familiar complaint that new ideas or skills do not transfer from training sessions to workplaces. This should come as no surprise. Traditional training efforts violate two key learning principles: learning is highly contextual and learning is social. As asserted in SoL's founding principles, people have an innate drive to learn if engaged with problems that have real meaning for them and with people with whom they must produce practical results. The reason that innovations like learning laboratories are so important is that they embed the learning process in the midst of the work process.

Type 2: Inter-organizational learning infrastructures

These support Type 1 infrastructures by linking people from different organizations to help, coach and support each other. As Edgar Schein says: 'Most radically new ideas and the skill sets or know-how that are needed to implement them are too complex to be acquired by practitioners from academics or consultants.' Schein argues that although consultants or outside researchers may be useful in the initial stages of a learning process (through, for instance, introducing new ideas or starting a learning process towards new capabilities) 'a second stage learning process is needed where the practitioners learn from others … who understand the opportunities and constraints afforded by the culture of the occupational community in which they operate' (Schein, 1995: 6–7). This same sentiment is expressed in SoL's principle of 'cross-organizational collaboration'.

Examples of SoL's inter-organizational infrastructures include the Annual Meeting, during which members reflect on progress in the community as a whole; capacity-building programmes open to all members; company visits (especially useful for new members); and periodic meetings hosted by member companies. The importance of these as community-building gatherings cannot be overstated. Participants in SoL's five-day 'Core Competencies of Learning Organizations' course frequently remark that they are surprised and relieved to discover how many other organizations struggle with the same problems. 'I thought we were the only ones who had this problem', said a sales manager from a Fortune 100 firm. 'It is really useful to discover that people from other very successful corporations have the same issues, and to see how they are wrestling with it.' Such gatherings can be surprisingly generative. Some of the OLC/SoL's most significant change projects were inspired by ideas generated from these cross-company visits and learning journeys. Today, SoL has a new sustainability consortium – a group of companies working together to apply organizational learning tools and principles in order to accelerate the development of sustainable business practices – in part because executives at the semi-annual Executive Champions' Workshop have spent the past two years exploring stewardship and the evolving role of the corporation. Similarly, one of the larger corporate SoL members has today a major company-wide 'reinvention' process that is, in many ways, inspired by what happened at OilCo in the mid-1990s. The executive VP of Marketing learned about OilCo's efforts from OilCo executives who hosted a SoL meeting in 1996. 'I was very impressed with the depth of conviction and willingness to experiment of the people (at OilCo)', said the executive. 'Two years later, when it became apparent that there was an opening for deep rethinking and renewal in our company, I remembered what I had seen at (OilCo).'

From our experience, creating effective inter-organizational infrastructures depends most of all on the quality of conversations that such infrastructures enable: their timeliness, relevance and depth. In all the examples cited above, a real effort was made to create an environment of safety and personal reflection, so that people focus on what they truly care about, rather than on making a good impression (as happens all too often in many cross-company meetings). The result is twofold: conversations that are candid and generative, and an evolving web of deepening personal relationships that is the manifestation of genuine community.

Type 3: Organization-transcending learning infrastructures

These support Type 1 and 2 infrastructures by creating the larger contexts, such as the formation of SoL itself. The creation of inter-organizational connections cannot be left to chance. However, there is a real dilemma as to who has the responsibility and ownership for making it happen. In addition to articulating a theory and a set of guiding ideas, the two-year process that led to the creation of SoL established a novel concept of organizing: a self-governing society based on equal partnership of companies, researchers and consultants. SoL is incorporated as a non-profit membership society with individual and institutional members in three categories: practitioner, researcher and consultant. It is governed by an elected council composed equally of the three types of members. The SoL organization exists to serve the SoL community in pursuit of its common purpose.

Moreover, the intent underlying SoL is not to create a single learning community but to establish a foundation that can allow for a global network of learning communities to emerge. The way that people in different parts of the world will pursue SoL's purpose and principles will vary naturally. Each SoL community, or fractal, represents a distinct embodiment of a common pattern, while also being unique. In enabling this sort of growth, SoL is seeking to embody a core growth principle from nature: unending variety of forms from simple building blocks. Unlike a franchise or other structure that is replicated, each SoL community has to generate itself out of its interpretation of SoL's purpose and principles. In effect, the commonality among the global community emerges from the underlying theory and guiding ideas, not from an imposed common form. While the commonality comes from adherence to the purpose and principles, the variety comes from the 'environment' from which each SoL fractal emerges.[3]

Throughout all of these changes, a consistent message is the importance of common purpose beyond self-interest and shared responsibility – the foundations for true community. Each group that incorporates a SoL assumes responsibility for its form, function, local strategy, staffing, budget and membership. The SoL global network provides help, mainly through interconnecting with other SoLs around the world. The SoL global network is itself governed by elected representatives from the member SoL communities. In this way, SoL very much resembles VISA, what Dee Hock sometimes calls a 'bottoms-up holding company'. But whereas a holding company is typically bound together by a common goal of business profit, the SoL community world-wide is bound together by the common purpose of building and sharing knowledge for organizational transformation.

Collaborative projects

Guiding ideas and infrastructures for learning are necessary conditions for community-building, but the process of community-building centres on people engaged in meaningful collaborative work. In order for learning communities to take root and continually to renew themselves, people must be excited about what they are doing together and accomplishing, not just about their common ideals and processes.

Yet, there are deep dilemmas in how such collaborative work comes about within a diverse, distributed learning community. On the one hand, if a centralized agent, like the SoL organization, tries to initiate collaborative projects, we have found that the response is lukewarm. All too often, the project focus reflects what a handful of people are committed to rather than where there is a genuine critical mass of commitment in the larger community. But 'self-organizing' cannot always be left to itself. Often, even though there is a common issue of broad and deep concern, little happens without help. In particular, if the issue area represents a long-term, systemic set of challenges, it may be the very type of issue which organizations find themselves unable to confront effectively, given the relentless pressures for day-to-day performance. Discovering and nurturing change initiatives where there is broad but latent commitment may prove to be one of the core competencies for effective community action research.

The newly formed SoL Sustainability Consortium may hold some keys to what is required for creating effective collaborative projects (Schley and Laur, 2000). Starting in 1995, several efforts initiated by a small group of consultant and research members to form such a consortium failed. In each case, there were individuals from member companies who participated and expressed interest. In each case, the meetings failed to generate momentum to carry the group forward. Finally, after a particularly disappointing meeting involving exclusively top managers, including several CEOs, from eight different companies, the organizing group was forced to rethink its efforts. Several conclusions were reached. First, while top managers were good at representing their organization, they were not necessarily very good at getting things done, at least not by themselves. The key was getting the right people together, not the right positions. Secondly, we were fragmented in our focus because several of the participating companies in each meeting were there to 'check out this sustainability stuff'. They were not deeply engaged already. This diminished energy for those who were already convinced and wasted time that might be spent on more concrete and action-oriented conversations. Third, we were talking too much at an abstract level and not connecting enough to concrete problems where people were already engaged and eager to learn.

What gradually emerged from these assessments was a distinct strategy. First, it was essential that the collaboration be initiated by practitioners, not consultants or researchers. Secondly, we needed the initiative to come from companies which already saw environmental sustainability as a cornerstone of their strategy. Third, we needed to make sure that those who came to the meetings were not only deeply interested in sustainability but had first-hand experience in achieving transformative breakthroughs as line managers. Only this would guarantee a sense of confidence that real change was possible.

We started by recruiting Interface to become a SoL member, a firm widely known in the USA for its commitment to recycling (Anderson, 2000). We then asked BP-Amoco, a founding member of SoL UK, to join as a co-convenor with Interface of the consortium. Jointly we developed an invitation that said that the purpose of this collaboration was to bring together companies for whom environmental sustainability was already a cornerstone of their strategy, or who were seriously moving in that direction. We did not want to have any more 'tire kickers'. We focused the meetings on real accomplishments and real struggles of the member companies and had the companies host the meetings. For example, the September 1999 meeting was hosted by Xerox, a world leader in design for re-manufacturing, and much of the meeting involved dialogue with team leaders of the 'Lakes project', a recently introduced, fully digitized copier that is 96 per cent re-manufacturable (Hotchkiss et al., 2000). Lastly, we handpicked attendees at the meetings to include some of the most experienced line managers with organizational learning tools and principles. After this new group had held two meetings, a host of collaborative projects began to develop spontaneously.

Obviously, there are strong parallels between the insights of this story and cornerstones of action research – like focusing on the issues which are most salient to practitioners and keeping working sessions aimed at concrete problems. But, the aim of also seeking to foster collaboration among practitioners from multiple firms greatly increases the complexity of the task. For example, striking a healthy balance between the concrete and the abstract is extremely challenging. In a collaborative setting, this balance must be achieved through identifying common learning imperatives across diverse organizational contexts. This requires that the practitioners operate more like researchers, stepping back from the idiosyncrasies of their organizational setting and pondering more generic issues. Lastly, collaboration, especially around helping one another through difficult change processes, is always about relationships. Probably the most important aim is to create a climate in face-to-face meetings where people begin to disclose their personal and organizational struggles, and feel comfortable sharing their genuine aspirations. For the SoL Sustainability Consortium, this began to happen at Xerox, through people talking in candid terms about their personal journeys, as well as their organizational challenges (Senge, 2000). When this started to happen, the meeting was no longer a typical business meeting, and a distinct level of trust started to form. Eagerness to work together arises as a natural by-product of perceived mutuality and trust. Without these, expressions of interest in learning together remain superficial, and little deep change is actually likely to happen.

Frontiers

As the SoL community begins to become established, several common themes are emerging that may constitute the beginnings of new theory, method and know-how.

1 Two sources of learning: reflecting the past or 'presencing' emerging futures

One insight from our more recent work is that there are two modes of both individual and organizational learning: reflecting on past experiences or 'presencing' emerging futures. These two modes of learning require different types of process, learning infrastructure and cognition.

The temporal source of reflective learning is *the past* – learning revolves around reflecting on experiences of the past. All learning cycles are variations of this type of learning. Their basic sequence is (1) action, (2) concrete experience, (3) reflective observation, (4) abstract conceptualization, and new action (Kolb, 1984).

The temporal source of emergent learning is *the future* or, to be more precise, the *coming into presence* of the future. In emergent learning situations, learning is based on a fundamentally different mode of cognition, which revolves around sensing emerging futures rather than reflecting on present realities (Bortoft, 1996). The basic sequence of the emergent learning cycle is (1) observe, observe, observe, (2) become still: recognize the emptiness of ideas about past or future, (3) allow inner knowing to emerge (presencing), (4) act in an instant, and observe again (Jaworski and Scharmer, 2000).

While organizational development and organizational learning have been mainly concerned with how to build, nurture and sustain reflective learning processes, our recent experiences suggest that companies are now facing a new set of challenges that require a new source of learning. These challenges are concerned with how to compete under the conditions of the new economy; namely, how to learn from a reality that is not yet embodied in manifest experience. The question now is how to learn from experience when the experience that matters most is a subtle, incipient, not-yet-enacted experience of the future (Scharmer, 1999).

The key difference between learning from the past and learning from emerging futures lies in the second and third steps – becoming still, and allowing inner knowing to emerge (presencing). These do not exist in the traditional learning cycles. Whereas reflective learning builds on inquiry-based dialogue and reflective cognition, learning through presencing is based on a different kind of awareness – one that Cszikszentmihalyi (1990) describes as 'flow', that Bortoft (1996) describes as 'presencing the Whole', that Rosch (2000) characterizes as 'timeless, direct presentation (rather than stored representation)', or that many people encounter in generative dialogue experiences (Isaacs, 1999).

Today, we find ourselves operating with both learning cycles. However, our main focus of work has shifted towards helping companies operate with possible leadership principles of emergent learning, like authenticity, vulnerability, and 'setting fields' for heightened awareness (Jaworski, Gozdz and Senge, 1997; Jaworski and Scharmer, 2000). These ideas are beginning to establish a foundation for a new approach to strategy as an emergent process, based on the capacity to 'presence' as well as to reflect.

2 From exterior action turn (explicit) to interior action turn (tacit)

As the source of learning expands from reflecting on experiences of the past to looking at emerging futures, the attention of managerial and research action must likewise expand, from focusing solely on exterior action to examining interior action. 'The success of an intervention depends on the interior condition of the intervenor' says Bill O'Brien (personal communication, November 10, 1998). The question is: how can action research adequately study the interior dimension of managerial action? Or, how can we integrate 'first-person research' (Bradbury and Reason, Conclusion; Torbert, Chapter 18) into the everyday routines of research and practice?

One example that highlights the interior action turn was recently given by a senior consultant considered to be one of the most outstanding interviewers in the SoL community. The deep-listening interview process developed by this consultant, which usually takes three to four hours for each interview, has turned out to be a life-changing event, in the assessment of many interviewees. Asked about the personal practices that allow such a unique conversational atmosphere, the consultant responded, 'The most important hour in this deep-listening interview is the hour *prior* to the interview', when the consultant opens his mind for the conversation. For this particular individual, this hour is always reserved for quiet preparation, which involves a combination of reviewing prior thoughts and meditation.

3 Three types of complexity

SoL's research agenda focused on helping leaders to cope with problems that are high on both dynamic complexity (Ackoff's 'messes') and behavioural complexity (Mitroff's and others' 'wicked problems'). We refer to this class of problems as 'wicked messes' (Roth and Senge, 1995). Today we believe a third dimension needs to be added: generative complexity.

Dynamic complexity characterizes the extent to which cause and effect are distant in space and time. In situations of high dynamic complexity, the causes of problems cannot be readily determined by firsthand experience. Few, if any, of the actors in a system are pursuing high leverage strategies, and most managerial actions are, at best, ameliorating problem symptoms in the short run, often leaving underlying problems worse than if nothing at all was done. *Behavioural complexity* describes the diversity of mental models, values, aims and political interests of the players in a given situation. Situations of high behavioural complexity are characterized by deep conflicts in assumptions, beliefs, worldviews, political interests and objectives.

These two types of complexity guided our research activities throughout the first half of the 1990s. However, during the course of the second half of the decade, many of SoL member companies found themselves moving into the business context of a new internet-based economy, and management and leadership teams faced the need continually to reinvent and re-position their business and themselves. In the new economy, *generative complexity* arises from the tension between 'current reality' and 'emerging futures'. In situations of low generative complexity we are dealing with problems and alternatives that are largely familiar and known – wage negotiations between employers and unions are an example of high dynamic and behavioural complexity but low generative complexity (non-obvious causality, different interests, given alternatives). In situations of high generative complexity we are dealing with possible futures which are still emerging, largely unknown, non-determined, and not yet enacted (non-obvious causality, different views, not-yet-defined alternatives).

In retrospect, throughout the 1990s, our research focus has steadily shifted from traditional 'wicked messes' of medium or low generative complexity to wicked messes that are also high in generative complexity. As also illustrated in Gustavsen's (Chapter 1) case of regional learning dialogues, the challenge in this kind of environment is how leaders can cope with problems that (a) have causes difficult to determine, (b) involve numerous players with different worldviews, and (c) are related to bringing forth emerging futures?

4 The shadow side of the new economy

Last, but not least, is the issue of the shadow side of the new global economy. We are increasingly aware that organizing around knowledge communities in the world of business is a double-edged sword. On the one hand, these patterns of relationships can become genuine communities as described above. On the other hand, many of these communities are part of a global economic structure that, at the same time, undermines the social and ecological foundations on which not only the economy but all social living operates (Schumpeter, 1962). We do not view knowledge-generating communities in the world of institutions as a substitute for more traditional communities that appear to be under great stress around the world (Castells, 1997). The question that follows from this is: how can we successfully participate in the current reality of business so that what we do does not undermine, but nurtures, the social, ecological and spiritual foundations of the world in which we live? This is emerging as a core question being addressed within SoL world-wide, as is evident in new developments like the SoL Sustainability Consortium.

Conclusion

It is widely recognized today that knowledge creation and learning have become keys to organizational competitiveness and vitality (de Geus, 1997, Brown and Duguid, 1998). Yet, knowledge creation is a very fragile process. Knowledge is an encompassing notion, embracing concept and capability, tools and tacit knowing. Knowledge is not a thing and is not reducible to things. It is neither data nor information, and cannot be 'managed' as if it were. Unlike traditional sources of competitive advantage, like patents, proprietary information and unique processes, it can be neither hoarded nor owned (von Krogh, 1998). Moreover, knowledge creation is an intensely human, messy process of imagination, invention and learning from mistakes, embedded in a web of human relationships. The more firms try to protect their knowledge, the more they risk destroying the conditions that lead to its generation. Thus, organizing for knowledge creation may be very different from organizing for traditional competitive advantage. Few managers and leaders have come to grips with these distinctions and the need for radical departures in organizing for knowledge creation. Community action research represents one approach to this challenge.

At its heart, community action research rests on a basic pattern of interdependency, the continuing cycle linking research, capacity-building and practice: the ongoing creation of new theory, tools and practical know-how. We believe this pattern is archetypal and characterizes deep learning at all levels, for individuals, teams, organizations and society. This is why we use the term 'fractals' to characterize different embodiments of the SoL concept, each enacting this common pattern in unique ways. The unifying feature of all is a commitment to integrate the knowledge-creating process to sustain fundamental social and institutional change, be it the local schools or multinational corporations.

Is community action research an idea whose time has come? It is too early to say. But one thing seems clear: Industrial Age institutions face unprecedented challenges to adapt and evolve, and we seriously question the adequacy of present approaches to the task. The well-being of our societies and many other of the living systems on the planet depend upon this.

Notes

Special thanks to Peter Reason, Hilary Bradbury, Peter Hawkins and Robin McTaggart for their valuable comments.

1 Founding corporate members of the MIT OLC included EDS, Federal Express, Ford, Harley Davidson, Hewlett-Packard, and Intel. Today, SoL members also include AT&T, BRAMCO, Detroit Edison, Interface, The Quality Management Network/Institute for Health-care Improvement; Royal-Dutch Shell, US West, the World Bank, the National Urban League, and Xerox Corporation.

2 Another, more contemporary, example is systems thinking, which is often cited as the most difficult of the five disciplines of organizational learning. This is easy to understand given that the basic concepts, though quite old, have never penetrated secondary and university education. The theoretical roots go back to basic ideas of feedback dynamics from the seventeenth century (e.g., James Watt's flyball governor), which had become well-established methods for engineering analysis by the mid-twentieth century, by which time they had only begun to be explicitly recognized within the social sciences (see Richardson, 1991). Moreover, non-linear feedback dynamics only became a significant subject of study in the past 30–40 years (Forrester, 1961; Waldrop, 1992). The net effect of these different historical currents is that we are only now at the onset of the development of practical tools for non-experts and large-scale capacity-building.

3 At present, over 20 SoL fractals exist or are organizing in Europe, North and Latin America, Africa, Asia and Australia. For information on the growing SoL network worldwide, see the web page: SoL-ne.org.

References

Anderson, R. (2000) 'Reflections on a transformational journey: a CEO's perspective', *Reflections*, 1 (4).

Argyris, C. and Schön, D. (1996) *Organizational Learning: a Theory of Action Perspective*. Reading, MA: Addison Wesley.

Bortoft, H. (1996) *The Wholeness of Nature. Goethe's Way towards a Science of Conscious Participation in Nature*. Hudson, NY: Lindisfarne Press.

Bradbury, H. (1999) 'Moving from the center to the periphery: a learning history for and about the Society for Organizational Learning'. Working Paper Series WP 99, Weatherhead School of Management, Department of Organizational Behavior, Case Western Reserve University, Cleveland, OH.

Brown, J.S. and Duguid, P. (1998) 'Organizing knowledge', *California Management Review*, 40 (3): 90–111.

Carstedt, G. (1999) 'About SoL', *Reflections*, The SoL Journal. Cambridge, MA: MIT Press. First issue: August 1999.

Castells, M. (1997) *The Power of Identity*. Malden, MA: Blackwell Publisher.

Csikszentmihalyi, M. (1990) *Flow. The Psychology of Optimal Experience*. New York: Harper Perennial.

Deming, W.E. (1982) *Out of Crisis*. Cambridge, MA: MIT Press.

Dumaine, B. (1994) 'Mr. Learning Organization', *Fortune*, 17 October: 147–57.

Forrester, J.W. (1961) *Industrial Dynamics*. Cambridge, MA: MIT Press.

Fuller, B. (1976) *Synergetics: the Geometry of Thinking*. New York: Macmillan.

Geus, A. de (1997) *The Living Company*. Boston, MA: Harvard Business School Press.

Hock, D. (1999) *Birth of the Chaordic Age*. San Francisco, CA: Berrett-Koehler.

Hotchkiss, M., Kelley, C., Oh, R. and Elter, J.F. (2000) 'The LAKES Story', *Reflections*, 1(4): 24–30.

Isaacs, W. (1999) *Dialogue, the Art of Thinking Together*. New York: DoubledayCurrency.

Jaworski, J., Gozdz, K. and Senge, P. (1997) 'Setting the field: creating the conditions for profound institutional change'. Working Paper, Society for Organizational Learning, Cambridge, MA.

Jaworski, J. and Scharmer, C.O. (2000) 'Leadership in the new economy: accessing another cognitive capacity'. Working Paper, Center for Generative Leadership, Hamilton, MA.

Kim, D.H. (1993) 'The link between individual and organizational learning', *Sloan Management Review*, Fall: 37–50.

Kleiner, A. and Roth, G. (1997) 'How to make experience your company's best teacher', *Harvard Business Review*, September–October: 172–7.

Kleiner, A. and Roth, G. (2000) *Oil Change*. New York: Oxford University Press.

Kolb, D. (1984) *Experiential Learning*. Englewood Cliffs, NJ: Prentice-Hall.

von Krogh, G. (1998) 'Care in knowledge creation', *California Management Review*, 40 (3): 133–53.

Lieber, R.B. (1997) 'AT&T: consultant junkie', *Fortune*, 135 (7): 160.

March, J.G. and Olsen, J.P. (1975) 'The uncertainty of the past: organizational learning under ambiguity', *European Journal of Political Research*, 3: 147–71.

Markova, D. (1999) 'Assessing to learn, learning to assess: a methodology for determining the effectiveness of short-term courses in personal mastery'. Unpublished paper, Society for Organizational Learning, Cambridge, MA. 16 June.

Nonaka, I. and Takeuchi, H. (1995) *The Knowledge Creating Company*. New York: Oxford University Press.

O'Brien, W. (1998) *The Soul of Corporate Leadership: Guidelines for Values-centered Governance*. Innovations in Management Series. Waltham, MA: Pegasus Communications.

Richardson, G.P. (1991) *Feedback Thought in Social Sciences and Systems Theory*. Philadelphia, PA: University of Pennsylvania Press.

Rosch, E. (2000) 'Spit straight up – learn something!: can Tibetan Buddhism inform the cognitive sciences', in B.A. Wallace (ed.), *Meeting at the Roots: Essays on Tibetan Buddhism and the Natural Sciences*. Berkeley, CA: University of California Press.

Roth, G. and Kleiner, A. (1996) 'The learning initiative at the AutoCo Epsilon Program'. SoL Learning History 18.009. Available through SoL-ne.org.

Roth, G. and Kleiner, A. (1999) *Car Launch*. New York: Oxford University Press.

Roth, G. and Senge, P.M. (1995) 'From theory to practice: research territory, processes and structure at the MIT Center for Organizational Learning', *Journal of Organizational Change Management*, 9 (1): 92–106.

Scharmer, O. (1999) 'Presencing: shifting the place from which we operate'. Paper, presented at the 1999 Academy of Management, Chicago, IL.

Schein, E. (1995) 'Learning consortia: how to create parallel learning systems for organizational sets'. SoL Working Paper 10.007. Available through SoL-ne.org.

Schein, E. (1999) *Process Consultation Revisited: Building the Helping Relationship*. Reading, MA: Addison Wesley.

Schley, S. and Laur, J. (2000) 'The SoL sustainability consortium', *Reflections*, 1(4): 22–30.

Schumpeter, J. (1962) *Capitalism, Socialism and Democracy*. London: HarperCollins.

Senge, P.M. (1990) *The Fifth Discipline*. New York: Doubleday Currency.

Senge, P.M. (1993) 'Transforming the practice of management', *Human Resource Development Quarterly*, 4 (1): 4–32.

Senge, P.M. (2000) 'Comments on the LAKES story', *Reflections*, 1(4): 30–1.

Senge, P.M., Kleiner, A., Roberts, C., Ross, R. and Smith, B. (1994) *The Fifth Discipline Fieldbook*. New York: Doubleday Currency.

Shewhart, W.A. (1931) *Economic Control of Quality of Manufactured Product*. New York: Van Nostrand.

SoL (1997) *Constitution*. Available through SoL-ne.org.

Waldrop, M. (1992) *Complexity: the Emerging Science at the Edge of Order and Chaos*. New York: Touchstone Books.

Wyer, J. and Roth, G. (1997) 'The learning initiative at Electro Components'. SoL Learning History. Available through SoL-ne.org.

18
The Practice of Action Inquiry

WILLIAM R. TORBERT

CHAPTER OUTLINE

Action inquiry offers a person, second-person and third-person types of research that each of us can conduct in the midst of our own ongoing practices at home or at work. First-person research in the midst of practice involves widening our awareness to include possible incongruities among our intent, our strategy, our actual performance, and our effects. Second-person research in the midst of a conversation or team meeting involves speaking in ways that encourage mutual inquiry and mutual influence. Third-person research in the midst of organizational practice can entail revisioning the collective's future, transforming strategies to meet the emerging era, or recrafting members' practices and existing assessment procedures. Action inquiry seeks, in each present moment, to integrate critical subjectivity, compassionate intersubjectivity and constructive objectivity in timely action.

Action inquiry is a research practice inspired by the primitive sense that all our actions, including those we are most certain about and are most committed to, are in fact also inquiries. Conversely, action inquiry is also inspired by the primitive sense that all our inquiries, including those we most painstakingly construct to detach ourselves as researchers, in so far as possible from biasing interests, are in fact also actions.[1]

Whether or not we imagine ourselves as inquirers at the outset of some semi-conscious action, even our most innocent and well-meant act sometimes elicits unexpected responses (e.g., 'You're fired!', 'If that's how you're going to be, I want a divorce'). Thus, when we act, we are also in part inquiring into an at least semi-intelligent cosmos (our fellow human beings are its nearest envoys to us). And, the main result of our action may be, not the consequence we had explicitly strategized, but rather the future amendment of our tactics (single-loop learning), or a broader (double-loop) reconstruction of life strategies ('I'm never going to be a victim again!').

Or, 30 years into some version of the vocation/practice of self-observation in action with others in the natural/social/spiritual environment – after millions of such self-observational moments and thousands of elongations of such moments with other inquirers – we may begin experiencing triple-loop learning. Triple-loop learning transforms not just our tactics and strategies but our very visioning, our very attention. This can be experienced as an epiphany, or as occasional epiphanies, or as a semi-continual *frisson* of analogies among moments of self-observation-in-action. My old friend interrupts me in one of my rare moments of loquacious enthusiasm, and with an unusually sharp tone that I instantly know is meant to 'raise' my attention, not make me defensive, says, 'Why must you so often reduce present pleasure by imagining a future programme of doing the same?'

If all our action and all our inquiry is, even if only subconsciously, action inquiry, how may we intentionally enhance the effectiveness of our actions and the destructiveness of our inquiry (destroying illusory assumptions, dangerous strategies and self-defeating tactics)? How may we do so individually, in our face-to-face groups and in the larger organizations and collectivities to which we belong? How may we do so in the very midst of the real-time actions of our everyday lives – here and now? To what degree need such inquiry be explicit to ourselves and to others at each moment?

If, to begin with, we try to bring just the first and simplest formulation of this question ('How may we inquire in the midst of the real-time actions of our daily lives?') into our daily lives, we immediately discover a fundamental difficulty. *We rarely remember to do so*. Moreover, we don't really know what to do when we do remember. We rarely experience ourselves as present in a wondering, inquiring, 'mindful' way to our own action. (If you try this apparently simple exercise for the rest of today or tomorrow, I believe you will see how rarely you 'see' yourself in action – especially if you make a mark in your calendar for the day after tomorrow, so that you remember to review the previous two days.)

Right now, for example, have you been present to the way you are reading – perhaps with a sharp question in mind, perhaps dully because this is just an assignment, perhaps flipping back and forth among the pages to get a sense of where this chapter is going? Is there a silent quality of seeing yourself seeing the page and seeing your thoughts absorbing, rejecting or conversing with these ideas, as well as listening to your breathing, tasting your tasting, and touching what you are touching? Is there a sense of presence to your sensing and to your reading? A common sensing? Was there prior to these questions? Will there be a page from now?

As much as we may like the idea of action inquiry, we rarely actively wish to engage subjectively in *first-person research/practice* in the present. At least, that's what I've found. When I first began to learn about the possibility of self-observation-among-others in Quaker meetings, civil rights demonstrations, Sufi dancing, Tavistock conferences, Buddhist retreats, *coitus interruptus*, etc., I was very excited by the idea and by the special experiences when practising with others under direction. But I could go days at a time in my everyday life without a single moment of intentional self-observation. Among all my teachers, as well as among all the members of my immediate circle of lifetime friends, I have known of none for whom it seemed easy to fashion her or his version of making-love-as-a-lifetime-act on a moment-to-moment basis. Geniuses have their special arts into which they pour their love – see the man who loved only numbers (Hoffman, 1998) – and they typically have equally strong shadows, arenas of daily life in which they are inattentive, unloving, ineffective. What does it take to wish to see and participate in every one of our moments, both the attractive and the unattractive, dispassionately, compassionately and passionately (Bennett, 1997; Raine, 1998; Marshall, Chapter 32)?

Not only are we individuals unpractised and unpolished in the domain of inquiry in the midst of our daily lives, but so also are our intimate relationships, our organizations, and social science itself. As practised during the past five centuries, the natural and social sciences do not provide research methodologies for generating mutually interpenetrating first-, second- and third-person action inquiries in the present – for studying the interplay among subjectivity, intersubjectivity and objectivity – except at frontiers that are being explored through books like this one. Rather, the natural and social sciences of the modern era are methodologies for conducting third-person inquiries about other things or people treated as 'outside' the researcher (Reason and Torbert, 1999; Sherman and Torbert, 2000; Torbert, 1991, 2000a). They study the preconstituted, externalized universe at the time of the study (including the preconstituted attitudes, beliefs or observations that are recorded during such a study).

Action inquiry also studies the preconstituted, externalized universe, sometimes in just the ways the social and natural sciences today do. But, in addition, action inquiry studies the internalizing and externalizing universe in the present, both as it resonates with and departs from the past, and as it resonates with and potentiates the future. Action inquiry studies three other 'territories of experience' in addition to the outside world, and it studies how all four interact. If one wishes to conceptualize and exercise across the 'four territory' way of differentiating the aesthetic continuum (Northrop, 1947), one can begin with the following words and numbers as pointers:

0	*Visioning* – The attentional/spiritual territory of inquiry-towards-the-origin/purpose/mission/undifferentiated-aesthetic-continuum, from which we may witness the present interplay among the other three territories.
1 or 2	*Strategizing* – The mental/emotional territory of theory, dreams and passions, where the essential dualism of communicating between origins and outcomes requires integration (the development of focus, soul, character, integrity, one-ness, $2^0 = 1$).
3	*Performing* – The sensual/embodied territory of practical, aesthetic, dialectically transforming performance (characterized by three primitive qualities – (i) energy, (ii) resistance (bodily limits, objects), (iii) intelligence (timely, enlightening action).
4	*Assessing* – The outside world territory wherein performance, its effects, and all things are observed, measured, evaluated.

The body of this chapter illustrates some specific first-person, second-person and third-person research/practices that characterize a present-centred, timeliness-seeking participatory action inquiry. Other recent publications further explicate the theoretical and methodological underpinnings of this approach (Torbert, 1999, 2000a). Because it is early in the history of this new kind of science, the following illustrations are offered without detailed analysis and will generate many questions (I hope). The illustrations are meant to point towards wide fields of study, not to define specific propositions precisely. More precisely, the different illustrations are meant to generate a *frisson* of analogies for attentive readers that calls them to join in a personal and collective re-visioning of both social science and social action during the next quarter-century and more.

First-person Research/Practice

In order for each of us to discover our own capacity for an attention supple enough to catch, at any moment, glimpses of its own fickleness, we must each exercise our attention. We may begin our first-person action inquiry from concerns to perform more effectively at work, or from a desire to transform some cycle of attributions, emotions and actions that is costing us happiness in love. But, as it evolves, our first-person action inquiry will either become increasingly energized by a concern for the quality of our moment-to-moment experience of ourselves (for myself as only I – or other disembodied presences within me – experience myself; for the quality of my aloneness), or it will cease to evolve.

At the outset, I cannot emphasize strongly enough how unknown such exercise is generally, nor how reliant we must therefore be on personal guidance by longtime practitioners of attention exercise in ongoing traditions of attentional inquiry. Reading about it does not generate the capacity for doing it. Reading about it does not even necessarily generate a very reliable wish to generate the capacity for doing it. Through Morris Kaplan, Stavros Cademenos, and other members of my sometimes joltingly diverse circle of lifetime friends (each engaged in his or her own versions of living inquiry as a lifetime practice), and through my longtime mentors John Pentland and Chris Argyris, I have found myself returning again and again to the influences of five distinctive traditions of research/practice. These traditions can be named gay Platonic political theory and practice (Butler, 1990; Kaplan, 1996), Buddhist practice (Cademenos, 1983; Trungpa, 1970; Wilber, 1998), Gurdjieffian self-study-with-others (Pentland, 1997; Vaysse, 1980), Quaker meetings (Nielsen, 1996), and Argyrisian confrontation (Argyris, 1965, Argyris and Schön, 1974). I have also sought out action/inquiry roles (as entrepreneur, consultant, researcher, teacher, spiritual aspirant, dean and Board member) in organizations that aspire not only to effective performance in conventional terms, but also to participate in transformational learning for their members and transformational change for their industry, science and/or social class (Fisher and Torbert, 1995; Rooke and Torbert, 1998; Torbert, 1976a, 1991).

All this effort can sound daunting (and my mentioning it can sound pretentious), but it is actually nothing more than what is motivated by my deepening questions. Moreover, any discerning observer will note how meandering, habit-ridden and forgetful I am. (Even I notice it sometimes!) So, I cannot imagine how anyone can generate awareness, mutuality and competence-expansion without: (a) eventually seeking direct tuition in some sort of meditative inner work; (b) seeking 'seeking friends'; and (c) framing one's own organizational roles as action inquiry opportunities. In this direction, one's whole life with others aspires towards a continual living inquiry.

The following journal entries offer some more situated illustrations of what ongoing (and offgoing) self-study-in-the-midst-of-action feels like to me after some thirty years' practice of specific disciplines. I offer episodes of leisure rather than episodes of work because I have mostly used work illustrations in previous writing and because first-person research/practice must first and foremost be a voluntary, leisurely pursuit if it is to go far.

6/28/97

My body stiffens in the chair. My heart is faint. My mind is confused and invaded by anxiety. My breath labors. As I notice this, I enter into my breath and it deepens. The pleasurableness of breathing out again, and then of following the cycle of in-and-out-breathing, begins to take over. My lower back softens, my shoulders round, my neck becomes my throat, liquefying.

My mind is emptying, increasingly engaged in a listening that welcomes the full synaesthesia of the traffic sounds outside, the computer's sounds as I tap, the smell of a Chinese dinner cooking downstairs, the caress of strands of memory, and I could go on …

But the phone is ringing and it may be one of my three sons …

… It was. (And I wrote more about that, but delete it here …)

6/29/97

This morning my story continues when I rise and read, in the 'Living' section of the *Boston Globe*, Donald Murray's column 'Write what you don't yet know,' which starts:

> Each year I live more lives. The hourly/daily experience becomes more complex, more deeply textured, more joyful, and more painful at the same time.
>
> There are no simple moments. I watch my granddaughter banging a block and she turns to me, smiling to share her delight in the drumbeat, and I see my daughter in her smile. Turning to her mother, my daughter, we smile and I see my mother in her smile – and in my mother's remembered smile, my grandmother with whom we lived. Four generations visited in a millisecond. (Quoted with the author's permission.)

Twenty-one years after beginning my own journal, I hear a resonance from Don Murray with the way my own experiencing increasingly functions. I want to share my journey in this world with you, Dear Reader, not because I want to create a model for others to follow, but because

I want to model following an idiosyncratic path that leads each of us more and more often into the inclusive present.

That's what I hear Don Murray so clearly doing in his ongoing construction and reconstruction of his living. He is documenting moments of presence – as in this case of experience of intergenerational smiles – smiles of joy and love – that, when perceived in relationship to one another, intensify one another toward a moment of purely sublimated ecstasy.

Or, to put the matter of modeling an idiosyncratic path in the even more paradoxical terms that it deserves, let me paraphrase Ursula LeGuin's translation of the beginning of the Tao Te Ching. 'Taoing,' she writes, begins with the realization that:

The path you can follow
Is not the real path.

7/1/97

This morning I was determined to treat myself better from the start.

Yesterday became a difficult day. I could not maintain my presence in a full and balanced way as I ventured forth to my office and appointed duties, and I suffered the loss. I felt anxious, feeling irrelevant and incompetently vulnerable. I was feeling allergic to all humankind up close, but was enough aware of my own sense of frustration not to become irritated with Reichi, who cooperated marvelously by moving mostly in her own orbit and accepting my slight gestures of gratitude and affection.

My best moment late in the day was a five minute period of pleasurably-paced pulling of weeds from our garden.

I had hoped Virginia's visit for dinner would resuscitate my sociability, but in the main it did not. I enjoyed her conversations with Reichi more than my own with her. And I felt cowed by the aspects of her that I most dislike – her tendency to overdo probing talk, and then when the other shies away, probing still further. She probes til I for one feel trapped (and her stories make me think others do as well). I become unwilling, as I became last night, to be coerced into further talk about being trapped.

Perhaps sucked out by my silence, Virginia roleplayed her version of my interior monologue as she left. As I was escorting her to her car, she had me making some blaming-annihilating comments about her. Her conversational move felt to me like a strong, semi-intentional bid to trick me into denying her attribution, thus getting into the conversation she wanted to continue (and I did not).

I was enough at-One with myself at this point not to 'meet her and raise' … but remaining quiet was hard and unrewarding work. She was suffering, and so was I. Why I, without question, preferred us to suffer separately than to join is beyond me.

So went yesterday's living inquiry into maintaining my presence in a full and balanced way – into remembering the **One** good I can always be doing – intentional listening – and, once doing that intentional listening, dividing it in **Two**.

I had already told myself to treat today more like vacation, before heading out this morning along the wooded path circling Cold Spring Park for my daily slow, twirling, running, swinging-on-the-rings, and balancing-on-the-beam ritual. But it was not until I passed the lake on the way back from the park that I realized that I could, and should – and even deserved to – truly name today as my first vacation day.

After all, as a professor, I'm not paid for July and August. And today *is* the first day of July. Certainly this is the day, if ever there be one, to shake off the cobwebs of petty professional functionalism and to discover whether there are any pure pleasures and inspirations left in this old rag by going swimming in the morning. My career was meant to make all my time my own, to be lived at whatever variable pace my sense of leisure chose, yet how hard to seize time is, moment by moment and day by day.

Daily rituals can serve as reminders in first-person research/practice. One kind of reminder is a set time for meditative exercises. Regular journalizing (three to four times a week) is another good early discipline for feeding a sense of identity in which inquiry in everyday life plays as big a part as any outwardly directed actions. Joseph Campbell (author of *The Hero with a Thousand Faces*) spoke of swimming in the morning and Scotch in the evening as his daily meditative rituals.

Here are a few further comments on how the foregoing journal excerpts illustrate first-person action inquiry. First-person research/practice witnesses and suffers gaps, such as the sudden phone call from my son interrupting my activity of journalizing. Each interruption can provoke an inquiry: to attend or not? If so, how to reorder my priorities while continuing to remain alert for interruptions that may be opportunities? Over time, how to transform incongruities among emergencies, short-term goals and routines, longer-term strategies, and lifetime character, vocation or mission?

Again, I witness and suffer the sense of difference with Virginia without conclusive interpretation (I later showed her the passage and we explored the matter further). Such participant-witnessed gaps or incongruities are a special kind of difference, invisible to conventional empirical science. The practice of action inquiry recognizes and deals with differences of identity across persons or groups (e.g., differences of race, gender, class, nation or religion). But the practice of action inquiry only really begins when one treats differences *within* one's own self, family, or a wider social system in which one participates (incongruities among vision, strategy, performance and outcome) as of greater concern than difference *from* others. Honig calls this kind of difference 'a difference that troubles identity from within its would-be economy of the same' (1996: 258). But sameness is not preferred to difference within identity action-logics that increasingly welcome inquiry and mutuality (Alexander and Langer, 1990; Cook-Greuter, 1999; Fisher and Torbert, 1995; Kegan, 1994; Overton, 1997; Torbert, 1991; Torbert and Fisher, 1992; Wilber, 1995).

Second-person Research/Practice

Since many of us spend repeated periods of our days in verbal exchanges, brief or prolonged, with others, a useful second-person research/practice is to adopt liberating speaking disciplines nested within the liberating listening disciplines illustrated in the previous section. Indeed, as listening through oneself both ways (towards origin and outcome) is the quintessential first-person research/practice, so speaking-and-listening-with-others (Heron, 1996; Isaacs, 1999; Senge et al., 1999) is the quintessential second-person research/practice.

Language itself cannot finally be understood as purely cognitive content, but rather always is written, uttered, heard, and (mis)interpreted as action within wider action contexts – a proposition that is beautifully argued in Pitkin (1972) and also explored in Torbert (1976a). If our intended meaning is incongruent with the content of what we say (if we do not mean what we say), if the content of what we say is incongruent with the pattern of what we actually do (if we do not do as we promise), or if what we actually do is incongruent with our effect on others (if we offer charity, but generate corruption), what we say means something very different from what it means when our intent, content, conduct and effect are mutually congruent. We generally seek congruity between intent and effect, though we sometimes believe that we can best do so by the manipulative/exploitative strategy of camouflaging our intent in what we say and how we perform (e.g., making promises we have no intention of keeping). However, language ceases to mean anything if its relation to intent, performance and outcome become random, and people lose trust in us if they interpret us as generating systematic incongruities that we are not willing to explore. Indeed, the meaning of language is based on the trusting premise of truth-telling (and one particularly depends on the premise of truth-telling when one lies). Thus, both second-person trust and truth-telling require a growing commitment to analogical harmony both down and up the ladder of abstraction. We can (but rarely do) publicly test with others whether they experience our actions from intent, through content and conduct, and into effect as harmonious. We can also publicly test (but rarely do) whether we have heard another's words and whether our inferences and assumptions about what they mean align with their intent (see Rudolph, Taylor and Foldy, Chapter 29).

Listening into the four territories of experience, we can gradually generate increasing plausibility, balance and analogical harmony in our use of four different 'parts of speech', emanating from the four different experiential territories named earlier. The four parts of speech can be named:

1 *Framing* – declaring or amending a possible shared sense of vision/intent for the occasion as a whole or for some fractal of the larger occasion;
2 *Advocating* – setting a goal, recommending a strategy, or making some other abstract claim (e.g., 'you're beautiful');
3 *Illustrating* – offering a concrete, visual picture/story based on observed performance; and/or
4 *Inquiring* – inviting any contribution or feedback from others about their response to one's speaking and associated conduct (Fisher and Torbert, 1995).

The very naming of these four parts of speech suggests how speaking is action and how, as speaking becomes more effective, it tends increasingly to move away from an exploitative/manipulative mode and towards mutually transforming action inquiry.

As observant participants in ongoing conversations with others, we may seek to balance the four types of speech in our own performances and seek to listen for and evoke the four types of speech from other conversants. Behind merely exercising and balancing these four complementary types of speech action lies the eternal question and lifetime practice of discovering what articulation congruently translates my (your) current personal, interpersonal and organizational experiencing into the frame/advocacy/illustration/inquiry that is most timely (across how many time horizons?) now. Such a practice can gradually transform an increasing proportion of our conversations from habitual, repetitive rituals into the transformational dances between the known and the unknown that true dialogue can be. The assessments generated by effective inquiry can either confirm the efficacy of the overall direction of the current action, or can generate slight changes in performance (single-loop feedback), a change in topic, timing or strategy (double-loop feedback), or a change in the framing assumptions of the occasion (triple-loop feedback) (Bradbury, 1998; Fisher, Rooke and Torbert, 2000; Torbert, 2000b). Whatever our original motivations for engaging in second-person research/practice, it either evolves into an increasingly mutual, loving listening, disclosing and confronting – for example Sedgwick's (1999) study of her therapy experience – or it devolves back towards habitual, unilateral behaviour.

Coitus interruptus is a second-person research/practice that exemplifies mutual, loving listening. *Coitus interruptus* is a Hindu, Tantric, spiritual practice, as well as a Tibetan Buddhist, Vajrayana spiritual practice. Most people who see the phrase *coitus interruptus* are, of course, unfamiliar with such practices and their purposes, and imagine instead that the phrase refers to some embarrassingly involuntary dysfunction amidst sexual engagement. But in spiritual practice that transforms erotic energy into something finer than just its physical, sexual expression, the intentional pause of *coitus interruptus* is a symbol (as all properly sublimated visible actions are) as well as a factual act. *Coitus interruptus* is a symbol of two (or even three or four) persons' ability to interrupt any pleasurable perspective and action for the higher and more generous pleasure of a more inclusive and more mutual awareness and interaction. Interweaving attentional, conversational and sexual intercourse (as Donne's love poems suggest) is an advanced form of second-person research/practice (see Torbert, 1991, 1993b, for further detail).

The daily newspaper shows us in how many ways our global civilization falls short of practising such increasing mutuality in relations among sects, tribes, nations, companies or genders. Such stories of unilateral violence – especially of the numbingly commonplace horror of rape – can touch each of us deeply, if we pause long enough to allow them to do so.

They touch the essence of our uncertain sexuality. And each of us is essentially uncertain sexually, in so far as we are truly sexual – truly erotic – at all. For the truly erotic impulse is spontaneous and relational, not pre-meditated and unilateral. The truly erotic impulse cannot know its proper form or enactment until it engages relationally. Truly relational engagement brings recognition of actual differences of power, status, development, etc. that influence the parties' actual mutuality at a given time. Truly relational engagement also allows the fullest realizable spontaneity among the players in mutually creating the pattern of this particular dance.

What, then, is going on when men abuse children or women? We are told by studies (Koss and Harvey, 1991; Raine, 1998) that the men more likely to rape have experienced more violence in their families of origin, view males as properly dominant, treat sex as a sport, the objective of which is to see how far you can go, and don't believe women mean 'No' when they say 'No.' This framing is the logical antithesis of second-person research/practice because it does not even invite single-loop feedback and learning, let alone double- or triple-loop feedback. In short, these men are not acting in truly inquiring, truly relational, truly erotic ways.

But it is not my intent to bash my fellow men. Instead, I would like to offer some positive images that point to the rewards of exercising mutual, non-violent power and inquiry rather than unilateral force (Heron, 1996; Senge et al., 1999). Perhaps the positive imagery of an unfamiliar sport can help us at the start to begin to envision sport, conversation and sexual engagement as predominantly collaborative inquiries rather than as predominantly competitions with winners and losers.

My Greek friend Stavros brought with him to this country two rather large and heavy wooden rackets. With the help of an old tennis ball, he has been teaching me 'pallette' over the past 22 years. (Today, one sometimes sees two persons with similar, but much smaller, rackets and little rubber balls on beaches.) The objective in pallette is for the two (or more) players to enter a mutual rhythm, so attuned to one another's skills as never to overtax them, so spontaneous and ever-changing as always to heighten one another's awareness, and so challenging as to stretch one another's capacities. One applauds the other's reach and challenge, appreciates the restful lobs, apologizes to the other and the god of the game for one's own miscreant shots, and marvels at how much such mutual games improve with age. Over the years, Stavros and I have played memorable games on pitch dark nights, over and around patchworks of tree branches, and amidst the ocean waves. Of course, we have never fully realized the objective, but we have become true peers and lifetime friends.

Stavros has been teaching his wife, Anne, pallette as well, over these many years, with the same effect. In the meantime, she and I – she much more than I – have been helping Stavros shape up his conversational game, for true conversation requires and generates this same mutuality, this same predominance of collaborative inquiry over competitiveness (Evered and Tannenbaum, 1992; Grudin, 1996; Sedgwick, 1999; Torbert, 2000b). Certainly, no conversation is occurring if any of the partners interprets what others say and acts on that interpretation without testing his or her interpretation publicly with the original speaker(s). (Look at that sentence carefully: few business or family conversations meet its test, and that explains a great deal of human misunderstanding, sense of betrayal and suffering.) For example, to suggest that one has some kind of private insight or right to interpret – unilaterally, without public testing – that another means the *reverse* of what she or he says ('Women don't mean "No" when they say "No"') is to undermine the very possibility of mutuality, the very possibility of conversation, the very possibility of human sociability. Whereas the statement 'Women don't mean "No" when they say "No"' treats women with utter contempt, it is the statement itself that deserves our deepest contempt, while whoever utters it warrants our most concerned confrontation.

Now, someone is sure to respond that he can document a particular case and provide witnesses to prove that someone once said (or that many people have often said) the reverse of what was meant. Good. Thank you. You have just publicly tested whether you have understood what I just wrote (although, had you been more aware that you were making an inference, you might have addressed me more inquiringly). This gives me the opportunity to try again to convey my meaning, for this response shows that I did not convey it the first time.

I did not say that no one ever says the reverse of what they mean. I believe that sometimes happens, for we are complex, uncertain creatures with only the most occasional and tenuous contact with what we ourselves truly wish. Hence, another may see evidence before we do that we are not doing as we truly wish, or are not saying what we truly mean. But this evidence may or may not be valid. Hence, it deserves public testing.

A wonderful conversational game of pallette is being played when a partner recognizes and acknowledges in an uncoerced fashion that he or she in fact means the reverse of what he or she originally said. (And such an acknowledgement properly represents anything but the end of the game.) But public testing of our interpretations rarely occurs in conversations for two reasons: first, because we rarely even realize that we are adding a questionable judgement to what we are seeing; and secondly, because we implicitly believe that public testing may be embarrassing and may reduce our control of the situation. These are in fact genuine risks (so long as our self-images are strongly tied to being right to begin with and to exercising unilateral, rather than mutual, control). It *does* require courage each time and oft-repeated practice to conduct public testing in a mutually liberating way. But when we do undertake this second-person research/practice, we begin to realize how much error, conflict and harm are generated by not doing so, and how much mutuality, trust and good will can be generated by public testing.

Ironically, anyone inclined to interpret that others mean the reverse of what they say should especially practice such interpretation and such public testing in sexual situations when the other says 'Yes'. For, there is much evidence to suggest that both men and women are more likely to say 'Yes' in sexual situations when at a deeper level they feel 'No' than vice versa.

This advice will no doubt sound ludicrous and unrealistic to those who treat sex as an exploitative sport, the objective of which is to see how far they can go. But even those who would like to believe that sex can be 'played' as a different kind of 'game', as a kind of mutual, conversational, sexual pallette – even those of us who would like to believe that sex can be an expression of collaborative inquiry and even of love – will feel intuitively how difficult meeting the demand for public testing of interpretations during sexual play is.

Certainly, listening for and testing interpretations publicly in the midst of sexual play, political action or a business negotiation is no simple, all-or-nothing process, with a pre-determined gambit to begin the game and a definitive sign that the game is over. Instead, it is a game that opens in many possible directions at every step in the play (Carse, 1986), requiring all our powers of judgement, intuition and care just when these are most likely to be dimmed by sexual desire, political conviction or the urgency of a business goal.

To play this kind of game – to do this listening – invites us and requires us to be more civilized than we ordinarily are – to wed the biological, the social and the spiritual in ourselves in a marriage that few of us ever achieve momentarily, let alone permanently. To play this game requires the actual and symbolic practice of *coitus interruptus*. More prosaically, this game is an advanced form of second-person research/practice.

Third-person Research/Practice

As the previous section illustrates, second-person research/practice presupposes and works to co-generate first-person research/practice. Similarly, one of the key characteristics of successful third-person research/practice is that it is an action inquiry leadership practice that presupposes first- and second-person research/practice capacity on the part of leadership. This leadership (which is not necessarily synonymous with the top executives of an organization) in turn creates organizational conditions where more and more of the members voluntarily adopt first- and second-person research/practices and join in the third-person research/practice of distributed leadership (Fisher and Torbert, 1995; Reason and Torbert, 1999; Rooke and Torbert, 1998; Torbert, 2000c). First-, second- and third-person research/practice mutually generate, require and reinforce one another because each is the preparation to welcome rather than resist timely transformation, at the personal, relational and organizational scale, respectively. These organizational conditions result from a kind of organizational design called 'Liberating Disciplines', wherein the leadership as well as other members are vulnerable to transformation (Torbert, 1991).

If the leadership is to lead in this direction, it must lead in learning and in modelling how to weave unilateral and mutual forms of power together so that the collective as a whole can rely less and less on unilateral forms of power and increasingly manifest mutuality. Both developmental theory and statistically significant empirical results in ten, multi-year organizational transformational efforts support the proposition that one must be willing to be vulnerable to self-transformation if one wishes to encourage ongoing, episodic transformation in others and in whole structures of activity (Rooke and Torbert, 1998). Whereas traditional forms of power (e.g., coercion, diplomacy, logistics, charisma) can be exercised unilaterally, transformational power can only be successfully exercised under conditions of mutual vulnerability.

But, virtually all third-person organizations and states today are dominated by relatively non-voluntary, non-mutual, unilateral power relations, even though there may be pockets and occasional democratic occasions of more mutual organizing. Hence, among the many skills, methods and theories relevant to third-person research/practice, perhaps the most important are those that concern the question of how to engage, motivate and gradually transform concentrations of unilateral power (Benhabib, 1996; Honig, 1996; Mansbridge, 1996; Torbert, 1991; Young, 1996). Over the past 50 years, however, most action research communities have been virtually allergic to 'power', assuming that exercises of power are inherently unilateral and therefore contrary to visions of voluntary, mutual decision-making. This 'allergy' to power has been sustainable only because action researchers have typically worked outside organizations (but this position has also severely reduced the potential influence of action research). In terms of gender stereotypes, men prefer their power unilateral, women prefer to ignore it. Traditionally, few have been eager to envision the long, voluntary, lifetime journey, with repeated backward somersaults through hidden trapdoors of transformation, that is required of persons, relationships and organized collectivities that aspire to full mutuality. The one action research school that does address issues of power directly is the 'Southern' participatory action research tradition inspired by Freire's *Pedagogy of the Oppressed* (1970) (see Gaventa and Cornwall, Chapter 6). But this tradition offers a rather blunt, bivariate theory of oppressive, top-down, unilateral, institutional power versus emancipating, bottom-up, mutual, people power, offering little insight into how to transform power itself.

There are many approaches to third-person research/practice currently being invented, and some are described by Gustavsen in Chapter 1 and Martin in Chapter 14 (see also, Reason and Torbert, 1999; Toulmin and Gustavsen, 1996). In addition, new forms of assessment, such as the Learning History, are being specifically invented to support individual, organizational, and distance learning simultaneously (Bradbury, 1999; see also Bradbury, 1998; Senge et al., 1994).

I will use another third-person research/practice method invented during the past quarter-century, a future scenario (Hawken, Ogilvy and Schwartz, 1982; Kleiner, 1996), as my primary illustration in concluding this chapter. The future scenario method, or research/practice, focuses primarily on the exercise of mutual power to co-construct the future, rather than on, say, the unilateral power of a positivist laboratory experiment for reflecting the past. This shift of perspective from using *data to pin down the past with a known degree of certainty* to using *data-driven stories hazily to floodlight a possible future* illustrates how fundamental the changes can be when research participates in generating mutually transforming power.

The particular future scenario presented below is chosen in part for its content, for it envisions one way in which the interweaving of third-, second- and first-person research/practices may begin to evolve into a globally influential process. This scenario was generated during a Board and senior management exercise in re-visioning the mission and long-term strategy of one of the largest and top-ranked health management organizations (HMOs) in the USA during the late 1990s. Guided by Collins's and Porras's *Built to Last: Successful Habits of Visionary Companies* (1994), the Board and senior management of this HMO developed a 100-year mission statement, a 25-year vision (summarized as becoming 'the most trusted and respected name in health care'), a five-year strategy, and an annual business plan with specific priority projects to be completed that year. The following 25-year vision was not created as a target, but rather as a *provocateur* of dialogue within the organization about fundamental issues in healthcare that invite creative responses.

Philadelphia Quaker Health in 2025

In 2025, Philadelphia Quaker Health is the most trusted and respected name in health care. It is one of the Nine Majors – the nine largest Not-for-Prophets (NFPs) in the world. (Of course, just as many for-profit entrepreneurial ventures fail, many organizations have failed in the attempt to create liberating developmental disciplines analogous to those of successful NFPs).

Philadelphia Quaker Health has close to one billion members, and, of these, nearly 100 million are fully vested. (Once fully vested, members' income and life care through death is guaranteed and at least half of their economic assets become fully integrated into PQH's Intergenerational Trust.)

Together, NFPs now account for approximately one-third of global annual revenues. Unlike for-profit corporations and government agencies, Not-for-Prophets have become global, multi-sector organizations by accepting the challenge of cultivating, not just the negative freedoms so well managed by the U.S. Constitution (under which all of the top 500 NFPs are incorporated), but also and in particular:

development of members and clients

the balanced adult

– eco-spiritual, social, physical, and *financial* –

Philadelphia Quaker offers personal budgetary options in regard to elective care for members who successfully maintain their health (and more than 80% of the membership in every age group of the octave does).

Currently, the *Mass-age Mess-age* unit receives the largest proportion of the elective budget.

'Friendly Quakers' – as we playfully call ourselves, whether we are doctors, business associates, member beneficiaries, or even mere clients of the enterprise – are all committed to personal, family, and organizational initiatives to increase good health and prevent disease. For example, every Friendly Quaker belongs to an 'Active Health Triangle.' The Triangles meet at least once every three weeks for exercise and conversation, to address each member's spiritual, organizational, and physical health dilemmas. In these Triangles members typically discuss their most perplexing and troubling issues and share suggestions, via the Web and the Intranet, about alternative resources they can access from other PQH services.

The opportunity to join a different Triangle each year is what initially attracts most clients to become members of PQH. As everyone is well aware, the Triangles shift membership each year based on the stated partner-preferences of each member. ('Free love,' new PQH members fondly imagine. As another of the Nine Majors advertises: *'Dreams do come true ... Dis-illusion-ingly ... Trans-form-ingly ...'*!!!)

Like the others of the Nine Majors in relation to their original sectors, Philadelphia Quaker Health is far and away the largest and most respected player in the health care industry globally. It is also a Liberating Discipline that generates enormous trust and longevity among its doctors, business associates, member beneficiaries, and clients. Indeed, the organization is more likely to choose to discontinue its relationship with members prior to their final, full vesting (after as many as 21 years) than the members are to discontinue their relationship with PQH.

In the wider global market and in the US political process, there is great controversy about the adult development orientation that all the successful Not-for-Prophets share. Spiritual, scientific, political, and economic fundamentalists – those who wish to preserve traditional forms of religious authority, empirical validity, individual rights, and property rights – tend to regard the Nine Majors as emanations of the Great Satan (the more so, as members of their own families join an NFP and their family inheritance is threatened).

Why do the Not-for-Prophets generate such contestation and consternation? Because the NFPs' 21-year vesting process for adults tests whether members will voluntarily undergo more than one developmental transformation, and these transformations challenge a person's inherited, fundamental, taken-for-granted beliefs and practices. For example, most of the Nine Majors put primary emphasis on Triangles and Quartets rather than Couples. Also, they divert wealth by inheritance from the blood family to the NFP community. Moreover – and worst of all from the perspective of the three dwindling monotheisms – they encourage 'Fast Forwarding' (a fasting and communal celebration process through which Senior Peers choose their time of death).

Religious and individual rights fundamentalists decry such transformational initiatives, arguing they are often cult-inspired or cult-manipulated (most people, though, think that's like the pot calling the fairy godmother black). In any event, the Nine Majors and the next 491 of the 'Good Life 500' have continued to gain market share by comparison to the Fortune 500, the global governmental sector, and the traditional religious and educational not-for-profits during the past twenty years.

The scenario envisions various institutions within Philadelphia Quaker Health that help its employees and other members to interweave first-, second- and third-person research/practice over their lifetimes. The scenario imagines that such Not-for-Prophet institutions help adults transform several times, from hardly seeking out single-loop learning to developing a taste for single-, double- and triple-loop learning. The institutions themselves are primarily guided, neither by the single-loop feedback of economic results (though positive results are necessary for the ongoing sustainability of the institutions), nor by the potentially double-loop feedback of members' political preferences (though each Not-for-Prophet will dwindle if its structure is not agreeable to its members). These Not-for-Prophet institutions are guided by their capacity (through many different Liberating Disciplines) for helping members develop to the point where they function as part of the increasingly widely distributed leadership that exercises single-, double- and triple-loop action inquiry in its first-, second- and third-person forms.

Conclusion

The foregoing 2025 scenario contemplates a social world in which a very large and increasing proportion of adults around the globe are engaging in a new kind of research/practice in their personal, relational and organizational lives. This 'living inquiry' seeks to integrate subjectivity, intersubjectivity and objectivity in moment-to-moment and lifelong actions that are timely and potentially transformational.

For millennia, we have had first-person meditational, devotional and martial arts research/practices to which only very small minorities of the world's population have committed (sometimes because these practices have been offered in the context of authoritarian institutions that have in practice demanded conformity more than inquiry and mutuality). During the twentieth century, there was an explosion of types of more or less disciplined and imaginative second-person research/practice dialogue (psychotherapy, 12-step meetings, sensitivity training, co-operative inquiry, etc.). At the dawn of the twenty-first century, the biggest missing link between now and the vision of large, decentralized 'Not-for-Prophets' in 2025 is a population of well-developed third-person research/practices, based on mutually transforming power, that make adult development through first- and second-person research/practices as common as child development today is.

This chapter attempts to reframe and re-vision the ends and the means of human action and human inquiry, indeed of human civilization. At best, its illustrations may generate questions that confront or confirm your assumptions about, and visions of, desirable personal, interpersonal, organizational and scientific conduct.

Note

1 A third inspiration for action inquiry accounts for the third word with which I usually characterize this approach nowadays – 'developmental action inquiry'. This primitive sense or intuition, which remains implicit throughout this chapter, is that the ultimate essence of efficient, effective, transformational, inquiring action is its unique, mythmaking timeliness, where 'timeliness' is understood to refer not just to an immediate effect or short-term consequence, but to a widening and deepening and transforming effect across ages of history (e.g., Socrates drinking the hemlock, or John Hancock signing the American Declaration of Independence). I begin to address the mysteries of six-dimensional time/space in Torbert, 1993a, 1991 (Chapter 15), 1993a (Lecture 5) and 1999.

References

Alexander, C. and Langer, E. (eds) (1990) *Higher Stages of Human Development*. New York: Oxford University Press.

Argyris, C. (1965) *Organizations and Innovation*. Homewood, IL: Irwin.

Argyris, C. and Schön, D. (1974) *Theory in Practice: Increasing Professional Effectiveness*. San Francisco, CA: Jossey-Bass.

Benhabib, S. (1996) *Democracy and Difference: Contesting the Boundaries of the Political*. Princeton, NJ: Princeton University Press.

Bennett, J. (1997) *Witness: an Autobiography*. Santa Fe, NM: Bennett Books.

Bradbury, H. (1998) 'Learning with the natural step: cooperative ecological inquiry through cases, theory, and practice for sustainable development'. Unpublished doctoral dissertation, Boston College Organizational Studies, Chestnut Hill, MA.

Bradbury, H. (1999) 'Moving from the center to the periphery: a learning history of and for the society for organizational learning'. *Working Paper Series WP 99*, Department of Organizational Behavior, Case Western Reserve University, Cleveland, OH.

Butler, J. (1990) *Gender Trouble: Feminism and the Subversion of Identity*. New York: Routledge.

Cademenos, S. (1983) 'The phenomenology of pain'. Unpublished doctoral dissertation, Brandeis University Sociology Department, Waltham, MA.

Carse, J. (1986) *Finite and Infinite Games*. New York: Free Press.

Collins, J. and Porras, J. (1994) *Built to Last: Successful Habits of Visionary Companies*. New York: HarperBusiness.

Cook-Greuter, S. (1999) 'Postautonomous ego development: a study of its nature and measurement'. Unpublished doctoral dissertation, Harvard Graduate School of Education, Cambridge, MA.

Evered, R. and Tannenbaum, B. (1992) 'A dialog on dialog', *Journal of Management Inquiry*, 1 (1): 43–55.

Fisher, D. and Torbert, W.R. (1995) *Personal and Organizational Transformation: the True Challenge of Continual Quality Improvement*. London: McGraw-Hill.

Fisher, D., Rooke, D. and Torbert, W.R. (2000) *Personal and Organizational Transformations: Through Action Inquiry* (revised edition). Boston, MA: Edge/Work Press.

Freire, P. (1970) *Pedagogy of the Oppressed*. New York: Seabury Press.

Grudin, R. (1996) *On Dialogue: an Essay in Free Thought*. Boston, MA: Houghton Mifflin.

Hawken, P., Ogilvy, J. and Schwartz, P. (1982) *Seven Tomorrows: a Voluntary History*. New York: Bantam.

Heron, J. (1996) *Cooperative Inquiry*. London: Sage Publications.

Hoffman, P. (1998) *The Man Who Loved Only Numbers: the Story of Paul Erdos and the Search for Mathematical Truth*. New York: Hyperion.

Honig, B. (1996) 'Difference, dilemmas, and the politics of home', in S. Benhabib (ed.), *Democracy and Difference: Contesting the Boundaries of the Political*. Princeton, NJ: Princeton University Press. pp. 257–77.

Isaacs, W. (1999) *Dialogue and the Art of Thinking Together*. New York: Doubleday.

Kaplan, M. (1996) *Sexual Justice: Democratic Citizenship and the Politics of Desire*. New York: Routledge.

Kegan, R. (1994) *In Over Our Heads: the Mental Demands Of Modern Life*. Cambridge, MA: Harvard University Press.

Kleiner, A. (1996) *The Age of Heretics: Heroes, Outlaws, and the Forerunners of Corporate Change*. New York: Doubleday Currency.

Koss, M. and Harvey, M. (1991) *The Rape Victim*. Newbury Park, CA: Sage Publications.

Mansbridge, J. (1996) 'Using power/fighting power: the polity', in S. Benhabib (ed.), *Democracy and Difference: Contesting the Boundaries of the Political*. Princeton, NJ: Princeton University Press. pp. 46–66.

Nielsen, R. (1996) *The Politics of Ethics*. New York: Oxford University Press.

Northrop, F. (1947) *The Logic of the Sciences and the Humanities*. New York: Macmillan.

Overton, W. (1997) 'Developmental psychology: philosophy, concepts, and methodology', in R.M. Lerner (ed.),

Theoretical Models of Human Development. New York: Wiley.

Pentland, J. (1997) *Exchanges Within.* New York: Continuum.

Pitkin, H. (1972) *Wittgenstein and Justice.* Berkeley, CA: University of California Press.

Raine, N. (1998) *After Silence: Rape and My Journey Back.* New York: Crown.

Reason, P. and Torbert, W.R. (1999) 'The action turn toward a transformational social science', Centre for Action Research in Professional Practice, University of Bath, and School of Management, Boston College.

Rooke, D. and Torbert, W.R. (1998) 'Organizational transformation as a function of CEOs' developmental stage', *Organization Development Journal,* 16 (1): 11–29.

Sedgwick, E. (1999) *A Dialogue on Love.* Boston, MA: Beacon Press.

Senge, P., Kleiner, A., Roberts, C., Ross, R. and Smith, B. (1994) *The Fifth Discipline Fieldbook: Strategies and Tools for Building a Learning Organization.* New York: Doubleday Currency.

Senge, P. Kleiner, A., Roberts, C., Ross, R., Roth, G. and Smith, B. (1999) *The Dance of Change: the Challenges to Sustaining Momentum in Learning Organizations.* New York: Doubleday Currency.

Sherman, F. and Torbert, W.R. (eds) (2000) *Transforming Social Inquiry, Transforming Social Action.* Norwell, MA: Kluwer Academic Publishers.

Torbert, W.R. (1976a) *Creating a Community of Inquiry: Conflict, Collaboration, Transformation.* London: Wiley Interscience.

Torbert, W.R. (1976b) 'On the possibility of revolution within the boundaries of propriety', *Humanities,* 12 (1): 111–46.

Torbert, W.R. (1991) *The Power of Balance: Transforming Self, Society, and Scientific Inquiry.* Newbury Park, CA: Sage Publications.

Torbert, W.R. (1993a) *Sources of Excellence: an Unorthodox Inquiry into Quality.* Cambridge, MA: Edgework Press.

Torbert, W.R. (1993b) 'Coitus interruptus: collaborative inquiry in sport, conversation and sex', *Collaborative Inquiry,* Centre for Action Research in Professional Practice, University of Bath, 11: 2–5.

Torbert, W.R. (1999) 'The distinctive questions developmental action inquiry asks', *Management Learning,* 30 (2): 189–206.

Torbert, W.R. (2000a) 'Transforming social science to integrate quantitative, qualitative, and action research', in F. Sherman and W.R. Torbert (eds), *Transforming Social Inquiry, Transforming Social Action.* Norwell, MA: Kluwer Academic Publishers.

Torbert, W.R. (2000b) 'The challenge of creating a community of inquiry among scholar-consultants critiquing one another's theories-in-practice', in F. Sherman and W.R. Torbert (eds), *Transforming Social Inquiry, Transforming Social Action.* Norwell, MA: Kluwer Academic Publishers.

Torbert, W.R. (2000c) 'The call to bridge knowledge and action: the response of the Boston College PhD program in Organizational Transformation', in F. Sherman and W.R. Torbert (eds), *Transforming Social Inquiry, Transforming Social Action.* Norwell, MA: Kluwer Academic Publishers.

Torbert, W.R. and Fisher, D. (1992) 'Autobiographical awareness as a catalyst for managerial and organizational development', *Management Education and Development,* 23 (3): 184–98.

Toulmin, S. and Gustavsen, B. (1996) *Beyond Theory: Changing Organizations through Participation.* Amsterdam: John Benjamins.

Trungpa, C. (1970) *Meditation in Action.* Boulder, CO: Shambhala Press.

Vaysse, J. (1980) *Toward Awakening.* New York: Harper & Row.

Wilber, K. (1995) *Sex, Ecology, Spirituality.* Boston, MA: Shambala Press.

Wilber, K. (1998) *The Marriage of Sense and Soul.* New York: Random House.

Young, I. (1996) 'Communication and the other: beyond deliberative democracy', in S. Benhabib (ed.), *Democracy and Difference: Contesting the Boundaries of the Political.* Princeton, NJ: Princeton University Press. pp. 120–36.

PART THREE
EXEMPLARS

19
Working Together, Learning Together: Co-operative Inquiry in the Development of Complex Practice by Teams of Social Workers

MARK BALDWIN

CHAPTER OUTLINE

This chapter provides an example of a co-operative inquiry. It describes the process of the inquiry and lessons learned by groups of social workers exploring the tensions between professional discretion and bureaucratic procedures in social welfare in the UK. Co-operative inquiry facilitated ownership of learning by practitioners, relieved their anxieties and demonstrated that co-operative inquiry can increase reflectiveness and lessen the negative effects of professional discretion.

This chapter provides an example of practice in one form of action research – co-operative inquiry (Heron, 1996; Heron and Reason, Chapter 12). It describes the process of and lessons that were learned from co-operative inquiries by two groups of social workers exploring the tensions between professional discretion and bureaucratic procedures in the implementation of a complex social policy in the UK. The chapter explores the reasons why this methodology was chosen, following misgivings about prior use of traditional qualitative research methodology. It is argued that co-operative inquiry facilitated ownership of learning by groups of social workers who were experiencing marginalization within their organization. This relieved their anxieties and provided lessons for policy implementation that could, if replicated, reduce the deficit effect of the unreflective use of discretion which has proved so undermining in other areas of policy (Lipsky, 1980).

Background

Social workers are front-line implementers of important social policies in the UK. These policies do not form a unified body of knowledge which instructs social workers how to act (Baldwin, 1997). Much of the guidance and managerial procedure is ambiguous or conflicting, and is also prescriptive (Lewis and Glennerster, 1996). Social workers, however, deal with complex interpersonal processes, assessing marginalized people's needs and negotiating 'packages' of care to meet those needs (Smale et al., 1993). To do this, they need to draw upon forms of knowledge in a reflective way (Smale et al., 1993). Evidence points to social workers using scope for discretion not to implement policy but to resist it (Ellis, 1993; Lipsky, 1980; Satyamurti, 1981). Such resistance comes in a context in which social workers have few opportunities to reflect upon the knowledge they engage when implementing systems such as assessment and care management. There is a tension between prescription and discretion, as well as a muddle around meaning and forms of knowledge for policy implementation. These tensions and the management of them within organizations provide the environment for this study.

Discretion in public policy implementation

Discussion in the literature on policy implementation (Clarke, Cochrane and McLaughlin, 1994; Hill, 1997a, 1997b; Hogwood and Gunn, 1984;

Hugman, 1991; Pressman and Wildavsky, 1973) about the role of discretion confirms that it exists, although most writers have a negative view of its effects. Rationalists, such as Hogwood and Gunn, insist their formula for top-down implementation would reduce policy deficit. Most other authors accept its inevitability within complex bureaucratic organizations.

There are two important versions of discretion. First, there is discretion as interpretation of rules within complex organizational procedures. Secondly, there is discretion as rule-breaking. In the latter version, workers use their scope for autonomy to act in a way that is outside of the statutory authority that defines the limits of their activities (illegal practice) or the rules – policy and procedures – of their employing organization. This tension between rules and discretion leads to an argument around legitimacy, democracy and accountability (Hill, 1997b). When front-line workers use their discretion they exercise power. It is important that organizations should have safeguards that track the use of discretion and ensure that workers are acting legitimately and with accountability. Workers also have a responsibility to reflect upon this. When social workers assess vulnerable adults, they are exercising a power which can affect the life chances of people already marginalized through disability, age and gender discrimination and racism. Unreflective use of discretion could, therefore, be discriminatory. Because 'combating' discrimination is a core value of social work practice, the use of discretion can raise the anxieties of ethical practitioners. There is no straight line from policy to front-line implementation and complexity of practice requires social workers to use their discretion to interpret the rules. The greater the degree of complexity, the more likely discretion will exist as both rule-breaking and interpretation. This means that the policy framework can be bent into different forms as the consequence of workers' discretion.

There is a distinction to be made between discretion as the unacknowledged habits of routine practice (Lipsky, 1980) and the deliberate and considered use of discretion in the process of decision-making. This distinction, of which I became aware in the process of inquiry described below, reveals a form of discretion that has not been acknowledged hitherto. This more positive form of discretion holds a creative potential for policy implementation. Considered use of discretion can be a positive part of front-line practitioners' work as they engage collaboratively with other stakeholders in the process of policy implementation. This analysis takes us beyond the tried and failed approaches to discretion which involve attempts to control it through autocratic management or technocratic procedures. It is in this context of exploring the positive use of discretion by front-line workers, such as social workers, that I engaged with two groups to both explore and practise the development of this positive form of discretion through co-operative inquiry.

Justification for co-operative inquiry as method

It is important that I acknowledge the reflexive journey during which traditional qualitative research interviews led to the use of co-operative inquiry. Prior to engaging with the co-operative inquiry groups, I carried out a series of semi-structured interviews with care managers in two local authorities. The use of this qualitative research methodology was a personal response to the environment in which I was engaged as a researcher – my 'socio-historical location' (Hammersley and Atkinson, 1995). This explains but does not justify the use of a methodology that, upon reflection, was not helpful in addressing my research questions. I wanted to elicit authentic responses not determined by interviewees' position as employees (organizational response) or as interviewees (researcher effect). I believe that my practice, using a semi-structured interview approach (Foddy, 1993; Lindlof, 1995; Silverman, 1993), was authentic within the limitations of the methodology, and the sense that I made of what I heard was of interest in a traditional academic sense. These interviews have helped me to understand that social workers acting as care managers do act with discretion in the way that is described by theorists such as Lipsky (1980). However, I now also know, with hindsight, what made the interviews problematic.

Reflecting upon these interviews revealed fundamental issues in research methodology. It does not matter how authentic and empowering I was if the issues of ownership and meaning of knowledge acquired through the interviews were not dealt with. I was shocked that only three interviewees replied to a request for a response to my report. It seems that the meaning that I gleaned from the interview transcripts either held little resonance for interviewees or, alternatively, so much that it was too painful to own. I have no way of knowing whether either of these conclusions is true, but I am left unable to claim that the interviews made any difference to the people whom they concerned, even if they helped me in my acquisition of knowledge. If the knowledge was not within the realms of their experience, what is termed 'experiential knowledge' (Reason and Bradbury, Introduction; Heron and Reason, Chapter 12), then it was not grounded in their actions and its validity is dubious. The knowledge expressed in the research report constructs a version of the real world which may have had little meaning for interviewees.

So, if scientific rationalism is a poor epistemological basis for implementation practice, is cooperative inquiry an alternative research methodology that could take into account the problems of ownership and meaning?

Co-operative inquiry as preferred method

Harre refers to the 'myth of certainty' (Harre, 1981: 8) in traditional positivist approaches such as mine described above. As a detached researcher, I was attempting to glean the truth from my research subjects. Positivist approaches are also based on the concept of dualism in which the researcher is separated from the researched (Reason, 1994a). But, what happens to ways of knowing which are not purely rationalist? Why ignore affective and behavioural knowing (Boud and Walker, 1993; Reason, 1994a)?

In a research process wherein the knower is separated from the known, both ontological and epistemological doubts are raised about the knowledge created. Claims to truth from a positivist framework have been weakened from a number of different angles. The dialectical process of reality creation (Freire, 1972) argues that we should consider both the concrete and the perception of the concrete. 'We choose our reality and our knowing of it' (Reason, 1994b: 332). Poststructuralist analysis suggests that language constructs reality (Potter, 1996; Rojek, Peacock and Collins, 1988) and that the 'discourse' that persuades people of its truth (Soyland, 1994) is what matters. 'What counts as true knowledge is ostensibly defined by the individual, but what is permitted to count is defined by discourse. What is spoken, and who may speak, are issues of power' (Parker, 1989: 61).

The participative worldview argues that human beings are engaged in 'co-creating their reality through participation' (Reason, 1994b: 324; Reason and Bradbury, Introduction). Relationship is fundamental to the creation of reality, and a methodology that separates the researcher from the researched denies that relationship. Ontologically, such a process would invalidate knowledge created, because it would not construct a reality that has meaning for the subjects of the research. The divisive epistemology of the positivist worldview separates and objectifies the subjects of research activity in much the same way that scientific managerialism and traditional social work objectify 'clients', and treat them as if they were the only reality to be dealt with, rather than constructs of persons created from particular forms of knowledge. Explanation is not reality itself, as scientific rationality would have us believe. Unless people participate in the construction of knowledge, the knowledge has no meaning for them. This is a question of power and politics in the research context (Reason and Heron, 1995), as it is in other areas of interest for this chapter – the management of discretion in social work practice and policy implementation. By engaging in a *co-operative* inquiry with social workers, the power to establish meaning was a democratic, shared process and not one imposed by an 'expert' researcher. Because of the dubious degree of validity in the previous interviews, I learnt that it was essential to use a participative approach for the next phase of empirical research. I chose co-operative inquiry (Heron, 1996) as most congruent with my research requirements.

Setting up the co-operative inquiry

In engaging with social workers in co-operative inquiry, I attempted a number of things. The first was to explore the current state of practice in the continuing implementation of community care policy. I was also interested in exploring co-operative inquiry as a methodology involving learning and practice development in a context of tension between prescription and discretion. Finally, as this was a participative venture, I wanted to respond to group interests.

The process started with a proposal to a social welfare organization, to feed back the findings from the original interviews, and to ask social workers to consider whether the findings were 'true for us?'. Workshop participants were concerned that bureaucratic process and resource constraint were still stifling professional discretion, effectively 'managing out' social work as a service. Practitioners felt that this undermined their role by marginalizing the knowledge, skills and values that underpin their practice which they claim could prevent the imposition of more restrictive alternatives such as residential care. The bureaucracy was experienced as an inefficient and ineffective process.

The two workshops ended with a description of co-operative inquiry as a way of investigating and working upon problems identified. After deliberation, two co-operative inquiry groups were formed. One was an established team of five hospital-based social workers (Hospital Group), and the other (Community Group) was formed from a disparate collection of social workers. The two groups met separately and I was offered the role of convenor. Both groups met eight times over a six-month period.

To what extent were these two groups co-operative inquiry groups in the way described by Heron and Reason in Chapter 12 and more comprehensively by Heron (1996)? Both groups agreed that the process should involve a co-operative approach. Members were involved in decisions about areas for investigation and methods that would be used in action and reflection stages. We progressed through cycles of action and reflection using a variety of methods for investigation and recording. I was asked to record reflective meetings, on the understanding that the notes would be drafts requiring unanimous approval. In hindsight, audio-recording of group discussions would have yielded more individuality and intimacy from the discussions, and its loss is regrettable. However, at the time, it was not felt to be an appropriate form of recording as there was suspicion about participants being 'allowed' by management to engage in these co-operative inquiry groups. Audio-recording was viewed as a more permanent record of their discussions which might have placed the participants in jeopardy. The role of facilitation meant that I could be convenor of the groups, facilitate discussion and play a role as 'devil's advocate'. I was not the only person to do this and my role as facilitator did not mean that I was in an exclusive leadership role. Rather, the groups were participative and democratic. With the exception of the recording issue (and I made every effort to ensure that recording was accepted by all involved), my view is that they were co-operative inquiry groups in the sense defined by Heron and Reason. We agreed that both groups should be closed to future involvement by others but inclusive, ensuring all members were present before proceeding. The level of commitment was very high and, except for one occasion, every session was fully attended. At the first meeting there was an 'ideastorming' session in which areas for exploration were discussed and selected for investigation. Prior to reconvening for the first reflective meeting, we decided what action would be taken and how it could be recorded.

It is interesting that the two groups chose similar areas for investigation, and that they were both largely driven by anxiety about the participants' performance as social workers within the Authority. There was, at the time, a question mark over organizational structure and staffing, so the future employment of some co-researchers was in doubt. We recognized the need to acknowledge and address anxiety as a powerful block to learning and practice development (Boud and Walker, 1993). It was argued that if anxiety was not tackled at the early stage it could sit silently in the room undermining commitment to mutual learning. It was also felt that a focus on practice issues over which the group had some control was more practical than looking at areas such as resource deficits, another area identified. Not only would research in the chosen area be more feasible, there was also a chance for successful outcome. We did not want to travel down any gloomy dead-ends.

The aim of meeting was to set up cycles of action and reflection to investigate the possibilities for practice development over time, within their restricted role as care managers, while at the same time exploring the use of discretionary social work practice. There was scepticism about this as professional discretion was believed to be in serious jeopardy within the new role of care manager imposed by a management agenda ruled by resource constraint rather than service provision. How achievable was practice development, using co-operative inquiry as the motivating force?

The process of co-operative inquiry

The groups met separately, for up to two hours at a time. We ensured the time was uninterrupted and that all members were present. The first meetings established ground rules around group processes, roles and confidentiality. We discussed the manner in which we were to relate to one another – avoiding personal comments but agreeing that problems would be addressed in the group rather than discussed outside. These deliberations are similar to those suggested in group-work literature (e.g., Brown, 1992) as good practice when establishing effective groups.

As indicated above, anxiety was recognized as a prime area for investigation in the initial 'ideastorming' sessions. The principal anxiety for both groups was a lack of consistency between individuals and between teams. How, inquirers wondered, would they know what agency practice requirements were? This question was a surprise, given that comprehensive guidance documentation existed. It was apparent that interpretation of guidance was varied and that this variation created anxiety. The next section focuses on the way one of the two groups tackled anxiety about consistency. Both groups had similar experiences so what follows provides a useful illustration of what can happen in such a co-operative inquiry.

Hospital Group Discussions

The Hospital Group focused on a specific bureaucratic procedure to investigate differences of practice. The document chosen was a form that had to be signed by a potential service user, to give consent for the social worker to contact third parties to seek information about the user. Consent was seen by the authority as good practice in that it reflected partnership. Social workers in the Hospital Group were concerned that requesting a signature was a threatening practice for some people. When they felt that to be the case, they did not ask for a signature, even though they knew they *ought* to. The mandated procedure is an example of the ethos of community care policy and the actual practice an example of the use of discretion. The use of social work discretion in the implementation of this procedure was thus the focus of inquiry. The group could investigate the extent to which policy was being undermined by their discretion.

The group devised a technique of investigation and recording. Every time one of the forms *should* have been completed, participants recorded the reason why they did or did not ask service users to sign the form. In effect, they were required to justify their actions, both to themselves and to their peers in the co-operative inquiry group. This provided an opportunity both to reflect-in-action ('why am I practising like this right now?') and to reflect-on-action ('why did I ask *that* person to sign the form but not *this* person?'). This was an example of Schön's reflective process of learning and practice development (Schön, 1987). This process was followed for three consecutive cycles of action and reflection. At the third meeting, one member of the group, acting as 'devil's advocate', questioned the purpose of continuing this exercise.

As a result of this challenge, and the discussion that followed, we opened an inquiry into the nature of intuition and reflection. As facilitator, I asked group members how they knew when it was the 'right' moment to ask someone to sign the form. The first response was 'I know intuitively when it is right'. We then deconstructed the concept of intuition, by continually asking *where* the knowing comes from. We identified the sources of knowledge, the theoretical perspectives, the social work values, the skills, as well as the assumptions and prejudices that often combine to make us act in a particular way. Prior to the group's engagement in co-operative inquiry, all this jumble of knowledge had combined to inform practice unreflectively. Every time we got to the bottom of intuition, defining it and describing it, we were left with something indefinable, which was labelled intuition! 'I just knew that I shouldn't push her on signing the form.' I described what I saw as a 'threshold technique' intuitively (at best) or unreflectively (at worst) being employed by group members. At some point they recognized that a particular individual met some undefined criteria that meant they could 'cope' with being asked to complete the required paperwork.

How did they know that they had crossed that threshold? What knowledge, what skills, were being employed to assist that decision? An exercise was developed, with a system of recording, to enable group members to utilize the threshold technique. This exercise encouraged social workers to maximize opportunities for participative practice. As a result, there was an increase in the numbers of forms signed without a consequent increase in service user or worker anxiety.

Upon meeting again and sifting out the propositions from the practical and experiential ways of knowing, we found that we had even more material to help in the definition of intuitive knowledge. Intuitive knowing was seen as an important aspect of creative understanding, although we agreed that it needed to be recognized and reflected upon because of the dangers of non-reflection. This process of reflection in and upon action enabled group members to differentiate the use of knowledge that was informed by the participatory and empowering values that they espoused in theory from the more unaware or stereotypical practice that they recognized occurred if they were *not* engaged in reflection. Discrimination is such a negative factor in contemporary social work ethos that it was anxiety-provoking to recognize their own potential for acting in discriminatory ways. It was also a salutary lesson to the group that they had so much opportunity for discretion. Practising with discretion but without reflection was recognized as ineffective or potentially oppressive.

The importance of reflection in and upon action had thus been established as a key to the maintenance of and the continuing development of 'good' practice in the light of new circumstances – such as the introduction of new policy or procedure. When, the group members asked themselves, did they have such opportunities to reflect upon their actions? How could they instil the discipline of reflection while engaged in relationship with service users? The co-operative inquiry group was providing such an opportunity, but what would happen when it finished?

The answer to these questions was raised in conjunction with another issue confronting the Hospital Group – the concerns that social work as a system of knowledge and values was being marginalized by the introduction of care management as method for assessing people's needs and planning their services. The Hospital Group recognized that social work was often the only service that could prevent informal supports breaking down and more restrictive services such as residential care becoming inevitable. How was it possible to protect available space for good quality assessments, develop a preventative service, and establish opportunities for reflection and practice development? This led us into exploration of workload relief and supervision. Group members recognized that supervision was an important arena for reflection and decision-making around workload management. The social workers relied upon their manager to give them space for good quality supervision, which was one forum, outside the co-operative inquiry, where they might establish some overview of consistency in their practice. How to encourage their manager to provide such supervision became a focus for one cycle of action and reflection. They also explored the possibilities for mutual aid when they felt stressed, and space for shared reflection upon work. Through these processes, team members gradually developed their own individual and collective techniques for replicating the most useful aspects of the co-operative inquiry in anticipation of its closure after six months.

Reflections and Conclusions

The purpose of co-operative inquiry is the mutual creation of owned and usable knowledge. In reflecting on the co-operative inquiries above, it is apparent that this purpose can be fulfilled by social workers investigating their practice in a participative framework. Both co-operative inquiry groups established new areas of understanding, some of them previously unrealised insights and others that were the result of revisiting and adapting formerly held knowledge. Unlike the knowledge created from the prior interviews, this knowledge held meaning for co-researchers which they were able to own and adopt in practice. The creation of knowledge in these groups thus had an effect on behaviour in the way that might be expected from an approach that is congruent with models of cyclical learning (Kolb, 1984) and reflective practice (Boud and Walker, 1993; Gould and Taylor, 1996; Schön, 1987).

As a system of investigation, co-operative inquiry has proved more effective than traditional qualitative approaches in facilitating the production of owned and usable knowledge. As street-level implementers, members of both groups recognized that they could use discretion to influence policy. They will be unable to differentiate whether this influence will be positive or negative unless they adopt a reflective approach. Co-operative inquiry can be successful in facilitating a process of learning in which participants incorporate different forms of knowledge into practice. It also provided us with propositional insights into the nature of discretion and reflection in organizational processes.

It is important to question whether these conclusions are idealistic. It could be argued that the co-operative inquiries were a one-off which will not change anything in organizations still wedded to scientific managerialism. There are counter arguments. First, co-operative inquiry was an experiment in the possibilities for engaging in reflection and learning for developmental practice and it proved successful in creating such opportunities, especially in a collaborative context. Such opportunities also set up an environment of dynamic and reflective use of discretion which is likely to force out unreflective discretion argued as normative within street-level bureaucrats' *modus operandi* (Lipsky, 1980). Such experiments require further investigation through replication in different settings to test out their effectiveness.

A second point concerns the practical developments that emanated from the groups' reflections. Workload management systems were explored as a method of freeing up social workers' time to engage in more preventative work. Such space also creates more opportunities for reflective evaluation like that provided in the co-operative inquiries. In addition, work was done on exploring effective ways of persuading first-line managers to offer developmental supervision replicating opportunities for reflection established through co-operative inquiry. Participants agreed to make better use of the participatory opportunities already available within the organization. These included the recording of unmet need which was an agency requirement. Participants realised the potential that the accumulation of their day-to-day practice could add to service developments. Following debate within the co-operative inquiry groups and with senior managers after their completion, prior scepticism about opportunities for participation in the organization gave way to a feeling that it was important to take such opportunities rather than dismiss them as tokenistic. None of these developments require additional agency resources.

Finally, looking beyond the advantages for group members individually and collectively, co-operative inquiry also revealed the degree to which participative investigation and learning can produce positive outcomes that are more consistent with policy intentions than traditional and coercive approaches to policy implementation and practice development based on the certainty principle of scientific rationality.

References

Baldwin, M. (1997) 'Key texts in community care: the analysis of discourse in government and government commissioned documents which relate to care management', *Social Work and Social Sciences Review*, 8 (2): 76–88.

Boud, D. and Walker, D. (1993) 'Barriers to reflection on experience', in D. Boud, R. Cohen and D. Walker (eds), *Using Experience for Learning*. Buckingham: Open University Press. pp. 73–86.

Brown, A. (1992) *Groupwork* (third edition). Aldershot: Avebury.

Clarke, J., Cochrane, A. and McLaughlin, E. (eds) (1994) *Managing Social Policy*. London: Sage Publications.

Ellis, K. (1993) *Squaring the Circle: User and Carer Participation in Needs Assessment*. York: Joseph Rowntree.

Foddy, W. (1993) *Constructing Questions for Interviews and Questionnaires: Theory and Practice in Social Research*. Cambridge: Cambridge University Press.

Freire, P. (1972) *Pedagogy of the Oppressed*. London: Penguin.

Gould, N. and Taylor, I. (1996) *Reflective Learning for Social Work*. Aldershot: Arena.

Hammersley, M. and Atkinson, P. (1995) *Ethnography* (second edition). London: Routledge.

Harre, R. (1981) 'The positivist–empiricist approach and its alternatives', in P. Reason and J. Rowan (eds), *Human Inquiry: a Sourcebook of New Paradigm Research*. Chichester: John Wiley. pp. 3–17.

Heron, J. (1996) *Co-operative Inquiry: Research into the Human Condition*. London: Sage Publications.

Hill, M. (ed.) (1997a) *The Policy Process: a Reader* (second edition). Hemel Hempstead: Prentice-Hall.

Hill, M. (1997b) *The Policy Process in the Modern State* (third edition). Hemel Hempstead: Prentice-Hall.

Hogwood, B. and Gunn, L. (1984) *Policy Analysis for the Real World*. London: Oxford University Press.

Hugman, R. (1991) *Power in Caring Professions*. Basingstoke: Macmillan.

Kolb, D. (1984) *Experiential Learning: Experience as the Source of Learning and Development*. Englewood Cliffs, NJ: Prentice-Hall.

Lewis, J. and Glennerster, H. (1996) *Implementing the New Community Care*. Buckingham: Open University.

Lindlof, T. (1995) *Qualitative Communication Research Methods*. London: Sage Publications.

Lipsky, M. (1980) *Street Level Bureaucrats: Dilemmas of the Individual in Public Services*. New York: Russell Sage Foundation.

Parker, I. (1989) 'Discourse and power', in J. Shotter and K. Gergen (eds), *Texts of Identity*. London: Sage Publications. pp. 56–69.

Potter, J. (1996) *Representing Reality: Discourse, Rhetoric and Social Construction*. London: Sage Publications.

Pressman, J. and Wildavsky, A. (1973) *Implementation*. Berkeley, CA: University of California Press.

Reason, P (ed.) (1994a) *Participation in Human Inquiry*. London: Sage Publications.

Reason, P (1994b) 'Three approaches to participative inquiry', in N. Denzin and Y. Lincoln (eds), *Handbook of Qualitative Research*. London: Sage Publications. pp. 324–39.

Reason, P. and Heron, J. (1995) 'Co-operative inquiry', in J. Smith, R. Harre and L. Langenhove (eds), *Rethinking Methods in Psychology*. London: Sage Publications. pp. 122–42.

Rojek, C., Peacock, G. and Collins, S. (1988) *Social Work and Received Ideas*. London: Routledge.

Satyamurti, C. (1981) *Occupational Survival: the Case of the Local Authority Social Worker*. Oxford: Blackwell.

Schön, D. (1987) *Educating the Reflective Practitioner*. San Francisco, CA: Jossey-Bass.

Silverman, D. (1993) *Interpreting Qualitative Data: Methods for Analyzing Talk, Text and Interaction*. London: Sage Publications.

Smale, G., Tuson, G., with Biehal, N. and Marsh, P. (1993) *Empowerment, Assessment, Care Management and the Skilled Worker*. London: HMSO.

Soyland, A.J. (1994) *Psychology as Metaphor*. London: Sage Publications.

20

The Early Mothering Project: What Happened When the Words 'Action Research' Came to Life for a Group of Midwives

PENELOPE A. BARRETT

CHAPTER OUTLINE

This chapter provides a snapshot of some reflective moments within an action research project that was informed by feminist principles and processes. It involved midwives as participants at a women's hospital working together to improve their practice. After six months of planning, the Midwives' Action Research Group set up an 'Early Mothering Group' for women in hospital before and following childbirth to meet together over morning tea and share stories. For both midwives' and mothers' groups, the therapeutic potential of women's ordinary talk emerged as a pivotal component of midwifery practice – yet mostly invisible within the prevailing biomedical, positivist frameworks that dominate healthcare today.

This chapter is an overview of the Early Mothering Project which I conducted with a group of midwives. Through telling my story and including pivotal, reflective moments, I will highlight how action research practice – informed by feminist processes – was applied within midwifery, leading to a change in practice that practitioners within this setting generated, implemented and evaluated. Doing research 'with', as opposed to 'on', people complements my own ideas about human relating which in turn have been shaped by the myriad of interactions and relationships encountered during my midwifery and nursing career. This connection is further strengthened when one considers the true meaning of the word 'midwife', which is 'with woman' (Bennett and Brown, 1993: 3).

Following my involvement in a 'classic (and heartening) Participatory Action Research piece of work' (Wadsworth, personal communication, 10 October 1997), I find myself in a unique position of being able to reflect on what happened when the words 'action research' came to life for a group of midwives at the Royal Hospital for Women in Sydney, Australia. Over a period of eighteen months, participants in a Midwives' Action Research Group (which became known as 'MARG') directed their action research work towards improving midwifery practice, enhancing women's satisfaction with their early mothering experiences, and facilitating women's access to informed choices. The change that MARG participants implemented provides a physical and temporal space once a week in the postnatal wards for childbearing women to talk to each other, share and reflect on experiences, learn from other women, and form supportive social networks during their stay in hospital.[1]

After six months of planning, MARG participants decided that the most significant offering the mothers' group could provide for women was time for *themselves* in hospital, either before or after birth. The Early Mothering Group was set up as a woman-centred place for mothers and mothers-to-be to meet together. Here, women share stories about birth or any other topic that arises. It is vitally important that midwives recognize emotional care as an integral component of midwifery practice, and the Early Mothering Group heightens midwives' awareness of this.

Groundings and Processes

Principles underpinning the project draw on threads woven through 'Groundings' and 'Practices', in particular, feminism, humanism and co-operative inquiry, which have been addressed by Maguire (Chapter 5), Rowan (Chapter 9), and Heron and Reason (Chapter 12) respectively. As feminist influences are multi-faceted and a variety of perspectives are encompassed within the term 'feminism', it is important for me to say what feminist ideas were significant in shaping the project and MARG activities. These relate to consciousness-raising, empowerment and evolution through sharing experiences, and a commitment to make women's voices more audible. I drew on Wheeler and Chinn's definition of praxis as '*values made visible through deliberate action*' (1991: 2, emphasis in original) to capture the essence of midwives' reflection on practice. Women in this project (including myself as researcher-midwife) exploited 'self-awareness as a source of insight and discovery' (Reinharz, 1979: 241).

Overview of the Action Research Design and Phases

Adapted from Kemmis and McTaggart (1988), the research design was flexible enough to allow for the evolution and refinement of processes which (as all action researchers know) can sometimes prove to be unpredictable, messy and emotionally charged. This incorporated:

- collaborating throughout the project with midwives in clinical practice at the Royal Hospital for Women;
- identifying concerns related to women's experiences of informed choice during the early mothering period;
- prioritizing these concerns and identifying a thematic concern/substantive problem related to practice;
- developing a plan of critically informed action to address the thematic concern and improve what is happening;
- observing the effects of the critically informed action in the context in which it occurs; and
- reflecting on and evaluating these effects as a basis for further planning, subsequent critically informed action and development of further action research cycles.

Through their conversation, midwives spun reflections about the action research activities and related topics into topic and issue threads during fortnightly (later monthly) MARG meetings. A reflective thematic analysis (Thompson and Barrett, 1997) of MARG 'field-tapes' helped me to understand the action research phases and processes.[2] Noting the patterns of conversation threads and their relationship to events as they unfolded, I identified five action research phases that evolved from midwives' action research work on the primary action plan (setting up the Early Mothering Group). These five phases incorporate: planning; implementing; evaluating; revise-planning; and continuing or discontinuing. Action research phases were connected by four processes – reflecting, learning, prioritizing and deciding – linking all facets of the research.

During the life of the project, phases wove into, through and spiralled around each other with a blurring of boundaries at the beginning and end of each and across MARG meetings. Doing action research mirrored life as it happened. This grounding in the messy reality reflecting the 'dailiness' of everyday events is, in essence, what action research provides in the way of an approach to generating fresh understandings and systematic changes in a practice-based discipline like midwifery. The findings are not only useful, but meaningful to those for and with whom the research is being conducted.

Everything that happened from the moment I was committed to the project became data; action research enabled information that may otherwise be overlooked, ignored or cast off (within positivist research) to become relevant within specific contexts. I kept a journal of events for discussion in later phases of the research. Along with midwives' ongoing reflections about their experiences, this proved helpful in generating understanding and insight about what was occurring. I have provided excerpts from my reflective journal and midwives' conversations (using pseudonyms) to illustrate pertinent points in the following discussions. Recording unexpected and less than favourable events became relevant in terms of revealing 'contestation and institutionalisation' across Kemmis and McTaggart's (1988) registers of 'language and discourses', 'activities and practices' and 'social relations and forms of organization'. Importantly, the milieu in which midwives and others functioned within the hospital was unveiled for comment and critique. Social and professional power relationships were revealed, and privilege assumed by members of certain groups (for example, doctors) over those of other groups (for example, midwives) was exposed and challenged.

Negotiating with Gatekeepers – the 'Hospital Ethics Committee Story'

Part of action research is to understand aspects which comprise the setting before change or improvement occurs, thus it was important to note the presence of institutional gatekeepers. One example of 'everything becoming data' relates to gaining entry to the institution. Even before formal data collection began at MARG meetings, the process of gaining Hospital Ethics Committee approval to conduct the study provided early insights into how access to the ability to generate knowledge about childbirth can influence the way women experience early mothering as carers and recipients of care.

The approval process involved a lot of negotiation on my part to convince powerful institutional gatekeepers that the research fulfilled all ethical criteria in relation to conducting human research, as it was seen to be methodologically different from medical research. Through reflection, I understood events and saw that difficulties were part of the research learning. I submitted the original proposal five months prior to writing the journal entries below, then waited two months for a response that requested methodological clarification (as opposed to ethical). In fact, there were no ethical problems with the proposal at all. My Ethics Committee experiences turned out to be an example of what interested me through an action research perspective; I learnt about power and my understanding of oppression within the organization grew. It is relevant to note that the composition of the Ethics Committee at the time included a number of medical officers and no midwives or nurses; neither was there any requirement for gender balance.

13 January 1992

Is this negative response from the Ethics Committee an example of midwives and nurses being oppressed? Or am I jumping to a simplistic conclusion? I think it is at least partially due to this. The Ethics Committee not only seems to fulfil an ethical role but also a gate-keeping role in hindering would-be researchers whose work doesn't fit the empirical-analytic framework and also which might reveal unpleasant truths about the setting …

13 February 1992, 11 pm

Why do I feel they are trying to block me in my research? I am sitting here crying because I feel so angry and frustrated about all this – it's just like the feelings I had in my nursing days when I felt I couldn't answer back or disagree with him [the doctor] for fear of either reprimand or ridicule. Is there something (as my soulmate Tony seems to be trying to tell me) so powerful about the social power relations between doctor and midwife or nurse that even though I am a PhD student I still feel impotent to act in face of their opposition. The other problem is, I don't know how or where to act, or what I can do to try and break out of this mould, if that's what I'm in.

What gives them the right to tell me which women I can or cannot have a conversation with on a voluntary basis for my research? Do they have a legal right? Or is it assumed power?

God I feel like tossing the whole thing in right now and going back to – what? –

The euphoria of success with the Hospital Ethics Committee waned within two weeks, when I was informed that I needed to ask the Senior Medical Staff Council for 'permission' to speak with the obstetricians' 'women' (the mothers). Again, through reflective journalling, I was able to step back and see beyond my immediate frustration. I came to understand that medical staff are influenced by a type of politics and power, just as midwives and nurses are. Further, I reflected on the role that loyalty between doctors plays in silencing those who are supportive and want to maintain good relationships with midwives and nurses, thus letting the more conservative doctors maintain power and control.

The Midwives' Action Research Group's (MARG's) Story

As participants took on their 'researcher-midwife' roles within the organization, the Midwives' Action Research Group evolved and became an entity – known about, spoken of, and referred to by personnel throughout all areas of the hospital. The group affectionately became known as MARG until it ceased meeting about 18 months following its inception. Co-incidentally, a midwife called Margaret later became the Early Mothering Group convenor. This provided a lovely rounding off to the whole evolutionary process as I gradually (and reluctantly) faded out of the 'action' picture to write up my doctoral dissertation (Barrett, 1998).

Once MARG had been set up, participants worked through the five action research phases. Some outcomes of the action research plan were sought after, while others emerged as unanticipated, yet rich sources of learning about the setting in which change was being implemented. In retrospect, the most important lessons participants learnt from reflecting on difficulties activating original ideas relate to being flexible and adaptable within given constraints as well as extending their lateral thinking ability.

Throughout these early months of MARG's existence, participants spent a great deal of time talking about midwifery practice with a focus on mothers' realities and needs, while reflecting on their own experiences as women and midwives. After about three meetings together, participants had established a level of trust and were openly sharing thoughts and insights about their lives and relationships. At these first three meetings I brought along a guideline and suggested structure for refining our 'thematic concern', a 'Table of Invention' which I had modified from the available literature (Kemmis and McTaggart, 1988). This remained under-utilized as participants identified their priorities and proceeded with decision-making for the primary action plan through spontaneous talking, listening, reflecting and learning with each other.

MARG participants spoke of aspects of practice that they thought could be changed and improved. Experiencing some tension between the need to guide and the need to let the group own the decision-making processes, I decided (on reflection) to be true to the egalitarian ideas upon which the project was based. I stepped back from directing the conversation, apart from gentle reminders along the way about the principles of action research and the realities of time available to undertake the primary action plan work. This sharing of power within the midwives' group was based on feminist process incorporating 'collectivity', 'sharing', 'letting go', 'diversity', 'consensus' and 'evolvement' (Wheeler and Chinn, 1991).

Some ideas for change and improvement that emerged related to providing more support for new fathers, setting up a midwives' peer support group, and changing some of the procedures in the antenatal clinic. Difficulties in meeting birth women's emotional needs (in particular those women who were hospitalized for complexities of pregnancy) surfaced as a practice issue. With the need for women to talk together becoming a pivotal concern, midwives spoke of providing a time and space for mothers in hospital to meet and chat during morning tea. Firm ideas were developed about rationale which supported the formation of an Early Mothering Group. For MARG participants, the idea of providing women time to talk to *each other* seemed an obvious and straightforward need that was not being met for them within these most crucial, early mothering days. As participants reflected (and were themselves enacting within MARG), women do this naturally. What MARG participants did was record the essence of how this talk was helpful in facilitating women's working through of some major life changes associated with childbearing.

The project proceeded with MARG participants sharing more of their stories as they became change agents, and it gradually emerged that the therapeutic potential of ordinary talk was part of MARG's experiences. MARG in a sense became the embodiment of the Early Mothering Group, with participants choosing to sacrifice a great deal of their own time and energy to see this action plan through. In relation to attending MARG meetings, Cath commented:

> You go and talk about things and you get professional support, which you don't get in the wards. It's different, more than just being (like) a maid. It makes it more of an important job for me, hearing all the other women, the way they talk and their interests ...

Ordinary Talk and Empowerment

Shared understandings led to insights about concepts such as 'empowerment' and 'informed choice'. Shared reflections were being incorporated into plans for action and woven into informing participants' practices, providing a mechanism for facilitating midwifery praxis. The idea that midwives could help women feel empowered through providing them with opportunities to share information about available choices parallels the imperative that I felt when negotiating the Hospital Ethics Committee process. Unless the generation and flow of information about options for care is unimpeded by predetermined standards about what constitutes 'legitimate' knowledge (for example, biomedical positivism being viewed as the only valid way of undertaking clinical research with childbearing women), a truly informed choice is not possible. MARG participants' understandings of empowerment were tied into realizing that they could challenge the status quo and implement a change to help make women's experiences more enjoyable. They would do this through promoting woman-centred practices like 'talk-time' which complement the routine care provided for mothers; adding strength to midwives' resolve that their fresh approach to improving practice within a large, medically-dominated institution was indeed worthy of feeling excited and empowered about. I recall thinking how much rehearsing MARG participants were doing during their own meeting conversations in preparation for facilitation of mothers' groups. The resolution of issues such as how to deal with interactional dynamics was unfolding from within MARG conversations.

Participants' understandings of empowerment were grounded in feeling strong and resilient from within – not needing the approval of those in positions of power to proceed and having enough information on which to base decisions. From an action research angle, difficulties became data. Reflections revealed how one kind of power – empowerment – can be viewed as positive and therapeutic, whereas another variety of power – related to control and gatekeeping – can lead to feelings of powerlessness and frustration. As MARG became an entity within the hospital and the Early Mothering Group evolved into a real change in practice, each group provided a framework for both empowering women and challenging the institutional structure. Didi emphasized the 'power from within' as being the key to feeling empowered:

> The only time I've ever felt really empowered [is] when I've got to the point where I don't even have to say, 'What do you think of this?' Because [only when] I feel so good about it myself ... do I find that I feel empowered.

Six months after their first meeting, MARG participants revealed the human vulnerability associated with being a change agent, along with some of the rewards. The need for action blended with feelings of hesitation and uncertainty as time for implementing the primary action plan drew near. Some of the midwives really wanted to get the mothers' groups up and running; however, others urged caution. As usual, the words of the midwives themselves proved to be the best guide for proceeding. Didi articulated things clearly in terms of hesitations with proceeding.

> I really believe that one of the biggest ways we're going to get anything done in this group is by gaining strength ourselves, through talking to each other, and getting really firm beliefs and strength in our own opinions ... I think the idea to me is that we will eventually have very firm ideas of the importance of what we're doing ... We haven't yet got feeling for the importance of what we're doing to the point where we're ready to stand up and take this action that we're talking about. I think that's why we haven't even had the meetings yet with the mothers. Because we haven't got that great feeling of how important it is. That's why we're here, because the women need support, and they're not getting it and we don't know how to go about giving it to them. So when we do know that, we'll be having morning tea with them. You know, it's going to be a brave thing that we do.

MARG participants were empowering *each other* through their talking and listening. As an extension to the action research work, participants saw that they might be able to have some input into planning for the new hospital that was in the process of being built. A year later, following MARG's written report to the hospital evaluating the Early Mothering Group, the Director of Nursing Services requested a copy of the full text of mothers' written comments (from the evaluation forms collected over an 11-month period). These would then be placed, 'where able ... into the Design Briefs for the new hospital (D. Thoms, personal communication, 30 March 1994). Empowerment was taking on meaning through midwives' praxis; it was not just an idealistic concept, but rather a process which MARG participants were living.

By the time that the Early Mothering Group first met, MARG conversations recorded the sense of unity being expressed by participants. Clear evidence that MARG had an identity arrived in the form of an invitation for Didi to attend a local Area Health Service seminar day, convened to ask women what they wanted in terms of services. Excitement grew about being seen as 'legitimate' not only by the hospital, but also by a local government agency.

Implementing the Change

The pragmatics of the Early Mothering Group had been ironed-out: a starting date; advertising; facilitation styles; its purpose; and the midwife-facilitator's role. Although on some topics MARG participants held different views, the feminist principles underpinning group processes within 'PEACE and Power' (Wheeler and Chinn, 1991), which value diversity in the group, were being lived out. Values were espoused and reflective, constructive debate ensued which made it easy for anyone within MARG to move their opinions back and forth without feeling as though they might be rejected by others in the group. Trust surfaced as a pivotal concern for MARG participants and in midwifery practice generally.

Involvement with mothers and others during the implementation phase added another pattern to the weave of the fabric, as women's conversation broadened to include mothers' words. The action plan was finally implemented shortly before MARG meeting 17, eight months after the first midwives' meeting. Earlier thoughts regarding possible similarities between MARG and the Early Mothering Group were coming to fruition as participants wove reflection about their experiences of facilitating mothers' groups into MARG meeting conversations. Fundamental similarities between midwives and mothers related to their under-acknowledged busyness (finding time and finding *a* time to meet) and difficulties with visibility and audibility in decision-making contexts. The key topic of helping women help themselves kept winding itself through MARG participants' conversation. Repeatedly, the theme of women's strength and potential for mutual support linked other topics together as both process and outcome. As Ann said in relation to dealing with difficult and powerful gatekeepers within the institution:

> You've got to stand your ground, have eye contact, be direct, hear what they say, and say, 'Now this is what I have to say'. And if you can do that, see yourself as an equal, see yourself as an advocate for women ... when I think I'm playing this role for the women who need this help, who can't themselves approach these people ... that's what gives me my strength.

Reflections on Power, Control and Change as a Source of Learning

Issues of power and control threaded through all MARG conversations. To facilitate implementation of the action plan, participants were open to possibilities for challenging some of the entrenched, *de facto* power assumed by gatekeepers within the hospital as this was encountered. Greater insight and fresh understandings crystallized as to the genesis and solution of problems. The 'Time-slot Story' – negotiating with a doctor who had been conducting a regular, longstanding group at the time MARG members wanted to hold the Early Mothering Group – tells of how institutionalized power was brought to light and successfully challenged.

By MARG meeting 20 (ten months since the first MARG meeting), the Early Mothering Group had become part of the hospital's: language and discourses; activities and practices; and social relations and forms of organization, following Kemmis and McTaggart (1988). With a name, an identity, a time-slot, and a physical space in one of the postnatal wards, MARG participants' ideas were validated as to the primary purpose and format for their action plan. The Early Mothering Group with a midwife-facilitator was established so that women could talk and listen to each other. Endorsement by the Director of Nursing Services was a significant factor influencing general acceptance within the hospital. In fact, shortly after arriving at the hospital to take up her new position, she joined MARG as a participant. Repeatedly throughout the project, collaboration and involvement (Kemmis and McTaggart, 1988) proved to be key principles underpinning success with action plan initiatives.

Talking, Listening and Learning with Women – Ordinary Talk as Therapeutic Process

MARG group processes would later be identifiable as primary therapeutic process-threads within the Early Mothering Group – debriefing, validation and catharsis. By making midwives' tacit knowing (Polanyi, 1983) more visible and voices more audible, possibilities within midwifery for opening up primary health promotion strategies were emerging. Within MARG over time, more conversations took place and mothers' evaluations of the action plan fed into ongoing events. Similarities between MARG and the Early Mothering Group became more obvious; each providing moments of intense emotion. Sharing stories, midwives and mothers processed happy and traumatic thoughts and experiences. The debriefing thread ran through participants' conversations when relating practice stories and mothers' talk of birth, generating strong feelings of identification and support. Laughter as catharsis emerged while telling both mothers' and midwives' 'horror' stories. Participants identified emotional and social care as an area of midwifery practice which could be improved, incorporating the idea of 'caring for the carers'. Midwives' skills in this sphere were being practised 'behind the screens' (Lawler, 1991). In other words, as with much of nursing's work, this important component of midwifery care was, in effect, 'invisible'.

The need for a midwives' support group, spoken of in previous meetings, was again articulated. The sense of belonging, safety, comfort and support that mothers said they gained by attending Early Mothering Groups was also felt by participants attending MARG; they wanted everybody around them, including the doctors, to benefit from groups like these. Participants yearned for other midwives to have access to the growth experiences that they had been exposed to through MARG meetings and Early Mothering Groups. At times it was as if MARG had always been part of everyday midwifery practice; it was comforting to know that participants would be there at the next meeting. There was so much to talk about now that the primary action plan was in full swing.

'It's Here To Stay'

After MARG meeting 22, I 'handed over' control of the group; travelling overseas facilitated this 'letting go' process but also removed me for some weeks from MARG. The group was primed for my absence as this had been part of our conversation for some time. I reminded participants that they were now in control of their own decision-making and direction. Didi volunteered to facilitate MARG in my absence, mastering the requisite skills for operating the audiotape recorder. Suitable meeting times and a roster for facilitating each mothers' group were arranged. During the ensuing weeks, the reality of participants' busyness, together with their energy and motivation to keep MARG going, was brought into sharp focus. In spite of difficulties, MARG was sustained by original and new members' commitment to the project. Constraints on midwives being able to practise fully as the women's advocate were discussed. Further to earlier reflections on power and empowerment, not only had participants experienced emotional pain and discomfort in being change advocates, but they had also gained personal satisfaction and a sense of shared accomplishment which led to an appreciation of what it actually felt like to *become* 'empowered'.

Following MARG meeting 26 (18 months after the first meeting), participants decided that they no longer needed meeting conversations transcribed, but rather that minutes of meetings would suffice. MARG processes of 'reflecting', 'learning', 'prioritizing' and 'deciding' continued after participants ceased recording their talk. During the data analysis phase of my doctoral research, I subsequently used the 26 MARG meeting transcriptions as the primary source of information for tracking – through participants' voices – what had happened in relation to changes in them as well as within the organization.

The reality of the change in practice that they had generated remained in the form of the Early Mothering Group. In other words, it was there to stay. MARG was now a part of the hospital practices – endorsed, approved of, and legitimate – with its own identity, having implemented an improvement in midwifery practice that was helping mothers enjoy their experiences of early mothering. As Didi commented:

> I remember in the beginning thinking it was important to tape, because it was like something really special that we had to have physical evidence of. And I thought we'd forget it or lose it or ... lose the importance or lose the spark that was keeping it going, if we didn't have it down on paper. But now I just feel today when we were talking about it at the meeting, I thought, 'We don't need to have physical evidence of it any more, because it's never going away. It's part of the institution. We have the support of the most powerful woman here. The most powerful nurse here is incredibly supportive, to the point of pushing it'. So I just think we don't need any hard evidence of it any more, because it's there! It's here to stay.

The Early Mothering Group was a tangible outcome of participants' hard work carrying out action research, not merely an intellectual exercise written up as a research finding. Prior to MARG's 30th (and final) meeting, participants helped me generate a coloured advertising poster symbolizing the mothers' group. Production was financially supported by the Director of Nursing Services and the posters were placed in strategic positions on all maternity wards.

The outcome of MARG participants' action research work lives on as testimony to the relevance for women of this change in practice. Presently, new mothers are invited on a voluntary basis to participate in a weekly Early Mothering Group, held on the postnatal wards. A midwife-facilitator maintains a relatively low profile in terms of directing the group. She is present in the role of another woman joining in with the others in conversation, being 'with' the women and providing advice only as solicited, as well as inviting the mothers to partake of refreshments such as coffee or a variety of teas, along with special 'non-hospital issue' biscuits/cookies. Sometimes the midwife-facilitator needs to spend more time with a woman who may have related an emotionally traumatic experience; there is also opportunity following each group for the midwife in charge of the unit to be made aware of any woman who may need special attention. It is not uncommon for the midwife-manager to suggest, for example, that 'Mrs X really needs to talk to someone, and would benefit from attending the Early Mothering Group'.

Conclusion – Weaving Change from the Threads of Feminist Process and Action Research

In the Early Mothering Project, midwives generated a reflectively informed change in practice. Understandings of feminist praxis were woven by MARG participants through their ordinary group talk, as they gained insight into and challenged some taken-for-granted aspects of social and professional power impinging on their ability to provide sensitive midwifery care. MARG participants shared stories and evolving understandings about practices, needs and realities. The richness of midwives' tacit knowledge patterned these conversations, while negotiating a way through various difficulties and dilemmas became a precious opportunity for 'wise learning' (Barrett, 1998: 369) about women's experiences in general and, more specifically, for the theme of this section of the handbook: midwives' research/practice. The research is significant for generating outcomes that are not only useful and relevant, but also meaningful for birth women.

The Early Mothering Group provides a space for women to share experiences and information, forming supportive social networks. Further, in legitimizing mothers asking questions and making choices for themselves, the group encourages active participation in making informed decisions rather than their being passive recipients of choices made by others. Many of the above-mentioned processes and benefits were also experienced by midwives participating in MARG. Both groups provided a framework for empowering women and challenging the prevailing medico-patriarchial institutional structure.

Notes

I wish to acknowledge the enthusiasm, energy and commitment that was freely given by MARG participants working together in this action research/practice – Rosemary Kennedy, Michelle Hill, Pauline Rowston, Susan Couper, Amanda Bartlett, Caroline (Dore) Homer, Barbara Ross, Deborah Thoms and Julie Rich – with special mention of those who were involved from MARG's beginnings – Fran Pekin, Marie Hiscock and Trish Panton. I also thank my husband, Tony Whitmore, and colleague, Associate Professor Rosalie Pratt, for helping me with the final drafting of this chapter, as well as my PhD supervisor, Professor Bev Taylor, for believing in me.

1 Women giving birth may choose to remain in the hospital's postnatal ward from an average of three to seven days, or alternatively go home with domiciliary midwifery support for about a week.

2 Field-tapes were audio-tapes of the 26 MARG meetings, with a transcript returned to participants at each subsequent meeting as a record of previous conversations for ongoing reflection.

References

Barrett, P.A. (1998) 'Early mothering – a shared experience: feminist action research with midwives and mothers'. Unpublished doctoral dissertation, School of Nursing and Health Care Practices, Southern Cross University, Lismore, NSW, Australia.

Bennett, V.R. and Brown, L.K. (eds) (1993) *Myles Textbook for Midwives* (twelfth edition). Edinburgh: Churchill Livingstone.

Kemmis, S. and McTaggart, R. (1988) *The Action Research Planner* (third edition). Geelong, Vic: Deakin University Press.

Lawler, J. (1991) *Behind the Screens: Nursing, Somology and the Problem of the Body*. Edinburgh: Churchill Livingstone.

Polanyi, M. (1983) *The Tacit Dimension*. Gloucester, MA: Peter Smith Publishers.

Reinharz, S. (1979) *On Becoming a Social Scientist: From Survey Research and Participant Observation to Experiential Analysis*. San Francisco, CA: Jossey-Bass.

Thompson, S.M. and Barrett, P.A. (1997) 'Summary oral reflective analysis (SORA): a method for interview data analysis in feminist qualitative research', *Advances in Nursing Science*, 20 (2): 55–65.

Wheeler, C.E. and Chinn, P.L. (1991) *Peace and Power: a Handbook of Feminist Process* (third edition). New York: National League for Nursing Press.

21

Learning with *The Natural Step*: Action Research to Promote Conversations for Sustainable Development

HILARY BRADBURY

CHAPTER OUTLINE

This chapter tells of action research with leaders of a Swedish environmental education organization named *The Natural Step*. It explores first-person research and the degree to which Bradbury's own commitment to environmental issues and research shaped this work. It also draws on 'second- and third-person research/practice' to work with the organization using a learning history method to generate a new insight for the organization's leadership with regard to their networking and educational efforts. The chapter shows how familiar academic tools such as interviewing and qualitative theory building can be drawn on as part of action research practice.

My chapter tells a tale of action research with leaders of a Swedish environmental education organization named *The Natural Step*. It is also a tale of my dissertation work. This tale is about 'second- and third-person research/practice' in that I used familiar academic tools while helping to generate a new agenda for the organization's leadership with regard to their networking and education efforts. It is, simultaneously, about my learning, or 'first person research/practice' (Torbert, 1997, Chapter 18), to the degree that my own commitment to environmental issues and research shaped this work.

Studying What Matters Most

I lived in Germany during what might be called the Green revolution of the early 1980s in which the Green party took seats in the elected *Bundestag*. My peers (I was a student of linguistics and philosophy) were quite ecologically minded. We conscientiously 'reduced, reused and recycled'! When I continued my graduate studies in the USA, moving into the more applied field of organizational behaviour, my intention to be involved in environmentally conscious projects slowly informed my thinking as I moved from the abstract conceptualization of philosophy to the active experimentation of management. My PhD programme at Boston College was designed for optimal learning, specifically about organizational change and transformation. It was clear, to me at least, that the general principles of change and transformation I was learning about would have much to do with the nature of change called for in our necessary societal turn to sustainable development. I theoretically linked practices at the micro-interpersonal level with more macro-institutionalized structures, following the logic of structuration (Bourdieu, 1977, 1991; Giddens, 1984). This structurated approach allows potent leverage points for change to become visible. I reasoned, for example, that developing interpersonal competencies of dialogue would be an important leverage point for the re-patterning of action among key stakeholders in the shift towards sustainable development; in other words, emergent change at the micro-level could shift the macro-dynamics of a system towards more sustainable practices.

My theoretical insights affected my own practices as I began to notice the quality of the process skills, for example, the ability to be in dialogue among those who publicly called for sustainable development. My experience in Germany was that business people and 'greenies' did not get along. Indeed in the 1980s there was a distance and certain mutual vilification between these groups. I noticed a suppression of opinions coupled with insistence on who is right and who is wrong. This linear approach was not especially fruitful; fruitful would mean thinking together through the complexity inherent in the present unsustainable state we have together created.

Working with the Founders and Leaders of *The Natural Step*: Sustainable Dialogue

I met the charismatic founder of *The Natural Step*, Dr Karl-Henrik Robèrt, while working at the MIT Center for Organizational Learning devoted to supporting the use of systems thinking for large-scale change in the organizational domain (see also Senge and Scharmer, Chapter 17).

The Natural Step had been envisioned by Robèrt as a partnership between business and environmental educators. This heralded new openness on both sides to working together. An important component of the partnership-building was the leadership of Robèrt himself, a gifted speaker and a Scandinavian pragmatist. His basic message was that business and the environmentalists need to talk and work together to solve our serious environmental problems. Robèrt had begun a process of educating the nation by convening scientists in search of common ground in the midst of the debates that are so often about our environmental problems. The scientists, under the guidance of Robèrt, developed a clear statement about environmental issues which resulted in a booklet sent to all Swedish households and schools. From this came requests for public lectures, the formalization of *The Natural Step* as a not-for-profit organization, and the development of professional networks to apply the scientifically valid information that *The Natural Step* was making available. Soon thereafter, *The Natural Step* developed a reportedly 'neutral set of scientifically based principles for sustainability', called 'the system conditions' which form the core of its education (see Table 21.1) and which are used to focus conversations about sustainability. Today *The Natural Step* is headquartered with a small office of about ten administrative staff in Stockholm. It operates, however, as a network of some 10,000 Swedes who seek to apply the insights of the system conditions in their professional arenas. (For a fuller account of *The Natural Step* please see Bradbury, 1998 or Bradbury and Clair, 1999).

I was interested in the dialogue, focused on the system conditions, which included 'thought-leaders' or 'culture creators' from both the economic and cultural sectors of society. I was happy to have found my dissertation site in *The Natural Step* in what I experienced as intellectual 'love at first sight'.

Emphasizing Process Skills

I hoped to find how basic organizational behaviour principles, that is, those of participation and good conversation, could create an architecture from within which practices in support of sustainable development would emerge to engage leaders from the cultural and economic sectors. My lens was therefore different from that of many others who have been more interested in the scientific and technological change aspects which underpin the work of *The Natural Step* (e.g., Natrass and Altomare, 1999). Soon I realized that I must inquire more into the invisible architecture of the diffusion of the conversations started by *The Natural Step*. I proposed to use an action research method I was co-developing with a group of scholars and practitioners, which is now called a 'learning history' (Roth and Kleiner, 1998). Having acquired funding, I approached Robèrt and asked if he and his colleagues would be interested in working with me, and hopefully learning something of value to them in the process. Robèrt, very much committed to facilitating others' engagement with the work of sustainable change, said 'yes, welcome!' I don't doubt that having independent funding possibly helped make me seem like an attractive action researcher also! Robèrt and those around him at the headquarters were very helpful to me in arranging to interview the key founders of *The Natural Step*, many of whom were business executives and some of whom lived in different European countries. I spent a few weeks in Sweden interviewing these folks, all the time mixing in with the enthusiastic core staff at *The Natural Step* headquarters. I was engaged in insider/outsider research (Bartunek and Louis, 1996) in that I was endeavouring to make my own research questions clear and then seeking dis/confirmation of what I was piecing together with the interviewees. I was also finding out about who else I needed to be talking to, if only informally, so as to get the 'real deal'.

I wanted to write a 'jointly told tale' (Van Maanen, 1988) in which the interviewees' voices would not be overshadowed by mine. I wanted also to develop a shared text for discussion among all the interviewees, as a form of feedback to the organization, which would offer a data basis for enfolding relevant theory for further generalizable conceptualization. To be engaged in action research for me meant therefore being involved in work that redistributed action and reflection among all people engaged in this change initiative concerning environmental

Table 21.1 *Scientifically-based principles of* The Natural Step

The 'four system conditions' below are described by *The Natural Step* as a compass for sustainable development. The system conditions allow for exploration of our actions and suggest other actions that will lead us to societal sustainability. They can be applied to all levels of society from individuals up.

System condition	*This means*	*Reason*	*Question to ask*
1 Substances from the Earth's crust must not systematically increase in the ecosphere.	Fossil fuels, metals and other minerals must not be extracted at a faster pace than their slow redeposit and re-integration into the Earth's crust.	Otherwise the concentration of substances in the ecosphere will increase and reach limits – often unknown – beyond which irreversible changes can occur.	Does your organization systematically decrease its dependence on underground metals, fuels and other minerals?
2 Substances produced by society must not systematically increase in the ecosphere.	Substances must not be produced at a faster pace than they can be broken down and integrated into the cycles of nature or deposited into the Earth's crust.	Otherwise the concentration of substances in the ecosphere will increase and eventually reach limits – often unknown – beyond which irreversible changes occur.	Does your organization systematically decrease its dependence on persistent unnatural substances?
3 The physical basis for productivity and diversity of nature must not be systematically diminished.	We should not harvest or manipulate ecosystems in such a way that productive capacity and diversity systematically diminish.	Our health and prosperity depend on the capacity of nature to reconcentrate and restructure wastes into new resources.	Does your organization systematically decrease its economic dependence on activities which encroach on productive parts of nature, e.g., over-fishing?
4 If we want life to go on we must have fair and efficient use of resources with respect to meeting human needs, because promoting justice will avert the destruction of resources that poor people must engage in for short-term survival (e.g., rainforest).	Basic human needs must be met with the most resource-efficient methods possible, and their satisfaction must take precedence over the provision of luxuries.	Humanity must prosper with a resource metabolism meeting system conditions 1–3. This is necessary in order to get the social stability and co-operation for achieving the changes in time.	Does your organization systematically decrease its economic dependence on using an unnecessarily large amount of resources in relation to added human value?

education so as to catalyse an outcome for the common good. With *The Natural Step* our goal was primarily to allow its leaders, who were so very busy in the world of action, to have an opportunity for reflection which might further inform and enhance this action.

My learning history work is influenced by the emerging practice of organizational dialogue, whose aim is to promote participants' ability to inquire into the values and assumptions from which they are operating (Isaacs, 1999). My developing a learning history is in support of such inquiry, also called 'double loop action inquiry' (Argyris, Putnam and Smith, 1985; Nielsen, 1996; Torbert, 1991). The manuscript itself is in two columns, one with the interviewees' narrative, the other with my reflections, embryonic hypotheses and commentary. It also devotes space to explaining ideas that may not be familiar to the reader or for introducing archival data. Overall it was intended to be reader-friendly and to promote conversation about its contents. I made efforts to offer supporting evidence for all phenomena discussed in the learning history. The design requirements of a learning history are predicated on learning and historical inquiry, and suggest the necessity of using a text to focus the conversation and experiential engagement with the issues at hand. This additionally allowed me, the researcher, to make work available for comment and criticism from the larger community of scholars and practitioners. In this case I later placed the document on a publicly accessible web site [http://www.sol-ne.org/Hilary Brad-NaturalStep-LH.html]. I have sought to write an engaging document, one which is not off-putting to people who are not involved in academic research. It is important to note that the document is introduced as an *open* document, one whose goal is only to anchor a conversation, not to capture a static truth.

I prepared for a dissemination workshop by sending the interview excerpts I wanted to use to the individual interviewees. In one case one interviewee asked me to omit a particular quote as it would be obvious to Swedish readers what well-known person was being referred to. I was reluctant to omit the quote. However, after a number of faxed iterations, we did reach agreement on how to preserve the essence of the quote while maintaining anonymity of the person under discussion. I asked each interviewee to review the material I wanted to use from her/his interview and I also sent a copy of the entire manuscript to them for further commentary so they could see the context in which I used the information they had shared.

The Value of Being an Engaged Historian in the Scholarly and Practitioner Arenas

Having created a manuscript acceptable to the interviewees and which I felt captured my own sense of things, I organized a dissemination meeting about six months after beginning my interviews in Stockholm. The most important result of the action research work with *The Natural Step* began with a realization that occurred to one of the interviewees during the dissemination meeting. As the text of the learning history was a tool for reflection for the community for whom it was written, it was important that the community gather to respond to it together.

I was given the name of an outside/neutral facilitator to whom I explained my dual objectives for the workshop, that is, dissemination and validation. The facilitator, whom I had spoken with on two occasions before meeting him on the morning of the workshop, practised facilitation using a self-described 'chaos orientation'. He was Danish and fluent in both Swedish and English. The meeting was held for the most part in English. The facilitator suggested that there be only a minimum of structure at the start and from there we would go where the conversation took us. We were invited to 'check in', that is, introduce ourselves and say a few words about where we would like to focus our attentions during the five-hour meeting. Following this, to the interviewees' surprise, we were each given scissors and fresh copies of the manuscript and were asked to cut out the parts from the manuscript that we each deemed to be the most important pieces of *The Natural Step* story. The interviewees, many people with natural science training, were then asked to arrange their pieces on the table by locating what they had cut out with others' pieces. All complied, some, albeit, with mild consternation; these expressed annoyance with what they felt was a kindergarten activity quite different from what they expected a research endeavour to be about. Following this we sat down to discuss our choices. One interviewee interjected, 'we are half way through this meeting and I am frustrated because usually when I go to a meeting I know what we are going to discuss. Here I do not.' I expressed my own frustration and invited the interviewee to say what he wanted to discuss. He replied: 'I have read this document carefully. There are a lot of concepts in one hat. I cut out the part about transformation. I realize that what is special about *The Natural Step* is the process [with which] they continually engage and transform the business leaders, it's not so much the content of the teaching as I had thought; it's this process which is always on going.' This comment struck a chord in each of us as indicated by the degree of energy with which people began to develop the idea concerning 'processual issues which undergird the work of *The Natural Step*,' and this focus defined the second half of the meeting. Another person present continued the theme of looking at *The Natural Step* as a *process of change* when he said he could now better understand the description of *The Natural Step* that is used by Paul Hawken in his best-selling book *The Ecology of Commerce* (1993). There Hawken balances emphasis of the technological aspects of *The Natural Step* with the social-processual aspects in his description. We began to reflect consciously on *both* the process of delivering *and* the content of *The Natural Step* message. The participants agreed at the end of the meeting that it had been a powerful one, full of insights on the matter of process which had not, hitherto, received so much explicit attention.

This insight proved valuable to the others present as more comments were offered which sought to grasp better the importance of the dialogic process by which the work of *The Natural Step* had been carried out. Leaders of *The Natural Step* thereby began to shift in their self-conceptualization from being 'tellers' of scientific information to being more consciously 'interlocutors', engaging with those interested in making sustainable development a focus of attention. One manifestation of this incorporation is contained in the description of a workshop designed by *The Natural Step* after the dissemination meeting. In addition to teaching the

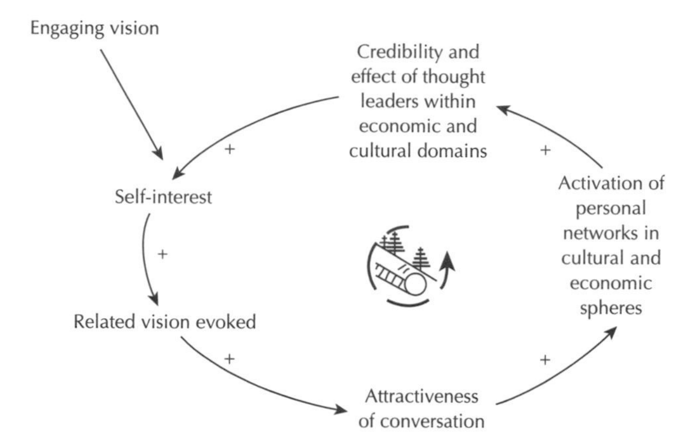

Figure 21.1 Conversations for sustainable development structuring societal change

principles of sustainability, representatives of *The Natural Step* facilitated a session called 'discussion in the pub'. The title of the new session is rather atypical for a Swedish business meeting and conveys the importance placed on facilitating good conversations.

The Use of Academic Skills in the Service of *The Natural Step*: Second- and Third-Person Research/Practice

The learning history contributes to the scholarly endeavour by offering a contextualized jointly-told tale, which has been both fact checked, but more importantly reflected upon, by those whose tale it is. From a hermeneutical point of view, this offers an improvement on qualitative research methods used in action research as it allows the words of individual interviewees to stand in their uniqueness and not be interchanged with the words of another from a different organizational context. And yet it does not simply reify difference, but rather, after presenting a thickly enough described context to allow uniqueness to emerge, higher order themes which seek similarity are also offered (Bradbury and Mainemelis, 1999).

By having each aspect of the learning history, and the action research project generally, be concerned with facilitating reflection on action – from conceiving the interviews as reflective conversations, to bringing the leaders (who sometimes did not know each other) together for conversation – the learning history offers a jointly-told tale (Van Maanen, 1988) of 'insider/outsider' research (Bartunek and Louis, 1996).

The causal loop diagram in Figure 21.1 summarizes our reflection on what lies at the core of the work of *The Natural Step*. A causal loop diagram is another tool used to aid reflection as we sought to clarify the underlying dynamics of the success of *The Natural Step*. At its heart we may see that dialogue acts as a catalyst for co-ordinating patterns of activity among people across the boundary of both the cultural and economic domains.

To read Figure 21.1, consider that the arrow means that the first variable causes the second, and the '+' sign next to the arrow means that the second variable changes in the same direction as the first. Catalysed by the founder's *engaging vision* of a sustainable society, *Self-interest* is often the initial point of attraction. For example, scientists reported their relief that Robèrt was getting noticed for saying what they had been trying to say for many years. Business people reported that *The Natural Step* education helped them respond to customer inquiries about the environmental impact of their products and offered direction for strategizing, given increasingly strict environmental regulations. Their work with *The Natural Step* allowed them see how following their self-interest also served the common good, thus evoking *a related vision* many people share of having their work be of substantial meaning for the world. Numbers of people, especially powerful people in business, getting involved made the conversation started by *The Natural Step* that much more *attractive*. In turn, those engaged in the conversations bring others into the conversation, and their *activation of personal networks in cultural and economic spheres* also increases. Finally, as more senior leaders in both the cultural and economic sectors become champions of sustainable development, *credibility and effect of thought leaders within economic and cultural domains* increases as a result of their impact on the culture in response to the *engaging vision* of creating a sustainable society.

This closes a 'reinforcing' or 'positive' feedback loop that will drive exponential growth in the size of the community promoting sustainable development. Around and around, like a rolling snowball (as the small picture signifies), the educational work will grow at a faster and faster pace, until it finds and reaches a limit.

I later enfolded into this data, the theories of structuration (Bourdieu, 1991; Giddens, 1984) and dialogue (Bakhtin, 1981) to develop more traditional academic papers to engage further with the wider scholarly community – which is a form of third-person research/practice. Ultimately, I came to call the reinforcing loop of diffusion in response to the early work of *The Natural Step*, 'Cooperative Ecological Inquiry' (Bradbury, 1998).

Reflection on First-person Research/Practice

My work with *The Natural Step* had changed me. I could see the connection between individual openness to inquiry and positive forces for large-scale change in society. I had also come across illustrations which cast aspersions on the dialogic nature of *The Natural Step*. One interviewee reported that 'some of the younger people working for *The Natural Step* are very arrogant and act as though "we've seen the light and you have not, we know the truth".' I realized that the work of real dialogue, both in my life and that of *The Natural Step*'s, is, much like all action research, always a work in progress.

In many ways this study, which is ostensibly about change in the social domain as effected by individuals in an organizational context, is also about the change that I, as a researcher, underwent and which therefore fashioned the lens which allowed me to tell the story I told. Bridging theory and real-life practice had become a research imperative. I laugh to think how disparaging I had been of the action paradigm not so very long ago, having been trained in the distancing assumptions of a philosophy-humanities education. As bridging knowledge and action became a desired option for me, I undertook more serious efforts to act in a consensus-seeking fashion myself, having begun my study of *The Natural Step*.

Conclusion

A premise of my work is: it is not enough to develop a 'technologically right solution' to our organizational environmental problems; we must also inquire into changing our individual and organizational behaviours so that such solutions can be meaningfully catalysed, implemented and sustained. My work with *The Natural Step* is about one way in which such change can occur. Dialogue and inquiry are central to this way. Sustainable development necessitates attention to both technological issues and issues of social process. To date, considerably more emphasis has been placed on the former.

The metaphor, or theory of change, which supports the work of radical transformation, as I have theorized it based on the case of *The Natural Step*, is that of continuous or organic change. This may be contrasted with a theory of episodic change (Weick and Quinn, 1999). With continuous change we presume that the human world, as we know it, is produced and reproduced by the innumerable acts and conversations that we undertake daily. In other words, that our world is structurated (Bourdieu, 1991; Giddens, 1984) in our micro-interactions. Change towards sustainability then requires intentional micro-changes catalysed through a logic of attraction by a compelling new vision and discourse. Before intentional change can be fostered, however, it helps to realize what reality we have co-created, however unintentionally. In Marshall McLuhan's words, we must endeavour as fish to see the water that we swim in. Our industrial world is not ecological or cyclical, the waste from one process is not the food for another, as architect Bill McDonough has suggested for design parameters that reach towards sustainability (McDonough, 1997). Instead we create waste, piles and piles of it, and, more dangerously, we create molecular waste (e.g., carbon dioxide from burning oil) which we cannot see. Our systems are linear and indeed were created when linear systems posed no obvious or immediate danger to our livelihood. Our systems need to change. Our ideas need to change. Our guiding images, those images which constitute our tacit feelings, need to change.

Some Implications of My Work

Action research can be of significant value in building capacity for, and in the study of, efforts in support of sustainable development. Action researchers can help further the conversations already underway through giving a common language to many of the transsectoral initiatives that include people from the cultural and economic realms, and then further telling these stories, be it through publication channels (which require further theoretical reflection) or through convening forums for public conversation.

Organization development-oriented action research can contribute to the fostering of sustainable development by facilitating dialogue spaces that allow for a multiplicity of perspectives. Ability to engage in dialogue, that is in developing an attitude of personal inquiry and social objectivity, may be thought of as the process equivalent of developing technological innovations to aid us in our quest for a sustainable state. Such process work is often overlooked and efforts requiring simple process interventions flounder in personality clashes that could be alleviated fairly easily through work which recognizes that people matter.

Action researchers can develop methods, such as the learning history I used, which keep us in dialogue with the mainstream of social science. This method derives from our need for an architecture to capture the historicity and continuity of organizational life, and the contingencies and decisions made through time. The learning history contributes to the field of action research in two primary ways. First, it offers an architecture which allows researchers and practitioners to act synergistically as 'engaged historians' (rather than change agents *per se*). It does this by bringing together the work of action and reflection through the meeting of the researcher with those engaged in action. Secondly, it emphasizes the use of text (usually de-emphasized in action research) as a springboard to communal dialogue that integrates reflection and action.

Graduate students can well afford to be engaged in the work they love if they attend both to the necessary 'rigour' of good social science as well as the necessary 'vigour' of work needed in the face of our quest for sustainable development. The tension between the two is creative and can bring fruit to our activism, by making it more robust and credible, and to our scholarship, by making it more relevant and engaged. Thus as scholars 'starting out' we bear witness to knowledge, within the paradigm of action research, being construed differently from other paradigms. Knowledge is about rendering useful interpretations for preferred action in the world, rather than simply knowing more 'facts' which are thought to describe an independent reality. In this sense action research can be understood as a part within the wider trajectory of pragmatism (see Rorty, 1989). This chapter is intended to exemplify for struggling graduate students that we need not give up on a desire to be in conversation with the legitimate academic mainstream because we are committed to using an action research approach.

Note

I wish to thank Bjørn Gustavsen for going beyond the call of duty with his input for suggested improvements to my chapter. Many thanks also to Peter Reason and Babis Mainemelis.

References

Argyris, C., Putnam, R. and Smith, D. (1985) *Action Science*. San Francisco, CA: Jossey-Bass.

Bakhtin, M. (1981) *The Dialogic Imagination*. Austin, TX: University of Texas Press.

Bartunek, J. and Louis, M.R. (1996) *Insider Outsider Research*. Qualitative Research Series. Thousand Oaks, CA: Sage Publications.

Bourdieu, P. (1977) *An Outline of Theory of Practice*. Cambridge: Cambridge University Press.

Bourdieu, P. (1991) *Language and Symbolic Power*. Cambridge, MA: Harvard University Press.

Bradbury, H. (1998) 'Learning with *The Natural Step*: cooperative ecological inquiry through cases, theory and practice for sustainable development'. PhD dissertation, Boston College, Ann Arbor, MI.

Bradbury, H. and Clair, J.A. (1999) 'Promoting sustainable organizations with Sweden's Natural Step', *The Academy of Management Executive*, 13 (4): 63–75.

Bradbury, H. and Mainemelis, C. (1999) 'Learning history and organizational praxis'. *Working Paper Series WP 99–21*, Weatherhead School of Management, Case Western Reserve University, Cleveland, OH.

Giddens, A. (1984) *The Constitution of Society: Outline of the Theory of Structuration*. Berkeley, CA: University of California Press.

Hawken, P. (1993) *The Ecology of Commerce: a Declaration of Sustainability*. New York: HarperBusiness.

Isaacs, W. (1999) *Dialogue and the Art of Thinking Together*. New York: Doubleday Currency.

McDonough, W.A. (1997) 'A boat for Thoreau, environmental challenges to business'. Paper delivered at the Environmental Challenges to Business Conference. University of Virginia, Virginia.

Natrass, B. and Altomare, M. (1999) *The Natural Step for Business: Wealth, Ecology, and the Evolutionary Corporation*. Gabriola Island, BC, Canada: New Society Publishers.

Nielsen, R.P. (1996) *The Politics of Ethics: Methods for Acting, Learning, and Sometimes Fighting, with Others in Addressing Ethics Problems in Organizational Life* (The Ruffin Series in Business Ethics) (ed. R.E. Freeman). New York: Oxford University Press.

Rorty, R. (1989) *Contingency, Irony and Solidarity*. Cambridge: Cambridge University Press.

Roth, G. and Kleiner, A. (1998) 'Organizational reflection: developing organizational memory through learning histories', *Organizational Dynamics*, 27 (2): 43–60.

Torbert, W.R. (1991) *The Power of Balance: Transforming Self, Society, and Scientific Inquiry*. Newbury Park, CA: Sage Publications.

Torbert, W.R. (1997) 'Developing courage and wisdom in organizing and in sciencing', in S. Srivastva (ed.), *Executive Wisdom and Organizational Change*. San Francisco, CA: New Lexington Press.

Van Maanen, J. (1988) *Tales of the Field*. Chicago, IL: University of Chicago Press.

Weick, K. and Quinn, R. (1999) 'Organizational change and development', *Annual Review of Psychology*, 50: 361–86.

22
Transforming Lives: Towards Bicultural Competence

GLORIA BRAVETTE GORDON

CHAPTER OUTLINE

Starting from the premise that 'all writing is autobiographical in some sense', this chapter brings 'life-world' under ongoing systematic scientific inquiry, drawing on personal experiences and exploring my experience as a 'Black woman' of African-Caribbean descent, educated and socialized in the UK. I show how embedding an inquiry process in my life was central to self-renewal. This chapter identifies links between the action research/inquiry process and the 'Black' (and *not* mainstream) liberation movement in the African Diaspora, showing how a particular approach to research brought these two schools of thought together.

> The responsibilities of the unvalued, the unheard, the silent, are greater than ever … It is not the size of the voice that is important: it is the power, the truth and the beauty of the dream … There is no such thing as a powerless people. There are only those who have not seen and have not used their power and will. (Okri, 1997: 101)

> To rediscover one's history is not only an act of self-discovery; it is an act of self-creation – a resurrection from the dead, a tearing away of the veil, a revelation of the mystery. (Wilson, 1993: 52)

I start with these quotes because they convey something deep and meaningful about who I am, the life experience from which I emanate as a 'Black British' woman of African-Caribbean descent. In addition they say something about how I experience the purpose of my life unfolding on a daily basis as I commit myself to ongoing personal and collaborative experiential action research/inquiry largely based on Torbert's action inquiry model (1991, Chapter 18; see also Torbert and Fisher, 1992). In this chapter I share some of the ways in which I have used the above processes as a means of 'living inquiry' or 'engaging in inquiry as a way of life'. In thinking about the nature of my research offerings in the context of this book, I draw on Marshall's (1984) work and her own acknowledgement that 'All writing is autobiographical in some sense'. As I bring my 'life-world' under ongoing systematic scientific inquiry, I too draw on my own personal experiences and understandings, allowing me also to engage in a powerful sensemaking process even as I break my own collusive silences. This life-world includes, in particular, my self/selves, my professional practice as a lecturer in a higher education institution, my family and my community/world. Of particular importance to me have been the social experiences of being 'Black' of African-Caribbean descent, educated and socialized in the UK (that is, 'Black British') as well as that of being a 'Black woman'. These dual experiences have been and continue to be challenging but 'silenced' human experiences with which I find myself needing to engage.

I was fortunate enough to enrol for my PhD at the Centre for Action Research into Professional Practice (CARPP) at the University of Bath, England. I say fortunate because the ethos of the Centre facilitates, for me, engagement with what is real in our lives rather than the 'ivory tower' type of research which can further alienate us from ourselves and our realities. During my PhD process I was to challenge myself to research into the 'crisis experience' (Outlaw, 1983) in which I was centred at the time. 'Towards Bicultural Competence: Researching for Personal and Professional Transformation' (the title of my PhD thesis) was my response to the issues which had been crystallized for me. What continues to be of interest to me was the fact that I was able, as a Black woman, to do this type of personally risky, institutionally challenging and yet life-enhancing research within the European academy, among a largely White cohort of fellow inquirers and an all White supervisory team. Potential problems related to race and culture were, I believe, to become secondary for me in the initial stages of my research as a result of the research opportunities I felt were provided by CARPP.

In order for you to be able to enter into the experience I share it is important for you to have an understanding of the 'Black British' cultural/racial experience so that you can understand the issues with which I was grappling at the time and continue to grapple with today (Bravette, 1994, 1996, 1997). To understand this experience more fully one would need to look beyond the official rhetoric of justice, equality, fairness and the existence of a meritocracy, to engage with the lived experience of what it means to be 'Black' in Britain in the late 1990s. This is an experience that I chose systematically to inquire into in order to gain personal understanding – simply living the experience did not mean that I understood it! A brief extract taken from my PhD thesis will provide some insights into this experience:

> The catalyst for this crisis had been my experience in the workplace as a black woman ... I was also increasingly becoming aware of a split in my psyche: a double consciousness (DuBois, 1903). A white consciousness (superego?) and a black (African) consciousness! ... It was a process in which I could have gone under as a result of the fear and powerlessness that I was experiencing. Would I crawl away and die, live a life of unresolved shame and much worse, pass that legacy on to my children, or would I as Freire & Shor (1987) argue, acknowledge my fear and then place limits on it? I chose the latter.
>
> I had become tired of ... the humiliating experiences of being devalued in comparison to white colleagues ... spoken down to ... lied to ... not accorded moral regard because of a perception of me as 'other' ... (Bravette, 1997: 34–5)

I intend two important contributions in this chapter: first, to show the systematic nature of my work to become a self-renewing organism through the embedding of an inquiry process in my life; secondly, to identify links between personal and collaborative action research/inquiry and the 'Black' (and *not* mainstream) liberation movement which includes the thinking of African-descended theologians, anthropologists, intellectuals, psychologists, educationalists and spiritual teachers. I share how my particular approach to research has enabled me to bring these two schools of thought together in order successfully to achieve changes (towards bicultural competence), demonstrating that a methodological approach exists which does not by necessity dehumanize us, its research population. As Akbar argues, research must be guided by a set of principles which ensure the ultimate utility of that research: 'The principle which must guide (Black) research must be an objective of self-knowledge and collective liberation.' (1991: 710).

Action Researching/Inquiring for Bicultural Competence

A key aspect of my work has been the development of the concept of 'bicultural competence' and then enacting it. DeAnda identified that:

> To become bicultural an individual must engage in a dual socialisation process. One acquires values, beliefs, communication and behavioural styles from a culture of origin as well as becoming exposed to the same dynamics of a majority culture. An ethnic minority will have success in becoming bicultural to the extent that information and skills needed for negotiating the mainstream culture are provided, commensurate with receiving affirmation for the basic values, beliefs and behavioural styles of one's minority culture. (DeAnda, 1984: 102)

My own concept of 'bicultural competence' (Bravette, 1994, 1997) was an attempt to depict the conscious and deliberate process of becoming bicultural, rather than merely making erroneous claims of biculturality as an automatic and defensive response to the realities of being 'Black' in White society. People of African descent *do not* receive affirmation for the basic values, beliefs and behavioural styles of their minority culture in British society. As a result, and this is particularly true for the many African Caribbeans who do not even like to be identified as being related to Africans, we tend to deny that culture.

Table 22.1 attempts to bring together the important components of the journey in which I have been engaged. In column one of the table I detail the key characteristics of engaging in action research and action inquiry which I found to be of critical importance to my ability to achieve the transformation that I was seeking. These key characteristics directed me to certain important processes that I would need to engage with if I was to achieve the 'bicultural competence' that I felt to be so desirable to my ability to negotiate successfully my way in British society. These processes I conceptualized into my five phase 'It makes SENSE Model' (Bravette, 1997) – column two of Table 22.1. The particular features of the SENSE model are detailed in terms of the essence of what I found necessary for me to do: that is, gain Self-knowledge, Educate myself for critical consciousness, Nurture my internal world, Seek support and Embed process in my life as a way of being. Achieving 'bicultural competence'

Table 22.1 *Personal and collaborative experiential action researching/inquiring for bicultural competence*

Action research characteristics	My sense strategy for bicultural competence	Parallel 'African' research strategy	Key sentiments of 'African' research strategy	Personal research outcomes
Double-loop or second order learning which strategically places the researcher and co-researchers, including their values, at the centre of the research and therefore under research scrutiny.	**Self-knowledge** – an increased awareness that I needed to know about myself historically, culturally, physically, psychologically, emotionally and spiritually in order to gain 'bicultural competence'.	*Black liberation psychologists*: Wade Nobles, Na'im Akbar, Josep Baldwin, Janet Helms; *Black women intellectuals*: bell hooks, Maya Angelou, Marimba Ani, Patricia Collins; *Black liberation theologists*: James Cone, James Cleage; *Black historians and anthropologists*: Cheik Anta Diop, John Henri Clarke, Chancellor Williams.	'Self-knowledge is the beginning of all knowledge.' Philosophical and cosmological considerations lead to decolonialization of the African consciousness and the realisation of life purpose. Self-determination results from self-knowledge and self-awareness leading to self-love and acceptance. Centred in one's own reality.	Ongoing engagement with the dynamic process of gaining self-knowledge and awareness in the following dimensions: Spiritually, Psychologically, Physically, Emotionally, Historically and Culturally. An enhanced awareness of the complexity of my own humanity facilitating a deeper awareness of the complexity of the human condition and our interconnectedness.
Critical theory and dialectical thought – the function of which is 'to break down self-assurance and self-contentment of commonsense, to undermine the sinister confidence in the power and language of facts …'.	**Education for critical consciousness** – an awareness that I was not only going to have to work with and acknowledge the external critics, but also, very importantly, my own internalized critic (superego). Choosing engagement with education for living and citizenship as opposed to the more traditional educational outputs of 'training'.	Molefi Kete Asante – 'Centricity'; Hilliard – 'Sankofa' (engaging in 'deep-thinking' and looking back in order to move forward). Hilliard – African-centred educational pedagogy.	Advocates the development of a politicized and critical African consciousness. Undoing 'miseducation'; removing the 'mask'; avoiding 'misorientation', 'disorientation', 'off-centredness' and 'marginalization'; cautiously weighing all information that is received.	Learning how to 'read the word and the world' critically from the centre of my reality as a Diasporic African woman. Broadening understanding and perspectives. Engaging in the ongoing process of becoming a critical thinker. Increased awareness of personal and social responsibilities. Increased awareness of wider oppressive forces.

(*Continued*)

Table 22.1 (*Continued*)

Action research characteristics	My sense strategy for bicultural competence	Parallel 'African' research strategy	Key sentiments of 'African' research strategy	Personal research outcomes
Emphasis on an **overarching value system**; ethical considerations; holism; recognition of a participatory universe. Spiritual values.	**Nurturing the internal world** – an acknowledgment of my previously devalued spiritual self; that inner knowing that had been repressed and denied in order to gain acceptance and achieve 'fit' in British society. Working with personal process in order to understand guiding belief and values.	Iyanla Vanzant; Oprah Winfrey; bell hooks; Wade Nobles's concept of 'Spiritness' vs the overused term of 'spirituality'.	Recommends the taking on of an optimal conceptualization system which places emphasis on the spiritual as well as the material. Also developing a philosophy, a concept, a framework for spiritual evolution and living.	Finding the centre of my reality enabled me to connect with my denied spirit/African consciousness. Focus on inner power and inner knowing (i.e., the devalued intuitive knowing). Finding congruence between inner and outer realities (authenticity). Working with my 'internalized oppressor'.
Collaboration; critical subjectivity; the acknowledgement of different ways of knowing (epistemology; ontology; axiology).	**Seeking support through networking** – an awareness of the need to move out of isolation in order to test out and share thinking and experiences with others. Putting work out for a wider audience to provide feedback.	Ra Un Nefer Amen – The Ausar Auset Society; Maulana Ron Karenga – Nguzo Saba (a value system for Diasporic Africans).	Recommends the building of an African community spirit which 'draws from tradition our cultural foundations of values and institutions … (adjusting) our traditions to fit and facilitate our movement in the African Diaspora'.	Realising the importance of community, unity, confirmation and affirmation whether as a person of African descent or as a woman, for example. A desire to work and learn in collaboration with others and to receive critical feedback from others.
Praxis – creating social change while developing a useable theory of knowledge from our practice.	**Embedding process in our lives** – an awarenesss of the need to remain open to new information and experiences.	Iyanla Vanzant	'the process teaches … (it) keeps you in the moment and you must be in the moment to fully experience the solution.'	More receptive to change and the possibilities of perspective transformation. Increased ability to take risks and be vulnerable.

for me means being competent not only in terms of my culture of residence but also, and very importantly, my culture of origin. Gaining competence in my 'culture of origin' was a significant challenge for me and meant that I was going to have to begin to connect and engage with that cultural experience and peoples I knew very little about. In column three of Table 22.1 I provide a (not inexhaustible) list of some of the key 'African' thinkers who have influenced my thinking and the liberation of my African consciousness. Very importantly, it will be noted, these thinkers were also pointing me in the same direction as the key requirements of the Action Research methodology with some of their key concepts and sentiments identified in column four. Column five details the important research outcomes which I am still claiming as my research progresses.

The Methods and their Features

Systematic action researching and inquiring enabled me to get in touch with the reality of my experiences as a woman of African-Caribbean descent, living in the UK since the late 1950s, in a way that I had been previously unable to do. Action research has been significant to me to the extent in which I have been introduced to the concepts of single-, double- (Argyris and Schön, 1974) and triple-loop (Torbert, 1998) learning. Double-loop learning required me not only to focus on the content of whatever it is that I am engaged in doing or studying but, very importantly, how I influence what I am doing or studying. This enabled me to begin to deconstruct my previously monolithic perspective on the world, my belief systems, taken-for-granted assumptions and the values that I espoused as compared to the values that I actually lived out on a daily basis. I found myself, for the first time, consciously at the centre of my thinking. As a person I became of *importance* – in stark contrast to what I had internalized from being socialized as a Black person in British culture. The experience of gaining these insights and eventually taking ownership has been a laborious but an ongoing process – a struggle to make *real* things I began to understand intellectually but had not known in any practical sense. I continue to seek to recreate myself, accepting Ghandi's idea that 'I must be the change that I want to see in the world' or even Hale's notion that 'society will be changed only to the extent that each of us transforms himself or herself' (1992: 75).

To this end I engaged in systematic action researching as developed by Kurt Lewin (1951) as a means to improve practice (McTaggart, 1991). The methodology consists of a spiral of cycles of action and research. Each cycle consists of five major stages (indicated in highlights below). An example of how I used the model to clarify my values and so engage in nurturing my internal world follows:

- *Planning and reconnaissance*. In this stage I acknowledged the dissonance between internal and external realities and made a commitment to myself to work with this dissonance. Important questions were: What values do I claim to be of importance to me? How do these espoused values compare with what I do in practice (my actual values in use)? Important values identified include: respect, equality, integrity, honesty, justice. This recognition led me to recognize the dissonance within my internal world where these values were concerned.
- *Action*. Having clearly articulated these values (they are no longer merely shadows in the recesses of my mind), I now intend to become consciously aware of myself acting them out in a variety of social contexts. Through deliberate action I will be able to define what these values mean for me in practice.
- *Observation*. This dimension required me to become mindful and to develop my noticing and participant observation skills which involved me, for example, in keeping a journal and/or using video and audio tapes in the classroom setting. I also found myself observing how variables, political contexts and oppressive social forces affect situations in which I intend to act. First-person research required me to observe myself: spiritually, emotionally, physically, psychologically, and assessing my impact on responses to the systems with which was I engaging.
- *Reflections*. This phase involved me in identifying the gap between what I claim and what I actually do! Realising for the first time the lack of integrity I manifest in my life as I choose personal survival over principles I claim to feel strongly about (my silences and therefore collusive behaviour). Realising the lack of self-respect that I show myself as a woman of African descent because of the racist stereotypes and beliefs that I have unconsciously internalized. Gaining insights into the reasons for the gaps between what I claim and what I actually do: fear; powerlessness; low self-esteem, etc.
- *Replanning*. Choosing what to work with and repeating the cycle in order to gain congruence in my internal world and begin the process of my self-transformation.

In the initial stages of my research much of my action researching was personal self-reflective work, enabling me to begin the process of clarifying what the issues were that I was going to have to work with. I found myself testing out the core and guiding beliefs that determined my life as well as beginning the process of testing my own taken-for-granted assumptions. This systematic approach to working with my personal values (detailed above), for example, was to enable me to have a new perspective on the world – somewhat like a new pair of eyes – and an enhanced clarity of vision. I have written about the experience of moving from an experience of being the 'walking dead' to being willing to engage with the world in a vital way, previously unknown (Bravette, 1997). This is, as I understand it, Torbert's notion of becoming more fully human, moving away from engaging with the world in an unconscious and automatic fashion (Torbert, 1991, Chapter 18).

Torbert (1991) highlights four territories of experience in which we need to develop simultaneous awareness, enabling us to engage in a 'kind of scientific inquiry that is conducted in everyday life'. In the following example I show how I have sought to develop my awareness in the four territories of experience identified by Torbert, opening up to the possibilities of change and an increased ability to take risks.

- *Purpose/vision.* A rehumanized world (the 'other' is me as a stranger!); spiritual evolvement; 'I must be the change I want to see in the world' (Gandhi); authenticity.
- *Strategy.* Self-knowledge/self-awareness (physical, emotional, psychological, spiritual, cultural, historical).
  Education for critical consciousness (booting out ignorance and automatic responses).
  Nurturing my internal world (my spirit).
  Support through collaboration with others (feedback).
  Embedding process in my life (being open to change).
- *Behavioural choices.* How am I living up to my purpose? What and how do I need to develop myself in order to achieve my goals? What is the gap between what I espouse and what I actually do? What do I need to do differently if I am to achieve my purpose? What choices do I have today?
- *Outside world.* Have I been able to make a connection with 'others'? Have I contributed positive energy to the world? Have I made reparations in those situations where I was responsible for contributing negative energy? Have I managed to challenge the thinking of others with whom I come into contact just through being 'who I am' and the way I am in the world? What do others have to say to me about how I am living, teaching, being, parenting, etc?

As a result of working with these processes I was able to realize my *passion/purpose* – the liberation of my consciousness as a woman of African-Caribbean descent! I was able to realise Mandela's words that as I liberate myself my very presence will liberate others. Very importantly I am now able to provide my three negatively stereotyped African-Caribbean sons with another vision and some practical tools for living and understanding their experience, as much as this is possible, in a society which devalues them on account of their Black skins.

In the following section I offer examples of how action researching and inquiring using the models detailed above enabled me to transform my perspectives and therefore ways of being in the world.

Self-knowledge: Silence

In seeking to deepen my awareness about myself and how I was in the world, especially with regard to my 'Blackness', a major issue that engaging in my PhD process threw up for me were my silences; silences which I was to come to realize were not necessarily of my own choosing. In exploring those silences – why I could not, would not, speak and therefore articulate my experiences of being 'Black', for example, in the world, even when I badly wanted to – I was taking up Lorde's (1984) call for turning silence into language and action. Before moving to language and action it was necessary for me to understand the nature of those silences. The conscious engagement with my silences made me aware that in my mind they were reflecting the 'mental inferiority' ascribed to Blacks in the Western world. I subjected my silences to systematic scrutiny in a similar fashion to that outlined for clarifying my values in order to understand better the dynamics which were feeding them.

- *Reconnaissance/plan.* Acknowledging my silences and the increasing discomfort I experience as a result of not speaking out around issues which are important to me. Researching to understand the nature of silence. Taking the decision to move out of silence. Identifying opportunities for informed action-taking.
- *Act.* Speak (or attempt to speak) in order to validate myself and my experiences and understandings in and of the world.
- *Observe.* Observe myself (how I am feeling, what I am thinking) and others (what effect are others having on me? To what extent am I being influenced by forces external to myself?) Observe the situation/context and the dynamics and variables at work.
- *Reflect.* Bring together what I have learnt from the literature and what has happened for me in practice. Draw out insights. Collaborate with others in the reflective process.
- *Replan.* Use practical wisdom gained, and propositional knowledge acquired, to improve my action-taking.

In addition, in coming into an understanding of my own silences I was to conceptualize silence as a *social construct*, critical to maintaining the societal taboo around race and racism in British society. The demand for silence around race was, I came to understand, tantamount to self-denial of my realities, including my 'Blackness'. In most cases this enforced silencing is further institutionalized within the system through the *self-silencing* born of frustration when it seems that the racial issue runs so deep and so wide as to make it unfathomable and a situation which, as Blacks, we must merely come to accept as our lot in life. When these two conceptions are further embedded in the structure of society through silencing as a *function of group processes* the Black individual can effectively become locked into silence through an insidious and unconscious process of self-preservation and social amnesia (Wilson, 1993). I was further to understand that the constant accusations of 'paranoia', 'persecution complex', 'having a chip on one's shoulder' directed at Black people who dare to raise the issue of race and racism were no more than the effective enacting of this silencing process. Exploring my practice enabled me to see that silence is a group's safety net and how the alienation and invisibility that I experienced, particularly in groups where I was in the token/solo role, were the natural outcome of this function. Coming into a heightened awareness of *patriarchy as a silencing force* was to be a newer experience for me as the important intersections between race and gender were crystallized alongside the collusive denial within the Black community that sexism is unimportant in the face of the racism that is experienced in White society. It was also important to me to recognize aspects of my silences within the context of *Black women, silence and resistance*, validating many of my personal experiences of silence being a place of protection, safety, strength and a behavioural mask just as it has been for African women at least since the days of slavery (Collins, 1991). Today I assess whether to be silent or not with the question: Do I come out of my silences wounded or as victor?

Education for Critical Consciousness

Educating myself for critical consciousness was the direct outcome of engaging with the process of gaining self-knowledge and awareness. As I become more alert to issues affecting my experiences in the world, I, by necessity, become more aware of and alert to the experiences of others. This means that I look at the world with different eyes, a more critically interested eye and from the centre of my reality – not any longer merely accepting but questioning. The discipline of action research was of vital importance to my living through the periods of chaotic anxiety-provoking unconnectedness and not becoming stuck with the feelings of anger and resentment which were so strong at the time.

The writings of other people of African descent (see Table 22.1) who had awakened to that experience were also vital to my continued wellbeing and motivation to move forward in that they affirmed my experiences and provided me with hope. They also showed me that I was not alone, my experiences at the individual level were symptomatic of the experiences of Africans at the macro-level. As a result of the process in which I was engaged I was able to come to my own understanding of Black–White relations in the world and to begin to identify clearly the links in the chain which needed attention if I was to move beyond the dysfunctional racial relationships which typify our world today. Table 22.2 was my conceptualization of the key issues identified as impacting on my world.

Chinweizu supports my own analysis when he argues that the impact of imperialist and racist historiography was far reaching 'for those who came to accept it, it bred complexes of racial inadequacy, a sense of fated inferiority, a belief in the congenital superiority of Whites, and a sense of pointlessness of the African initiative' (1987: 80). Lukes's (1974) third dimension of power illustrates this point when he discusses the insidious use of the socialization process in preventing people from questioning their lot in life (silence as a social construct!). From my own practice the lack of competence and feelings of inadequacy that I felt within myself can be directly related to a sense of not being 'good enough' based on Western standards of what is 'good'!

Conceptualizing the above contemporary position of Africans in the world and beginning to recognize how it was being perpetuated in my own life-world enabled and challenged me to engage with this cycle to break self-perpetuating links strategically. Stepping outside of my monocultural allegiance to British culture to explore and understand the fundamentals of another culture (my culture of origin) enables me to develop a critical perspective on British culture and my own reality. Having considered the Black predicament I was pushed to consider what the contemporary White (European) predicament might look like and identified the following cycle – a necessary corollary to the contemporary Black (African) predicament (see Tables 22.2 and 22.3).

The understanding that I have gained from the conceptualization of both of these cycles enables me to make choices in terms of *how I want* to be in the world as well as the *responsibilities* I believe I have, and then to challenge myself into action through the systematic use of the action research cycle. The process of action researching and inquiring

Table 22.2 *The contemporary Black (African) predicament*

The contemporary Black (African) predicament started with
The social construction of Race as a concept
and the development of the ideology of
'White Supremacy' and its corollary 'Black Inferiority'
both of which have become normalized in the Western world today and are kept in place by the tools of:
Christianity/Western culture/hegemonic discourse
all three of which are effective in maintaining the status quo and result in the
Creation of the 'dysfunctional' African personality
an aspect of whose experience is by necessity
Black (African) Self-denial
The denial of one's essence (Blackness) can only result in
A legacy of shame
which then feeds into the myth of an inferior race and the cycle repeats itself with the idea of the racial inferiority of Black (African) people gaining in potency for both Blacks and Whites

Table 22.3 *The contemporary White (European) predicament*

The contemporary White (European) predicament started with a need for power, domination and control which led to:
The social construction of 'Race' as a concept
and the development of the ideology of
'White Supremacy' and its corollary 'Black Inferiority'
both of which have become normalized and actively perpetuated in the Western world today, kept in place by:
Christianity/Western culture/hegemonic discourse
all three of which are effective in maintaining and perpetuating the status quo and the illusion of White supremacy and result in the
Creation of an egoistical Western personality
an aspect of whose experience is by necessity
Delusionary self-aggrandisement and a denial of the facts of their history
The denial of truth (facts) and integrity can only result in
A legacy of fragmentation from and projection on to other weakened groups
which then feeds into the myth of a superior race and the cycle repeats itself with the idea of the racial superiority of White (European) people gaining in potency, especially as the cycle of Black inferiority is also being enacted, for both Blacks and Whites

also enables me to acknowledge my fears and then, as Freire argues, to place limits on them. Here I acknowledge the fear (not unfounded) which leads many Blacks to pretend not to have seen or to be in denial of the racism at work in order to ensure personal survival. What this also acknowledges is the conscious/unconscious collusive and complicit involvement of Blacks, like myself, in the daily enactment of racism (Laing, 1961). As a result of the above, daily changes are taking place in my life because of the challenging self-reflective work with which I am engaged.

Conclusions

I have found action researching/inquiring to be powerful transformational tools which, coupled with my own strong motivational drive for intentional self-transformation, greatly accelerate my learning and development. The experiences that I have shared are the result of a conscious engagement with my own life-world and the systems that I influence, enabling me to become a self-renewing organism as I challenge myself to live more consciously according to the spiritual values that I now realize I am passionate about. I have moved from a position of being a silent and unheard victim in the world to a place where I fully agree with Okri that 'there is no such thing as a powerless people. There are only those who have not seen and have not used their power and will' (1997: 103). I continue to face many challenges in life and now measure my success according to the extent to which I am able to make positive contributions to our world rather than where I am positioned on the occupational ladder or the size of my salary. I am a strong advocate of first-person research, including action inquiry, because of its inherent requirements for those using the methodology to engage with what is *real* for them in the world as they seek to achieve social change. This form of researching is particularly relevant to the needs of people of African descent and the issues that we are facing, based on our own unique history and social experiences. I can see the wider use of it, too, in Britain today, for those individuals and institutions who are serious in their intent to grapple with the serious charge of institutionalized racism levelled by MacPherson (1999) at London's Metropolitan Police in the wake of the Stephen Lawrence inquiry. As for me, ongoing systematic engagement with the methodology today still enables me to extend my own personal boundaries, moving beyond yet another comfort zone that I had been accepting as a limitation. Today I am still engaged in the 'act of self-creation – a resurrection from the dead, a tearing away of the veil, a revelation of the mystery' that I am and the potential that I have and never knew when I was nothing more than a 'Black British' woman! Current issues that I am inquiring into in my life-world are moving me forward and challenging me to engage with the experiences of what it means to be a Black *woman* in the world in a way that I have not previously done to date – crystallizing the processual nature of action inquiring. As a woman of African descent I accept Segal's call that coming from the unique African experience that I do 'infused by oppression and suffering ... [I am] ... *charged with a special responsibility, to remember and remind*: to redeem that past with a creative meaning' (1995: xii, emphasis added). Engaging with first-person research enables me to keep this at the forefront of my mind and, therefore, consciously on purpose.

References

Akbar, N. (1991) 'Paradigms of African American research', in R.L. Jones (ed.), *Black Psychology* (3rd edition). Hampton, VA: Cobb & Henry Publishers.

Argyris, C. and Schön, D. (1974) *Theory in Practice: Increasing Professional Effectiveness*. San Francisco, CA: Jossey-Bass.

Bravette, G. (1994) 'Black women managers and participatory action research'. Paper given to *World Congress 3 on Action Learning, Action Research and Process Management*, University of Bath, England.

Bravette, G. (1996) 'Reflections on a black woman's management learning', *Women in Management Review*, 11 (3): 3–11.

Bravette, G. (1997) 'Towards bicultural competence: researching for personal and professional transformation', PhD dissertation, University of Bath, England.

Chinweizu, (1987) *Decolonising the African Mind*. Lagos, Nigeria: Pero Press.

Collins, P.H. (1991) *Black Feminist Thought: Knowledge, Consciousness and the Politics of Empowerment*. London: Routledge, Chapman & Hall.

DeAnda, D. (1984) 'Bicultural socialisation: factors affecting the minority experience', *Social Work*, March/April: 101–5.

DuBois, W.E.B. (1903) *The Souls of Black Folk*. London: Signet Classics.

Freire, P. and Shor, I. (1987) *A Pedagogy for Liberation: Dialogues on Transforming Education*. Basingstoke: Macmillan.

Hale, C.S. (1992) 'Psychocatabolism and the dark night of the self', *Journal of Humanistic Psychology*, 32 (1): 6–19.

Laing, R.D. (1961) *Self and Others*. London: Penguin Books.

Lewin, K. (1951) *Field Theory in Social Science: Selected Theoretical Papers*. New York: Harper & Row.

Lorde, A. (1984) *Sister Outsider*. New York: The Crossing Press Feminist Series.

Lukes, S. (1974) *Power: a Radical Review*. Basingstoke: Macmillan.

MacPherson, W. (1999) *The Stephen Lawrence Inquiry: Report of an Inquiry by Sir William MacPherson of Cluny*. London: The Stationery Office Limited.

McTaggart, R. (1991) *Action Research: A Short Modern History*. Victoria, Australia: Deakin University.

Marshall, J. (1984) *Women Managers – Travellers in a Male World*. Chichester: John Wiley & Sons.

Okri, B. (1997) *A Way of Being Free*. London: Phoenix.

Outlaw, L.T. (1983) 'Philosophy, hermeneutics, social-political theory: critical thoughts in the interest of African Americans', in L. Harris (ed.), *Philosophy Born of Struggle*. Dubuque, IA: Kendall/Hunt Publishing Company Limited.

Segal, R. (1995) *The Black Diaspora*. London and Boston: Faber & Faber.

Torbert, W.R. (1991) *The Power of Balance: Transforming Self, Society and Scientific Inquiry*. Newbury Park, CA: Sage Publications.

Torbert, W.R. (1998) 'Developing wisdom and courage in organizing and sciencing', in S. Srivastva and D. Cooperrider (eds), *Organizational Wisdom and Executive Courage*. San Francisco, CA: New Lexington Press.

Torbert, W.R. and Fisher D. (1992) 'Autobiographical awareness as a catalyst for managerial and organizational development', *Management Education and Development*, 23 (3): 184–98.

Wilson, A.N. (1993) *The Falsification of Afrikan Consciousness: Eurocentric History, Psychiatry and the Politics of White Supremacy*. New York: Afrikan World InfoSystems.

Further Reading (African Literature – Table 22.1)

Asante, M.K. (1993) 'Racism, consciousness and Afrocentricity', in G. Early (ed.), *Lure and Loathing: Essays on Race, Identity and the Ambivalence of Assimilation*. Harmondsworth: Penguin.

Asante, M.K. (1998) 'The Afrocentric idea in education', in W.L. Van Deburg (ed.), *Modern Black Nationalism: From Marcus Garvey to Louis Farrakhan*. New York: Temple University Press.

Helms, J.E. (1990) *Black and White Racial Identity: Theory, Research and Practice*. Westport, CT: Greenwood Press.

Hilliard, A.G. (1984) *Kemetic Concepts of Education: the African Perspective of Education*. London: Hackney Black Peoples Association.

Hilliard, A.G. (1995) *The Maroon within Us*. Baltimore, MD: Black Classic Press.

hooks, b. (1981) *Ain't I a Woman: Black Women and Feminism*. London: Pluto Press.

hooks, b. (1989) *Talking Back: Thinking Feminist, Thinking Black*. Boston, MA: South End Press.

hooks, b. (1993) *Sisters of the Yam: Black Women and Self-Recovery*. London: Turnaround.

hooks, b. (1995) *Killing Rage, Ending Racism*. Harmondsworth: Penguin.

Karenga, M. (1988) 'The Nguzo Saba (The Seven Principles): their meaning and message', in W.L. van Deburg (ed.), *Modern Black Nationalism: From Marcus Garvey to Louis Farrakhan*. New York: New York University Press.

Karenga, M. (1988) *The African American Holiday of Kwanzaa: a Celebration of Family, Community and Culture*. Los Angeles, CA: University of Sankore Press.

Nobles, W.W. (1991) 'African philosophy: foundations for Black Psychology' in R.L. Jones (ed.), *Black Psychology*. Hampton, VA: Cobb & Henry Publishers.

Ra Un Nefer Amen (1990) *Metu Neter Vol 1: the Great Oracle of Tehuti and the Egyptian System of Spiritual Cultivation*. New York: Khamit Corp.

Vanzant, I. (1993) *Acts of Faith: Daily Meditations for People of Color*. New York: Simon & Schuster.

Vanzant, I. (1995) *The Value in the Valley: a Black Woman's Guide through Life's Dilemmas*. New York: Simon & Schuster.

Vanzant, I. (1996) *Faith in the Valley: Lessons for Women on the Journey to Peace*. New York: Simon & Schuster.

23
Action Research to Develop an Interorganizational Network

RUPERT F. CHISHOLM

CHAPTER OUTLINE

This chapter describes the year-long action research process used to develop a network organization from 14 widely dispersed rural local business incubators in a large region of Pennsylvania. It describes how participants invented, discovered and applied action research to develop the system and capture learnings from the process. The study was guided by theories of interorganizational networks, and drew on developmental conferences as part of its methodology. It argues that action research must be tailored to specific situations and that this requires extensive involvement with system members and other stakeholders.

This chapter covers the year-long action research process used to develop a network organization from 14 widely dispersed rural local business incubators in a large region of Pennsylvania. Coverage emphasizes how participants invented, discovered and applied action research to develop the system and capture learnings from the process.

Three influences converged in 1993 to trigger the network development process: several incubator managers recognized potential benefits from building the 14 independent incubators into a regional network; a primary funding organization felt that increased linkages would improve the management of individual units; outside funds became available for a computer-based information system to link local incubators. These convergent events led to developing a funding proposal, submitting it to the Center for Rural Pennsylvania, and receiving a one-year grant to conduct the network development process.

This chapter comprises four sections: (1) concepts that guided the process; (2) key action steps and the grounding of them in action research; (3) impacts of the network development process; and (4) conclusions.

Guiding Concepts

Action research

An action research (AR) approach provided one conceptual base for developing the network. Essentially, AR, as we define it, involves engaging in repeated cycles of diagnosing, planning, implementing, collecting and analysing data on outcomes, discussing outcomes with system members, reaching conclusions and defining new sets of action steps. In short, the process is highly cyclical. A second notable feature of AR is an orientation to system development or improvement. In the present case, building a loosely-linked network among independent local incubators comprised the general development goal. Action research also attempts to generate knowledge of a system, while, at the same time, trying to change or develop it (Lewin, 1946). Ideally, this leads to developing a system that is continuously learning from experiences, learning how to learn, and creating conditions (structures, processes and culture) that support and foster learning. Developing such a learning system increases its capacity to deal with greater complexity and a changing environment (Huber, 1991). Action research also attempts to contribute to general knowledge about systems and the dynamics of changing them.

Great variety exists in the forms of action research used to meet the development goals and contextual requirements of various situations (Elden and Chisholm, 1993). Analysis of AR applications in quite different systems in several countries identified five dimensions for examining action research cases: (1) system level of target system (from group to transsocietal); (2) organization of the research setting (from tightly organized to loosely organized); (3) openness of the AR process (from closed to open); (4) intended outcomes of AR (change goals and purpose); and (5) researcher role (from expert to co-inquirer). Chisholm and Elden (1993) describe these dimensions in much greater detail than space permits here. They also use them to analyse a set of diverse cases. In brief, AR provides a general approach for developing systems and organizations. To be effective, each project must tailor the process to meet development goals and contextual requirements of the specific situation.

In the present case, following the AR approach required incubator managers to take an active role in the development process. Their role was to define network goals and participate directly in devising ways of developing the system to reach them. Managers also furnished the energy for development and provided information about the realities of carrying out business incubation work in their region. This knowledge was essential to designing and conducting an effective network development process and in shaping key features of the emerging system.

Research team members had primary responsibility for proposing designs and facilitating events that would help incubator managers discover how a network organization could enhance work of their incubators and general economic development in the region. Specific elements of the research role involved designing and facilitating meetings, collecting and feeding back information, monitoring and helping manage the overall network development process, and creating ways for members to learn from the development process. Consistent with the AR approach, all phases of the development and research process involved collaborating closely with network members through a steering committee.

Interorganizational network

The network construct has emerged as a key form of organization in the late twentieth century (Chisholm, 1996, 1998). This project used the socio-ecological perspective of interorganizational networks (Finsrud, 1995; Trist, 1983, 1985) to conceptualize and guide the development process. From the ecological perspective, the basic orientation of individual member organizations is to the higher level purpose that binds the set of organizations together (Trist, 1983). Organizations form networks to enable them to deal with meta-problems that single members cannot handle alone.

Loose-coupling of members to the network comprises another feature of these systems. Members represent independent organizations that are physically dispersed and only meet as needed to conduct activities required to carry out the network purpose. Belonging to a network is voluntary with minimal formal organizational structures and processes to help make involvement permanent. Networks also rest on a horizontal rather than a hierarchical organizing principle: all members are equal and none has a superior–subordinate relationship with another.

Network organizations are controlled by members, not by a centralized source of power. Members are responsible for developing a purpose, mission and goals, and for initiating and managing projects and work activities. The organization is self-regulating (members direct and control activities) and rests upon a shared understanding of the basic issue or meta-problem. In short, the organization *is* the ways members devise to relate to each other as they work to influence key aspect(s) of the external environment in an identified way. A shared vision orients network activities to the larger environment. Continuously maintaining this orientation at the domain level is critical.

In brief, the socio-ecological view provided the basic features of the type of system we were attempting to develop. Action research provided the process used to develop the system with the specific features required for it to function effectively in the existing environment. Action research was essential in all aspects of development work.

The Development Process

The development process comprised having incubator managers engage in a series of designed activities during the project year. Each activity or event aimed to help members understand the nature and potential of the network and move the emerging network closer to emerging system development goals. Development resulted from a shared understanding of these goals, information on the state of the network and its linkages to the external environment, and planning and taking action based on new appreciations (Vickers, 1968). Active member participation in devising development interventions and activities was designed to increase members' understanding and learning about the network and its potential and to build this understanding and learning into the emerging system. Greater understanding was expected to increase both network and individual incubator effectiveness.

Action steps in developing CN Group network

The major steps involved in developing the incubator network are listed below.

- Research team conceptual planning activity (November 1993–31 December 1994).
- Planning meeting (7 January 1994).
- Plan visits to local incubators and draft interview-survey questionnaire.
- Steering Committee (SC) meeting (17 February 1994).
- Visits to local incubators (7–18 March 1994).
- Prepare for first development conference – design work, discuss with SC, make final arrangements, etc.
- First development conference (11–13 May 1994).
- Steering Committee meeting (17 June 1994).
- Network members work on items identified at May development conference.
- Design and plan second development conference.
- Second network development conference (22–23 September 1994).
- Work on action items – network members work on items identified previously.
- Steering Committee meeting (16 November 1994).
- Design and plan third development conference.
- Third network development conference (1–2 December 1994).
  - Follow-up on action items.
  - Future of CN Group.
  - Complete second assessment questionnaire.
  - Evaluate network development process.
  - Future individual incubator assessment process.
  - Policy recommendations to state government.
- Data analysis; prepare and distribute report on third development conference.
- Feed back comparative findings from two surveys to network members (February 1995).

Early work in late 1993 involved conceptualizing the network development process. Later, the research team discussed the scope of the development process and its goals, assessed the current state of linkages among incubators, and defined a tentative strategy and first steps for building the network. Several daunting questions persisted during this early period: How important was participation in a regional network to local managers and were they willing to devote the time and energy required to develop it? What was the client system and who was the contact person(s) for it? To what extent did the 14 incubator managers experience already being part of a network and were they satisfied with this involvement? Would the proposed development process actually work? How would incubator managers experience actual engagement in the AR process? One nagging feeling lay beneath these specific questions: given all the unknowns, was it possible to develop a new network system in the short time period available?

Setting up the Steering Committee

Our approach required close collaboration among the research team, members of the network, and several outside stakeholders during all phases of the development process. To foster this collaboration, participants in the January planning meeting formed a Steering Committee (SC) whose role included: managing the development process; providing a means for stakeholders to give ongoing input into the development process; providing continuous communications and linkages among the groups and key individuals. Consistent with socio-technical systems theory (Pasmore, 1988), using a steering committee builds participation by key parties directly into the AR process and requires system members to take responsibility for change. The Committee consisted of three local incubator managers, three representatives of external stakeholders and the three-member research team.

Linking with the system

Using the AR process meant cycling through steps of diagnosing, planning, implementing, collecting and analysing data on outcomes, discussing outcomes with system members, reaching conclusions and defining new sets of action steps. For example, participants in the January planning meeting clarified researcher and member roles, discussed project goals, began to form as a working group, and adopted a tentative strategy and first action steps. They also discussed membership and role of the Steering Committee and ground rules for the development process. In effect, this meeting dealt with many organizational development (OD) entry/linking-up issues (Cummings and Worley, 1993; Weisbord, 1973).

Researchers took results of this meeting, added details to the action plans, devised a tentative process for visiting and collecting data from each incubator, drafted an interview questionnaire and brought these to the February Steering Committee meeting for discussion and modification. At this one-day meeting participants refined plans for interview visits, revised the questionnaire and worked out the logistics and scheduling of incubator visits. They also worked on questions about the development process and continued to develop working relationships among members.

Visits to local incubators

Visits to the 14 incubators comprised the first direct contact of the research team with all members of the potential network. Incubator managers on the SC helped plan and arrange incubator visits, informed local managers about the purpose of the meetings, and responded to their many questions. Each visit began by getting acquainted with the manager, learning about local incubator operations and discussing the purpose of our visit. An interview guide and short survey questionnaire were designed to help develop the network and, in the process, generate data about it. The interview-discussion process attempted to cause managers to reflect on current relationships among the 14 incubators and to begin thinking about the possibility of developing a new network organization. Phases of the process were: (1) identifying current images of the CN Group; (2) defining existing relationships among the 14 incubators; (3) describing the existing state of the CN Group as a network organization; and (4) triggering thinking about the future potential of the network by identifying features and functions of an ideal network.

In general, incubator managers were friendly and answered questions and discussed their local operations freely with the researchers. At the same time, they were unclear about what the intended network would be, their role in it, and how it might benefit their local incubator. Nevertheless, managers expressed a general willingness to participate in development activities.

Development Conferences

Three conferences comprised major interventions in developing the incubator network. These conferences took place in May, September and December 1994 in 'neutral' facilities located in different parts of the region. Each conference lasted between two and three days. Space limitations prevent describing each conference in detail. Hence, this chapter gives a fairly detailed description of only the first conference and a much less complete account of the third conference.

First development conference

Nine incubator managers participated in the first conference. Network development goals, Steering Committee members' knowledge of past and present relationships among incubator managers, information from researcher visits to local incubators, and OD/system development concepts provided material for designing the conference. Search conference principles (Emery and Emery, 1978; Emery and Purser, 1996) guided much of the overall design.

Introduction

Activity started with an introduction, statement of general conference goals, an overview of activities, and a review of conference guidelines and ground rules. Guidelines that stressed the creative, holistic, future-oriented nature of the development process helped constructively channel participants' behaviour during discussions.

Exploring general trends

Following search conference concepts, participants began work by identifying future trends in the general environment that would likely affect the US economy. This activity focused attention on the macro-level and helped members see the importance of environmental forces on the network. In all, they identified more than 30 broad economic, political, social, technological, demographic, global issues and environmental trends. This two-and-a-half-hour discussion provided the context for later development work and grounded the work at the ecological level.

Sharing perceptions of existing relationships

During the next conference phase, managers reviewed the data collected during the March visits to the incubators. (A second survey was conducted at the third development conference in December.) This activity introduced reality to the network development process by sharing managers' perceptions of the nature and current state of the system. Data showed that most of the incubator managers associated the CN Group with another organization (e.g., the state incubator association), or were confused about its identity in some other way. Managers had a general lack of clarity about network identity and functions.

Identifying network goals

Following discussion of data generated and broad areas for possible work, managers finally selected three goals for future work and developed ways of addressing each: developing a CN Group presentation to the state board of the principal funding agency; implementing a computer information system; and improving communication among local incubators.

Conference activity also included a two-hour workshop on diagnosing current local incubator operations. Each manager agreed to conduct a preliminary in-depth analysis of his or her incubator using the model and guidelines from the workshop. Discussing preliminary plans for the second development conference and assessing conference work also took place at the end of the meeting.

Steering Committee meeting

Applying the AR approach, the Steering Committee met in the middle of June. Meeting midway in the project year provided a timely opportunity to assess development work done so far, capture learnings and plan future action steps. A representative of a second external stakeholder organization joined the committee at this meeting. Specific work during the meeting involved reviewing and updating general project goals, reviewing development work conducted so far, assessing development progress, identifying learnings from the development process and planning the second development conference.

Committee members indicated that they had learned several things by being involved in developing the network. These included recognizing that there is a need for the network and that there is more to do, learning that the network role is to function as an action organization ('we can be a powerful group') and realizing that more work can be accomplished by working as a group than by working as individuals. Members also experienced a qualitative change in 'how we related to each other at the end of the first development meeting' compared with relationships before the conference. This feedback suggested that system members had begun to understand and value the network and that progress was being made in developing it.

Work to design, plan, conduct, capture learnings from and follow up on the first conference illustrates the AR approach used throughout the network development process. Each conference and key action step was designed jointly by the Steering Committee and the research team. And each event built upon information generated and learnings from earlier development work. Ongoing work and contacts among SC members, among the SC and other incubator managers, and with the research team provided further boosts to developing the network.

Third development conference

The third development conference presented a last opportunity to work directly with members on developing the network. Steering Committee/research team discussion led to conducting the following work at the conference: reviewing progress on action items from the September development conference; discussing future CN Group actions to foster and expand incubation; discussing future development of the network – what is required to continue development and how will the development process continue after current funding ends on 31 December; evaluating the process of developing the CN Group as a network; generating feedback on impacts of the development process and completing questionnaires on the state of network (repeating the March questionnaire). To conserve space, coverage only includes brief discussion of work on extending incubation activity, future development of the network and evaluating the process of developing the CN Group.

Future network development

Managers identified the CN Group as a catalyst for incubation in the state and stated that without the group the Pennsylvania Incubator Association would cease to exist. They also expressed a strong need to continue the CN Group and identified several requirements to maintain the network in the future: regular meetings; facilitation (internal or external); shared goals and work plan; funding – having adequate internal or external funding; commitment of members. Participants agreed to work out ways of meeting these requirements.

Extending incubation work

Managers voiced strong concerns about the existence of several pseudo-incubators – 'incubator' organizations that do not offer real incubator services to clients. Participants concluded that the CN Group should initiate action to create a professional certification process for incubator managers and local incubator organizations. Members felt that this would improve the role of incubators in economic development, increase linkages with incubators in other regions of the state, and show continuing CN Group leadership in incubation. Participants defined steps for working on this and agreed on a specific completion date. Managers also expressed a need to reach out to the 30-plus other incubators in Pennsylvania to help improve the quality of incubation services and identified the state incubator association as a way to reach these managers. Group members agreed to draft a short telephone survey questionnaire and to work with the association to conduct a survey of all local incubators.

Network development process

During the next phase of the conference, participants evaluated the network development process.

Managers completed a brief questionnaire individually and listed their responses on flip chart sheets under each question. I facilitated group discussion of responses. Members readily engaged in discussing responses and appeared energized by having an opportunity to reflect and comment on the development process itself. After the conference, the research team analysed individual written responses, grouped comments in emergent categories, summarized the data and shared it with network members in the conference report and feedback session.

Impacts of the Network Development Process[1]

Three sources provided data for determining the effects of the network development process: (1) assessing the network development process itself; (2) comparing the results of the March and December questionnaires; and (3) observing critical incidents during the development process.

Assessing the network development process

Reviewing the year-long effort was intended to surface important aspects of the development process, to increase understanding of what had taken place, to help incorporate these learnings in the network, and to provide qualitative information on the meaning of the development process to participants. Questions started at the individual incubator level and proceeded to the successively higher levels of region, state and incubator industry. Researchers designed questions to stimulate thinking and collect data. Specific questions asked for managers' perceptions, feelings and expectations about network development *before* and *after* the development process, key positive (and negative) outcomes for his or her local incubator, positive and negative outcomes for economic development in the CN region and beyond, and learnings from participating in network development activities.

Overall, responses to these questions showed much positive change. Before the project, managers lacked clarity about the purpose and nature of the network and were cautious or indifferent about expectations. At the same time, several managers expressed interest in developing the network and some scepticism or suspicion about the real purpose of the development effort. Responses about current views of network development indicated a sharp contrast to members' reactions before the development process began. Group members stated that they recognized the current worth of the network, its future potential and had increased clarity about the nature and role of the network.

Managers identified education, stronger relationships among incubator managers and development of the computer information system as positive outcomes for their local incubators. Participants expressed that they had broadened their understanding of how other organizations could help them and also gained knowledge and information to use in helping clients. Members also experienced being more fully integrated into the network and stated that this enhances information sharing and giving support. Managers mentioned no negative outcomes. Members saw 'greater professionalism', 'closer networking' and 'better internal management practices' as positive outcomes of the development process for the region. In addition, several participants saw the network as the advocate for state business incubators.

Understanding the importance of the network comprised the most important learning for members – 'We share a common fate and face similar problems'. Managers also saw the incubator group as having the capacity to influence future funding of state incubators. In addition, members showed a strong belief in the importance of the network by indicating a desire to continue working to develop it. Overall, members indicated that they had experienced success by participating in the development process and expected further positive outcomes from future work.

Questionnaire findings

The questionnaire used during the March visits to incubators and at the December development conference contained both open-ended and Likert scale questions. The process served two purposes: (a) data gathering – systematically collecting data about managers' perceptions of the state of the network before and after development work; and (b) development – engaging managers in a process of reflecting on existing relationships among CN Group members and of stimulating thinking about new ways of relating to each other and to external stakeholders. Discussion also helped foster learning and model the learning process as a key feature of the network.

Analysis of answers to open-ended questions about the purpose, image and functions of the CN Group showed that managers greatly increased their understanding of the identity and role of the network. While most managers confused the CN Group with another organization and expressed a lack of clarity about its identity in March, none did in December. By December, they also saw the network more as a system that could make a difference in advancing incubation to support economic development. Responses regarding key network functions indicated a clear shift towards activities that support improved professional practices and develop the incubation industry as a whole.

Questionnaire responses showed that virtually all measures of the internal dynamics among the 14 incubators improved between March and December 1994. Managers reported large increases in facilitating communications, fostering learning among members, providing opportunities for incubator managers to share experiences and developing new ways of member co-operation. Members' clarity of CN Group goals also increased substantially during the development process.

The external orientation of members also showed a substantial increase from the beginning to the end of development work. Managers indicated that the network increasingly helped members gain understanding of the economy and outside world, provided information about 'best practices' from outside the CN Group, and helped maintain 'state-of-the-art' knowledge/skills.

Observations

Observing events provided a third way of understanding and assessing the development process. Four observations stood out. First, participation in the development conferences increased greatly from the first to the third meeting. Nine managers participated in the first, 12 in the second, and all 14 in the third conference. Apparently, managers recognized that something positive was happening and word spread to this effect.

The second dealt with network identity. As reported above, findings showed that initially much confusion and ambiguity existed in members' minds about the network. An incident at the first development conference also demonstrated this phenomenon. Towards the start of activities, individuals had difficulty talking about the network and confused it with several other groups or organizations. And, for the first day and a half of the conference participants openly refused to call the network by name, despite the difficulty this caused during discussions. They felt that using a name would separate the CN Group from other incubators in the state. In the absence of a name, I invented 'no name group' to refer to the network. Gradually, however, members began to use 'CN Group' spontaneously and a conscious decision to adopt it was unnecessary. By the third conference, members used the term freely and showed a sense of pride in the Group, its activities and accomplishments.

A third notable observation concerned a multimedia presentation to the state board of the primary funding organization in early September. Members generated the idea of developing the presentation during the first conference. Members worked as a group, individually, within their teams, and in pairs over a two-month period to develop the multimedia presentation. They also enlisted production help from a local technology centre. Feedback from state board members was positive. De-briefing of the experience during the second development conference indicated that individuals had gained several insights from involvement. For example, one person stated that 'there is strength in numbers – we impressed them by the size of our group'. Others expressed the importance of working together as a total group to produce the presentation. CN Group members were surprised at board members' low level of knowledge about incubation and concluded that they needed to become more active in continuously educating and providing information to their local boards and other key stakeholders.

Working on the presentation also had a major impact on network members' perceptions of themselves as a group. Members expressed elation from having succeeded in a difficult, important task. One member's statement that 'this is the first time we really had to pull together to do something for all of us' captured the general feeling. Developing and delivering the presentation was important in building the network organization through member collaboration on an important real-life activity. Success also symbolized a new stage in the development of the CN Group.

Observation also showed that network members became increasingly proactive in developing plans to influence a growing number of critical outside organizations during the development process. The previous paragraph described the Group's first activity of this type. Work at the second development conference extended plans for actively engaging key external stakeholders to several additional individuals, groups and organizations (i.e., the state economic development association, a gubernatorial candidate, the state department of commerce and key state legislators). Overall, a growing feeling of the importance of expanding to influence stakeholders occurred at the meeting. At the December development meeting, members extended their focus to include other incubators in the state beyond the CN region. The Group's plan to develop certification processes for local incubator managers and local incubator organizations illustrates this larger network role. Since these would be the first professional certification processes in the USA, the network had expanded its target to influencing business incubation nationally. In brief, as the network development process progressed, CN Group members extended their definition of work to include a larger number of stakeholders and expanded their scope of thinking to include the state and the USA as a whole.

Conclusions about Using Action Research for Network Development

Several conclusions about AR stem from the present case. A brief description of these follows. First, action research can bring about considerable progress in developing an interorganizational network from 'scratch' in a fairly short period of time. The development process started in a highly ambiguous situation virtually at ground zero. Potential network members had little understanding of a 'network' or how it might help them reach individual incubator goals and higher-level goals for the region. Despite this, most managers were willing to engage in a process to explore the possibility of developing the network. By engaging in the jointly designed and managed development process they learned the importance of the network, how they shared a common fate and experienced similar problems. Relationships among managers improved and their perspective moved from an internal towards an external focus. Becoming more proactive accompanied these changes. Overall, the action research process brought about many positive outcomes in developing the CN Group as a network system.

Secondly, it is possible to integrate research with taking action to develop a network. A common criticism of traditional AR studies is that there is too much emphasis on action, too little on research. In the case of the CN Group, the research process was a critical part of the total network development process – the two were tightly linked and one aspect would not have occurred without the other. From the beginning, the action research team had to create ways of learning about the system while, concurrently, helping system members discover new ways of thinking about and relating to each other and the external environment. Asking questions, discussing and reflecting on responses and designing activities that required members to behave in new ways were primary modes of conducting development work. Interview visits with each local incubator manager illustrate this approach. Having members involved in an in-depth analysis of the development process *per se* is another example. So, conducting research was an ongoing part of developing the CN Group; this was essential to action taking and member learning.

Thirdly, the socio-ecological network model provided an effective way to conceptualize, plan and take action. Features of this model complemented the action research process. For example, orienting development of the CN Group to the total network or ecological level was essential to having local incubator managers break their frame of thinking about going it alone or relating to only one or two other incubator managers and begin to conceive of higher-level regional and state-wide issues. 'Loosecoupling' gave members room to participate and explore new ways of working together without a threat to the identity and autonomy of their local incubator organizations. And, member control of all network activities reduced fears of working together and helped assure the relevance of development work. Other features of the socio-ecological view of networks also contributed to progress in using AR to develop the CN Group. However, space constraints prevent further description.

Finally, several foci of action research were used, invented or discovered to develop the CN Group as a network. The most apparent type involved designing processes that generated systematic information about overall system functioning or a specific activity (e.g., feeding back interview/questionnaire findings to CN Group managers during the first development conference). This process grounded the network development process in members' perceptions of the then existing situation. Repeating the survey feedback process towards the end of active work with the group provided information on changes in perceptions and attitudes, and on outcomes of the development process. It also contributed to members' learning about the nature of the network, its development and future potential.

The AR approach also requires researchers/ system members to be alert for opportunities to design events that incorporate the spirit and form of the process. Holding a Steering Committee meeting shortly after the first development conference modelled the AR process. Design of the meeting required participants to assess work done so far, re-examine development goals, identify learnings and make them part of the emerging system, and plan next action steps. Research team members believed that committee members' participation would help advance their understanding of AR and how to use it to develop the network and institutionalize the approach in the system.

Developing inter-organizational networks involves another form of AR: identifying situations that arise spontaneously and offering possibilities for increasing understanding and action. One event at the second development conference illustrates such an opportunity. As described earlier, network members were startled by the lack of knowledge and understanding their board members had about local incubator work to foster economic development. This event provided an opening for researchers to help members expand awareness of the importance of external organizations to the future success of local incubators and the network. A simple question 'What other organizations or groups are important to the future success of incubators?' triggered much discussion. At the end, managers had identified several additional stakeholders (e.g., legislators, a gubernatorial candidate, state commerce department) and made plans to contact them. Initiating these contacts with individuals who were fairly remote from managers' everyday operations represented a new type of awareness and activity for network members.

What emerges from this brief review of using AR to conceptualize, plan and conduct network development is that the process is messy and hard to define precisely. Instead, action research emerges as a creative free-form process. The types of action research required to support developing interorganizational networks fall towards the open, complex and difficult-to-manage ends of three of the conceptual dimensions outlined earlier in the chapter (Chisholm and Elden, 1993). Hence, considerable latitude exists for designing and carrying out AR in particular settings. Effective action research reflects key features of the context in which it occurs. Tailoring AR to specific situations requires extensive involvement with system members and other stakeholders.

To conclude, instead of being a special activity, action research provides an approach towards network development. It is an ongoing process of planning, taking action, questioning, reflecting, searching and capturing learnings. Questioning, reflecting and building learnings into the network can occur during any phase of the total action research process. Using action research to develop networks emphasizes proactive engagement and invention, not reactive adjustment and application. Ideally, as a result of the development process, the approach increasingly pervades every network member, group and activity, and becomes an integral part of the thinking and behaviour of network members and a key value of the system culture.

Note

1 Complete findings appear in Chisholm, 1998: 142–55.

References

Chisholm, R.F. (1996) 'On the meaning of networks', *Group and Organization Management*, 21 (2): 216–35.

Chisholm, R.F. (1998) *Developing Network Organizations: Learning from Practice and Theory*. Reading, MA: Addison Wesley.

Chisholm, R.F. and Elden, M. (1993) 'Features of emerging action research', *Human Relations*, 46 (2): 275–98.

Cummings, T.G. and Worley, C.G. (1993) *Organization Development and Change*. Minneapolis-St Paul, MN: West.

Elden, M. and Chisholm, R.F. (1993) 'Emerging varieties of action research', *Human Relations*, 46 (2): 121–42.

Emery, M. and Emery, F.E. (1978) 'Searching', in J.W. Sutherland (ed.), *Management Handbook of Public Administration*. New York: Van Nostrand Reinhold. pp. 257–301.

Emery, M. and Purser, R.E. (1996) *The Search Conference: A Powerful Way for Planning Organization Change and Community Action*. San Francisco: Jossey-Bass.

Finsrud, H.D. (1995) 'How about a dialogue? Communication perspective meets socio-ecological perspective', in O. Eikeland and H.D. Finsrud (eds), *Research in Action*. Oslo: Work Research Institute.

Huber, G.P. (1991) 'Organizational learning: the contributing processes and the literatures', *Organization Science*, 2 (1): 1–13.

Lewin, K. (1946) 'Action research and minority problems', *Journal of Social Issues*, 2 (4): 34–46.

Pasmore, W.A. (1988) *Designing Effective Organizations: the Sociotechnical Systems Perspective*. New York: Wiley.

Trist, E.L. (1983) 'Referent organizations and the development of interorganizational domains', *Human Relations*, 36 (3): 269–84.

Trist, E.L. (1985) 'Intervention strategies for interorganizational domains', in R. Tannenbaum and F. Massarik (eds), *Human Systems Development: New Perspectives on People and Organizations*. San Francisco, CA: Jossey-Bass.

Vickers, G. (1968) *The Art of Judgement*. London: Chapman and Hall.

Weisbord, M. (1973) 'The organization development contract', *Organization Development Practitioner*, 5 (2): 1–4.

24
Participatory Research and Education for Social Change: Highlander Research and Education Center

HELEN M. LEWIS

CHAPTER OUTLINE

Highlander, an adult education centre in the southern Appalachian Mountains of the USA, has been a resource and gathering-place for grassroots groups involved in struggles for social and political change since 1932. Highlander developed democratic, participatory educational methods similar to what is now called participatory action research, methods based on the experiential knowledge of participants. This chapter gives an account of the principles of Highlander's work and two examples from practice.

Highlander Research and Education Center (Highlander), New Market, Tennessee is an adult education centre located in the Southern Appalachian Mountains of the USA. Highlander has been a resource and gathering place for grassroots groups in Appalachia and the rural South since 1932. The Center has been involved in the major social movements for social justice in the region since that time: labour organizing in the 1930s and 1940s; Civil Rights movements of the 1950s and 1960s and Appalachian movements around strip mining, coal mine safety and union reform in the 1960s and 1970s. In the 1980s and 1990s work at Highlander involved groups not only in Appalachia and the South but extended nationally and internationally. The work has also included environmental issues, community-based development, the effects of globalization, issues of economic justice and democratic participation. Highlander's pedagogy, based on the experiential knowledge of participants, included democratic, participatory, educational methods similar to what is now called participatory action research.

The communities in which Highlander has worked have included those in the coalfields of Appalachia, African American communities in the rural South, coastal communities of South Carolina, Native American communities from North Carolina to Oklahoma and more recently Hispanic migrant communities from Florida to Tennessee. Highlander staff have also worked with logging communities of Oregon, Native American communities of the Dakotas, and communities in Nicaragua, southern Africa, Malaysia and the maquilidora region of Mexico.

Early History of Highlander

Originally established as the Highlander Folk School by a group of young men and women, mostly from the Southern USA, who in the middle of the Depression sought to establish a school to educate adults for social and political change in the South, Myles Horton, James Dombrowski and Don West were the three main founders of Highlander. Although Dombrowski and Don West left Highlander early to develop other organizations, Horton stayed with Highlander until his death in 1990. All three founders were greatly influenced by social gospel theology, Christian socialism and populist politics of the times.

Horton had grown up in a poor Tennessee, sharecropping family that valued education and experienced the economic realities of the Depression and the exploitation of rural communities. He had taught summer Bible school in the mountains where he found abject poverty and wasted land. He had learned that outside owners siphoned off the rich minerals, cut and hauled away the trees and left the locals with next to nothing. He was in New York amid the stock market crash, jobless bread lines and labour strikes. For Horton and his co-founders the Depression exposed the fundamental unreality of the American dream and they became convinced that a new social order was needed. They became interested in unions and the first work of Highlander focused on the labour movement. Horton and Jim Dombrowski attended Union Theological Seminary where they were influenced by faculty members Harry Ward, whose book, *On Economic Morality and the Ethic of Jesus* (1929), called for a Christian Socialist economy, and Rheinhold Neibuhr, who headed the Fellowship of Socialist Christians. Horton later attended the University of Chicago and was influenced by sociologists Robert Park and Lester F. Ward and Jane Addams of Hull House (Peters and Bell, 1987).

Highlander Education Philosophy

Seeking a model for his educational work, Myles Horton spent a year in Denmark studying Danish Folk Schools. He was influenced by the Danish Folk Schools where people learned from their own experiences and related their education to life problems. While in New York, Horton learned from the progressive educators, John Dewey and George Counts. Other influences on the educational programme of Highlander included New Deal programmes, populist and socialist politics, including Fabian socialists and Karl Marx. Horton said: 'I was not so much interested in Marx's conclusions, predictions and prophesies as I was in how you go about analyzing and envisioning society' (M. Horton, with Kohl and Kohl, 1990: 42). Critical analysis of one's experiences became a major part of the educational work.

Highlander's education methods evolved through working with people and communities marginalized and underserved by the mainstream economy. Horton recalled how in the early days, despite their intellectual commitment to participatory educational practices, the young 'teachers' tended to follow the patterns learned from their educational experiences and lecture the students. They found this did not produce understanding, reflection or action so they 'learned from the people' and developed a method which was participatory and transformational.

Highlander's philosophy insists that for institutional change to be effective solutions must come from the people who are experiencing the problem and who will be directly affected by the action taken. Grassroots leaders and community organizations are strengthened through an educational process that allows people to analyse problems, test ideas and learn from the experience of others (Highlander Research and Education Center, 1989; Oldendorf, 1989). In this way, the Highlander pedagogy is similar to that developed by Paulo Freire in Brazil through the use of literacy education with peasants and the poor of Sao Paulo (Horton et al., 1990).

Zilphia Mae Johnson came to Highlander as a student volunteer. She was a trained musician and interested in labour organizing. She became Myles's wife and an important member of the staff. She added her skills to introduce drama, dancing and music to the curriculum and community life. An educational programme evolved from Zilphia's work that integrated cultural expression in the educational work (for the history of Highlander, see Adams, 1972, 1975; Glen, 1988, 1993; A. Horton, 1989; M. Horton, with Kohl and Kohl, 1990). At Highlander, the use of culture for vision, hope and spiritual renewal was combined with the critical analysis of people's experiences to produce their pedagogy.

Highlander first became involved in the labour movement and the education of labour union organizers and members. Highlander became a school for unemployed, striking workers and impoverished mountain workers. In Wilder, Tennessee, the site of a particularly brutal and dangerous coalminers' strike, Horton was arrested and charged with 'coming here and getting information and going back and teaching it'. Myles always said it was the only time he was correctly charged when arrested. The critical analysis of this 'information', the experiences of the workers, combined with dramatic skits and music, which included rewriting familiar gospel songs for the picket lines, became the core curriculum of the labour education programme. This same technique served the Civil Rights movement and the development of 'We Shall Overcome', which became the rallying song of the Civil Rights movement.

'We Shall Overcome' resulted from a participatory, collective experience using the cultural experiences of the people working for change. Striking food and tobacco workers sang an old hymn on the picket line in Charleston, South Carolina. They brought the song to a workshop at Highlander in 1945. The original song had undergone some changes on the picket line and had been rewritten to be less other-worldly and more politically oriented in its message. 'I will be all right' and 'the Lord will see us through' became 'we will organize', and 'we will overcome'. Zilphia slowed the song to anthem speed and the group began to add verses. Zilphia began to sing and teach it around the South and later groups in the Civil Rights movement changed the rhythm to have more of a beat and added verses. 'We Will' was changed to 'We Shall' as Pete Seeger began to sing it with social movement groups. Guy Carawan of the Highlander staff took it to the picket lines of the Civil Rights movement where new verses and singing styles were added. This revision from different cultural experiences resulted in a traditional hymn with additional words, drawn from current issues and situations that took on revised musical harmonies and rhythm. People all over the world, who are seeking to make social changes, sing 'We Shall Overcome' (Carawan and Carawan, 1990a, 1990b, 1996).

The Civil Rights Movement

Highlander played a major role in the Civil Rights movement, not only with the song 'We Shall Overcome' but the development of Citizenship Schools which began in the coastal islands of South Carolina. These were literacy schools to teach African Americans to read and write in order to vote. They became the basis of the 'freedom schools' and voter registration movements in the Civil Rights movement. An estimated 100,000 black adults learned to read, write and register to vote through the Citizenship Schools. Based upon a specific need, to read in order to register to vote, the literacy training used the learners' own situation and need to develop the curriculum. State governments required Black registrants to read and interpret State Constitutions in order to vote so these became the text, along with registration forms, other catalogue forms and information from the students' work and everyday life. Teachers were peers and local leaders who taught in a democratic, non-authoritarian way. In 1961, when Highlander was closed by the state of Tennessee as an attempt to curb civil rights activity, the Citizenship Schools were moved from Highlander to Martin Luther King's organization, Southern Christian Leadership Conference. Septima Clark, a Highlander staff person, moved to Atlanta, Georgia to direct the programme and Citizenship Schools were spread all over the South.

Highlander then moved from its original location in Monteagle, Tennessee, to Knoxville, Tennessee, and changed names from Highlander Folk School to Highlander Research and Education Center. Along with its changed name and location, Highlander's mission shifted to the Central Appalachian coalfields and the rural communities of Tennessee, North Carolina, Virginia, West Virginia and Kentucky.

Participatory Research at Highlander

The term 'participatory research' did not enter the vocabulary of Highlander staff until the 1970s. Communities where Highlander staff worked began to organize around issues of environmental pollution and health problems, corporate ownership of land and minerals, taxation and occupational safety issues which required information often limited to professionals. John Gaventa and Juliet Merrifield joined the staff of Highlander and developed the library into a resource centre to provide research assistance to community groups and to train citizens to do their own research and participate more effectively in public policy decisions. John Gaventa remembered a workshop at Highlander in 1976: 'I first heard the words "participatory action-research" 20 years ago when I was working at Highlander. We met some folks who after hearing about our work said, what you do is called participatory research. So we grasped it then because all of sudden, aha! we had something to call our own work' (Williams, 1997: 83).

Research projects among community groups in the coalfields began to document the economic and environmental records of coal companies, occupational safety issues and legislation and the interlocking relationships between corporations and public officials. Community groups such as Bumpass Cove, Tennessee, and Yellow Creek, Kentucky, which were fighting toxic waste dumps, sought out Highlander's assistance. Residents wanted to understand the toxic chemicals and the health effects which were causing problems in their communities. They used their findings in community education and other skills acquired at Highlander for organizing. Later they became the educators for many other communities dealing with chemical companies, toxic waste disposal sites and the resultant health problems.

The Bumpass Cove Story

Bumpass Cove, a former zinc and manganese mining community, is in a fairly remote, mountainous area of east Tennessee (see Merrifield, 1989, for a fuller version of the Bumpass Cove story). The last remaining mine shut down in 1961. A creek flows through the community into the Nolichucky River where many people used to fish. Springs or wells provide drinking water to the residents but downstream the river supplies drinking water to the small towns of Jonesborough and Greenville. Since the mines closed down residents were either unemployed, living off the land or travelled long distances to work in factories. Therefore residents were pleased in 1972 when a company called Bumpass Cove Environmental Control and Mineral Co. announced plans to resume mining and to backfill the mined areas with a household garbage landfill. The mining never happened, but the landfill meant a few jobs for valley residents – working in the company office or driving the trucks which brought the garbage to the site.

Soon after the landfill began operations, people in the valley began to notice strange things happening.

Trucks would come into the landfill at night, without lights. A barrel rolled off a truck on to the side of the creek, and all the vegetation around it died. An incinerator started to emit noxious smoke and fumes. Later the residents would learn that the incinerator was unlicensed. Some of the people who lived beside the only road up the Cove began to suffer new illnesses. One woman's daughter began to have serious asthma attacks, especially when she was playing outside in the yard beside the road where the trucks came through.

Most people ignored what was happening. There were jobs at stake, and they could not believe that the government would allow any serious threats to their health. But Hobart Storey, who had worked in the mines when they operated and had spent much of his life roaming and hunting the hills around the Cove, began to notice changes among the wildlife. He found animals dead for no apparent reason and realized that birds were disappearing. He began to write letters to the Tennessee Department of Public Health, asking what was going on with the landfill and requesting that they investigate. His handwritten letters were filed, but were not acted upon.

Hobart Storey was ignored not only by the officials, but also by his fellow residents. The more he talked about the problems he saw, the more people dismissed him as a 'crazy old man'. Surely the Department of Public Health would not allow dangerous materials to be placed in their community. But slowly the evidence began to gather. One man died of a raging fever after hunting in the hills and drinking from a spring there. Doctors would not go public, but privately said they thought the death was from poisoning. Hobart and another community resident used a home movie camera to document the trucks bringing barrels into the landfill, the barrels left split open on the hillside. But still most people in the community could not believe in the seriousness of the problems the landfill was causing. A crisis finally precipitated action.

One Saturday night in spring 1979 a flood washed barrels out of the landfill into the creek and downstream into the Nolichucky River. The next morning when people attended church in the Cove, the fumes were so strong that some people passed out. The local Red Cross ordered the evacuation of the community, and finally people mobilized.

On Monday morning most of the community was out on the road blocking the way of the landfill trucks. When the trucks later tried to by-pass the blockade via a dirt road, that road was strewn with nails. The county government co-operated by putting a weight limit on a bridge that effectively excluded the landfill trucks. No trucks reached the landfill and the company, three months later, finally closed the landfill.

Much later, scientists from the state health department admitted what Hobart Storey had known all along: hazardous chemicals had been placed in the landfill, although it was licensed only for domestic garbage. The chemicals had already begun leaching out of the landfill into groundwater and the creek.

Soon after the community organized and stopped the landfill from operating, a small group of residents came to a Highlander workshop which brought together people from communities across Tennessee who were experiencing hazardous waste problems. The excitement they shared is common to many Highlander workshops, they found that they were not alone, that other communities shared their problems and frustrations, and had knowledge from their experiences to share.

Later, a couple from Bumpass Cove travelled to the Nashville offices of the State Department of Public Health. They found the Department's files in 'a terrible mess', but after a couple of days' work obtained photocopies of internal memos and correspondence between the landfill operators and officials documenting the chemicals which had been buried in the landfill.

Much of the material found was couched in technical and scientific terminology. They were unable to assess the significance of their findings. Several residents came to Highlander to use the library facilities with the goal of compiling a list of chemicals that had been placed in the landfill during its operation.

Juliet Merrifield of the Highlander staff and the Bumpass Cove group went through the mass of correspondence, memos and test reports, and made a 3 × 5 inch card each time they found a mention of a chemical having been dumped, or found in tests. They also made a card for each request to dump material. It was later borne out by Health Department comments that these materials had in fact been dumped at Bumpass Cove.

In order to find out what the potential health effects were of the list of chemicals, they went to chemical directories, medical dictionaries and *Webster's Dictionary*. The chemical directories gave information on potential health effects, results of animal testing done, and any standards for workplace exposure to the chemical. The medical dictionaries helped them figure out what the symptoms really meant. 'Apnoea', for example, turned out to be loss of 'consciousness'. And the dictionary helped translate the words of the medical dictionaries into language they could understand.

Some of the people conducting the research were high school drop-outs. None were trained health scientists. They would have been regarded as scientifically illiterate by the 'experts' employed by the State Health Department. But they had the incentive to struggle with difficult material. Their health was at stake. They were able to overcome the barriers placed in the way of their understanding by obscure language, remote sources and lack of scientific training. What came out of the exercise at Highlander was a list of chemicals suspected to have been dumped at the Bumpass Cove landfill and with their potential health effects. The impact was much more than a list. For the first time people began to feel that they had some control over the information and a feeling of power *vis-à-vis* the experts. Their feeling was soon strengthened by a confrontation with the Health Department inspector.

The Health Department had agreed to sample water in several drinking wells in the Cove which were close to the landfill. An inspector then visited the citizens' organization to report on the findings at one well in particular, which was only 200 yards from the landfill. In a standard technique, he reeled off a list of chemicals with long names that had been found in the samples from the well and then hastened to reassure the citizens that these chemicals were harmless. The citizens pulled out their copy of a chemical directory which the Highlander staff had sent home with them, looked up the names of the chemicals, and challenged the inspector. 'This book says this chemical may cause liver damage, that one affects the central nervous system.' The inspector left speedily, and the citizens, while disturbed by the nature of the information they had found, felt empowered to have been able to challenge an 'expert' on his own ground.

This small experience contributed to the citizens' growing feeling that they knew what the scientists did not, and that they had a right to speak out on what they knew.

Highlander continued to do this kind of research training with citizens' groups, both in the field of environmental and occupational health and in other issue areas.

Appalachian Land Study

One of the first Highlander projects that was called 'participatory research' was a major collaborative Land Study Project developed at Highlander by John Gaventa and Billy Horton of the Appalachian Alliance (Appalachian Land Ownership Taskforce, 1981; Gaventa and Horton, 1981). Although local residents knew that outside corporations owned most of the land and minerals in the coalfields of Central Appalachia, this had never been documented. No studies had ever been made to determine the ownership patterns. Most local tax assessors relied on the coal companies' declarations in order to develop their tax assessments. There was growing interest by community groups to change the tax structures and assess the land and minerals at a fair rate. About 100 grassroots 'researchers' were mobilized and trained to gather data about land and mineral ownership from tax rolls and deed books in their home communities throughout the coal mining region of Appalachia. The absentee and corporate ownership of land and minerals of the region was documented. The data became the tools of organized community groups working for fair taxation.

The research became a means of popular action itself. By controlling knowledge, the citizens were then empowered to confront the power structure. Statewide organizations were formed which began to develop legislative strategies to change the tax structures. When people began to see themselves as researchers, they developed many ingenious methods of gaining information. They also learned to use their own water sampling kits, video cameras, and computers to get and compile the information they needed. Because those who are experiencing the problem were the ones researching it, they had many sources of information in the community which were not available to the professional researcher.

Economic Education

Through participatory action research at Highlander people learned about economics and how to assess community needs and resources to begin community-based development. Highlander staff combined this approach with the Highlander pedagogy of beginning with people's own experiences. Community members used their own and others' oral histories to analyse their past development history as well as their family employment histories and they began to understand the economic changes which they had experienced (Lewis and Gaventa, 1988; Lewis et al., 1986). Asking questions of grandparents, parents and peers about their work and means of survival, and then charting those responses, became a way of understanding broad economic changes through people's own experiences. The people could then begin planning for development that would be more just and democratic or would preserve some of the means of survival that had been part of their community and family history.

Community members developed surveys and interviewed several hundred people in each community. The survey not only gathered data but also mobilized local discussions and consideration of their problems. Collective analysis of survey results helped develop research skills and became a way to state and prioritize problems to be addressed.

Visual portrayals, community mapping and drawing were ways of describing current problems and relationships in the community, as well as articulating visions for the future. Some communities developed elaborate maps of every street, house, business and other structures and young people made photographs throughout the community and then drew their vision of changes for the future.

After their analysis of community resources and needs, community members carried out interviews of powerful decision-makers within the community, including bankers, industry heads and county planners. Having reclaimed the community knowledge about the economy, grassroots people stood their ground against the diagnosis of the 'experts'. Since the community definitions of needs usually contrasted dramatically with those of the power-holders, participants analysed why the 'official' bodies failed to reflect their own needs.

Cultural components became part of the curriculum and the learning process. At the community level, economic knowledge cannot be separated from other ways of knowing. Some communities developed theatre from the oral histories to tell the story of changes in the community and hopes for the future. People wrote poems and songs. In some communities Bible studies were used to talk about the economy, and to analyse and understand community experiences to develop values and visions of what should be done. Some communities developed history books and museums in the community to tell their story. (See Hinsdale, Lewis and Waller (1995) for an account of participatory research with a community doing community development.)

What We Learned

Through the years Highlander has changed issues and some of the operation styles. Today there are problems of plant closures and de-industrialization instead of problems of beginning industrialization; absentee transnational corporations have replaced the local coal, timber or textile barons. Yet some of the basic problems of exploitation of resources and people remain the same. Highlander's tradition, acknowledging and respecting people's culture, helps develop and recover local knowledge. Residents overcome dominant knowledge structures through oral histories which have been denigrated or suppressed. Bumpass Cove and Yellow Creek both discovered that songs and poetry written about the pollution problems helped organize and educate around the problem. Communities used their cultural expressions in their gatherings and celebrations as an affirmation of their identity. Their old songs and stories are also a window on their past and present fears and beliefs.

The process of people gaining control over knowledge and skills normally considered to be the monopoly of the experts is empowering and produces much more than information. One of the lessons from Bumpass Cove is that people who must live with toxic chemicals may recognize their effects long before scientists ever get around to studying them, and that they do so through observing changes in phenomena well known to them. They may see their children's health deteriorate or the wildlife and natural phenomena becoming endangered. Residents may not know these phenomena in the same way as scientists, or use the same concepts and language to describe them, but they do understand them. Scientists must learn to acknowledge and respect their knowledge.

Bumpass Cove also shows that the prevailing myth of science as the domain only of trained experts may discourage many people, persuading them that what they know is not valid. The belief that science is politically neutral persuades people that scientists would not allow bad things to happen to them. Such beliefs and deference to the experts allow science to be used to buttress political power and to disempower ordinary people. When people begin to research their own problems they begin to feel that they have some control over the information, a feeling of power *vis-à-vis* the experts. They strengthen that feeling when they confront the experts such as the Health Department or other government officials and discover they knew what the scientists did not. They recognize their right to speak out on what they know.

The Highlander staff found participatory action research an effective tool whenever there is a strong personal incentive to get the information. And people have devised their own creative ways of gaining access to information they need. They may raid corporate garbage cans, remove labels from chemical containers or research the contents in the library. Highlander and similar organizations have an important role to play in systematizing and giving validity to people's knowledge. Collaborative learning at Highlander helped people gain access to information about problems that affect them and to interpret and present their results. People carried out their own health surveys, documented suspected problems and gave validity to common knowledge. Juliet Merrifield remembers:

> Prior to work in Bumpass Cove our staff had done research on chemicals and their health effects *for* people and given them the results, but had not systematically taught them how to gain access themselves to the information they needed. Without that step, little empowerment took place. People might have the information they needed for a particular fight but they were no better equipped to confront the next one. They had not changed any of their perceptions about themselves *vis-à-vis* the scientific experts. It was only when the citizens themselves knew how to get information they needed that they felt able to challenge the experts on their own grounds, and felt that what they themselves knew could be validated. The importance of that became apparent to us with the Bumpass Cove experience. (Merrifield, 1989: 24)

When people learned how to do their own research, they began to recognize that experts are not the objective, unbiased, disinterested purveyors of truth. Scientists often use 'science' to impress or hide political decisions as 'scientific'. 'Science' is not accountable and responsible to the needs of ordinary people but serves the power-holders. Highlander was able in some cases to find scientists who would join with citizen or worker groups to address their problems. Physicians worked with communities to develop health surveys which would be accepted as legitimate. Scientists worked with communities to study water and air pollution. In these relationships between scientists and people in communities with the problem these crucial questions have to be asked:

- Who determines the need for the research?
- Who controls the process of research and makes decisions along the way which affect its outcome?
- Who controls the dissemination of results?
- Where does accountability lie? (Merrifield, 1989: 29)

Highlander tends to work most often without reliance on co-operative scientists, instead collaborating with communities and relying on people's knowledge and to help systematize and analyse their knowledge. This knowledge is found to be closer to the 'truth' than the theoretical scientific knowledge. A community that is experiencing an environmental and occupational health problem, that is exposed to toxic chemicals, know they are affected even when the 'scientific' instruments for measuring these effects are inadequate. Unfortunately, 'science', as controlled and used by power-holders, refuses to accept people's knowledge and demands scientific proof of harm before action can take place. Science must begin to meet the needs of ordinary people rather than the power-holders and become a constructive and humane science.

Note

Thanks to the staff of the Highlander Center and members of my class, Collaborative Community Research, Appalachian State University for suggestions and editing assistance.

References

Adams, F. (1972) 'Highlander Folk School getting information, going back and teaching it', *Harvard Education Review*, 42 (4): 433–56.

Adams, F. (1975) *Unearthing Seeds of Fire: the Idea of Highlander*. Winston-Salem, NC: John F. Blair.

Appalachian Land Ownership Taskforce (1981) *Land Ownership Patterns and Their Impacts on Appalachian Communities* (Vols 1–7). Washington, DC: Appalachian Regional Commission.

Carawan, G. and Carawan, C. (1990a) *Been in the Storm So Long*. Washington, DC: Smithsonian/Folkways.

Carawan, G. and Carawan, C. (1990b) *Sing for Freedom: Songs of the Civil Rights Movement*. Bethlehem, PA: Sing Out Publications.

Carawan, G. and Carawan, C. (1996) *Voices from the Mountains, Life and Struggles in the Appalachian South*. Athens, GA: University of Georgia.

Gaventa, J. and Horton, B. (1981) 'A citizens' research project in Appalachia, USA', *Convergence*, 14 (3): 30–42.

Glen, J.M. (1988) *Highlander, No Ordinary School, 1932–1962*. Lexington, KY: University Press of Kentucky.

Glen, J.M. (1993) 'Like a flower slowly blooming: Highlander and the nurturing of an Appalachian movement', in Stephen L. Fisher (ed.), *Fighting Back in Appalachia*. Philadelphia, PA: Temple University Press. pp. 31–5.

Highlander Research and Education Center (1989) *Highlander Research and Education Center: an Approach to Education Presented through a Collection of Writings*. Highlander Research and Education Center, 1959 Highlander Way, New Market, Tennessee 37820.

Hinsdale, M.A., Lewis, H. and Waller, M. (1995) *It Comes from the People: Community Development and Local Theology*. Philadelphia, PA: Temple University Press.

Horton, A.I. (1989) *Highlander Folk School: a History of its Major Programs, 1932–1961*. New York: Carlson Publishing.

Horton, M., Freire, P., Bell, B., Gaventa, J., and Peters, J. (eds) (1990) *We Make the Road by Walking: Conversations on Education and Social Change*. Philadelphia, PA: Temple University Press.

Horton, M., with Kohl, J. and Kohl, H. (1990) *The Long Haul: an Autobiography*. New York: Doubleday.

Lewis, H.M. and Gaventa, J. (1988) *The Jellico Handbook: a Teacher's Guide to Community-based Economics*. Highlander Research and Education Center, 1959 Highlander Way, New Market, Tennessee 37820.

Lewis, H.M. et al. (1986) 'Picking up the pieces'. *Working Paper Series, Vol. 4*, Highlander Research and Education Center, 1959 Highlander Way, New Market, Tennessee 37820.

Merrifield, J. (1989) 'Putting the scientists in their place: participatory research in environmental and occupational health'. *Working Paper Series, Vol. 12*, Highlander Research and Education Center, 1959 Highlander Way, New Market, Tennessee 37820.

Oldendorf, S.B. (1989) 'Vocabularies, knowledge and social action in citizenship education: the Highlander example', *Theory and Research in Social Education*, Spring, 17 (2): 107–20.

Peters, J.M. and Bell, B. (1987) 'Horton of Highlander', in Peter Jarvis (ed.), *Twentieth Century Thinkers in Adult Education*. New York: Croom Helm. pp. 243–65.

Ward, H.F. (1929) *On Economic Morality and the Ethic of Jesus*. New York: Macmillan.

Williams, L. (1997) *Grassroots Guide to Participatory Research*. Knoxville, TN: Community Partnership Center, University of Tennessee.

25

Creative Arts and Photography in Participatory Action Research in Guatemala

M. BRINTON LYKES
in collaboration with the Association of Maya Ixil Women – New Dawn, Chajul, Guatemala

CHAPTER OUTLINE

This chapter represents a collaborative effort among a religiously, linguistically, politically and generationally diverse group to re-thread community in rural, post-war Guatemala. The Association of Maya Ixil Women – New Dawn (ADMI) has developed five projects, including three economic development projects, an educational programme for children between the ages of 6 and 12, and a local library. The Photo Voice project described here is an integral development within ADMI's work and illustrates how the arts and photography within the context of participatory action research serve as resources to tell a story of war and its effects while facilitating personal and community change, thereby improving the quality of community life in a post-war context of persistent poverty.

In 1992 I visited Chajul, a rural town in the Guatemalan Highlands where my friend Maria grew up. Chajul and the neighbouring towns of Cotzal and Nebaj constitute the Ixil Triangle. It was one of the sites of atrocities committed during Guatemala's 36-year war, including massacres, the scorching of villages, disappearances and widespread displacement and exile (CEH, 1999; Falla, 1994; ODHAG, 1998; Stoll, 1993). A group of six Chajulense women had organized themselves as a Women's Committee. Knowing of my previous community-based field research and training activities in Guatemalan war zones (Lykes, 1994, 1996; Melville and Lykes, 1992), Maria hoped that I might accompany them in their efforts to rebuild their community, improving their lives and those of others in their town.

The extremely unequal distribution of land contributed to uprisings in the 1960s and 1970s that were met by subsequent repression. Years of war did not improve economic or social conditions in this Central American country. Only 54 per cent of the rural population has access to safe, clean water; 57 per cent to health services. Fifty-one percent of the rural population is below the absolute poverty level, defined as the income level below which a minimum nutritionally adequate diet plus essential non-food requirements is not affordable. Total adult literacy in Guatemala is 65 per cent; yet there are only 79 literate women for every 100 literate men and rates of illiteracy are considerably higher for women and men in rural areas. School enrolments are also notably lower for girls than boys, in part due to the disproportionate responsibilities girls and women bear as household heads and helpers (United Nations Children's Fund, 1997, 2000).

The Ixil[1] of Chajul are one of 21 Mayan groups in a country of approximately 11 million inhabitants, 51 per cent of whom are under the age of 18. The Ixil women of Chajul formed a women's committee within a context of ongoing violence, persistent poverty, limited educational opportunity and inadequate healthcare. In my previous work I had responded primarily to the ongoing threats of war and its destructive impacts on individual and community life (Lykes, 1994, 1996, 1997; also, see below). In Chajul I was invited to work with local protagonists who sought a more integrated approach to the multiple realities of rural poverty and war while addressing its particular impacts on women and children (see Lykes et al., 1999, for a description of the development of the committee and, subsequently, of the Association of Maya Ixil Women – ADMI). In this chapter I represent aspects of this work to illustrate how the arts and photography serve as resources in participatory action research with local women seeking to improve the quality of community life in response to the effects of war and extreme poverty.

Thirty-six Years of War: the Context for PAR

Much has been written about how contemporary warfare destroys the fabric of social life, affecting families, communities, institutions and social life in general. Others have addressed the symbolic aspects of terror and trauma and its effects within and across generations. Those destructive forces and their wake mark individuals in differing ways, distorting perception, suspending many in unresolved grief, and terrorizing and traumatizing others. Children and their parents are forced to 'choose' fight or flight (Martín-Baró, 1994), joining military or guerilla organizations or fleeing their homes, even their countries. Institutionalized racism and economic inequality destroy the material and spiritual fabric of everyday life among people who have inhabited a land for centuries (see Graça Machel/UN Study on the Effects of War on Children, 1998; Lykes, 1994, 1996 for reviews of this literature).

The engendered nature of war's violence has only recently been highlighted and the case of Guatemala is no exception (see, e.g., Agger, 1994; Aron et al., 1991; Lykes et al., 1993). The Archdiocesan-sponsored report on violations of human rights/ ODHAG, *Nunca más* [*Never again*] (1998, Vol. 1), and the official United Nations-sponsored report of the Commission for Historical Clarification/CEH (1999) documented thousands of gross violations of human rights, including the destruction of more than 400 rural villages, many in the Ixil Triangle. Interviews with some women and with key informants told of repeated rapes of girls and women, the brutalization of foetuses torn from pregnant women's stomachs, the torture and killing of girls and women, and of children in front of their mothers, mothers in front of their children. Many women were impregnated, giving birth to children frequently rejected by their communities and, sometimes, by the mothers themselves (ODHAG, 1998: 91–2). The women of Chajul and its surrounding villages were no exception to this violence.

Despite this brutality, women were more likely than men to survive and face the burdens of the psychosocial and material consequences of this violence. Many responded by creating and leading human rights organizations while others contributed to the sustenance and growth of their families and communities where women in rural areas are now tending large animals, preparing fields for planting, chopping wood and participating in local religious and political organizations. The Women's Committee in Chajul represented one collective response to these atrocities.

Arts, storytelling and healing: antecedents to the work in Chajul

My earlier work in Guatemala was developed to respond to some of war's realities. It drew heavily on creativity and the arts as resources in psychosocial, community-based work. In collaborations with Argentine colleagues from the Solidarity Movement in Mental Health (MSSM) and Guatemalan colleagues from the Association of Community Health Services (ASECSA) we developed training programmes for community leaders that sought to accompany child and youth survivors of war, particularly in rural Mayan communities with little to no access to health or mental health resources. Our modality of work sought to weave traditional resources of storytelling, play and dramatization (Freidel, Schele and Parker, 1993; Montejo, 1991) that gave expression to Mayan spirituality and traditional beliefs (Cojti Cuxil, 1991) with children's natural gifts for self-expression through movement, play and drawing. The group-based workshops were spaces for facilitators (in their training experiences) and participants (children and youth) to enact the unspeakable stories of violence and destruction that they had survived or witnessed. The group's processes, as well as its 'performances' through drawings, collages, stories, dramatizations and masks, constituted survivors' previously silenced 'stories', opportunities for interpreting the past through the enactment and re-enactment of horrific events, their effects and responses to them. As group facilitators we stood alongside participants, in solidarity with their experiences, critical of the government and military responsible for such violence (see Lykes and Liem, 1990, among others, on the non-neutrality of the psychologists working in these contexts).

In one exercise participants were invited to play with words, that is, to turn two unrelated cognates into protagonists and create a story (Rodari, 1987). One group worked with the words 'oreja [ear/spy]' and 'duck'. An affectionate duck shared with his community, 'defended the little ones' and 'called [them] to organize themselves', whereas a 'crafty duck', the 'oreja', 'killed [the affectionate duck] ...

to take his leadership and finish off the ducks' organization, which was his main objective' (Lykes, 1996: 170–1). Deeply experienced and ongoing ethnic and racial tensions were re-presented through the less threatening activities of animals. Mayan participants and observers believe that animals participate in all aspects of material and human life, thus transforming what appears to be a 'child's story' to a lesson 'about us, about our people'. The duck-as-spy embodied the experience of the threat of betrayal from 'one of our own', symbolizing the lack of trust that prevailed in 1991 when this story was created (see Goudvis, 1991; Lykes, 1994, 1996, 1997).

The group was a context in which some began to re-thread relationships, re-encountering themselves in a space of relative security. These creative workshops were developed by facilitators and participants and constituted a preventive strategy, a resource for health promoters, childcare workers and educators to engage their own creativity to develop psychosocial assistance for children and youth in their communities. Those working as facilitators of the groups were local residents, members of the community and survivors of the same violence that had affected the children and youth participating in the workshops.

To evaluate our training and community-based group work we collaborated in developing a four-country participatory research project in 1990. The texts created in group-based activities with children and youth were 'read' by group facilitators and collaborating researchers to clarify changes that occurred through the processes as well as to assess the contributions of the groups' 'productions' to local community life. Through documentation and analysis in four Latin American contexts affected by war and state-sponsored violence we developed 'thick descriptions' of the experiences of some child and youth survivors and assessed the relative contributions and limitations of this intervention modality for 'creating a better future' (Goudvis, 1991; Lykes et al., 1994).

Peace Processes And Local Communities

A negotiated settlement between the guerrilla forces (URNG) and the Guatemalan government in December 1996 has created alternative spaces in which survivors are giving more direct expression to the multiple effects of this 36-year war. In Chajul, women have been using creative resources, such as those described above, and photography and participatory research methods (see below), to create a public testimony, a PhotoVoice, that witnesses to the atrocities committed against the Maya Ixil and K'iche' and contributes to their development of individual and collective responses to health and educational needs of women and children in their communities.

Photography and participatory research as resources for healing and change

The Association of Maya Ixil Women – New Dawn (ADMI) grew out of the committee of six women with whom I began to work in 1992. With technical assistance from Guatemalan ladinos and Maya, ADMI has developed five projects in addition to the one described here, including three economic development projects, an educational programme for children between the ages of six and 12, and a local library (Lykes et al., 1999). Their work represents a tentative re-threading of community among a religiously, linguistically, politically and generationally diverse group of women. I have served as a consultant to this work, providing workshops similar to those described above and others focused more explicitly on organizational development and psychosocial issues that the women of ADMI have encountered as they occupy new roles within their organization and the wider community.

As a group of primarily Ixil-speaking women, very few of whom speak Spanish and even fewer of whom can read and write in any language, we sought methods for working together that would facilitate the participation of all yet also enable us to communicate within and beyond our borders. Inspired by the work of Chinese rural women, *Visual Voices: 100 Photographs of Village China by the Women of Yunnan Province* (1995), the women of ADMI decided that they wanted to use photography to develop a public record of their lives, to 'tell the story of the violence' and also their story as women responding to the war and its effects. They hoped to prevent future violence by speaking out, and, through storytelling, to build connections with other women in Guatemala and beyond who were engaged in similar processes. As important, they sought new skills and resources to develop economic and psychosocial resources for their communities.

The workshops I had been facilitating since 1992 integrated Freirian pedagogical and analytical techniques (Freire, 1970), creative resources, indigenous practices (e.g., weaving, religious ceremony and oral histories) (see, e.g., Lykes, 1994, 1996; Zipes, 1995), and PAR strategies (Fals Borda, 1988; Fals Borda and Rahman, 1991; Maguire, 1987). Two photographic methods, 'PhotoVoice' (Wang and Burris, 1994; Wang, Burris and Xiang, 1996; Wang, 1999) and 'talking pictures' (Bunster and Chaney, 1989) served as important resources that we incorporated into our existing group processes to consolidate a PAR method that fit the needs articulated within the group. We developed an iterative process of data collection and analysis; women 'analyzed as they photographed'. Photographers recorded their own life stories, sometimes assisted by a facilitator, through paired interviews among the 20 participants. They photographed life in Chajul and travelled to neighbouring villages, photographing women and their families. Through recording multiple stories of daily living, that is, of war, its effects and ongoing poverty, they developed sensitivities to the various forms of violence experienced in the wider municipality as well as analyses of the complex challenges facing the region as it develops recovery strategies in the wake of war's trauma.

A village girl

Taking pictures and telling stories: data collection and analytic processes

Once we had completed an orientation and training programme that included the self-identification of 20 of ADMI's more than 65 members as participants of PhotoVoice (see, Lykes et al., 1999), each of the participants received an automatic camera and began to take pictures. The thematic focus of each roll was decided in workshops involving all participants. Our initial topic, work, was based on our understanding of the challenges facing women and children in Chajul and had been an ongoing topic in my workshops with ADMI since 1992. Later topics – women and their families, health and illness, religion, culture and traditional practices, the war and its effects, the harvest, and the work of ADMI – were drawn from analyses of the photographs as the process developed.

The process

Each photographer selects five to seven pictures from each roll of 24 developed photos. She then 'tells the story' of each picture to a small group including two to four other participants. She includes her particular reasons for choosing this picture, as well as any stories that she may have been told by the person she photographed. In a second round of analysis, we form groups of five to seven women who select two to four pictures from the previously selected individual photographs, now clustered topically. These group analytic sessions have been particularly mobilizing and motivating. Through careful planning and the scaffolding of experiences within the group discussions (Rogoff, 1990; Vygotsky, 1986), women have developed strategies for clustering ideas, identifying similarities and differences between and across photos, and constructing holistic analyses of clusters of photographs. They have explored possible proximal and distal causes for the problems represented in any given picture and hypothesized causal sequences. For example, an initial story told about a young barefooted girl, carrying wood, described her desire for a chocolate covered banana and her need to sell the wood on her back in order to secure money to buy her treat.

Subsequent group-based analyses revealed that this school-age child had been forced to sell the wood to bring home cash, thereby entering a market economy. In contrast, the photographers' experiences as child-workers included gathering wood to heat their homes or to cook the family's food. In their analyses, the women calculated the cost of the child's treat and the money she would get for selling the wood. They concluded that the bulk of the funds she secured would be used to enable the family to buy necessary goods for basic survival. Others in the group suggested that the load of wood was 'overly burdensome for a small child' and that the child's labour 'deprived her of access to education'. Comments about her torn skirt, lack of shoes, and dirty face were offered as other indices of family poverty, a lack of hygiene and neglect.

The hanged woman

Writing stories of war and its effects: words and pictures

Among the photographs selected for analysis are many depicting the war and its effects. One picture and the stories told by the woman being photographed, as well as others who analysed it, exemplify the direct effects of the war on the women and children of Chajul. The story that accompanies this second photograph is based on an interview that one of the women in PhotoVoice conducted with a grandmother who had returned to her village after having been forced to move into the town of Chajul during the early 1980s. Her husband and son had been killed in the war and she and her daughter and grandchild sought refuge in the town. Lacking food and income, her daughter left the town one day in search of plants from their home village that would provide soap for cleaning and leaves and roots for cooking. She went with her mother's blessings and under the protection of a military patrol that was scouting in the area. The patrol, ambushed by guerillas who killed some of the soldiers, accused the young mother of having set up the ambush and arrested her. The following day, despite the grandmother's pleas on behalf of her still-nursing grandchild, the young woman was brought to the town square. Church bells were rung and once all the townspeople had gathered in the town square, the daughter was summarily hanged from the balcony of the town hall. The brutal murder, a 'lesson' to the townspeople about 'collaboration with the guerilla', served also to instill fear and silence.

The picture-taking and interview, PhotoVoice, enabled this grandmother to share her losses with a member of her community who accompanied her process of mourning that had been suspended, a grief that had been frozen (Ulloa, 1990). Others from the PhotoVoice group had witnessed the hanging and in their analysis group they shared conflicting stories of what they 're-membered' of this day. Fear had terrorized the community and a silence enshrouded the event. The storytelling and analysis process offered an opportunity to reconstruct the events, to create a shared story. Several members of the group volunteered to interview others in the community to establish the precise date on which this event had occurred and to situate it within the town's public history, thereby ensuring that the next generation would know what had happened from those who had survived who now dared to speak publicly about their suffering, their deep loss and their anger. This process, these pictures and stories, and many like them, create a context for grieving but also for building towards a different future.

These analyses are recorded and, with the pictures, were presented to the larger group where they are subject to re-analysis by other participants and/or to further elaboration through drawing, dramatization and storytelling. In this latter context participants explore possible solutions to the problems identified at the individual and collective level, thereby also developing a shared vision for change. The latter work is then summarized in the notes from each workshop and forms important data from which priorities for future work are developed. We have selected approximately 60 pictures from among several thousand and crafted short stories from the pages of interviews and analyses that we have developed over the past two years to create *Voces e Imágenes* book (Women of PhotoVoice/ADMI & Lykes, M.B., in press). There are four chapters, including the violence and its effects, culture, women and their families and ADMI. Ana Caba, one of the participants in PhotoVoice, and the Co-ordinator of ADMI, described the significance of this project in the following way:

> The project PhotoVoice is very important for us because as the name says it is photographs and voice, the voice, which explains the photograph and thereby is a guide, a road, which is guiding us in the search for a solution to our needs as women. Through the photographs we will develop a book, which can be read, and those who read it can come to better understand women's ways of doing work, women's needs, children's problems. These same women are working with photography and telling their stories. A picture is not the same as telling a story; the picture is there; you can see the reality, and we can seek additional support for our work [with these pictures] ... With the project of PhotoVoice we are observing that we women and others who have suffered from the violence and have lived those experiences of violence are able to remember it, and this is very important, because there are many who are growing up now who did not live this suffering and don't think it existed because they did not see it. In contrast, there are many people like ourselves who live and suffer this in our own flesh, and we are remembering it. When we interview a person who has suffered this and also seen her family die, well, there is a relief for them to be able to tell their story to another person [in their community]. One thinks that they are also asking for relief and that they are also asking that this violence, that this war, never return. Through PhotoVoice we are also seeking a means whereby the international community can offer its help so that this violence, will never happen again. For us then this project is very important.

Selected challenges encountered in PAR crossing borders

We have encountered multiple challenges and problems during these seven years of collaboration and most recently in the development of PhotoVoice (see also, Lykes et al., 1999). The introduction of cameras and of outside collaborators into this rural Mayan community entails challenges and incongruities including: (1) multiple cameras and outside collaborators from afar in an impoverished community; (2) non-Spanish-speaking, non-professional and mostly illiterate women as photographers and authors; and (3) photographs of spontaneous activities as the 'subject/object of investigation'.

Economic realities

Project participants have been enthusiastic about the work and delighted with the 'outcomes'. However, as the local co-ordinators absorbed the realities of the budget we had co-constructed, including the costs of cameras, film development, tape recorders, transcriptions of recorded group sessions, etc., there were frequent debates about the allocation of funds within our two-year grant. Equally tense for all were moments when the professionals associated with the project, who received stipends or honoraria and transportation funds that far exceeded those paid to local co-ordinators, were challenged to justify our remuneration. This was made more complex by my own previous decisions to contribute my time without remuneration and a lack of transparency in the real costs of our collaborative work prior to our having received funding for the PhotoVoice project. The extreme poverty in which many participants live and the fact that only a few local women in leadership were benefiting financially from the project created additional tensions that continue to be debated. Finally, we were all too aware that this project cannot easily be self-sustaining in Chajul.

Women and gender in rural Mayan community

The 20 women who are part of the PhotoVoice team identify themselves as photographers and as researchers. Several of the older women in the group marvel at the skills they have developed and the contributions they have made despite their illiteracy and limited language skills. Many who argued several years ago that they could not speak Spanish have become bilingual translators and interpreters. Through picture-taking and reflections on their pictures these women have 'stepped outside' their daily lives and developed a new respect for themselves as women as well as for each other. These changes in self and in self-identifications have not gone unnoticed by men in the community, some of whom have been very supportive of women's emerging contributions to the community. Others, including husbands of some of the younger women, have resisted the project, interfering in their wives' participation and sometimes disrupting the group's work.

Efforts to situate PhotoVoice as a community project have contributed to establishing ADMI as a resource to the wider community and the mayor has affirmed the women's rights to take pictures within the community and its villages. The processes involved in negotiating these rights and the support they reflect have contributed importantly to personal growth for many of the women and to the organization's development. The journey has been more costly for some women and some have not been able to participate as fully as they might have liked because of spousal resistance. In contrast some of the older widows within the group have exhibited a newfound humour about their plight, teasing younger women about 'not having to ask permission from men' since they are 'without husbands'. The project's 'successes' underscore the need to develop interventions that create opportunities for men to explore the multiple and varied challenges for them as their wives, mothers, sisters and daughters engage new roles and identities.

Formal versus spontaneous photography: the othered's self

Maya are represented widely in photo essays, magazines and postcards. Tourists and professional photographers alike struggle to capture 'the exotic Mayan customs' for expensive 'coffee table' books or postcards whereas male Guatemalan photographers (*los ambulantes*) rove among county fairs to take formal family shots or offer themselves for hire to record weddings and funerals (Parker and Neal, 1982). Space does not permit a fuller analysis of these local histories of photography but the women of PhotoVoice and the wider community members who have allowed their pictures to be taken for this community project are very aware of its contradistinction to other experiences of 'being photographed'. This 'local history' further contextualizes the transgressive nature of what these Mayan women photographers have created through PhotoVoice, highlighting another incongruity and contributing, I think, to the transformative nature of the project for the photographers as well and the communities of Ixiles and K'iche's who have been photographed. These contradictions and incongruities underscore the ways in which any collaboration in which outsiders enter a community with resources not heretofore available represents an intervention in that community and generates consequences for the project, its participants and the community more widely.

Conclusions: Photography as Art, as Resource for Healing, as Research Strategy

Drawing, dramatization, storytelling and photography have been employed by local Mayan communities to recover the stories of war, reflect upon its effects and re-thread community. PhotoVoice offers an important alternative both at the level of the photograph and, as importantly, at the level of storytelling and analysis. The process of taking pictures within one's local community became an opportunity to develop individual and collective stories that had heretofore been silenced or spoken only privately to outside researchers or human rights workers. The photograph creates its own story and becomes a site for wider participatory storytelling and analysis. It re-presents the photographer's perspective or point of view but then becomes a stimulus for the group's reflections, discussions, analyses and re-presentations. The fixed image serves as a catalyst for an ever-widening discussion of the differing realities that are present within these Mayan communities.

The stories and subsequent analyses of the photographs have contributed to our developing a shared understanding of some of the multiple causes of 'the violence' and its local effects while contributing to healing and recovery processes within the group and beyond. Based on these understandings, ADMI is enhancing its current programmes and developing new ones that respond to the needs of women and children in their community and beyond. Participants with fifth- or sixth-grade formal schooling have honed analytic skills that were multiplied through small-group work with other photographers with considerably less formal education. As significantly, a core group has participated in training designed to prepare them for assuming all roles within the research process as well as strengthening their local women's organization. They have developed computer skills, become data recorders and systematizers, and learned how to balance the projects' financial accounts. Several have written grant proposals to support some of the new programmatic initiatives that have evolved from this ongoing work. Others have spoken publicly in national forums about their work. Most recently, they have established a team of 'technical assistants' from among the 20 participants in the PAR project who are beginning to work with women in some of the villages surrounding Chajul to help them establish women's groups in their communities and begin to develop community-based projects that will improve their lives and the lives of their families. Others represent ADMI in national efforts to pressure the government to fulfil promises made to Mayan communities as part of the Peace Accords.

This project represents one effort to combine the uses of art and creativity that have heretofore characterized the work of only a few psychologists, on the one hand, and sociologists and anthropologists on the other. The former have tended to use drawing, play and dramatizations within the confines of counselling and psychotherapy (see Jennings, 1992; Krauss, 1983; Landy, 1993) and neither linked these resources to research nor attended to the ways in which they intersect with local community practices and politics. The latter have tended to focus more specifically on the photograph as a resource for documenting social reality, complementing the researcher's focus on local communities as 'objects' of study (Caldarola, 1985). The work described here draws on both of these traditions as well as work by professional photographers (Duarte, 1998; Ewald, 1985, 1992, 1996; Franklin and McGirr, 1995; Spence and Solomon, 1995) and social scientists (Worth and Adair, 1972; Ziller and Smith, 1977; Ziller, Vern and Camacho de Santoya, 1988) who have put cameras in the hands of local communities, inviting them to document their own reality. Finally, this work shares some commonalities with the small number of social scientists who have recently begun to use the arts and storytelling as resources in the resolution of conflict (Liebmann, 1996) or in community organizing and social change work (Rappaport, 1998; Wang et al., 1998). The work represented here thus seeks to incorporate the best of these resources with practices from participatory action research to enhance the participants' capacity to facilitate personal and community change.

Notes

I thank, first and foremost, the many women, men and children of Chajul whose lives give meaning to the work presented here. Although this chapter focuses on the protagonism of the women of the Association of Maya Ixil Women (ADMI), it would not have been realized without the support and collaboration of many others. María Caba Mateo, María Victoria Menchú and Ubaldo Ruiz provided technical support and personal assistance. Joan W. Williams, M. Luisa Cabrera and Angela Shartrand contributed significantly to the PhotoVoice project. PhotoVoice has been generously supported by a grant from the Soros Foundation–Guatemala, a sabbatical leave from Boston College and technical support from the town of Chajul. Finally, my thanks to Ramsay Liem, Catherine M. Mooney and Vicky Steinitz for helpful comments on earlier versions of this chapter.

1 A full discussion of ethnic and interethnic relations within Guatemala is beyond the scope of this chapter. The Ixil are one of the smaller groups nationally yet make up the majority of the population in Chajul whereas a less numerous group locally, the K'iche', belong to one of the four largest Mayan groups. Most of the small stores in Chajul are owned by K'iche's and ladinos. The term 'ladino' is used synonymously with the term 'mestizo', referring today to both descendants of the Spaniards and those who are either born of mixed parentage and/or have assimilated to the dominant, mixed cultural group. Although scholars and activists argue for more flexible understandings of the categories Maya and ladino, they nevertheless underscore the profound impact of racism on life within Guatemala (Bastos and Camus, 1996; Warren, 1999), including the disproportionate genocidal killings and disappearances of Maya during Guatemala's nearly 36-year war.

References

Agger, I. (1994) *The Blue Room: Trauma and Testimony among Refugee Women, a Psycho-social Exploration* (trans. M. Bille). London: Zed Books.

Aron, A., Corne, S., Fursland, A. and Zewler, B. (1991) 'The gender-specific terror of El Salvador and Guatemala: post-traumatic stress disorder in Central American refugee women', *Women's Studies International Forum*, 14: 37–47.

Bastos, S. and Camus, M. (1996) *Quebrando el silencio: Organizaciones del pueblo maya y sus demandas (1986–1992) [Breaking the Silence: Maya Organizations and their Demands (1986–1992)]*. Guatemala: Facultad Latinoamericana de Ciencas Sociales/FLACSO.

Bunster, X. and Chaney, E.M. (1989) 'Epilogue', in X. Bunster and E.M. Chaney, *Sellers & Servants: Working Women in Lima, Peru*. Granby, MA: Bergin & Garvey Publishers. pp. 217–33.

Caldarola, V.J. (1985) 'Visual contexts: a photographic research method in anthropology', *Studies in Visual Communication*, 11 (3): 33–55.

CEH/Commission for Historical Clarification [Comisión para el Esclarecimiento Histórico] (February 1999) *Report of the CEH* [On-line]. Available: http://hrdata.aaas.org/ceh. Guatemala: CEH.

Cojti Cuxil, D. (1991) *Configuración del pensamiento político del pueblo Mayan [Configuration of Political Thought of the Mayan People]*. Quetzaltenango, Guatemala: Asociación de Escritores Mayances de Guatemala [Association of Guatemalan Mayan Writers].

Duarte, C. (1998) *Cameristas: Fotógrafos Mayas de Chiapas/Mayan Photographers*. Mexico: CIESAS.

Ewald, W. (1985) *Portraits and Dreams: Photographs and Stories by Children of the Appalachians*. New York: Writers and Readers.

Ewald, W. (1992) *Magic Eyes: Scenes from an Andean Girlhood*. Seattle, WA: Bay Press.

Ewald, W. (1996) *I Dreamed I had a Girl in My Pocket: the Story of an Indian Village*. Durham, NC: Double Take Books.

Falla, R. (1994) *Massacres in the Jungle: Ixcan, Guatemala, 1975–1982* (trans. J. Howland). Boulder, CO: Westview Press.

Fals Borda, O. (1988) *Knowledge and People's Power*. New Delhi: Indian Social Institute.

Fals Borda, O. and Rahman, M.A. (eds) (1991) *Action and Knowledge: Breaking the Monopoly with Participatory Action Research*. New York: Apex Press.

Franklin, K.L. and McGirr, N. (eds) (1995) *Out of the Dump: Writings and Photographs by Children from Guatemala* (trans. K.L. Franklin). New York: Lothrop, Lee & Shepard.

Freidel, D., Schele, L. and Parker, J. (1993) *Maya Cosmos: Three Thousand Years on the Shaman's Path*. New York: William Morrow and Co.

Freire, P. (1970) *Pedagogy of the Oppressed*. New York: Seabury Press.

Goudvis, P. (1991) *Trabajando para un Futuro Mejor: Talleres Creativos con Niños [Working for a Better Future: Creative Workshops with Children]* [Film]. (Available from the author).

Graça Machel/UN Study on the Effects of War on Children (1998) *Peace and Conflict: Journal of Peace Psychology*, 4 (4). Entire issue.

Jennings, S. (1992) *Dramatherapy*. London & New York: Tavistock/Routledge.

Krauss, D.A. (1983) 'Reality, photography, and psychotherapy', in D.A. Krauss and J.L. Fryrear (eds), *Phototherapy in Mental Health*. Springfield, IL: C.C. Thomas. pp. 41–56.

Landy, R.J. (1993) *Persona and Performance: the Meaning of Role in Drama, Therapy, and Everyday Life*. New York/London: The Guilford Press.

Liebmann, M. (ed.) (1996) *Arts Approaches to Conflict*. London: Jessica Kingsley Publishers.

Lykes, M.B. (1994) 'Terror, silencing, and children: international multidisciplinary collaboration with Guatemalan Maya communities', *Social Science and Medicine*, 38 (4): 543–52.

Lykes, M.B. (1996) 'Meaning making in a context of genocide and silencing', in M.B. Lykes, A. Banuazizi, R. Liem and M. Morris (eds), *Myths about the Powerless: Contesting Social Inequalities*. Philadelphia, PA: Temple University Press. pp. 159–78.

Lykes, M.B. (1997) 'Activist participatory research among the Maya of Guatemala: constructing meanings from situated knowledge', *Journal of Social Issues*, 53 (4): 725–46.

Lykes, M.B., with Caba Mateo, A., Chávez Anay, J. Laynez Caba, I.A. and Ruiz, U. (1999) 'Telling stories – rethreading lives: community education, women's development and social change among the Maya Ixil', *International Journal of Leadership in Education: Theory and Practice*, 2 (3): 207–27.

Lykes, M.B. and Liem, R. (1990) 'Human rights and mental health in the United States: lessons from Latin America', *Journal of Social Issues*, 46 (3): 151–65.

Lykes, M.B., Brabeck, M.M., Ferns, T. and Radan, A. (1993) 'Human rights and mental health among Latin American women in situations of state-sponsored violence: bibliographic resources', *Psychology of Women Quarterly*, 17: 525–44.

Lykes, M.B. and multiple co-authors (1994) *Trauma Psicosocialy adolescentes Latinoamericanos: formas de acción grupal [Psychosocial Trauma and Latinamerican Youth: Forms of Group Actions]*. Santiago, Chile: ILAS.

Maguire, P. (1987) *Doing Participatory Research: a Feminist Approach*. Amherst, MA: Center for International Education.

Martín-Baró, I. (1994) *Writings for a Liberation Psychology: Ignacio Martín-Baró* (ed. and trans. A. Aron and S. Corne). Cambridge, MA: Harvard University Press.

Melville, M. and Lykes, M.B. (1992) 'Guatemalan Indian children and the sociocultural effects of government-sponsored terrorism', *Social Science & Medicine*, 34 (5): 533–48.

Montejo, V. (1991) *The Bird Who Cleans the World and Other Mayan Fables*. Willmantic, CT: Curbstone Press.

ODHAG/Oficina de Derechos Humanos del Arzobispado de Guatemala [Office of Human Rights of the Archdiocese of Guatemala] (1998) *Nunca más: Informe proyecto interdiocesano de recuperación de la memoria histórica [Never Again: Report of the Interdiocescan Project on the Recovery of Historic Memory]* (Vols 1–5). Guatemala: ODHAG.

Parker, A. and Neal, A. (1982) *Los Ambulantes: the Itinerant Photographers of Guatemala*. Cambridge, MA: MIT Press.

Rappaport, J. (1998) 'The art of social change: community narratives as resources for individual and community identity', in X.B. Arriaga and S. Oskamp (eds), *Addressing Community Problems: Psychological Research and Interventions*. Thousand Oaks, CA/ London: Sage Publications. pp. 225–46.

Rodari, G. (1987) *La gramática de la fantasia: introducción al arte de inventar historias [The Grammar of Fantasy: Introduction to the Art of Inventing Stories]*. México: Ediciones Comamex.

Rogoff, B. (1990) *Apprenticeship in Thinking: Cognitive Development in Social Context*. New York: Cambridge University Press.

Spence, J. and Solomon, J. (1995) *What Can a Woman Do with a Camera?* London: Scarlet Press.

Stoll, D. (1993) *Between Two Armies in the Ixil Towns of Guatemala*. New York: Columbia University Press.

Ulloa, F. (1990) 'Lecture'. University of Buenos Aires, Faculty of Psychology, October.

United Nations Children's Fund (1997) *The State of the World's Children 1997*. New York: Oxford University Press.

United Nations Children's Fund (2000) *The State of the World's Children 2000*. New York: Oxford University Press. Accessible: http://www.unicef.org/

Visual Voices: 100 Photographs of Village China by the Women of Yunnan Province (1995) Yunnan, China: Yunnan People's Publishing House. (Available from Dr Caroline Wang, University of Michigan, Ann Arbor, MI, 48109.)

Vygotsky, L.S. (1986) *Thought and Language* (trans. A. Kozulin) (newly revised edition). Cambridge, MA: MIT Press. (Original translation in 1962.)

Wang, C. (1999) 'PhotoVoice: a participatory action research strategy applied to women's health', *Journal of Women's Health*, 8 (2): 185–92. See also http://www.photovoice.com/

Wang, C. and Burris, M. (1994) 'Empowerment through photo novella: portraits of participation', *Health Education Quarterly*, 21 (2): 171–86.

Wang, C., Burris, M. and Xiang, Y.P. (1996) 'Chinese village women as visual anthropologists: a participatory approach to reaching policymakers', *Social Science and Medicine*, 42 (10): 1391–400.

Wang, C., Wu, K.Y., Zhan, W.T. and Carovano, K. (1998) 'Photovoice as a participatory health promotion strategy', *Health Promotion International*, 13 (1): 75–86.

Warren, K. (1999) *Indigenous Movements and their Critics: Pan-Mayanism and Ethnic Resurgence in Guatemala*. Austin, TX: University of Texas Press.

Women of PhotoVoice/ADMI and Lykes, M.B. (in press) *Voces e Imágenes: Mujeres Maya Ixiles de Chajul/Voices and Images: Mayan Ixil Women of Chajul*. Guatemala: Magna Terra.

Worth, S. and Adair, J. (1972) *Through Navajo Eyes: an Exploration in Film Communication and Anthropology*. Bloomington, IN: Indiana University Press.

Ziller, R.C. and Smith, D.E. (1977) 'A phenomenological utilization of photographs', *Journal of Phenomenological Psychology*, 7 (2): 172–82.

Ziller, R.C., Vern, H. and Camacho de Santoya, C. (1988) 'The psychological niche of children of poverty or affluence through auto-photography', *Children's Environments Quarterly*, 5 (2): 34–9.

Zipes, J.D. (1995) *Creative Storytelling: Building Community, Changing Lives*. New York: Routledge.

26

The Art of Clinical Inquiry in Information Technology-related Change

JOE MCDONAGH AND DAVID COGHLAN

CHAPTER OUTLINE

It is well documented that large-scale investments in information technology (IT) not only fail to deliver much-promised business value but actually result in under performance and failure in a large number of cases. Such poor outcomes are due primarily to the failure of both the executive and IT communities to consider the human and organizational dimensions of IT-related change. We describe a case in which one of us worked as a clinical researcher in an IT-related change initiative working in a collaborative interventionist mode to facilitate change. The case particularly illustrates the value of clinical inquiry in fostering a more integrated approach to the introduction of IT while concurrently providing deeper knowledge concerning the role of diverse communities in shaping such change over time.

While the effective introduction of information technology (IT) into work organizations necessitates the pursuit of an integrated approach to change that concurrently attends to economic, technical, human and organizational considerations, it remains that the pursuit of such integration is inordinately difficult. On closer inquiry it emerges that this dilemma is rooted in the behavioural patterns of polarized occupational groups that have vested but divergent interests in exploiting IT. By way of attending to this dilemma this chapter identifies distinct challenges in the pursuit of integrated IT-related change and illustrates the role of clinical inquiry in addressing these challenges. In particular the art of clinical inquiry is explicated (see also Schein, Chapter 16), as are the dual roles of clinical researchers in shaping effective social action and developing robust social theory.

The Challenge of IT-related Change

Consideration of the role of information technology in contemporary work organizations is very complex. One must consider the economic, technical, human and organizational elements of organizations with respect to IT (McDonagh, 1999a). Economic issues drive both the rationale for investing in IT, the amount invested and the return on that investment. Technical issues address the design of the technical system and its capability to deliver. Human and organizational issues focus on how IT is used by individuals and teams and how it is integrated into the wider organization and managerial system (Coghlan, 1998). The distinctive challenge of IT-related change, therefore, is to integrate economic, technical, human and organizational aspects of change (McDonagh, 1999a, 1999b).

Notwithstanding this integrative challenge, it remains that most IT investment decisions are dominated by economic and technical foci (Lunt and Barclay, 1988; More, 1990). Yet, such foci are unlikely to feature prominently when IT fails to deliver, as it so often does. Technical failure, as in hardware and software, accounts for no more than 7 per cent of IT-related failure (Isaac-Henry, 1997). Many researchers bear witness to the fact that it is the human and organizational aspects of a technology that are responsible for its effects, not the economic and technical aspects (Clegg and Kemp, 1986; Hirscheim, 1985).

Given the prevalent attention to economic and technical issues in IT-related change, it is not surprising that the process of introducing IT into work organizations has posed significant challenges, frequently resulting in reports of persistent under-performance and failure (Clegg et al., 1996; Hirscheim, 1985; Tomeski and Lazarus, 1975). Clegg and others (1996) provide startling evidence to show that 40 per cent of IT projects fail or are abandoned completely, 80 per cent are delivered late and over budget, and 90 per cent fail to deliver espoused business benefits. The percentage of IT initiatives which actually deliver business value in accordance with agreed performance criteria is disappointing. Indeed, empirical research over the last three decades bears witness to the fact that outcomes from IT investment initiatives are poor with no more than 10 per cent of such initiatives delivering promised business value (McDonagh, 1999a).

As an explanation for why IT-related change has been so problematic, Schein (1992) proposes that the challenge of introducing and exploiting IT in organizations is essentially a cultural one. He argues that executive management and IT specialists, as embodied in their respective occupational communities, can be viewed as two sub-cultures, each with its own set of assumptions about the nature of information, learning and organization.

Reflecting on the diverse sub-cultures of the executive and IT communities, it is no surprise to discover that the challenge in IT-related change is frequently framed in terms of inter-community conflict. Unfortunately, this is a rather predictable outcome considering the manner in which each community addresses the introduction of IT (McDonagh, 1999a, 1999c). Each community assumes a limited perspective on the introduction of IT: executives assuming an economic focus and IT specialists a technical focus. Each community shares a predilection to design people out of rather than into systems. Similarly, each community shares a genuine lack of knowledge concerning the human and organizational aspects of IT-related change. Considering the power and influence that these communities exert on the process of introducing IT into work organizations, the task of integrated change seems daunting.

Given this cultural divergence between the executive and IT communities, the pursuit of a more collaborative approach to the introduction of IT is imperative since it enhances the prospect of a more integrated approach to the introduction of IT. Notwithstanding that, achieving such integration is inordinately difficult since the seeds of IT-related under-performance and failure are nurtured and sustained in the respective frames of reference and concerns of the executive and IT communities. We identify several distinct challenges in the pursuit of integrated IT-related change.

Diverse forms of knowledge and expertise as embodied in the executive and IT communities need to be integrated. Diverse requirements and demands that the executive and IT communities place on the process of introducing IT into work organizations need to be accommodated. Diverse bases of power and influence which the executive and IT communities mobilize to shape the introduction of IT need to be balanced. An inclusive approach to change based on principles of partnership and participation needs to be crafted. The case study that follows usefully illustrates both the challenges set out above and the manner in which they may be researched.

The Case of Sematron

Sematron (a fictitious name) is a large commercial enterprise with interests in Europe, North America and Asia. It makes extensive use of information and communication technologies (IT) and considers such technologies as pivotal to the ongoing development and operation of the enterprise's core activities. Indeed, the role of such technologies has become increasingly critical as the enterprise strives to increase both efficiency and operational throughput. Historically, the corporate IT function has been charged with delivering an integrated IT infrastructure that is capable of supporting managerial and operational activities in the enterprise at large.

In the summer of 1995, as part of an executive development programme, a group of senior managers was assigned responsibility for an IT infrastructure initiative with the intention of delivering a coherent framework for the deployment of IT systems for the following five years. The group, consisting of corporate executives, corporate IT specialists and other senior managers, met on a frequent basis in order to progress the infrastructure initiative which was one of six initiatives involving senior management as part of the executive development programme. By the spring of 1996 the IT infrastructure group was in disarray and had become bogged down in ongoing conflict and dissent between group members.

Recognizing difficulties with both group dynamics and the nature of the task being addressed, Sematron invited me[1] to act as an external process consultant to support the group in addressing both its own internal dynamics and the substantive issue of IT infrastructure. Encounters between myself and the IT infrastructure group were revealing. Several patterns of behaviour were particularly evident.

Corporate IT appeared to place little value on the views and perspectives of senior management who, it believed, was inept and incompetent at addressing IT-related issues. Corporate IT believed that it knew the most appropriate IT infrastructure for the organization and that engaging with senior management as part of the IT infrastructure group was futile since such managers were unlikely to have anything worthwhile to add. Indeed, corporate IT believed that the lack of commitment from senior management in the past was sufficient grounds for rejecting its present overtures emanating from the wider executive development programme. The delivery of a coherent infrastructure was, in the view of corporate IT, a technical challenge that it was adept at addressing. Unlike corporate IT, which was unrelenting in its views on the technical nature of IT infrastructure, senior managers were intensely frustrated at their inability significantly to influence corporate IT's approach to the development of an appropriate IT infrastructure for the future. Indeed, unlike corporate IT which spoke with a unified voice, senior management appeared to speak with a multiplicity of voices reflecting rather diverse perspectives on the nature of IT infrastructure. In the absence of clarity, corporate IT believed that it knew the most appropriate way forward as IT infrastructure was its bailiwick when all was said and done.

Corporate IT believed that the IT infrastructure initiative offered the possibility of investing in the latest information and communication technologies and in particular offered an unrivalled opportunity of introducing a seamless environment where all technical systems would be truly integrated. Such a vision was far removed from the concerns of most senior managers who complained bitterly about the lack of IT systems to support managerial and operational activities adequately. Such concerns appeared to find little favour with corporate IT since it believed that a superior technical infrastructure was an imperative prior to addressing the concerns of senior management. Indeed, corporate IT was unwilling to relent on its demands since it considered senior management as being incapable of elaborating on either its precise needs or the precise nature of IT infrastructure. Furthermore, it appeared to corporate IT that many of the demands of senior management were incongruent and that such demands reflected the personal aspirations of individual managers rather than the actual needs of the enterprise. Confronted with a diverse set of apparently conflicting demands from senior management, corporate IT was intent on championing its own cause and wilfully engaged in a process with the intent of attending primarily to the technical aspects of IT infrastructure.

Corporate IT believed that it had the legitimate right to dictate the technical aspects of the IT infrastructure. In attending to this challenge it chose to keep the IT infrastructure group in the dark and wittingly pursued a strategy that involved delivering its proposals for the future directly to the deputy chief executive with responsibility for IT. While most of the group believed that corporate IT was truly capable of subverting the group's deliberations, no one believed that corporate IT would actually outwit the group and attempt to by-pass it completely. Faced with the onslaught of a narrow, highly technocratic agenda, senior management appeared rather powerless when attempting to influence the direction of the IT infrastructure initiative. The predilection of corporate IT to focus almost exclusively on technical considerations was exceptionally problematic for senior management who appeared to have a distinct lack of IT parlance. That lack of IT parlance served progressively to weaken the influence of senior management while concurrently ostracizing its concerns in the deliberations of the IT infrastructure group. In the words of one senior manager, 'we were ill equipped to attend to the immediate challenge and naive to think that we could create the future as equal partners with corporate IT'.

The difficulties between corporate IT and senior management as outlined above were giving rise to a torturous process for the IT infrastructure group with intense distrust and suspicion between group members. Indeed, such distrust and suspicion had permeated the organization for well over two decades and was therefore nothing new for group members. Unfortunately, it all too frequently resulted in the collapse of group initiatives at Sematron with group members becoming intensely frustrated and dispirited, giving rise to apathy and ultimately rending apart both groups and their respective initiatives.

Reflection

Reflecting on the Sematron case, it emerges rather succinctly that the essential challenge for me was to help the organization while simultaneously attending to the development of robust social theory. The insight that this was action research, and in particular clinical inquiry, emerged as the change initiative unfolded. Theory development was of particular importance in this case since our understanding of the role of senior management in shaping the introduction of IT was largely underdeveloped with extant research focused almost exclusively on the roles of the chief executive officer and the chief information officer (Feeney, Edwards and Simpson, 1992; Jarvenpaa and Ives, 1991; Raghunathan and Raghunathan, 1988, 1989, 1993; Thong, Yap and Raman, 1996). Such a narrow focus precludes consideration of the possibility that other executives shape the introduction of IT.

Contributing to effective social action necessitated fostering a collaborative approach to IT-related change based on principles of partnership and participation. Of particular importance in this regard was engaging both executive management and corporate IT specialists in a deliberately crafted inclusive process that encouraged participants to shape collectively an appropriate IT infrastructure that fulfilled their diverse requirements and demands. Interestingly, such collaboration was a relatively new experience for Sematron and had rarely been applied to IT-related issues in the past.

Over time I developed a deeper understanding of the organization, its members, and its experiences with IT. From the outset I sensed that the pursuit of a more collaborative approach to the introduction of IT would be a difficult process considering the prevailing climate within the organization. That climate was permeated with intense discord and conflict both within the executive management team and between corporate IT and senior management.

In general the atmosphere was characterized by an extremely negative attitude to IT with corporate IT being perceived as 'control' freaks who would ultimately derail any initiative grounded upon principles of partnership and participation. Corporate IT was deemed to have for too long exercised what was seen to be excessive power and influence over IT-related change, resulting in the process being considered intensely political. The failure of earlier initiatives to redress this perceived imbalance of power was generally considered to be a bad omen for the future. This negative attitude was not confined to IT alone but equally extended itself to executive management. Executives were considered to be incompetent in addressing IT-related issues, having long abandoned any direct interest in matters of this nature. Similarly, many executives attracted scorn due to their unwillingness to provide adequate leadership and example.

Reflecting on the nature of the organizational climate, it was imperative that I was sensitive to the potential clash between the dominant autocratic approach to the introduction of IT and the emerging desire for a more democratic approach as espoused in the executive development programme. With this in mind I believed that the investigative approach had continuously to address a range of challenges as they were unfolding. I could see that they needed to craft a collaborative approach where executive management, IT specialists, and other senior managers could contribute simultaneously to the development of an appropriate IT infrastructure. There was a need to create space for individuals and diverse groups to express themselves freely without fear of reprisal or recrimination. Explicating past experiences with IT with a view to learning how to introduce IT with greater effect was essential. Engaging individuals and diverse groups in identifying and addressing the challenges involved in moving forward was critical. Uncovering diverse perspectives and opposing views about IT infrastructure was essential with a view to generating a shared perspective on the way forward. Ways of surfacing antagonism, bickering and hostility that had the potential to impede the development of an effective IT infrastructure were of prime importance. In short, shaping an integrative approach where the technical, human, economic and organizational aspects of IT-related change were attended to in a systemic manner was fundamental.

Addressing these challenges throughout the IT infrastructure initiative involved various interventions as described by Reddy (1994). I engaged in *cognitive-based interventions* through continuous questioning and probing both at individual and group levels. Significant energy was devoted to capturing the knowledge and expertise of individuals and groups with a view to generating shared perspectives on both the past and the way forward. I regularly utilized *activity-based interventions* at both individual and group levels and also inter-level dynamics as a way of framing past experiences and generating ideas on how to move forward (Rashford and Coghlan, 1994). For example, I set individuals and groups the task of clarifying the essential nature and scope of IT infrastructure and then reconciled individual and group differences in this regard. I used *behaviour description interventions* by describing what I had observed at both individual and group levels. At times I reflected the *emotions* or feelings observed at both individual and group levels. I attempted to make sense of observed behaviour by way of offering plausible hypotheses or *interpretations*. Such hypotheses were based on my knowledge and expertise and were intended to stimulate dialogue rather than being 'truth' in an objective or analytic sense.

The investigative skills involved in pursuing interventions of the nature outlined above were many and varied. They involved observing individuals and groups in both formal and informal settings. They involved listening intently and being willing to probe and question with a view to understanding thoroughly both what was and what was not being said. They regularly involved summarizing and challenging what was said at both individual and group levels. Beyond this it was imperative that I remained easily accessible, impartial, non-judgemental and politically astute at all times.

As the organization's trust in me increased my involvement with the organization deepened over time. This resulted in many organizational members at all levels treating me as a confidant with whom they were willing to express their deeper thoughts about the organization and its approach to the introduction and exploitation of IT among other things. This gave rise to endless fortuitous meetings in hallways, restaurants, and local hotels and taverns. Such meetings generated enormously rich data for investigative purposes.

Over time, key social actors involved in the IT infrastructure initiative increasingly recognized that the initiative would not progress without the deployment of external expertise. As my relationship with the organization deepened it offered a basis for negotiating a way forward that was acceptable to all concerned, albeit that that involved significant compromise. Senior management was particularly appreciative of the opportunity to consider the introduction of IT in a wider context that proactively embraced the organization's overarching strategic objectives while not requiring it to demonstrate a deep knowledge of IT. Similarly, corporate IT was appreciative of the opportunity to attend to the deep technical aspects of IT infrastructure in the knowledge that senior management's concerns were being adequately accommodated as part of the overall change process.

From my perspective, the key to building a deep relationship with both senior management and corporate IT lay in the development of a deep understanding of their respective differences along with a rich understanding of the organizational context in which change was being progressed. No attempt was made on my part to downplay or eliminate significant differences. Rather, the intent was to make explicit the diverse interests of key social actors while concurrently harnessing the diverse forms of knowledge and expertise that energized such differences. Indeed, the process of explicating diverse interests was frequently a private rather than public process. Once significant differences were understood by diverse social actors, the process of going public with a negotiated compromise was relatively straightforward since I was generally viewed as trustworthy, impartial and working for the common good of the organization and its members.

Ultimately, the outcome of the clinical inquiry process at Sematron was twofold. First, by way of contributing to effective social action, I brokered a political compromise that delivered significant value for both the executive and IT communities alike. The concentration on attending to strategic challenges and ensuring that investments in IT were strategically focused was of paramount importance to executive management. The concentration on an appropriate technical infrastructure was critical for IT specialists with their concentration on the proposed deployment of new computing and communications software applications and supporting hardware.

Upon reflection, the essential challenge for me when contributing to effective social action was to attend simultaneously to both the content and process of integrated change. More specifically, the key to achieving such a political compromise lay in my ability to facilitate the integration of diverse forms of knowledge and expertise that executive management and IT specialists use to shape the introduction of IT while concurrently facilitating the integration of diverse requirements and demands that executive management and IT specialists place on the process of introducing IT. It equally lay in my ability to reconcile the diverse bases of power and influence that executive management and IT specialists use to shape the introduction of IT, while simultaneously nurturing a collaborative approach to change based on principles of partnership and participation.

Secondly, by way of contributing to social theory, I was committed to gaining an understanding of the role of executive management in shaping the effective introduction of IT. By being prepared to engage with 'practitioners over things that actually matter to them' (Eden and Huxham, 1996: 526), I was able to gain insights into the behavioural patterns of executive management in IT-related organizational change, insights that are not readily forthcoming in many positivist approaches to inquiry.

The Appeal of Clinical Inquiry

Within experiential paradigms of action research, clinical inquiry has hitherto received relatively limited attention. Clinical inquiry is particularly concerned with the observation, elicitation and reporting of data which are available when the researcher is engaged by an organization to help manage change or solve some perceived problem (Schein, 1987, 1993, 1995). Its core elements are threefold. First, clinical researchers are present in the organization at the organization's behest, because the organization wants help and is therefore more likely to reveal important data. Secondly, clinical researchers are expected to intervene which allows new data about the client system to be surfaced. Thirdly, the richness of the data allows clinical researchers to develop insights into the client system.

In clinical inquiry the essential challenge for clinical researchers is to embrace concurrently the twin roles of researcher and process consultant (Gummesson, 1991; Schein, 1999). As process consultants, clinical researchers attempt 'to release the client's own resources through self-diagnosis and self-interventions' (Gummesson, 1991: 32). At the same time, because clinical researchers are working in the process consultation mode, they enable the generation of useful knowledge, of 'what really goes on in organizations' (Schein, 1993: 703).

The appropriateness of clinical inquiry to the IT infrastructure initiative at Sematron was not the product of a deliberate choice prior to the initiation of the relationship between the organization and myself. Rather, its appropriateness unfolded over time as the relationship between the organization and myself deepened with key social actors disclosing their thoughts about the organization and its experiences with IT. Upon reflection, the quality and depth of the relationship combined with my role suggested that this approach to collaborative inquiry was consistent with that espoused in clinical inquiry.

Clinical inquiry is particularly suited to IT-related organizational research. It enables inquiry and intervention into the distinct challenges we have previously identified. Clinical inquiry is capable of facilitating *the integration of diverse forms of knowledge and expertise* that executive management and IT specialists use to shape the introduction of IT. Clinical researchers proactively embrace the distinctive perspectives on IT-related change as embraced by the executive and IT communities. In essence, that involves attending to the executives' concentration on issues of strategy and organization, and more specifically to the strategic fit between the organization and its macro-economic environment. It equally involves attending to the technocratic nature of the IT specialists' role with its distinctive parlance and interest in pivotal aspects of information systems engineering. Clinical researchers' knowledge of strategy, organizational behaviour and software systems engineering enables them to understand the worldviews of the executive and IT communities and their respective influences on IT-related change.

Clinical inquiry is capable of facilitating the *integration of diverse requirements and demands* that executive management and IT specialists place on the process of introducing IT. Clinical researchers are capable of supporting the executive community by way of explicating its requirements to exploit IT in a manner that impacts positively on strategic performance and attends to the pursuit of strategic integration. Similarly, clinical researchers are capable of supporting the IT community by way of explicating its requirements for clarity in the process of information systems engineering. Indeed, the process of clinical inquiry enables the development of a shared dialogue between the executive and IT communities (Isaacs, 1999; Schein, 1999).

Clinical inquiry is capable of *reconciling the diverse bases of power and influence* that executive management and IT specialists use to shape the introduction of IT. Clinical researchers embrace the role of negotiator when addressing this distinctive challenge. Inevitably, this may involve significant compromise for both the executive and IT communities alike, since addressing the collective requirements and demands of both communities may not be feasible when all known constraints on change are accounted for. Clinical researchers rightfully recognize the diverse bases of power and influence and seek to negotiate a way forward that delivers added value to both communities and is deemed acceptable to them. Clinical researchers do not take sides between conflicting groups, rather they build a trusting relationship with all parties so that they can act as brokers of inquiry, co-operation and compromise (Kakabadse, 1984).

Clinical inquiry is capable of *nurturing a collaborative approach to change* based on principles of partnership and participation. Recognizing the rightful place of diverse forms of knowledge and expertise along with diverse requirements and demands, clinical researchers proactively cultivate a collaborative approach to change that accommodates the political realities of organizational life. Indeed, this is accomplished in a manner that attends to the introduction of IT in an integrated manner, concurrently attending to economic, technical, human and organizational considerations (McDonagh, 1999a, 1999b).

The clinical approach to IT-related change offers unrivalled opportunities for gaining deep insights into the complex nature of such change. More particularly, such insights arise from attempts to integrate different forms of knowledge and expertise, attempts to integrate diverse requirements and demands, attempts to reconcile diverse bases of power and influence, attempts to craft a collaborative approach to change and, finally, the role of clinical researcher as a hired facilitator of change.

From the Sematron case we can extrapolate and affirm some generalizations which, confirm the diverse nature of both the executive and IT communities, confirm the political nature of IT-related change, and account for the complex and multifaceted nature of IT-related change.

In summary, clinical inquiry affords researchers the opportunity to develop insider knowledge of organizations (Evered and Louis, 1981). By being invited to help the organization to manage change or solve some perceived problem, clinical researchers are privileged with an intimate knowledge of what really goes on in organizations. Through their interventions, this knowledge unfolds as outcomes are studied and further interventions are planned and implemented. In the case of IT-related change, where the cognition and power of diverse occupational groups create complex organizational dynamics, clinical inquiry offers valuable, if not essential, opportunities for both the effective management of change and the generation and dissemination of important and useful organizational knowledge and theory.

The Sematron case study set out in this chapter represents a small part of a more comprehensive and detailed longitudinal case study of IT-related change that provides a retrospective account of change between 1970 and 1993 and a real-time account of change between 1995 and 1998 (McDonagh, 1999a). The use of clinical inquiry in IT-related change at Sematron provided rich and deep insights into the role of executive management in shaping strategic change over time.

Note

1 Joe McDonagh was invited to act as process consultant on the basis of his past experience with both IT and Sematron.

References

Clegg, C.W. and Kemp, N. (1986) 'Information technology: personnel, where are you?', *British Journal of Psychology*, 85: 449–77.

Clegg, C.W., Axtell, C., Damodaran, L., Farbey, B., Hull, R., Lloyd-Jones, R., Nicolls, J., Sells, R., Tomlinson, C., Ainger, A. and Stewart, T. (1996) 'The performance of information technology and the role of human and organizational factors'. Report to the Economic and Social Research Council, UK.

Coghlan, D. (1998) 'The interlevel dynamics of information technology', *Journal of Information Technology*, 13 (2): 139–49.

Eden, C. and Huxham, C. (1996) 'Action research for the study of organisations', in S. Clegg, C. Hardy and W.R. Nord (eds), *Handbook of Organizational Studies*. Thousand Oaks, CA: Sage Publications. pp. 526–42.

Evered, R. and Louis, M.R. (1981) 'Alternative perspectives in the organizational sciences: "Inquiry from the inside" and "inquiry from the outside"', *Academy of Management Review*, 6 (3): 385–95.

Feeney, D.F., Edwards, B.R. and Simpson, K.M. (1992) 'Understanding the CEO/CIO relationship', *MIS Quarterly*, December: 435–47.

Gummesson, E. (1991) *Qualitative Methods in Management Research*. Thousand Oaks, CA: Sage Publications.

Hirscheim, R. (1985) *Office Automation: a Social and Organizational Perspective*. Chichester, UK: Wiley.

Isaac-Henry, K. (1997) 'Management of information technology in the public sector', in K. Isaac-Henry, C. Painter and C. Barnes (eds), *Management in the Public Sector: Challenges and Change*. London: Thomson. pp. 131–59.

Isaacs, W. (1999) *Dialogue and the Art of Thinking Together: a Pioneering Approach to Communicating in Business and in Life*. New York: Bantam.

Jarvenpaa, S.L. and Ives, B. (1991) 'Executive involvement and participation in the management of information technology', *MIS Quarterly*, June: 205–27.

Kakabadse, A. (1984) 'Politics of a process consultant', in A. Kakabadse and C. Parker (eds), *Power, Politics and Organizations: a Behavioural Science View*. Chichester, UK: Wiley. pp. 160–83.

Lunt, P.J. and Barclay, I. (1988) 'The importance of organizational considerations for the implementation of information technology', *Journal of Information Technology*, 3 (4): 244–50.

McDonagh, J. (1999a) 'Exploring the role of executive management in shaping strategic change: the case of information technology', PhD dissertation, University of Warwick, England.

McDonagh, J. (1999b) 'Addressing the enduring dilemma with IT: the role of action-oriented inquiry', Fifth American Conference on Information Systems, Milwaukee, Winsconsin, 13–15 August, 698–700.

McDonagh, J. (1999c) 'When information technology fails to deliver: the role of occupational groups', Annual Conference of the British Academy of Management, Manchester Metropolitan University, Manchester, England, 1–3 September, 691–703.

More, E. (1990) 'Information systems: people issues', *Journal of Information Science*, 16: 311–20.

Raghunathan, B. and Raghunathan, T.S. (1988) 'Impact of top management support on IS planning', *Journal of Information Systems*, 2 (2): 15–23.

Raghunathan, B. and Raghunathan, T.S. (1989) 'Relationship of the rank of information systems executive to the organisational role and planning dimensions of information systems', *Journal of Management Information Systems*, 6 (1): 111–26.

Raghunathan, B. and Raghunathan, T.S. (1993) 'Does the reporting level of the information systems executive make a difference?', *Journal of Strategic Information Systems*, 2 (1): 27–38.

Rashford, N.S. and Coghlan, D. (1994) *The Dynamics of Organisational Levels: a Change Framework for Managers and Consultants*. Reading, MA: Addison Wesley.

Reddy, W.B. (1994) *Intervention Skills: Process Consultation for Small Groups and Teams*. San Diego, CA: Pfeiffer.

Schein, E.H. (1987) *The Clinical Perspective in Fieldwork*. Thousand Oaks, CA: Sage Publications.

Schein, E.H. (1992) *Organizational Culture and Leadership* (second edition). San Francisco, CA: Jossey-Bass.

Schein, E.H. (1993) 'Legitimating clinical research in the study of organizational culture', *Journal of Counseling & Development*, 71: 703–8.

Schein, E.H. (1995) 'Process consultation, action research and clinical inquiry: are they the same?', *Journal of Managerial Psychology*, 13 (6): 14–19.

Schein, E.H. (1999) *Process Consultation Revisited: Building the Helping Relationship*. Reading, MA: Addison Wesley.

Thong, J.Y.L., Yap, C. and Raman, K.S. (1996) 'Top management support, external expertise and information systems implementation in small businesses', *Information Systems Research*, 7 (2): 248–67.

Tomeski, E. and Lazarus, H. (1975) *People-oriented Computer Systems: the Computer in Crisis*. New York: Van Nostrand.

27

Participatory Action Research in Southern Tanzania, with Special Reference to Women

MARJA-LIISA SWANTZ, ELIZABETH NDEDYA AND MWAJUMA SAIDDY MASAIGANAH

CHAPTER OUTLINE

The two cases in this chapter are part of a large rural development programme in which participatory principles have been applied within administrative practice and extension work in southern Tanzania. Participation has provided an environment of continuity in the local context in which participatory action research (PAR) has become people's tool for reflection and action. The first case illustrates how development workers apply PAR with a women's group. It leads the women to make a simple analysis of their own economic situation and to decide to acquire credit for brick production. In the second case, fishing communities struggle to engage the authorities in a fight against dynamite fishing. They have adopted participation as a tool for resistance against indifferent or corrupt authorities, thus creating space for their own initiatives in an environmental struggle.

The cases presented in this chapter are part of a large rural development programme in which participatory principles have been applied as part of the administrative practice and extension work in Mtwara and Lindi regions in southern Tanzania. Participation as an agreed principle has provided an environment of continuity in the local context in which participatory action research (PAR) has become people's tool for reflection and action.

PAR has a 30-year history in Tanzania. After independence, the country had adopted a political programme which aimed at people's participation in their own development (*Arusha Declaration*, 1977; Nyerere, 1968: 106–44). Initially, PAR was developed in support of the national politics based on *ujamaa* socialism. It was applied in extensive action research projects which aimed at supporting rural development in the midst of radical restructuring of rural areas, with negative effects on the rural population (Swantz, 1973, 1975a, 1975b; Swantz and Jerman, 1977).

In practice, participatory principles were not implemented in the country's political programme as initially intended, but the articulated rhetoric of 'people's participation in their own development' familiarized leaders as well as commoners with the language of participation. This is an asset today, when PAR is being implemented in a different political context.

PAR was initially developed in close co-operation with the university departments in Dar Es Salaam, but it did not become a generally applied approach within the universities of Tanzania. Social sciences followed closely the models taken from Western academies and they did not include methodology for action research (AR), still less for PAR; consequently, the teachers did not risk adopting it into their teaching of research methodology. Within the externally supported development projects, development was conceived mainly as a technical and economic process. To no one's surprise, they were not ready to adopt participation as a determining concept. After three decades of disappointing results, the so-called 'donor' agencies were ready to experiment with participatory approaches on a small scale and, finally, towards the end of the 1990s to include them as a basic requirement for development assistance projects. Participation became a slogan after the donor flagship, the World Bank, started promoting it.

In a small way, the two women's projects described in this chapter illustrate larger issues in the present phase of developing PAR. On the one hand, participation has, at least rhetorically, become part of the implementation of development programmes based on people's own planning. The first case illustrates this acceptance on the part of development officers and represents one way of assisting people to make their own simple analysis of their own situation. On the other hand, villagers have adopted participation as a tool for resistance against indifferent or corrupt authorities. They have created space for their own initiatives in the struggle for their own rights. The second case is an example of this.

In the small women's group, where women were trying to find a way for self-support, the district leaders and technical staff were in support of the participatory approach. The second case is about inappropriate fishing practices, specifically the use of dynamite in fishing, which was of much concern to fisherfolk because of the damage and injury it caused. However, the authorities placed total blame for this practice on the fisherfolk, thereby covering their own neglect to take action. No one could be unaware of what was happening since frequent explosions could be heard by all. The fishing communities knew that relatively few, mainly young fishermen, were able to get hold of dynamite from the protected stores, and drew their own conclusions that there was corruption within the government circles. PAR made it possible for the fishing communities to come out into the open with their suspicions, to organise themselves and bring about effective government action against dynamiting. Women's struggle was part of the larger movement, but in addition, they had their own problems to analyse.

The two women's projects are small flashes of how a participatory environment induces women's active involvement in an analysis of their own situation and how the public exposure of women enables them to take part in consequent planning and implementation. It is highly significant that they make their analysis and planning within a participatory administrative practice which the women, their facilitators, as well as the village leaders and government officials, have adopted – or are in the process of learning. This takes place in the context of a systematic application of participatory methods, derived initially from the Participatory Rural Appraisal (PRA) and applied with active support from the highest regional authority. These tools have been adapted and further developed in local and district planning. In a hierarchical, bureaucratic system the support from higher authorities is a necessity if participation is to become a general approach.

The long-time use of participatory action research in various programmes and projects and the promotion of participatory philosophy in general in Tanzania must be seen as significant background factors leading to the present participatory development. Encouraged by the experience in the south, the President of the Republic, himself originating from Mtwara region, initiated a process of spreading the participatory approach and tools to all the ministries. The Permanent Secretaries of all the ministries holding workshops were involved in PRA training in which the Regional Commissioners from the southern regions and Tanzanian and foreign participatory facilitators, including agricultural and planning officers versed in participatory methods, introduced to them the participatory principles.[1]

Involvement of the highest level of the ministerial, district and regional personnel in participatory principles and tools opens a door to participatory analysis and long-term political development. It facilitates a co-operative exploration of participants from different levels into issues introduced by either side. It also reveals the extent to which participation can work as a political country-wide, operational principle. This operational experience of participation as an integral part of the government administration and extension work in two regions, applied in programmes, projects and organizations initiated by citizens, offers a wide, still largely unused opportunity, to research the political, operational and theoretical implications connected with the use of the participatory principle and participatory research as part of it. The new six-year phase at present starting offers an opportunity for an extensive participatory assessment of the extent to which it is possible to apply PAR as an integral part of the local government reform programme, which in recent years has been encouraged in Tanzania as well as in other developing countries by the governments and external agencies alike.

In the south-eastern regions, participation, as the ruling principle in the development programme and people's own PAR as part of it, has been facilitated by the Rural Integrated Project Support (RIPS) programme, supported at present for the seventh year by the Finnish development agency.[2] It is a multi-sectoral programme with a broad perspective, with no direct involvement in running projects. It is based on an ongoing learning process through analysis and action in implementing bottom-up participatory development. The government policies meet locally developed initiatives half-way. In this kind of a climate people have been facilitated to do their own research and analysis but other researchers have also conducted environmental and social research in cooperation with the population making use of a variety of research methods acceptable to all the participants. Self-analysis in groups is part of a larger AR process in which action takes preference over reports and written plans. Media has also been used in the form of self-conducted radio programmes and videos taken in support of the quest for people's, especially women's, rights and opportunities.

I itemize briefly the main components which I see to be prerequisites to adequate and appropriate application of successful participatory action research in the context of rural development:

- Commitment to a long-term process by different participants.
- A context in which participation becomes an accepted and practised political principle for analysis, planning and action in local government.
- An allowance for multi-dimensional development which requires a multidisciplinary approach to PAR and incorporates people's own analysis and research.
- Concession that people's participation in the transformation of their own life situation is likely to involve them in a political process.
- The understanding that methods used in introducing a participatory process, such as PRA tools, are to be only initial tools in a continuing participatory process, of which research is part.
- The understanding that no research should be allowed to use approaches and methods which conflict with participatory principles, even if all the research conducted in the research area needs not to be participatory to the same extent. All researchers and actors must conceive themselves to be part of the larger participatory process which facilitates their presence in the communities, even if they use hard science methods. They should recruit their local partners in the participatory mode.

Participatory Research to Explore Women's Potential for Credit: a Case Study of Muungano Women's Group, Ruangwa, Tanzania (*Elizabeth Ndedya, Mtwara*)

Background and objective

This case study of Muungano Women's Group in Ruangwa district of Lindi region presents a situation where a participatory analysis was used with members of a women's group to enable them to access credit. The women decided to initiate group activities to generate income for themselves and their families. They found brick-making to be most profitable of the village activities and decided to go for it, although culturally brick-making in this area was a men's activity.

Many times when money was available for lending to the women for their economic activities, the system was that the technical staff prepared all the groundwork on behalf of the women. This included writing up project proposals, prioritization and decision-making. Even the applications were made on the women's behalf. Generally this meant deciding on the size and kind of credit on the women's behalf. This was the result of a deep-rooted belief, to a certain extent also a fact, that women are poor, often illiterate and ignorant about administrative procedures. Leaders who have been educated to believe that only knowledge based on higher education is valid did not think that simple women could do these things on their own. In such situations women have received services which were not relevant to their situation, simply because somebody decided that this was what they needed. In some cases women have been given larger loans, which they cannot pay back, as solutions to their problems, when what they needed was just information and advice. Therefore this participatory analysis was carried out with the women to enable them to make an exploration of the potential opportunities and constraints and to take the decisions themselves whether or not to apply for credit for carrying out economic activities.

One of the rural facilitators to this participatory analysis was working with the Rural Integrated Project Support (RIPS) programme, the other one was a community development officer. The purpose of the RIPS programme is to strengthen both formal and informal rural institutions to empower the poor, men and women, young and old. Therefore, one of the roles of RIPS facilitators is to assist different groups of people, men, women and youths within communities, in using participatory methods to analyse their development situations and come up with development plans for implementation.

In this case study, facilitators on their regular field tours were asked by the community development officer to visit Ruangwa village. First they met the village community development and extension officers, who later took them to the village leaders. After a few words of introduction, the extension officers, together with the village leaders, organized a discussion between the women's group and the visiting team. This informal meeting was held at the premises where the women carry out their activities. The visiting team was able to meet with four group members during the discussion.

Methodology

The women went through the whole process of analysis of their own issues with the facilitators. This was an occasion of mutual learning by doing, the women were able democratically to prioritize their activities and use the information generated during the exercise for making decisions to set out and plan further their activity and learn to budget for it. By the end of the day they were able to discover their opportunities, assess their potential for carrying out their project using credits and also identify the kind of service they needed. The whole process consisted of the following steps:

1 Building rapport

Before the actual work began, the facilitators had to build rapport with the group members so that they would understand that the visitors had not come to tell the women what to do and how. This is a crucial step so that what follows does not slip into the traditional hierarchical community development procedure of people passively listening and nominally accepting what the community developers have to say. First, all those present were seated informally on the ground and all, including the facilitators, introduced themselves by saying their names and a few words about their families and everyday life, mentioning also their educational background.

The first member to introduce herself was Hakika Mkupa, who was the group leader. Hakika had completed seven years of primary education, was married and had three children. Then Haiti Libudi said she had completed four standards, was married and had five children. They were followed by Maudi Kaojoa who was a widow with two children and had not been to school. The last woman to introduce herself was Hadija Mathayo. She had completed primary education and was married with two children.

2 Analysis

Hakika Mkupa, as the leader of the group, told us that their group was initiated in 1994. The idea came from the members themselves who were by then six in number. After they had discovered that generating income by carrying out economic activities alone was difficult, they wanted to try to do it in a group, which was also encouraged by the community development officers.

Hakika told the facilitators that they had discussed among themselves what the most profitable activity would be in their village. After some discussion, they reached a consensus that brick-making would be best and they decided to go for it, even though they did not have the required expertise. It did not worry them so much, since there were youth in the village who had been making bricks and earning good income. This was an opportunity for them. They approached the youths and requested training in brick-making, which the youths agreed to do on free terms. After the training, another problem cropped up: they did not have tools to work with. The youths even volunteered to lend them their tools.

Hakika went on to explain that during the first year, 1994, they were able to make 5,000 bricks which they sold at 15 TSh each. They realized 75,000 TSh which was shared among themselves. Asked by the facilitators why they did not use this money to solve the problem of working tools, Hakika said the women badly needed the money to solve family issues.

The following year no bricks were made. According to Hakika, no bricks were made because there were only three members committed to group activities, one member simply dropped out saying she could not continue with brick-making because she found it to be tedious work. Another member fell sick during the brick-making season and a third member was mourning for her husband who had passed way. The three remaining members thought that without their friends they could not make bricks. When the rainy season came, Hakika went on, the three members decided to divert from brick-making to agriculture and cultivated one and a half acres of maize. The facilitators wanted to know why they opted for cultivating maize. In response to that, Hakika said tilling the land is something they have learnt since their childhood, it is something that one can do even by herself. The maize field did not earn them anything because the planted maize seeds were eaten by rodents and no replanting was done.

In 1996, the group with four members decided to resume the brick-making project. This decision was made after realizing that the price for one brick had gone up to 30 TSh. And this is when the facilitators met them. They had already set up a target of making 600 bricks.

3 Further analysis and generation of issues

Hakika, assisted by her colleagues, told the facilitators that their group started with nothing in terms of money but banked on their energy. Therefore working tools was their major constraint. As a result they were again forced to borrow working tools from the youth, this time on the condition that they make bricks for the youth. The women complained that their project created a big gender issue because everybody in the village laughed at them saying 'brick-making is for men'. This could be one of the reasons why there was a poor attendance during brick-making days.

Record-keeping was another constraint which was not directly mentioned by the group. As the individual members were interviewed by the team, they realized that they could not remember details about their group activity because they depended on their memories, most of the useful information was forgotten.

Table 27.1 *Assessing the needs*

Issue	Respondent 1	Respondent 2	Respondent 3	Score	Rank	Priority	Activity flow ranking
Lack of working tools	000	00000	0000	12	2	2	3
Poor attendance	0	000	0000	8	4	4	4
Lack of capital	000000 00000	000000	0000 0000	25	1	1	1
Demoralization/ sex abuse	00	00	00	6	5	5	4
Inadequate record-keeping	000	0000	00	9	3	3	2

Ranking of the issues

During this part of the analysis, the role of the facilitators was to assist the women to set out their priorities so that they dealt with one constraining issue at a time. The idea of using participatory rural appraisal tools for ranking was introduced by the facilitators, in order to make the discussion more visible and enable the women to see clearly their situation. At this point a matrix was drawn on the ground and used to rank the constraining issues. Three out of the four members were provided with 20 stones each and were asked to rank the constraints according to their individual opinion and without consulting one another draw the results in the matrix table on the ground. The results are shown in Table 27.1.

Analysis by the respondents

After the individual ranking was completed, the facilitators' role was to assist the women to reach a consensus. They asked each of the three respondents to explain to the others why they had ranked the items in the way they had. All the respondents were given a chance to explain their scoring. As the Table 27.1 shows, there were no great discrepancies. All three women said that the main problem was capital. They scored lower for tools because they could be bought once there was capital. Attendance was an issue, but would be improved if there was capital.

The first woman believed in commitment of few members rather than having many non-committed members. This first respondent scored higher for capital (11) than others because she thought with good initial capital a lot of problems would be solved. Tools could be bought, motivation would be high and it would influence attendance and none of the members will respond to the abusing words because then they will be earning more money. The second woman thought that when the group performs better and earns more it will attract other women to form groups and this will end the abuse by men. The third respondent said that working tools was not a big issue for her because they could continue borrowing them from the youths. If they had the capital, then they could buy the working tools and attendance would improve. A lot of activities would be carried out and the training on record-keeping would be meaningful because then there would be a lot of things to record.

In the discussion afterwards it became clear that they all believed the record-keeping was a constraint to them. If they were to continue, then it would not be possible for them to keep all the information about their group in their heads. 'Please train us', they all said finishing their analysis.

This analysis of the matrix was later followed by a general discussion by all the members. The discussion was very long, with facilitators chipping in when necessary. In the beginning the members thought that capital was their main constraint. As the discussion went on, they discovered that the two constraints on the matrix (lack of capital and lack of working tools) in principle were really the same thing. Basically, they needed money and working tools were what they were going to spend the money on. So they all agreed to work straight on the lack of working tools. At this point they even noted how they were being exploited by the youths when they had to make bricks for them in order to borrow their working tools. They also reached the consensus about their need for training on record-keeping. They realized that lack of this skill made them count the bricks each time they wanted to know how many bricks they had sold. They had never kept records nor did they know what records to keep and how to do it.

Table 27.2 *Estimating the costs*

Working tools	Number required	Cost per item	Total cost
Buckets	4	4,000/=	16,000/=
Hand hoes (big size)	4	2,000/=	8,000/=
Timber	4	3,000/=	12,000/=
Big knives	4	2,000/=	8,000/=
Spades	2	5,000/=	10,000/=
Transport moulds	2	5,000/=	10,000/=
Total			64,000/=

5 Planning and decision-making

With assistance from the facilitators the women worked out how much money was required to purchase the working tools. The outcome is shown in Table 27.2. Working out the budget together was an important exercise. After this budget was completed, the facilitators assisted the women to identify the source this money would come from. They asked them a set of questions in order to find out whether they were able to raise this amount of money or not. They did not respond to these questions immediately, but discussed among themselves in their local language. After a very short discussion Maudi, on behalf of the others, said, 'We do not have any savings; where to take the money from? We are going to ask for a loan.'

The fact that the women went straight for loans did not impress the facilitators. As mentioned earlier, loans sometimes become a burden. They wanted to know for sure if the women really were not able to raise the needed money. The women identified their other sources of income. They mentioned agriculture, sales from local brew and sales of their labour, but they did not think that the income from these sources would allow them to make any savings and sometimes it was not enough even for their daily needs. The facilitators continued to explore whether there were any traditional systems for borrowing money. According to the women, these systems used to be there but due to changes in the society, they no longer worked because people had lost trust in one another. Therefore after this discussion the facilitators agreed with them that they would go for a loan.

The next step was to identify the lending institutions and see whether the women could access them. They were aware that some banks provided an opportunity for women to access credits but were ignorant of the procedures. They asked the village Community Development Officer (CDO) to lead them through the loan process. According to them, the CDO had been working very closely with them and they commended her for the good job she was doing to create awareness on important issues like explaining to them the importance of forming groups and encouraging them to ignore the abuse by men. Here the CDO chipped in, 'If you want me to assist you to access credit you must first assure me that you will pay it back and think through how you are going to do it.' Hakika, their leader, said, 'We now know how much we need for purchasing the working tools, therefore we will make sure that we reach our target to produce 600 bricks. If we sell them at 30 shillings each, we will be able to repay and have something left over for ourselves.' It was agreed that the CDO would assist the women to access credit and she promised to train them in record-keeping.

Lessons gained

This small case study helps us to see that if women are assisted to do this kind of simple analysis, they are capable of sharing their experience and can develop a better understanding of the kind of support and service they need. Often their lack of self-confidence arises from very little things which community workers overlook both in their training and in exhorting the women to do something. For this reason, it is important that training and analysis go hand in hand with practical action. The case also shows the importance of training the workers in a participatory way in action. Women often lack the organizational ability or knowledge to plan their income-earning projects in such a way that they have continuity. The whole process is first of all about equality, believing in the women and giving them their chance, treating them as adult, mature people. People who act as advisors or facilitators, whether ordinary planners or community workers of different categories, need to learn simple, concrete ways of working in a participatory manner with people, facilitating analysis which can grow into important research in co-operation with researchers and institutions specializing in participatory research. The right kind of communication guides women to use their knowledge and to acquire new skills, it empowers them and creates a new kind of awareness.

Participatory Action Research, Analysis and Planning with Women in Fishing Communities *(Mwajuma Saiddy Masaiganah, Bagamoyo)*

Background

Fisherwomen have been active participants in action research and analysis for the improvement of their own livelihood systems in south-eastern Tanzania. In 1993, RIPS (Rural Integrated Project Support programme), in collaboration with FTP (Forest Trees and People) programme, conducted participatory training for selected district and regional staff of the two regions in six villages of Mtwara District. This was part of the participatory planning phase for the long-term co-operation of RIPS with the districts in the two south-eastern regions. I had recently joined the programme and could bring into it my experience from the earlier participatory research projects in which I had participated.

Analysis of problems

When villagers analysed their problems and resources using and modifying participatory rural appraisal (PRA) tools in Msangamkuu fishing village, a peninsula jutting into the Indian Ocean, they brought up as the major problem the diminishing size of the catches. They credited to the degrading conditions of the marine environment caused by intensive dynamite fishing. Other fishing villages later came up with the same problem. The fishermen were forced to go to far away waters in search of fish. The method particularly useful for analysis was the ranking of problems. Participants divided into several small groups and mentioned their problems which were then written on small cards and placed in matrices of large squares drawn on the ground. Twenty large seeds were distributed to one in each group. They were divided in the proportion suggested by the participants in the group into the squares indicating problems. The squares with seeds were then ranked according to the numbers of seeds in each of them. The causes of the problems were then also ranked in the similar manner. The exercise can continue with aspects which the participants bring up and consider relevant. An important aspect that arose was who in the village participated in what kind of fishing and on what basis. An examination of this aspect revealed the small share of the youth in the resources needed for fishing. Women were given the sticks to do the drawing and they explained the reasons why the seeds were put in the places they were. The women were also asked to do a separate exercise, depending on the number of people present and the felt need for a specific women's analysis.

What highlighted the effects of the problem most was the *mobility map* drawn by the group of fishermen from Msangamkuu. It showed that they went as far as to Mozambican islands in the south and the northern part of Tanzania to do the fishing. The discussions that followed were a key to the long process which resulted in electing a committee and finally in the founding of the *Shirikisho*, meaning Confederation of fisherfolk in coastal villages.

After ranking the causes and effects of the problems, dynamite fishing was seen to be the worst cause of reduced catches. Men dynamite in the area openly, not caring the least who is around. This practice was done mostly by young men who seemed to be desperate because they did not own any fishing gear and got their catches by diving for reef fish. Some of these young men were used by wealthy boat-owners in the villages, who let them use their boats to do fishing for them and who gave them dividends. The youngsters also said openly that they used dynamite because they could get money more easily than practising normal fishing. Yet they blamed the government for not making the gear available at affordable prices and for not taking strict measures for the safe-keeping of the dynamite.

All the villagers blamed the 'big shots', '*wakubwa*', who own boats without gear but are well equipped with chill boxes and sometimes with weapons like guns, and provide dynamite as a means of fishing. They claimed that there were men who provide the villagers with dynamite in the villages and who collect the fish. When the chill boxes are full they distribute or sell the remaining dynamite to the villagers. The villagers elaborated these stories, saying that there was no way the villagers could get the well-guarded supplies of dynamite, intended for public works like road building, unless people in the government machinery were involved.

Women affected

Misete near Mtwara town was one of the villages in which participatory training was conducted. It became very clear that fisherwomen there were affected even more than the men. They were not only confronted with dynamiting but also faced another problem which particularly affected them as women. Because of the degrading seabeds, men had started fishing with small meshed nets along the shores, catching even the juvenile fish in the waters which earlier were left for women's fishing. Women were bitter because women's fishing was done wading on foot in the waters close to the shore while the men used boats which women could not afford. They called for government action because fish was scarce as the result of illegal practices. It rendered women jobless and robbed them of their main source of cash income and daily source for food. One woman put it into words:

> Men fish in our waters, women's waters, waistline waters. They use boats and we go by our feet. We do not fish at night, only day time because we do not have fishing lights, we cannot afford them. If we had fishing lights, we could do wonders at night.

In January 1994, RIPS supported a workshop in one of the fishing villages, Sudi, in order to give the fishermen and women in the individual coastal villages an opportunity to analyse their problem in a broader perspective. Two representatives were invited from each of the 12 villages. Only one village, Misete, sent a woman. The participants did a thorough analysis of the problems, the causes of the degradation of livelihood and the environment, and the opportunities and ways available for going forward in their villages. The participants composed a Sudi Declaration, *Azimio la Sudi*, condemning the illegal practice of dynamiting, and a Sudi Committee was formed. Sudi is a Swahili word meaning 'pride, good luck'. The name was given to the village by one Arab trader who visited the area during the colonial times, stayed there for a while, built a mosque and conducted prayers, and then planted a coconut tree in front of the mosque. In appreciation of the good people in that village, he said that '*hii ndiyo sudi yangu*', 'this is my only pride, the only good luck I have had'.

A documentary video was made of all the discussions and proceedings, and visits to the scenes of action by the staff of the Mtwara Media Center. The Sudi Committee could make use of it in their effort to influence the villages by using the video. They assisted in creating environment committees in almost all the coastal villages in Mtwara, Lindi and Kilwa districts for the implementation of the tasks listed in the Sudi Declaration. As the process continued, the committee members visited villages and gathered from fishermen and women systematic information on the situation, which gave added value to their own voices.

Outcome of Sudi Declaration and the women's cry, 'Not in our sea'

After eight months I made a follow-up visit to the active participants in each village, looking at the effect of the Declaration and people's reaction to the Committee members' own research of the situation. We found out that the dynamiting had gone down during the first months after the workshop because people feared that action might be taken by the government. After they realized that no action followed, dynamiting increased again. The Sudi Committee decided to travel to Dar Es Salaam and Zanzibar in the autumn of 1994 to visit the Attorney General, the Minister of Natural Resources and Tourism and the Director of Fisheries, the Minister of Work of the mainland and the corresponding offices in Zanzibar. The committee showed the video they had made and told of the results of their own research. They also visited Chwaka village in Zanzibar where they discussed environmental issues with the fisherwomen and men. This visit was important because we could see how they had turned to seaweed farming due to fish scarcity as a result of environmental destruction. The trip was successful in creating greater awareness among the leaders, yet it failed to bring about any results since, on returning home, no change was seen in spite of all the promises the officers had made. The dynamiters increased the speed of dynamiting and the availability of dynamite was like buying cheap sweets in a street shop.

During this period, two villagers, one youth of 25 years with a wife and two small children and another man with two wives and ten children, were victims of dynamiting, the former having both legs and the latter one arm amputated. As a result, more women became concerned that this might happen to their men and families and cause their livelihood systems to be disturbed. Women showed their discontent of the use of dynamite. In words of a woman in Misete: 'When they come to blast here, we tell them we don't want them here. Go to Pemba or Mikindani but here you cannot come, not in our sea.'

The video, showing also the affected victims and women fishing with small catches, got its name from this woman's words: '*Bahari yetu, hatutaki*', 'Our sea, we do not want'. From this point on women were hand in hand with men in the committees in the efforts to stop dynamite fishing. They said, 'Men rob us of our fish by fishing in our waters, they really rob us totally and leave us with nothing at all'.

We can see from the discussion above that dynamiters included both insiders and outsiders, coming from nearby villages and from distant places like Dar Es Salaam. They travelled a long way to the south because this was the only place with plenty of fish. The women in Misete did not want the young men who came from other villages to come.

Other efforts were made to find alternatives for the fishing communities, yet maintaining their touch with the sea. Such was a seaweed farming project in pilot villages. A woman marine biologist from the Marine Biology Institute in Zanzibar, who was specializing in seaweed farming, was called. With her, women's groups walked into the sea at low tide surveying the seabed for the suitability for seaweed-growing and learning from her to recognize what conditions were needed for the seedlings to flourish. They began to plant seaweed and became actively involved first in selling seedlings and later selling seaweed for the export trade. This gave the women promising prospects for alternative ways of earning income. In return for payments from selling seaweed, women could get credit to buy shrimp fishing nets and thereby keep in fishing business which was what they really wanted.

Evaluation workshop: attitude and policy changes

In December 1996, after realizing that their efforts had not brought the results they had hoped, the Sudi Committee decided to conduct an evaluation workshop and asked RIPS to support it. This time the Committee invited to the workshop an equal number of men and women from all the coastal villages in the three districts of Mtwara, Lindi and Kilwa, all the district and regional officials from the Natural Resources and Fishing Departments, all District Council chairpersons and their secretaries, the Members of Parliament from the coastal constituencies, the Marine Police and the District and Regional Police Commanders. The marine research component was brought in by Frontier Tanzania Ltd., an organization doing sea exploration in co-operation with RIPS and involved in giving the villages quantitative data. The qualitative information had been gathered by the villagers themselves with some guidance from us, who were involved in recording the study results. A Frontier Tanzania representative showed audio visuals, and told participants that in Mnazi Bay alone they could record 144 blasts in one day. The pictures gave evidence of the degrading seabed/coral reef and it caused grave concern. Some participants were given a chance to go out and use an underwater video camera to see the reef and to compare corals suffering from blasting with a virgin reef.

During the process, women shared their views equally with men, and their determination was quite astounding which was new to men in fishing communities. The findings showed that the Sudi Committee and the villagers had done a good job, but there had been little or no co-operation from the government organs. In particular, the judiciary and the police were given zero ranking on the elimination of corruption which, according to both women and men, played a big role in explaining why the efforts of arresting transgressors were to no avail. Women and men made their assessments separately.

The birth of a Confederation and struggle for the participation of the higher authorities

I list here a few of the decisions made by the workshop to step up their activities. It was agreed that gender and age were to be considered in electing Committee members. As a consequence, one older member was replaced and six new members were elected to the Committee. In addition to the Sudi Declaration it was decided to establish a Southern Zone Confederation on Environmental Protection and to register it with the authorities to make its work stronger and enable it to operate independently. The registration was completed in 1997. It was also decided that a delegation would go to the Parliament and to see the Prime Minister to air their discontent.

I went to Dodoma with this delegation of five, as the second woman. During the discussions with the Prime Minister and some Members of Parliament the MPs from the total Southern Zone went, with one voice, on record to fight the issue and the issue was then discussed in depth. The woman minister and elected Member of Parliament from Masasi in Mtwara region finally expressed herself in the following words:

> If we had followed the process of creating awareness of our people, and if the government had listened and done its part, we would not be crying now the El Nino effects. Awareness could have been created among our people and the destruction of the environment could have been arrested. To blame the El Nino effect is due to our ignorance about these issues. The process of active participation and research is the right way that we should follow to get ourselves out of this mess.

Both parties recognized that as the dynamiters were among the villagers and known by them, the committees in the villages should be used to name them and to take the list to the Prime Minister's Office. The woman member, Mwanashuru Mzee, on behalf of the whole team from the South, presented the documentary video to the Prime Minister and told him, after seeing it, to take necessary action, before it is too late and before the people become too tired to do work which does not bring any fruit.

A list of over 500 names of dynamiters was presented to the Prime Minister in less than a month's time. He made a trip to the South where he read out some of the names from the list that was presented to him. He then instructed the regions to see to it that the practice was stopped.

Changes in the Fisheries Act and policy changes in the government system

A combination of self-analysis, guided self-survey, research in marine conditions, and intense process of supported action led to results. Action research made women and men aware of their situation and their power to act and to speak out. The government had to take action and to change some sections in the Fisheries Act. They also made some adjustments in the fines and jail sentences, because the existing rules made it easy to let the criminals go after they had been brought to the police, even if they had dynamite in their hands but they had not been caught while they were in the act of dynamiting. The Environment Department in the Vice President's Office is taking the matter more seriously than before and the Ministry of Natural Resources and Tourism, in collaboration with the Defence Ministry, has deployed soldiers in most villages along the coast, changing them every three months. They work in cooperation with the village environmental committees. The involvement of the Defence forces is due to the Civil Rights Act of the Defence Forces and not to the use of authoritarian power. Ideally, they work under the guidance of the village government and in close collaboration with the people, although in practice suspects can be beaten before evidence is brought to bear.

In writing this story one would think that success can be effected with comparative ease. The fact is that it required much courage from those who stepped forward to list and expose names and to initiate the fight against environmental destruction. They could be threatened and some faced losing their position in committees and specific jobs. The measures taken were politically sensitive and involvement in citizens' action could be seen as a measure against the higher leadership. That my contract was discontinued and not renewed later cannot be totally separated from my participation in the fishing communities' action which turned against the government authorities. One has to make choices when and in which conditions it is appropriate to engage in citizens' movements and actions critical of the ruling cadres, and also to think ahead where the potential partners and supporters of the action are. One has to be aware also of how one's own position relates to the action. There is a time when one has to retreat into the background and appear only in one's writings or in contacting specific people and offices.

As a postscript, we can add a recent message received from Mtwara, sent by the Information and Liaison Officer, Gratian Luhikula, from the Tanzanian Coastal Management Partnership after their recent visit to Mtwara:

> Today we can share with the reader information from my recent Mtwara and Lindi trip. Everyone there is happy that the dynamite fishing has been completely eliminated. With a community participatory approach being applied in the two regions, dynamite fishers are not only surrendering to local and village governments, but also taking a leading role in monitoring and patrolling the coast to make sure no outsiders carry out the illicit fishing. A sense of ownership within the community is prevailing. The theme is: *bahari yetu, hatutaki* – we don't want anybody to tamper with OUR SEA! Some 229 people have voluntarily surrendered their bombing tools and material, including 112 kg TNT Magnum buster, 202 kg Ammonium nitrate, 120 detonators and 26 fuses.

The RIPS programme manager confirms the message by adding that he has not heard dynamiting for a year while earlier it could be heard many times daily.

Conclusion

The extent to which we can speak about participatory action *research* is a question which arises in reading the case studies. How far is it necessary to draw lines between more formal action research and analysis which people make for their own benefit? If the questions are answered on the basis of traditional scientific criteria, research is hardly applicable as a term for people's practical analysis. Much of the knowledge useful to common people, whether educated or not, is commonsense practical knowledge which is relevant to their situation and to their livelihood. In the case studies people's particular knowledge is drawn out, systematized and utilized when facilitators and government officers responsible to the communities make use of their own generalized knowledge based on experience and education. Mutuality of learning is crucial here. This kind of participatory analysis, resulting in action, does not usually go under the term research, yet it has all the ingredients and the setting of action research. For me personally, this kind of work with people offers a research situation within which I gain more complete knowledge of the researched problem than I would if I followed the orthodox rules of science.

If the initial setting which the participatory administrative system at present potentially offers is more systematically utilized in the two regions, it could offer opportunities for exciting innovative PAR which would integrate originally non-participatory hard science research into a participatory mode. This development is in fact taking place when the researchers from the Naliendele Agricultural Research Institute in Mtwara have become aware of the possibilities that the participatory environment gives them. Several staff members have moved to work within the regional participatory framework and have co-operated with RIPS.

One illustration of applying local participatory research is a cashew research project initiated by a natural scientist with agricultural officers working with RIPS within the participatory regional programme. Primary school students and teachers are engaged in innovative research through daily observation, recording and manual cleaning off of mildew in the budding leafy branches of cashew trees with the aim of reducing to a minimum the use of expensive and destructive sulphur and increasing production manifold. This is original research, the results of which are of great interest to the parents of students and the population at large. The production has increased with greatly decreased expense, making it possible also for poorer farmers to engage themselves in cashew production.

So far such co-operation is left for individual scholars to discover as an opportunity available to them. University departments as institutions do not have the flexibility or the tradition for linking up their research with what is going on locally.[3]

Notes

1 In implementing the programme, training was done by utilizing the PRA tools and principles developed by Robert Chambers. Chambers took part in two training workshops for the officials from the ministries.

2 The Ministry for Foreign Affairs of Finland, Department for International Development Co-operation, in 1992 made a long-term commitment to support a participatory programme referred to as RIPS (Rural Integrated Project Support). In its initial stages the Institute of Development Studies, University of Helsinki (the writer included), because of its long-time experience in PAR and its familiarity with the south-eastern regions, was incorporated into an 18-month participatory planning of the new programme and, as researchers, we have continued in parts of the programme.

3 The introduction and conclusion were written by the first author.

References

Amalric, F. (ed.) (1998) *Sustainable Livelihoods: Communities as Seeds of Change*. London: Sage Publications.

Arusha Declaration (1977) Dar Es Salaam: Dar Es Salaam Printers.

Masaiganah, S.M. (1998) 'The stories, Tanzania: gender roles and culture in the Mtwara region', *Development Journal*, 41 (3): 58–60.

Norad, Oslo (1986) *The Role of Women in Tanzania Fishing Societies*. University of Dar Es Salaam: Institute of Development Studies, Women Study Group.

Nyerere, J.K. (1968) *Socialism and Rural Development in Ujamaa: Essays on Socialism*. Dar Es Salaam: Oxford University Press. pp. 106–44.

RIPS (1998) *Paths for Change. Experiences in Participation and Democratisation in Lindi and Mtwara Regions, Tanzania*. Rural Integrated Project Support (RIPS) Programme Phase II. Helsinki: Oy Finnagro Ab.

Swantz, M.-L. (1973) 'Research in action as a programme for university students'. Service Paper 7, Bureau of Resource Assessment and Land Use Planning, University of Dar Es Salaam.

Swantz, M.-L. (1975a) 'Research in action at Dar Es Salaam', *Overseas Universities*, 22: 19–22.

Swantz, M.-L. (1975b) 'The role of participant research in development, Bureau of Resource Assessment and Land Use Planning'. Research Report No. 15 (New Series). Also in *Geografiska Annaler*, Vol. 57, Ser. B, 1976: 2, Stockholm.

Swantz, M.-L. and Jerman, H. (eds) (1977) 'Bagamoyo Research Project Jipemoyo: Introduction to its general aims and approach', in *Jipemoyo, Development and Culture Research 1/1977*. Seven volumes in the series Jipemoyo, Development and Culture, 1977–1989.

28
Six Street Youth Who Could …[1]

ELIZABETH WHITMORE AND COLETTE MCKEE

CHAPTER OUTLINE

This chapter describes how a team of youth, staff members and an outside methodologist designed and conducted a participatory evaluation of a downtown Drop-In Centre for street-involved youth. After summarizing what the team did and how, we explore some of the key lessons learned. These include aspects of effective team building, the importance of flexible time limits, finding ways to tap into 'other' knowledge (specifically PRA techniques), struggling with some ethical issues and maintaining quality.

A Drop-In Centre for street-involved youth, in a Canadian city, had been running for four years and it was time to evaluate its services. The Centre's mission and clientele were controversial. Some people felt that a safe place to 'hang out' met the initial needs of street-involved youth and allowed staff to reach out informally, build trust, and intervene effectively in crises. Others wanted more structured activities and stricter rules, while still others thought the Centre attracted 'high risk' youth to the area and wanted it shut down completely. The evaluation, initiated by the youth-serving agency and a local school of social work, identified four objectives:

- To involve youth in designing and implementing an evaluation to measure the impact of Drop-In services.
- To improve service delivery to youth.
- To collaborate with community members on long-term solutions to help integrate street youth into the community.
- To make the evaluation instrument available to other youth centres.

In this chapter, we describe what we did, the process we used, and the mix of methodology. We then discuss the lessons that emerged from the experience.

Background

Part of a large youth service agency with offices throughout the city, the Drop-In Centre provides support services to 'high-risk,' street-involved youth. Open ten hours daily, 365 days a year, the Centre offers free services: a hot lunch, showers, laundry, referral to other agencies and crisis counselling.

An average of 80 youth visit the Centre daily. The majority are marginalized by poverty, have histories of abuse, lack education and employment skills. Often they attempt to overcome these barriers and avoid their problems through criminal activity and drug and alcohol misuse. Because the Centre was staffed by only three front-line workers, the large numbers of clients facing serious issues created a chaotic environment that raised concerns about safety.

A participatory approach was chosen for the evaluation because:

- Street-involved youth were assumed experts in their own lives. Because they mistrust adults in general, especially those in authority, a peer-to-peer approach would yield better data and a deeper understanding of the key issues.
- The evaluation offered an opportunity to engage six street-involved youth in an empowering process – to build skills in evaluation,

interviewing, public-speaking and writing, while developing confidence and self-esteem.

- It was an opportunity to reach the wider street-involved youth population so that they too would have a stake in the process and in any recommended changes.

Adapting a Framework

We approached this evaluation from the perspective of *acompañamiento* or 'accompanying the process' – a phrase used by Latin American development workers to describe a relationship with communities, groups and individuals that fosters mutual support, trust, a common commitment and solidarity (Clinton, 1991). Implicit in this are the concepts of 'empowerment' and participation. Development partnerships promote people as active architects of their own change processes rather than passive recipients of development assistance. In a context of North–South partnerships, this approach makes it clear that the (Southern) partners own and control the process: 'It is we who accompany *their* process' (Wilson and Whitmore, 1995).

This approach is based on six principles:

1. *Non-intrusive collaboration*. Decisions, however different from our own, must be respected; the host retains ownership of the process and the results.
2. *Mutual trust and genuine respect*. All people have the ability to understand and deal with their own realities. With time and patience, trust can be built among people from different cultures, classes, races or ages.
3. *Solidarity*. All humanity is connected in a common journey and a shared destiny.
4. *Mutuality and equality*. All participants in a collaboration should make their interests, agendas and goals explicit. Everyone's interests are important.
5. *A focus on process*. A partnership requires emotional as well as intellectual involvement, informal interaction that goes beyond a detached working relationship and respects others' cultures, ways of relating and construction of time.
6. *Language as an expression of culture and power*. Language is not just a technical matter; it is a way of understanding and dealing with the world.

These principles formed the basis of the team's work and guided us through the inevitable ups and downs of the process. The youth needed considerable support at the beginning, but decisions were made by consensus and the process gradually became theirs. It took time to build trust and a collaborative relationship. We were able to reach a level of solidarity, an understanding that the group depended on all of us supporting and taking care of each other. We began by having each person declare his or her interest and why he or she wanted to be part of this project. We focused on process: using check-ins and check-outs, paying attention to individual and collective needs, building in incentives, abandoning the day's agenda when necessary to deal with pressing emotional concerns. And we paid attention to language, avoiding words that mystified or excluded and appreciating the power of words to respect or offend.

Getting Started

Our first task was to build an effective team of six youth, two staff members (Colette and Rick) and one outside evaluation methodologist (Bessa). The staff members were known and trusted by the youth. Their role was to assist and support the youth throughout the evaluation.

The youth went through a standard recruitment process: posters throughout the Centre advertising the positions, an application, interviews, and final selection by Colette, Rick and Bessa. The criteria for selection included a one-year commitment, current or past participation as a Drop-In client, and an expressed interest in learning how to evaluate a programme. In terms of gender, race and language (French/English), we sought to reflect the wider street-involved youth population. Also, the youth team members were affiliated with different street sub-groups that tend to compete with each other and don't mix much. All at least had some knowledge of others in the group, which was both a plus (familiarity) and a minus (preconceptions about each other).

This project was funded by an Ontario government foundation, allowing the youth to be paid as participants, for release time of staff and the outside methodologist and for general expenses. Like the youth, Rick and Colette had no evaluation experience but extensive experience with street culture. Bessa had limited knowledge of the street culture and its diverse youth affiliations. These limitations were seen as a benefit, 'leveling the playing field' for all team members. Each type of expertise was valued and acknowledged throughout the evaluation project.

The project began in February 1997. The group met two afternoons a week at the Drop-In. The team first established ground rules: attending meetings only when sober, 'parking' personal issues at the door, maintaining confidentiality and being punctual. The team established some routines from the onset, an important one being a 'check-in' and 'check-out' at every meeting. This provided a transition in and out of each meeting. The 'check-in' focused on how people were feeling, whether they were tired, in a good or bad mood. The 'check-out' was a space to review our time together, clear up misunderstandings and to say whatever needed to be said so that ill feelings were not carried over to the following meeting or worst yet, played out on the street.

At the beginning, the team devoted considerable time to doing warm-up exercises designed to get to know each other, and to build trust and commitment. We rotated selection and leadership of these exercises, getting everyone used to being in a facilitator role and to see their peers as equals in leadership roles. The exercises were balanced with a focus on task as Bessa got us started on what evaluation was all about and how to go about it.

The team also had snacks (or meals) which was itself an exercise in negotiation and compromise. Food was seen as an important part of the process as the youth were living in poverty and often came hungry. Responsibility for getting the food was rotated among everyone and had been built into the budget. Oreo cookies were regarded by the youth as one of the four major food groups.

Another team-building aspect was the monthly outing which was planned as a group. These outings were designed for fun and relaxation, something street youth do not have a lot of. We went bowling, played mini-golf and pool, and went out for supper together. Every three months, we used part of the outing to reflect on how we were doing. This gave us the opportunity to appreciate what was going well and to recognize and try to change what was not.

Design and Data Collection

The evaluation began with the team considering three questions: 'What do we want to know?', 'How will we find out?' and 'Who do we need to talk to?' (Barnsley and Ellis, 1992). Bessa introduced a variety of methods and ways of approaching evaluation. Through brainstorming, the design gradually took shape. The team decided to use questionnaires to survey youth who used Drop-In services, youth who did not use the services, the business community, agency staff, other youth-service agencies, the police, and the security staff at an adjacent shopping mall.

The team worked together and in small groups to develop the initial questionnaire (for youth who used Drop-In services). Framing questions that would get the information they wanted was a lengthy process, with many drafts and re-drafts and the need for encouragement to maintain interest. Once this first questionnaire was complete, it set the framework for all the others.

Though the youth felt a sense of ownership of this process and the questionnaires, they got bored with surveys and felt isolated from their Drop-In peers. As their motivation flagged, they looked back to Participatory Learning and Action (PLA) whose credibility they had originally questioned. PLA evolved from research methods commonly used to appraise villages and communities in developing countries. It is distinguished by its shared visual representations and analysis by 'local' people through tools such as mapping, ranking, sequencing, semi-structured interviews. The intent is to 'pass the stick' – a phrase derived from using sticks to draw on the ground – so that people themselves take over the process (Chambers, 1997: 106). Now they were more open to trying alternative methods: group mapping, direct matrix ranking and semi structured interviews. The youth worked together to develop tools that would fit the Centre milieu and engage other street-involved youth. When the tools were ready, each session was advertised in the Drop-In, with pizza as an incentive for participation.

Data Analysis

A similar (iterative) process was established for data analysis, 'walking through' responses to open-ended questions to learn the principles and techniques of analysis. The youth worked in pairs to describe and summarize the data, usually with Bessa, Rick or Colette. Then we collectively developed themes/categories. All information was recorded in writing so the whole team could discuss it.

Reporting

The team produced a formal report, a 'Kit' and participated in community and academic presentations about their work. The formal written report was produced by everyone brainstorming the contents, Bessa drafting each section, submitting it for feedback to the team, and re-drafting. The result was a thorough, well-crafted document. The youth took the main role in community and academic presentations. Sharing their expertise publicly helped them gain confidence and pride in their hard work and the impressive results.

Perhaps the most interesting reporting mechanism was 'The Kit,' a colourful guide for other youth evaluators.[2] 'The Kit' was designed and produced entirely by the youth team members. After the team collectively brainstormed the contents – 'how', 'what', and 'tips' – the youth worked on each section individually or in pairs and truly 'owned' the final product.

Results

The impact of the evaluation has been extensive. The agency's Board of Directors and upper management took the recommendations seriously and legitimized the process through their support. There have been dramatic changes at the Drop-In – a redesigned management structure, a new youth advisory committee with power to oversee the implementation of the evaluation recommendations, and strengthened relationships with businesses and the police. Most of all, expectations for staff and youth have been clarified, resulting in a new atmosphere of optimism, respect and mutual responsibility.

Lessons Learned

Building an effective team

The team should include staff members who are known and trusted by the youth

Ongoing staff support was crucial in helping the youth cope with life issues and in motivating them to complete the evaluation tasks. The outside 'expert' did not have the time, expertise, or – most of all – trust to handle the daily concerns and all-too-frequent crises. There were several instances of potential and actual violence. The staff played a key role in preventing or defusing the situation. The agency had clear rules and procedures; the staff knew what to do and did it.

This presented a dilemma (even a potential conflict of interest) for staff members on the team. Can an evaluation be trusted if 'insiders' are so heavily involved? Can critical comments in an evaluation be seen as reflecting team members' personal opinions? What if the evaluation reveals problems with management? In this case, the staff members balanced these loyalties with utmost integrity. Committed to a thorough evaluation and to youth empowerment, they put their own opinions and loyalties aside. They contributed their knowledge and understanding of the agency, but were careful to frame their contributions as additional information or context, rather than as fact. They fully respected the integrity of the data. The bottom line is that, without staff members on the team, the evaluation simply would not have happened.

An outsider with evaluation expertise plays an important role on the team

In this case, the evaluation methodologist served as technical expert and teacher, providing guidance, support and structure (Preskill and Torres, 1998).

Youth need to be full team members

This means shared decision-making and control of both the process and the product – 'passing the stick'. Building this sense of ownership takes time, patience, skill and the commitment of management to convince sceptical youth that change can actually result from their efforts. Using everyday language (as opposed to jargon) demystifies the process and allows full participation.

'People' skills are essential tools in participatory evaluation (Burke, 1998)

Really listening, supporting, understanding group dynamics, organizing, facilitating and problem-posing are not normally a part of evaluator training, but should be (Mertens, 1994; Whitmore, 1994).

Build in fun!

Though hardly a new idea, fun is essential to keeping people together and completing tasks.

Seek flexible time limits

Flexible time limits allow participants to 'own' more fully the process without compromising the quality of the final product. How much time is needed will depend on who they are, the other demands in their lives, their levels of knowledge and skill, and how much they want to be involved. Flexibility often bumps up against funder or management demands for short-term, 'measurable' outcomes, resulting in superficial or even erroneous conclusions.

Learning the principles, techniques and language of evaluation can be complicated. For many participants, most of this will be new and short time-frames limit their participation. In this case, fully engaging the youth required that task and process be blended in each session. Sometimes rigid timelines and agendas had to be abandoned to deal with personal or group crises if the team was to continue working productively. When there were more stringent time pressures, the adults tended to take over, compromising the empowerment of the youth and possibly the validity of the findings (Kirkhart, 1998).

Having the time and resources to do a thorough job is a rare luxury. Fortunately, the budget was sufficient and flexible. Enough time (however that is decided) needs to be built into project design, and managers and decision-makers need to trust the team and allow it to work (overtime, if needed). The project began with a year's time-frame in mind; it ended up taking 18 months from the first announcement to the completion. The extra six months were crucial in assuring the high quality of the final report and finishing 'The Kit'. Had the team been pushed to produce the report earlier, the youth would not have been able to participate fully in the writing, and the purposes of the exercise would have been defeated – producing a high-quality evaluation report and empowering the youth in the process.

Tapping into 'other' knowledge

The interactive (PLA) methods yielded detailed, reliable and valid data by engaging both the youth on the team and the broader population of street-involved youth in the process (Chambers, 1997). The mapping and matrix exercises enhanced their sense of ownership and their commitment to seeing that changes were actually implemented. Accountability was enhanced because decision-makers knew that an informed constituency was watching and expecting follow-through on the report's recommendations for change.

Conventional techniques (especially surveys, experiments, control groups) are often inappropriate for this population which has been excessively 'studied' by outsiders. Street-involved youth have been 'surveyed to death' in recent years and are reluctant to fill out yet another form or answer yet more questions. The 'subjects' are likely to become resentful and resist in subtle ways (not answering questions truthfully or seriously) and not-so-subtle ways (refusing to respond at all). Surveys assume literacy, and many street-involved youth have low literacy skills. The questions are often framed by 'experts' who have limited understanding of street culture. Reliance on control groups ignores the transiency of life on the streets; surveys and experiments may not be able to compensate for the mistrust among street youth around being 'used' for someone else's purposes. These techniques tend to further objectify and disempower an already marginalized group. So why did the youth decide, initially, to do primarily surveys? This seems to have been a contradiction, given that they complained of being over-surveyed. Yet, this was the technique most familiar to them and perhaps they felt it was more legitimate.

The absence of a demand for rigid, pre-specified 'measurable results' meant that we could develop our own measures and frame the results in our own way. We were not pressured to fit our work into someone else's 'slots' (Smith, 1987, 1990). 'The Kit' was an unanticipated result. It is the youths' representation of what they learned; its style, content and graphics speak to young people. While the content is solid and rigorous, its presentation is boisterous, colourful, full of life and humour (Chambers, 1993).

Ethical issues

Several incidents during this project raised ethical dilemmas around questions of confidentiality. The first dilemma had to do with sharing information about internal staff or management politics with users of services. This issue arose as a result of the inexplicably low response rate to the written staff survey. Colette and Rick were aware of internal dynamics that could account for the problem, but neither the youth nor Bessa knew about these dynamics or the history behind them. Recognizing that the situation needed to be understood if the evaluation was to have any validity, the team decided that Bessa should conduct a combination of individual interviews and focus groups with staff.

Her first challenge was to establish enough trust with the interviewees that they would disclose what was going on. Staff members were understandably wary, given that two of their colleagues and the youth team members would be privy to the information. Assuming that she succeeded in learning the answers, the next challenge was to determine the extent to which it would be appropriate or helpful to share internal staff and management politics with the youth. Would such 'raw' information undermine their confidence in the agency and agitate a clientele who tend to operate 'close to the edge'? Would the youth honour their commitment to confidentiality when it came to information about staff factions and internal battles among people who were their counsellors in times of crisis? On the other hand, would withholding the data imply that the youth could not be trusted?

The team decided that Bessa would craft her findings into a set of general themes. This would avoid implicating any individual staff member while capturing the essence of the problem in a form that could be readily shared with the team and included in the final report. This process not only worked well but appears to have been a positive factor in moving the staff and agency towards constructive change.

A second dilemma related to the mapping exercise in which youth drew a map of the downtown area and specified spots where drugs were sold and street prostitutes were operating. How much of this information should be shared with the police and other authorities? The team decided to summarize the data in the report, protecting the confidentiality of the information and of the youth, while respecting the value and importance of the picture they painted through that exercise.

The overall parameters of these ethical issues are not unusual. All organizations have internal issues that need to be handled with discretion. Professionals working with marginalized populations invariably struggle with the balance between maintaining confidentiality and seeming to endorse illegal activities revealed by their clientele. There are no universal answers; as in this evaluation, the best possible solutions must be sought for particular circumstances.

Maintaining quality

Attention to quality was carefully built into the process. However, along with conventional guidelines to ensure technical rigour, the definition of quality was reframed to encompass inclusiveness and issues of power and control as well. This effort yielded its own set of lessons:

Use appropriate tools

The combination of conventional and PLA methods yielded more comprehensive data and a deeper level of analysis than conventional methods alone would have (Migotsky, 1998). For example, the difference in results between the written survey of youth and the youth focus groups provided the basis for rich discussion which deepened our understanding (Greene and Caracelli, 1997). The written survey of youth yielded poor (incomplete, unreliable) data. The PLA exercises, on the other hand, belonged to the youth. The interactive process was more 'youth-friendly'; the interest and enthusiasm of the respondents spoke for itself. They could express individual views while also taking part in the larger discussion. They felt that their opinions really did count, and in the (sometimes raucous) sessions they became truly engaged in the evaluation and its outcome.

Set the evaluation tasks within the capacity of the team members

In teaching the team how to conduct an evaluation, Bessa broke down the tasks so that the youth could handle them. She introduced some technical terms (instruments, sample and stratified random sample) once they had mastered a concept. Though jargon was generally avoided, the ability to use carefully selected technical terminology helped legitimize the youths' work.

By collaboratively analysing qualitative data, the youth learned how to summarize responses, recognize themes and patterns, and weave these together into a coherent whole. The iterative process – between the raw data and the emerging themes; among different data sources; and between the small groups analysing one set of data and large-group discussion of findings, impressions, and tentative conclusions – enhanced their understanding of the data and the quality of our findings. It also contributed enormously to their sense of ownership. The computer-generated data turned out to be less useful, yielding responses that were sometimes contradictory, sometimes nonsensical. Though the quantitative data certainly were part of the process and stimulated much discussion, the computer as a tool for analysis did not work well. In the context of teamwork, it was an individuating task; the machine just did not *engage* people in the process.

Identify and address biases

We used a number of techniques to get at biases. For example, after developing a draft questionnaire about problems and issues at the Drop-In Centre, the youth team members interviewed each other. We then discussed the assumptions/biases implicit in their responses and the importance of neutrality in interviewing and in analysing data. The discussion was then broadened to consider such questions as: 'What have other youth experienced?' (raising issues of gender, race, sexual orientation, sub-group membership, age), 'What do "most youth" think?', 'Who are "most youth"?' We could then tease out the hidden biases in the discussion. Role plays brought out positive and negative attitudes towards particular respondent groups.

Triangulating data sources and methods built in a 'check and balance' for bias. Similarities and differences of viewpoints helped the youth appreciate the importance of respecting people's views, however different they might be from their own. At first, for example, they reacted angrily to the negative views of the Drop-In and street-involved youth expressed by some businesses, the police and the security people. Later, they were able to recognize the legitimacy (and even validity) of these views as part of the 'whole' picture.

Carefully balance ownership and technical quality

How much should/can the 'experts' revise or edit the work done by participants? Do we rework poorly framed questions or revise what others have worked so hard to construct, however technically flawed? The issue here is one of ownership as well as quality; and the balance can be delicate. In most instances, the team was able to compromise so that questions were worded in a 'youth-friendly' way but would elicit useful answers. Without the foundation of trust and mutuality that the team had so carefully built, we could not have done this effectively.

The big challenge came in writing a well-framed, well-articulated formal report that would stand up to scrutiny by sceptical audiences (the agency board and staff, the business community, and funders). Most of the youth on the team had less than a high school education and could not realistically be expected to write such a report. So how to do this and still maintain their sense of ownership (Whitmore, 1991)? The key was having enough time – time to draft each section, time to go over it as a group, to correct inaccurate information and to get a sense of how this report should look. The youth picked up a number of inaccuracies, since they had done the analyses and knew the data backwards and forwards. One youth, after insisting that she 'did not read', went over the analysis with a fine-tooth comb and picked up factual, grammatical and spelling errors! Gradually, the report came together; the youth created the graphs and charts, assembled the appendices and designed the cover page. Everyone was fully invested in it and wanted to 'get it right'. They deservedly felt very proud of their solid, fully credible product. In addition, because the youth had participated in and fully understood the contents of the report, they could answer detailed questions about it from board members and others who attended their presentations.

Conclusion

In this project, we sought to 'accompany the process' of the youth participants who evaluated services designed for their benefit. It was indeed their process and we were fully conscious of our role as supporters and teachers. It is hard to do; it is so easy to slip into taking over, especially when others are insecure, inexperienced and impatient with the process. As noted above, the keys were sufficient time, adequate resources, a lack of rigid rules around measuring 'results', the consistent presence of trusted staff, and a solid commitment to 'pass the stick' to the youth.

Notes

1 This chapter is dedicated to the memory of G.

2 We would like to thank everyone involved for their participation and support. These include the youth (Karen, G, Tammy, Iffie and Bobbi), those youth who participated in the focus groups, Rick Perley (the other staff member on the team), Dan Paré and Denise Vallely, Youth Services Bureau of Ottawa-Carleton, and members of the evaluation sub-committee (Mark Totten, Diann Consaul and Ken Hoffman). We acknowledge the generous support of the Trillium Foundation for funding this project. We are grateful to Pat Maguire and Ann Buxbaum for their editorial assistance.

References

Barnsley, J. and Ellis, D. (1992) *Research for Change: Participatory Action Research for Community Groups*. Vancouver, BC: The Women's Research Centre.

Burke, B. (1998) 'Evaluating for a change: reflections on participatory methodology', in E. Whitmore (ed.), *Understanding and Practicing Participatory Evaluation. New Directions for Evaluation,* No. 80. San Francisco, CA: Jossey-Bass. pp. 43–56.

Chambers, R. (1993) 'Notes from alternatives to questionnaire survey workshop'. Institute for Development Studies, University of Sussex, England.

Chambers, R. (1997) *Whose Reality Counts? Putting the Last First*. London: Intermediate Technology Publications.

Clinton, R.L. (1991) 'Grassroots development where no grass grows: small-scale development efforts on the Peruvian coast', *Studies in Comparative International Development*, 26 (2): 59–95.

Greene, J.C. and Caracelli, V.J. (1997) 'Advances in mixed-method evaluation: the challenges and benefits of integrating diverse paradigms'. *New Directions for Evaluation*, No. 74. San Francisco, CA: Jossey-Bass.

Kirkhart, K.E. (1998) 'Validity and evaluation use: an integrated theory'. Paper presented at the annual conference of the American Evaluation Association, Chicago, IL.

Mertens, D.M. (1994) 'Training evaluators: unique skills and knowledge', in J.W. Altschuld and M. Engle (eds), *The Preparation of Professional Evaluators: Issues, Perspectives and Programs. New Directions for Evaluation*, No. 62. San Francisco, CA: Jossey-Bass. pp. 17–27.

Migotsky, C. (1998) 'Empowerment evaluation coupled with traditional approaches: triangulation or just headaches?'. Paper presented at the American Evaluation Association, Chicago, IL.

Preskill, H. and Torres, R.T. (1998) 'Transformative learning and evaluation use'. Panel discussion at the American Evaluation Association Conference, Chicago, IL.

Smith, D. (1987) *The Everyday World as Problematic*. Toronto: University of Toronto Press.

Smith, D. (1990) *The Conceptual Practices of Power*. Toronto: University of Toronto Press.

Whitmore, E. (1991) 'Evaluation and empowerment: it's the process that counts', *Empowerment and Family Support Networking Bulletin*, 2 (2). Ithaca, NY: Cornell University Empowerment Project.

Whitmore, E. (1994) 'To tell the truth: working with oppressed groups in participatory approaches to inquiry', in P. Reason (ed.), *Participation in Human Inquiry*. London: Sage Publications. pp. 82–98.

Wilson, M. and Whitmore, E. (1995) 'Accompanying the process: principles for international social development', *Canadian Journal of Development Studies*, 16 (1): 55–66.

PART FOUR

SKILLS

29

Collaborative Off-line Reflection: a Way to Develop Skill in Action Science and Action Inquiry

JENNY W. RUDOLPH, STEVEN S. TAYLOR AND
ERICA GABRIELLE FOLDY

CHAPTER OUTLINE

How can action researchers loosen entrenched thought patterns so they can learn new ways of acting, seeing and inquiring? This chapter describes a method of collaborative off-line reflection that encourages participants to examine their current ways of thinking and behaving, to generate alternatives, and to experiment with new approaches. It illustrates the method by applying it to a case involving familiar dilemmas of leadership.

How does a person loosen the bonds of firmly held beliefs and entrenched thought patterns enough to learn new ways of acting, seeing and inquiring? Action researchers need these capabilities to conduct themselves on-line in ways that enhance inquiry and valid information. Action science (Argyris, Putnam and Smith, 1985) and action inquiry (Fisher and Torbert, 1995; Torbert, 1991) offer both theory and technique to build these skills. Action science (AS) and action inquiry (AI) are meant primarily to help reshape action on-line, in the moment. However, reflecting and changing in the moment is enormously difficult for most people. This chapter highlights the intermediate step of learning to reflect, off-line, on our thoughts, feelings and actions, and the results they produce. Collaborative off-line reflection is one step in an iterative, ongoing learning practice that includes experience, off-line reflection and experimentation with newly designed approaches. Off-line reflection is not only for people who identify as action researchers; it is useful for anyone who wishes to enhance his or her capability for effective action in complex social situations.

Reflecting on practice off-line helps build AS/AI skills in at least three ways. First, off-line reflection gives one distance in time and space to analyse and re-experience feelings and thoughts, actions and results that may have been imperceptible or confusing in real time. Secondly, it provides a practice arena in which to build skill with action science/inquiry tools where mistakes have little or no adverse impact. Thirdly, it allows one to experiment with different ways to phrase interventions, a crucial step in adopting new behaviours that feel authentic.

This chapter illustrates a process by which the three authors (and many students of AS/AI before us) conduct research to improve their own effectiveness. Working with others gives the reflective practitioner (see Schön, 1987) a variety of perspectives on the situation and future options that can help break through established patterns of seeing and acting that are often invisible to us. In this group approach to offline reflection, we usually explore the challenges faced by one group member, and help him or her devise new approaches to similar dilemmas in the future. This process of thinking through one person's challenges helps all members of the reflection group explore ways to improve their effectiveness in action.

The chapter also offers a specific illustration of how Dana (a pseudonym for one of the authors), could resolve dilemmas common to power-holders in any organization. Dana is not conducting action research in the example presented here; she is trying to run her organization effectively. The action research described is our collaborative effort to understand and recraft her way of acting.

Collaborative off-line reflection starts with one group member writing a case about a problematic situation s/he faced. The case includes a brief orientation to the situation, actual or remembered dialogue from the situation, and a 'left-hand column' that captures what the case-writer thought and felt, but may not have said. The case below portrays dilemmas that Dana faced in how to set strategy for her organization.

Dana's Case: 'Butting Heads'

Dana was the director at *Action on Changing Technology* (ACT), a union-based coalition that addressed the occupational health effects of computer technology. When this conversation took place, Dana had been the director for less than a year. Anne, the other person in the case, pre-dated Dana at the organization by about a year and a half. Anne hadn't wanted the director position. Anne was very smart organizationally and politically, despite her youth.

Dana had a lot of respect for her and relied on her heavily, especially when she first took the director's post. At the time of this conversation, there were two other staff members, Miriam and Fred. Dana had hired both of them several months after she arrived. Though Dana was the director, all decisions of any importance were made collectively.

Anne and Dana had a very good relationship for the first few months after Dana arrived, but at some point it began to get strained. More and more often, their conversations would reach an impasse. In the following example, typical of the pattern, Dana and Anne argue about what sites are appropriate targets for their organization's help. Miriam and Fred were present, but quiet, in the following exchange.

Dana's thoughts and feelings	What Dana and Anne said
	Dana: What are some other potential sites?
	Anne: A while ago we talked to some people at Phoning, Inc. Maybe we can check back with them.
That's not a good idea. Why is she suggesting it?	*Dana*: You mean the telemarketing group in Western Mass? They do good stuff, don't they? They only take progressive clients.
	Anne: Well, they don't treat their phoners very well.
She's missing the point.	*Dana*: They're a tiny outfit and they're basically on our side. Maybe if we had infinite resources, but we don't.
	Anne: I don't see what all that has to do with it. There are workers there working under bad conditions. They could use our help.
Shit, are we going to butt heads again? Her purist politics drive me nuts.	*Dana*: The enemy is not the director of Phoning, Inc.
	Anne: Maybe he's not your enemy, but maybe he's my enemy!
Why do we get like this? Why does it get so tense? Why do we fall into this pattern over and over?	*Dana*: But that's not strategic.

Tools of the Trade

The point of working through a case is to help the casewriter (and others) see how s/he is stymied and to avoid similar problems in the future. The learning pathways grid (see Figure 29.1) provides one overarching framework that guides this work.[1] The work group sits together with copies of the case and a flip-chart version of an empty grid. Using the tools described below, we analyse the case and fill in the grid with observations about Dana's frames, actions and results (see Table 29.1). 'Frame' in this setting refers to the ways the casewriter understands and feels about the situation. Frames can run the gamut from if–then decision rules (if someone is yelling, then withdraw) to an amorphous sense, for example, of what is safe, right, rational or polite behaviour.[2]

The left-hand column, described above, the learning pathways grid (Action Design, 1993) and the ladder of inference (Argyris, Putnam and Smith, 1985) are three tools we use here. Moving around the grid step-by-step helps us clarify both the impasse Dana finds herself in and how she got there. The goal of the reflection process is to address the mismatch between the desired and actual results, which filling in the grid reveals. The grid helps illuminate some of the sources of this

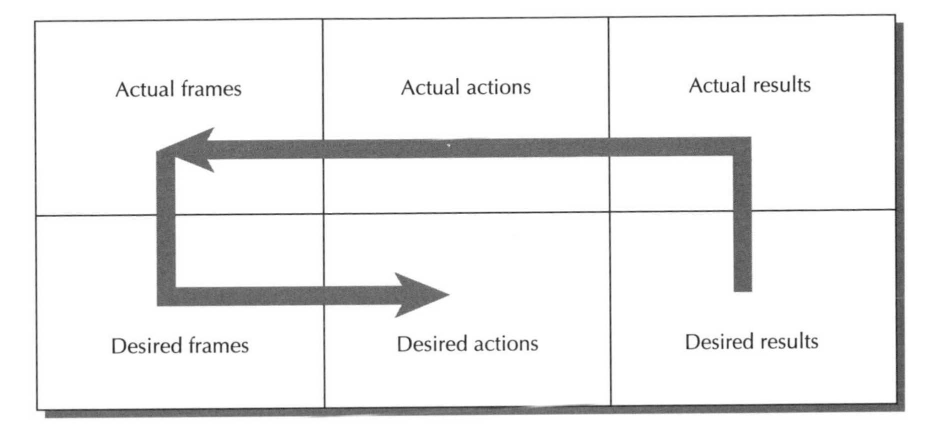

Figure 29.1 The learning pathways grid

Table 29.1 *Case summary using the learning pathways grid*

Dana's actual frames	Dana's actual actions	Actual results
1 Anne has purist politics and these are the wrong standards for the organization. 2 If I'm wrong, then my credibility (as the boss) is shot. If I'm wrong, then maybe I shouldn't be the boss. 3 It's my responsibility to handle this tough strategy question (alone). 4 If I admit I was mistaken, then I lose face.	• Advocate own point of view but don't inquire about others'. • Keep reasoning hidden. • Appeal to abstract standard of being 'strategic' about which there is no consensus.	• Deadlock: Dana's view does not prevail and there is no real dialogue. • Frustration.
Dana's desired frames	**Dana's desired actions**	**Desired results**
1 I respect Anne and her views. 2 I'm not solely responsible for the strategic direction of the organization. 3 Real dialogue about strategic direction enhances my credibility. 4 I'm willing to experiment to get a better outcome.	• Dana inquires about Anne's view. • Dana makes her own reasoning public and inquires about other people's views. • Dana publicly reflects on her and Anne's conflict and asks for help.	• Dana's point of view prevails. • Harmony in the group. • Real dialogue in the group.

mismatch: we examine what actions seem to have led to the actual outcomes and the way Dana framed the situation that would lead her to act the way she did. We then help the casewriter develop alternative frames and role play new actions that could surface, transcend or transform the dilemma s/he faces.[3]

The ladder of inference is a 'schematic representation of the steps by which human beings select from and read into interaction as they make sense of everyday life' (Argyris, Putnam and Smith, 1985: 57). For the most part, this process is automatic and unconscious. That is why it is so powerful and potentially so dangerous. At the bottom of the ladder is some observable data: a live conversation, a transcript, answers on a questionnaire, a newspaper account, facial expressions or other behaviours. At the first rung, we unconsciously make some choices, attending to some data and ignoring others. At the next rung we name the data in a way that makes sense to us; next we draw an inference about the (incomplete) data. We connect that inference with other theories we have – thus integrating it into our larger way of understanding the world – and decide what to do. As an example, let's look at an interaction between Sal and Elizabeth, work colleagues. Sal comes up to say hello to Elizabeth. As he does so, he both smiles warmly and takes a quick glance at his watch. Elizabeth, who tends not to think of herself as very important, notices the glance at the watch, rather than the smile. She assumes Sal is busy or late and doesn't have time to talk. Even though she would like to talk to Sal, she just says a quick hello and moves on. Sal wonders why Elizabeth was not very friendly to him.

The ladder shows how an existing frame (I am not very important) can influence what data we attend to (the glance at the watch) and what inferences we draw from that data (Sal is busy). It also shows how automatic inferences can lead to undesirable results (Sal and Elizabeth missing a chance to connect). That same dynamic is continually present in conversations. As we analyse the case, we try to make explicit the reasoning that takes the casewriter, and us, the case analysers, up the ladder.

Analysing the Case

Desired results

What did Dana want to get out of this interaction? The left-hand 'What I thought and felt' column of the dialogue often provides clues about the casewriter's desired results. Below we consider some of the results Dana seems to care about in this scenario.

Dana's point of view prevails

Dana's left-hand column suggests she thinks Anne's nomination of a target site for an educational effort is wrong-headed. Dana thinks, 'That's not a good idea' and 'She's missing the point.' In the spoken dialogue Dana attempts to set Anne straight, exclaiming, 'The enemy is not the director of Phoning Inc.', and when Anne retorts that maybe he *is* Anne's enemy, Dana's rejoinder is 'But that's not strategic.'

What is the right sort of target, as far as Dana is concerned? We get a hint that it is *not* a small, progressive organization when Dana attempts to turn aside Anne's suggested target by saying, 'They do good stuff, don't they? They only take progressive clients?' and 'They're a tiny outfit and they're basically on our side.' When we analysed the case with Dana and noted these patterns, we asked her if she could clarify why she said these things. She said she wanted to influence the group to identify targets that fit *her* criteria.

Harmony

Dana also seems to be bothered by the conflict between herself and Anne. She thinks to herself, 'Shit, are we going to butt heads again?' and 'Why do we get like this? Why does it get so tense?' When we queried Dana about this, she said she wanted a harmonious discussion that would help the organization move forward.

Real dialogue

By this time in our conversation about Dana's case, the irony of Dana wanting a harmonious discussion in which only her point of view was allowed to prevail was plain to all of us, especially Dana. In hindsight, Dana noted that she had another goal in the conversation which was less obvious to her at the time and which seemed to have been overridden by her desire to have her viewpoint prevail. That other desired outcome was 'to have a real dialogue'. 'What is a real dialogue?' we asked. Dana said a real dialogue would be one in which Anne and Dana share their views fully, listen to each other and negotiate actively.

Actual results

There are a host of actual outcomes here, but we will focus on two: deadlock about what organizations to target and frustrating conflict.

Deadlock

Dana's point of view does not prevail and there is no real dialogue. Rather, there is a deadlock between Dana and Anne about what to do next. It is easy to see their argument degenerating into the sort of schoolyard argument that goes back and forth with duelling assertions and no inquiry:

'It is strategic!'
'Is not!'
'Is too!'

Frustrating conflict

Dana and Anne's argument leaves Dana frustrated, 'Why do we fall into this pattern over and over?' and hot under the collar, 'Her purist politics drive me nuts!' It's easy to imagine that they are angry with each other, and that hostility is rising. Our case analysis conversation with Dana confirmed that our imaginings are on target.

Dana's challenge: a mismatch between desired and actual results

When we compare Dana's desired results with the ones she got, we get a clear picture of the challenge facing Dana. In this case, the actual results are almost the exact opposite of what Dana hoped for. Instead of having her point of view prevail, she and Anne are deadlocked. Instead of real dialogue, they have duelling assertions. Instead of harmony, they have simmering frustration. How did this happen?

Actual actions

Dana's main strategy seems to be advocating her view strongly, and not inquiring about other people's views. Though the dialogue starts with Dana's question 'What are some other potential sites?', from then on Dana advocates her point of view and makes only one shallow inquiry about Anne's comments, 'You mean the telemarketing group in Western Mass?' It is hard to see how one can foster real dialogue without asking any real questions. Unless she inquires of Anne or anyone else in the room 'What makes you think it is important to target such-and-such?' they are likely to keep their reasoning to themselves.

Dana also keeps her reasoning to herself by advocating her positions unilaterally without inviting scrutiny of them. Throughout most of the dialogue Dana asserts her inference that Phoning Inc. is not a good target, and does not invite others to comment on this view or offer theirs. Dana does begin to make her reasoning public by implying what criteria would exclude organizations from being targeted: '[Phoning Inc. is] a tiny outfit and they're basically on our side.' She also begins to explain some of her reasoning for having to pick and choose among targets: 'Maybe [we could target them] if we had infinite resources, but we don't.' But she seems to offer these statements as a way to buttress her own view and doesn't explain that they illustrate her reasoning or invite others to share their views.

Dana implies that her organization should act 'strategically', a standard about which the group clearly has not yet reached consensus. Yet she does nothing to move the dialogue to ground where consensus could be developed.

In sum, Dana contributes to the outcomes of deadlock and conflict by advocating a lot, inquiring little and keeping her reasoning opaque. Why does she do this? Her cognitive and emotional framing of the situation offers some clues.

Actual frame

What may have led Dana to act the way she did, especially when those actions led to outcomes she didn't want? One way to understand her actions is to examine the words, deeds and thoughts in the case and make inferences about how Dana framed her role and the situation, and check these inferences with Dana. The casewriter's collaborators ask questions like, 'What were you thinking and feeling that led you to act in such-and-such a way?' We describe two of the frames we generated by this process below.

Anne has purist politics and these are the wrong standards for the organization

If Dana wanted real dialogue, how do we explain her failure to promote dialogue by inquiring about what Anne was thinking? One possible explanation is that she dismisses Anne's 'purist politics' and then appears to dismiss whatever else Anne has to say. She neither inquires into nor does her left-hand column reflect any consideration of Anne's point of view. As we discussed this pattern with Dana, we came to the conclusion that she was operating with a frame something like this: 'If someone evinces purist politics (which are stupid) then disregard (and don't inquire about) what they say.'

Dana elaborated her view when we queried her about it: She believed that an organization with limited resources has to pick its battles; Anne's interest in a small, progressive, non-profit organization was way off target. Rather, Dana's organization should be focusing on large corporations that had unions or union-organizing potential. Thus, her organization could leverage its interventions by strengthening both the labour movement and efforts to reduce workplace injury. In Dana's mind, Anne's idea should be derailed as quickly as possible.

If I'm wrong or my view of strategy is incomplete, then my credibility is shot

Dana never invites comment on her own views despite her stated desire to have real dialogue. Why not? As we analysed the case together, Dana said she worried that if others noticed that her strategy was incomplete or wrong, her credibility as the director of the organization would be undermined. She didn't realize she held these frames and was surprised by them. Here are some of the other assumptions that made up Dana's frame:

- Since I'm the boss, I'm supposed to be right and if I'm not right then maybe I shouldn't be the boss.
- It's my responsibility to handle the burden of this tough strategy question (alone).

Given these assumptions, it is easy to see how threatening Dana might find it to open up any discussion of her views. In Dana's mind, such a discussion would not simply have been about organizational strategy but, by implication, about her suitability to lead her organization.

Argyris, Putnam and Smith note that people tend to condemn mistakes when they view them as a sort of crime (1985: 287). We see this frame at work in Dana's assumption, stated as we examined the case together, that 'Once I've committed myself to a view, if I backtrack then I lose face.' For Dana to be embarrassed or ashamed about changing her mind, she also has to believe that it is wrong to be wrong.

Desired frames

Reframing how one sees a situation is one path (and sometimes the only path) to generating new, more effective behaviours (Watzlawick, Weakland and Fisch, 1974). Reframing is a process in which the same old situation is cast in a new light. The process of writing down and discussing one's own actual frames often prompts memories of less salient contrasting ones. In addition, baldly stating one's own frames often highlights the ridiculously high or low standards to which we hold ourselves and this is often enough to jar us loose from them. We don't mean to imply that adopting a new frame is easy, but reflecting on frames as we have done here often provides both a strong impetus to change them, and ideas on what changes to make. Below we suggest reframes for each of the actual frames Dana held.

Actual frame: Anne has purist politics and these are the wrong standards for the organization

Reframe: I respect Anne and her views

At first blush, this reframe sounds like a Pollyannaish reversal of Dana's earlier dismissal of Anne's purist politics. In fact, however, we discovered that Dana frequently relied on Anne, who had been at the organization 18 months longer, for advice and knowledge about the field. In our off-line reflection, Dana said, 'I really do respect Anne, I just have to move this to the front of my mind.' This view of Anne is much more likely to make Dana curious about her views, and willing to inquire about them.

Actual frame: If I'm wrong or my view of strategy is incomplete, then my credibility is shot

Reframe A: I'm not solely responsible for the strategic direction of the organization

Dana knew that other people in the organization had useful perspectives on its mission and direction. In fact, when we analysed the case together, she noted that there was a good possibility that the strategy would be improved by discussing it. She could reframe her role as orchestrating processes to help surface the best possible strategy. Seen in this way, she could share the burden of developing an effective strategy. There was an important side effect of this reframe. Dana then realized that having her view prevail wasn't the result she really wanted. She didn't want her view to prevail at the expense of learning about other views. However, she wanted her view to be considered seriously along with others.

Reframe B: Real dialogue about strategic direction enhances my credibility

If Dana's role is to orchestrate a process that helps develop the best possible strategy, then she could now view such discussion as enhancing her stature as the leader of the organization.

Actual frame: If I admit I was mistaken, I will lose face

Reframe : I'm willing to experiment to get a better outcome

Once Dana was willing to relax her grip on the strategy development process, she recognized that, 'It's more important to me to have communication with Anne than to stick rigidly to my criteria for what is 'strategic' and totally dictate the strategy of the organization.' Put another way, Dana was willing to admit her strategy might not be the right one and explore other ways of developing strategy. Specifically, as Diana Smith often puts it (Smith, 1996), she was willing to entertain the 5 per cent possibility that Anne had something useful to say and pursue that possibility with 100 per cent of her effort.

Desired actions

We have analysed the 'Butting Heads' case, diagnosed some of the obstacles Dana faces in achieving outcomes she wants, and made some prescriptions about ways she might reframe the problem she faces (see Table 29.1 for a summary). We now turn to the process of crafting new ways for Dana to act. The goal is to devise approaches that are more likely to lead to the results Dana really wants, like having a real dialogue, having harmony in the group, and identifying targets that are strategically important. The first step in helping casewriters generate new ways of acting is to devise and write down new conversational approaches and phrases that they could use to express themselves. The second step, and it is a crucial one, is having casewriters role play these new actions. We find this is particularly useful in helping them try on the new frames, and in using the often-unfamiliar phrases that accompany them.

Dana inquires about Anne's view

One simple innovation, but only a start, would have been for Dana to ask Anne, 'Why do you see Phoning Inc. as a good target?' immediately after Anne suggested it. If Anne felt Dana was asking the question in good faith, the whole deadlock might have been avoided. If, however, we believe either that Anne might be suspicious of Dana's motives or would give reasons with which Dana wouldn't agree, then another approach might be necessary.

Dana makes her own reasoning public and inquires about other people's

Once the conflict between Dana and Anne surfaced, Dana could initiate a new dialogue with a brief introduction about where she wants it to go, then assert her view of what is strategic, and *then* inquire about what Anne and the others there (Miriam and Fred) see as strategic:

> I'd like to share my current view of our organizational strategy and then hear other people's views. I think if we work together on this, there's a good chance we could come up with a better strategy than the ones each of us are individually carrying around in our heads. Would you all be willing to brainstorm together? [*She then would check for agreement or comments and then, if appropriate, move on to say*] … My view of our strategy is that we have limited resources that we need to leverage. The best way to leverage them is by focusing on for-profit corporations who may be doing other things we oppose and where we can dovetail with other groups – unions, environmental groups, whatever. Now I'm open to influence on this view. How do others see it?

This approach does not explicitly address Anne and Dana's conflict. It does, however, encourage open discussion of all views and it invites the silent Miriam and Fred into the conversation. Bringing other views into a two-person argument often shifts the conversational ground in helpful ways.

Given that Dana and Anne have butted heads before and have a certain amount of animosity towards each other, there's a possibility that ignoring their conflict may not work. In that case, Dana could try something like the following.

Dana publicly reflects on her (and Anne's) conflict and asks for help

Dana could describe what she sees happening and invite others in the group to help her figure out a better approach:

> I feel in a dilemma here. On the one hand, I really want us to target the organizations I think are right. On the other, when I push my view I think that contributes to a pattern that Anne and I repeat over and over that has stymied us in the past: I say my view, then she says hers, and we don't seem to have much of an impact on each other. I'm not getting my way, she's not getting hers and we are all just stuck. I think I'm open to influence on what the right strategy is. I believe if we worked together, we might actually come up with a better strategy than the ones Anne and I are individually carrying around in our heads. Would others of you be willing to give this a try?

This approach has two advantages. Like the first intervention, it invites the silent Miriam and Fred into the conversation. Secondly, it describes the deadlock. Though the reader may now think this dynamic obvious, to the actors mired in the situation, simply having someone describe what is happening often helps them see a way through it.

Conclusion

We started this chapter contending that off-line reflection is one step towards better on-line action research in complex social interactions. We have described the first step, the off-line reflection process itself, examining the frames, actions and results of a specific past situation and inventing specific new ways to act. The off-line reflection process helps the casewriter and his or her co-investigators see the unintended consequences of the casewriter's action patterns and what frames motivated those patterns in a specific setting. But what impact does this off-line reflection have on later practice? Of her experience with this case Dana says: 'This case has changed the way I feel about authority and credibility. Realizing that, as the boss, I didn't always have to be right was enormously reassuring!'

How can off-line reflection lead to skilled reflective action on-line? First, it heightens on-line awareness of how people, including oneself, often produce consequences they do not want by falling into action patterns that backfire, driven by their own unrecognized frames. One of us now notices that:

> When I find myself or someone else being judgemental, upset or frustrated, I now have the habit of asking myself, how am I (or s/he) framing this situation that would make me (him/her) feel this way? I then either try on different frames till I find one that might help me get a more productive view of the situation or start exploring what the other person's frame might be.

Secondly, it alerts one to one's own idiosyncratic responses and frames as one acts. One of us remarks that:

> Surfacing my own (often subconscious) frames in cases where I found my own behaviour problematic has

> given me cues to pay attention to and an arsenal to draw on in real time. For example, when I notice that I am being extremely rational, I realize that this probably also means that I am angry. I can then look at some reasons for my anger based on the various frames that I have uncovered in off-line reflection. This level of awareness is often then enough to allow me to handle the situation in a much more effective way.

Finally, collaborative off-line reflection increases confidence in one's own ability to diagnose and transform frustrating situations on-line. Dana found that:

> Rather than seeing such incidents [as she and Anne being stuck] as intractable and inevitable, I have a much clearer sense of action patterns I tend to fall into and what frames motivate those patterns. This helps me take a step back and try something different.

Our goal was to show how off-line reflection will help action researchers and others develop useful habits of attention and analysis, develop new ways to phrase interventions and give them an opportunity to see how inferences about their own and others' actions are formulated. Turning a clear eye on ways of acting that we often do not particularly admire takes courage, and we hope we've emboldened others to try it. Lastly, we hope to have conveyed the moment-to-moment excitement of this reflection process, as well as the big benefits for later action.

Notes

We would like to thank Diana McLain Smith for getting us started in action science/action inquiry and Bill Torbert for his role in keeping us going. John S. Carroll, Sandy Kendall, Charles Parry and Robert Putnam all provided feedback that improved this chapter.

1 The term 'learning pathways' (see Action Design, 1996) refers to a framework by which we can recraft our actions by examining connections and mismatches among results we achieve, actions we take, and mental frames we hold.

2 These if–then rules illuminate people's 'theories-in-use' (Argyris and Schön, 1974), rules that guide their action. These are distinct from espoused theories of action, things they say they believe.

3 We would like to acknowledge Kenlin Wilder who skilfully orchestrated the first analysis of this case and introduced the three authors to the learning pathways grid.

References

Action Design (1993) *Advanced Institute Training Materials*. Weston, MA: Action Design.

Action Design, (1996) *Organizational Learning in Action: New Perspectives and Strategies*. Weston, MA: Action Design.

Argyris, C. and Schön, D. (1974) *Theory in Practice: Increasing Professional Effectiveness*. San Francisco, CA: Jossey-Bass.

Argyris, C., Putnam, R. and Smith, D.M. (1985) *Action Science: Concepts, Methods and Skills for Research and Intervention*. San Francisco, CA: Jossey-Bass.

Fisher, D. and Torbert, W.R. (1995) *Personal and Organizational Transformations: the True Challenge of Continual Quality Improvement*. London: McGraw-Hill.

Schön, D. (1987) *Educating the Reflective Practitioner: Toward a New Design for Teaching and Learning in the Professions*. San Francisco, CA: Jossey-Bass.

Smith, D.M. (1996) 'Class lectures, January–May'. Carroll School of Management, Boston College doctoral seminar, *Consulting Theory and Practice*.

Torbert, W.R. (1991) *The Power of Balance: Transforming Self, Society, and Scientific Inquiry*. Newbury Park, CA: Sage Publications.

Watzlawick, P., Weakland, J.H. and Fisch, R. (1974) *Change: Principles of Problem Formation and Problem Resolution*. New York: Horton.

30
On Working with Graduate Research Students

PETER REASON AND JUDI MARSHALL

CHAPTER OUTLINE

Since collaborative action research is a personal, political and social process, this chapter argues that it is important to work with the emerging *process* of inquiry as much as with the content. This chapter suggests some ways to look at the first-person aspects of inquiry and reflects on a process-oriented approach to research supervision.

Since the early 1980s with our colleagues at Bath we have worked with graduate students within the experiential, collaborative and action-oriented approaches to inquiry which are represented in this handbook. Our students adopt a range of first-, second- and third-person approaches, drawing on different methodologies and perspectives at each stage of their inquiry. They may be 'living life as inquiry' (Marshall, 1999), filling their life with self-reflective practice and borrowing from perspectives such as action science (Argyris, Putnam and Smith, 1985) and action inquiry (Torbert, 1991). They may set up co-operative inquiry groups engaging others fully as co-researchers (Heron and Reason, Chapter 12). They may attempt to develop processes of inquiry within whole organizations and communities. Whichever approaches they adopt, their work will be rooted in their own and others' experience, be based on attempts to establish collaborative relationships with others, and be action-oriented. Our students are typically competent, mature people – consultants, managers, nurses, doctors, social workers, police women and men, teachers – who wish to examine and develop some aspect of their personal and professional lives, to transform the quality of relationships in their organization and community, to explore and confront questions of race, gender and class in our society, and so on.

As we wrote earlier:

> All good research is *for me*, *for us*, and *for them*: it speaks to three audiences … It is *for them* to the extent that it produces some kind of generalizable ideas and outcomes which elicit the response 'That's interesting!' from those who are concerned to understand a similar field (Davis, 1971). It is *for us* to the extent that it responds to concerns for our praxis, is relevant and timely, and so produces the response 'That works!' from those who are struggling with problems in their field of action. It is *for me* to the extent that the process and outcomes respond directly to the individual researcher's being-in-the-world, and so elicit the response, 'That's exciting' – taking exciting back to its root meaning, to set in action. (Reason and Marshall, 1987: 112–13, original emphasis)

Because we believe that research in this mode is a personal, political and social process, in working with our students we have increasingly realized that it is important to work with the emerging *process* of inquiry as much as with the content (indeed, our students often know more about the content of their inquiry than we do). In particular, we believe that developing the *personal process* of inquiry, the first-person research process, is the basis from which our students reach out to create a wider influence. In this chapter we describe our perspectives on research as a personal process, and sketch the principles of process-oriented supervision which we have developed.

Research as Personal Process

We can think about the personal process of research from three interrelated perspectives: first, from an existential perspective as the here-and-now struggle with one's being-in-the-world; secondly, from a psychodynamic perspective which views current patterns of experience and behaviour as rooted in unresolved distress from earlier (often childhood) experiences; and thirdly, from a transpersonal perspective which views individual experience as a reflection of archetypal patterns of the collective unconscious.

From the existential perspective individuals are 'thrown' into the world, confronted with a set of issues – problems or life opportunities – with which they have to deal, and creating their life through the choices they make in the face of these issues. An individual's being is affirmed by and arises out of his or her choices, so that in the extreme, we are our choices. A central existentialist concern is the relation of being to non-being: the individual's sense of being is enhanced by the courage of his or her choice-making in the face of a world which is in the end unknowable and unpredictable; in contrast non-being is a consequence of avoiding such choices (Hampden-Turner, 1970; May, 1961).

So people come to research with their life issues, with the opportunities offered to them by their gender, class, age, race, employment status, and so on, with the need to deal with careers and relationships in various states of development and decay, and confronted by birth, death and illness and by the challenges of a planet in political and ecological disarray. Often they come to the university as a kind of retreat, with a need to take stock and make sense of their life and experience so far. Life can be seen as a series of commitments to certain ways of being: we make a choice, and live out that choice more or less completely. Yet there comes a time when we turn *against* the old ways of being, when our existing life pattern seems inadequate, when we need to affirm and develop other, neglected sides of our being, and make new choices.

> Carlis Douglas started her PhD inquiries with the intention of exploring the application of equal opportunities policies and practices in British organizations. As she reflected on the project she had undertaken, she realized over time that a more pressing question was how Black professional women like herself could thrive, rather than simply survive in their organizational lives – a phrase she took as inspiration from the Black woman poet Maya Angelou. (see Douglas, 1999)

A psychodynamic perspective complements the existential by pointing out that many of the limitations on being here-and-now have their roots in childhood experience.

> The theory here is that people in our sort of society carry around a good deal of unresolved distress – grief, fear, anger – from past experience, especially from the very beginnings of life and from childhood; and that there is a tendency for this to be projected out unawarely into all sorts of present situations, distorting perception of a situation and/or behaviour within it. (Heron, 1982: 8; see also Heron, 1988)

From this view of individual psychological development, we argue that researchers often choose (consciously or unconsciously) research topics which will re-stimulate old patterns of distress and invite a renewed attention to restrictive patterns: it is as if we are not content with our distorted experience and behaviour. Many theorists of human development have suggested that human beings have a natural tendency or drive towards full realization of the self; we suggest that, in the choice of research topic and inquiry process, the researcher moves into the anxiety of old distress, and that this is (intentionally or unintentionally) a bid for personal development.

When this happens, the inquiry process obviously offers an important opportunity to move through and beyond old limiting patterns. Unfortunately, as Devereaux (1967) pointed out, the usual response to the re-stimulated anxiety is defensive, so that we project our anxiety out on to the research situation, thus distorting our perspective in a way similar to the effect of counter-transference in psychotherapy. Maslow (1966) has shown how this defensive attitude pervades science. Yet this does not have to be so: if researchers are committed to the pursuit of rigorous critical subjectivity (see Heron and Reason, Chapter 12), if they are prepared and able to use their subjectivity as part of the inquiry process, if they have the skills and support to manage and transcend this re-stimulated distress, the response can be creative and developmental.

All inquirers need to explore how their unaware distress and psychological defences distort their inquiry. Some systematic method is needed which is powerful enough to reach into the unconscious, draw the distress into awareness and either resolve it or allow it creative expression – this might be psychotherapy or a discipline of spiritual development. A fundamental practice many students draw on is autobiographical and creative writing (Goldberg, 1986). However, we have also discovered that the very discipline of the inquiry process, in particular the cycles of action and reflection supported by a group of colleagues engaged in a similar process, is a developmental process in its own right.

> For a long time at the beginning of her research Jill was unable to be clear about her work. She wanted to explore the role of emotions in training groups, but beyond that was often not capable of expressing her ideas. Interactions in the postgraduate research group often brought on tears, and she became curious that she was nearly always menstruating at the times of the group sessions. At first we were concerned and frustrated with her lack of clarity, but as we worked together, with the

> help of the rest of the group, she realized the tension that had always existed between her emotional, intuitive ways of knowing and the rational forms of knowledge that had always been demanded of her at school and college. Together we realized that an important part of her work was to produce a 'watery' thesis full of 'fluid knowledge'. Tears and menstrual flow became positive signs of knowing flowing. Sometime following this realization Jill started to become immensely productive, writing at length with flow and creativity. (see Treseder, 1996)

A third perspective through which we can view human development is the transpersonal. The self may be approached through the imaginal world (Avens, 1980; Hillman, 1975); it may be seen as a reflection of different archetypal patterns – 'primordial psychic processes transformed into images, where consciousness can grasp them' (Hampden-Turner, 1981: 46). Imaginal work 'eschews causal connections', which it sees as 'literalisms which may trap the psyche' (Hillman, 1985). Rather, it works through multiple imaginal perspectives, different matrices, metaphors and myths to view, deepen and interconnect. As Hillman says, the task of imaginal psychology is soul-making, honouring one's inner spirit or daimon (Hillman, 1975, 1996). It is important to honour this way of working and to be open to a variety of patterns through which imaginal knowing can emerge and take shape. Students experiment often with storying and re-storying their lives, drawing on myths and other imaginal forms to do this.

Thus, from this perspective we can see the inquiry process as part of the discovery and realization of the self in one of its archetypal forms, and as such as an expression of the collective unconscious. The task then becomes that of exploring the images of the archetype arising in the researcher's unconscious – for example, in dreams and fantasy – and manifesting them through the inquiry process. The importance of the transpersonal process lies not in the 'correctness' of its imagery, but in the challenge it throws out to the materialistic and rational world in which we live. It draws our attention to the unconscious as an essential source of creativity and to the reality of our imagination. It offers the possibility of integrating a knowing from psyche or soul with our knowing from intellect and experience.

Rob Weston, when challenged about whether his work showed adequate systematic application, argued that he felt he was manifesting the Hermes/Trickster archetype, who flits from idea to idea, moves between upper and lower worlds, is a bearer of new ideas, and 'loves to give others the ideas or tools to do a job, and then leave them to do the dirty work'. Later Rob wrote:

> Looking at the past two years from here/now, I can see that it is not quite the case that I have been 'living out the trickster archetype.' It feels, right now, more as if I have been danced – or had my strings pulled, puppet-like – by him!
>
> Dancing with Hermes the Trickster has been, to say the least, a mixed blessing. By his nature, he bestows gifts of great beauty one moment and trips one up in front of a puddle of slurry the next. Working with this archetype has frequently been agonisingly painful. Yet, as is his way, he has helped me to move between the worlds, the worlds of the pre-midlife dolt and the emergent (bruised and confused) man. (Weston, 1999: 19)

Process-oriented Supervision

Given our view that research is not an impersonal, external and solely intellectual endeavour, but rather a complex personal and social process, rather than concentrate on providing 'expert' advice on the content and methodology, our primary attention in supervision is on students' life energies as they engage with their research. We seek to facilitate the personal learning in research, and so help people realize *their* potential project which has relevance to their lives. In our view, good research is an expression of a need to learn and change, to shift some aspect of oneself.

We believe that the quality of this personal process is the foundation for quality in all aspects of the research, including its intellectual creativity. While we do all the things that are usually expected of a research supervisor – we teach methodology, make suggestions as to what students might read, debate ideas, become excited and involved in the content of the research – we hold that they are always secondary to the underlying process of nurturing the student's developing competencies both in understanding and in effective action.

Thus we approach supervision intending to pay attention to a wide range of themes or 'strands of concern'. We see our role as helping bring into the foreground, to make *figural*, those themes which currently require attention and to help the student work with them. In order to achieve this we hold the intention of scanning internally and externally for clues about issues behind those being discussed: incongruities, aspects of the research which are currently being neglected, and so on. We generally surface our ideas and intuitions as suggestions or possibilities, for the student and us to consider.

Over the years we have identified some key themes which can be seen as developmental tensions or dilemmas in the unfolding life of the researchers. The supervision role is to help focus these, affirm them as significant and aid the students in working with them. It is seldom our intention to help them gloss over the issue or resolve it by adopting a solution from outside themselves, although this can occasionally be a choice we all explicitly, and usually temporarily, make. We may therefore at times be experienced as unhelpful. But we see it as vital that students stay in charge of their own research, for only then can they tap and benefit from the life process it expresses. We currently work with groups of about five graduate students as well as one to one, and encourage everyone present to contribute to an exploration of these themes.

Engaging with the project: what is this research about in students' lives?

As we have argued above, the motivation to research may arise from existential commitments in students' lives: they are committed to work with issues of race or gender, to manage in ways that are collaborative and inquiring, to address the crisis of ecological sustainability. Often they know intuitively or tacitly what it is they want to research, but their definition of the project is typically too loose, too formal, too presented for outside consumption to really take off. The project needs to touch their heart in some way if it is to sustain them over the several years required. Engagement may come in stages, with a progressive deepening of appreciation that the research has life relevance. It may occur early on in the process, or arrive much later. The feeling of lack of engagement may haunt the project for a while, lurking in the background but somehow difficult to address. There may be a sudden 'Aha!' experience as the student realizes what their research is really about for them. Sometimes full engagement never happens, so the student is left with a competent yet unexciting (for them) project.

Engaging with the personal process of inquiry

As we argued above, engaging in the inquiry process may touch on old hurts and re-stimulate old patterns of response. While the supervisor is not a psychotherapist and the research peer group is not a therapy group, both need to find a willingness lovingly and attentively to sit with the disturbance, to help find its creative edge, to interrupt when it is acted out unproductively.

Research in this mode may take people to the edge of their capabilities and beyond, so from time to time most pieces of research hit a more major crisis – a life issue arises which will not go away, cannot be resolved in the relatively short term. At these times it is important to acknowledge the significance of what is happening, to affirm it as a longer-term process, and to attempt to allow space for the issue to find its own resolution.

Engaging in the learning community

Good research cannot be done alone: we each need to be with others who can support and challenge our work, to be affirmed as inquiring persons and to know where we stand in relation to others. We have in the past emphasized the importance of other people acting as 'Devil's Advocates' (Heron, 1988) and as 'friends willing to act as enemies' (Torbert, 1976). Maybe in this we have not emphasized enough the need for 'friends willing to act as friends': inquiry can be a difficult and lonely path, and we need all the support we can get.

To serve these several purposes, we have established postgraduate research groups for teaching, supervision, support and appropriate critique. Working in this way requires attention to group dynamics, and the *manner* in which students engage with their peers – their response to the issues of inclusion, control and intimacy which arise in the group (Srivastva, Obert and Neilson, 1997) – can provide important cues for the development of students and their inquiries.

Mirroring

Thus the research community itself can become part of the field of inquiry. What is going on in the students' projects may be mirrored in the supervision sessions, in the relationship with the supervisor, and in the relationship with peers in the research community. This may require as much attention as other aspects of the research.

Relations with authority and self-authority

We are senior academics with considerable reputations in our field; we are also seen as *standing for* the authority of the scientific and academic establishment. For both these reasons we are often invested with unrealistic power and insight; we are also a potential authoritarian threat. There is at times a distressing and difficult process: students initially express undue reverence for us or rebel; they then decide that we too are far from perfect and not particularly threatening. This is hopefully followed by a realistic assessment of our position as rather more experienced but certainly not infallible co-inquirers.

Even when students seem to have taken on personal responsibility for their inquiry and to have recognized their previous attribution of authority externally, it is interesting how easily the pattern of de-authorisation can recur. Any mention of examiners, for example, can swiftly trigger it. It then helps to have other students around who can notice and challenge this.

Developing an appropriate methodology

Closely related to the last point, it is our experience that even though our students join us because of our reputation for non-traditional methodologies, they often still seem to have absorbed a 'received' view of science. That is, maybe unconsciously, they believe that there is some 'true' or 'correct' methodology for the problem that they are studying, and that there is some authority who holds the key to this.

The methodologies we teach are best seen as sets of general principles and heuristic devices which can be adapted creatively to different research issues. They raise questions rather than offer answers, and we see ourselves as working to help students create and frame strategies for themselves, always seeking the appropriate method and form to the circumstances. However, sometimes students think that they have to adopt one of the methodologies that we teach; they may, for example, feel inadequate as researchers until they have done a 'proper' co-operative inquiry. Sometimes insecurity about 'getting it right' is more covertly expressed, and we have to explore whether this is an issue.

Moving from internal to external engagement

Co-operative inquiry has been called 'research *with* people' and a 'process of learning through risk-taking in living'. To conduct this kind of inquiry the initiating researcher must establish quite long-term collaborative relationships with a group of people. This form of research engagement is usually far more demanding than interviewing or using a questionnaire. Similarly, methods such as action inquiry require that students engage critically and authentically with their own experience in relation to others. There is something about embarking on research that can make people feel inadequate and unskilled. This feeling of inadequacy can take many different forms – intellectual, interpersonal, emotional, empirical, entrepreneurial and so on.

The step of moving from conception to active engagement is sometimes quite difficult. Students need to be bold enough to take this step and clear enough about their own purposes to express these to possible collaborators, and yet to be open enough to other people's interests to enter into dialogue. Entering this engagement phase raises all kinds of practical questions about the amount of time and commitment required, whether others are as interested in the inquiry questions as the students, and whether the latter feel sufficiently skilled and self-valuing to proceed. If researchers also think that they should do the project perfectly, they feel even more inhibited.

Moving from action to reflection and intellectual development

A contrasting pattern is for students to prefer active engagement and dive into this early in the inquiry. This may well be their preferred style of learning, but it has both benefits and costs which we then discuss with them. Sometimes the reflective aspect of the research is repeatedly neglected as more action opportunities arise; then we become particularly suspicious and challenging. Sometimes students are wary about their ability to work conceptually and so will avoid moving on to explore theoretically.

Developing intellectual competence

The intellectual theme is often a focus of particular concern for postgraduate research students. There are several reasons for this. Studying for an MPhil or PhD carries a lot of social kudos, and therefore anxiety. The latter qualification, particularly, is seen as a pinnacle of academic achievement in a society which over-values the intellectual. This can draw out immensely driven and competitive behaviour in some people. But so many people's intellectual self-confidence has been damaged and undermined in earlier life. They come to us with all the appropriate qualifications, but not trusting their abilities to think for themselves, or believing that their kinds of conceptual thinking – perhaps because they seem more intuitive or emotion-related – are somehow not legitimate.

Another intellectual challenge that most students face is that there seem to be so many ideas around, so much that has to be read and known, that they can become swamped by other people's frameworks and thus have no space to develop their own. Other people's thinking often acquires an undue weight of apparent authority by being published in books and referred to in cryptic phrases by other students and supervisors. We do not believe all-encompassing literature searches are necessarily relevant, especially as many of our students will be exploring the intersections of different academic topic areas, making this an impossible task. We do look for engagement in depth with relevant and stimulating theoretical sources. What the limits of this should be is another topic of ongoing debate and negotiation between us.

The intellectual competence required for *nontraditional* forms of research is particularly problematic because it involves the skill of stepping outside the framework of one's own thinking. Frameworks of understanding serve as temporary resolutions as we participate in creating our worlds. We need them, but also need to 'hold them lightly', and be ready to discard them when they are in danger of becoming rigid and reified. We often think of this in terms of Bateson's levels of learning (Bateson, 1972). While Learning II takes place within a framework of knowledge, Learning III moves beyond and looks over the boundaries of frameworks. The latter is a pretty tall order, because it involves going beyond the bondage – and thus beyond the safety – of a particular paradigm, and importantly also beyond the taken-for-granted sense of self (see also Kegan, 1994; Torbert, 1991).

Communicating

When it comes to writing about their research, many students encounter problems. Most often they reexperience doubts about their competence – 'I can't write' – or worry that they cannot tell the full story of the research because it is too personal or too challenging of mainstream ideas – 'I can't write *that*!' Many will be concerned about who will read their theses – parents and work colleagues, especially – and do not want to disclose truths they have learnt through the inquiry process which would disrupt or shock particular audiences. Often academic spectres emerge, partly to allay such anxieties, and the writing becomes dry, cryptic, distanced, defensive – and so very different from the lively and sometimes chaotic process of research.

We work with students to help them find their authentic voices and forms for expressing the research. We particularly encourage people to start writing early on in their inquiry to keep a continuing record of their developments, and to write for themselves first in an uncensored way to see what emerges. Later they may make protective choices about what to include in their theses, often able to comment reflectively on the boundary of privacy they have chosen.

The Supervision Process

As we mentioned above, while as research supervisors we do recommend reading, debate ideas, teach methodology and engage in other more traditional activities, our attention and interest centres on these issues of personal process. What kinds of behaviour do we engage in?

Noticing and reflecting

We try in all our supervision engagements to cultivate a dual attention. While our primary attention may be focused on an issue of theory or methodology, we attempt at the same time continually to ask ourselves, 'What else is going on?'; we try to pay attention to cues in our own and the students' behaviour that might hint at other issues. We share our wonderings and our observations with our students as freely as we are able.

Making the mirror conscious

As we believe strongly that the supervision process and students' participation in the postgraduate groups mirror the research process, we try to make this connection conscious by asking explicit questions about potential connections, and by pointing out links as we see them.

Scanning for other themes

Quite often we find that students may be attending primarily to one aspect of the inquiry when we suspect that the key issue resides in another. This may involve over-concern for methodological or intellectual subtlety as a means of avoiding a more personal issue that the work is throwing up. Noticing and questioning what is not being attended to is one of our most important functions as supervisors. It involves commenting on the framing of the research rather than becoming trapped within it.

Using a range of intervention strategies

Our style of working requires us to use a range of intervention strategies and to be able to move between them flexibly and with appropriate timing – and we do not always do this skilfully. We believe we use far more facilitative than authoritative interventions (Heron, 1999; see also Wadsworth, Chapter 31) – although our students may not interpret us as doing so. We are particularly aware of needing to integrate support and challenge in our responses to people's work, and to build relationships robust enough to take open feedback, in both directions.

Noticing, or leaving open to question, our own personal, political and social processes

What we bring to supervision is obviously a vital aspect of the relationship, and it is important that we work to be clear about our agendas and their potential impacts. It helps to have others around – both staff and other students – who can point out when we may be working our issue rather than helping the students.

Issues of authority

We find many challenges in managing our own authority as educators and as academics. We believe strongly that we both have a lot to offer: we have developed a particular range of perspectives on the conduct of inquiry; we have strong and clear opinions about issues of epistemology and methodology; we are both forceful personalities who want to be influential. We try to draw attention to our use of authority when we notice it arises, to frame it as a question to be explored rather than a given condition.

Conclusion

This chapter sketches some of the issues we have been increasingly aware of over the past ten years and have discussed informally many times; articulating this perspective has helped us clarify our views of our practice. By making our view of our practice explicit both to existing and potential students we hope we will all heighten our awareness so that our inquiry process becomes more fully part of our lives and our practice continually develops.

Note

This chapter borrows liberally and adapts from earlier papers (Marshall and Reason, 1994; Reason and Marshall, 1987). We deeply appreciate the willingness of our graduate students to learn with us over these many years, and are grateful in particular for a close and long-term collaborative colleagueship with Jack Whitehead and more recently with Donna Ladkin.

References

Argyris, C., Putnam, R. and Smith, D.M. (1985) *Action Science: Concepts, Methods, and Skills for Research and Intervention*. San Francisco, CA: Jossey Bass.

Avens, R. (1980) *Imagination is Reality*. Dallas, TX: Spring Publications.

Bateson, G. (1972) *The Logical Categories of Learning and Communication: Steps to an Ecology of Mind*. San Francisco, CA: Chandler.

Davis, M.S. (1971) 'That's interesting! Towards a phenomenology of sociology and a sociology of phenomenology', *Journal of the Philosophy of Social Science*, 1: 309–44.

Devereaux, G. (1967) *From Anxiety to Method in the Behavioural Sciences*. The Hague: Mouton.

Douglas, C. (1999) 'From surviving to thriving: Black women managers in Britain'. Unpublished PhD dissertation, University of Bath, Bath.

Goldberg, N. (1986) *Writing Down the Bones – Freeing the Writer Within*. Boston, MA: Shambhala Publications Inc.

Hampden-Turner, C. (1970) *Radical Man*. London: Duckworths.

Hampden-Turner, C. (1981) *Maps of the Mind*. London: Michell Beazley.

Heron, J. (1982) 'Empirical validity in experiential research', Human Potential Research Project, University of Surrey, Guildford.

Heron, J. (1988) 'Validity in co-operative inquiry', in P. Reason (ed.), *Human Inquiry in Action*. London: Sage Publications. pp. 40–59.

Heron, J. (1999) *The Complete Facilitator's Handbook*. London: Kogan Page.

Hillman, J. (1975) *Revisioning Psychology*. New York: Harper Colophon.

Hillman, J. (1985) Comments at an Oxford Seminar organised by the Champernowne Trust.

Hillman, J. (1996) *The Soul's Code: In Search of Character and Calling*. New York: Random House.

Kegan, R. (1994) *In Over Our Heads: the Mental Demands of Modern Life*. Cambridge, MA: Harvard University Press.

Marshall, J. (1999) 'Living life as inquiry', *Systematic Practice and Action Research*, 12 (2): 155–71.

Marshall, J. and Reason, P. (1994) 'Adult learning in collaborative action research: reflections on the supervision process', *Studies in Continuing Education: Research and Scholarship in Adult Education*, 15 (2): 117–32.

Maslow, A. (1966) *The Psychology of Science*. New York: Harper & Row.

May, R. (1961) *Existential Psychology*. New York: Random House.

Reason, P. and Marshall, J. (1987) 'Research as personal process', in D. Boud and V. Griffin (eds), *Appreciating Adult Learning*. London: Kogan Page. pp. 112–26.

Srivastva, S., Obert, S.L. and Neilson, E. (1997) 'Organizational analysis through group processes: a theoretical perspective', in C.L. Cooper (ed.), *Organizational Development in the UK and USA*. London: Macmillan. pp. 83–111.

Torbert, W.R. (1976) *Creating a Community of Inquiry: Conflict, Collaboration, Transformation*. New York: Wiley.

Torbert, W.R. (1991) *The Power of Balance: Transforming Self, Society, and Scientific Inquiry*. Newbury Park, CA: Sage Publications.

Treseder, J. (1996) 'Bridging incommensurable paradigms in organizations'. Unpublished PhD dissertation, University of Bath, Bath.

Weston, R. (1999) 'Digging for gold'. Unpublished MSc dissertation in Responsibility and Business Practice, University of Bath, Bath.

31
The Mirror, the Magnifying Glass, the Compass and the Map: Facilitating Participatory Action Research

YOLAND WADSWORTH

CHAPTER OUTLINE

In this chapter I describe the move from being 'the researcher' to becoming 'facilitator of our co-researching'. I discuss what I did as a facilitator over a number of years in a large piece of participatory action research, and from this articulate six key facilitation capabilities, showing also how these can be applied to a snapshot of the micro practice of part of a day. The conclusion draws out the differences between the working practices of 'the researcher' in a conventional piece of research and those of a 'facilitator of participatory action research'.

Can you love or respect the people and assist their/our inquiry without imposition of your will
Can you intervene in the most vital matters and yield to events taking their course
Can you attain deep knowing and know you do not understand
Conceive, give birth and nourish without retaining ownership
Trust action without knowing outcome
Guide by being guided
Exercise stewardship without control …

(Interpretation of words attributed to Lao Tzu, *c.* 550BC)[1]

From the Royal 'We' to the Achieved 'We'

My discomfort grew, during the early years of my career, with the mantle of the scientific 'We' and the presumptive and ultimately unscientific ventriloquism that it authorized: of speaking for the lives and realities of 'our' subjects without them being actively present in that process. The discomfort propelled many of us to shift from being the deemers and certifiers of Truth, to being the facilitators of inquiry processes for others to come to their own truths-for-the-purposes.

In reclaiming the 'I' as critical to inquiry, we also came to real-ize the deeply intersubjective nature of truth-construction *per se*. For example, in this paradigm, active engagement – far from distorting truth – may become the only way to get at certain truth/s. Thus 'I' becomes a node or knot in an extended iterative feedback network, cybernetic system or new 'community of science'. In this sense the task of 'facilitation' of inquiry may also be understood as more shared, and the nature, extent and quality of the sharing in turn determining the nature of the outcome. On the other hand, the more the tasks are centralized, the more the challenge to any nominal facilitator/s' capacity to democratize the effort and assure the collective construction which constitutes an important source of trustworthiness and 'objectivity'.

The genuine achievement of a sense of 'we' or 'us' becomes then an indicator of this trustworthiness: 'starting' with the group making its own selection of facilitator, and continuing through to 'an end' when any write-up not only contains no surprises to the collaborating inquirers but is actively embraced by them/us as expressing theory and new practice already trialled. Or when an analysis is so resonant that any of the participants can independently reproduce it in other forums. It is reflected now also in my mistrust of a 'truth' unless

I can know and judge the context, level and kind of participatory processes that were engaged in to produce it. This includes needing evidence of participation of the relevant 'others', including those who might have been a 'them' at the outset of the inquiry.

Thus the more that research admits to its processes all who are relevant or have an interest, the task of facilitation may be a more collective undertaking shaped by the micro-actions of all participants who are, to greater or lesser extents:

- observing and surfacing the discrepancy that drives the inquiry;
- talking with others critically interested in or affected by it;
- framing and asking questions about it;
- being interested and involved in the answering;
- developing interpretations, new theories, answers and subsequent action-proposals;
- trying them out, and so on.

Conceptually we might think of two kinds of facilitation – the first where we carry out these things for ourselves, and a second where we 'keep watch' and take actions to ensure these things are happening for others, individually and collectively.

Given that the quality of an inquiry can be depleted if participants are not themselves actively inquiring, one of the important skills of a nominal facilitator is to divine for and assist the maximum energetic self-pursuit of the questions and answers by the largest number of people possible. In my experience, when this works, participatory research 'takes off' and the facilitator or co-ordinator may need only lightly to hold the shape of the emergent design.

Applying Facilitation Skills

In my own work I characteristically practise in one of two kinds of ways. One is as a largely hands-off consultant to other people's inquiry efforts (including other people's facilitation of other people's inquiry efforts). In this work my most useful contribution is usually at the outset where I assist in the shaping, framing, conceptualization and design. This is primarily 'compass' work involving close divination of guiding values and practical purposes, an assessment of interest and energy levels, time, money and people resources, creative drawing on a bag of techniques and iteratively checking for resonance. There is a lot of intense listening, probing, questioning, clarifying, offering, watching for the response and being guided by it, and then listening, probing, questioning, etc. again. The people – having got to their own 'YES!' – usually do the rest. I might do many of these in a year.

The second facilitation practice is more long term and involves me in developmental efforts with one group or organization over a period of at least several years. It is much more an 'ours', I am much more in the thick of it and I usually feel like I am 'knitting socks on 24 needles'. Below I describe one experience that started as the former (a single consultancy session) and grew into an example of the latter (for six years, over a period of a total of eight years).

The particular story I tell about my part in facilitating the large, complex and lengthy 'U&I' inquiry project represents a specific and negotiated constellation of skills and tasks in response to the particular situation – in turn resting on my level of mastery (or lack of it) of various key capabilities I describe later.

It is also worth observing that I have not found this an easy chapter to write. Not only do presumptuous claims of the immodest Royal 'I' (as in 'I did this' 'I did that') sit uncomfortably with a hard-won 'we', but the irony is that the more any of us work to facilitate inquiry, the more all our store of exemplars, working techniques, methods, decision-rules, built capabilities and practical experiences, collected in the course of thousands of hours of observing, listening, responding, talking, asking and thinking seem to have – and probably need to have – largely disappeared into our relatively inaccessible mental filing cabinets of intuitive, unconscious tacit knowing!

Facilitating the Understanding and Involvement (U&I) Project

Facilitation tasks	**From questionnaire survey …**
Listen.	It all started as a quite modest and conventional effort.
Examine the seed and the ground in which it is taking root.	The co-ordinator of the small but activist Statewide peak organization for mental health service-users rang to ask for advice about conducting a questionnaire opinion survey of patients at a large central city psychiatric hospital that had sought their involvement. The survey seemed to be the next step after a previous study conducted by an external contract researcher.
Compass work – guided by the critical reference perspective (Wadsworth,	When asked to give comments on the proposed exit survey I could have done just that – made that conventional 'expert' intervention – and that could have been the end of the matter.

1997a (1st edn), 1997b: 12-18, Epstein and Wadsworth, 1994), namely here: consumers.

Instead I arranged to meet with the co-ordinator and other service- users involved with the organization and, rather than just going ahead quickly, we talked. This talk, like all talk throughout any project, is a form of 'getting to know you' – ostensibly about the topic, but simultaneously we are checking for each other's trustworthiness, beliefs, values, *modus operandi*, and so on. As well, if I am working with a genuine consumer organization, such as this was, I will check for desire to work with staff (and if it is staff or management of an organization, I will check for levels of desire to work with consumers – and quite often make it a condition of my facilitation that consumers, usually more than one, meet with us).

Further compass work – detecting the deeper purposes and the state of existing, desired and alienated connections, and the strength of the driving energies.

People talked of their experiences of questionnaire surveys as not really telling *their* stories, and also typically not being acted on. On probing, it emerged that they wanted staff to *understand* their situation by putting themselves in the consumer's situation – so they would see the need for change, and then work out how to do this with the input and active *involvement* of consumers.

The conditions which indicated a special need for a facilitation-of-participation style were present. There was ambivalence, perspectives were often divergent even radically so, and were additionally not clearly understood by each other; they were varied within and across the major stakeholding groups, and it was a persistent problem that seemed to defy solution. The situation cried out for the involvement of all those concerned – staff and consumers – and thus the *Understanding, Anytime* project commenced (McGuiness and Wadsworth, 1991). Further probing revealed that consumers preferred to speak face to face about their experiences in their own words as a way of doing justice to the rich meanings of their 'whole' stories.

... to dialogic design

Shaping, focusing – cutting away extraneity; assisting with research methods, staff selection.

Subsequently the initial idea, about a self-completed questionnaire survey for patients being discharged, transformed into an idea for some kind of participatory evaluation conducted in dialogue with staff. A college-based Nursing Department was originally to conduct the staff side of the study, but this did not eventuate. The consumer organization then offered to conduct both a series of informal interviews with a total population of all inpatients at one ward admitted during a one-week period late in 1990, and match this with a series of consumer-perspective questions to staff.

Framing questions. Noticing. Cultivating respect/ connectedness. and magnifying glasses. Shape dialogue as a design: mirrors

The consumer discussions heard people's experiences of coming to, being in and then leaving the ward, and the staff were asked consumer-perspective strategic questions about what they were trying to achieve for consumers, what they were up against, how they knew if they achieved useful things for consumers, and so on.

The material from each of the two groups was then swapped and further discussions arranged to reflect on it. In this way people became the researchers of their own and each others' experiences.

The results of these reflections were swapped once more before time and funds ran out and the process came to a temporary halt.

Systems-thinking to make dialogue permanent. Contribute to research grant application.

Many were extremely interested in what staff and consumers had to say. However the consumer organization was concerned with how these kinds of reflective and illuminative conversational processes might *continue* in busy daily work to the point of innovating new practice – especially as they seemed to have ended in this instance just as they were really beginning.

One cycle ends ...

To examine how to build in such talk and dialogue between

staff and consumers as a permanent element of any mental health services, a further four-year project – the *Understanding and Involvement (U&I)* project commenced.

Building research, building understanding

... another begins. The process of facilitation repeats ... and 'scales up' with new grounding, identifying a 'sample' and the emergent questions ... building further connectedness and mutual knowing.

The U&I project began with a process of 'organic referral' to make contact with about 60 staff and consumers located in a range of strategic spots in the hospital, associated area mental health services, and regional and central offices of the relevant government department. Our questioning about possible consumer evaluative methods had to be responsive also to volunteered talk about the 'culture' or context of acute psychiatric services and broaden to encompass themes such as power, fear, violence, stigma, etc. (The 'our', 'us' and 'we' in this account is, variously, a core group of the four of us in the research *Work Team* [of whom three were service-users]; this was part of, and worked with, a *Collaborative Committee* of about 14, of whom half were staff and half were consumers. The service-users were also part of a paid *Consumer Consultants' Group* of around 15; and in turn all three of these groupings were part of a *Network* of eventually around 200 people who either took part in the research or an element of it or retained an interest in it.)

What people said was circulated as discussion papers to the 60 who had taken part (Epstein and Wadsworth, 1994). We also needed a way to cross-fertilize the ideas and opted for short, multi-coloured, monthly project bulletins that reported to the network on the project's various tentacles of activity and mini action research projects throughout the second year. We later concluded that this network was crucial in the eventual 'gelling' of both our own understandings and also the subsequent new policy and funded programme directions for mental health service consumer participation.

Building in the resources, by which more energies can be kindled. Creating reflective pools in which to explore hunches, chart new maps.

Meanwhile the U&I project office (located in the hospital's clinical services building) became something of a safe space for increasing numbers of consumers attracted to the project. We noticed that both this office and a research advisory committee – which had metamorphosed into a Staff–Consumer Collaborative Committee wanting to talk about the issues – were doing some rather unique things that also needed to be found a time and place as part of the fabric of consumer feedback/staff–consumer communication. Particularly they seemed to operate as a special place for 'deeper talk' in a way that did not easily happen in the press of daily practice. We realized this was an essential mechanism in its own right if old closed-loop or single-loop thinking was to be replaced by double-loop learning that could retrieve and transform the more fundamental assumptions driving practice (Argyris, 1993).

Stepping back to let the critical energies ground themselves.

Alongside the development of the Collaborative Committee, it soon became clear the consumers in the project needed to meet as a consumer-only panel. This panel also metamorphosed, becoming a Consumer Consultants' Group in which consumers began to articulate the contribution they could make to assist the system, hear the experiences of consumers and make changes. The group functioned continuously to strengthen and support their own ways of speaking and acting and to build confidence and certainty about these ways. This nurturing of discourse or 'native language' meant truths could be spoken that otherwise could not. In this way a new resource was created to supply a self-trained cadre of consumers ready, willing and able to engage with, and contribute to, the mental health services system.

Compass work – detecting flat energy – and knife work to carve out a new inquiry design element. Systems thinking.

Meanwhile back in the wards, we initially thought we would be seeing small groups of staff establishing standard small action research or quality assurance projects – inquiring into consumers' views and co-reflecting on their practice. A small number of projects did eventuate, and they were circulated in the inquiry network, but for the most part staff were polite (and sometimes wary) but overwhelmingly busy elsewhere. We then tried a different tack. To mimic the first stage of an inquiry, we decided to try to supply staff with a free and confidential voice to say what questions they would like to ask of consumers concerning the methods which had arisen in the initial round of discussions. The Medical Director and Director of Nursing Services signed a cover letter urging staff to respond to this survey as an official Quality Assurance exercise.

Observing energies ignite ... but then detecting new blockages.

Expecting only a small response we instead got 100 staff (a 50 per cent response rate) volunteering more than 1,400 questions they would like to put to consumers. Yet when we went back to each of the wards with the questions staff had nominated, we again encountered the 'melting away': the paradox we eventually theorized whereby staff 'want to hear from consumers' but also seemingly 'don't want to hear from consumers'.

More map-making.

While we deepened our theory about what structural aspects we were up against, we had eventually to conclude that the transformative energy was not able to come from staff alone in sufficient degree to be effective.

With time running out, and with the urging of two influential staff members combined with the energy bubbling in the Consumer Consultants' Group, we began trialing the involvement of consumers as catalysts for ensuring consumer views were fed back into the wards.

Energies run ... ignite, are shaped and fuelled.

Immediately we got movement. Sympathetic staff had something to work with, the activities were not too elaborate, and the processes did not have to end. We were able to research and develop a range of methods (Wadsworth and Epstein, 1996a) including:

Shape the resources into systems elements.

- Satisfaction/end-of-stay questionnaire surveys.
- Special purpose 'spot' surveys on specific topics.
- Complaints procedures and feedback mechanisms (e.g., suggestion boxes).
- Group discussions, ward community meetings, focus groups and dialogues.
- History and case storytelling; self-written case records.
- Advocacy by others (e.g., community visitors, case advocates).
- Interpersonal sensitive communication/conversation
- Involvement of ex-consumers as systems consultants and consumer representatives (e.g., on wards and to management processes such as staff selection, policy, ethics, training and programme review committees).
- Patient involvement in their own treatment plans, including access to medical and nursing records.
- Consumer involvement in planning and policy meetings.

Scaling-up the system

Systems thinking, compass and process work to expand the connections ... and track the lode-bearing seams and lines of greatest energy

Yet we found that things had to change at all levels and throughout the system if change for any individual service-user on any single ward was to be achieved and sustained. We understood this not as a simple matter of 'research followed by implementation' but that the research was *of* the implementation efforts to *and least resistance.*

'build in' something do-able system-wide.

Work with the initial ward extended and expanded upwards, outwards and iteratively: to all wards in the hospital, then to the Area Mental Health Service, other area services, to the region and state and finally federal levels of government policy and funding administration. Despite the incessantly paradoxical nature of people's commitment to consumer participation, we then began to watch systemic change take place.

More systems thinking ... and bigger maps are drawn, charting the new territory revealed. Full summer flowering ... and a rich harvest.

Eight years and two projects later (attracting a total of a quarter of a million dollars of research funds), consumer–staff collaboration had developed a comprehensive working model and valuable new theory regarding paradox and its origins as well as regarding the conditions needed to involve consumers. The model was taken up and funded in one hospital and area mental health service, and then elements of it were taken up in other Area Mental Health Services.
A statewide Consumer Participation Policy was associated with this work, as well as follow-up projects on dialogue and a statewide government funding programme to employ consumers as quality improvement consultants in every area mental health service (recently re-funded for the third year). The consumer consultants' group is a continuing and independently incorporated organization which has also now produced its own systems-evaluation book. The project also won two national awards – one from the Australasian Evaluation Society for pioneering evaluation literature, and the other a prestigious Mental Health Services gold award for a partnership project.

New managers let the tree die.

While our work of course does not account for everything that followed, the detailed documentation does indicate the extent and nature of its contribution during the active phase of the project. However, an evaluation for which funding had been won was never conducted (on the grounds either that some staff 'didn't want it' and that it was 'unscientific' or that it wasn't valued), thus bringing the project to a premature end.

Map-making.

The U&I research made a theoretical contribution in setting out to explain why there were so many limits to staff wanting to experiment with ceding even modest power to consumers. We came to understand the mental health system as *paradoxical* – as one which society has established both to help its citizens to health, healing and recovery and to 'manage' its own helplessness and fear in the face of anxiety, uncertainty, distaste and perceived social difference. In effect the system represents a concentration of these. Staff may respond to consumers with their own negative feelings, resorting to language and other coercive, exclusionary or distancing practices *at the same time* as being called on (and wanting) to respond in a caring and healing way. Subsequently, there may be defensive explanation and resort to the legal reserve powers that the system makes available, and the cycle of complaint thus continues (Wadsworth and Epstein, 1998).

We saw that a more healthy system would rest on there being sufficient amounts of contemplative, reflexive and restorative practice to counter the constant tendency to second-guessing and unresponsive practices. Ironically, the peer supports and resources for staff and consumers are missing to the extent the system goes on protecting itself from 'intelligence information' from consumers and from staff. This is the chicken and the egg of a system that can only hear feedback if it basically knows it is of a pretty good standard, but will only get to that pretty good standard with consumer and staff feedback ...

Drawing out the Key Facilitation Capabilities

Among the hundreds of micro-skills drawn on in the above work, I want to draw out six key areas that I now think are crucial to the success of facilitating collaborative inquiry. For those who find metaphor a useful device, these six capabilities or elements of facilitation may be thought of as ground, air, fire, wood, metal, water, respectively. Their cyclic and sequential nature – like that of action research *per se* – may also usefully be thought of as analogous tothe cycle of the seasons, or to the cycle of life *per se*. At the risk of a feat of supreme abstract reductionism, they are as follows.

Knowing self, knowing others

The primary capability is, I think, the extent and ways in which we can know others and know our own selves (including surfacing what is conscious and unconscious, discussable and undiscussable). The metaphors of the mirror and the magnifying glass are key tools in this capability (Wadsworth, 1997b). Not only does this now seem to me to be the way of ensuring our inquiry efforts are well-grounded, but also I think marks the boundaries of the extent – and limits – to our facilitation efforts. In a way our work in the 'outer projects' rests on how far we get with our 'inner project'. For example, knowledge and acceptance of one's own 'inner diversity' may be a key to knowing and accepting diversity among others.

With insight and observation, we are better able to 'know our turf', detect the lay of the land, chart the nature of the territory, and follow the layers and lode-bearing seams. We are better able to ground our knowledge of when to do what (and when not to do what), to know what we feel and think and what others feel and think, and to serve as a well-earthed basis from which to take creative risks. Radars and geiger counters might be other useful metaphoric tools for this element of the work and Denis Cowan's 'self as sonar pulse' – sending out probes which reflect back the person's current position and possible direction – also touches on this matter nicely (ACTLIST email discussion group, 8 March 1998, 9:07:55). This capability is also a pathway to self and mutual regard – to 'capacity-build' a culture of respectful response in which people are questioned and understood and acted towards in mindful relation.

The resulting descriptions, models, concepts and theories are the maps we make of the charted territory.

In the U&I project, no one emerged the same person as when they began, and the achievements and limits of the project reflect our individual journeys in ways told only so far superficially in the last pages of the final U&I volume (Wadsworth and Epstein, 1996b). The gift from one member of staff to me in the last days of the project of a copy of *The Velveteen Rabbit* – the story of a battered journey to 'truth' – represents for me in a non-trivial way what we went through individually and collectively.

Real-izing inter-connectedness

A second capability is to make real, in numerous ways, the existing and potential ways in which our own inner and outer diverse and grounded natures are related to one another. This includes our being able to connect with each other in shared experience, breathing life or an *esprit de corps* into each other and our collective inquiry. While the spaces and places between us can separate us, it is these same spaces and places that are needed for 'arc-ing' (Goff, 1998: 178–83) to take place across, for the purposes of connecting us. Tasks include identifying and bringing together all relevant participants or stakeholders through inclusive processes of 'organic' or 'naturalistic recruitment', and emergently knitting together inquiry groups and inquiry networks. It rests on the use of ecological, hermeneutical or 'big picture' systems thinking to assist us to see the way we are together in the world and to enable us to draw the best theoretical 'maps' by which we can navigate until better ones are found.

In the U&I project, we found and inclusively built groupings of people to sustain the mutual inquiry. This included the core group who shared the critical reference group perspective and the inquiry's questions, and the wider network that included the spectrum of players, perspectives and value-interests. We found a place (both practically and/or conceptually) for every consumer and staff member who was interested to maximize the energies running and also, as a practical test, to see if every consumer's feedback and every staff member's effort could contribute to service improvement. We then worked to facilitate the needed dialogue within and between the various stakeholder/participant groups (Guba and Lincoln, 1989: 72–33; 204–214; Wadsworth, 1998c).

Identifying the new growth and driving energies

Next is a capability to be able to 'divine' (Wadsworth, in Fitzgerald and Wadsworth, 1996) accurately the sparks of life or the sources and currents of energy both in those who are in our collaborative inquiry field as well as within ourselves. It is these energies which are essential to commence and then drive the inquiry and the participation and action forward and prevent them losing purpose and direction. Critical to this is being able to set the compass of the relevant *'critical participant group/ stakeholder perspective'* which needs to be held and trusted to illuminate the particular and relevant discrepancies between 'is' and 'ought', and guide the emergent design.

Facilitating an inquiry process is in many ways to be an 'energy-worker'. Working with the energies (and the blocked energies) by continuously responding to them is how we are able to get *movement* – the shifts, the insights, the expansion and innovation to 'make the road by walking' (Horton and Freire, 1990). Or, when 'navigating' by embodied energy in the form of emotion (Wadsworth, 1997b; also Small, 1997), we can sense when people are 'jumping to proceed', 'fired up', or 'flat' and energy-sapped.

To achieve this, the U&I project needed to find ways to ensure it would remain driven by consumer energies but also ignite staff energies on this joint journey. This prefigured the policy being sought for all consumer-responsive human services work, namely how to start from 'where consumers were at' and respond to *that*, rather than start from professional theory and practice and attempt to achieve consumers' compliance with these. To this end, the purpose, form and direction were initiated by a consumer organization in response to the hospital's request. The consumer organization selected and employed a consumer research officer, two part-time consumer researchers and myself as a consumer perspective (but non-service user) research consultant on design. We then employed a further 23 part-time consumers as casual researchers and consultants over its four years. The project attempted to model consumer-driven/staff collaborative inquiry by ensuring consumers shaped all phases of the project, including selection and asking of questions, analysing and synthesizing results and deciding on the findings and in collaboration with staff.

Nevertheless many staff did not engage actively. Yet when processes worked more 'from staff's side' and staff's energies would ignite, it would be consumers who would melt away as staff reverted to their own comfortable and familiar discourse, sometimes unwittingly offending consumers (and then feeling specially wounded if this was brought to their attention). At critical moments each literally could not bear to hear the other. If the gap was rarely bridged from staff to consumers, it was also not a matter of finding 'middle ground'. To do so was to risk never ending in the consumer perspective territory that was the whole point of the inquiry. Instead, it seemed to be a matter of facilitating the achievement and holding of a consumer discourse *and* then trying to connect with the staff's.

There were countless further small changes as the 'divining' of energy led to different strategies and various iterations of the emergent project.

Resourcing the effort

Every inquiry effort needs nutrition or fuel for growth: ideas, experiences, perceptions, notes, transcriptions, summaries, perspectives, concepts, new language, theories and creative ways of doing and being; questions (and a permissive culture of questioning and speaking), the responses of selves and others, other people's answers, models, hunches and intuitions; logics, methods for finding out things, exercises, mechanisms, visual methods, newsletters, research techniques, write-ups, electronic lists, organizational and group and process knowledge, knowledge of histories, economies, politics, ethics, dynamics, emotions, various disciplines and professions, similar and diverse people to contribute, supporters, 'critical friends', insiders, outsiders and commentators. All of these can be sought out, foraged, collected, accumulated and offered for consumption by those with the driving energies.

In the U&I project we drew on an extensive range of methods and techniques to resource the process, assisting consumers and staff to employ these themselves (as well as using them in some cases directly myself). They included: community development, group work, evaluation logic, theory-building, naturalistic testing, interviewing, ethnography, case studies, brainstorming, questionnaire surveys, focus group-type discussions, dialogue, co-counselling-type listening techniques, small business management, scribe/writing and records-keeping, storytelling, strategic questioning, systems thinking and reflexivity. As well I brought historical knowledge of the specific mental health and broader human services sectors and knowledge of the public policy process, and then added to these resources by formally consulting widely to identify new methods, practices, etc. I also co-held a big picture that was first built and then applied as a resource to the next cycles of inquiry.

Shaping the inquiry

If the 'grounding' is the time for inquiry *to yield and take in*, then there are also times throughout the cycles of inquiry when there is a need *actively to go forward and shape*: to focus on the essential nub of the inquiry, to be selective and to cull extraneity (while remaining grounded and mindfully open to redefining what is 'extraneity'), to intervene to make 'climbing frames' of linked conceptual 'namings', to make underlying logic or assumptions or explanatory theory-in-use explicit, and challenge new growth so that what survives is strong, to remove any dead wood and generally to shape in substance and timing all that is done and proposed.

Shaping the emergent inquiry enables the inquiry questions to be addressed so as to meet effectively the needs of those with (or with an interest in) the critical driving energies. The accuracy, flexibility and responsiveness of this capacity rests on resonance with the common ground of values and assumptions and on the strength of the trust and connectedness between those involved. Further around an inquiry cycle, it involves discriminating between competing ideas and theories until the agreed interpretations and theoretical 'maps' emerge that in turn shape the processes and outcomes in the next action steps.

If done skilfully, and circumstances allow it to be done responsively from the outset, it can be a gentle process. If the tasks of grounded-shaping are neglected or the environment has responded already with irrelevance or rejection, then the tasks may only be accomplished with more noticeable discomfort and even pain, calling for even higher risk-taking.

Accompanying the transformative moments

The potential and actual moments of change that mark the move between the cycles of observation, questioning, inquiry and thought into new cycles of different action, observation, etc. call for thoughtful 'companioning'.

The requirements here are to assist in the making of space and time for deeper and more creative levels of individual and collective contemplation and dialogue to break out of single-loop into double-loop thinking (Argyris, 1993), to envision, imagine, invent, conceive, and to have faith and trust in the possibility and probability of change. It also requires comfortableness with both stormy and becalmed waters as well as with deep reflective pools of sometimes uncomfortable silence between the seeing-then and the seeing-now, and confidence in the emotions stirred in the body – individual and politic – when painful discrepancy is realized and then addressed. And it needs special resources and methods to aid reflection, contemplation and creativity (such as time and space *per se*, journaling, trusted 'critical friends'). Transformation calls on the facilitator to construct and 'hold' the needed liminal spaces and the safe-holding 'containers', and be driven to probe and feel the ways through the barriers, get leverage over the hurdles and around the road-blocks.

The transformative element then calls for the new ideas or ways to be translated into new practice, and the cycle repeats as that becomes the new 'ground' to be examined.

Once the 'spaces' have been created, the task is to ensure they remain 'built in'. In ensuring the 'parallel universe' of the U&I spaces (drawing on Schein, 1988) remained in the mainstream service system's structures, we worked to make them prefigurative. We constantly asked: How will this survive the end of the project? Who will carry out this function? How will this element be funded? Where in the organization does this 'fit'? We reviewed, reflected on and evaluated everything we did – successes and setbacks – asking How did that go? Did anything change? What did people do as a result of that? Who learned or did what differently after being involved in this? We did this directly, face to face, by written feedback sheets, phone-arounds, asking people to ask others, routine 'check-outs' after every meeting, and so on. We also kept up the momentum for transformation, treating setbacks as 'useful data', projecting an expectation that staff were well-meaning and consumers had valuable things to contribute, keeping going, having courage to go back and ask again when knocked back, keeping the conversations going with as many people as we could, being around, and sitting with silences after asking staff questions that were outside the currently accepted discourse.

A Micro-snapshot of Facilitation Practice – the Project Office

In terms of the key capabilities just described, the following is a snippet of the daily micro-facilitation and compass work that built the larger shape of the U&I project. The scene focuses on the last phase of implementation when our project office transformed into something of a collaborative 'living laboratory' or crucible for reflecting on, developing and testing ideas and practice. In the final months of active fieldwork, every Tuesday, a busy schedule of meeting after meeting saw small groups of consumers and staff coming in and out of the office to work together.

The project office provides an interesting 'text to read' for signs of the hand of facilitation. What is noticeable is the achievement of an atmosphere of communication about matters rarely given time on busy acute units. It displays a combination of 'chance' elements, naturalistic learning, and the way in which such a slightly chaotic and unpredictable environment, characterized by (relatively) high levels of trust and collaboration, yielded more accurate and rich insights and deeper theory later found useful in numerous other services. In among the energetic 'business' are gems of deeper dialogue and communication about theoretical issues as well as about some deeply confidential ones touching on core issues of fear and shame. Facilitation both shaped this and observed the working conditions for alliance, the barriers and enablers of the changed practices we were working towards, and the strengths and weaknesses and opportunities and threats on which we gradually built our working understandings and shaped 'the model' – adding and subtracting elements – to take account of them.

The text is drawn from a research work team member's day book (Wadsworth and Epstein, 1996c: 4–5). This also testifies to the need in a research project – if a published account for a wider audience is considered desirable – for meticulous note-taking in the midst of active 'real life'. Unlike William Foote Whyte in his famous account of retiring to the toilet to make his observations of 'street corner society', these notes were taken in open view of all participants, and at times under hilarious circumstances as we attempted to 'stop the real life' as one of us, mostly me, would ask '*has* that been recorded?' and leap to a notepad or journal to record it. The write-up rested on hundreds of pages of such journals, day books, files of notes and audiotape transcriptions.

Facilitation tasks	**Part of a day-in-the-life of the project office**
	9.30am
Present 'fuel' for 'energies'. Introduce a reflective pool regarding map-making, map-use.	[Two casual paid staff–consumer researchers] and [a staff member] began discussing our consumer participation programme implementation action plan … There is a side discussion evaluating our technique of using – and repeatedly re-using – about half a dozen large poster sheets which record progress made, decisions reached, activities to be undertaken and diagrammatic theory/conceptual models of what we are doing. The view was expressed by those present that they work effectively to retain our 'corporate memory' in a reliable and consistent way, and that they make it easy for newcomers to see where we are 'at' and for participants to be able to take the sheets and tell the story themselves (to new audiences) …
Encourage ear to the ground – to direct the compass ('everything is data').	[Consumer researcher] recounts how she ran into [a senior hospital executive member] at a consumer art show, and unexpectedly received valuable feedback about how [that person] was seeing the project. This gave confidence to a decision for us to write to [that executive member] about [another issue troubling us] …
	10.00am
Connect ground to map of methods and resources.	[A nurse unit manager] pops in to mention a proposal to research consumer involvement in the writing of their own case records while in hospital. (Later in the day, it is suggested the nurse might work with the to-be-appointed Staff–Consumer Consultant and is asked if s/he would like it raised as a project for the Consumer Participation Implementation Committee meeting that afternoon …)
Encourage ground work.	[A consumer who has worked as a casual consultant for the project] is on the phone and updates us on the Internet debate about forcible treatment …
Some metalwork.	[A former co-investigator on the project] rings to report on a letter from a senior hospital clinician associated with our project, apparently indicating a surprising lack of understanding about the requirements for genuinely involving consumers in a writing project. We co-draft a response …
	11.30am
A reflective pool; link to the bigger picture	[A consumer who has come for the project meeting] hands me a written reflection on his/her role in the project for use in the write-up …
	11.45am
Connect new local groundwork.	[Three staff and two more consumers, the latter being paid sitting fees] join us for a meeting of the evaluation research Project Committee. They have come early and there is more informal talk. The meeting starts over half an hour late.
	12.40pm
Weave more elements into the inquiry design.	At the meeting, among other updates, there is a discussion about complaints procedures, a matter being strongly pursued by a sub-group of two staff and several consumers involved in our project …

1.15pm

Actively yield (yin) to the 'fired up' energies.

When the meeting ends, two more consumers and one more staff person come for the special meeting to discuss Complaints Procedures. [Two consumers] and [one member of staff] stay, while [three consumers] and [Non-Government Organization representative] from the previous meeting leave. I go and do photocopying to remove myself from this nascent committee's self-running …

Observe

I return to an active self-sustaining discussion and work at my desk in the background on other things (including a mailout to wider network participants which is slow work given there is a personal post-it yellow note written for most of them). From time to time I record the group's exchanges in the discussion for our files where they throw new light on any matter to do with consumer feedback. The group is also taking its own notes for our project write-up.

Scribe work.

Connecting.

Observe. Check for connectedness. 'Read' the embodied discrepancy. Watch/listen intently. Go forward (yang) ... use systems thinking, driving perspective, hold respect/ connectedness

Just then [a male consumer] new to our project, arrives. I see his head ducked down, eyes not meeting anyone's. He tells quickly and almost inaudibly of his search (at the Admissions Reception counter) for the meeting. Apparently he found himself submitting to the receptionist's request to give his name and address and DOB and was told some of his patient record when it came up on her computer screen. I read clear enough signs of shame and suppressed hurt and I intervene in the discourse (of bravado) to move it into research mode by reframing the discrepancy: a hospital reception employee has encountered a visiting hospital project consultant who is seeking information about a meeting room, transforming him into a patient and casually or unwittingly breaking confidentiality. I ask what it had taken for 'the system' (including he and the person on the desk) to have had this extraordinary exchange. As the shame/cynicism lift, he reflects on what had made the event happen. The now curiosity-driven discussion traverses the current hospital and service-provider culture, including power relations, purposes, policies, historical context, etc. It also includes a reflection on why not seeing the event as extraordinary is part of the system we are discussing.

Map-making.

Notice cascade of energy blockage-removal.

Groundwork.

In the continued (and now more easily permissible) discussion of how the complaints system operates, [a female consumer] then reveals being given shock treatment against her will, suffering subsequent loss of memory and staff refusing her a complaints form. Staff had said she was 'OK now' so there was no need. People register the discrepancy and then consider how to 're-write the script' of what staff could alternately have done and said. [One consumer] a travel agent, suggests normal hotel (guest feedback) practice as a more respectful analogic practice.

Strategic questioning.

Chart territory.

Reflection.

Systems thinking. Some yang, some yin. Some more reflection.

The rest of the day is spent in de-briefing and a further implementation meeting with managers. There is further generation and testing of ideas, the making of observations, some moving forward, some strategic yielding, some sitting with a pool of fears and some further collective analysis.

Conclusion

It has struck me that there is a certain irony in my experience of co-facilitating the U&I project, given the repeated criticism of participatory action research as 'easy', 'lacking rigour' and 'unscientific' and given that it drew on every store of knowledge, experience, logic, evidence-based reasoning, record-keeping and retrieval, writing capacities and emotional intelligence that I had, not to mention stretched me to almost indescribable limits of personal endurance. But perhaps it is no surprise that

Table 31.1 *A comparison of standpoints: 'The Researcher' and 'The Facilitator'*

The researcher	The facilitator of research
The inquiry is the researcher's inquiry.	The inquiry is more or less the participants' inquiry.
The stakeholders are the researcher's subjects, or they are recipients of the researcher's final report.	The stakeholders are participants and co-researchers with the facilitator.
The researcher conducts a usually one-off, time-limited inquiry, implementing a research plan established and agreed at the outset.	The facilitator assists an iterative, emergent inquiry that might be more or less continuous and responsive. Often longer-term, over time.
The researcher (or/and their assistant/s) selects the methods and the questions, asks the questions, interprets and analyses the data, draws conclusions, makes recommendations and writes up the report.	The facilitator involves and works with the co-researchers to choose the methods and questions to be asked of (and possibly by) the co-researchers, and circulates the responses among them; together they interpret, analyse and draw conclusions and decide on new actions, and then experiment with these, selfmonitoring them, and so on.
The researcher sees disparities of power as irrelevant, or accepts them as inevitable, works around or avoids them as much as possible.	Disparities of power require the facilitator to design strategies so that all people may both speak and be heard accurately.
The researcher remains at arms' length from each stakeholder, examining the operation of the variables 'through a microscope'.	The facilitator enters into an engaged, intersubjective process with the participants, and together they hold up mirrors and magnifying glasses to themselves and each other.
Worst possible results are 'getting it wrong' and being rejected as 'academic' or vilified as 'subjective' or 'political' (or, worse, you don't ever know the impact); or you leave behind simmering resentment from those who never felt heard.	Worst possible results are that self-understandings are still not achieved and the group or organization is left with its status quo practices and conflicts. (Facilitator vilified as not having come up with 'the answers'!)
Best possible results are you get it right and are lauded as 'objective'!, although it may either not be different from what was thought, expected or planned at the outset, or it may have been used to introduce changes wanted only by one or some parties (who had the power to make them).	Best possible results are new insights are gained by all the relevant players and are more or less quickly applied in practice without need for executive direction. (But it never gets written up!) Over a sequence of cycles, more and more desirable changes are a result of the inquiry.

participatory and action-oriented forms of research call forth more and new skills given their peculiar suitedness to conditions of greatest uncertainty, conflict or undiscussability of people's perceptions, beliefs and truths, as well as to identifying the conditions for successful change. Yet I am also acutely aware that, in the micro-world of everyday practice, we all do this differently (see for example, Goff, 1998, compared to our U&I work; or Hall, 1996).

The stories of our various trajectories from non-participatory to participatory, from untrustworthy 'objectivism' and unilluminating abstract reductionism to the resonance and depth of qualitative inquiry, and from the uselessly shelved (or hurtfully applied) reports to the vibrantly fruitful, are important to the understanding of why we now do what we do. The specificity of all these journeys illuminates the specificity of our current personal styles associated with our biographies, education, discipline or profession, and biological and ancestral inheritance. All this social software and embodied hardware combine to make a distinctive approach with characteristic preferences and features.

Yet, despite our differing styles and practices, there is a growing mass of us who have come, overall, to reject a certain mainstream approach to inquiry and truth-formation which belong to 'the researcher', and to embrace another where the researcher becomes an active facilitator of – and more or less co-researcher in – collective inquiry processes. I summarize these main shared elements in Table 31.1. Capturing the sense of the facilitation style in the right-hand column is the Australian Aboriginal educator Lilla Watson's observation: 'If you've come to help me you're wasting your time. But if you've come because your liberation is bound up with mine, then let us work together' (Wadsworth, 1997a: 17).

Notes

This chapter draws on some material from an unpublished conference paper on process facilitation and two papers published locally (Wadsworth, 1998a, 1998b; Wadsworth et al., 1999). It acknowledges the support of a Research Fellowship with the Victoria University of Technology, of which the consultancy facilitation study was a part. I acknowledge also various personal and electronic list (notably Bob Dick's AR-list) discussions about facilitation that have taken place over the past two years, and the particular contributions of Penny Barrett, Denis Cowan, Susie Goff, Susan Hall, Bill Harris, Deborah Lange, Judith McMorland, Paul Murray, Judith Newman, Michael Patton, Eileen Piggot-Irvine, Shankar Sankaran (also for reminding me of Lao Tzu's #10), Jack Whitehead and Bob Williams. I take responsibility for what I have made of it all. The original U&I research, used here as an example of facilitation, was funded by the Myer Foundation, the Victorian Health Promotion Foundation, the State Government of Victoria and the Royal Melbourne Hospital. Permission for its use kindly granted by the Victorian Mental Illness Awareness Council.

1 Here I draw on five different translations/interpretations of Passage #10 from the Tao Te Ching to create this interpretation for the purpose of this chapter: S. Mitchell (1998) *Tao Te Ching: A New English Version*. New York: Harper Perennial, p. 17; D.C. Lau (1963) *Lao Tzu*. Harmondsworth: Penguin Classics, p. 14; Chu Ta-Kao (1976) *Tao Te Ching*. London: Mandala Books/Unwin, p. 22; U.K. LeGuin (1997) *Lao Tzu Tao Te Ching: a Book about the Way and the Power of the Way*. Boston, MA: Shambhala, p. 13; and W. Byner (1986) *The Way of Life According to Lao Tzu*. New York: Perigee Books/Putnam, p. 38.

References

Argyris, C. (1993) *Knowledge for Action: a Guide to Overcoming Barriers to Organisational Change*. San Francisco, CA: Jossey-Bass.

Epstein, M. and Wadsworth, Y. (1994) *Understanding and Involvement (U&I): Consumer Evaluation of Acute Psychiatric Hospital Practice. Vol. 1: A Project's Beginnings* ... Melbourne: Victoria Mental Illness Awareness Council.

Fitzgerald, L. and Wadsworth, Y. (1996) '(Coonara Action Research Taskforce) CART – from the horse's mouth', *Community Quarterly*, 40: 24–9.

Goff, S. (1998) *Restraint of Love: Participatory Action Research into the Meaning of Violence to Young People*. Lismore, NSW: Southern Cross University Press.

Guba, E. and Lincoln, Y. (1989) *Fourth Generation Evaluation*. Newbury Park, CA: Sage Publications.

Hall, S. (1996) 'Reflexivity in emancipatory action research: illustrating the researcher's constitutiveness', in Ortrun Zuber-Skerritt (ed.), *New Directions in Action Research*. London: The Falmer Press. pp. 28–48.

Horton, M., Freire, P., Bell, B., Gaventa, J. and Peters, J. (eds) (1990) *We Make the Road by Walking: Conversations on Education and Social Change*. Philadelphia: Temple University Press.

McGuiness, M. and Wadsworth, Y. (1991) *Understanding, Anytime: a Consumer Evaluation of an Acute Psychiatric Hospital*. Melbourne: Victoria Mental Illness Awareness Council.

Schein, E.H. (1988) *Process Consultation: its Role in Organization Development* (Vol. 1). Reading, MA: Addison Wesley.

Small, W. (1997) 'Keeping emotion out of it?' The problem (and promise) of the investigator's feelings in social research', *The Australian Journal of Social Research*, 4 (1): 97–118.

Wadsworth, Y. (1997a) *Everyday Evaluation on the Run*. London: Allen & Unwin.

Wadsworth, Y. (1997b) 'Navigating by embodied emotion through large-scale systems change: setting out to get consumer feedback into a human services system'. Unpublished paper to the Australian Sociological Association Conference, Wollongong, 9–12 December.

Wadsworth, Y. (1998a) 'Engaging the client in the consultative process: consumer feedback in a mental health organisation'. Unpublished paper to the Australian Psychological Society National Conference, Melbourne, 4 October.

Wadsworth, Y. (1998b) 'The U&I Project as an illuminative action research case story', in Jennifer Angwin (ed.), *The Essence of Action Research*. Geelong, Vic: Deakin University Press. pp. 25–36.

Wadsworth, Y. (1998c) 'Coming to the table: some conditions for achieving consumer-focused evaluation of human services by service-providers and service users', *Evaluation Journal of Australasia*, 10 (1&2): 11–29.

Wadsworth, Y. and Epstein, M. (1996a) *Understanding and Involvement (U&I): Consumer Evaluation of Acute Psychiatric Hospital Practice. Vol. 2: A Project Unfolds* ... Melbourne: Victoria Mental Illness Awareness Council.

Wadsworth, Y. and Epstein, M. (1996b) *Understanding and Involvement (U&I): Consumer Evaluation of Acute Psychiatric Hospital Practice. Vol. 3: A Project Concludes*. Melbourne: Victoria Mental Illness Awareness Council.

Wadsworth, Y. and Epstein, M. (1996c) *Orientation and Job Manual for Staff–Consumer Consultants in Mental Health Services*. Melbourne: Victoria Mental Illness Awareness Council.

Wadsworth, Y. and Epstein, M. (1998) '"Building in" dialogue between consumers and staff in acute mental health services', *Systemic Practice & Action Research Journal*, 11 (4): 353–79.

Wadsworth, Y., Epstein, M., Findlay, R. and Somerville, M. (1999) 'What was the model the U&I project came up with?', *New Paradigm*, VICSERV Newsletter, February: 5–12.

32
Self-reflective Inquiry Practices

JUDI MARSHALL

CHAPTER OUTLINE

This chapter offers a selective account of the author's principles and practices of self-reflective inquiry. Three frameworks are outlined as parallel attentional disciplines: inquiring through inner and outer arcs of attention; engaging in cycles of action and reflection; and being both active and receptive. Glimpses of inquiry in action are then offered, using attendance at an international conference as illustration. Themes of inquiry as political process and as life process are explored. Researchers are invited to pay attention to research intentions and how they are formulated and unfold. Some form of self-reflective practice is advocated as a necessary core for *all* inquiry.

This chapter seeks to show something of my version of the principles and practices of self-reflective inquiry. I first outline some of the attentional disciplines I use and aspire to. I then illustrate inquiry in action, drawing on my story of attending the American Academy of Management Annual Meeting in Chicago in August 1999. Through this material I explore themes of research as political process and as life process, and advocate paying attention to inquiry intentions.

I see having some version of self-reflective practice as a necessary core for *all* inquiry. For example, anyone engaging in collaborative research needs robust, self-questioning disciplines as their base.

Inquiry Requires Attentional Disciplines

In this section I outline some of my disciplines of inquiry. These are open frames rather than rigid behaviour patterns. I seek to pursue them with soft rigour, determined and persistent, but not obsessive. Part of inquiring is making judgements about when to be focused and directed and when to be open and receptive. I have learnt about these practices from my own experience and deliberate development, and from working with postgraduate researchers on our programmes at the University of Bath (Marshall and Reason, 1998). Each person's inquiry approach will be distinctive, disciplines cannot be cloned or copied. Rather, each person must identify and craft his or her own qualities and practices. The questioning then becomes how to do them well, how to conduct them with quality and rigour appropriate to their forms, and how to articulate the inquiry processes and sensemaking richly and non-defensively.

All of the practices I discuss here can be used generatively, appropriately, or degeneratively, inappropriately. There are no objective standards for making such judgements and as the inquirer I cannot be fixed in my evaluation. I work with this questioning, seeking to develop my craft of inquiry and my abilities to notice, reflect on and adjust my approach. In this chapter I am not claiming that I always inquire well and skilfully.

Below I offer one major and two ancillary, *parallel*, framings which emphasize the dynamic processes of inquiry.

Inquiring through inner and outer arcs of attention

A key notion for me is that of engaging in inner and outer arcs of attention and of moving between these. In my own development as an inquirer I have especially paid attention to the inner arcs, seeking to notice myself perceiving, making meaning, framing issues, choosing how to speak out and so on. I pay attention for assumptions I use, repetitions, patterns, themes, dilemmas, key phrases which are charged with energy or that seem to hold multiple meanings to be puzzled about, and more. I work with a multi-dimensional frame of knowing; acknowledging and connecting between intellectual, emotional, practical, intuitive, sensory, imaginal and more knowings.

Scanning, for breadth, and tracking, for sustained curiosity, are words I currently favour to describe *how I work with inner arcs of attention*; I value the terms' multiple associations. Note-taking is essential to this stream of inquiring. I use notebooks and different coloured pens or pencils for over-writing previous notes, alongside computer-based writing. When the scanning and tracking processes are working well, this is not 'just' a stream of consciousness in the moment, unbounded. At its best, it is a discipline, a craft, a developed process. Then I can show the workings of my sensemaking processes, up to a point. Awareness has its limits, as noted below. Also, taken out of real time, some (most?) of the richness of perception and breadth of associative thinking is lost. But reporting it all would not only be impossible but also too self-absorbed. And as I select from the noted and remembered array, there is another process of self-talk. How much of that should I report?

I note how presumptuous it is to say that I do all this, as if I am claiming self-awareness when this is a highly contentious notion. Any self-noticing is framed and conducted by selves beyond the screen of my conscious appreciation. (The conscious self sees an unconsciously edited version of the world, guided by *purposes*. 'Of course, the *whole* of the mind could not be reported in a *part* of the mind' (Bateson, 1973: 408).)

And simultaneously I note that reporting this level of detail about what I think/feel/sense also seems so trite. Doesn't everyone do this self-tracking and deconstruct their own potential narratives with a critical eye as they go along? (If people do, perhaps they devalue such practices. Do they respect, hone and extend them as their craft?) These may be the fine details of self-reflective practice, but they seem strange out there on the page, and they are more ephemeral and to be worked with in the moment than any descriptions may imply.

Also, reporting this internal activity makes some people concerned that I am a worrier or self-punishing, especially when I then ponder the integrity or good form of my actions. But mostly my inquiring is a compelling aspect of being inquisitive, curious and open to testing self and others; it is fun, engaging, interesting and playful, and opens me to opportunities for learning. However, I do also need to know when to leave aspects of my life 'unprocessed' in these terms.

Pursuing outer arcs of attention involves reaching outside myself in some way. (The inner attentions are operating simultaneously.) This might mean actively questioning, raising issues with others, or seeking ways to test out my developing ideas. Or it might mean finding ways to turn issues, dilemmas or potential worries into cycles of (explicit – to me) inquiry in action, perhaps seeking to influence or change something and learning about situation, self, issues and others in the process.

Sometimes the outer arcs of attention are deliberately about engaging with other people, often to inquire with them collaboratively. I might tailor forms of collaborative researching to the situation and my purposes. But some of my testing is not seeking joint exploration or affirmation from others. Sometimes this would be inappropriate or unlikely, for example if my approach comes from a more critical theory or political frame. Then I might need to monitor and critique my sensemaking without direct confirmation; being disconfirmed by others may be significant in its way. So my researching is not necessarily consultative.

Note-taking takes on a slightly different form when looking outwards. The self-tracking continues, but another, more emphasized, attention runs alongside, aiming to do sufficient justice to what is going on around me, and/or what is being said by others. I seek to still myself to allow me to be more receptive. I note what is happening, interested in pattern, form as well as content. I take verbatim notes of what people say, not every word but keeping track as best I can, noting what seem to be key phrases or ways of formulating meanings, minimizing translating into my languages and frames. I know, however, that my perception is selective, and sometimes my abilities to process 'incoming' material lose engagement, becoming mechanical only, or break down altogether. There may be relevant reasons for this, which become material to be worked with in their own right. So my internal self-tracking remains an important, dual attention.

As I work, I hold in mind the notion of thick description (Geertz, 1973) as my aim. I seek some qualitative robustness of material to work with and as a base for tentative interpretations. And I am strategic, targeting my questing and questioning to engage with selective depth or selective difference as I think appropriate. What outer arcs of attention are appropriate and possible is topic- and context-related. Finding appropriate contexts, to offer discord as well as accord, is part of the craft of inquiry.

And so I juggle and balance and move emphasis between inner and outer arcs of attention, seeking an alive interplay, a generative, appropriate combination and dynamic.

Engaging in cycles of action and reflection

The second parallel frame that I use to image inquiry is that of cycling between action and reflection. At its clearest this may mean planning to engage in some action or exploration, becoming immersed in the chosen territory in an appropriate way, noting as I go along, and then taking a step back and reflecting on what I have experienced and done, later moving on again to plan another cycle of engagement. This is a classic action research format, with the potential to be tailored to inquirer, topic and situation in a multitude of ways. The rhythm and discipline of moving back and forth between action and reflection in some way or another seems to generate its own momentum, and so to enhance different forms of attention and of behavioural experimentation (Marshall and Reason, 1998; see also Reason and Marshall, Chapter 30). It can become a way of life, a form of inquiring (professional) practice.

There is simplicity in this notion, and many choices that can be made. And in my experience the dynamics are seldom quite so clear-cut as the above description implies. The inner and outer tracking of attentions continues throughout, the emphasis and combination shifting as I go. As I inquire, I am partly making choices about when to move from action into reflection or vice versa, and what combination of outer and inner attentions to hold. And I sometimes find myself doing these things without apparent conscious intent, and notice how my inquiring is unfolding, as if of its own volition, and then have the choice to challenge or consent to this. Tracking these movements between states and forms of activity is a key aspect of self-reflective inquiring. Rowan (1981; see also Chapter 9) describes the researcher as moving repeatedly round a project cycle of being, project planning, encounter and communication, involving phases of thinking and making sense, moving inwards and outwards. His description is rich for its attempt to articulate how any state the researcher occupies eventually becomes insufficient or is transcended in some way and how moving on therefore seems appropriate. As I notice or shape them, I might judge these movements, these shifts of consciousness, appropriate, generative, or inappropriate, degenerative. (And in retrospect, I might interpret them differently.) Is moving from reflection into trying something out, for example, a valuable testing or a flight from issues which I find too challenging? Is dwelling in reflection an avoidance of difference or of having my frames challenged? No rules of practice can resolve these dilemmas; they must be engaged in the process of inquiring.

I find the notion of cycles, of moving between, of checking back and forth, helpful. If I am static or repetitive within a frame in my process this requires attention.

Being both active and receptive

As I reflect on my practice, I realise how informed I have been – intellectually, but also fundamentally in my behaviour and being – by notions of agency and communion I drew from David Bakan many years ago. I was researching women in management and wanted to depict styles and choices of human functioning without labelling them narrowly 'masculine' or 'feminine' (Bakan, 1966; Marshall, 1984, 1989). I offer these notions briefly as a third parallel frame on the dynamics of living inquiry.

Agency and communion are potentially complementary coping strategies for dealing with the uncertainties and anxieties of being alive. Agency is an expression of independence through self-protection, self-assertion and control of the environment. Communion is the sense of being 'at one' with other organisms or the context, its basis is integration, interdependence, receptivity. I take from this frame another combining of approaches. I will push, pursue, shape, persist in a path of inquiry. And I will treat what happens and how I find myself acting and speaking as potentially meaningful, as having the possibility of 'in-forming' me, that is of giving shape to my way of seeing, not simply imparting information in frameworks already established. These complementary tendencies are always in dialogue, sometimes in tension, sometimes combining with fluidity. At my best, then, I am both directed and open/receptive, testing this dynamic combination in the moment.

Enacting Inquiry

In the following sections I turn to key aspects of enacting inquiry. To show some glimpses of myself as a self-reflective practitioner, I briefly report a recent time of intense inquiring, which was rich with ideas about research. I use a thematic approach to contain the narrative.

Inquiring with intent

Inquiry involves intent, a sense of purpose. This may be held tacitly. There may be multiple intents, in accord or discord. Often intents unfold, shift, clarify or become more complex. Working with this aspect of inquiry is vital to self-reflective practice.

Often these days I state overtly that an issue, event, theme, dilemma or whatever is an inquiry for me. This is a deliberate means to keep my questioning open and to help it develop. Doing so heightens my attention inwards and sharpens my external testing of developing ideas and of my own practice in action. It gives me a frame for noting my ever-provisional sensemaking as I proceed, articulating it – to self and others – as part of the process of inquiry. I use such practices to guide and support me in living my life as inquiry as well as to study 'topics' as an academic researcher (Marshall, 1999).

The illustration of inquiring I shall use in the rest of this chapter shows some of these aspects of multiple, unfolding intents. I shall therefore introduce it here.

In August 1999 I attended the Annual Meeting of the American Academy of Management, held in Chicago. This became an important experience of inquiring for me, with several dimensions. First, I went to Chicago because I was invited to join people I respect in a potentially exciting session (Symposium 218: *Feminism/Otherness: Celebrating Journeys of Change and Discovery on the 50th Anniversary of Beauvoir's* The Second Sex *and the Verge of a New Millennium*).

When I accepted this invitation in December 1998, I was explicit to myself and others that I would *also* use the event as a gently important inquiry in my life, because it offered a valuable opportunity and would force me into some needed decision-making. There is a research study which I have been contemplating for some time but have not yet initiated. I wanted to think it through in the context of what other researchers are doing, and decide whether to proceed. This testing was my foreground inquiry intention.

The research interest is what 'generativity' (loosely defined and subject to critical scrutiny as a concept) means in mid-life (and a little later), and how this affects current women and men managers and professionals, their notions of career, the ways they shape their lives and how they contribute to their organizations. A cluster of related themes and questions have held energy for me, and I have been acquiring relevant references, ideas and conversations. (To illustrate: Notions of generativity are often framed as sacrifice, as giving to future generations, perhaps through mentoring. Are these applicable to women who have adopted relationally-based approaches throughout their lives? Is some measure of self-assertion more their theme in mid-life [Gallos, 1989]? What is happening to people who are seeking to be effective social change agents from inside-outsider positions [Meyerson and Scully, 1995]?) I wanted to see whether these ideas would stand scrutiny or dissolve as meaningful research topics, whether they are worthwhile or too indulgent, perhaps too related to my own life questioning.

This process of worrying away at whether to engage in a particular research area and how to formulate my expression of interests is an element in my self-reflective practice. I need to know that a potential inquiry project is viable, meaning sufficiently energizing for me and well-conceived in terms of issues. I will give this process of coming to research plenty of time, I will let the ideas grow, and seek to notice if they have withered or some aspect of their formulation is wrong, incongruous in some way. I will engage in active questioning of others and myself as part of this testing, tracking how my explicated and more tacit inquiry intents change or persist.

The potential research area of generativity has been around for several years. People encourage me, say these are interesting issues. But the study has not yet started to fly properly, to engross me. Maybe I am too busy with other things. But maybe there is something more remiss than that. I wonder if this could just be comfortable narrative-based research with privileged people, and therefore vacuous in a way. I have become impatient yet again for the world to change, and yet my learning is that small wins are all I can potentially influence (Marshall, 1999; Meyerson and Scully, 1995).

In the background, as context to this specific project, I was also carrying questions about who I am as an academic these days. I have been over-busy with administration and teaching during recent years and have done relatively little focused research and writing. I pine for these activities, but sometimes wonder whether I should struggle to resurrect my researcher self or should concede to current forces, let my professional life be what it is, and pay more attention to the quality of my life generally.

As I suggested earlier, inquiry requires appropriate settings. The conference in Chicago was a potentially rich and compressed territory for me, and had resonance with my various questions. The Academy of Management (AOM) is a professional association of management educators and practitioners, based in the USA but with world-wide membership and influence. It is an important institution in terms of making meaning in management scholarship. Its Annual Meeting takes a theme to which submissions are directed and is attended by thousands of people. There are multiple, parallel streams and activities. It is an important gathering for finding out about current scholarship and advanced organizational practice, and for debating the relative importance of issues. It is an opportunity to meet old friends, make new ones, network, be seen; it is a time to account for our professional lives. It incorporates individual and collective ambivalence and tension as well as connection. I decided to use it as a deliberate opportunity for inquiry.

I carried my inquiry intents more unconsciously than consciously from December 1998 onwards. I was amused to find that even as I travelled to Chicago my sense of inquiring was highly active, as if seeded eight months earlier.

Doing inquiry

What do I mean by conducting inquiry in this setting? There were many mutually relevant activities, enacting the inquiry practices described above.

I explored through engaging with the world and people I encountered, and through tracking my reflections, thoughts and feelings. I took notes during conference sessions and in my own reflective spaces. Some tracked material, experiences and ideas relevant to the inquiry intents introduced above. I also followed other arising issues, images, puzzles. I experienced connections with other people, some a surprise and delight, and also distance and separation. I reflected on these. As I talked to people I sometimes fed my questions and emerging ideas into our conversations, learning from hearing my voice on the issues as well as from the replies, comments and life experiences I heard back. One aspect which contributed to my sense of compressed and meaning-rich living in Chicago was the synchronicity I experienced several times in meeting people of relevance to my curiosities, which in that crowded, diverse gathering seemed most fortuitous. The synchronicity of certain encounters, and their right-timing to contribute to my ongoing inquiring, seemed amazing, breath-taking, thrilling. This does not mean that just because things happen they are very meaningful, symbolic. Rather they are 'stuff' to be worked with, respected, fully engaged through inner and outer arcs of attention. (As is not-happening, sluggishness, etc. – these are just other forms.) I am reminded of two of Brew's (1988) axioms of phenomenological research: 'entertain the possibility that everything is relevant', immediately moderated with 'if you think you know, look again'. Combining these attentions provides another potential inquiry rubric.

One of the ways that I will judge whether the opportunities which arise are to-the-point is through my experience of inquiry as a physical and intuitive, as much as an intellectual, sensing for me. Tracking is partly judging the quality of my inquiry practice in the moment. I know the signs of engaged inquiry: I feel physically alert and multi-sensing, I breathe fully, I think/feel, I am agile as I move within and between inner and outer arcs of attention, I 'find'/experience ways of speaking which both question openly and pursue. And when I have been thus engaged for a while, I may rest back and notice that I am thoroughly tired, almost immobilized. And then I must respect this receding of energy, not push, know that it will not be permanent (although I may fear it might be) and allow what comes next. And so inquiry involves oscillations of whole-person movement, bringing as much attention as possible into the states and dynamics engaged.

In following sections I shall report some of my experience of Chicago through two themes. This is a highly selective account, in which I want to give fleeting glimpses of the conference, a form appropriate to my experiencing and memories.

Research as political process

Noting the many ways in which research is political process was a strong theme for me throughout the conference. This is not a new realization, but was striking and became elaborated in Chicago. Elsewhere I have written:

> Research is also 'political process' in many ways. Who researches and how; whose experience is researched and how that is named or categorised; what discourses gain currency and hold power; what forms of inquiry and writing are favoured by 'mainstream' power-holders; and much more are political issues. 'Creating knowledge' is political business. Living practice is thus politicised. (Marshall, 1999: 158)

My concerns about the political nature of research took various forms. I attended several Research Methods Division sessions on qualitative and interpretive research. I enjoyed these and felt at home to some extent, but also coming from a different place. During question times and discussions there was much reference to the unacceptability of interpretive and qualitative methods in US academia. (These seem tame labels for research to me.) I had a sense of embattled, enmeshed people, hostile journals, limited mainstream frames, and needing to fight for legitimacy and space. I was amused/dispirited that one questioner suggested publishing in books and in European journals, identifying these as more open to interpretive approaches. The UK's regular Research Assessment Exercises now devalue these places to publish ('international', meaning US, journals are the ideal); we are being systematically assessed into more orthodoxy. The next five-year census period closes in December 2000 and so is on our minds.

One answer to proving the rigour of qualitative research advocated at the sessions was to locate oneself in a tradition (such as hermeneutics or ethnography), and be faithful to its originating texts and ideas. I agree strongly that people should not use research terms without substance, but am concerned that adopting a tradition could become inappropriately defensive, imposing alternative orthodoxies, not engaging with the dilemmas of fully living qualitative, interpretive, action-based forms of researching. And I saw that some lone qualitative researchers felt beleaguered within their organizations, unsupported – but also un-challenged by people of sufficiently like kind – likely to play out roles of defence, flamboyant radical or something else. As I processed all these impressions I both positioned myself in these debates and wondered how they are shaping emerging methods, fearing that their embattled nature may encourage restricted orthodoxy in new guises. I would rather see energy directed at developing diverse ways of doing research well that is simultaneously political, personal, intellectual and frame-challenging. But it is all very well for me to advocate such 'risks', and to support such developments in those whose context of assessment I can influence; it seems many people are operating in potentially hostile territory.

As I moved on through the conference I became especially sensitive to exciting and potentially radical content – about race, gender, identities, inter-minority relationships and so on – clothed in orthodox-seeming method. I found myself explicitly questioning presenters about the research approaches they were using. Were they committed to traditional methods or (appropriately?) playing safe? Is it too confronting to use qualitative, participative, self-reflective, action-based inquiry approaches with potentially contentious issues? At times, often, I think we have to take the radical path in content *and* method, to make a double leap. Otherwise the limitations in orthodox methods stifle the radical potential of inquiry.

One aspect of my inquiring in Chicago was where I placed myself in the multitude of offered activities, reflecting my own politics as a scholar. I especially felt pulled between informing myself about current 'mainstream' thinking on change (a core topic at the meeting) and attending sessions which reflected my interests in difference, marginality, ecology, race, feminism and related issues. The latter seemed to be positioned towards the edges of the Programme, not (yet?) much incorporated into mainstream thinking. I became increasingly wilful about what sessions to attend as time went on, gravitating towards the latter stream and appreciating the stronger sense of questioning and politics/power there. Alternative, more vibrant and challenging, notions of change were being debated. I felt affirmed by acknowledging my own interests and positioning, and by having them depicted back to me through my journey through the conference.

As I developed and tested these various strands of thinking about research as political process, I used some to question and comment in sessions. I monitored my own voice and phrasing, reflecting on this, and benefited from other people's affirmation or recognition of the issues I raised. The notion of *researcher as social activist* began to frame up for me and excite me. I started to write this phrase in my notes, repeating it, as I listened/thought. It is not an innovative idea, but was whole, clear and forceful for me at the time. It became a collecting place for the themes I had been tracking, signalling the need for us to comport ourselves with awareness, including questioning whether we collude with dominant frames – of research, managerial norms, societal values and so on – as we create our lives as scholars. Such questioning may seem unusual or contentious in a management research setting. It raises issues about the skills required for such researching. And, at the same time, I wonder, much as I enjoy the notion, whether seeing oneself (myself) as an agent of potential social change is somewhat grandiose.

Tracking generativity

Reflecting on my potential project on generativity was a major thread of my experience in Chicago. Issues of research as political process became thoroughly interwoven with the topic area.

Attending sessions to do with careers contributed to this thinking. Informal conversations were also highly relevant, and offered opportunities to work the issues simultaneously as academic questions and as potentially relevant to my own life situation. I talked with people, many of them women – some known, some newly met – about our work and lives. These conversations provided a valuable intertwining and moving between aspects of self, sometimes with a hint of pleasure like a Starbuck's coffee or a walk outside. In these conversations I was fully my professional self and also fully 'me'.

My initial reason for attending the AOM also contributed significantly to my reflections on generativity. The invitation to explore Simone de Beauvoir's life and work was truly a gift. My notes testify to its importance, and to the many dimensions of relevance. For example, commentators such as Moi (1994) have noted how Beauvoir's work illustrates the interconnections of the personal, professional and intellectual. This sense of the scholar, manager or professional as a multi-faceted person seems central to any understanding of generativity. Also, Beauvoir's positioning as a member of the intellectual elite in France in her time is noted, and how unusual and pioneering this was for a woman. Her life raises questions relevant to those who are potentially diverse and yet can now claim membership of the dominant group. Commentaries on Beauvoir suggest that her positioning simultaneously enabled and disabled her. Her access meant that she could be an independent intellectual, and yet in some ways she over-identified with prevailing, male-based, notions of desirable human qualities, and was unable to see the way she was marginalized as a woman by the ideas she identified with. I saw similar issues reflected in sessions at the AOM, for example, as relevant to successful women now in mid-career, and as challenges for researchers who might want to adopt methods seen as radical, but fear for their careers.

Several key moments in Chicago brought together my thinking about generativity as a potential project. There was a relaxed, engaging conversation with a woman academic after dinner, about our lives, decisions and pathways. I articulated some of my choices, my life quality standards. I was interested in her, younger, approach. I was struck by a phrase she used, that the work is more important than the job position, the latter is just the opportunity. Yes!!

The first session I attended the next day was entitled *Careers as Life Journeys* (496). The first paper – 'The mid-life transition of professional women: an external and internal recalibration' – was the material of the previous night's conversation in academic form, its themes and sentiments recognisable, especially in the notion of 'recalibrations', despite the mechanical language. The other papers in the session were also interesting. I thought that mid-life women seem to be in safe hands (Gordon, Beatty and Whelan, 1999), that I might not need to do my study.

And, thirdly, in these pivotal fragments, the theme of research as political process appeared in the centre of this thinking. A young researcher I was introduced to wants to research careers using notions of agency and communion (Marshall, 1989). I heard my comment back – that these notions can seem too individualistic, too voluntaristic and need to be set in a wider political appreciation – as advice to self as well as to her. And so I came to realise strongly that I need to build a sense of political issues into the core of any research I might do next. Stories of 'generativity', for example, would need to be embedded thoroughly in (interpersonal, social, political, organizational) contexts and questionings of contexts.

Inquiry as Life Process

In earlier papers on inquiry I have sometimes started by describing research as partly 'personal process', noting how we draw on our lives and their themes to inform our inquiries. This labelling has value, yet it maintains some sense of separated selves; as if I could be not-personal, a relic perhaps of objectivity. I currently prefer the notion of *inquiry as life process*, respecting how inquiring is a core of my being, and that my full (multiple) being is involved in any 'researching' I undertake.

I am very aware, for example, that in Chicago there was a parallel track of my own career/life questioning to which I have referred in this chapter. My notebook shows this developing, often with a circled J attached or at an angle to other text to mark it. In my inquiry practice I recognize this parallel stream, allow it and have ways to work with it. I do not see it as detrimental to my academic scholarship – far from it. Looking inwards (which includes this life reflection and is far more than that) is essential to bringing attention to how I look outwards and act. How to work with this generatively, rather than being self-absorbed or self-indulgent, is a key challenge of self-reflective practice. I explore some principles of intertwining inquiry in life more fully elsewhere (Marshall, 1999).

When I initially agreed to attend the AOM, I thought the possible project on generativity would be my focus. But my learning in Chicago was broader than this. Whether I do the study I had envisioned matters less now than *how* I would do it, or anything else I approach. Through the compressed experience of the conference, I re-connected with my attachment to inquiry and re-valued issues and dilemmas about researching that concern me. This sense of renewed commitment and possibilities could be read as part of my route to seeking generativity, an answer to my second inquiry question in a way.

But this journey has not been about me alone, interwoven though it is with my autobiography. I am a selective lens for reflecting issues of politics in the legitimation of some kinds of research and academia and the potential marginalization of others. Acting, as I believe I do, somewhere on the margins (but relatively close-in compared to others), I use myself and my position, I test my courage and my contribution. This story shows some challenges of doing so. And the material from Chicago continually points me also at the more general picture, the scene in which researchers who are non mainstream seek to conduct themselves with integrity, to live creatively, and to have effects.

In Chicago I was learning as I went along but let my original questions de-focus while I was in the midst of the conference. By its close, I felt that they had been explored and I had some key directions and further puzzles to work with, expressed more through a relaxed, reflective sense of self than through statements about what I had 'learnt'. I still do not know whether I should research generativity as a topic, but my own senses of purpose have been enhanced. Sometimes inquiring brings what I invite, but not in the form or realm I anticipate.

References

Bakan, D. (1966) *The Duality of Human Existence*. Boston, MA: Beacon Press.

Bateson, G. (1973) 'Conscious purpose vs nature', in G. Bateson (ed.), *Steps to an Ecology of Mind*. London: Paladin Books. pp. 402–14.

Brew, A. (1988) 'Research as learning'. Unpublished PhD dissertation, University of Bath, Bath.

Gallos, J.V. (1989) 'Exploring women's development: implications for career theory, practice, and research', in M.B. Arthur, D.T. Hall and B.S. Lawrence (eds), *Handbook of Career Theory*. Cambridge: Cambridge University Press. pp.110–32.

Geertz, C. (1973) *Interpretation of Cultures*. New York: Basic Books.

Gordon, J.R., Beatty, J.E. and Whelan, K.S. (1999) 'The midlife transition of professional women: an external and internal recalibration'. Paper delivered at the

Academy of Management Annual Meeting, Chicago, IL, August.
Marshall, J. (1984) *Women Managers: Travellers in a Male World*. Chichester: Wiley.
Marshall, J. (1989) 'Re-visioning career concepts: a feminist invitation', in M.B. Arthur, D.T. Hall and B.S. Lawrence (eds), *Handbook of Career Theory*. Cambridge: Cambridge University Press. pp. 275–91.
Marshall, J. (1999) 'Living life as inquiry', *Systemic Practice and Action Research*, 12 (2): 155–71.
Marshall, J. and Reason, P. (1998) 'Collaborative and self-reflective forms of inquiry in management research', in J. Burgoyne and M. Reynolds (eds), *Management Learning*. London: Sage Publications. pp. 227–42.
Meyerson, D.E. and Scully, M.A. (1995) 'Tempered radicalism and the politics of ambivalence and change', *Organization Science*, 6 (5): 585–600.
Moi, T. (1994) *Simone de Beauvoir: the Making of an Intellectual Woman*. Oxford: Blackwell.
Rowan, J. (1981) 'A dialectical paradigm for research', in P. Reason and J. Rowan (eds), *Human Inquiry*. Chichester: John Wiley. pp. 93–112.

Conclusion: Broadening the Bandwidth of Validity: Issues and Choice-points for Improving the Quality of Action Research

HILARY BRADBURY AND PETER REASON

In this chapter we will address questions of quality and validity. How do action researchers, both individually and together with co-researchers, address the questions 'am *I* doing good work?' and 'are *we* doing good work?' This chapter weaves five dimensions of the participatory worldview articulated in the Introduction together with reflections and questions which emerge for us from the contributions in this handbook. These questions and the subsequent choice-points they pose, allow us to consider issues of validity and quality in action research work. We hope to build a bridge between academic concerns about validity and more reflexively practical questions about the work of action research.

For the academic community, we see this chapter on the issue of quality as initiating and sustaining an engaging conversation among action researchers and between action research and non-action researchers. For while the issues and questions which provoke choice-points in our work obviously inform the work of action research, we believe they may also be extended to a conversation about validity in other types of research work. We hereby join the lively debate that has been referred to as 'the fertile obsession' with validity (Lather, 1993). In joining this debate to add voices from action research we hope to broaden the 'bandwidth' of concerns associated with the question of what constitutes good knowledge research/practice.

We are aware that the possibility of even having standards or criteria of validity has been questioned in this era of postmodern loss of legitimacy (Lyotard, 1979). Kvale (1989) has questioned the validity of the very question of validity, that is to say, raised a question as to whether we are foolishly trying to fit the qualities of action research into a traditional discourse about validity whose concerns have little to do with those of action research. Wolcott (1990) has argued for dismissing validity altogether, precisely because the discourse is inextricably bound to the ideals of positivism. Schwandt (1996) has also bid a 'farewell to criteriology', where criteriology has meant a uniform set of measures. In light of those important concerns we say that our purpose in this chapter is with continuing about validity which emerges from our concern for continuing an ongoing and important dialogue. We hope that a shared and no doubt growing vocabulary, providing clarity about common-ground and disagreement, can only improve both the quality of our work and collegial relationships in action research. To some measure we hereby also stand upon the shoulders of the scholars who have preceded us in their concern for continuing but shifting the dialogue about validity from a concern with idealist questions in search of 'Truth' to concern for engagement, dialogue, pragmatic outcomes and an emergent, reflexive sense of what is important.

Lincoln (1995), in calling for a profusion of validities that emerge from the context of a given study, began a shift in the discourse about the *nature* of criteriology (i.e., what they are) to their *function* (i.e., what they engender). Lather has continued this trajectory as 'a rehearsal for a new social imaginary out from under scientism'. Lather writes 'our framing is shifting validity from a discourse about quality as normative to a discourse of relational practices' (2001). Habermas (1979; and see Kemmis, Chapter 8 for a fuller description), posits that truth results from an emancipatory process, one which emerges as people strive towards conscious and reflexive emancipation, speaking, reasoning and co-ordinating action together, unconstrained by coercion. And so we follow a number of scholars by taking up a point well made by Gustavsen (Chapter 1): our concern in this chapter is not with getting the labels of the criteria 'very right' but with extending a useful conversation about getting valuable work done well. Thus this chapter is about drawing attention to important choices that an action researcher must make through raising questions and pointing to exemplars of good practices offered in the handbook.

In what follows we will identify the types of important issue which emerge from a participatory worldview. We then draw on the chapters of the handbook, especially those from the Exemplars and Practices sections, to suggest the types of question and subsequent choice-points which are core to action research. These questions offer us a solid starting-point for understanding the many choices that we face in making our work worthy of the label 'good'. Of course no one action research project can be 'perfect' in the sense of responding to all the issues we note. Some concerns are simply more pressing in particular contexts. We do hope, however, that each action researcher can use the questions we raise as a reminder of the issues that deserve our attention. We hope that the action researcher and the action research community can make their choices clear so as to allow a conversation so that increasingly, better action research work will develop.

Choice-points for Action Research

Each theory of the way the world is gives rise to particular ways of *seeing the world*. In the Introduction we have argued that action research emerges from a participative way of seeing or acting in the world in which we find ourselves always in relationship. As a starting-point we need to be concerned, therefore, with both the quality of our theory and with our holistic, everyday, lived experience. Gustavsen writes that 'both our theoretical worlds and our life world [or lived experience] are necessary and cannot be substituted. More theory cannot fill the vacuum of a lack of experience and more experience cannot bring more order into an uninterpreted world' (1996: 94). Such concerns lead us into the following five broad issues, already discussed in the Introduction, within which we may begin to articulate choice-points for good action research.

A participative worldview draws our attention to the qualities of the participative-relational practices in our work. Issues of interdependence, politics, power and empowerment must be addressed at both micro- and macro-levels, that is, in inquiring relationships in face-to-face and small-group interaction, about how the research is situated in its wider political context. In particular, we must pay attention to the congruence between qualities of participation which we espouse and the actual work we accomplish, especially as our work involves us in networks of power dynamics which both limit and enable our work (Gaventa and Cornwall, Chapter 6). A mark of quality in an action research project is that people will get energized and empowered by being involved, through which they may develop newly useful, reflexive insights as a result of a growing critical consciousness. They may ideally say 'that was our research and it helped us to see ourselves and our context anew and to act in all sorts of new ways'. We may therefore say that as action researchers we must ask questions that inquire into and seek to ensure quality of participation and relationship in the work.

As we participate with people, oriented by our shared concerns and interests, the practical outcome of our work is important. Thus a series of pragmatic questions must be asked of action research work such as: 'is the work useful/helpful?', 'Do people whose reputations and livelihoods are affected act differently as a result of the inquiry?' We acknowledge that what is considered 'helpful' or 'useful' is itself not at all a straightforward issue – as Stephen Kemmis shows us in Chapter 8 by distinguishing between technical, practical and emancipatory outcomes – and must be explored reflexively by those who are participating, which in turn informs the relational process. Ideally, people's response to action research work is 'that worked' or that was 'helpful'. We may therefore say that as action researchers we must ask pragmatic questions about outcome and practice in our work and consistently strive to be reflexive about this. By this we mean that while we may begin in a mode of 'single-loop inquiry' (Argyris and Schön, 1996[1978]), seeking merely to get things accomplished, we must proceed appropriately to 'doubleloop inquiry' (Argyris and Schön, 1996[1978]) in which we ask questions about the value of the very things we are seeking to accomplish.

As we participate, our knowledge of the world includes, but is never limited to, conceptual or intellectualized forms of knowledge, most often associated with the traditional academic enterprise. Action research recognizes the importance of conceptual knowledge while also consciously engaging in extended forms of epistemologies which we noted in the Introduction. We may ask how different ways of knowing, be they aesthetic or presentational, representational, experiential, as well as more theoretical-conceptual, have been drawn on or allowed to surface in our work? How have they informed the ways in which the work itself is represented?

Often, action research practice is described in terms of cycles of action and reflection (e.g., Heron and Reason, Chapter 12; Marshall, Chapter 32) so that there is a development of both understanding and practice as the cycling develops. Certainly, a basic tenet of action research is that any new understandings must be grounded in experience/experiment. It is argued that there should be a heightened awareness of the relationship between purpose, strategies and practices (Torbert, Chapter 18) and that action should be congruent with espoused theory (Friedman, Chapter 11).

Each particular way of knowing raises questions concerning quality in its own right. How well is an inquiry experientially grounded? How is it embodied in sensuous knowing? What is the appropriate form of presentation given the audience? Is it aesthetically elegant? Is it conceptually clear to all involved? Does it promote further knowing by raising new questions, or by allowing us to 'see through' old conceptual frameworks so that these are newly experienced as more limiting than enabling? By drawing on and integrating diverse ways of knowing, ideally people will say of action research work, 'that is true, that is right, that is interesting, engaging, thought provoking'. And as action researchers we must ask about how the palette of extended ways of knowing is acknowledged in and by our work.

Inquiry methods – including those described in the Practices section – may be seen as an outgrowth of epistemology in service to the research question. We must therefore ask why certain methods are chosen, how well they have been pursued and whether they are indeed congruent with the participative orientation of the action research work? As Hall (2001) points out, participatory research is an attitude, a way of creating knowing in action, possibly even a way of life, not just simply a method. So a question for action researchers is whether they have drawn on the different methodological traditions appropriately and creatively in the context of their own work.

Since our work together includes the co-mingled aspects of reflecting and acting, we must take time to ask questions about the value and worthwhileness of our work. It is not enough to do good work if the work itself is not of real importance – indeed, we believe it important that researchers take the risk of asking big questions, be it as simple as stopping with one's co-researchers to inquire 'so why are we doing this work? and why this way?' Sometimes it will be obvious what is important – stopping children being poisoned, or an ecology being damaged; at other times it is far more complex – in the holistic medical project referred to by Reason in Chapter 12 (see also Reason, 1988), participants continually debated the relative merits of power-sharing with patients, developing a complementary range of clinical treatments and bringing spiritual disciplines into medical practice, for there was not time to attend to everything. We may ask as action researchers how our work calls forth a world worthy of human aspiration, so that ideally people will say that 'work is inspiring, that work helps make me live a better life'.

Our fifth broad issue concerns thinking through the developmental quality of our work through its history and into the future. First-person research/practice (see the Preface for a detailed explanation) is a lifetime's project, as Bill Torbert and Judi Marshall show us (Chapters 18 and 32 respectively). Second-person collaborative inquiry is something that has to be grown over time, moving from tentative beginning to full co-operation. Participatory action research is emergent and evolutionary: you cannot just go to a village or an organization or a professional group and 'do it', but rather the work evolves (or does not) through mutual engagement and influence. Further, because we are participating in work of enduring consequence, we must attend to the question of viability in the longer term (third-person research/ practice). We must therefore ask whether the work was seeded in such a way that participation could be sustained in the absence of the initiating researcher? We must create a living interest in the work.

Action research is a potent orientation to change and transformation. Before intentional change can be fostered, however, it helps to realize, at an individual, group and community level, that the reality we have co-created, however unintentionally, can be re-patterned in participative inquiry. In thinking of our institutions as emergent in our activities and therefore continuously changing, we suggest that the human world as we know it is produced and reproduced by the innumerable acts and conversations that we undertake daily. This is not to conflate large systems with aggregates of individual actors acting consciously; we must recognize that systems have their own logic. However, a structurationist view (Bourdieu, 1977; Giddens, 1984) offers a logic from which to commence the work of change by implicitly asserting that systems are not totalizing, and that conscious, action-oriented people, especially those working and reasoning together, can indeed achieve systematic and systemic change through time. What seems important in action research, which leaves new institutional patterns in its wake, is its ability to integrate the three manifestations of work: for oneself ('first-person research practice'), work for partners ('second-person research practice') and work for people in the wider context ('third-person research practice'). The integration of these three approaches to action research suggests a logic of continuous change, which supports the work of radical transformation of patterns of behaviour which support a world worthy of our lives. Ideally, people involved in emerging and enduring work will say 'This work continues to develop and help us' and other people will say, 'can we use your work to help develop our own?' We may say that as action researchers we must ask questions about how our work has emerged and developed over time, whether it is sustainable into the future, and how it will influence related work.

These five issues, about relationships, practical outcomes, extended ways of knowing, purpose and enduring consequence, are quite demanding on action researchers. Before paralysis or emotional overload strikes, it is important to remember that action research is emergent and along the way is probably concerned with one broad issue more than another.

We can also say that in a pluralist community of inquiry – whether it be a face-to-face inquiry group, an organization, or a community – different individual members are likely to hold different questions with different degrees of interest. Some will be most concerned with relationships, some with action, some with understanding, some with raising awareness. To the extent that dialogue is encouraged between these different perspectives the quality of the inquiry will be increased. We would argue that it is important for the action research team or community of inquiry as a whole to take time regularly for reflection on the choice-points made along the way and the possible need for re-orientation from time to time.

Some action researchers (e.g., Heron, 1996) have argued for the primacy of one issue above all others – in Heron's case it is to suggest the 'primacy of the practical'. We take the position that the issues are choice-points and that the action researcher is thus 'partial' as a result of the material circumstances in which each finds her/himself. Perhaps it is not by accident that it is those using action research and writing a dissertation (see Baldwin and Bradbury, Chapters 19 and 21 respectively) who particularly emphasize the issue of conceptual-propositional integrity. Others, much longer in the field, and perhaps thereby more able to define their own relationship to academic forms of knowledge, have privileged pragmatic concerns (see Swantz, Ndedya and Masaiganah, Chapter 27). Both sets of action researchers attend to issues of pragmatic outcome and conceptual-propositional integrity, but they do so in different measures.

An Examination of the Issues and Choice-points with Reference to Exemplars and Practices

Before we begin a necessarily sequential discussion of each issue, let us note at the outset that there is overlap among the five issues, which is evident in many chapters. For example, the issue of quality in participation and relationships can strongly impact upon the quality of useful, pragmatic outcomes. McDonagh and Coghlan (Chapter 26), for example, use clinical inquiry (see Schein, Chapter 16) to be helpful to an organization seeking to introduce a new system of information technology. Given the reluctance of the information technology specialists to consider the actual people who would work with the new system, the intervention described sought to increase the participation of those making decisions about the system. In this case, participation led to a more useful information technology system because it was more widely shared and understood. So while we may recognize the overlap in the five issues, we discuss chapters as particular exemplars of only one or two issues. This is a matter of necessary simplification; it also correctly suggests that all action research is circumscribed by particular interests, that is, our work is always 'partial' (Haraway, 1984) or 'partisan' (Gustavsen, 1996).

1 Quality as Relational Praxis

Bessa Whitmore and Colette McKee (Chapter 28) write about their work with youths living on the street. They involved the youths as full members of an inquiry-evaluation group convened to assess a youth service centre. Content knowledge differed among the group members which allowed for mutual respect. For example, Bessa as a university-based researcher knew about 'science', while the youth themselves knew, and over time were willing to tell, about life on the streets. Thus participation guaranteed faithfulness to the phenomenon under study. Even the ostensibly mundane activities, such as deciding about snacks, were taken as an opportunity for participation. The importance of full participation led to particular decisions, for example, allowing the evaluation to be submitted after the project deadline so as to allow for the full participation of the youth who were working on a different timetable. It also allowed for a better product, written to capture the energy, colour and youthful spirit of the group.

Whitmore and McKee pay explicit attention to developing the quality of relationships within the group. Cooperative inquiry is thus informed with real attention to the issue of congruence between the process and cooperative spirit of the inquiry, such that appropriate participation and authority is made possible.

Ann Martin (Chapter 14) stresses the need to expand the bounds when we think about whom to invite to participate and when. Martin suggests that all large-scale efforts, such as future search or open space, may really only qualify for the label 'action research' when all who are participating have an opportunity to be a part of the planning.

These chapters raise some possible questions about quality and relational-participation. We might therefore ask with regard to this issue whether the action research group is set up for (eventual) maximal participation? Furthermore, we may wonder to the degree possible, whether opportunities are used to allow all to feel free to be fully involved? When push comes to shove, whether serious decisions are made on the principle that the best decision is one that maximizes participation? Whether especially less powerful people are helped by their experience of participation in inquiry?

2 Quality as Reflexive-Practical Outcome

Marja-Liisa Swantz, Elizabeth Ndedya and Mwajuma Saiddy Masaiganah (Chapter 27) assert a pragmatic concern with the work of participatory action research (PAR). Swantz writes 'much of the knowledge useful to common people, whether educated or not, is commonsense practical knowledge, which is relevant to their situation and to their livelihood. Research is therefore for people's own benefit not as an answer to questions [of curiosity] posed by scientific criteria.' In this chapter we learn of literally life and death situations, improved by women's use of PAR. Through PAR women got the skills they desperately needed, such as organization and representation, analysis and calculation, prioritizing and decision-making, as well as access to resources. Over all, the women experienced heightened self-efficacy through their empowerment and new awareness, albeit not without a cost. Similarly Lykes (Chapter 25) works to help repair the lives of women after the trauma of war. Ostensibly using the method of photo narratives, she is also allowing women to tell their stories and come to terms with the hardship and pain they have endured in such a way that leaves them better off.

In reading these chapters we are awed at the ability of research tools to have enduring positive impact upon patterns of patriarchy, poverty and disenfranchisement. We are led to ask whether, in principle, our more ordinary work also has pragmatic consequence. Levin and Greenwood (2001) write of Dewey's term 'warranted assumptions'. This emerges from the notion that people with real material issues at stake (jobs, reputations, livelihoods) are willing to act on what has been learned in the course of their research. An important question to ask, therefore, is whether the research is 'validated' by participants' new ways of acting in light of the work? In the simplest sense people should be able to say 'that was useful – I am using what I learned!'

3 Quality as Plurality of Knowing

3a Quality through conceptual-theoretical integrity

Mark Baldwin (Chapter 19) tells of developing a theory about the use of appropriate discretion in the context of social work. Hilary Bradbury (Chapter 21) builds on the insights of structuration (Bourdieu, 1977; Giddens, 1984), to anchor sustainable development in its dynamo of attractive conversations in personal networks. Both are concerned with propositional-conceptual integrity and that the efforts at theorizing be anchored in people's experience. Theory is used to bring more order to complex phenomena, with a goal of parsimonious description so that it is also of use to the community of inquiry. It was Kurt Lewin who said that theory is practical, not that it *should* be practical, merely that it *is* practical! Indeed without theory, one's practice is impoverished.

Victor Friedman (Chapter 11) reminds us that knowledge in action research often derives from deep knowledge of one case; how then can we consider generalizing our findings? A well-written study can be used by fellow inquirers with similar concerns to 'see as if' and illuminate their own situations. This honours the notion of a community of inquiry among action researchers. Friedman further reminds us that the world is immensely complex, and that as a result, just to get by, we always have a theory of practice which can be explicated as 'if, ... then, ... because'. He suggests that we be humble in keeping with our ignorance of all that could be known and cultivate a rigour of uncertainty. What we know is really just a hypothesis about reality. Of course good interpretations are those that are more reasonable than others. And reasonableness can be tested in community, that is, whether others also act as if they think the hypothesis is reasonable. Thus the propositional issue is always connected to the others – whether the theory is reasonable and practical becomes an important question as a result.

In developing conceptual-theoretical integrity we may wish to draw on current qualitative and ethnographic practices of making sense of data (Denzin and Lincoln, 1994, 2000). We might also ask if our new theory allows us to re-see the world, or see through taken-for-granted conceptual categories that are oppressive or no longer helpful. Lewis (Chapter 24) shows us that the notion that ordinary people are too ignorant to work with scientific information is simply not true.

3b Quality through extending our ways of knowing

Action research respects and works with many epistemologies. Helen Lewis's chapter (Chapter 24) tells us about the residents of Bumpass Cove, whose interest in finding out about the environmental toxins in their community started, as with all work at Highlander, with an experiential knowing that something was amiss, and led to a venerable form of knowing, that based on scientific facts. However, the chapter also tells of the use of song and dance as artful ways of expressing and continuing knowledge. Traditional knowledge can bring power to hitherto poorly educated people in that it allows them to question successfully the practices of the powerful.

Penny Barrett (Chapter 20) also emphasizes how her inquiry is based in the midwives' experience as professional women practising in a medically dominated institution, and was 'grounded in feeling strong and resilient from within'. This experience is developed and expressed within the group in 'ordinary talk', as the group found less need for formal academic sensemaking processes. While for Barrett the inquiry led to a PhD, for the midwives in MARG, it led to a new form of practice and some change in the institutional forms of the hospital.

Mienczakowski and Morgan's work (Chapter 15) suggests the use of theatre as a way in which researchers may present their work and have additional data and its impact verified in the presence of the co-inquirers.

In seeing that the outcome of inquiry can be a shift in ways of being in the world, and in the development of new skills, we are liberated from the tyranny of having to 'write up' everything. And in asking about how our work responds to the aesthetic-representation issue we are offered a chance to be creative and to liberate the creative impulses of those with whom we work. Conversation and paper writing are valuable tools, but the worlds of theatre, dance, video, poetry and photography invite us to be inspired in the service of better theory and practice.

3c Quality through methodological appropriateness

Jenny Rudolph, Steve Taylor, and Erica Foldy (Chapter 29) offer us a clearly described method for enhancing our appreciation of the gap between our espoused theory and our actual practice. This relies on engaging with others in systematic inquiry about conclusions drawn in any given conversation. Thus inquiry is placed at the centre of personal and small-group research practice. It might be seen as foundational steps towards building larger infrastructures based on inquiry.

While Mark Baldwin draws directly, and appropriately, on co-operative inquiry, Gloria Bravette Gordon (Chapter 22) draws widely on action science, action inquiry and liberationist writings to develop a form of inquiry which suits her particular needs. Bessa Whitmore and Colette McKee (Chapter 28) work within the traditions of PAR but draw on a wide range of methodologies, changing them over time to suit the evolving needs of the group and its inquiry.

If we are animated by a worldview of participation and seek to have congruence between our theory of reality and our practice, then our selected methods must also be relational and be able to describe a relational worldview (Bradbury and Liechtenstein, 2000). We imagine that they will provide a systematic way of engaging people on issues of importance, drawing on many ways of knowing in an iterative fashion.

4 Quality as engaging in significant work

As we review the inquiry project reported in this volume, we are struck that while all contributors are concerned with addressing questions they believe to be significant, few pay *explicit* attention to inquiring into what is worthy of attention, how we chose where to put our efforts. Three chapters stand out as exceptions to this.

Bill Torbert (Chapter 18) and Judi Marshall (Chapter 32) give accounts of their first-person inquiry practices, the many techniques and disciplines they draw on for increasing reflexive attention, asking questions about the relationship between practice and purpose. They illustrate ways in which we can bring ongoing consciousness to the fundamental question of whether or not we ought to be doing what we are doing at all. At the heart of both chapters is the issue of accessing self-inquiry that pushes us always to ask about the values we hold and the value of the work with which we engage.

In a different fashion, the account of appreciative inquiry offered by Jim Ludema, David Cooperrider and Frank Barrett (Chapter 13) draws attention to the very questions which animate our research. They suggest it is more worthwhile to articulate the positive, life-enhancing qualities in a situation and to amplify these, than to seek the problems and try to solve them. It is thus better to ask appreciative questions than critical questions so as to catalyse a constructive inquiry. The emphasis here is on asking the right research question so that we are convening a process which will generate the outcome we want.

While few other contributions explicitly address what is worthwhile, it can of course be argued that any participative form of inquiry, well-grounded in the everyday concerns of people, will necessarily be worthwhile. This is particularly so if it moves beyond addressing simply technically-oriented questions towards engagement with emancipatory questions – in which case people's capacity for asking questions of deeper significance is developed. It is arguable that as inquiry groups cycle between action and reflection over time they move from surface concerns to more fundamental issues – for example that the people involved at Highlander (Lewis, Chapter 24) start with pressing practical concerns and increasingly move towards greater self-direction both individually and in community. However, we note the absence of explicit, critical attention to this: we see few direct accounts of this kind of transformation. Since the action research community as a whole is committed to bringing an attitude of inquiry towards questions of fundamental importance, we would do well to find ways to address the question of what purposes are worthy of attention more direct.

5 Emergent Inquiry towards Enduring Consequence

Marja-Liisa Swantz (Chapter 27) refers to the three decades of participatory research in Tanzania, involving people in their communities, academia and government. She emphasizes the importance of a longer-term commitment from these different parties. The collaborative PhD projects reported by Mark Baldwin, Penny Barrett and Hilary Bradbury extended over many months of developing engagement in which the quality and focus deepened over time. Action research in all its forms is a long-term, evolutionary, emergent form of inquiry.

Peter Park (Chapter 7) argues that in addition to creating objective knowledge of social conditions, action research also strengthens community ties, and heightens transformative potential through critical consciousness. The simultaneous pursuit of these three goals makes action research a holistic activity addressing key human social needs, which may be unique among social change activities. Seeing social change as a research activity forces us to think of community ties and critical awareness as forms of knowledge.

We have noticed the repeated criticisms of existing institutional structures, especially universities. We are interested to note that action research seems to thrive where institutions have been intentionally created to support, sustain and legitimate it. The Society for Participatory Research in Asia and the Highlander Research and Education Center; the Work Research Institute in Norway; and our own institutional homes, the Department of Organizational Behavior at Case Western Reserve University and the Centre for Action Research in Professional Practice at the University of Bath, all offer good examples of ongoing institutions from the civic, the quasi-governmental and the academic realms which sustain action research practice.

Senge and Scharmer (Chapter 17) show that the work of action research is best accomplished when there is a new structure that allows for the meeting in a community of practice of organizational academics, consultants and managers. Such meetings are not easy in our usually fragmented organizational structures, in which managers rarely spend time with scholars.

We noted earlier that the integration of first-, second- and third-person research/practice correlates well with emergent and enduring consequence. Penny Barrett offers an example of integrating the three approaches of action research. Beginning from her own experience, as captured in a journal, she moves to action with a group of midwives, eventually leaving behind the 'Midwives' *A*ction *R*esearch *G*roup' after she must move on. Similarly, Senge and Scharmer tell us of the Society for Organizational Learning, which also combines the three approaches to action research. Now operating in many countries throughout the world ('third-person research practice'), the work developed out of practices of 'personal mastery', drawing on the action science work of Chris Argyris ('first-person research practice', see especially Torbert, Chapter 18, and Marshall, Chapter 32), in addition to systems thinking, etc. and developing methods such as the learning history (Bradbury, Chapter 21) to bring a more creative and inquiring orientation to work with others.

The integration of the three aspects of action research (first-, second- and third-person) suggests that sustaining the work of action research is often the outcome of a logic of structurated action in which the dyadic or small-group micro-engagement of people working on a project together convened around an area of mutual concern manifests in an ongoing new patterning of behaviours at a more macro-level. We may call the latter a new infrastructure in that it structures new patterns of behaviour even after the action researcher has left the scene. Thus new behaviours are created and can begin to alter institutional patterns of behaviour, albeit slowly. One may start off with, and build upon, small wins (Marshall, Chapter 32).

Broadening the Bandwidth of Validity Concerns in Research/Practice

In this review we make no pretence of being comprehensive – indeed, to do so would be to fall into the totalizing and essentialist trap of seeking to provide a new set of firm criteria for validity. We know that this is neither possible nor desirable because each piece of inquiry/practice is its own work of art, articulating its own standards. What we hope we have done is sketch out the basis for some of the questions that need to be asked by an individual action researcher and by action research communities.

We reassure the reader that no action research project can address all issues equally and that choices must be made about what is important in the emergent and messy work of each action research project. As we suggest above, making explicit the questions of what is important to attend to is itself often part of good action research. This might be done by reviewing the issues, choice points and the questions that they raise and deciding where to put the weight of attention. This may be the task of an individual action researcher acting alone. We invite a PhD student using action research to include a review of the strengths and weaknesses of the work in relation to the issues and choice points we are raising. On the other hand, a facilitator of an action research project will wish to share this work with his or her inquiry colleagues; the role here is educative, to explore the choice points with them so they can together decide which are most relevant. Of course, in a participative inquiry, which has emerged in its fullest sense as not *with* people but research *by* people, responsibility for exploring these issues will rest with the community as a whole.

We believe it is helpful to address all questions if only to say why one is more important than the other. Thus when next asked how big one's 'n' was or what to do about the fact that one's data must be considered contaminated by interests or that the co-inquirers were all self-selected, the action research may refer to the differing axiomatic assumptions in action research which arise from a worldview and lived experience of participation. We suggest that the action researcher seek to expand the conversation about validity to include the broader bandwidth of considerations that inhere in research/practice in search of a world worthy of our lives.

In summary

We have suggested that there are five interrelated issues, which together provoke eight choice-points in action research. Questions of quality and validity in research involve encouraging debate and reflection about these issues among all those involved. The following list is intended as a mnemonic device for action researchers starting and continuing to develop a world worthy of human aspiration. These questions will hopefully provoke many others as appropriate to the needs and desired outcomes of the action research work undertaken.

Issues as choice-points and questions for quality in action research

Is the action research:

- Explicit in developing a praxis of relational-participation?
- Guided by reflexive concern for practical outcomes?
- Inclusive of a plurality of knowing?
  - Ensuring conceptual-theoretical integrity?
  - Embracing ways of knowing beyond the intellect?
  - Intentionally choosing appropriate research methods?
- Worthy of the term significant?
- Emerging towards a new and enduring infrastructure?

References

Argyris, C. and Schön, D. (1996 [1978]) *Organizational Learning*. Reading, MA: Addison Wesley.

Bourdieu, P. (1977) *An Outline of Theory of Practice*. Cambridge: Cambridge University Press.

Bourdieu, P. (1991) *Language and Symbolic Power*. Cambridge, MA: Harvard University Press.

Bradbury, H. and Liechtenstein, B. (2000) 'Relationality in organizational research: exploring the space between', *Organization Science*, 11 (5): 565–88.

Denzin, N.K. and Lincoln, Y.S. (eds) (1994) *Handbook of Qualitative Research*. Thousand Oaks, CA: Sage Publications.

Denzin, N.K. and Lincoln, Y.S. (eds) (2000) *Handbook of Qualitative Research* (second edition). Thousand Oaks, CA: Sage Publications.

Giddens, A. (1984) *The Constitution of Society: Outline of the Theory of Structuration*. Berkeley, CA: University of California Press.

Gustavsen, B. (1996) 'Development and the social sciences: an uneasy relationship', in S. Toulmin and B. Gustavsen (eds), *Beyond Theory. Changing Organizations through Participation*. Amsterdam: John Benjamins. pp. 5–30.

Habermas, J. (1979) *Communication and the Evolution of Society* (trans. Thomas McCarthy). Boston, MA: Beacon Press.

Hall, B.L. (2001) 'I wish this were a poem of practices of participatory research', in P. Reason and H. Bradbury (eds), *Handbook of Action Research: Participative Inquiry and Practice*. London: Sage Publications. pp. 171–8

Haraway, D. (1984) 'Situated knowledges: the science question in feminism and the privilege of partial perspective', *Feminist Studies*, 14 (3): 575–99.

Heron, J. (1996) 'The primacy of the practical', in *Qualitative Inquiry*, 2 (1). Special issue edited by Peter Reason and Yvonna Lincoln.

Kvale, S. (1989) 'To validate is to question', in S. Kvale (ed.), *Issues of Validity in Qualitative Research*. Sweden: Studentliteratur. pp. 73–92.

Lather, P. (1993) 'Fertile obsession: validity after poststructuralism', *The Sociological Quarterly*, 34 (4): 673–93.

Lather, P. (2001) 'Validity, as an incitement to discourse: qualitative research and the crisis of legitimation', in V. Richardson (ed.), *Handbook of Research on Teaching* (fourth edition). Washington DC: American Education Research Association.

Levin, M. and Greenwood, D. (2001) 'Pragmatic action research and the struggle to transform universities into learning communities', in P. Reason and H. Bradbury (eds), *Handbook of Action Research: Participative Inquiry and Practice*. London: Sage Publications. pp. 103–13.

Lincoln, Y.S. (1995) 'Emerging criteria for quality in qualitative and interpretive research', *Qualitative Inquiry*, 1 (3): 275–89.

Lyotard, J.-F. (1979) *The Postmodern Condition: a Report on Knowledge* (trans. Geoff Bennington and Brian Massumi). Manchester: Manchester University Press.

Reason, P. (1988) 'Whole person medical practice', in P. Reason (ed.), *Human Inquiry in Action*. London: Sage Publications. pp. 102–26.

Schwandt, T. (1996) 'Farewell to criteriology', *Qualitative Inquiry*, 2 (1): 58–72.

Wolcott, H. (1990) 'On seeking and rejecting validity in qualitative research', in E. Eisner and A. Peshkin (eds), *Qualitative Inquiry in Education: the Continuing Debate*. New York: Teachers College Press. pp. 121–52.

Index

abstraction/abstractness meaning 109
academic research 198–9
academic skills 240–1
Academy of Management 338
accompanying process 298
accountability 80, 222, 301
action 9, 17
  co-operative inquiry 151
  continuation 173
  and participation 1–2, 18, 74, 77
  reflection and (cycles) 77, 145–6, 223–5, 247–8, 255, 316, 336–7, 344, 349
  reflective knowledge 89
  responsibility for 172
Action on Changing Technology 308
action inquiry 75, 238
  collaborative off-line reflection 307–14
  practice 207–16
action research 1–2
  characteristics 2
  clinical inquiry 3, 185–94
  community 4, 195–205
  dialogue *see* dialogue
  diverse origins 2–4
  Early Mothering Project 228–34
  ethnodrama 176–82
  feminism 60–7
  humanistic approach 106–15
  inter-organizational network 253–61
  large-group processes 166–74
  origins 38–40
  paradigms 4–7
  pragmatic 3, 347
  primary purpose 2
  quality 8, 12, 343–50
  race in US discourse 3, 49–58
  relevance of critical theory 94–105
  social constructivism 5, 65, 112, 249
  systems thinking 117–27
  The Natural Step 236–42
  theory and practice 17–25
  validity of 8, 12, 193, 343–50
  in the workplace 38–47
  see also appreciative inquiry; co-operative inquiry; collaborative action research; experiential action research; participatory action research; systems thinking
action science 8
  collaborative off-line reflection 307–14
  defining 131–2
  distinguishing features 131–42
action turn 2
actions, soft systems thinking 122
Active Health Triangles 215
active/receptive approach 337
activity-based interventions 282
advocating 211
affectivity (in knowing others) 87
African American Women in Defense of Ourselves 56
African Americans, US discourse 3, 49–58
African Caribbeans 243–51
Against Method 28
agency 73, 74, 300, 337, 340
agreements, development 18
alienation 6, 11, 110–11
All Our Kin 54
alternativists 137–40
American Sociological Association 52, 55
amplifying loops 118, 119
anthropology 28, 54–5, 119
Apollonian inquiry 148
Appalachia 29, 71, 85, 262, 266
applied systems thinking 119–20
appreciative inquiry 155–65, 348
arcs of attention 335–6, 339
Aristotle 3, 9, 32
arts, Photo Voice project 269–76
Arusha Declaration 286
assessment process 208
Association of Black Sociologists 55
Association of Community Health Services Guatemala 270
Association of Maya Ixil Women 269–76
Atman Project, The (Wilber) 106
attention 335–6, 339
  quality of 9
audiences (ethnodrama) 178, 180–3
Australia 30, 102, 177, 182
authenticity 108, 109, 112, 114, 122, 150
authority 318, 320–1
authorship 54
autobiographical writing 316
autocratic groups 39
autonomy 89, 99, 112, 222
awareness building 77–8

Baddies, Grubs and the Nitty Gritty 179–80
balancing loops 118, 119
beauty 11–12
behaviour 38, 39–40, 41, 120, 133, 320–1
behaviour change 30, 39, 79
behaviour description interventions 282

behavioural choices 248
behavioural complexity 204
behaviourism 108
being 8–9, 110, 112, 316
Between Facts and Norms 102, 103
Bhoomi Sena (Land Army) 28
bias 53, 67, 72, 84, 87, 193, 302
bicultural competence 243–51
binaries 62, 156
biological determinism 62
Black feminism 64
Black liberation movement 243–51
Black Liberation Social Science Movement 51
  examples from research tradition 53–5
  links to action research 52–3
black sociology 49–58
bodymind 8, 87–8, 108, 112
boundary-crises 97, 101, 102
bracketing 150
brick-making project 288–92
British Coal Board 41, 42
British Holistic Medical Association 146
Bumpass Cove 264–6, 267, 348
Bunju village (Tanzania) 28
business incubators 253–61
Busting project 177–8, 182
Buttings Head case 308–13

Calico Mills 42
capacity-building 159–63, 171, 197, 198, 201
capitalism 27, 32, 34, 171
Career Project 64, 65
Careers as Life Journeys 341
Cartagena World Congress 27, 32, 33, 34
Cartesian dualism 8, 27, 62
Cartesian worldview 5, 10
case studies 46
cashew research project 295–6
catharsis 181, 233
Caucus of Black Sociologists 52, 55
causal loop diagram 240
CEH 269, 270
Centaur consciousness 106–8, 109
Centre for Action Research into Professional Practice 243
Chajul (Guatemala) 269–76
change
  continuous 241
  institutional 33, 79, 263
  IT-related 279–84
  micro and macro-level 78–80
  organizational 3, 4, 50, 62, 79, 155, 164–5, 166
  proposals 123
  Real Time Strategic 169, 171
  theory of action 135
  see also behaviour change; social change
chaos 34, 46, 151, 197
Characteristics of Socio-Technical Systems 43–4
Chicago 339–41
Chinese language 87–8
choice points 137, 343–50
Citizenship Schools 264
Civil Rights Movement 50–1, 52, 262, 263–4
client-initiated inquiry 188–91
clients 30
clinical inquiry/research
  definition/dimensions 3, 185–94
  IT-related change 279–84
closed boundary inquiries 148
closed systems thinking 43
CN Group 255–61
co-inquiry 52
co-operative inquiry 3, 75, 144–52, 229, 319
  in social work 221–6
coal industry 41–2
cognitive science 108
cognitive turn 5, 6
cognitive-based interventions 282
coitus interruptus 211–12
collaborative action research
  authentic 150
  experiential 243–51
  graduate research students 315–21
  interactive 191–2
collaborative off-line reflection 307–14
collaborative projects 202–3
collusion 150
colonization of lifeworld 100–1
command-and-control bureaucracies 156, 164
commitment 28, 29, 30, 200
Committee on Racial and Ethnic Minorities in Sociology 55
communication 110, 111, 320
Communication and the Evolution of Society 96
communicative action 19
  and action research 101–2
  theory development 102–3
  theory of system and lifeworld 96–101
communicative learning 168
communicative space 61, 103–4
communion 8, 337
communitarianism 195–205
communities of inquiry 4, 131–42
communities of practice 132–3
community
  action research 195–205
  building 200
  development 4, 46, 75, 84, 86
  dialogues 167
  erosion 156–7
  groups (Highlander projects) 262–8
  projects Photo Voice 269–76
  see also learning communities
community action committees 52
Community Development Officer 291
Community Group 223–5
community of inquiry 346
compass work, U&I project 323–5, 326
competence
  bicultural 243–51
  emotional 150
  intellectual 319–20
complexity 204
complexity theory 4, 126
comprehensiveness, vs. simplicity 109
conceptual knowledge 344

conceptual models 123
conceptual-theoretical integrity 347–8
conceptualization 170–1
conferences 18, 20–4, 43, 57, 74, 118–19, 168–70, 256–8, 260
conflict 34, 62, 72, 135–41
congruence 150
connected knowing 9
Connecticut State Inter-Racial Commission 40
conscientization 9, 30, 89
consciousness 8, 11, 52, 89, 317
  critical 72–3, 84, 245, 248, 249–51
  humanism and 106–8, 109
  raising 9, 10, 64
consciousness-raising (CR) groups 64
consensus 76, 96, 99, 103, 104, 150
constitutive meaning 122
constructionist theory 3, 5, 6, 7
  appreciative inquiry 155–65, 348
  social constructivism 65, 112, 249
Constructivist Research 33
consultants 198, 199, 201
Consultations with the Poor project 78
contemplation 109, 110
contract research 189
control 4, 133, 232–3
control groups 301
convergence (co-operative inquiry) 150
Convergence conference 74
conversations 61, 88, 155, 212
  containment of 156
  MARG project 228–34
  positive 163
  sustainable development 236–42, 347
core values 102, 222
corporate IT 279–84
Cosmopolis 5
cosmos, nature of 8
counterpartal role inquiries 147
courage, fear and 108–9
creation-centred spirituality 11
creative writing 316
creativity 317
crises 99
criteriology 343
critical action research 95–6, 101–2
critical awareness 124, 125
critical consciousness 72–3, 84, 245, 248, 249–51
critical ethnodrama 176–82
critical incident questionnaire 173
critical intellectuals 34
critical reflection 168
critical subjectivity 149, 246, 316
critical systems thinking 124
critical theory 18, 40, 86, 88–9, 90, 94–105, 245
critical thinking 3
critique, relational consequences 156–7
cultural deficit 157
cultural reproduction 98, 99, 100, 101
culture 97–9, 191
Curriculum Studies 97
cybernetic theory 118–19

Dana (case study) 307–14
dance 348
Dar Es Salaam 286, 293
Dark Ghetto 53–4
Deakin University 30, 94–5, 96
Death of White Sociology, The 49–50
debate 125
decision-making 44, 46, 72, 76, 152, 222, 291
deconstruction 6, 7, 34, 112, 247
deep listening interview 204
deep participation 86
defensive attitude 316
deficit-based vocabularies 157, 163, 164
democracy 3, 25, 32, 34, 120, 164, 222
democratic dialogue 19–20, 56–7
democratic groups 39
demography 186
Department of Army Psychiatry 40
descriptive inquiries 149
design, socio-technical systems 44
design phase 158, 160, 162, 172–3
desirability, change proposals 123
destiny phase 158–9, 160, 162–3
development
  conferences 18, 256–8, 260
  organization 3, 46, 50, 102
  process (CN Group) 255
devolution technique 31
dialectical thought 245
dialogic design (U&I project) 324–6
dialogue 39, 84, 148, 158, 346
  community 167
  conferences 18, 20–4
  Dana (case study) 310, 311
  democratic 19–20, 56–7
  ground rules 173
  in *The Natural Step* 237, 241
  see also conversations
difference 210
differentiation 100
Dionysian inquiry 148
discourse 6, 18–19, 21–2
discovery phase 158, 160, 161
discretion 221–2
distress management 150
divergence (co-operative inquiry) 150
double-loop action inquiry 238
double-loop learning 135, 207, 215, 245, 247
doubt 135
Dream of the Earth, The 127
dream phase 158, 160, 161–2
dreams 317
Drop-In Centre 297–303, 346
DuBois-Johnson-Frazier Award 55
dynamic complexity 204

Early Mothering Project 64, 228–34
ecological perspective 10–11, 120–1, 254, 260
Ecology of Commerce, The 239
economic education (Highlander) 266–7
economic systems 97, 100
economy, global 204–5

education 34, 38
critical consciousness 249–51
environmental 236–42
Highlander philosophy 3, 263–4
interventions/facilitation 189–90, 193–4
educational action research, social change 262–8
educative imperative 10
ego boundaries 106, 107
emancipatory action research 2, 9, 30, 95–6
emancipatory knowledge 85
emergence 117, 118
emergent learning 203, 204
emotional competence 150
emotions 282
empathy 86
emphasized femininity 114
empiricism 29, 95, 108, 114
empowerment 10, 151, 267, 298
feminist research 64, 65, 67
knowledge and 72, 74, 76–8
shared reflections 231–2
energies, driving/divining 328–9
engagement 4, 28, 212, 318, 319, 336–7
enlightenment 25, 95, 179, 4, 5, 31, 86–7
Enterprise Development (2000) 20
environment
Bumpass Cove 264–6, 267, 348
causal texture 120
rural development 286–96
social ecology 43
sustainable development 236–42, 347
epistemological individualism 108
epistemological turn 9, 84
epistemology 3, 4, 8–9, 11, 28, 29, 89, 145, 345
extended 7, 9, 33, 149
equality 298
espoused theories 134, 135
espoused values 247
ethics 114–15, 301–2
clinical inquiry 189
ethnodrama 181, 182, 183
ethnodrama 57, 176–82
ethnogenetic emancipatory ethos 34–5
ethnography 6, 41, 46, 176, 187, 347
evaluation tasks 302
everyday experience (of women) 66
existential perspective 3, 316
existential psychotherapy 111–12
experience 1–2, 5
territories of 208, 248
experiential action research 3, 57, 176–82, 243–51
experiential knowing 9, 11, 145, 149
experiential knowledge 109, 222
Highlander projects 3, 262–8, 349
experiential learning 89
clinical inquiry 3, 185–94
community action research 4, 195–205
humanist approach 106–15
experiments 17–18, 39, 42, 186–7
expert consulting 189, 199
expertise 72, 76, 280, 300
experts 30, 46, 72, 267, 297, 300
exterior action turn 204

facilitation (clinical inquiry) 189–90
facilitator 168, 170, 174, 224, 239, 288, 290
of participatory action research 322–34
falsifiability 134
fantasy 317
fear, courage and 108–9
feasibility, change proposals 123
feedback/feedback loops 23, 118, 187, 241
femininity 113, 114
feminism 3, 6, 50, 89–90
action research 60–7
Early Mothering Project 228–34
knowing 9
field theory 38, 40
first-person research 172, 204, 251, 349
practice 208, 209–11, 345
The Natural Step 241
fishing community (Tanzania) 292–5
flows 118
Forest Trees and People 292
foundationalism 5
4-D model 158
fractionation level, work 44
framing 171–2, 211
Frankfurt School 28
freedom 73, 75
freedom schools 264
friendship 87
Frontier Tanzania 294
frontiers, community research 203–5
functional knowledge 85
functional rationality 97
functionalism 25, 29
future scenario method 214
Future Search 167
futures, emerging 203, 204

gender 3, 62–3, 65
Mayan community 274–5
see also men; women
general systems theory 118, 119
generalizability 33, 141
generative complexity 204
generativity 338, 340–1
global economy 204–5
global inquiry (case study) 159–63
Global Relief and Development Organization 159–63
global uniformizations 34
Going Home From Hospital 169, 171, 173–4
government, legitimacy 10
graduate research students 315–21
Great Depression 5, 262
grievances, power and 72
grounded theory 177
group interaction inquiries 147
group therapy 40
group-based inquiries 147

groups 3, 39, 41, 103
 inquiry in 151–2
 training (T groups) 3, 187–8, 190
 see also co-operative inquiry
Guatemala 269–76

Habermas, Jürgen 94–105
Harlem 51
Harlem Youth Opportunities Unlimited 53
Harwood experiments 39
Hawthorne studies 187
he-man 113–14
healing 11, 126
 Chajul project 270–1, 271–2, 275–6
health
 Bumpass Cove 264–6, 267, 347
 ethnodrama 176–82
 holistic medicine 146, 147, 148, 152
 MARG project 64, 228–34, 348
health visitors study 145–6, 148
hegemonic masculinity 113
hegemony 6, 72
hermeneutics 85, 86, 95
Hermes/Trickster archetype 317
hierarchies, power/weakness 74, 75
Highlander Research and Education Center 3, 262–8, 349
Highly Indebted Poor Countries programme 78
Hill-Thomas controversy 56
historiography, imperialist 249
holism 108
holistic medicine inquiry 146, 147, 148, 152
holons/holarchy 112–13
Hospital Ethics Committee 65, 230, 231
Hospital Group 223–5
How We Think 38
human activity systems 123
human emancipation 124
human rights 270, 274
human systems 121–2, 158, 192
humanism 5, 34, 108, 229
humanist approach 3, 106–15
hypothesis testing 141

I-thou/I-It 108
IDAC Documentation Centre 28
identity 63, 87
if-then rules 137–40
illocutionary claims 86
illustrating 211
imaginal work 317
IMF 78
immaturity 109
imperialist historiography 249
inclusion 77, 163–4
India 42
indigenous knowledge 3
individualism 108
individuation 97–9, 101
Indonesia 78
Industrial Age institutions 195, 196, 205
industrial democracy 120
industrial dynamics 119
Industrial Revolution 4
inference, ladder of 134, 308, 309–10
information technology 346
 -related change 279–84
informative inquiries 145, 148, 152
infrastructures 200–2
inquiry 84
 attentional disciplines 335–7
 client initiated 188–91
 Dewey's concept 135
 enacting 337–41
 as life process 341
 and participation 1–12
 researcher initiated 186–8
 see also action inquiry; appreciative inquiry; clinical inquiry/research; co-operative inquiry
inquiry cultures 148–9
inside inquiries 147
Institute of Development Studies 79
Institute of Labour Studies 28
Institute of Popular Culture 28
institutional change 33, 79, 263
instrumental learning 168
instrumental rationality 29
integration 98–101, 111–12, 279, 281–3
intellectual competence 319–20
intellectual development 319
intent 211, 337–8
intentional change 241, 345
inter-connectedness 328
inter-organizational learning 201
inter-organizational network 253–61
Interface 203
interior action turn 204
International Council for Adult Education 30
internship 189
interpersonal ethics 115
interpretation(s) 18, 134, 141, 222, 282, 347
interpretive knowledge 85–6, 88
interpretive research 95, 132, 134
interpretive thinking 122, 123–4
interrelatedness 117, 118, 120, 121
intersubjectivity 208, 215
intervention(s) 320
 educational 189–90, 193–4
 emancipatory action research 95
 IT-related change 282
 large-scale 171–2
 total systems 124, 125–6
interview, deep listening 204
intimacy 88
intra-organizational learning 200–1
intuition 8, 225, 348
involved observer 53–4
Ixil (of Chajul) 269–76

joint inquiry 187, 188
joint optimization 42
Journal of Consciousness Studies 106, 109
Jubilee 2000 Campaign 78
justice 96
 social 33, 50, 52, 61, 262

key facilitation capabilities 328–30
Kit, The 299, 301
knowing
  in Chinese 87–8
  forms of 75, 88, 145
  intuitive 225
  nature of 9–10
  others 87, 328
  quality as plurality of 347–9
  self 328
  ways of 2, 12, 149
  see also epistemology
knowing-in-action 195
knowledge
  in action research 2, 347
  creation 52, 65, 67, 168, 195–205, 221–6
  feminist research 66
  forms of 9, 84–90
  indigenous 3
  and participatory research 83–91
  power and 6, 71–80, 90, 124
  reflective 9, 88–90
  relational 9, 86–7, 88, 90
  representational 9, 85–6, 88, 90
  science and 29
  systems thinking 117
  see also experiential knowledge; meta-knowledge; practical knowledge; scientific knowledge; tacit knowledge
Knowledge and Human Interests 94
knowledge-constitutive interests 95–6

labour market parties 18, 20, 24
labour movement 263
ladder of inference 134, 308, 309–10
laissez-faire groups 39
Land Study Project 266
language 31, 298
  Chinese 87–8
  communities of practice 132–3
  unconditional questions 156, 158–9, 163
language turn 2, 4, 5–7
large-group processes 166–74
large-scale change 79–80
lawful relationships 120, 121
leaderless group method 41
leadership 39–40, 41–2, 174
  Buttings Head case 308–13
  third-person research 213
learning
  action research 168
  double-loop 135, 207, 215, 245, 247
  emergent 203, 204
  experiential *see* experiential learning
  history method 237, 238–9, 240, 242
  large-scale intervention 171–2
  mutual 224, 288, 295
  organizational 44, 119–20, 142, 166, 167, 196, 199–203
  ownership 221
  reflective 173, 203, 204
  second order 245
learning *cont.*
  single-loop 135, 199, 207, 215
  The Natural Step 236–42
  triple-loop 207, 215
  see also self-learning
learning communities 4, 164, 195–205, 318
learning laboratories 200–1
learning organization 39, 119–20
learning pathways grid 308–9
Learning region programme 21–2
legitimacy 10, 46, 71, 100, 103, 222
lesbian feminists 63, 64
Liberating Disciplines 213
liberationism 3, 10, 31–3
life philosophy, PAR as 31
life process, inquiry as 341
lifeworld 86, 87, 96–101
  bicultural competence 243–51
linguistics *see* language
listening 88
local policies 78–9
Logos-Mythos technique 31, 32
LOM programme 19, 20
longwall method 120
loose-coupling 254, 260
love 87, 88, 208, 211

macro-level PAR 78–80
Macy conferences 118–19
magnifying glass metaphor 328
maps/map-making 133, 137–40, 266, 292, 301
  U&I project 326, 327
Marcus Garvey Movement 51
Marriage of Sense and Soul, The 109
Marxism 3, 25, 89, 102
masculinity 62–3, 113
matrix exercise 301
maturity 109
meaning 11–12, 122, 125
mechanism/mechanistic science 108
mediating discourse 18–19, 21
  generation of relationships 21–2
men
  he-man 113–14
  masculinity 62–3, 113
  patriarchy 90, 249, 347
mental ego stage 107, 112, 113
mental models 120, 126
meta-intentionality 150
meta-knowledge 199
meta-narratives 6, 7, 28, 34
methodological complementarity 124, 125
methodologies 319, 348
micro-level PAR 78–80
Midwives' Action Research Project 64, 148, 228–34, 349
military selection process 40–1
mind and matter 8
mind/heart 87–8
mindfulness 3
Minority Fellowship Program 55
mirrors/mirroring 318, 320, 328

MIT Center for Organizational
Learning 196–7, 237
mixed role inquiries 147
mobility map 292
modernism 4, 5, 6
modernity 97–101
monitoring 80
moral responsibility 34
morality/moral values 89
mothers 64, 228–34, 348
Moynihan report 51, 52
multidisciplinary work 33
multiple identities 63
multiple interpretations 134
multiple perspectives 173
mutual learning 224, 288, 295
mutual understanding 96, 98, 99, 103, 104, 171
mutuality 87, 212, 298
Muungano Women's Group 288–92

nascency 179
National Autonomous University 28
National Health Service 148
National Institute for Working Life (in Sweden) 21
National Science Foundation 200
National Seminar on Action Research 94
National Union of Farmers 43
Natural Step, The 236–42
Negro Family: a Case for National Action 51, 52
networks 20–1, 23, 80
inter-organizational 253–61
neutrality 29
New Left 64, 66
NGOs 3, 28, 159–63
NIMO denial 126
non-attachment 150
non-intrusive collaboration 298
Nordvest-Forum 20
North Country Food Security 168–9, 174
Norway 17, 18, 42
Norwegian Industrial Democracy Projects 42–3
Not-for-Prophets (NFPs) 214–15
note-taking 336
noticing (in supervision process) 320
NTL Institute for Applied Behavioural Science 40

object, subject and 8, 30–1, 32
objective knowledge 6, 84
objectivity 29, 53, 208, 215
observation stage 247
observations, (CN Group) 259
ODHAG 269, 270
off-line reflection 307–14
Office of Executive Specialist 55
officer selection process 40–1
OilCo Learning Centre 200, 201
ontology 8, 61, 84, 223
open boundary inquiries 148
Open House (case study) 135–41
Open Space 167, 172
open systems theory 43, 45, 118, 120
operational rationality 29

oppression 6, 18, 61, 63, 75, 96, 126
see also pedagogy of the oppressed
optimal state 112
order, chaos and 151
organic intellectuals 31
organizational capacity-building 158–60
organizational change 3, 4, 50, 62, 79, 155, 164–5, 166
organizational deficit 157
organizational development 3, 46, 50, 102
organizational learning 44, 119–20, 142, 166,
167, 196, 199–203
organizations, systems thinking 118, 121–2, 123–4
orientational directives 20
other/others 248, 275, 323
knowing 87, 328
knowledge (tapping into) 301
self and 9, 10, 73, 168, 274
outside inquiries 147–8
outside world 208, 248
overlapping networks 23
ownership 221, 222, 247, 300, 301, 302–3

panexperientialists 8
paradigms 4–7
alternative 32–3
participant observation 177, 187
participant observers 54
participation 298, 346
action and 1–2, 9, 18, 74, 77
external 148
inquiry and 1–12
soft systems thinking 122
Participation in Human Inquiry 126–7
participative medical practitioners 7
participative research 2, 3, 10
participatory action research
facilitating 322–34
feminisms 60–7
knowledge and 83–91
Photo Voice project 269–76
power/knowledge in 71–80
for social change 262–8
in social theory 27–35
in Tanzania 286–96
Participatory Learning and Action 299, 301, 302
Participatory Poverty Assessment Process 78
Participatory Rural Appraisal 3, 33, 62, 65,
287, 290, 292
participatory worldviews 2, 4–12, 223
issues and choice-points 343–50
partnership 159–63, 298
past, reflecting the 203
paternalism 159–63
pathology 193
patriarchy 90, 249, 348
pedagogy of the oppressed 10, 28, 77, 214
peer review 198
pejorative perspective 51, 52
performance/performing 208
ethnodrama 176–82
personal attitudes 79
personal mastery 120, 127

personal process of inquiry 315–17, 318
personality 97–9
phenomenology 108
Philadelphia Quaker Health 214–15
Philosophical Discourse of Modernity, The 99, 102–3
philosophy of the subject 102–4
Photo Voice project 269–76
phronesis 3, 32
planning, societal 43
poetry 181, 267
political action 34
political dimension, participation 10
political process, research as 339–40
political systems analysis 124
political-legal systems 97, 100
politics 72
popular action 77, 266
popular knowledge 75
positive questions 155–65
positive relationships 163–4
positivism 4–5, 6, 7, 29, 46, 52, 75, 194, 223, 343
positivist science 3, 4, 7, 85, 132, 134
postgraduate research groups 318, 320
postmodernism 3, 4, 6, 7, 28, 34, 97, 112
poststructuralism 6, 7, 97, 103, 223, 348
power 18, 112
  balance/imbalance 10, 173
  feminist perspective 65, 66–7
  and gender 62
  and knowledge 6, 71–80, 90, 124
  MARG project 232–3
  over 74–5, 90
  transformational 213–14
  unilateral 214
  within 73, 90
practical action research 95
practical knowing 1, 2, 9, 11
practical knowledge 149, 197, 198
practice, theory and 17–25, 29–30, 104, 347
pragmatic action research 3, 124, 347
pragmatic linguistics 86, 87
pragmatists 137–40
praxis 30
  critical theory 3, 89, 90, 102
  experiential action research 246
  MARG project 229, 232, 234
  quality as relational 346–7
  and reflection 77
  systems thinking 121, 125
pre/trans fallacy 106
presencing 203, 204
presentational knowing 9, 149
primary outcomes 149, 152
privilege 10
problem-solving 3, 10, 38, 77, 84, 95, 131, 133, 199
process 125, 239, 298, 315–21
process consultants 283
process consultation 190–1
professionalism 74–5
progress 126
project office (day in the life of) 330–2
projects 110, 111
propositional knowing 9, 149
provocative propositions 162
psychodynamic perspective 316–17
psychological contract 185–91, 193
psychology 3, 40, 108, 111, 112, 317
psychospiritual development 106–8, 113
psychotherapy 3, 107, 111–12, 185, 316
public policy (implementation) 221–2
public spheres 100–1, 103
purpose 11–12, 12, 29, 170, 208, 248, 337–8
purposive rational action 98

qualitative research 12, 114, 222, 339
quality
  of action research 8, 12, 302, 343–50
  monitoring for 80
Quality Management 198
quantitative research 114
quantum metaphor 8
questionnaires 75, 173, 258–9, 323–4

race/racism 10, 248–50, 270
  in US discourse 3, 6, 49–58
radical epistemology 145
radical practice 150
rational-purposive action 97
rationality 31, 86, 87
  functional 97
  instrumental 29
  scientific 222–3
  technical 132
real, making 328
Real Self 106–8, 109, 111–13, 115
Real Time Strategic Change 169, 171
Real Time Strategic Planning 172
reality 4, 6, 7, 8, 77, 110, 223
  social 122, 168, 275
reason 29, 38, 86
receptive/active approach 337
receptivity 109
reconnaissance/plan stage 247
record-keeping 289, 290
reductionism 108, 117, 118, 126
reference groups 31
reflecting (in supervision process) 320
reflecting the past 203
reflection 142
  and action *see* action
  in action research 168
  co-operative inquiry 151
  collaborative off-line 307–14
  continuous 170, 173
reflective inquiry 3
reflective knowledge 9, 88–90
reflective learning 173, 203, 204
reflective performance 176, 178
reflective practitioner 307
reflective thinking 38
reflexivity 7, 67, 114, 179, 344, 347
Reformation 4
reframing 150, 312
regimes of truth 73

relational ecological form 10–11
relational knowledge 9, 86–7, 88, 90
relational praxis 12, 346–7
relations of ruling 66
relationship-building event 22, 23
relationships 10, 21–5, 44, 73, 164–5
Renaissance 4, 5
replanning stage 247
representation 6
representational knowledge 9, 85–6, 88, 90
repression 34, 73
Republican Era (United States) 55
research
  by practitioners 94
  cycle 109–11, 114–15, 144–52, 329
  with people *see* co-operative inquiry
  personal process 315–17
  political process 339–40
Research Center for Group Dynamics 40
research cycling 150
researcher
  as facilitator 168, 170, 174, 224, 239
  initiated inquiry 186–8
respect 298
responsibility 34, 89, 174, 251
rhetorical impact, of critique 156–7
rich pictures 122–3
rigorous testing 33, 134, 141
rituals 210
roles, (humanistic approach) 107, 111–14
root definitions 123
Rosca Foundation 28
rule-breaking 222
rural areas
  development (Tanzania) 286–96
  Participatory Rural Appraisal 33, 62, 65, 287, 290, 292
  Photo Voice project 269–76
Rural Integrated Project Support 287, 288, 292, 293, 294
Rural School District 169–70, 171, 172, 174

sacralization 11, 109
same role inquiries 147
Sandanista revolution 31
scaling up process (U&I project) 326–7
scanning (supervision process) 320
schizophrenia 181–2
science 10, 126, 267–8
  humanistic approach to 108–9
  knowledge and 29
  positivist 3, 4, 7, 85, 132, 134
scientific management 41, 46, 223
scientific rationality 222–3
scientific research 4, 34
scientism 3, 29, 30
scripting (ethnodrama) 178–81
search conferences 18, 43, 167, 168–70
second order learning 245
second-person research 172, 211–13, 345
  The Natural Step 240–1
secondary outcomes 149, 152

selective perception 141
self
  knowing 328
  other and 9, 10, 73, 168, 274, 275
  Real 106–8, 109, 111–13, 115
self-actualization 100, 111, 112
self-analysis, in groups 287–8
self-authority 318
self-awareness 8, 12, 229
self-creation 8, 251
self-directed group therapy 40
self-education 95
self-help groups 3
self-images 108
self-interest 240
self-knowledge 245, 248–9
self-learning 77
self-objectivity 30
self-observation 208
self-organizing systems 100–4, 164
self-realization 316, 317
self-reflection 12, 168
self-reflective inquiry 335–41
self-reflective projects 95
self-reflexivity 67
self-reinforcing learning communities 164
self-silencing 249
self-understandings 96
Sematron 280–1, 283, 284
Senior Medical Staff Committee 65
SENSE model 244–7
senses, knowing through 88
separated knowing 9
sex/gender distinction 62
sexism 10, 56, 249
sexuality 56, 212–13
shaping the inquiry 329–30
shared vision 120
silence 72
  self-knowledge and 248–9
  voice and 64–6, 156
simplicity 109
sincerity 86, 87
single product event 22, 23
single-loop learning 135, 199, 207, 215
skills
  academic 240–1
  action research 141
  developing 305–14
  facilitation 323
  inquiry 149–51
Skinnerism 25
social action 89
social awareness 124, 125
social capital 80
social change 43, 52, 57, 74, 103
  action research 10, 168
  empowerment 76–8
  knowledge and 76–8, 84
  participatory research for 262–8
social constructionism 62, 112
social constructivism 5, 65, 112, 249

social democracy 3
social ecology 43
social entropy 119
social ethics 115
social experimentation 134–5
social hierarchy 157
social integration 98–101
social justice 33, 50, 52, 61, 262
social macro-subject 102–4
social movement 72–3, 78, 79–80, 90
social phenomena 117
social reality 122, 168, 275
social science
  gap between social practice and 132
  strategies 174
  systems thinking in 117–18
social theory 27–35
social workers 221–6
socialism 34, 286
socialization 97–9, 101
society 18, 97–9, 101
Society for Organizational Learning 197, 199–203, 204, 350
Society for Participatory Research in Asia 3
socio-ecological perspective 120–1, 254, 260
socio-technical systems 38–47
soft systems thinking 122–3
solidarity 66, 100, 157, 270, 298
Solidarity Movement in Mental Health 270
song 263–4, 267, 348
Southern Christian Leadership Conference 264
Southern Zone Confederation on Environmental Protection 294
space(s) 8, 79, 328, 330
spectator knowledge 109
speech 211
speech act 86, 88
spirit 11–12
spirituality 3, 126, 127
spontaneous will 112
stakeholders 122, 222
Steering Committee (CN Group) 255, 256, 257, 260
Steering Committee (Open House) 136
steering media 99, 100
stereoscopic vision 100
storytelling 267, 270–1, 272, 273, 275
strategy/strategizing 174, 208, 248
strength-resiliency model 55
structuration 236, 241, 345, 347, 350
structure 125
Structure of Scientific Revolutions, The 4
subject
  -client relationships 186–8
  and object 8, 30–1, 32
  philosophy of 102–4
subjectivity 149, 208, 215, 246, 316
substantive social theory 97
suchness/suchness meaning 109
Sudi Declaration 293–4
suicide, fictionally-constructed 182–3
supervision, process-oriented 317–21
surveys 75, 187, 301
Sustainability Consortium 201, 202, 203
sustainable development 236–42, 347
Sweden 17, 18, 20, 21, 42
Swedish Office for European programmes 21
symbolic interactionism 181
symbolic reproduction 98, 99, 100
symmetric reciprocity 30, 167
synchronicity 339
synergy 117, 120
system conditions 237, 238
system dynamics 119–20
system and lifeworld theory 96–101
system principle 120
systematic action research 247–8
systematic restitution 31
systemic thinking 117–18, 121, 122, 126
systems functioning 101–2
systems idea 124
systems theory 100
systems thinking 3, 117–27
  socio-technical systems 38–47

T-groups 3, 187–8, 190
tacit knowledge 9, 198, 199
tacit theories 133
talk (MARG project) 64, 228–34, 348
Tanzania 3, 28, 286–96, 349
Tavistock Institute 2–3, 25, 38, 40–3, 120, 193
teachers 102
team building 298–9, 300
team learning 120
technical action research 95
technical rationality 132
technological determinism 46
technological progress 126
technology 10, 30, 126, 192
text/textuality 6
theatre of cruelty 181
theoretical complementarity 124
theoretical inspiration, action research 3–4
theories of action 133, 134
theories of practice 132
theories in practice 133, 134, 140
theories-in-use 134
theory
  and action 89
  and practice 17–25, 29–30, 104, 347
Theory of Communicative Action, The 97, 99–100
Theory and Practice 94
thick analyses 53
thinking phase 110
third-person research 172, 345
  practice 213–15
  The Natural Step 240–1
Thirty Years War 5
Thoughts and Conclusions 30
three dimensional view, of power 73–4
threshold technique 225
time, space and 8
Tomorrow's Tomorrow: the Black Woman 54
topic choice 158
  (GRDO case) 159

total systems intervention 124, 125–6
touching 88
tracking 339, 340–1
training, T-group 3, 187–8, 190
transformational action 61
transformational power 213–14
transformative inquiries 145, 148–9, 152
transformative learning 168
transformative moments 330
transformative process 101, 123, 197, 200, 213
transpersonal 106–7
transpersonal perspective 317
transpersonal psychology 3
tree metaphor, learning 197
Triangle Theatre (Coventry) 177
triangulation 177, 183, 302
triple-loop learning 207, 215
trust 5, 211, 298, 301
truth 5, 6, 18, 29, 30, 75, 322
  communicative action 98
  emancipatory process 343
  experiential knowledge 268
  and justice 96
  philosophy of the subject 102, 103
  positivism 223
  see also regimes of truth
truth-telling 211
turbulence 120
turn-to-action 61
Twilight: Los Angeles 57

uncertainty 43, 347
unconditional positive questions 155–65
unconscious 317
uncoupling, of system and lifeworld 99–100
understanding 2, 6, 85, 86, 122
  mutual 96, 98, 99, 103, 104, 171
Understanding and Involvement (U&I)
    Project 323–34
uniformity 34
unilateral power 214
Union of Radical Sociologists 52
Union Theological Seminary 263
United States, race in discourse 3, 6, 49–58
universities 102

validity 33, 132
  of action research 8, 12, 193, 343–50
  claims 96, 99, 181
  procedures 146, 149–50
value systems 89, 246
value-free science 109
values 109
verstehen (understanding) 86
vertical alliances 80
Vienna Circle 5
violence 34
VISA 200, 202
vision/visioning 208, 248
vivencia 31, 32
voice
  ethnodrama 176
  silence and 64–6, 156

war (Photo Voice project) 269–76
warranted assumptions 347
weaving industry (India) 42
welfare state 97, 100
well-being 2
western thought, evolution of 5
Whole System Event 169
wholeness 126, 127
women
  MARG project 228, 230–2, 233, 234
  Photo Voice project 269–76
  use of PAR, Tanzania 286–96
  see also femininity; feminism
Women's Research Centre 66
words, Chinese language 87, 88
Work Environment Fund 18
Work-Out 167
workplace (socio-technical systems) 38–47
World Bank 3, 78, 287
World Congress (Cartagena, 1977) 27, 32, 33, 34
World Council of Churches 28
World Symposium of Action Research 31
worldviews 123, 137
  see also participatory worldviews

Yellow Creek 264, 267
youth, street-involved 297–303, 346